Perspectives on Marriage

—— A Reader ——

SECOND EDITION

Edited by

Kieran Scott
Fordham University

Michael Warren
St. John's University

New York   Oxford
OXFORD UNIVERSITY PRESS
2001

Oxford University Press

Oxford   New York
Athens   Auckland   Bangkok   Bogotá   Buenos Aires   Calcutta
Cape Town   Chennai   Dar es Salaam   Delhi   Florence   Hong Kong   Istanbul
Karachi   Kuala Lumpur   Madrid   Melbourne   Mexico City   Mumbai
Nairobi   Paris   São Paulo   Singapore   Taipei   Tokyo   Toronto   Warsaw

and associated companies in
Berlin   Ibadan

Published by Oxford University Press, Inc.,
198 Madison Avenue, New York, New York, 10016
http://www.oup-usa.org

Oxford is a registered trademark of Oxford University Press

Library of Congress Cataloging-in-Publication Data
Perspectives on marriage : a reader/edited by Kieran Scott and Michael Warren.—2nd ed.
      p. cm.
    Includes bibliographical references.
      ISBN 0-19-513439-7 (pbk. : alk. paper)
        1. Marriage—Religious aspects—Catholic Church. 2. Catholic Church—Doctrines. I.
Scott, Kieran. II. Warren, Michael

    BX2250 .P415 2001
    248.4—dc21
                                                                    99-052929

Printing (last digit): 9 8 7 6 5

Printed in the United States of America
on acid-free paper

To Connie and Ellen,
who continue to teach us the meaning of marriage

Acknowledgments

Robert Miller, executive editor at Oxford University Press, encouraged us to embark on this second edition. Elissa Morris, editorial assistant, patiently ushered us through numerous earlier proposals. Christine D'Antonio, project editor, skillfully shepherded the manuscript through the copyediting, design, and production stages. Drs. German Martinez, Gerald Vigna, Robert Brancatelli, and Rose Zuzworsky offered invaluable suggestions for deletions and additions. Patti Troy, graduate assistant at Fordham University, worked tirelessly in assembling the final manuscript. Without their generous help, this revised edition would never have been published.

CONTENTS

PART FOUR

Attitudes toward Sexuality

PART EIGHT

Spirituality of Marriage

PART NINE

Interreligious Perspectives on Marriage

Introduction

Kieran Scott
Michael Warren

This book arose from a need recognized for several years by many teachers of the university-level course in the theology of marriage. During a casual conversation, we expressed a zest for the course, while deploring the lack of any single resource-rich reader. There were fine books about aspects of marriage, but no single resource approaching marriage from a variety of angles. This book is an attempt to address that need.

While assembling the materials for this volume, we asked colleagues about their marriage courses and found a variety of approaches to the topic: some more theological, some more sociological, some psychological, but all seeking to catch the serious attention of students. Almost all combined a theological perspective with a social science one. In asking these persons about the sort of reader that might be helpful, we concluded that variety should be a key component.

Born of such background, this book should not be intended as a course outline, and we warn against letting the book's contents design the marriage course. Instead, the book should be used the other way around: the vision of the course should determine what here might be useful in a particular approach to marriage. This reader offers a series of excursions into various aspects of marriage. We suspect what gives special life to the course in marriage is the artistry worked out by particular teachers examining marriage from insightful angles based on their own study and gifts.

This second edition taps into the insights and promptings we received from those who took up the first edition with such appreciation. We found some of the material in the original 1993 edition to be too theoretical or abstract for our students, and we tended to avoid using it. We wondered what others using the book might have to say about what parts of the book they used and what they avoided. We contacted a sampling of teachers using the book to get their advice on a possible revised edition. Their help was indispensable for working out the shape of this edition.

Most teachers of the university-level course in the theology of marriage see their efforts as an academic enterprise, not a ministerial or church one. They seek to disclose historical traditions, including religious ones, affecting marriage, while attending to recent social and cultural shifts in attitudes toward the practice of marriage. Still, an academic course dealing with the religious dimensions of marriage will have some things in common with church efforts in ministry to marriage. One of these is concern for marriage preparation.

Despite the fact that more and more young people have come to question whether a "legal" or formal marriage is necessary or even advisable, students continue to crowd into the theology of marriage courses looking for insight and wisdom about a troubled institution. They know the stakes for them in this enterprise—however they may choose to approach it—are quite high. Bristling in the midst of our students are all the important dilemmas about what it means to be alive at this moment in history. Our goal in this reader is to press them with radical questions and humanizing perspectives that have important consequences for their futures. If they become more thoughtful about the issues and more constructive about their decisions, our efforts will be well rewarded.

Any course that puts marriage in a religious perspective has the possibility of contesting some currents in contemporary culture that are hostile to enduring commitments—hostile to the kind of love ethic needed for successful parenting over the long haul, and hostile to the wider networks of support needed for families in the future. While some religious assumptions about marriage need critique, many religious convictions offer a radically humanizing view of the marital relationship, quite different from some of the depictions of marriage found in current film and television fare.

The readings in this collection contest various assumptions about marriage, including many recently created by a consumerist culture and some being challenged from within religious traditions themselves. Careful reading will spark earnest, if not heated, discussion and some conflicts over basic points of view. Many of the underlying, larger issues cannot be settled in a semester.[1] We expect many students will leave their courses with lingering questions needing continuing reflection: the seeds of emancipatory practice.

We recognize the variety of academic levels in what we have gathered here. Some readings are historically "dense" and will need careful preteaching before being read. Others make use of theologically sophisticated concepts that will also need explanation before becoming accessible to many students. Other fare is less weighty but not less important. We have included several popularizations of first-rate social science scholarship. The ideas and issues in such essays should not be dismissed as "magazine pop psychology," since they make accessible for serious and informed discussion sophisticated research conducted, in some cases, over several years.

Our hope is that the resources and ideas found here provide some part of a foundation for joyous, and struggling, life commitments.

Those familiar with the first edition of *Perspectives on Marriage* will immediately note both what has been carried over from the first edition and also the deletions and additions that make up this new edition. In some cases readings have been shortened and simplified or even moved to a different section. Each reading continues to be followed by questions for discussion and, in some cases, titles for further study.

Part 1, "Marriage in Historical Perspective," brings together a rich set of materials on marriage in the Jewish and Christian tradition. This material is indispensable for acquiring a developmental sense of religious teaching on marriage.

Part 2, "Contemporary Perspectives on the Theology of Marriage," presents marriage as a basic Christian sacrament, a sign of God's presence.

Part 3, "Marriage: Meanings and Transitions," raises some questions young people have about marriage and offers an approach to marriage as a process of growing together.

Part 4, "Attitudes toward Sexuality," is the longest section, with several provocative readings on the basic assumptions we bring to our relationships.

Part 5, "Communication, Conflict, and Change," is presented as a key section on the issue of conflict and conflict-resolution in marriage. All students are familiar with the problems it sets out, but not so many will have considered the kinds of changes in attitudes and behavior it calls for. The difference between conflict and violence is a key matter in these readings.

Part 6, "Getting beyond Stereotypes," looks at issues raised by the contemporary women's and men's liberation movements.

Part 7, "Divorce and Annulment," acknowledges the failure, at times, of the marital ideal and its effects on people's lives. Canonical and theological perspectives on divorce and remarriage are offered, and probe the dilemma remarriage poses for Catholics seeking ecclesial belonging.

Part 8, "Spirituality of Marriage," is a new section on what it might mean to actually live out a deeply religious marriage in a time of consumerism.

Part 9, "Interreligious Perspectives on Marriage," is offered for the many students living in an increasingly multicultural and multireligious nation who bring to the marriage course questions about interreligious marriage.

Our metaphor for this revised volume is the wedding feast, a moment of hope and joy that unity is possible, that the Spirit of God can reveal itself through human self-gifting. These readings themselves represent for us a kind of intellectual feast on the question of marriage, a question at the heart of what it means to be human.

NOTE

1. See the wise overview of marriage preparation from a religious perspective found in: Pontifical Council for the Family, "Preparation for the Sacrament of Marriage," *Origins* 26:7 (4 July 1996): 97/99–109. A key point in this document is its recognition that marriage preparation starts in infancy and continues right up to marriage.

PART ONE

Marriage in Historical Perspective

CHAPTER 1

Marriage in the Bible

Michael G. Lawler

We all have attitudes toward marriage that have been socially shaped for us within our own lifetime. We can easily tend to think of marriage as it is today— or even as it is depicted for us today in movies and television. Marriage has been imagined for us by our own parents, by the behavior of other married people we know, and by the many literary, TV, and film depictions of it.

The following essay is an account of the religious imagination of marriage, particularly the Jewish and the Christian imagination of what it could and should be. Some will find the account unbelievable, perhaps almost shocking. Not all those who call themselves Jews or Christians are aware of the quite radical approach to the marriage relationship their faith calls for.

This essay calls for careful reading. The best way to read it is to have read immediately beforehand the passages from the Old and New Testaments the author refers to and then to have them open before you while reading this important account of the profound Jewish and Christian understanding of marriage.

Questions for Discussion

1. The author stresses the differences between Israel and its neighbors in their understanding of sexuality and marriage. What differences are highlighted here, and exactly why are they so different?

2. Of the Israelite understanding of marriage, do you find any features that are still not widely accepted today—say, in the way marriage is presented in movies and on television?

3. Is the author claiming that marriage is the analogy for understanding our relation to God or that our relation to God is the analogy for understanding marriage?

4. Were Hosea living today, some would say he was "hung up" on Gomer or, in more psychological terms, "obsessed" by her. Obsession is not a beautiful thing. How would you explain the beauty of Hosea's commitment to Gomer, and what is its religious significance?

5. In more than one place, the author stresses that covenant love in the Bible is "not the same as a passionate affection for a person of the opposite sex." Does the author's approach make covenant love seem dull or unexciting? What is his point in this emphasis?

6. In dealing with New Testament passages about marriage, the author spends the most time dealing with several verses in Ephesians. Why does he see these verses as so significant? If the ideas of these verses were actually lived out, what difference would they make in the way people "love" one another?

7. Mutual giving way is an important concept here. What might be some examples of this mutual giving way in an actual marriage? Could you describe five situations in which it might take place?

8. What did you make of the author's claim "If marital love exists only inchoately on a wedding day, as it surely does, indissolubility also exists only inchoately. Marital love is . . . a task to be undertaken"?

As in all other matters, the biblical teaching on marriage should be seen in the context of the Near Eastern cultures with which the people of the Bible had intimate links, specifically the Mesopotamian, Syrian, and Canaanite. It is not my intention here to dwell on these cultures and their teachings on marriage and sexuality. They were all quite syncretistic, and a general overview sufficiently gives both a sense of the context and their specific distinctions from the Jewish Bible.

Underlying the themes of sexuality, fertility, and marriage in these cultures are the archetypal figures of the god-father and the goddess-mother, the sources of universal life in the divine, the natural, and the human spheres. Myths celebrated the marriage, the sexual intercourse, and the fertility of this divine pair, legitimating the marriage, the intercourse, and the fertility of every earthly pair. Rituals acted out the myths, establishing a concrete link between the divine and the earthly worlds and enabling men and women to share not only in the divine action but also in the efficacy of that action. This is especially true of sexual rituals, which bless sexual intercourse and ensure that the unfailing divine fertility is shared by man's plants and animals and wives, all important elements of his struggle for survival in those cultures.[1] In Mesopotamia, the divine couple is Ishtar and Tammuz; in Egypt, Isis and Osiris; in Canaan, Ashtarte (or Asherah) and, sometimes, Eshmun. After the Hellenization of Canaan, Eshmun is given the title of Adonis.

MARRIAGE IN THE OLD TESTAMENT

The biblical view of sexuality, marriage, and fertility makes a radical break with this polytheistic perspective. The Old Testament, whose view of marriage I do not intend to treat fully here but only as it provides the basis for the New Testament view of Christian marriage, does not portray a god-goddess couple, but only Yahweh who led Israel out of Egypt and is unique (Deuteronomy 6:4). There is no goddess associated with him. He needs no

Pages 5–22 are reprinted with permission from *Secular Marriage: Christian Sacrament*, copyright © 1985 by Michael G. Lawler, published by Twenty-Third Publications, P.O. Box 180, Mystic, CT 06355.

goddess, for he creates by his word alone. This God created man and woman, "male and female he created them and he named *them 'adam*" (Genesis 5:2). This fact alone, that God names male and female together *'adam* (that is, earthling or humankind), founds the equality of man and woman as human beings, whatever be their distinction in functions. It establishes them as "bone of bone and flesh of flesh" (Genesis 2:23), and enables them "therefore" to marry and to become "one body" (Genesis 2:24). These details are taken from the early Yahwist creation account. But the much later priestly account which we find in Genesis I also records the creation of male and female as *'adam* and the injunction given them to "be fruitful and multiply and fill the earth" (Genesis 1:28).

Equal man and woman, with their separate sexualities and fertilities, do not derive from a divine pair whom they are to imitate. They are called into being by the creative action of the sovereign God. Man and woman *'adam*, their sexuality, their marriage, their fertility are all good, because they are the good gifts of the Creator. Later Christian history, as we shall see, will have recurring doubts about the goodness of sexuality and its use in marriage, but the Jewish biblical tradition had none. As gifts of the Creator God, who "saw everything that he had made and behold it was very good" (Genesis 1:31), sexuality, marriage, and fertility were all good, and belonged to man and woman as their own, not as something derived from some divine pair. When looked at within this context of creation-gift, all acquired a deeply religious significance in Israel. That is not to say that they were sacred in the sense in which the fertility cults interpreted them as sacred, namely, as participation in the sexuality and sexual activity of the divine pair. In that sense they were not sacred, but quite secular. But in another sense, the sense that they were from God and linked man and woman to God, they were both sacred and religious. "It was not the sacred rites that surrounded marriage that made it a holy thing. The great rite which sanctified marriage was God's act of creation itself."[2] It was God alone, unaided by any partner, who not only created *'adam* with sexuality and for marriage but also blessed him and them, thus making them inevitably good.

Man and woman together are named *'adam*. They are equal in human dignity and complementary to one another; there is no full humanity without both together. Human creation, indeed, is not complete until they stand together. It is precisely because man and woman are equal, because they are *'adam*, because they are "bone of bone and flesh of flesh," that is, because they share human strengths and weaknesses, that they may marry and become "one body" (Genesis 2:24). Among the birds of the air and the animals of the field there "was not found a helper fit" for the man (Genesis 2:20), and it is not difficult to imagine man's cry of delight when confronted by woman. Here, finally, was one who was his equal, one whom he could marry and with whom he could become one body.

That man and woman become one body in marriage has been much too exclusively linked in the Western tradition to one facet of marriage, namely, the genital. That facet is included in becoming one body, but it is not all there is. For *body* here implies the entire person. "One personality would translate it better, for 'flesh' in the Jewish idiom means 'real human life.'"[3] In marriage a man and a woman enter into a fully personal union, not just a sexual or genital one. In such a union they become one person, one life, and so complement one another that they become *'adam.* They enter into a union which establishes not just a legal relationship, but a blood relationship which makes them one person. Rabbis go so far as to teach that it is only after marriage and the union of man and woman into one person that the image of God may be discerned in them. An unmarried man, in their eyes, is not a whole man.[4] And the mythic stories,[5] interested as always in aetiology, the origin of things, proclaim that it was so "in the beginning," and that it was so by the express design of God. There could be for a Jew, and for a Christian, no greater foundation for the human and religious goodness of sexuality, marriage, and fertility. Nor could there be a secular reality better than marriage for pointing to God and his steadfastly loving relationship with Israel. That was the next step in the development of the religious character of marriage.

MARRIAGE AS COVENANT SYMBOL

Central to the Israelite notion of their special relationship with God was the idea of the covenant. The Deuteronomist reminded the assembled people: "You have declared this day concerning Yahweh that he is your God and Yahweh has declared this day concerning you that you are a people for his own possession" (Deuteronomy 26:17–19). Yahweh is the God of Israel; Israel is the people of Yahweh. Together Yahweh and Israel form a community of grace, a community of salvation, a community, one could say, of one body. It was probably only a matter of time until the people began to imagine this covenant relationship in terms drawn from marriage, and it was the prophet Hosea who first did so. He preached about the covenant relationship of Yahweh and Israel within the biographical context of his own marriage to a harlot wife, Gomer. To understand his preaching, about marriage and about the covenant, we must first understand the times in which Hosea lived.

Hosea preached around the middle of the eighth century B.C. at a time when Israel was well established in Canaan. Many Israelites thought that the former nomads had become too well established in their promised land, for as they learned their new art of agriculture they learned also the cult of the Canaanite fertility god, Baal. This cult, which seriously challenged their worship of Yahweh, was situated in the classic mold presented earlier, that of the god-goddess pair, with Baal as the Lord of the earth, and Anat as his wife (and sister). The sexual intercourse and fertility of these two were looked upon as establishing the pattern both of creation and of the fertile intercourse of every human pair. The relationship of human intercourse and its fertility to that of the divine couple was acted out in temple prostitution, which required both *kedushim* and *kedushoth,* that is, male and female prostitutes. These were prohibited in the cult of Yahweh (Deuteronomy 23:18), and any

Jewish maiden participating in temple prostitution was regarded as a harlot. It was such a harlot, Gomer, that Hosea says Yahweh instructed him to take for his wife (1:2–3).

It is quite irrelevant to the present discussion whether the book of Hosea tells us what Hosea did in historical reality, namely, took a harlot-wife and remained faithful to her despite her infidelity to him, or whether it offers a parable about marriage as steadfast covenant. What is relevant is that Hosea found in marriage, either in his own marriage or in marriage in general, an image in which to show his people the steadfastness of Yahweh's convenantal love for them. On a superficial level, the marriage of Hosea and Gomer is just like any other marriage. But on a more profound level, it serves as prophetic symbol, proclaiming and realizing and celebrating in representation the covenant relationship between Yahweh and Israel.

The names of Hosea's two younger children reflect the sad state of that relationship: a daughter is Not Pitified (1:6), and a son is Not My People (1:9). As Gomer left Hosea for another, so too did Israel abandon Yahweh in favor of Baal and become Not Pitied and Not My People. But Hosea's remarkable reaction proclaims and makes real in representation the remarkable reaction of Yahweh. He buys Gomer back (3:2); that is, he redeems her. He loves her "even as Yahweh loves the people of Israel, though they turn to other gods" (3:1). Hosea's action towards Gomer reveals and makes real in representation the action of Yahweh's unfailing love for Israel. In both cases, that of the human marriage symbol and of the divine covenant symbolized, the one body relationship had been placed in jeopardy. But Hosea's posture both is modeled upon and models that of Yahweh. As Hosea has pity on Gomer, so Yahweh "will have pity on Not Pitied," and will "say to Not My People 'you are my people,'" and they will say to him, "Thou art my God" (2:23). The covenant union, that between Hosea and Gomer as well as that between Yahweh and Israel, is restored. A sundering of the marital covenant relationship is not possible for Hosea because he recognized that his God is not a God who can abide the dissolution of covenant, no matter what the provocation. He believed what the prophet Malachi would later proclaim: "I hate divorce, says Yahweh, the God of Israel . . . so take heed to yourselves and do not be faithless" (2:16).

There are two possibilities of anachronism to be avoided here. The first is that overworked word *love*. In its contemporary usage, it always means a strong affection for another person, frequently a passionate affection for another person of the opposite sex. When we find the word in our Bible it is easy to assume that it means the same thing. But it does not. Covenant Love, of which Hosea speaks and which we read of first in Deuteronomy 6:5, is not a love of interpersonal affection but a love that is "defined in terms of loyalty, service and obedience."[6] When we read, therefore, of Hosea's steadfast love for Gomer and of Yahweh's faithful love for Israel, we ought to understand loyalty, service and obedience, and not interpersonal affection. The second possibility of anachronism rests in the hatred of divorce proclaimed by Malachi. "In the circumstances addressed by Malachi, what God hates is the divorce of Jew and Jew; there is silence about the divorce of Jew and non-Jew."[7] The post-exilic reforms of Ezra and Nehemiah require the divorce of all non-Jewish wives and marriage to Jewish ones. Malachi speaks for this period. The divorce of Jewish wives is hated, but the divorce of all non-Jewish ones is obligatory. As we shall see, Paul will adapt this strategy to the needs of his Corinthian church, and it continues to be a crucial factor in the Catholic strategy toward divorce in our day.

What ought we to make of the story of his marriage that Hosea leaves to us? There is a first, and very clear, meaning about Yahweh: he is faithful. But there is also a second, and somewhat more mysterious, meaning about human marriage: not only is it the loving union of a man and a woman, but it is also a prophetic symbol, proclaiming and making real in representative image the steadfast love of Yahweh for Israel. First articulated by the prophet Hosea, such a view of marriage recurs again in the prophets Jeremiah and Ezekiel. Ultimately, it yields the view of Christian marriage that we find in the New Testament.

Both Jeremiah and Ezekiel present Yahweh as having two wives. Israel and Judah (Jeremiah 3:6–14). Oholah-Samaria and Oholibah-Jerusalem (Ezekiel 23:4). Faithless Israel is first "sent away with a decree of divorce" (Jeremiah 3:8), but that does not deter an even more faithless Judah from "committing adultery with stone and tree" (Jeremiah 3:9). Israel and Judah are as much the harlots as Gomer but Yahweh's faithfulness is as unending as Hosea's. He offers a declaration of undying love: "I have loved you with an everlasting love; therefore, I have continued my faithfulness to you" (Jeremiah 31:3; cf. Ezekiel 16:63; Isaiah 54:7–8). The flow of meaning, as in Hosea, is not from human marriage to divine covenant, but from divine covenant to human marriage. The belief in and experience of covenant fidelity creates the belief in and the possibility of fidelity in marriage, which then and only then becomes a prophetic symbol of the covenant. Yahweh's covenant fidelity becomes a characteristic to be imitated, a challenge to be accepted, in every Jewish marriage. Malachi, as we saw already, puts it in a nutshell: "I hate divorce, says Yahweh . . . so do not be faithless" (2:16).

MARRIAGE IN THE NEW TESTAMENT

The conception of marriage as a prophetic symbol, a representative image of a mutually faithful covenant relationship is continued in the New Testament. But there is a change of dramatis personae, from Yahweh-Israel to Christ-Church. Rather than presenting marriage in the then-classical Jewish way as an image of the covenant union between Yahweh and Israel, the writer of the letter to the Ephesians[8] presents it as an image of the relationship between the Christ and the new Israel, his church. This presentation is of such central importance to the development of a Christian view of marriage and unfortunately has been used to sustain such a diminished Christian view that we shall have to consider it here in some detail.

The passage in which the writer offers his view of marriage (EPH.5:21–33) is situated within a larger context (EPH.5:21–6:9) which sets forth a list of house-hold duties that exist within a family at that time. This list is addressed to wives (EPH.5:22), husbands (EPH.5:25), children (EPH.6:1), fathers (EPH.6:4), slaves (EPH.6:5), and masters (EPH.6:9). All that concerns us here is, of course, what is said of the pair, wife/husband. There are two similar lists in the New Testament, one in the letter to the Colossians (3:18–4:1), the other in the first letter of Peter (2:13–3:7). But the Ephesians' list is the only one to open with a strange injunction. "Because you fear Christ subordinate yourselves to one another"[9]; or "give way to one another in obedience to Christ"[10]; or, in the weaker translation of the Revised Standard Version, "be subject to one another out of reverence for Christ."[11] This junction, most commentators agree, is an essential element of what follows.

The writer takes over the household list from traditional material, but critiques it in 5:21. His critique challenges the absolute authority of any one Christian group over any other, of husbands, for instance, over wives, of fathers over children, of masters over slaves. It establishes a basic attitude required of all Christians, an attitude of giving way or of mutual obedience, an attitude which covers all he has to say not only to wives, children, and slaves, but also to husbands, fathers, and masters.[12] Mutual submission is an attitude of all Christians, because their basic attitude is that they "fear Christ." That phrase probably will ring strangely in many ears, clashing with the deeply rooted Augustinian-Lutheran claim that the basic attitude toward the Lord is not one of fear, but of love. It is probably for this reason that the Revised Standard Version rounds off the rough edge of the Greek *phobos* and renders it as *reverence*. But *phobos* does not mean reverence. It means fear, as in the Old Testament aphorism: the fear of the Lord is the beginning of wisdom (Proverbs 1:5; 9:10; 15:33; Psalms 111:10).

The apostle Paul is quite comfortable with this Old Testament perspective. Twice in his second letter to the Corinthians (2 Cor. 5:11 and 7:1) he uses the phrase *fear of God*. In his commentary on Ephesians, Schlier finds the former text more illuminating of Ephesians 5:21.[13] But I am persuaded, with Sampley, that the latter is a better parallel.[14] Second Corinthians 6:14–18 recalls the initiatives of God in the covenant with Israel and applies these initiatives to Christians, who are invited to respond with holiness "in the fear of God" (2 Cor. 7:1). The fear of God that is the beginning of wisdom is a radical awe and reverence that grasps the mighty acts of God and responds to them with holiness. In 2 Corinthians 6:14–17 that holiness is specified as avoiding marriage with unbelievers; in Ephesians 5:21 it is specified as giving way to one another. That mutual giving way is required of all Christians, even of husbands and wives as they seek holiness together in marriage, and even in spite of traditional family relationships which permitted husbands to lord it over their wives.

As Christians have all been admonished to give away to one another, it comes as no surprise that a Christian wife is to give way to her husband, "as to the Lord" (EPH.5:22). What does come as a surprise, at least to the ingrained male attitude that sees the husband as supreme lord and master of his wife and appeals to Ephesians 5:22–23 to ground and sustain that un-Christian (superior) attitude, is that a husband is to give way to his wife. That follows from the general instruction that Christians are to give way to one another. It follows also from the specific instruction about husbands. That instruction is not that "the husband is the head of the wife" (which is the way in which males prefer to read and cite it), but rather that "in the same way that the Messiah is the head of the church is the husband the head of the wife."[15] A Christian husband's headship over his wife is in image of, and totally exemplified by, Christ's leadership over the Church. When a Christian husband understands this, he will understand the Christian responsibility he assumes toward the woman-gift he receives in marriage as his wife. In a Christian marriage, spouses are required to give way mutually, not because of any inequality between them, not because of any subordination of one to the other, not because of fear, but only because they have such a personal unity that they live only for the good of that one person. Mutual giving way, mutual subordination, and mutual obedience are nothing other than total availability and responsiveness to one another so that both spouses can become one body.

The way Christ exercises headship over the church is set forth unequivocally in Mark 10:45: "The Son of Man came not to be served but to serve, and to give his life as a ransom (redemption) for many." *Diakonia*, service, is the Christ way of exercising authority, and our author testifies that it was thus that "Christ loved the church and gave himself up for her" (Ephesians 5:25). A Christian husband, therefore, is instructed to be head over his wife by serving, giving way to, and giving himself up for her. Headship and authority modeled on those of Christ does not mean control, giving orders, making unreasonable demands, reducing another human person to the status of servant or, worse, slave to one's every whim. It means service. The Christian husband-head, as Markus Barth puts it so beautifully, becomes "the first servant of his wife."[16] It is such a husband-head, and only such a one, that a wife is to fear (v. 33b) as all Christians fear Christ (v. 21b).

(In this section of Ephesians) the reversal of verses 22 and 25 in verse 33 is interesting and significant. Verse 22 enjoined wives to be subject to their husbands and verse 25 enjoined husbands to love their wives. Verse 33 reverses that order, first commanding that husbands love their wives and then warmly wishing that wives fear their husbands. This fear is not fear of a master. Rather it is awe and reverence for loving service, and response to it in a love-as-giving way. Such love cannot be commanded by a tyrant. It is won only by a lover, as the church's love and giving way to Christ is won by a lover who gave, and continues to give, himself for her. This is the author's recipe for becoming one body, joyous giving way in response to, and for the sake of, love. It is a recipe echoed unwittingly by many a modern marriage counselor, though we need to keep in mind that the love the Bible urges upon spouses is not interpersonal affection but loyalty, service, and obedience. That such love is to be mutual is clear from v. 21, "Be subject to one another," though it is not stated that a wife is to love her husband. The reasons that the writer adduces for husbands to love their wives apply to all Christians, even those called wives!

Three reasons are offered to husbands for loving their wives, all of them basically the same. First of all, "husbands should love their wives as [for they are] their own bodies" (v. 28a); secondly, the husband "who loves his wife loves himself" (v. 28b); thirdly, "the two shall become one body" (v. 31b), a reading which is obscured by the Revised Standard Version's "the two shall become one." There is abundant evidence in the Jewish tradition for equating a man's wife to his body.[17] But even if there was no such evidence, the sustained comparison throughout Ephesians 5:21–33 between Christ-Church and husband-wife, coupled with the frequent equation in Ephesians of church and body of Christ (EPH.1:22–23; 2:14–16; 3:6; 4:4–16; 5:22–30), clarifies both the meaning of the term *body* and the fact that it is a title of honor rather than of debasement.

Love is always essentially creative. The love of Christ brought into existence the Church and made its believers "members of his body" (v. 30). In the same way, the mutual love of a husband and a wife brings such a unity between them that, in image of Christ and Church, she may be called his body and his love for her, therefore, may be called love for his body or for himself. But it is only within the creative love of marriage that, in the Genesis phrase, "the two shall become one body" (Gen. 2:24). Prior to marriage, a man did not have this body, nor did a woman have this head. Each receives a gift in marriage, a complement neither had before, which so fulfills each of them that they are no longer two separate persons but one blood person. For each to love the other, therefore, is for each to love herself or himself.

The second reason offered to a husband for loving his wife is that "he who loves his wife loves himself" (EPH. 5:28B, V. 33A). Viewed within the perspective I have just elaborated, such reasoning makes sense. It makes even more Christian sense when one realizes that it is a paraphrase of the great commandment of Leviticus 19:18, cited by Jesus in Mark 12:31: "You shall love your neighbor as yourself." Ephesians, of course, does not say that a husband should love his neighbor as himself, but that he should so love his wife. Where, then, is the link to the great commandment? It is provided through that most beautiful and most sexual of Jewish love songs, the Song of Songs, where in the Septuagint version the lover addresses his bride nine separate times as *plesion*, neighbor (1:9, 15; 2:2, 10, 13; 4:1, 7; 5:2; 6:4). "The context of the occurrence of *plesion* in the Song of Songs confirms that *plesion* is used as a term of endearment for the bride."[18] Other Jewish usage further confirms that conclusion, leaving little doubt that the author of Ephesians had Leviticus 19:18 in mind when instructing a husband to love his wife as himself.

The great Torah and Gospel injunction applies also in marriage: "you shall love your neighbor as yourself." As all Christians are to give way to one another, so also each is to love the other as himself or herself, including husband and wife in marriage. The paraphrase of Leviticus 19:18 repeats in another form what had already been said before in the own-body and the one-body images [of Ephesians]. What the writer [of Ephesians] concludes about the Genesis one-body image, namely. "This is a great mystery, and I mean in reference to Christ and the church" (v. 32), will conclude our analysis of this central teaching of the New Testament on marriage.

"*This* is a great mystery," namely, as most scholars agree, the Genesis 2:24 text just cited, "the two shall become one body." The mystery, as the Anchor Bible translation seeks to show, is that "this (passage) has an eminent secret meaning," which is that it refers to Christ and the Church. All that has gone before about Christ and the Church comes to the forefront here: that Christ chose the Church to be united to him, as body to head; that he loved the Church and gave himself up for her; that the Church responds to this love of Christ in fear and giving way. Christ who loves the Church, and the Church who responds in love, thus constitute one body, the Body of Christ (Ephesians 1:22–23; 2:14–16; 3:6; 4:4–16; 5:22–30), just as Genesis 2:24 said they would. The writer is well aware that this meaning is not the meaning traditionally given to the text in Judaism, and he states this forthrightly. Just as in the great anithesis of the Sermon on the Mount, Jesus puts forward his interpretations of biblical texts in opposition to traditional interpretations ("You have heard that it was said to the men of old . . . but I say to you"), so also here the writer asserts clearly that it is his own reading of the text ("*I* mean in reference to Christ and the church," v. 32b).

Genesis 2:24: "That is why a man leaves his father and mother and clings to his wife, and the two of them become one body," was an excellent text for the purpose the writer had in mind, for it was a central Old Testament text traditionally employed to ordain and legitimate marriage. He acknowledges the meaning that husband and wife become one body in marriage; indeed, in v. 33, he returns to and demands that husband and wife live up to this very meaning. But he chooses to go beyond this meaning and insinuate another. Not only does the text refer to the union of husband and wife in marriage, but it refers also to that union of Christ and his church which he has underscored throughout Ephesians 5:1–33. On one level, Genesis 2:24 refers to human marriage; on another level, it refers to the covenant union between Christ and his Church. It is a small step to see human marriage as prophetically representing the covenant between Christ and his Church. In its turn, the union between Christ and Church provides an ideal model for human marriage and for the mutual conduct of the spouses within it.

Ephesians is not, of course, the only New Testament passage to speak of marriage and of the relationship between husband and wife. Paul does so in 1 Corinthians 7, apparently in response to a question which the Corinthians had submitted to him. The question was: "Is it better for a man to have no relations with a woman?" (7:1). The answer is an implied yes, but not an absolute yes. "Because of the temptation to sexual immorality, each man should have his own wife and each woman her own husband" (7.2). Marriage is good, even for Christians, he seems to say, as a safeguard against sexual sins, a point he underscores again in vv. 5–9. I do not wish to dwell, however, on this unenthusiastic affirmation of marriage. I wish only to highlight the equal relationship Paul assumes in marriage between a husband and a wife, a relationship he makes explicit in vv. 3–4. "The husband should give to the wife her conjugal rights, and likewise the wife to her husband. For the wife does not rule over her own body, but the husband does; likewise the husband does not rule over his own body, but the wife does."

A modern Christian might seize (as did medieval canonists seeking a precise legal definition of marriage) on Paul's dealing with marital sexual intercourse as an obligation owed mutually by the spouses to one another. But his contemporaries would have seized on something else, something much more surprising to them, namely, his assertion of strict equality between husband and wife in this matter. As Mackin puts it, correctly: "A modern Christian may wince at finding the apostle writing of sexual intercourse as an obligation, or even a debt, owed by spouses to one another, and writing of husbands' and wives' marital relationship as containing authority over one another's bodies. But Paul's contemporaries—at least those bred in the tradition of Torah and of its rabbinic interpreters—would have winced for another reason. This was Paul's assertion of equality between husbands and wives, and equality exactly on the juridical ground of authority and obligations owed."[19]

The author of 1 Timothy 2:8–15 also has something to say about the attitudes of men and women, laying down somewhat disproportionately what is expected of men (v. 8) and women (vv. 9–15). Of great interest in this text are the two traditional reasons he advances for the authority of men over women and the submission of women to men. The first is that Adam was created before Eve, and the other that it was Eve, not Adam, who was deceived by the serpent. Here the submission of women to men, and therefore of wives to husbands, is legitimated by collected stories of the mythical first human pair. For his part, the author of 1 Peter 3:1–6 requires that wives be submissive to their husbands "as Sarah obeyed Abraham" (v. 6). Such widespread views on such Old Testament bases were common in the Jewish world in which the Christian church originated, which makes the attitude of the writer to the Ephesians all the more surprising.

The Old Testament passage that the writer chooses to comment on is one which emphasizes the unity in marriage of the first pair, and therefore of all subsequent pairs, rather than their distinction. He embellishes it not with Old Testament references to creation and to fall, but with New Testament references to the Messiah and to his love. This leads him to a positive appraisal of marriage in the Lord that was not at all customary in the Jewish and Christian milieu of his time. While he echoes the customary *no* to any form of sexual immorality (5:3–5), he offers a more-than-customary *yes* to marriage and sexual intercourse. For him marriage means the union of two people in one body, the formation of a new covenant pair, which is the gift of both God who created it and his Christ who established it in the love he has for the church. So much so that the Christian marriage between a man and a woman becomes the prophetic symbol of the union that exists between Christ and the Church.

This doctrine does not mythicize marriage as an imitation of the marriage of some divine pair, nor does it idealize it so that men and women will not recognize it. Rather it leaves marriage what it is, a secular reality in which a man and a woman seek to become one person in love. What is added is only this, simple and yet mysteriously complex. As they become one body-person in love, they provide through their marriage a prophetic symbol of a similar oneness that exists between their Christ and their Church.

QUALITIES OF CHRISTIAN MARRIAGE

The qualities of Christian marriage already appear from our biblical analysis. The root quality, the one that irradiates all the others, is the fulfillment of the great Torah and Gospel injunction: "You shall love your neighbor as yourself" (Leviticus 19:18; Mark 12:31; Matthew 19:19). The Apostle Paul instructed the Romans that every other commandment was "summed up in this sentence, 'You shall love your neighbor as yourself'" (13:9). It is an instruction that holds true even, perhaps especially, in marriage, *Love*, of course, is a reality that is not easy to specify in words. It has a variety of different meanings. In Christian marriage love between the spouses, in fulfillment of the great commandment, is so radically necessary that in our time the Roman Rota, the Supreme Marriage Tribunal of the Roman Catholic Church, has ruled that where it is lacking from the beginning a Christian marriage is invalid.[20] That is how important Christian love is between Christian spouses.

We recall here that covenant love in the Bible is a love that is defined in terms of loyalty, service, and obedience, not in terms of interpersonal affection. The Letter to the Ephesians specifies that the love that is demanded in a Christian marriage is that kind of love. It is, first, love as mutual giving way, love as mutual obedience. The love of the spouses in a Christian marriage is a love that "does not insist on its own way" (1 Corinthians 13:4), a love that does not seek to dominate and control the other spouse. Rather is it a love that seeks to give way to the other whenever possible, so that two persons might become one body. There are individuals whose goal in life appears to be to get their own way always. The New Testament message proclaims that there is no place for such individuals in a marriage, least of all in a Christian marriage. That is not to say that there is no place in a marriage for individual differences. It is to say only that spouses who value getting their own way always, who value the domination of their spouses, who never dream of giving way, will never become one person with anyone, perhaps not even with themselves. In a Christian marriage, love requires not insisting on one's own way, but a mutual empathy with and compassion for the needs, feelings, and desires of one's spouse, and a mutual giving way to those needs, feelings, and desires when the occasion demands for the sake of, and in response to, love. Love that is exclusively *eros* is not the kind of love that is apt to ensure that two persons should become one body.

Love in a Christian marriage is, secondly, love as mutual service. All Christians are called to, and are sealed in baptism for, the imitation of Christ, who came "not to be served but to serve" (Mark 10:45). It cannot be otherwise in Christian marriage. In such a marriage there is no master, no mistress, no lady, no lord, but only mutual servants, seeking to be of service to the other, so that each may become one in herself/himself and one also with the other. This is required not just because it is good general counsel for marriage, but specifically because these Christian spouses are called in their marriage both to be imitators of Christ their Lord and to provide a prophetic symbol of his mutual servant-covenant with his church. For Christian spouses their married life is where they are to encounter Christ daily, and thereby come to holiness.

The love that constitutes Christian marriage is, finally, steadfast and faithful. The writer to the Ephesians instructs a husband to love his wife "as Christ loved the church." We can be sure that he intends the same instruction also for a wife. Now Christ loves the Church as Hosea loves Gomer, steadfastly and faithfully. A Christian husband and wife, therefore, are to love each other faithfully. This mutually faithful love, traditionally called fidelity, makes Christian marriage exclusive and permanent, and therefore an indissoluble community of love. On the question of indissolubility I want my position to be clear. Christian marriage is indissoluble because Christian love is steadfast and faithful. Indissolubility is a quality of Christian marriage because it is, first, a quality of Christian love. If marital love exists only inchoately on a wedding day, as it surely does, indissolubility also exists only inchoately. Marital love, as mutual giving way, as mutual service, as mutual fidelity, as mainspring of indissoluble community, is not a given in a Christian marriage but a task to be undertaken. It has an essentially eschatological dimension. *Eschatological* is a grand theological word for simple and constant human reality, namely the experience of having to admit "already, but not yet." Already mutual love, but not yet steadfast; already mutual service, but not yet without the desire to control; already one body, but not yet one person; already indissoluble in hope and expectation, but not yet in full human reality; already prophetic representation of the covenant union between Christ and his church, but not yet totally adequate representation. For authentic Christian spouses, Christian marriage is always a challenge to which they are called to respond as followers of the Christ who is for them the prophetic symbol of God.

SUMMARY

Four things we have seen in this chapter need to be underscored. First, human marriage is not an imitation of the eternal marriage of some divine couple, but a truly human, and therefore truly secular, reality which man and woman, *'adam*, hold as their own as gift from their Creator-God. In the giving and receiving of this gift, the Giver, the gift and the recipient are essentially and forever bound together. Secondly, this bond is explicated by the prophet Hosea, who brings into conscious focus the fact that marriage between a man and a woman is also the prophetic symbol of the covenant union between Yahweh and his people. Thirdly, the author of the letter to the Ephesians further clarifies the symbolic nature of marriage by proclaiming "a great mystery."

The great mystery is that as a man and a woman become one body-person in marriage, so also are Christ and his Church one body-person, and that the one reflects the other. From such thinking Roman Catholic theologians will be led slowly to declare that *human* marriage, on occasion, may be also *Christian* sacrament. Fourthly, Christian marriage is both a covenant and a community of love between a man and a woman, love that does not seek its own, love that gives way, love that serves, love that is steadfastly faithful. Because it is a covenant and a community of steadfast love, it is a permanent and exclusive state and a prophetic symbol of the steadfast covenant and community of love between Christ and his Church. That Christian marriage is such a reality, though, is not something that is to be taken blindly as being so. Rather it is something that in steadfast continuity is to be made so. Permanence is not a static, ontological quality of a marriage, but a dynamic, living quality of human love on which marriage, both human and Christian, thrives.

QUESTIONS FOR REFLECTION AND DISCUSSION

1. In your judgment, what is the radical distinction between the ancient Jewish mythology about sexuality, marriage, and fertility and that of the peoples surrounding them in the ancient Near East? Does that distinction make any contribution to the mythology you hold about those same realities?

2. If you believed that sexuality and marriage were gifts of God, would that be enough for you to say that they related you to God? If you believed they were gifts of God, would that be enough for you to say that they were sacramental? If yes, in what sense?

3. Do you look upon marriage as sacramental? What does *sacramental* mean to you?

4. The two great commandments in Judaism and Christianity prescribe the love of God and the love of neighbor. According to the letter to the Ephesians, how are these commandments to be lived in a Christian marriage?

5. What does it mean to you to say that a man and a woman become one body in marriage? Do you understand their one-body relationship to be a legal or a kind of blood relationship? If it were a kind of blood relationship, how would you go about getting a divorce?

NOTES

1. For more detailed information see M. Eliade, *Patterns in Comparative Religion* (London: Sheed and Ward, 1979); E. O. James, *The Cult of the Mother-Goddess* (London: Thames and Hudson, 1959).

2. E. Schillebeeckx, *Marriage: Secular Reality and Saving Mystery*, Vol. 1 (London: Sheed and Ward, 1965), 39.

3. F. R. Barry, *A Philosophy from Prison* (London: SCM, 1926), 151. Cp. Schillebeeckx, *Marriage*, 43; Markus Barth, *Ephesians: Translation and Commentary on Chapters Four to Six. The Anchor Bible* (New York: Doubleday, 1974), 734–738; X. Leon—Dufour (ed.), *Vocabulaire de Theologie Biblique*, 2nd ed. rev. (Paris: Cerf, 1970), 146–152.

4. See Richard Batey, "The *mid sarx* Union of Christ and the Church," *New Testament Studies* 13 (1966–67), 272.

5. For a discussion of whether the term *myth* should be applied to any biblical passage, and for a suggestion of alternative language, see John McKenzie, "Myth and the Old Testament," CBQ 21 (1959), 265–282.

6. William L. Moran, "The Ancient Near Eastern Background of the Love of God in Deuteronomy," CBQ 25 (1963), 82.

7. Bruce J. Malina, *The Testament World: Insights from Cultural Anthropology* (Atlanta: John Konox, 1981), 110.

8. It is of no interest to any thesis in this book whether the Apostle Paul was or was not the author of Ephesians, and so I do not deal with that disputed question, referring only to *the writer*. Those who require information on the question may consult any of the modern commentaries.

9. Markus Barth, *Ephesians*, 607.

10. *The Jerusalem Bible* (London: Darton, Longman and Todd, 1966).

11. *The Holy Bible: Revised Standard Version* (London: Nelson, 1959).

12. Barth, *Ephesians*, 609.

13. Heinrich Schlier, *Der Brief an die Epheser* (Düsseldorf: Patmos, 1962), 252.

14. J. Paul Sampley, *And the Two Shall Become One Flesh: A Study of Traditions in Ephesians 5:21–33* (Cambridge: Cambridge University Press, 1971), 119–121.

15. Barth, *Ephesians*, 607.

16. Ibid., 618.

17. Cf. Sampley, *Two Shall Become One Flesh*, 33.

18. Cf. Ibid., 30. See 30–34; cp. Barth, *Ephesians*, 704–708.

19. Theodore Mackin, *What Is Marriage?* (New York: Paulist, 1982), 56.

20. Cited in Paul F. Palmer, "Christian Marriage: Contract or Covenant?" TS 33 (1972): 647–648.

CHAPTER 2

The Primitive Christian Understanding of Marriage

Theodore Mackin, S.J.

Most people understand marriage only within the customs of their own day and are thus unable to consider the arbitrariness of many marriage customs. Thus, our own socially determined customs take on a kind of sacredness unable to be questioned. Theodore Mackin's description of the Jewish marriage customs of Jesus' day helps us see how differently various societies can go about the tasks and duties of marriage. Even more important, this account helps us understand the way Jesus himself would have thought of marriage and then suggests how unusual his contemporaries would have found the fact that he himself did not marry.

The specific roles of women and men in marriage, the role of families in determining whom one would marry, and the centrality of having children are all matters that make the following essay fascinating. This essay could open up discussion of the subtle ways some of these ideas, attitudes, and customs are still with us in a time when they seem so foreign.

Further Reading

In Mackin's book, *What Is Marriage?*, readers will find an equally fascinating description of a later period: "Christian Marriage in the Roman Empire," pp. 67–79.

S ince it is accurate enough to date the establishing of the community of Jesus' followers as a church within the decade 27–37 A.D., we may put the end of the second Christian generation at the turn of the first century. By that time two major traditions, the Jewish and the Hellenistic-Roman, had formed the character of early Christian life in community. By the end of these sixty years the confluence of these two traditions in Christianity was complete. Each had had time to make its contribution to Christian life in full strength. Each had conditioned the other. And even though the first communities of Jesus' followers in Palestine had been destroyed, or at least dispersed, during the devastation of Judea and the siege of Jerusalem by the Roman army under Vespasian and then Titus in 68–70, the Jewish influence continued past that date because the first Christian communities outside Palestine had been formed mainly from the synagogue communities scattered around the eastern half of the empire. Consequently, though the Hellenistic-Roman character eventually overwhelmed at least Jewish custom as the Jewish portion of the Christian population dwindled, the Jewish vision of marriage left its effect in the early Christian consciousness. It is this vision that we must seek to understand first.

PALESTINIAN JEWISH MARRIAGE CUSTOM

Among Jesus' people marriage was regarded as obligatory. The male who had reached eighteen years but had not yet married could be compelled by a court to do so. While girls, as also boys, could not be married before puberty, the former were ordinarily married as soon as they reached it, which was set at twelve years and six months. Thirteen was the earliest age at which a boy might marry. These early ages for marrying hint clearly at the meaning of Jewish marriage in Palestine at that time. It was for family decisively and in multiple ways. The principal motive for marrying was to provide children so as to preserve the husband's family, to keep his and his father's name from dying out, to keep the tribe, the nation itself as the people of God in existence— withal to honor the ancient covenant commitment with Yahweh to be a light to the nations. Since infant mortality was high and life-expectancy low even for those who survived until adulthood, it was important that the childbearer marry at the onset of puberty so as to bear as many children as possible.

Hesitant belief in personal survival beyond death reinforced this tradition. If a man had no heirs, even if he had daughters but no sons, he risked having his name die out; the memory of him might vanish and be lost to his people forever and in every way. Hence marriage was before all else what Christian tradition would later call an *officium*, a dutiful vocation, a vocation motivated by *pietas*, loyal loving concern for one's parents and one's people. The Jewish people itself had already been given and had accepted the *officium* mentioned earlier, to be a light to the nations. Obviously it could be faithful to this vocation only if its sons and daughters bore and nurtured children.

The Jewish people of Jesus' time were not a defining people in the Western sense of assigning an entity to generic and specific categories of existence. But if one were to ask in terms of these categories about the essence of marriage among this people, no more exact answer could be given than that it was an abiding relationship between a man and a woman intended mainly although not exclusively for children.

Although the negotiations between the two families to settle the dowry and the *mohar* (the bride-price given by the husband-to-be to the girl's father) were contractual in form, the marriage itself was not thought of as a contract. For one thing an element essential to a contract was missing. The mutual consent by the contracting parties themselves to the exchange of a contractual good was deemed ated their children's marriages; the wills of the fathers held good for those of their children. The latters' marital consent was more an obedient acceptance of the partners chosen for them, although loving parents took their children's desires into consideration, especially if the desire were against the tentatively chosen partner. Thus the marriage was a covenant between two families. It was made orally by the parents, but by Jesus' time the covenant was confirmed legally in writing.

The preferred source wherein to search for spouses for one's children was one's own relatives, within those forms and degrees of kindred permitted marriage by Torah and the traditions of the fathers. Marriage between uncle and niece was not uncommon; the girl's father found a husband for her among his own brothers. Marriage of cousins was common. This marrying within the family gained two understandable advantages. One could be less uncertain about the quality of a spouse in the uncertain human enterprise of marrying. And there was less likelihood of divorce if a dissatisfied husband had to answer to his brother for dismissing the latter's daughter from his house. And if she did fall victim to divorce, there was considerable comfort for her in having to fall back only to a family she had never really left.

When the girl married she became a member of her husband's family. Since he owed obedience to his father as long as the latter lived, so too did his wife. She became in effect her father-in-law's newest daughter. Often enough the newly married pair, especially if they were quite young, lived in the paternal household. When they did, the young wife took her place as an added daughter in the household managed by her mother-in-law under her father-in-law's authority.

THE RELIGIOUS REALITY OF JEWISH MARRIAGE

Was this marriage a religious reality or was it secular? The question would have been meaningless for a Jew of Jesus' time, for he simply recognized no division in life between these two realms. All of life for him was religious because all the world came from the hand of God. Getting married was one form of faithful response to God's covenant invitation to his people Israel. Marriage in turn was God's gift to men and women as part of his creation. According to the creation poem of Genesis his work of creating came to its climax in the sexually differentiated pair who were given the *officium* of using their sexuality in order to populate the earth and rule it. According to the Genesis parable of the garden the sexually different and therefore desirable creature, the woman, was given to the man as God's gift to him to relieve his loneliness. He made them two and sexually different expressly so that they could become one—even "one flesh," one person before God and the people. The sexual uniting was holy because it was God's creation and given as his gift. Yet it was of this world and worldly, not sacred in the sense of the ancient fertility cults' sexuality interpreted as participation in genital activity of the gods. It was not sacred precisely because it was created and therefore creaturely in substance. It was created by a supra-sexual deity, therefore by one who could not be imitated sexually and in this way bribed by sexually magic ritual.

Because in the parable of the garden God "brought the woman to him" (the man) as a gift to relieve his loneliness, marriage at least in this ancient tradition could only with difficulty be constructed as a contract. An added difficulty against this was the fact that the most excellent religious model for the husband-wife relationship proposed by the prophetic tradition could hardly be contractual. This was the husband-bride relationship of God to Israel pictured by the prophets Hosea (1:1–3:35), Jeremiah (2:1–2), and Ezekiel (16). Common acceptance of this religious metaphor as a normative model, where it was done, overweighed the husband's authority in the marriage severely. The model presumed the wife's infidelity and need to be disciplined; it gave the husband a divine warrant to discipline her. But for this reason alone the model blocked the possibility of seeing Jewish marriages as contracts. As the bride Israel could not negotiate with God, could not in justice hold him to contractual conditions, neither could the Jewish wife with her husband. She could expect and demand that he care for her, protect her, forgive her, but none of these as obligations in justice. As God had promised these to Israel only out of love and in sovereign freedom, so, according to this model, the wife could expect these from her husband only as a gift of his love freely given.

I have said that the marriage itself was not understood as a contract, and that where this prophetic model was in the forefront of awareness, any temptation to understand a marriage contractually was suppressed. But given the contractual nature of the marriage arrangements, especially as these were detailed in the *ketuba,* the inclination to think of the relationship as contractual must have been strong. But since the pre-marital agreement had been struck not between the spouses but between the families, the inclination was to think of these as the contractors.

The solemnization of the Jewish marriage was, in the senses I have explained above, both religious and nonsacral. The *kiddushin,* the year-long trial period (literally "the sanctification"), was sealed and begun with the handing over of the *mohar* to the bride's father. The boy and girl were dedicated to one another and held to sexual fidelity. The bride's intercourse with a third person during that year, but only hers, was considered adultery. In the northern Israel the two were forbidden intercourse with one another until after the wedding feast. In the south, in Judea, betrothal and marriage were in effect the same in permitting intercourse.

The wedding feast lasted a week. All of it was deemed religious, as I have said, but the core of the "liturgical" part of the celebration was a series of seven benedictions read by the father of the groom. No part of the feast took place in either temple or synagogue. No priest, levite or rabbi had a part in it as an exercise of his office. It was a family affair, supervised and conducted by parents. It was private in that sense but thoroughly public in the sense that the entire village might join in the celebration. Since the groom's father presided over the celebration, it ordinarily took place in his home. The bride's father gave her away, and the groom's father took her for his son. The ceremony ended and climaxed with the groom's leading his bride in procession to his home. If he was quite young, this would be his parents' home.

Joachim Jeremias supplies more detail when describing the condition of women and wives in Jesus' time:

> The wife's first *duties* were household duties. She had to grind meal, bake, wash, cook, suckle the children, prepare her husband's bed and, as repayment for her keep . . . to work the wool by spinning and weaving. . . . Other duties were that of preparing her husband's cup, and of washing his face, hands and feet. . . . These duties express her servile relationship with her husband; but his rights over her went even further. He laid claim to anything his wife found . . . as well as any earnings from her manual work, and he had the right . . . to annul her vows. . . . The wife was obliged to obey her husband as she would a master—the husband was called *rab*—indeed this obedience was a religious duty. . . . This duty of obedience went so far that the husband could force a vow upon his wife, but any vows which put the wife in a discreditable position gave her the right to demand divorce before the court. . . . Relationships between children and parents were also determined by the woman's duty of obedience to her husband; the children had to put respect for their father before respect for their mother, for she was obliged to give a similar respect to the father of her children. . . .
>
> Two facts are particularly significant of the degree of the wife's dependence on her husband:
>
> (a) Polygamy was permissible; the wife had therefore to tolerate concubines living with her. Of course, we must add that for economic reasons the possession of several wives was not very frequent. Mostly we hear of a husband taking a second wife if there was dissension with the first, but because of the high price fixed in the marriage contract, he could not afford to divorce her. . . .
>
> (b) The right to divorce was exclusively the husband's. . . . In Jesus' time (Matt. 19:3) the Shammaites and Hillelites were in dispute over the exegesis of Deut. 24:1, which gives, as a reason for a man divorcing his wife, a case where he finds in her "some unseemly thing," *'erwat dabar*. The Shammaites' exegesis was in accord with the meaning of the phrase, but the Hillelites explained it as, first, the wife's unchastity' (*'erwat*) and, secondly, something (*dabar*) displeasing to the husband; either gave him the right to put away his wife. . . . In this way the Hillelite view made the unilateral right of divorce entirely dependent on the husband's caprice. From Philo (*De spec. leg.* III, 30) and from Josephus (*Ant.* 4.253), both of whom knew only the Hillelite point of view and championed it, it appears that this must already have been the prevailing view in the first half of the first century A.D. However, reunion of the separated parties could take place; also by reason of divorce there was a public stigma on the husband as well as on the wife and daughters . . . ; then, too, when he divorced his wife, the husband had to give her the sum of money prescribed in the marriage contract; so in practice these last two facts must often have been obstacles to any hasty divorce of his wife. As for his

wife, she could occasionally take things into her own hands and go back to her father's house, e.g., in the case of injury received. . . . But in spite of all this, the Hillelite view represented a considerable degradation of women.

. . . to have children, particularly sons, was extremely important for a woman. The absence of children was considered a great misfortune, even a divine punishment. . . . As the mother of a son the wife was respected; she had given her husband the most precious gift of all.

As a widow too a woman was still bound to her husband, that is, if he died without leaving a son. . . . In this case she had to wait, unable to make any move on her side, until the brother or brothers of her dead husband should contract a levirate marriage with her or publish a refusal to do so; without this refusal she could not remarry.

The conditions we have just described were also reflected in the prescriptions of religious legislation of the period. So from a *religious* point of view too, especially with regard to the Torah, a woman was inferior to a man. She was subject to all the *prohibitions* of the Torah (except for the three concerning only men . . .), and to the whole force of civil and penal legislation, including the penalty of death. . . . However as to the *commandments* of the Torah, here is what was said: "The observance of all the positive ordinances that depend on the time of the year is incumbent on men but not on women."

As a woman's religious *duties* were limited, so were her religious *rights*. According to Josephus, women could go no further in the Temple than into the Courts of the Gentiles and of the Women. . . . During the time of their monthly purification, and also for forty days after the birth of a son . . . and eighty days after the birth of a daughter . . . they were not allowed even into the Court of Gentiles. . . . By virtue of Deut. 31:12 women, like men and children, could participate in the synagogue service . . . but barriers of lattice separated the women's section. . . . In the liturgical service, women were there simply to listen . . . Women were forbidden to teach. . . . In the house, the wife was not reckoned among the number of persons summoned to pronounce a benediction after a meal. . . . Finally we must record that a woman had no right to bear witness, because it was concluded from Gen. 18:15 that she was a liar. Her witness was acceptable only in a few very exceptional cases, and that of a Gentile slave was also acceptable in the same cases . . . e.g., on the remarriage of a widow, the witness of a woman as to the death of the husband was accepted.

On the whole, the position of women in religious legislation is best expressed in the constantly repeated formula: "Women, (Gentile) slaves and children (minors)." . . . like a non-Jewish slave and a child under age, a woman has over her a man who is her master . . . and this likewise limits her participation in divine service, which is why from a religious point of view she is inferior to a man.

From a distance of nineteen and a half centuries it is impossible to know with certainty how much this subservant condition of wives in Jesus' time among his people was due simply to the customs of a patriarchal culture, and how much was the consequence of husbands' asserting the lordship they had found granted them in Genesis 3:16b. No doubt the two causes converged and reinforced one another; custom and inclination were justified by what was taken to be a divine decree. And insofar as the decree was understood to be a warrant to punish, the punishment was thought in turn to be for the violation of a covenant. That the violation was also thought to have the first husband's manipulable need as one of its contributing causes could not have diminished the inclination to punish.

CHAPTER 3

Marriage in the Western Churches

Joseph Martos

⌦⌦

The history of marriage in the Christian church is as complicated as it is important. Marriage was influenced by shifts in society, in philosophy, in theology, and in church organization. Joseph Martos's detailed examination of this history is worth careful study for the light it sheds on the questions religious people still ask about marriage today. Martos shows us where certain ways of thinking about marriage came from, helping us reflect on them in the light of these origins.

"Marriage in the Western Churches" explains the gradual shift from secular to ecclesiastically governed marriages. In part, the conflict between Roman and Germanic marriage traditions led to more church control. As differing understandings of what constituted a marriage had to be resolved, so did various understandings of what the sacrament of marriage meant. These matters were settled only to an extent, since we find these controversies still with us today. Understanding these origins helps us reexamine marriage today.

There developed in Christian churches two church traditions regarding marriage. The one we will consider here developed not in the East but in the western half of the Roman Empire, and it developed along quite different lines from the Eastern tradition.

Initially in the West, as in the East, marriage between Christians involved no distinct wedding ceremony. A Christian marriage was simply one that was contracted between two Christians by their mutual consent and lived "in the Lord." In the fourth century, however, once Christians could practice their religion openly, bishops and priests were sometimes invited to wedding feasts and to bestow their blessing on the newly wedded couple after the family marriage ceremonies were concluded. Sometimes this blessing was given instead during a eucharistic liturgy a day or more after the wedding itself. As in the East, the priest's blessing was usually given as a favor to the family or as a sign of his approval on the marriage; it was not a standard or universal practice. In some places the bishop or priest occasionally participated in the wedding ceremony itself by draping a veil over the newly united couple, a custom that was parallel to the practice of garlanding in the East. Bishop Ambrose of Milan even insisted that "marriage should be sanctified by the priestly veil and blessing" (*Letters* 19), but there is no other evidence that the veiling was ordinarily done by a cleric during this period.

Shortly before the end of the fourth century, however, Pope Siricius ordered that all clerics under his jurisdiction must henceforth have their marriages solemnized by a priest, and Innocent I at the beginning of the next century issued another decree to the same effect. Around the year 400, then, the only Christians who had to receive an ecclesiastical blessing on their marriage were priests and deacons.

AMBROSE AND AUGUSTINE

Ambrose was also the first Christian churchman to write that no marriage should be dissolved for any reason, and to insist that not even men had the right to remarry as long as their wives were alive. "You dismiss your wife as though you had a right to do this because the human law does not forbid it. But the law of God does forbid it. You should be standing in fear of God, but instead you obey human rulers. Listen to the word of God, whom those who make the laws are supposed to obey: 'What God has joined together, let no man put asunder'" (*Commentary on Luke* VIII, 5). Ambrose would not even allow divorce and remarriage in the case of adultery. And his firm stand on the permanence of marriage was taken up by one of his converts to Christianity, Augustine, later the bishop of Hippo in North Africa and one of the greatest influences on the early schoolmen in the Middle Ages.

Augustine's attitude toward marriage was an ambivalent one. On the one hand he viewed it as a beneficial social institution, necessary for the preservation of society and the continuation of the human race, and sanctioned by God since the creation of the first man and woman. On the other hand he saw sexual desire as a dangerous and destructive human energy that could tear society apart if it were not kept within bounds. As a young man he had had two mistresses and a child by one of them, but he had also been attracted by the moral asceticism of the Manichean religion, to which he had belonged for a time. He was the first and only patristic author to write extensively about sex and marriage, and in the end he affirmed that marriage was good even though sex was not.

That attitude was common among the intellectuals of his day. The stoic philosophers taught that strong impulses should be controlled in order to have peace of soul and harmony in society and that the only justification for intercourse was to produce offspring. The Manicheans and other Gnostics were often sexual puritans, condemning sensuality as evil and even forbidding marriage among the devout members of their sects. Christian ascetics like the hermits and monks of the desert sought to quench the desires of the flesh in order to free their minds for prayer and mediation. A number of the fathers of the church, including Gregory of Nyssa and John Chrysostom, taught that intercourse and childbearing were the result of Adam and Eve's fall from grace, and that if they had not sinned God would have populated earth in some other way. Virginity for both men and women was exulted as the way of perfection for those who sought first the kingdom of God and wished to devote themselves to the things of the Lord. In Augustine's mind sexual desire was evil, a result of original sin, so those who gave in to it cooperated with evil and committed a further sin, even in marriage: "A man who is too ardent a lover of his wife is an adulterer, if the pleasure he finds in her is sought for its own sake" (*Against Julian* II, 7).

According to Augustine, therefore, only those who remained unmarried could successfully avoid the sin that almost always accompanied the use of sex. Those who were married usually committed at least slight sin when they engaged in sexual intercourse, but they could be excused as they did it for the right reason. "Those who use the shameful sex appetite in a legitimate way make good use of evil, but those who use it in other ways make evil use of evil" (*On Marriage and Concupiscence* II, 21). And for Augustine, as for the stoics, the only fully legitimate reason for having sexual relations was to produce children.

Children were thus the first of the good things in marriage that counterbalanced the necessary use of sex. Another was the faithfulness that it fostered between a man and a woman, so that they did not seek sex for pleasure with other partners. These two benefits could even be found in pagan marriages, said Augustine, but Christians also received that benefit that was mentioned by Paul in one of his epistles: it was a sacred sign, a *sacramentum*, of the union between Christ and the church. Augustine read the New Testament in Latin, not Greek, and in Ephesians 5:32 Paul's word *mysterion* had been translated into Latin as *sacramentum*. Augustine took it to mean that marriage was a visible sign of the invisible union between Christ and his spouse, the church. But he also saw a deeper meaning in the word by understanding it in the sense that a soldier's pledge of loyalty was called a sacramentum. It was a sacred pledge of fidelity. In this sense it was something similar to the sacramental character that Christians received in baptism. Just as baptism formed the soul in the image of Christ's death and resurrection, so marriage formed the soul in the image of Christ's fidelity to the church; and just as Christians could not be rebaptized and receive another image of Christ, so spouses could not remarry and receive another image of his fidelity. The sacramentum of marriage was therefore not only a sacred sign of a divine reality but it was also a sacred bond between the husband and wife. And like the sacramentum of baptism it was something permanent, or nearly so: "The marriage bond is dissolved only by the death of one of the partners" (*On the Good of Marriage* 24).

It was this invisible sacramentum, argued Augustine, that reminded Christians that they should be faithful even to a partner who was not. Marriage between Christians therefore should not be disrupted even in the case of adultery; instead, like the prophet Hosea in the Old Testament, Christians should try to win back their erring spouses. If it happened that the visible sign of this union was broken by their being separated, they still had no right to remarry, for the invisible sign of their union, the bond that was formed in the image of Christ's union with the church, remained. And if they did take another partner while their first spouse was still living, the sacramentum of their first marriage marked them as adulterers.

Augustine presented a strong theological case for the prohibition of divorce and remarriage, and the council of Carthage that he attended in 407 reflected his position by forbidding divorced men as well as divorced women to remarry. It would be some centuries, however, before the Latin church would turn to Augustine's writings to justify an absolute prohibition against remarriage by either spouse while the other remained alive.

Jerome, a scripture scholar and contemporary of Augustine, spoke out strongly against remarriage after divorce, but he spoke out much more strongly in the case of women than men. He took Christ's words in the Bible as an absolute prohibition for women: "A husband may commit adultery and sodomy, he may be stained with every conceivable crime, and his wife may even have left him because of his vices. Yet he is still her husband, and she may not remarry anyone else as long as he lives" (*Letters* 55). But for men who had divorced unfaithful wives he had a different warning: "If you have been made miserable by your first marriage, why do you expose yourself to the peril of a new one?" (*Commentary on Matthew* 19). He even insisted on scriptural grounds that a man should not continue to live with an adulterous woman, although he was equally insistent that nothing but adultery was a valid reason for separation.

In the opinion of Innocent I, those who divorced by mutual consent as the civil law allowed were both adulterers if they remarried, regardless if they were men or women. He was equally clear in affirming that a woman who had been legally dismissed for adultery could not remarry as long as her husband was alive, but he apparently held that a husband in that case could remarry. Around the year 415 he wrote to a Roman magistrate about a woman who had been carried off by barbarian invaders sometime before and had returned later, only to find her husband remarried. Claiming to be his rightful wife, she appealed to her bishop and Innocent agreed with her: "The arrangement with the second woman cannot be legitimate since the first wife is still alive and she was never dismissed by means of a divorce" (*Letters* 36). Presumably if her husband had divorced her (since women in captivity were usually violated), Innocent would have considered the second marriage legitimate.

Later in the century bishops began to get even more involved in marriage cases as the Germanic invasions led to a breakdown of Roman civil authority. The council of Vannes in France decided that husbands who left their wives and remarried without providing proof of adultery should be barred from communion. And a similar council at Adge in 506 imposed the same penalty on men who failed to justify their divorce before an ecclesiastical court before they remarried. At the close of the patristic period in the West, then, Christian bishops were becoming legally involved with marriage, and there was still no universally recognized prohibition against divorce and remarriage for both sexes. And apart from Augustine, no one spoke of marriage as a sacrament.

FROM SECULAR TO ECCLESIASTICAL MARRIAGE

With the coming of the Dark Ages in Europe after the fall of the Roman Empire, churchmen were called upon more and more to decide marriage cases. Centuries before, Constantine had given them authority to act as judges in certain civil matters, and now that authority grew as the regular judicial system collapsed. Bishops also began to issue canonical regulations about persons who should not marry because they were too closely related. Initially the churchmen simply adopted the prevailing Roman customs, although they sometimes added prohibitions that were found in the Old Testament. Later they incorporated the customs of the invading Germanic peoples into the church's laws. These customs varied somewhat from tribe to tribe, but generally speaking persons who were more closely related than the seventh degree of kinship (for example, second cousins) were not allowed to marry legally.

Moreover, just as the bishops had earlier accepted Roman wedding customs, so they now also accepted the marriage practices of the Germanic peoples who settled within the old Roman provinces. Again these varied from tribe to tribe, although they, too, followed a general cultural pattern. Marriages were basically property arrangements by which a man purchased a wife from her father or some other family guardian to be his wife. The arrangement involved a mutual exchange of gifts, spoken and sometimes written agreements between the groom and the bride's guardian. In many places brides were betrothed ahead of time in return for a token of earnestness such as a small sum of money or a ring from the prospective husband, which would be forfeited if the marriage did not take place as agreed. On the wedding day the guardian handed over the woman and her dowry of personal possessions to her new husband, and received the bride-price as compensation for the loss her family incurred by allowing her to leave it. After the wedding feast that was celebrated by the relatives and other witnesses to the marriage, the bride and groom entered a specially prepared wedding chamber for their first act of intercourse, which formally sealed the arrangement.

Throughout this early period, then, marriage was still a family matter similar to what it had been in the Roman Empire, and the clergy was not involved in wedding ceremonies except as guests. Bishops in their sermons and letters tried to impress their people with the Christian ideal of marriage found in the New Testament, and they sometimes urged them to have their marriages blessed by the clergy, but again this blessing was not essential to the marriage itself. In some places it was given during the wedding feast, in others it was a blessing of the wedding chamber, and in others it was a blessing during a mass after the wedding. Some bishops in southern Europe also suggested that the Roman custom of veiling the bridal couple should be done by a priest, but it was not a very common practice.

Just as churchmen were not officially involved in weddings, so also they were not officially involved in divorces when they occurred. However, some divorces ran counter to accepted Christian practices, and when they occurred those who were responsible for them had to confess their sin and do penance for it. The penitential books from the early Middle Ages show that divorce was more accepted in some places than others, but almost all allowed husbands to dismiss unfaithful wives and marry again. An Irish penitential book written in the seventh century instructed that if one spouse allowed the other to enter the service of God in a monastery or convent, he or she was free to remarry. The penitential of Theodore, archbishop of Canterbury in the same century, gave the following prescriptions: a husband could divorce an adulterous wife and marry again; the wife in that case could remarry after doing penance for five years; a man who was deserted by his wife could remarry after two years, provided he had his bishop's consent; a woman whose husband was imprisoned for a serious crime could remarry, but again only with the bishop's consent; a man whose wife was abducted by an enemy could remarry, and if she later returned she could also remarry; freed slaves who could not purchase either spouse's freedom were allowed to marry free persons. Other penitential books on the continent contained similar provisions.

The penitential books contained only unofficial guidelines to be followed in the administration of private penance, but conciliar and other church documents contained more official regulations. Again, these were not uniform, and ecclesiastical practices during this period ranged from extreme strictness to extreme laxness, but at least they show that there was no universal prohibition against divorce. In Spain the third and fourth councils of Toledo in 589 and 633 invoked the "Pauline privilege" in allowing Christian converts from Judaism to remarry. Irish councils in the seventh century allowed husbands of unfaithful wives to remarry, and although the council of Hereford in England advised against remarriage it did not forbid it. In eighth-century France the council of Compiègne allowed men whose wives committed adultery to remarry, and it allowed women whose husbands contracted leprosy to remarry with their husband's consent. In 752 the council of Verberie enacted legislation that allowed both men and women to remarry if their spouses committed adultery with a relative, and it prohibited those who committed the sin from marrying each other or anyone else. It also permitted a man to divorce and remarry if his wife plotted to kill him, or if he had to leave his homeland permanently and his wife refused to go with him. Pope Gregory II in 726 advised Boniface, the missionary bishop to Germany, that if a wife were too sick to perform her wifely duty it was best that her husband practice continence, but if this was impossible he might have another wife, provided that he took care of the first one. Boniface himself recognized desertion as grounds for divorce, as well as adultery and entrance into a convent or monastery. Other popes of the period, however, protested against what they considered to be unlawful divorces, and the Italian council of Friuli in 791 strictly forbade divorced men to remarry even if their wives had been unfaithful.

One reason why churchmen became involved in marriage and divorce cases, especially after the popes started sending missionaries into northern Europe, was the difference between Roman and Germanic marriage customs. According to Roman tradition marriage was by consent, and after the consent was given by either the spouses or their guardians the marriage was considered legal and binding. In the Frankish and Germanic tradition, however, the giving of consent came at the betrothal, and the marriage was not considered to be completed or consummated until the first act of intercourse had taken place. Moreover, it was customary for parents to consent to the marriage of their children months and even years before they would begin to live together as husband and wife. This was particularly prevalent among the nobility, who often arranged such marriages as a means of securing allies or settling territorial disputes between them. But it sometimes happened that one of the betrothed spouses would undermine the parental arrangement by marrying someone else before the arranged marriage could be consummated. Bishops who were asked to settle these and similar cases could follow either the Roman or the Germanic tradition in coming to their decision. Under Roman law the arranged marriage was the binding one and the subsequent marriage was adultery, but according to Germanic custom the arrangement between the parents was only a nonbinding betrothal and the second marriage was the real one. Even before any marriage was arranged young people might consent to marry and then claim that they were not free to marry the partners their parents picked out for them, whereupon the parents might appeal to the episcopal court for a decision. In still other cases people sought to rid themselves of unwanted spouses by claiming that they had secretly contracted a previous marriage, which would make their present marriage unlawful. The legal question that had to be decided in each case was: which marriage was the real marriage? And underlying the practical matters was the more theoretical question: are marriages ratified by consent or by intercourse? For a long time there was no uniform answer to that theoretical question, and both episcopal and royal courts decided the practical matters according to which tradition they were accustomed to follow.

As Charlemagne initiated legal reforms in his European empire, both church and civil governments made an effort to impose stricter standards for marriage. Late in the eighth century the regional council of Verneuil decreed that both nobles and commoners should have public weddings, and a similar council in Bavaria instructed priests to make sure that people who wanted to marry were legally free to do so. In 802 Charlemagne himself passed a law requiring all proposed marriages to be examined for legal restrictions (such as previous marriages or close family relationships) before the wedding could take place. When the false decretals of Isidore were "discovered" in the middle of the ninth century, they contained documents purportedly from the patristic period aimed against the practice of secret marriage. A decree attributed to Pope Evaristus in the second century read, "A legitimate marriage cannot take place unless the woman's legal guardians are asked for their consent, . . . and only if the priest gives her the customary blessing in connection with the prayers and offering of the mass." Another decree represented the third-century pope Calixtus as saying that a marriage was legal only if it was blessed by a priest and the bride-price was paid. The proponents of reform in the Frankish Empire used these spurious documents to support their efforts to outlaw secret marriages, and they were partially successful. Laws were passed making marriages legal only if guardians gave their consent and were present at the wedding.

In the meanwhile, however, Rome continued to follow its own tradition. In 866 Pope Nicholas I sent a letter to missionaries in the Balkans who had asked about the Greek church's contention that Christian marriages were not valid unless they were performed and blessed by a priest. In his reply Nicholas described the wedding customs that had become prevalent in Rome: the wedding ceremony took place in the absence of any church authorities and consisted primarily in the exchange of consent between the partners; afterward there was a special mass at which the bride and groom were covered with a veil and given a nuptial blessing. In Nicholas's opinion, however, a marriage was legal and binding even without any public or liturgical ceremony: "If anyone's marriage is in question, all that is needed is that they gave their consent, as the law demands. If this consent is lacking in a marriage then all the other celebrations count for nothing, even if intercourse has occurred" (*Letters* 97). According to Rome, then, it was the couple's consent, not their betrothal by their parents or their blessing by a priest, that legally established the marriage.

Charlemagne had wanted Roman practices to become normative in his empire, and in the years that followed, a Roman-style nuptial liturgy sometimes began to be included in the festivities that followed a wedding, though it was never very prevalent. Moreover, the pope's insistence that only consent constituted a marriage was initially ignored or largely unknown in the rest of Europe. Hincmar, the bishop of Rheims during this period, decided a number of marriage and divorce cases among the Frankish nobility, and he generally followed the opinion of the false decretals that legal marriages had to be publicly contracted. He also followed the Germanic tradition in ruling that marriages had to be consummated by sexual intercourse, and he allowed that people who had been given in marriage but who had not yet lived together could be legally divorced.

For a while, divorce regulations in northern Europe became more stringent under the impetus of ecclesiastical reform. As early as 829 a council of bishops at Paris decreed that divorced persons of both sexes could not remarry even if the divorce had been granted for adultery. By the end of the century a number of other councils in France and Germany passed similar prohibitions, and the penitential books were revised accordingly. But at the same time in Italy, popes and local councils continued to allow divorce and remarriage in certain circumstances, especially adultery and entering the religious life. Then in the next two centuries the trend in northern Europe reversed itself, and councils at Bourges, Worms, and Tours again allowed remarriages in cases of adultery and desertion.

During this same period, moreover, ecclesiastical courts were slowly gaining exclusive jurisdiction over marriage and divorce cases. As Charlemagne's short-lived empire dissolved into a disunited array of local principalities, more and more marriage cases were appealed to church tribunals. Eventually the secular courts came to be bypassed altogether, and by the year 1000 all marriages in Europe effectively came under the jurisdictional power of the church.

CHURCH CONTROL OF MARRIAGE CEREMONY

There was as yet no obligatory church ceremony connected with marriage, but in the eleventh century this began to change. In order to ensure that marriages took place legally and in front of witnesses, bishops invoked the texts of Popes Evaristus and Calixtus in the false decretals to demand that all weddings be solemnly blessed by a priest. It gradually became customary to hold weddings near a church, so that the newly married couple could go inside immediately afterward to obtain the priest's blessing. Eventually this developed into a wedding ceremony that was performed at the church door and was followed by a nuptial mass inside the church during which the marriage was blessed. At the beginning of this development the clergy was present at the ceremony only as official witnesses and to give the required blessing, but as the years progressed priests began to assume some of the functions once relegated to the guardians and the spouses themselves, and many of the once secular customs in the wedding ceremony became part of an ecclesiastical wedding ritual.

By the twelfth century in various parts of Europe there was an established church wedding ceremony that was conducted entirely by the clergy, and although there were numerous local variations it generally conformed to the following pattern. At the entrance to the church the priest asked the bride and groom if they consented to the marriage. The father of the bride then handed his daughter to the groom and gave him her dowry, although in many places the priest performed this function instead. The priest then blessed the ring, which was given to the bride, after which he gave his blessing to the marriage. During the nuptial mass in the church itself the bride was veiled and blessed, after which the priest gave the husband the ritual kiss of peace, who passed it to this wife. In some places the priest also pronounced an additional blessing over the wedding chamber after the day's festivities had concluded.

Along with the church's liturgical and legal involvement in marriage came a growing body of ecclesiastical laws about premarriage kinship, the wedding ceremony itself, and the social consequences of marriage and divorce. The medieval system of government and inheritance emphasized property rights and blood relationships arising from marriage, making it important for ecclesiastical judges to know who was legally free to marry, who was married to whom, and who could have their marriage legally dissolved. In the eleventh century the discovery and circulation of the Code of Justinian led to increasing acceptance of the idea that marriage came about by the consent of the partners, and this idea was reflected in the new rituals for church weddings in which the priest asked the bride and groom, not their parents, for their consent to the marriage. But the growth of the consent theory also led to an increase in the number of secret marriages, which brought legal difficulties about the legitimacy of children and their right to inherit their father's property, as well as pastoral difficulties when women and children were deserted by men who claimed they had never intended to establish a marriage.

In response to these difficulties some church lawyers defended a different theory about when a marriage legally took place, based on the old Germanic notion that intercourse was needed to ratify a marriage. As it was taken up and developed by the law faculty at the University of Bologna, this theory proposed that a real marriage did not exist unless and until the couple had sexual relations. But the opposing theory, that consent alone made a marriage, also had its staunch defenders, mainly at the University of Paris.

Around 1140 Francis Gratian published his collection of canonical regulations known as the *Decree* in which he tried to bring some order into the sometimes conflicting decrees and decisions of popes and councils dating from the patristic era. He was aware of the two schools of thought about what constituted a marriage, and he tried to harmonize them by suggesting that the consent of the spouses or their parents (in the case of betrothal) contracted a marriage and that sexual intercourse completed or consummated it. His opinion was that a marriage could be legally dissolved before it was consummated but not afterward, and in this respect he sided with the Bologna school. But he also agreed with the Paris school's contention that a binding marriage could be made in secret, without any public ceremony or priestly blessing. In his opinion such a marriage would be illicit or illegal because it flouted the laws of the church, but it would nonetheless be a real marriage, initiated by consent and consummated by intercourse.

Gratian's work clarified but did not settle the issue. In Italy, for example, church courts continued to dissolve marriages if it could be proven that no sexual relations had taken place, but in France the courts refused to dissolve any marriage once the partners' consent had been given. It was not until later in the twelfth century, when a noted canon lawyer of the period became Pope Alexander III, that a definitive solution was worked out and legislated for the whole Latin church. Because it offered a clearer criterion of an intended marriage between two individuals, Alexander sided with the ancient Roman practice that was defended by the Paris school, and he decreed that the consent given by the two partners themselves was all that was needed for the existence of a real marriage. This consent was viewed as an act of conferring on each other the legal right to marital relations even if they did not occur, and so from the moment of consent there was a true marriage contract between the two partners. In and of itself it was an unbreakable contract, but since the church had jurisdiction over it by the power of the keys, it could also be nullified or annulled by a competent ecclesiastical authority if sexual relations between the spouses had not yet taken place.

The decision of Alexander III became the legal practice of the Catholic Church. It was reinforced by further papal decrees in the thirteenth century and has remained in effect in canon law through the twentieth century. With the exception of the "Pauline privilege" by which non-Christian marriages could be dissolved if one of the spouses converted to Catholicism, henceforward the church would grant no divorces whatever. Henceforward the marriage bond would be considered indissoluble not only as a Christian ideal but also as a rule of law. Henceforward if Catholics wanted to be freed from their spouses they would have to prove that their marriage contact could be nullified, declared to be nonexistent, either for lack of intercourse or for some other canonically acceptable reason.

But the pope's decision and the support it received in subsequent centuries did not rest only on the practical needs of ecclesiastical courts. Rather, the indissolubility of Christian marriage in the mind of Alexander and later churchmen rested also on a firm theological ground, the sacramentality of Christian marriage. For it was precisely around this time—the late twelfth century and the early thirteenth century—that marriage came to be viewed as one of the church's seven official sacraments.

MARRIAGE AS A SACRAMENT

What Francis Gratian did for canon law in his *Decree*, Peter Lombard did for theology in his *Sentences*. Lombard's collection of theological texts did not solve many of the theological problems of the Middle Ages but it did go a long way toward defining what they were and how they should be treated. Marriage was treated in the section on the sacraments, for by this time in mid-twelfth-century France there was an established Christian ritual for marriage that was not unlike the other rituals that Lombard classified as sacramental.

When the book of *Sentences* was first published, however, many theologians still had difficulty in accepting the idea that marriage was a sacrament in the strict sense that was then being developed, and Lombard himself believed that it was different from the other six sacraments in that it was a sign of something sacred but not a cause of grace. One reason for the difficulty was that marriages involved financial arrangements, and if marriage was counted as a sacrament like the others it looked like grace could be bought and sold. Another reason they hesitated to call marriage a sacrament was that it obviously existed before the coming of Christ, and so it could hardly be said to be a purely Christian institution like the other six. But the third reason was the most crucial, and it was that marriage involved sexual intercourse.

Throughout the early Middle Ages most churchmen held virginity in higher esteem than marriage. On the one hand Christians could not deny that God had told Adam and Eve to increase and multiply, and so marriage itself had to be good. But on the other hand marriage, as Paul said, distracted one from the things of the Lord, and he seemed to suggest that people should marry only if they could not quench the fire of sexual desire. So marriage in the Middle Ages was often viewed negatively as a remedy against the desires of the flesh rather than positively as a way to become holy, and those desires themselves were viewed as sinful or at best dangerous. Some bishops who blessed newly married couples recommended that they abstain from intercourse for three days out of respect for the blessing; others told them not to come to church for a month after the wedding, or at least not to come to communion with their bodies and souls still unclean from intercourse. Most writers held that sexual activity motivated by anything but the desire for children was sinful, but most of them also believed that even here children could not be conceived without the stain of carnal pleasure.

So the Western theological tradition through the eleventh century taught that marriage was good even though sexual activity was usually sinful. Three things happened in that century, however, that forced them to reexamine that view. The first was the rise of a religious sect in southern France that, like the Manicheans in the patristic period, taught that matter was evil and so marriage was sinful because it brought new material beings into the world. The Albigensians did not accept the Christian concept of God, they denied the value of church rituals, and their leaders attacked the Catholic clergy as corrupt, so they were first denounced and later burned as heretics. And in combatting the Albigensian view of marriage, Christian writers began to propose more strongly than before that intercourse for the sake of having children was positively good. The second thing that happened during this century was the development of a Christian wedding ritual that, by the presence of the clergy and the blessing they gave, implied that the church officially sanctioned sexual relations in marriage. And the third thing was the rediscovery of the writings of Augustine on marriage in which he developed the idea that marriage was a *sacramentum*. To the early schoolmen it seemed to suggest that marriage was a sacrament in the same way that baptism and the Eucharist were sacraments.

Augustine had taught that marriage was a *sacramentum* in two ways. It was a sign of the union between Christ and his church, and it was also a sacred pledge between Christ and his church, and it was also a sacred pledge between husband and wife, a bond of fidelity between them that could not be dissolved except by death. It was something like a character or imprint on the souls of the spouses that permanently united them, and it was this permanence of their union that symbolized the eternal union of Christ and the church. It seemed to the schoolmen, therefore, that the Christian marriage ritual should be open to the same kind of analysis that they gave to the other sacraments, namely that in marriage there was a sacrament, a sacred sign, a *sacramentum et res*, a sacramental reality, and a *res*, a real grace that was con-

ferred in the rite. It took most of the twelfth century for the scholastics to satisfactorily fit marriage into the scheme, but by the time they did it the
Catholic concept of sacramental marriage had become the theological basis
for the canonical prohibition against divorce.

DEFINING THE SACRAMENT

But what was the sacramental sign in marriage? At the beginning it seemed
to many of the schoolmen that it should be the priest's blessing, since in the
wedding ritual it corresponded to the part that was played by the priest in
the other sacramental rites. Later, others suggested that it should be the physical act of intercourse between the spouses, since this physical union could be
taken as a sign of the spiritual union between the incarnate Christ and his
spouse, the church. Still others felt it should be the spiritual unity of the married couple, since this union of wills was closer to the actual way that Christ
and the church were united with each other. However, each of these suggestions met with difficulties and had to be abandoned. It was objected that the
priest's blessing could not be the sacramental sign because some people were
truly married even though they never received the blessing, for example,
people who married in secret. The schoolmen who still believed that sexual
relations even in marriage were venially sinful objected to intercourse's
being considered the sign because this would paradoxically raise a sinful act
to the dignity of a sacrament. And it was objected that the union of wills in
the married life could not be the sacramental sign because sometimes this
spiritual unity was minimal at the beginning of a marriage and altogether
lacking later on.

Eventually, because of the growing acceptance of the consent theory of the
canon lawyers, the sacramentum in a sacramental marriage came to be viewed
as the consent that the spouses gave to each other at the beginning of their
married life. This mutual consent was something that had to be present in all
canonically valid marriages, even those that were unlawfully contracted in
secret. Both the canonists in Paris and Pope Alexander in Rome insisted that
a real marriage existed from the moment that the consent was given, and theologians such as High of St. Victor argued that a real marriage would have to
be possible even without consummation in intercourse since according to tradition Joseph and the Virgin Mary had been truly married even though they
had never had sexual relations. In addition, locating the sacrament in mutual
consent kept it within the wedding ritual for most Christian marriages, and it
made it possible to look upon the union of wills in a happy marriage life as a
"fruit" of the sacrament even if it was not the sacrament itself.

But the greatest theological consequence of seeing the act of consent as
the sacrament in marriage was that it made it possible to regard the marriage
contract or bond as the *sacramentum et res*. According to canon law the bond
of marriage was a legal reality that came into existence when the two spouses
consented to bind themselves to each other in a marital union. Now, in the-

ology, the bond of marriage could also be understood as a metaphysical reality that existed in the souls of the spouses from the moment that they spoke the words of the sacramental sign. Following the lead of Augustine, the scholastics argued that this metaphysical bond was unbreakable, since it was a sign of the equally unbreakable union between Christ and the church. It was not, as in the early church, that marriage as a sacred reality should not be dissolved; now it was argued that the marriage bond as a sacramental reality could not be dissolved. According to the church fathers the dissolution of marriage was possible but not permissible; according to the schoolmen it was not permissible because it was not possible. Thus the absolute Catholic prohibition against divorce arose in the twelfth century both as a canonical regulation supported by sacramental theory, and as a theological doctrine buttressed by ecclesiastical law. The two came hand in hand.

Even through the beginning of the thirteenth century, however, many theologians found it hard to admit that marriage as a sacrament conferred grace like the other sacraments. The traditional view of marriage was that it was more of a hindrance than a help toward holiness, a remedy for the sin of fornication rather than a means of receiving grace. Many theologians accepted Augustine's idea that original sin was transmitted from one generation to the next through the act of intercourse, and so even sexual relations for the sake of having children were often seen as a mixed blessing. Alexander of Hales was the first medieval theologian to reason that since marriage was a sacrament and since all the sacraments bestowed grace, then marriage must do so as well. But William of Auxerre believed that if any grace came from marriage it must be only a grace to avoid sin, not a grace to grow in holiness. William of Auvergne and Bonaventure both agreed that the effect of the sacrament must be some sort of grace, but both of them also held that the grace came through the priest's blessing.

Nevertheless, under the influence of reasoning like Alexander's and the desire to fit all the sacraments into a single conceptual scheme, theologians from Thomas Aquinas onward admitted that the sacrament gave a positive assistance toward holiness in the married state of life. That grace was first of all a grace of fidelity, and ability to be faithful to one's marriage vow, to resist temptations of adultery and desertion despite the hardships of married life. It was also even more positively a grace of spiritual unity between the husband and the wife, enabling him to love and care for her as Christ did the church, and enabling her to honor and obey him as the church did her Lord. It was true, of course, that even non-Christians could be faithful to one another and achieve marital harmony, but for Aquinas Christians were called to an ideal constant fidelity and perfect love that could not be attained without the supernatural power of God's grace.

Aquinas also realized as did the other scholastics that marriage existed long before the coming of Christ, but for him this was no different from the fact that washing existed before the institution of baptism or that anointing existed before the sacraments that used oil. It was thus, like the other sacraments, something natural that had been raised in the church to the level of a sacramental sign through which grace might be received. But this also meant for Aquinas that the sacrament in marriage was not just the act of mutual consent in the wedding ritual but the marriage itself, which came into existence through the giving of consent, was sealed by the act of intercourse, and continued for a remainder of one's life. As a sacramental sign it was therefore permanent, as was the sacramental reality of the marriage bond that was created by consent and made permanent through consummation. As a natural institution marriage was ordered to the good of nature, the perpetuation of the human race, and was regulated by natural laws that resulted in the birth of children. As a social institution it was ordered to the good of society, the perpetuation of the family and the state, and was regulated by civil laws that governed the political, social, and economic responsibilities of married persons. And as a sacrament it was ordered to the good of the church, the perpetuation of the community of these who loved, worshipped, and obeyed the one true God, and was regulated by the divine laws that governed the reception of grace and growth in spiritual perfection. The "matter" of the sacrament was therefore the human reality of marriage as a natural and social institution since this was the natural element, like water or oil, out of which it was made. And the "form" of the sacrament consisted of the words of mutual consent spoken by the spouses, since these were what signified the enduring fidelity that would exist between them, just as it existed between Christ and the church.

Most of the other things that Aquinas had to say about marriage—and this was true of the other schoolmen as well—had to do with the ecclesiastical regulation of marriage, with the laws governing who may and may not lawfully marry, with regulations regarding betrothal and inheritance, and so on. For marriage in the Middle Ages was viewed not so much as a personal relationship but as a social reality, an agreement between persons with attendant rights and responsibilities. Thus Aquinas and the other thirteenth-century scholastics occasionally spoke of marriage as a contract, and in the centuries that followed the legal terminology of canon law was further incorporated into the sacramental theology of marriage.

John Duns Scotus, for instance, conceived of marriage as a contract that gave people a right to have sexual relations for the purpose of raising a family, and from this he drew the inference that intercourse in marriage was legitimate not only for begetting children but also for protecting the marriage bond. A woman was bound in justice to give her husband what was his by right, he reasoned, and so she had to grant his requests lest he be tempted to bring discord into the marriage by satisfying his desires with someone else. Other theologians in the fourteenth and fifteenth centuries also came to accept this argument, and by the sixteenth century it was commonly taught that not every act of intercourse had to be performed with the intention of having children. Married people could ask for sex without blame, provided they did it not out of lust but only to relieve their natural needs.

Scotus was also the first theologian to teach that the minister of the sacrament was not the priest but the couple that was getting married. According to canon law people who wed without a priest were validly married even though they went about it illegally, and according to theology people who were validly married received the sacrament. It followed, therefore, that the bride and groom had to be the ones who administered the sacrament to each other when they gave their consent to the marriage. In the fourteenth and fifteenth centuries this view became more widely accepted, but even in the sixteenth century some theologians still maintained that the priest was the minister of the sacrament, for in many places the priest not only handed over the bride to the groom during the wedding ceremony but he also said, "I join you in the name of the Father and of the Son and of the Holy Spirit."

One thing that did not change, however, was the official prohibition against divorce. In the decree that was drawn up for the Armenian Christians during the Council of Florence in 1439, marriage was listed among the seven sacraments of the Roman church and explained as a sign of the union between Christ and the church. It adopted Augustine's summary of the goods of marriage as the procreation and education of children, fidelity between the spouses, and the indissolubility of the sacramental bond. It granted that individuals might receive a legal separation if one of them was unfaithful, but denied that either one of them could marry again "since the bond of marriage lawfully contracted is perpetual."

Nonetheless, Christians in certain cases did separate and remarry. The hierarchy no longer allowed divorces but ecclesiastical courts were now empowered to grant annulments to those who could prove that their present marriage was invalid by canonical standards. If a married person could show, for example, that he had previously consented to marry someone else, the court could decide that the first marriage was valid even though unlawful and that the present marriage was therefore null and void. Marriage within certain degrees of kinship was also regarded as grounds for an annulment even after years of marriage. But the closeness of prohibited relationships varied in different parts of Europe, and so a marriage that might be upheld in one country might be annulled in another. And if the blood relationship or secret marriage was difficult to prove, ecclesiastical courts were sometimes open to being persuaded by financial considerations, generously but discreetly offered.

PART TWO

Contemporary Perspectives on the Theology of Marriage

CHAPTER 4

Christian Marriage: Basic Sacrament

Bernard Cooke

It was only in the late twelfth and early thirteenth centuries that marriage came to be officially regarded as a sacrament. The Council of Trent (1563) and Vatican II (1962–65) reaffirmed this official teaching. However, relatively early in the history of Christianity, marriage was regarded as a sacrament in the broader sense. The marriage ceremony was only one important element within a larger sacramental process. Bernard Cooke retrieves this ancient perspective, which receded with the legalism of the Counter-Reformation.

The starting point for sacramental reflection is the human context of love and friendship. In filial and loving relationships, God's presence unfolds. Marriage is a paradigm of human friendship and personal love. It touches the most basic level of life. It is, as the author suggests, the basic sacrament of God's presence to human life. In their relationship to one another, the couple are a sacrament for each other, for their children, and for all who come to know them. They "give grace" to one another.

The reader will find in this essay the best of personalistic philosophy, the sacraments viewed as process, and marriage contextualized in a redemptive setting of love and friendship.

Questions for Discussion

1. What is meant by "uncreated grace"?
2. Why can we say that human love is the most basic sacrament?
3. What is the revelation expressed in Gen 1:10?
4. How do we know that God is personal? What does "personal" mean when applied to God?
5. When and how was the sacrament of Christian marriage instituted?
6. The Christian couple are the sacrament of marriage. Explain.

In the traditional short definition of Christian sacrament, the third element is a brief statement about the effectiveness of sacraments: "Sacraments are

Pages 79–94 are reprinted with permission from *Sacraments and Sacramentality,* copyright © 1985 by Bernard Cooke, published by Twenty-Third Publications, P.O. Box 180, Mystic, CT 06355.

sacred signs, instituted by Christ, to give grace." Sacraments are meant to do something. What they do is essentially God's doing; in sacraments God gives grace. Before looking at the sacramentality of human friendship and of marriage in particular, it might help to talk briefly about the kind of transformation that should occur through sacraments.

In trying to explain what sacraments do, we have used various expressions: celebrants of sacraments "administer the sacraments" to people; people "receive sacraments" and "receive grace" through sacraments; sacraments are "channels of grace." The official statement of the Council of Trent, which has governed Catholic understandings for the past four centuries, is that "sacraments contain and confer grace."

The traditional understanding of grace and sacraments would include at least the following. The grace given was won for us by the death and resurrection of Jesus. Without depending upon misleading images such as "reservoir" or a "bank account," it seems that there must be some way that the graces flowing from Jesus' saving action are "stored up" so that they can be distributed to people who participate in sacraments. The grace given in sacramental liturgy is, at least for baptized Christians, a needed resource if people are to behave in a way that will lead them to their ultimate destiny in the life to come.

Beneath all such formulations—which we are all familiar with in one form or another—there lurks a basic question: What is this "grace" we are speaking about? It is all well and good to say that we receive the grace we need when we come to sacramental liturgy, and that we receive it in proportion to our good will. But what do we have in mind when we use this word "grace"? We have already begun to see that "sacrament" should be understood in a much broader sense, one that extends far beyond the liturgical ceremony that is the focus of a particular sacramental area. Now, with grace also, a deeper examination leads us to the conclusion that grace touches everything in our lives; it pervades everything we are and do.

In trying to get a more accurate notion of grace, it might help to remember a distinction that was sometimes made in technical theological discussions, a distinction that unfortunately received little attention and so was scarcely ever mentioned in catechetical instructions about grace. This is the distinction between "uncreated grace" and "created grace."

"Uncreated grace" refers to God himself in his graciousness towards human beings; "created grace" refers to that special ("supernatural") assistance God gives to humans to heal and strengthen them and to raise them to a level of being compatible with their eternal destiny. For the most part, our previous theological and catechetical explanations stressed created grace as a special help that enabled persons to live morally good lives, an assistance to guide and support them when they faced temptations. There was also a frequent reference to "the state of grace," the condition of being in good relationship to God and therefore in position to move from this present earthly life to heaven, rather than to hell. But there was practically no mention of uncreated grace.

During the past few decades, there has been a renewed interest in and study of grace. We have learned to pay much more attention to uncreated grace, that is, to the reality of God who in the act of self-giving and precisely by this self-giving transforms and heals and nurtures our human existence. Along with this new emphasis on God's loving self-gift as *the* great grace, there has been more use of the notion of "transformation" to aid our understanding of created grace. Under the impact of God's self-giving, we humans are radically changed; this fundamental and enduring transformation of what we are as persons is created, sanctifying grace.

In various ways, sacraments—in their broader reality as well as in their liturgical elements—are key agencies for achieving this transformation. Though the effectiveness of the different sacraments is quite distinctive, each area of sacramentality touches and changes some of the significances attached to human life. As these significances are transformed, the meaning of what it is to be human is transformed; our human experience is therefore changed, and with it the very reality of our human existing.

This process of transformation is what we now turn our attention to, hoping to discover what sacraments are meant to accomplish in the lives of Christians.

SACRAMENT OF HUMAN FRIENDSHIP

Explanation of the individual sacraments traditionally starts with baptism. Apparently it is the first sacrament Christians are exposed to, and the one all the others rest upon; it is the one that introduces the person to Christianity, etc. However, as we attempt to place the sacraments in a more human context, there is at least the possibility that we should begin with another starting-point. Perhaps the most basic sacrament of God's saving presence to human life is the sacrament of human love and friendship. After all, even the young infant who is baptized after only a few days of life has already been subjected to the influence of parental love (or its lack), which in the case of Christian parents is really the influence of the sacrament of Christian marriage.

Sacraments are meant to be a special avenue of insight into the reality of God; they are meant to be words of revelation. And the sacramentality of human love and friendship touches the most basic level of this revelation. There is a real problem in our effort to know God. Very simply put, it seems all but impossible for humans to have any correct understanding of the divine as it really is. God is everything we are not. We are finite, God infinite; we are in time, God is eternal; we are created, God is creator. True, we apply to God the ideas we have drawn from our human experience; we even think of God as "person." But is this justified? Is this the way God is?

Some fascinating and important discussion of this problem is going on today among Christian philosophers, but let us confine our approach to those insights from the biblical traditions. As early as the writings of the first chapter of Genesis (which is part of the priestly tradition in Israel that found final form around 500 B.C.), we are given a rich lead. Speaking of the creation of humans by God, Genesis 1:19 says that humans were made "in the image and likeness of God." That is to say, somehow the reality of human persons gives us some genuine insight into the way God exists. But the passage continues—and it is an intrinsic part of the remark about "image and likeness"—"male and female God made them." This means that the imaging of God occurs precisely in the relationship between humans, above all in the interaction of men and women. To put it in our modern terms, some knowledge of the divine can be gained in experiencing the personal relationship of men and women (and one can legitimately broaden that to include all human personal relationships).

The text provides still more understanding, for it points out that from this relationship life is to spread over the earth; humans in their relation to one another (primarily in sexual reproduction, but not limited to that) are to nurture life. And humans are to govern the earth for God; they are to image and implement the divine sovereignty by this nurture of life that is rooted in their relationship to one another. As an instrument of divine providence, human history is meant by the creator to be effected through human community, through humans being persons for one another.

Though the first and immediate aspect of the relationship between Adam and Eve as life-giving is their sexual partnership, the text does not confine it to this. Rather, Genesis goes on to describe the way Adam's own human self-identity is linked with Eve's. As Adam is given the chance to view the other beings in God's creation, he is able to name them, but he is unable to name himself until he sees Eve. The very possibility of existing as a self is dependent upon communion with another.

Implicit in this deceptively simple biblical text is a profound statement about the way human life is to be conducted. If life is to extend to further life, either by creating new humans or by creating new levels of personal life in already-existing humans, it will happen on the basis of people's self-giving to one another. And, if women and men are truly to "rule" the world for God, they will do this by their love and friendship, and not by domination. To the extent that this occurs, the relationship of humans to one another will reveal the fact that God's creative activity, by which he gives life and guides its development (in creation and in history), is essentially one of divine self-gift. Humans have been created and are meant to exist as a word, a revelation, of God's self-giving rule; but they will function in this revealing way in proportion to their free living in open and loving communion with one another.

Whatever small hint we have regarding the way God exists, comes from our own experience of being humanly personal. Our tendency, of course, is to think of the divine in human terms, even carrying to God many of the characteristics of our humanity that obviously could not apply directly to God, for example, changing our minds as to what we intend to do. Excessive anthropomorphism has always been a problem in human religious thinking and imagination; we have always been tempted by idolatry. Even today, when our religious thinking has been purified by modern critical and scientific thought, we still fall into the trap of thinking that God exists in the way we think God does. This does not mean, however, that we must despair of ever knowing God. On the basis of biblical insights (like those in Genesis 1:19 and even more in New Testament texts grounded in Jesus' own religious experience) we can come to some true understanding of God by reflecting on our own experience of being personal.

For us to be personal—aware of ourselves and the world around us, aware that we are so aware, relating to one another as communicating subjects, loving one another, and sharing human experience—is always a limited reality. We are personal within definite constraints of time and place and happenings. Even if our experience as persons is a rich one, through friends and education and cultural opportunities, it is always incomplete. For every bit of knowledge there are immense areas of reality I know nothing about; I can go on learning indefinitely. Though I may have a wide circle of friends, there are millions of people I can never know; I can go on indefinitely establishing human relationships. There are unlimited interesting human experiences I will never share. In a sense I am an infinity, but an infinity of possibilities, infinite in my completeness. Yet, this very experience of limitation involves some awareness of the unlimited; our experience of finite personhood points toward infinite personhood and gives us some hint of what that might be.

GOD REVEALS SELF AS PERSONAL

What lets us know the divine is indeed personal in this mysterious unlimited fashion is the fact (which as Christians we believe) that this God has "spoken" to humans; God has revealed, not just some truths about ourselves and our world, but about God's own way of being personal in relation to us. God in the mystery of revelation to humans is revealed as someone. What this means can be grasped by us humans only through our own experience of being human together. In our love and concern for one another, in our friendships and in the human community that results, we can gain some insight into what "God being for us" really means. These human relationships are truly insights into God, but not just in the sense that they are an analogue by which we can gain some metaphorical understanding of the divine. Rather, humans and their relationships to one another are a "word" that is being constantly created by God. In this word God is made present to us, revealing divine selfhood through the sacramentality of our human experience of one another.

One of the most important results of this divine revelation and genuinely open relationships to one another is the ability to trust reality. This might seem a strange thing to say, for reality is a given. Yet, the history of modern times has been one of growing uncertainty and strong distrust of the importance and goodness and even the objective reality of the world that surrounds us, the world of things and especially the world of people. Great world wars, among other things, have made many humans cynical about human existence and have made many others unwilling to admit that things are as they are. There is abundant evidence that our civilization is increasingly fleeing towards fantasy, taking refuge in a world of dreams, so that it does not have to face the real world. It is critically important, perhaps necessary for our sanity, that we find some basis for trusting life and facing reality optimistically and with mature realism.

Most radically, a culture's ability to deal creatively with reality depends on its view of "the ultimate," of God. We must be able to trust this ultimate not only as infinitely powerful but also as infinitely caring, as compassionate and concerned. The only ground, ultimately, for our being able to accept such an incredible thing—and when we stop to reflect, it is incredible—is our experience of loving concern and compassion in our human relationships. If we experience the love and care that others have for us, beginning with an infant's experience of parental love, and experience our own loving concern for others, this can give us some analogue for thinking how the ultimate might personally relate to us. Jesus himself drew from this comparison. "If you who are parents give bread and not a stone to your children when they ask for food, how much more your Father in heaven. . . ."

Experiencing love in our human relationships makes it possible for us to accept the reality of our lives with a positive, even grateful attitude. And this in turn makes it possible for us to see our lives as a gift from a lovingly providential God. If we have friends, life has some basic meaning; we are important to them and they to us. What happens to us and them makes a difference; someone cares. If love exists among people, there is genuine, deep-seated joy, because joy shared by people is the final dimension of love. If this is our experience of being human, then our existence can be seen as a good thing and accepted maturely and responsibly.

All of this means that our experience of being truly personal with and for one another is sacramental; it is a revelation of our humanity at the same time that it is a revelation of God. This experience of human love can make the mystery of divine love for humans credible. On the contrary, if a person does not experience love in his or her life, only with great difficulty can the revelation of divine love be accepted as possible. Learning to trust human love and to trust ourselves to it is the ground for human faith and trust in God.

To say that human love is sacramental, especially if one uses that term strictly (as we are doing), implies that it is a mystery of personal presence. Obviously, in genuine love there is a presence of the beloved in one's consciousness; the deeper and more intimate the love, the more abiding and prominent is the thought of the beloved. To see this as truly sacramental of divine presence means that human love does more than make it possible for us to trust that God loves us. The human friendships we enjoy embody God's love for us; in and through these friendships God is revealing to us the divine self-giving in love. God is working salvifically in all situations of genuine love, for it is our consciousness of being loved both humanly and divinely that most leads us to that full personhood that is our destiny. Such salvation occurs in our lives to the extent that we consciously participate in it, in proportion to our awareness of what is really happening and our free willingness to be part of it.

It is instructive to note that when Jesus, immediately after being baptized by John, was given a special insight into his relationship to God as his Abba, the word used in the gospel to describe his experience of his Father's attitude towards him is the Greek *agapetos*, "my beloved one." This was the awareness of God that Jesus had, an awareness of being unconditionally loved, an awareness that became the key to human salvation. And John's Gospel describes Jesus at the last supper as extending this to his disciples. "I will not now call you servants, but friends."

MARRIAGE, PARADIGM OF FRIENDSHIP

Among the various kinds of human friendship and personal love, the one that has always been recognized as a paradigm of human relationship and love, and at the same time a ground of human community, is the relation between husband and wife. There is considerable evidence that humans have never been able to explain or live this relationship satisfactorily, basic and universal though it is. In our own day, there is constant and agitated discussion of the way men and women are meant to deal with one another, and there is widespread talk of a radical shift taking place in the institution of marriage. As never before, the assumptions about respective roles in marriage are being challenged. Marriage is seen much more as a free community of persons rather than as an institution of human society regulated for the general benefit of society; equality of persons rather than respect for patriarchal authority is being stressed. And with considerable anguish in many instances, people are seeking the genuine meaning of the relation between women and men, and more broadly the relationship of persons to one another in any form of friendship.

Questioning the woman-man, and especially the husband-wife, relationship is not, of course, a new phenomenon. As far back as we can trace, literature witnesses to the attempt to shed light on this question. What complicates the issue is the merging of two human realities, sexuality and personal relatedness, in marriage, a merging so profound that people often are unable to distinguish them. We know, however, that in many ancient cultures there was little of what we today consider love between spouses; marriage was a social arrangement for the purpose of continuing the family through procreation. In not a few instances, there was so pronounced a cleavage between love and sexuality that the wife was considered the property of her husband and she was abandoned if she proved unable to bear him children. If men sought human companionship, they sought it outside the home. Apparently the marriages in which something like a true friendship existed between wife and husband were relatively rare.

SACRAMENTALITY OF MARRIAGE IN ISRAEL

In ancient Israel an interesting development began at least eight centuries before Christianity. Surrounded as they were by cultures and religions that worshipped the power of human sexuality, the Israelites assiduously avoided attributing anything like sexuality to their God, Yahweh. At the same time, these neighboring erotic religions were a constant temptation to the Israelites; the great prophets of Israel lashed out repeatedly against participation by Israel's women and men in the ritual prostitution of the Canaanite shrines. In this context it is startling to find the prophet Hosea using the example of a husband's love for his wife as an image of Yahweh's love for his people Israel.

Apparently, Hosea was one of those sensitive humans for whom marriage was more than a family arrangement; he seems to have had a deep affection for his wife, Gomer. The love was not reciprocated; his wife abandoned him for a life of promiscuity with a number of lovers; perhaps she became actively involved in some situation of shrine prostitution. At this point, Hosea was obliged by law to divorce her, which he seems to have done. But then "the word of the Lord came to Hosea," bidding him to seek out and take back his errant wife. And all this as a prophetic gesture that would reveal Yahweh's forgiveness of an adulterous Israel that had gone lusting after false gods.

Once introduced by Hosea, the imagery of husband-wife becomes the basic way in which the prophets depict the relationship between Yahweh and the people Israel. Tragically, the image often has to be used in a negative way. Israel is the unfaithful spouse who abandons Yahweh to run off with "false lovers," the divinities of the surrounding fertility religions. Yet, despite this infidelity on Israel's part, Yahweh is a merciful God who remains faithful to his chosen partner. "Faithful" becomes a key attribute of this God of Israel. Yahweh is a faithful divinity who keeps his promises to Israel. And the husband-wife relation becomes in the prophetic writings an alternative to the king-subject relation that the rulers of Israel and Judah (for their own purposes) preferred as a way of describing the covenant between Yahweh and Israel.

Our particular interest, however, is not the manner in which the use of the husband-wife imagery altered Israel's understanding of the covenant between people and God. Rather, it is the manner in which, conversely, the use of imagery began to alter the understanding of the relation between a married couple. If the comparison husband-wife/Yahweh-Israel is made, the significance of the first couplet passes into understanding the significance of the second couplet, but the significance of the second passes also into understanding the first.

The understanding the people had of their god, Yahweh, and of his relationship to them, the depth and fidelity of his love, the saving power of this relationship, slowly became part of their understanding of what the marriage relationship should be. Thus, a "Yahweh-significance" became part of the meaning of married relatedness. The sacramentality of the love between husband and wife—and indirectly the sacramentality of all human friendship—was being altered. It was, if we can coin a term, being "yahwehized." The meaning of God in his relationship to humans became part of the meaning of marriage, and marriage became capable of explicitly signifying and revealing this God. This meant that human marriage carried much richer significance than before; it meant that the personal aspect of this relationship was to be regarded as paramount; it meant that the woman was neither to be possessed as property nor treated as a thing; it meant that the marital fidelity was expected of both man and woman. Thus the "institution of the sacrament of marriage" begins already in the Old Testament.

MARRIAGE AS A CHRISTIAN SACRAMENT

With Christianity another dimension of meaning is infused into this relation between wife and husband, the Christ-meaning that comes with Jesus' death and resurrection. Several New Testament passages could be used to indicate this new, deeper meaning, but the key passage probably is the one in Ephesians that traditionally forms part of the marriage liturgy.

> Be subject to one another out of reverence for Christ. Wives, be subject to your husbands as to the Lord; for the man is the head of the woman, just as Christ also is the head of the Church. Christ is indeed the savior of the body; but just as the Church is subject to Christ, so must wives be subject to their husbands. Husbands, love your wives, as Christ also loved the Church and gave himself up for it, to consecrate it . . . In the same way men are bound to love their wives, as they love their own bodies. In loving his wife, a man loves himself. For no one hates his own body: on the contrary, he provides and cares for it; and that is how Christ treats the Church, because it is his body, of which we are living parts. Thus it is that (in the words of scripture) "a man shall leave his father and mother and shall be joined to his wife, and the two shall become one flesh." (5:21–32)

In dealing with this text it is important to bear in mind what the author of the epistle is doing. As so often in the Pauline letters, the purpose is neither to challenge nor to vindicate the prevailing structures of human society as they then existed. Just as in other cases the Pauline letters do not argue for or against an institution like slavery, the passage in Ephesians takes for granted the commonly accepted patriarchal arrangements of family authority without defending or attacking them; in a patriarchal culture all authority is vested in the husband-father. However, Ephesians insists that in a Christian family this authority structure must be understood and lived in an entirely new way. The relation between the risen Christ and the Christian community must be the exemplar for a loving relationship between the Christian couple.

This text contains a rich treasure of sacramental and Christological insight that has scarcely been touched by theological reflection. Mutual giving of self to one another in love, not only in marital intercourse but also in the many other sharings that make up an enduring and maturing love relationship, is used in this passage as a way of understanding what Jesus has done in his death and resurrection. He has given himself to those he loves. His death was accepted in love as the means of passing into a new life that could be shared with those who accept him in faith. Jesus' death and consequent resurrection was the continuation of what was done at the supper when Jesus took the bread and said, "This is my body (myself) given for you." Ephesians 5 tells us that we are to understand this self-giving of Jesus in terms of the bodily self-giving in love of a husband and wife, and vice versa, we are to understand what this marital self-gift is meant to be in terms of Jesus' loving gift of self in death and resurrection.

One of the most important things to bear in mind in studying this text is that Jesus' self-giving continues into the new life of resurrection. Actually, his self-giving is intrinsic to this new stage of his human existence. The very purpose and intrinsic finality of his risen life is to share this life with others. The risen Lord shares this resurrection life by sharing what is the source of this life, his own life-giving Spirit. For Jesus to exist as risen is to exist with full openness to and full possession of this Spirit. So, for him to share new life with his friends means giving them his own Spirit. What emerges from this Spirit-sharing is a new human life of togetherness, a life of unexpected fulfillment, but a life that could not have been reached except through Jesus freely accepting his death. So also, a Christian married couple is meant to move into a new and somewhat unexpected common existing, which cannot come to be unless each is willing to die to the more individualistic, less unrelated-to-another, way of life that they had before.

Christ's self-giving to the church is more than the model according to which a man and woman should understand and live out their love for each other. The love, concern, and self-giving that each has for the other is a "word" that expresses Christ's love for each of them. The fidelity of each to their love is a sign that makes concretely credible their Christian hope in Christ's fidelity. In loving and being loved, each person learns that honest self-appreciation which is the psychological grounding for believing the incredible gospel of God's love for humankind. In their relationship to one another, and in proportion as that relationship in a given set of circumstances truly translates Christ's own self-giving, the couple are a sacrament to each other and a sacrament to those who know them.

In this sacramental relationship, a Christian man and woman are truly "grace" to one another; they express and make present that uncreated grace that is God's creative self-giving. Though there certainly is mystery in this loving divine presence, it is revealed in the new meanings discovered in the lived relationship between Christian wife and husband. The trust required by their unqualified intimacy with one another and the hope of genuine acceptance by the other, which accompanies this intimacy, help bring about a new level of personal maturity. But this trust and hope are grounded in the Christian faith insight that open-ended love can lead to new and richer life. Perhaps even more basically, a Christian couple can commit themselves to this relationship, believing that it will not ultimately be negated by death. Instead, Christian hope in risen life supports the almost instinctive feeling of lovers that "love is stronger than death."

Psychological studies have detailed the ways a truly mature married relationship, one that integrates personal and sexual love, fosters the human growth of the two people, and it is not our intent to repeat such reflections here. But these same studies point also to the indispensable role that continuing and deepening communication with each other plays in the evolution of such a relationship. In a Christian marriage the communication is meant to embrace the sharing of faith and hope in that salvation that comes through Jesus. The Christian family is meant to be the most basic instance of Christian community, people bonded together by their shared relationship to the risen Jesus.

All of us can think of marriages where this ideal has been to quite an extent realized, where husband and wife have over the years supported and enriched one another's belief and trust in the reality and importance of Christianity. Various challenges can come to Christian faith, if it is real faith and not just a superficial acceptance of a religious pattern. These challenges can change shape over the years, they can come with suffering or disappointments or disillusionment or boredom, they can come to focus with the need to face the inevitability of death. At such times of crisis, when faith can either deepen or weaken, the witness of a loved one's faith and hope is a powerful and sometimes indispensable preaching of the gospel.

Perhaps the most difficult thing to believe over the course of a lifetime is that one is important enough to be loved by God. Nothing makes this more credible than the discovery of being important to and loved by another human. The fidelity of one's lover, not just in the critically important area of sexual fidelity but also in the broader context of not betraying love by selfishness or exploitation or pettiness or dishonesty or disinterestedness or insensitivity, makes more credible the Christian trust in God's unfailing concern.

One could go on indefinitely describing how a Christian couple "give grace" to each other, because the contribution to each other's life of grace (their being human in relation to God) involves the whole of their life together. The sacrament of Christian marriage is much more than the marriage ceremony in the church; that ceremony is only one important element in the sacrament. Christian marriage is the woman and the man in their unfolding relationship to each other as Christians; they are sacrament for each other, sacrament to their children, and sacrament to all those who come to know them. The meaning of what they are for each other should become for them and others a key part of what it means to be a human being.

SUMMARY

If we restrict "sacrament" to certain liturgical rituals, it is logical to think of baptism as the initial sacrament. If, however, we realize the fundamental sacramentality of all human experience and the way Jesus transformed this sacramentality, there is good reason for seeing human friendship as the most basic sacrament of God's saving presence to human life. Human friendship reflects and makes credible the reality of God's love for humans; human friendship gives us some insight into the Christian revelation that God is a "self."

Within human friendship there is a paradigm role played by the love between a Christian wife and husband. Building on the transformation of a marriage's meaning that began with the Israelitic prophets, Christianity sees the love relationship of a Christian couple as sacramentalizing the relationship between Christ and the church, between God and humankind. God's saving action consists essentially in the divine self-giving. This is expressed by and present in the couple's self-gift to each other; they are sacrament to each other, to their children, and to their fellow Christians. This sacramentality, though specially instanced in Christian marriage, extends to all genuine human friendship.

CHAPTER 5

Models of Marriage:
A New Theological Interpretation

German Martinez

Lyn Burr Brignoli

In this previously unpublished essay, Martinez and Brignoli bring us beyond the theological analogy between worship and marriage so ably described (by Martinez) in the first edition to this volume. This theological discussion reflects a broad vision of the sacramentality of marriage, one that emphasizes the quality of the personal relationship. The core components of this intrinsic sacramentality are seen through the lens of the metaphor of worship, and through the use of models. This deepens and broadens our perspective. The analogy of worship allows us to glimpse the complexity of the marital experience, while the linguistic framework of models allows us to examine its core values and salient features.

The theme of the first part of the essay ("Marriage as Worship") is captured well in the old Anglican wedding rite: "With my body I thee worship." A coherence exits between marriage and Christian worship from a fourfold perspective: symbolic action, depth of meaning, self-transcendence, and salvation as an end. Marital life is seen as an icon, a grammar of godly love. Some practical implications of this analogy are suggested.

In the second part of the chapter ("Models of Marriage"), the authors do for marriage what Avery Dulles does for the church in his minor classic *Models of the Church*. Five distinct but interrelated and complementary models are proposed as ways of seeing the core values of marriages. These models (vocation, communion, covenant, sacrament, and partnership) open up a variety of legitimate interpretations of marriage, especially in different cultural contexts.

This intertwining of worship and models reclaims marriage as a calling, a basic sacrament, and ultimately as a mystery.

Questions for Discussion

1. How is the central meaning of Christian marriage captured in the pledge: "With my body I thee worship"?
2. How can the analogy of marriage and worship lay the foundation for a spirituality of marriage?
3. What model of marriage do you see as most fruitful in our time and place?
4. The authors describe marriage as a call to enter a crucible, "a call to strip away all barriers to *authenticity*." What are some practical implications of this call?

5. Jesus asked: "Can you drink the cup of my life with me?" This question, the authors claim, could be asked by married couples of each other. What could this questions mean for married life today? Do you agree or disagree with the authors' interpretation?

6. How could the model of marriage as covenant be a form of prophetic resistance in a culture of divorce?

The theology of the sacramentality of marriage has reached a major watershed in our time, equal in importance to its classical formulation during the High Middle Ages. During the twelfth century the church proclaimed the canonical components of the "institution" of marriage, which, for the first time, determined its sacramentality. Today we are coming full circle, back to the anthropological and theological foundations of marriage, which reflects a broader vision of the sacramentality of marriage, one that emphasizes the *quality of the personal relationship* in which two people are sincerely giving one another the gift of themselves, understandably a decisive factor for true happiness in marriage.[1]

In our contemporary society marriage is a foundering institution, at least in the Western world where it has been subjected to the most radical and rapid changes in the last decades. If the sacrament of marriage is in crisis today, it is not only due to the collapse of traditional value systems and the desacralization of the "institution," but also because marriage never has had a central position in Christian theology and praxis. A number of theologians, including Karl Rahner[2] along with members of the Catholic hierarchy,[3] have acknowledged that our theology of marriage is deficient both in its specific and in its broad-based understanding of marriage. As Walter Kasper stated,

> There is no area of human life more important for personal happiness and fulfillment and in which faith and life are so intimately connected as that of marriage. Yet it is very disturbing that there is hardly any other sphere of human life today in which the discrepancy between the official teaching of the Church and the convictions and practice of very many Christians is so great as in questions of sexuality and marriage. Many practicing Christians find the Church's teaching if not hostile to life, then at least very remote from life today.[4]

Thus, what is needed is a credible, contemporary theological perspective of marriage, one rooted in revelation, yet valid in our present world's cultures, so that we may develop new pastoral approaches to the crisis facing marriage today. A theological perspective of marriage must integrate the full complexity of its core values into a multifaceted, *real-life experience*.

It is most essential that we view marriage, first of all, as a human experience, as well as one that takes place in a particular historical and cultural context. As Theodore Mackin puts it, "The marriage sacrament, like all sacraments, has as its matrix a complex human experience. And there is no understanding of the sacrament unless we first understand its matrix-experience."[5]

Historically, the church's vision of *sacrament* has been progressively shrinking since the late Middle Ages, resulting in our present-day minimalist formulation that severely constricts our understanding of marriage, for example. In light of this, this chapter will be concerned mainly with a contemporary vision of the core components of the sacramentality intrinsic to marriage, seen through the lens of the metaphor of *worship*, and through the use of *models*, which allows us to expand considerably the depth and breadth of our perspective.

The *analogy of worship* allows us to glimpse something of the rich complexity of the marital experience, for just as we cannot describe *love* (whether of God or spouse) empirically, neither can we describe marriage; moreover, the metaphor provides a foundation for a genuine Christian theology and spirituality of marriage. Worship is not only the true setting, but it becomes the very context of the sacrament of marriage, since at the heart of worship lie the day-to-day struggles and aspirations of human life lived out in the mystery of God's presence.

In addition, a relevant theology of marriage must also integrate its *core values*, which we will call the *models of marriage*. The purpose of these models is to allow us to examine the salient (major) realities that are simultaneously intertwined in this most complex experience.

MARRIAGE AS WORSHIP

Marriage, like worship, is fundamentally symbolic in nature. While the conjugal partnership is, on one hand, a sign with complex meanings and levels of reality, on the other, it is the symbolic expression of something higher and transcendent. We can compare marriage to Christian worship in that both rely heavily on (1) *symbol and image* to convey (2) *deeper meaning*, both offer the possibility of (3) *self-transcendence*, and for both their end is (4) *salvation*—all four elements are present. Thus, marriage is in itself true worship; it is, in fact, the most basic and original act of worship.

"Love," says L. Mitchell, "whether of God or the girl next door is all but impossible to express except through outward symbolic action, that is, through ritual acts. The same is true of friendship, respect, or for that matter, hatred or contempt. We kiss, shake hands, shake our fist, turn our backs. These are ritual actions. They are all around us in our daily lives."[6]

Whether we are in love with God or with our spouse, we speak in the language of ritual, because what we have to say is so profound and so complex that only words combined with symbols or images can help us express all that we can see, feel, and consciously understand about love. Then by drawing us into our *whole* selves, that is, into the "unspeakable" mystery of God himself where, paradoxically, we "lose" or transcend ourselves, can we more fully say, "I love you."

In fact, God's touching us deeply and wholly as individuals is related to conjugal intimacy; this correlation is, indeed, the core of marital spirituality.

Just as an individual can only find his or her "true" self in God—an outcome of worship—so too the couple can only find authentic validation in God.

The pledge of the old Anglican wedding rite, "With my body I thee worship," speaks profoundly of the central meaning of the analogy. Like worship, which etymologically means "ascribing worth to another being," marriage is the total validation of the other in the devotion and service, celebration and mystery of a relationship.[7]

The implications of the analogy of marriage to worship are far-reaching. For example, one of the fallouts of the feminine movement in the West is that all the tedious tasks traditionally performed by women are taken at face value; women see themselves as degraded by them. If instead women could perceive washing dishes, and so forth, as symbolic ritual, in the same way that the Mass is a ritual, these tasks would be enormously fulfilling, and thus the marriage would have more meaning. In the same way, if we were to understand the Mass merely at face value, divorced from divine presence and meaning, it too would appear repetitive, even absurd. The same argument could be applied to men who might participate more in the so-called feminine tasks in the household with an attitude of entering into the ritual. Thus, competition between men and women for jobs with "prestige" would become a nonissue. Just as the experience of worship engages the whole person, so too marriage is the total gift of self, not a mutual accommodation of fifty/fifty, but 100 percent commitment from each spouse; like the ritual of the Mass, which connects us to all people of faith (in all time), these household tasks connect the spouses with all married people.

When we lose sight of the *meaning* underlying the tangible signs and symbols of ritual, an authentic, transcendent experience is diminished or even missed altogether. Conversely, when too much importance is attributed to the external symbols themselves, the larger significance is lost. For example, if the water pitcher breaks when the priest is washing his hands during the liturgy, the *meaning* of the celebration of the Lord's Supper in all its elements is not "broken." In the same way, when a crisis arises in marriage, the spiritual foundation, or the *transcendent* undergirding of the marriage is not "lost" or diminished. But in our contemporary, predominantly secular and individualistic society, especially in the West, which relies so strongly on "material evidence" and "self-fulfillment," we have become disconnected from an authentic experience of marriage, one that includes a faith vision, because we have lost touch with both its symbolic gestures and the mysteries they imply.

While we have merely touched on the analogy of marriage as worship, there are many other dimensions to the comparison that can be played out in all aspects of the relationship. In specific Christian terms, the bestowal of the marital embrace and the sharing of one eucharistic cup and bread intersect in the mystery of the cross, which is the paradigm of Christian worship. Certainly, the salient feature of the analogy points to an inherent sacramentality in marriage that is both rich and diverse.

Whether in worship or in marriage, sacramentality in the full sense begins with human experience. Thus, marriage sacramentality is anchored primarily in the conjugal love relationship. While friendship, as well as passion and unconditional love, intimacy and communication, respect and forgiveness, self-control and responsibility, and the totality of a committed partnership are all part of the experience of the couple, these experiences are not unique to Christian marriage. Nevertheless, Christians have an opportunity to live in a way that allows them to be constantly renewed, however, because of God's liberating love poured forth in Christ, although the sacramental or transcendent potential of the relationship may not always be realized.

The marriage relationship embodies both human and divine realities, not only because all creation is potentially sacramental, but because marriage itself both signifies and makes mystery present. It is, in fact, as Walter Kasper sees it from a biblical perspective, "the grammar that God uses to express his love and faithfulness."[8] In fact, marriage is a sacrament not because it is a sign of Christ's love for his church. It is a sign of Christ's love for his church because it is, in itself, a sacrament; that is, a natural sign of salvific actualization and self-transcendency that can express the core of the Christian mystery.

In our Christian orientation the concept of sacrament cannot be separated from its broader *natural* meaning. That is, Christian sacramentality emphatically rejects the false dichotomy between the sacred and profane; instead, it acknowledges the presence of "the holy" in whatever has secular value. Thus, all the mundane tasks of marriage are holy in and of themselves because the central focus of marriage is in fact God's creative and redemptive action in Christ in which both spouses share. Herein lies the wider natural meaning of the sacramentality of Christian marriage. Marriage, like sacramental worship, can only be expressed in the whole of life. Since divine grace permeates all of human existence, it follows that the life of every faithful person, indeed of every couple, is sacramental—a holy union of the divine and human.

David Thomas graphically summarizes the symbolic importance of marriage sacramentality:

> Christian marriage is, therefore, a genuine sign/symbol/sacrament that God's presence, love, and power are present in the real world, and that the married can, if willing, make God quite real in bed, board, babies, and backyard.[9]

MODELS OF MARRIAGE

Since the traditional concept of what we call *sacrament* may be too narrow and/or too static to adequately express an understanding of the rich complexity of marriage, we propose, instead, several overlapping models that taken together embrace the core values and reflect "the heart" of the sacramentality of marriage, and thus allow us to approach the depth and breadth of its sacramental mystery. Thus, in reflecting on marriage as a dynamic process, and in understanding marriage to be all-embracing and lifelong, we propose the following predominant models that express the inherent symbolic nature of marriage:

Vocation

Communion

Covenant

Sacrament

Partnership

It is important to note, however, that these models are complementary and open to a variety of legitimate interpretations, especially in light of different cultural contexts.

The use of these five models offers a radical shift from the traditional approach where marriage is emphasized as sacrament in the narrow sense. As a result of this single-minded focus, the church has overemphasized the *indissolubility* of marriage, and thus has neglected its many other essential facets. In this new approach, using symbolic models, "marriage as sacrament" is but one dimension. Moreover, these models must be considered together to adequately describe Christian marriage; they cannot be considered in isolation. Thus, it seems preferable to refer to marriage as a *sacramental mystery* rather than simply to state that "marriage is a sacrament."

In this chapter we will approach each symbolic model as a fundamental dimension of the sacramentality of marriage.

MARRIAGE AS VOCATION

Forming an intimate partnership and a family is a dynamic process, whereby a man and a woman separate from their original families, build a shared world, and commit to one another for life. In practice this process, which entails complex human and religious elements, occurs as a gradual transition in two distinct phases: the engagement and the wedding. From a purely anthropological perspective, marriage is a rite of passage; theologically speaking, marriage is a sacrament of initiation.

Scholastic medieval theologians recognized the contractual aspects of the marriage bond as being key. Thus, the traditional Catholic scholarship on marriage is focused on the wedding ceremony itself as an initiatory sacrament. What follows is a reflection on marriage as a rite of initiation, but seen from the broader sacramental perspective of marriage as vocation; as such, this particular initiation lasts a lifetime.

The word *vocation* means call. Thus, theologically speaking, marriage is the divine call by which spouses are fitted and empowered to form an intimate community of persons able to love and serve. John Chrysostom (fourth–fifth century) spoke of the sacramentality of marriage as a vocation of spiritual sacrifice where husband and wife are each ministers in their priestly vocation offering life and love to each other.[10]

More recently the church's emphasis on "the universal call to holiness" reminds us that God's call to be holy is not confined to a monastic or celibate elite; but rather, it has raised an awareness that marriage (and family life) is indeed a vocation in and of itself; marriage is just as valid a path to holiness as is a call to the priesthood. In fact, marriage is the vocation par excellence, for here the spouses are God's cocreators in the gift of new life, and thus in the child's first experience of love.

In today's foundering secular culture, the church, in promoting a better understanding of marriage as an ongoing process or an *initiation into a vocation,* can play a decisive role in strengthening the sacrament of marriage. Moreover, the church can make use of the experiences of married people, and, therefore, of marriage itself, as a major arena for creating Christian consciousness—in particular for developing an understanding of what it means to be "called" by God and to live out that special "calling." When, for instance, serious problems surface in marriage, the spouses, who understand the nature of their particular calling, can live in the midst of even extraordinary difficulties in a way that brings hope and strength to both partners.

Another way to envision the vocational aspect is to see marriage as a call to enter a crucible; it is a call to strip away all barriers to *authenticity.* For example, inevitably, two people who have been deeply hurt in childhood come into marriage with a woundedness that eventually takes over; woundedness is relating to woundedness. Each spouse, unconsciously hidden in a "false self," is protecting him/herself from past hurts. The husband lashes out, that is his defense. The wife withdraws, that is her defense. The husband reacts because the wife has touched the raw nerve endings; he laughs inappropriately when in pain. The paradox is that it seems comfortable to remain behind the "safety" barriers, but the kingdom of God is not hidden, it is out in the open. As, for example, the wife learns to open herself because she can take her hurt to the cross, she begins peel off her "false self." It is a hard fight. Every fiber in her wants to stay closed. But whenever the spouses are *vulnerable* to one another, they allow God to meet them there. Thus, marriage becomes that earthen vessel that can withstand "the heat" of melting away the disguises. Both partners, by allowing themselves to become vulnerable, can mature and grow in authentic love, which *is* God's love.

While, historically, baptized Christians have long recognized that marriage is a holy state and, thus, have considered it sacramental (albeit not in the technical and restricted sense that the ecclesiastical wedding ceremony conferred after the twelfth century), traditionally, family rituals and customs surrounding courtship and marriage were essentially rites of initiation. Referring to the later development both of the sacramental status and of the initiatory nature of the marriage rite, J. Martos states:

> Wedding ceremonies are always sacramental, at least in the broad sense of being celebrations of the sacred value of marriage, whatever it may be in a given culture, as well as in the sense of being rituals of initiation to a new style of life which is honored and meaningful, supported by social custom and religious tradition. In these same ways Christian wedding ceremonies have always been sacramental, for they have celebrated the sacred value of marriage in a Christian culture, and they have initiated men and women into

a style of life that was to be modeled on the relationship between Christ and the church.[11]

However, the art of courtship, which in the past involved extended families along with their traditional values and social customs, has been lost to a large extent today. Thus, as a faith community we truly need an initiation process to mark the transition from engagement to marriage, not only because it is a significant life-passage, but more important because the cultural and familial supports of past generations are no longer in place.

An initiation process, as such, can also provide an opportunity for the church to create a more effective program for *marriage preparation*. Since marriage is not only a religious experience, but also one that marks a stage in human development, it behooves us to include important insights from the human sciences in marriage preparation as well.

For example, the seminal work of Arnold van Gennep, *Les Rites de Passage*, which became a landmark in cultural anthropology, provides a model of initiation in three parts: *Rites of Separation, Rites of Liminality,* and *Rites of Incorporation*.[12] These rites serve several purposes—helping an individual to become integrated into a cultural community, symbolizing the beginning of the new life, and offering meaning in the process of the transformation. These rites, in fact, correspond to the deep structures of marriage: The rites of separation are the betrothal, which involves a provisional commitment to a future marriage. The rites of liminality correspond to the engagement, a period of preparation culminating in the rite of incorporation, the wedding celebration.

Christian tradition teaches us two important lessons: First, the entire ongoing process of marriage is a rite of passage (an anthropological reality). Secondly, the nature of the marital union and conjugal life as a whole is sacramental (a theological reality), which stems not from the wedding rite, but from the consecration of the bridal pair at baptism. The gradual divorce between the former home-based family rituals and the newer church wedding of the last centuries has "led to a secularization of the domestic and its alienation from the realm of the sacred, now identified with the church," state two experts of the historical marriage rites. They rightly affirm that "the renewal of Christian marriage, then, would seem to be inseparable, finally, from the renewal of baptismal consciousness and from the profound consequences that will flow therefrom not only for the life of the family, but for the structures of the Church itself. Thus we shall have come full circle, back to the baptismal foundations of 'marriage in Christ' with which the Church's theology of marriage began."[13]

Bringing to mind an awareness of the baptismal foundations of marriage, that is, as being a "marriage in Christ," requires a shift in mentality and style that will depend to a great extent on the church; the family is too vulnerable in today's secular atmosphere to provide the kind of support and insight required. Our traditional remedial approach to marriage, based primarily on church doctrine, no longer seems valid. Instead, the church today needs to create a new process of phased initiation, beginning with engagement and continuing through the first years of marriage. Kenneth Stevenson supports "a three-stage marriage liturgy to be inaugurated, not as an optional extra, but as the norm from which shorter versions of the scheme would derive their existence."[14]

The recently restored Rite of Christian Initiation of Adults (RCIA) offers the theological model and the ritual framework of a three-stage preparation and celebration of marriage. Pope John Paul II echoed this new understanding of the dynamic nature of marriage when he envisioned it as a "journey of faith, which is similar to the catechumenate," and thus the pastoral care of the family is to be regarded as a progressive action "step by step in the different stages of its formation and development."[15]

Consequently, solemnization of the wedding in church (the rite of incorporation) is not enough, because it is only part of the longer process of *realizing* the marital vocation. While the church cannot disregard the canonical requirements, its role should be primarily theological and pastoral, so that a total ministry to marriage may offer a concrete, existential vision of the spouses' vocation. The initiation process is, in fact, integral not only to the human complexities of marriage, but also to its sacramental nature.

MARRIAGE AS COMMUNION

Communion—the mutual sharing of the gift of self—is a fairly recent idea in the history of the theology of marriage. The preconciliar theology of the past approached marriage from the point of view of a juridical contract, one that existed solely for the purpose of mutual support and for biological procreation. The notion of marriage as one of the seven sacraments of the faith came about historically as an *extrinsic* addition.

It is the European existential philosophies, by focusing on individual consciousness, that have contributed to the new and more profound perspective of marriage, one that recognizes its sacramentality as an *intrinsic* element. In particular, the philosophy of "existence as dialogue" (where one's existence is predicated on dynamic interchange) has influenced theologians such as K. Bath and K. Rahner, for example, who offer a more personal, less objective interpretation of the sacraments. By reaching back to the existential roots of a person's experience, and by emphasizing the quality of the personal relationship, marriage becomes, according to a more recent definition, "the intimate community of life and love."[16]

Interestingly, the concept of "marriage as communion" is present in the patristic writings, especially in the Eastern patristic tradition, which understands marriage from the broader level of *sacrament as mystery*. John Chrysostom, who calls marriage the "sacrament of love," sees the intimate union of the spouses as integrated in the eternal redemptive mission of Christ.[17] The African writer Tertullian offers an inspiring, even poetic spirituality of the communion of the marriage partners: "They are brother and sister, both servants of the same master; nothing divides them, either in flesh or in spirit.

They are, in very truth, two in one flesh; and where there is but one flesh, there is also but one spirit."[18]

In taking into account the evolution of "marriage as communion," we must also consider social and cultural anthropological perspectives, which condition not only the spiritual, but also the ethical dimensions of marriage. Classical theology did not go beyond Boethius's definition of a person at the beginning of the Middle Ages: "An individual substance of rational nature."[19] This rationalistic view has persisted in spite of the more contemporary view of the whole person who exists and is, moreover, defined within dynamic, human relationships. Consequently, our traditional theology of marriage is weak because it has not taken into account an individual person as a dynamic, social being; it also lacks an adequate theological consideration of sexuality.

Thus, our present understanding—through the symbolic model of both "marriage as communion" and "marriage as a living sign of salvation" presented by *Gaudium et Spes*—reflects a paradigm shift: The contemporary vision of marriage expands from the covenantal base to interpret marriage as an intimate partnership operating from a center of love; it presents a positive view of sexuality, and stresses the dignity and freedom of the human person.

A contemporary perspective of biblical revelation provides the foundation for a theology of "marriage as communion." The archetypes in Genesis where man (and subsequently woman) is created in the "image of God" point to the interpersonal nature of the man-woman relationship, as well as to the "goodness" of the body and of the sexual relationship.

The Bible also witnesses in a unique way to the transcendent quality of the origin of human beings; the individual is both "other" and yet completely dependent on the creator. Hence, dialogue with God becomes the only hope of liberation from the primordial chaos. In this way God-*agape* is the source of life and goodness in the marital communion—the "I-Thou" of dialogue and reciprocity described by Martin Buber—which is dynamically enclosed by, and moves toward the ultimate mystery, God himself: "extended, the lines of relationship intersect in the eternal you."[20] In this way the communion between husband and wife points to the innate sacramentality, and thus to the saving reality of marriage at its very core.

As G. van der Leeuw wrote: "The old primitive world knew marriage as a sacrament in the literal sense of the word. This implies that in some ways the end of marriage is not mutual comfort or procreation, but salvation to be found through it."[21]

An image of a cup comes to mind when we think of marriage as the loving communion of two people. In the eucharistic meal, sharing "the cup" draws us into loving communion with one another, as well as into the place where we are touched by God. We refer to the eucharistic cup as "the saving cup" or "the cup of blessing." When Jesus said to Zebedee's sons, "Can you drink this cup that I am going to drink?" (Matt 20:20–23), Jesus was referring to the agony of his suffering along with his resurrected life.[22] Jesus was asking a question that a married couple might well ask each other: "Can you drink the cup of my life with me?" Or, just as important, "Can you share in all my pain and sorrow, as well as in the joy and successes of the past that have contributed to who I am today?" The extent to which the couple can drink the cup of each other's lives is the extent to which they can enter into a tremendous freedom. And conversely, the extent to which they refuse to imbibe the substance of their partner's life, is to refuse, in a paradoxical way, the freedom that authentic communion brings. This is because at the same time that the partners share, totally and completely, the cup of each other's lives, they are also sharing in the transcendent life, the lifeblood of Christ, which is the sacramentality that marriage accords.

For example, a daughter-in-law who shuns her abusive father-in-law is pushing away "the cup" of her husband's life. When she accepts the difficult reality, she enters deeply into her husband's life, allowing the possibility of the transcendent love of Jesus to re-create not only her own relationship with her father-in-law, but also the relationship with her husband. While the father-in-law may not actually change, the wife and her husband can experience a deep communion of sharing their lives in such a way that "the cup" of pain and resentment becomes "a cup of blessing" to them both.

Thus, the marital "cup" is in a real sense like the eucharistic chalice. Here "communion" is the lifeblood through which transcendent love of God infuses the ordinary circumstances of life. We call it a graced relationship whenever those marital realities of happiness or sadness are lived authentically. God is hidden in them.

Finally, communion and sacrament imply one another; neither is compete without the other. The church's current theology of marriage, which stresses the intrinsic connection, can be summarized as follows: marriage is God's creative reality raised to the dignity of a *sacrament*; established as a covenant of intimate communion of life and love; by which the spouses *signify* and *share* in the mystery of love and fidelity between Christ and the church.[23]

MARRIAGE AS COVENANT

While it is a symbol, marriage is also a reality. (As we have noted, the symbolic is real.) When it is lived as mutual self-giving and intimate sharing between a man and a woman in faithful love, marriage exemplifies the ideals of the biblical concept of covenant. Moreover, because the union of the two partners goes beyond any notion of a human contract, marriage is, in fact, "a paradigm of human relationship and love"[24] and, thus, is covenantal in its core.

Inspired by the nuptial symbolism of the covenant, Paul sees in the marital union an image of Christ's love for his church (Eph 5:32), and uses "the language of the sacramental sign-value."[25] Following the same line of theological thinking, patristic theology drew insights from the biblical paradigm to describe marriage as the "image and likeness" of God's covenant with humanity, and perceived in marriage a particular way of living out the

Christ-church spousal mystery. Tertullian, who saw in the conjugal union an image and symbol of the divine covenant, writes: "If you accept Christ and the church, you must also accept what is His image, symbol and sacrament."[26] Thus, the ancient, as well as the patristic view of "marriage as covenant," is based on scriptural revelation, and is, therefore, sacramental, albeit not in the technical sense of later medieval theology.

Since *covenant* is the graced and intimate personal encounter between God and his people fulfilled in Christ, as such, it is the cornerstone of Christian sacramentality, especially the sacramentality of marriage: Marriage is, in fact, *the sacramental covenant.* This covenantal partnership, a human mystery, is in itself a way of holiness, that is, a saving reality, as the church teaches: "the conjugal covenant instituted by the Creator which already is in a true and proper sense a journey toward salvation,"[27] is expressed by the ritual celebration and living out of the sacrament "in spirit and in truth."

The intrinsic relationship between covenant and marriage is rooted in the history of salvation in a double sense: (1) *symbolic* and (2) *archetypal.*

On the one hand, the symbolic language opens up a new dimension to the reality of God. By God's initiative people come closer to God and are introduced into the divine mystery. In this way marriage is part of God's transcendent mystery. But adhering strictly to the symbolic perspective of marriage offers some pitfalls. For example, because marriage shares in the contingencies of the ever-changing and unpredictable human journey, it provides a potentially fallible symbol of God's forever infallible love.

Tibor Horwath has pointed out two major difficulties in applying the idea of covenant in a symbolic way to the human mystery of marriage: (1) equality is not implied in the biblical notion of covenant (the Aramaic word *berith*), and (2) covenant is a changing concept in Scripture.[28] In fact, God and Israel were unequal partners. This concept has led some to conclude that marriage is not "an image of the covenantal relationship between God and Israel as symbolized in the prophetic literature."[29] Certainly, a symbolic perspective should not be exaggerated, and cannot be taken literally. But, nevertheless, *the heart of the symbolic message of the covenant,* in light of our faithful interpretation of revelation, can provide a source of meaning and strength for the contemporary partners as they live out the relationship in all its ethical demands. In this regard the life-creating and salvific message of the biblical covenant is most relevant in contemporary religious consciousness.

On the other hand, the biblical covenant also represents the archetypal model of Christian marriage. Conjugal love is modeled on the faithful and compassionate initiative of God's covenantal love, whose ultimate prototype (*in the archetypal sense*) is the marriage of Christ and his bride, the church, in which Christ sacrifices everything for her, even his life. Thus, God has freely given to his people the total gift of himself. It is this event, *Christ's Pasch,* which grounds the sacramental covenant of marriage, and thus makes it the archetypal model of Christian marriage. Moreover, it is the couple's faith, as expressed in their lives, that renders them a people of the covenant, and consequently makes their union a sign and a Christian sacrament of the covenant.

Speaking from the perspective of God's presence and action in creation, Karl Rahner is decisive in regard to the salvific dynamics of marriage: "The unity between Christ and the church is the ultimate cause and origin of the unity of marriage."[30] This "great mystery" is the foundation of the marriage sacrament. Moreover, marriage, like each of the sacraments, receives its transforming power from the paschal event: The spouses find here both *the archetype* of their marital spirituality, and a source of transforming spiritual power.

When we think of the biblical concept of *covenant*, an image that comes to mind is a rainbow, the sign given to Noah. At sea, a rainbow can be a spectacular sight. But all sailors know that the conditions of earth must join with the conditions of "heaven" to produce a rainbow. The weather has to be just right—the humidity and the brightness of the sunlight. It is as if God is speaking to us of marriage by saying he will bless us, but we need to bring something into the marriage also. That something is our faith that marriage is a sacred bond. For example, most couples start out feeling the promise of faith. But often, after a while, when problems arise, the promise appears to be broken. Instead of a place of love, the home becomes a place of anger where hurt is piled on top of hurt. At this juncture, many, if not most, couples split up. However, it is at this point that the *covenantal* aspect of marriage becomes most significant. Courageous trust, not that the wife, for example, trusts in her husband, but her trust in the *larger meaning of the marriage* allows her to live in the *transcendent* dimension of the relationship, believing that God is somehow present in the brokenness. It can be a time of active "waiting" for the Lord, albeit a painful time when counseling may be essential, but it can also be a profound spiritual experience, even a time of healing. But, without active *faith*, covenant has no meaning.

Finally, the biblical concept of covenant, which provides an integrated vision of the spirituality of marriage, is reflected in the wedding liturgy. From ancient times, the rite of marriage, replete with all its symbolic themes, has been shaped from the biblical model of the covenant, and where, according to tradition, the covenant of the Eucharist is the seal of the covenant of marriage. The Eastern liturgies are far more eloquent in their mystical and profoundly spiritual view of marriage. The intimate connection and dependence among the nuptial, paschal, and eucharistic mysteries flow from the Christ-church covenantal theme.

MARRIAGE AS SACRAMENT

As noted earlier, the idea of marriage as one of the seven sacraments of the church was elaborated on by the eleventh-century scholastic theologians, and later adopted officially by the medieval hierarchy in the following century. This concept, however, was not an ecclesiastical invention, but stemmed from the broader meaning of the sacrament as *mystery*, proposed by the early church fathers, especially Augustine, who spoke about the three foods of marriage: *offspring, faithfulness*, and *sacrament*. At the same time Augustine acknowledged that marriage of non-Christians was also a "sacrament-bond" of a sacred and mysterious reality, which, nevertheless, called to mind the fullness of the revelation of the Christian mystery. What follows is a reflection of the two different, although not separate, dimensions of "marriage as sacrament": (1) *human mystery* and (2) *saving reality*. This discussion will point to those specific elements of marriage that define it as a profoundly Christian sacrament.

HUMAN MYSTERY Faithful love is the core of the marital partnership and the heart of its meaning; it is this which renders marriage a primary and universal symbol. Moreover, since marriage is common to all peoples, regardless of cultural or spiritual orientation, it is the original, universal sacramentality known to human life, and is acknowledged, as such, by all religions. Thus, the sacramental mystery of marriage is anchored fully in a human reality; it is a *radically human sacrament*.

From the perspective of its rich biblical, anthropological relevance, however, marriage is essentially a sign, not only of life, but of the whole of life. Its meaning is the salvation of a personal community. It cannot be reduced to a sacred function or ritual, because it is a sign in all its human fullness and transcendent reality. In acknowledging that all human experience is potentially sacramental, and is transformed by Christ, Bernard Cooke calls marriage a basic and key sacrament of the saving presence of God to human life.[31]

The sacramental mystery of marriage, as stated above, is anchored in a human reality, which is, nevertheless, open to the transcendent. While love and friendship are part of the committed partnership, these elements are not unique to Christians. But, as noted earlier, Christians have the opportunity to live in a way that allows the constantly renewing love of Christ to liberate them, and, thus, affords them the possibility of realizing the transcendent quality of the partnership. While the centrality of conjugal love constitutes the human foundation of the sacrament, when two Christians marry, God is present within their human partnership. Thus, the partnership has been subsumed by the redeeming force of Christ, who is part of creation and head of it (Col 1:16). David Thomas extends the sacramental meaning to five distinct, although related, aspects of Christian marriage: the sexual, the creative, the loving, the ecclesial, and the spiritual—which are organically related and mutually interdependent.[32]

From this perspective the sacramental sign-value of marriage is all-embracing and life-long. Marriage is an all-embracing *symbol* and a *reality* because of the centrality of committed love, which makes it a paradigm of an interpersonal relationship. This intimate partnership establishes the couple in a mutual, faithful, fruitful, permanent, and public union. Thus, love and sexuality, procreation and caring, intimacy and communication, and all the hopes and struggles of the intimate and familial lives of the spouses are not just natural phenomenon, but are salvific mystery.

SAVING REALITY Marriage is not only a radically human sacrament, it is also a sacrament of faith. The human values of the partnership constitute the "matter" of the sacrament and its sacramental root, which is fundamentally related to the experience of mystery. This mystery is called *sacrament*, a saving reality in the specific Christian sense, for "the Lord encounters Christian spouses through the sacrament of marriage."[33] While considering the baptismal character of marriage, Scheeben points out that there is an essential and intrinsic relationship between sacramental marriage and the mystery of the spousal relationship of Christ and the church. Marriage participates actively and effectively in that fundamental mystery.[34] In this regard marriage is, in itself, a natural sacrament, that is, a radical hope of salvation and an actual means to it.

The theology of the sacramentality of marriage recognizes three fundamental dimensions of its sacramentality: (1) *marriage is a natural sacrament* in its own right instituted by God; (2) *marriage is a covenantal sacrament,* and as such is a prophetic symbol of the community of grace and salvation between Yahweh and Israel; and (3) *marriage is an essentially Christian sacrament,* as revealed by Jesus, who has redeemed human beings, each to live as "a new creation."

What then is the full meaning and unique reality of Christian marriage? What makes this natural sacrament a specifically Christian sacrament? Once more, the key to the sacramental reality is not in the act of marrying itself, but occurs before this, specifically in the baptismal consecration, in which a Christian is inaugurated into a personal relationship with Jesus and incorporated into the Body of Christ. The sacraments of Christian initiation (baptism of water and the Spirit and Eucharist) are the true foundations of marriage, because through faith the baptized person participates in transcendent self-giving by means of the sanctifying presence of Christ. It is in this newness in Christ, and by means of an ongoing relationship with Christ, that the Christian couple is, in fact, in the words of Karl Rahner, "the very fulfillment of the Church."[35]

The "new creation" that we are "in Christ" is the essence of Christian sacramentality. The specific elements of Christian marriage stem from this Christ-church spousal relationship. Consequently, *faith, baptism,* and *community,* respectively, constitute the personal, ontological, and ecclesial qualifications of the Christian sacramentality of marriage. Baptism is the foundation on which the intimate partnership of the spouses is built in the image of Christ, and through which the partnership becomes (ontologically) a "new way of being" in the church. (The personal and covenantal orientations of marriage, noted previously, include and presuppose the institutional and contractual aspects, although the latter are subordinate to the personal, covenantal dimensions of marriage.)

The sacrament of marriage is not only a public commitment, but it is also a concrete expression of the universal sacrament of the church. Consequently, we celebrate the rite of marriage, the sacramental sign, before the community. We celebrate not to make marriage holy, but because it is already holy, and, as sign of faith, it demands a public and ecclesial expression. The need for a symbolic and sacramental celebration does not come from outside, but from life itself, which is sustained by sharing in the divine source and the redeeming love of Christ.

The sacrament of marriage, thus, becomes a particular actualization of the baptismal vocation. This is exactly what the wedding ritual implies: the permanent manifestation and actualization (anamnesis) of the new covenant of Christ. The sacramental reality remains in the life of the couple, who continue to represent the mystery and to be a sacrament to one another, to their family, and to the community of faith. They are the "fleshed out" sign of God's love to the world.

In this regard the couple is called to experience one another as "speaking" a *word* about God. As Thomas Merton expressed it: "God utters me like a word containing a partial thought of Himself."[36] In fact, if every human being is a *word of God*, if only we can *listen* to that *word*, certainly in marriage, particularly in difficult times, the spouses are called to enter into a deeper dimension of trust in that *word of God* that each one of us is. In this way, the spouses become sacraments to one another. However, in marriage, as in any intimate relationship, such as a parent with a child, for example, we can either express some aspect of God's *healing* presence, just as we can also abuse the intimacy to be destructive, preying on each other's vulnerabilities. For example, a husband who has been abandoned by his mother at birth may have serious difficulty trusting his wife. For the wife this can be as painful as it is for her husband. In her frustration it might be tempting to retaliate when he hurts her, he perhaps always testing, "Will you leave me too?" But rooted in Jesus' love she can offer herself in unconditional love, forgiveness, and compassion. In so doing, she allows not only the possibility of healing her husband, but more important, allows herself to be healed, as she becomes more fully grounded in Christ's love.

In conclusion, this study of "marriage as sacrament" has emphasized two dimensions of sacramentality: the interpersonal marital relationship whose essence is *love,* and the ecclesial dimension, through which the marriage is specifically Christian—namely, in *faith, baptism,* and *community.*

MARRIAGE AS PARTNERSHIP

The Second Vatican Council's (1963–65) well-known definition of marriage as an "intimate partnership of married life and love," cited above, represents a paradigm shift in the Catholic theology of marriage, away from the overly canonical and rationalistic view of the past, to today's emphasis on the "whole" person. Contemporary theology thus takes into account what happens in the total life experience of the couple, and finds here the essence of the sacramentality of marriage. Although the models we have previously considered, such as "marriage as communion," have included the partnership aspect, this symbolic model examines the conjugal union against the background of the sacramentality of all of creation, and envisions marriage as *a process.* This model, therefore, includes the whole of family life, for "the family reveals marriage as a social sacrament."[37]

While complementary to the other models we have considered, such as the covenant, "marriage as partnership" incorporates in a unique way the phenomenological approach to sacramentality. As Merleau-Ponty points out, "the real has to be described, not constructed or formed."[38] Thus, we do not add the sacramental dimension to marriage, but rather, it is already part of the human experience. As Leonardo Boff stated, it is difficult to see how the classical theology of marriage applies the concept of sacrament to the fact of marriage. The sacrament is not something added to marriage, but marriage as a human order possess a sacramental character inherent in it which speaks of its intrinsic sanctity.[39]

Therefore, while the conjugal partnership is the anthropological foundation of marriage, it is also its sacramental root, for "this relationship is the sacrament first and foremost and in its own right."[40] In their total, mutual self-giving, the couple symbolizes God's life-giving gift of himself (grace), which is always available to the spouses to transform and heal their marital relationship. In this regard, the whole of the spouses' life together, including the earthy and sexual sides, is not profane, but is graced.

Echoing the patristic revival, Vatican II presented the "Church as the sacrament of the world," where the world is the object of God's redeeming grace. Speaking from a phenomenological view of sacramentality, Karl Rahner presented the sacraments as revelatory events illuminating the sacredness of all of life, and pointed out that the "secular" world is from the outset always encompassed with God's communication of himself: "The world is permeated by the grace of God . . . The world is constantly and ceaselessly possessed by grace from its innermost roots, from the innermost personal center of the spiritual subject."[41] The concepts of the *cosmic grace of God* and of the *cosmic sacrament* imply both the fulfillment and the heart of the Christian mystery.

If all of life is "graced," marriage is especially so, because of its nuptial connotations, which is symbolized in the spouses' sexually differentiated bodies. As John Paul II teaches: "The human body, with its sex, and its masculinity and femininity, seen in the very mystery of creation, is not only a source of fruitfulness and pro-creation . . . but includes right 'from the beginning' the nuptial attribute, that is, the capacity of expressing love in which the man-person becomes a gift—by means of this gift—fulfills the very meaning of his being and existence."[42] In their willingness to surrender to one another, the spouses are truly a gift of "grace," a healing sacrament to each other, for they make present God's gift of himself. (Due to human frailty, however, this sacramental potential may remain unfulfilled.)

For example, the Song of Songs portrays playful lovers in an idealized way. However, in reality a lasting, loving physical relationship evolves slowly, with ups and downs, and not without some anguish or misunderstanding. Nevertheless, the deep truth that the Song of Songs alludes to is that the body through its senses understands what reason cannot grasp, that is, it understands on a transcendent level. It points to the mystery of meeting the Lord through the senses, just as in the worship liturgy we are encouraged to experience him: "*O taste and see that the Lord is good.*" Thus, in marriage the sexual act for people of faith becomes a way to know God, not through "ideas" but through experience; we meet the body of God with our bodies. Frequently, the sexual encounter can lift us out of our pettiness, even heal us. For example, small hurtful remarks or behaviors can eat away at the relationship, and then a sensitive kiss or caress washes over us, and we are renewed in love. Indeed, whenever we are fully present to each other in love, we are changed by the meeting.

It is important to note that there are no formulas for "successful" sexual intimacy; in fact, it is demeaning to conjure up a "quick fix" or a "one-size-fits-all" mentality for any aspect of the marriage partnership.

Finally, from the perspective of the new anthropology that stresses the concept of *process*, the partnership model provides a vision of the couple as a dynamic entity with a past, a present, and a future: A partnership is sustained and grows—if it does grow—but also, and inevitably, the couple lives with paradox and uncertainty in the process of growing and "becoming." In simple terms, the sacramentality of the partnership is never something fully accomplished, because partnership is a journey, an ongoing, shifting reality, not a static commodity.

The emphasis on the quality of the personal relationship, which is evolving, is not opposed to the ecclesial dimension of marriage. This "becoming" aspect, or the calling to *become* holy (vocation), does not render the covenantal bond less "real," but rather revitalizes it; it does not deny, but reaffirms the ontological foundation of the sacramentality of marriage. From the above perspectives, Bernard Cooke examines the question of indissolubility of Christian marriage: "To put it in biblical terms, a Christian marriage, like any other created realities, does not exist absolutely; like anything in creation, particularly anything in human history, a marriage exists eschatologically; it is tending toward its fulfillment beyond this world. However, the fact that it does not yet have in full fashion the modalities—such as indissolubility—that should characterize it does not mean that it is devoid of them. A Christian marriage is indissoluble, but short of the eschaton it is *incompletely indissoluble* . . . already realizes to some degree the indissolubility which can mirror the divine fidelity to humans, but it cannot yet lay claim to the absoluteness which will come with the fullness of the Kingdom. Similarly, two Christians can be very genuinely and sacramentally married, but they are still being married to one another; their union can become yet richer and stronger."[43]

This historical vision thus implies the larger, indeed the lifelong *process of sacramentality*, which cannot be reduced to the wedding rites. Indeed, the process of sacramentality consists of three phases: *baptismal, celebrative,* and *eucharistic.* Baptism, the primary and initiatory sacrament, is the foundation of marriage, and thus constitutes the preparatory phase of the sacramentality of marriage; the wedding rite, the public and ecclesial actualization of the dignity and holiness of marriage in Christ, is the celebrative phase; and the Eucharist, "the source and climax of the Christian life," is the continuing phase, which provides nourishment for spiritual formation, "bread for the journey." While there are many other important considerations in preparing for the vocation of marriage, nevertheless, an active participation in the sacramental life, which extends to every facet of life, is the core of the specific Christian call of the couple. As in the case of each of the seven sacraments, the popular language of the church ritual conveys the deeper reality of the Christian faith: We are *made* Christians, but we are also to *become* Christians.

> Our language of *getting* betrays a *reification* or *thingification* of sacrament. Actually sacraments are ritual celebrations, steps in a process of growth. Specifically, for our discussion of marriage, one simply cannot *get married*. Two persons can *grow married, become married,* or *become divorced* (or, I suppose, *remain stagnant*). The sacramental ritual is a step in a process . . . again, the goal is to engage in the mystery of *becoming married*.[44]

The contemporary theological perspective that embraces the concepts of *the process* and *the history* of the partnership must also take into account what the human sciences, specifically psychology, have to say about the complex interaction of the marriage partnership. In particular, the psychological constructs of *togetherness* and *individuality* "offer a common sense view of how marriages change and mature. Like the oceans, marriages are dynamic with tides rising and falling on a consistent, sequential basis."[45] For example, when the couple grows older, eventually the children leave home, and a different kind of partnership emerges. Only a view of the partnership that integrates this dynamic sacramentality, or sacramentality that is "in process," with the many other modern aspects of the different stages of the marital, family journey, can approach the wholeness and reality that is the fulfillment of grace.

NOTES

1. The following essay is new in its theological framework and some important insights, but derives much of its content from German Martinez's book, *Worship: Wedding to Marriage* (Washington, D.C.: Pastoral Press, 1993).

2. Karl Rahner, *Theological Investigations,* vol. 10 (New York: Herder and Herder, 1973), p. 199.

3. Peter J. Elliot, *What God Has Joined . . . The Sacramentality of Marriage* (New York: Alba House, 1990), p. vii.

4. Walter Kasper, *Theology of Christian Marriage* (New York: Seabury, 1980), pp. 1–2.

5. T. Mackin, "How to Understand the Sacrament of Marriage," in *Commitment to Partnership: Explorations of the Theology of Marriage,* ed. W. P. Roberts (New York: Paulist, 1987), p. 34.

6. Leonel L. Mitchell, *The Meaning of Ritual* (New York: Paulist, 1977), p. xii.

7. James F. White, *Introduction to Christian Worship* (Nashville: Abingdon, 1981), p. 25.

8. Kasper, *Theology,* p. 27.

9. David M. Thomas, *Christian Marriage: A Journey Together* (Wilmington: M. Glazier, 1983), p. 203.

10. John Chrysostom, *Homily 9 on 1 Timothy* (PG 62:546).

11. Joseph Martos, *Doors to the Sacred: A Historical Introduction to Sacraments in the Catholic Church* (Tarrytown, N.Y.: Triumph Books, 1991), pp. 386–387.

12. Arnold van Gennep, *Rites of Passage* (1909; reprint, Chicago: University of Chicago Press, 1981), pp. 10–11.

13. Mark Searle and Kenneth W. Stevenson, *Documents of the Marriage Liturgy* (Collegeville, Minn.: The Liturgical Press, 1992), pp. 270–271.

14. Kenneth Stevenson, *To Join Together: The Rite of Marriage* (New York: Pueblo Press, 1987), p. 192.

15. Pope John Paul II, *On the Family (Familiaris Consortio)* 65: *Origins* 2 (1981) 459.

16. Pastoral Constitution of Vatican II, *Gaudium et Spes,* 47–51.

17. John Chrysostom, *Epistola I ad Cor.* 9.3 (51:230); Henri Crouzel, "Le mariage des chretiens aux premiers siecles de l'eglise," Esprit et vie 83 (1973) 87–91.

18. Tertullian, *Ad uxorem 2,* VIII, 6 (CCL 1:395), trans. J Quasten, *Patrology,* vol. 2 (repr. Westminster, MD: Christian Classics, 1983) 303.

19. "An individual substance of rational nature"; see Ch. Schultz, "Der Mensch als Person," in *Mysterium Salutis,* vol 2, pp. 637–656.

20. M. Buber, *I and Thou* (New York: Ch. Scribner's Sons, 1970) 123.

21. G. van der Leeuw, *Sakramentales Denken* (Kasel, 1959) 152. The following statement of Pope Leo XIII is relevant in this respect: "Since marriage is a divine institution, and, in a certain sense, was since the beginning a prefiguration of the Incarnation of Christ, a religious quality is an ingredient in it, a quality which is not adventitious, but inborn, not bestowed upon it by human beings, but built-in (*Arcanum Divinae,* in *Acta Apostolicae Sedis* 12 [1879] 392).

22. Cf. Henri Nouwen, *Can You Drink the Cup?* (Notre Dame, Ind.: Ave Maria Press, 1996).

23. *Ordo Celebrandi Matrimonium, Editio Typica Altera,* (3-19-1990) Introduction.

24. Bernard J. Cooke, *Sacraments and Sacramentality* (Mystic, Conn.: Twenty-Third Publications, 1983), 20.

25. Denis O'Callaghan, "Marriage as Sacrament," *Concilium* 55 (1970): 107.

26. Tertullian, *De Monogamia* XA. 1-2 (PL 2:994)

27. *Familiaris Consortio* 68; *Origins* 11 (1981) 459.

28. Tibor Horwath, "Marriage Contract? Convenant? Community? Sacrament of Sacraments—Fallible Symbol of Infallible Love, Revelation of Sin and Love," in *The Sacraments: God's Love and Mercy Actualized,* ed. Francis A. Eigo (Villanova, Pa.: Villanova University Press, 1979), pp. 148–151.

29. Francis Schüssler Fiorenza, "Marriage as a Sacrament in Current Systematic Theology," in *Systematic Theology: Roman Catholic Perspectives* (Minneapolis: Fortress Press, 1991), p. 332.

30. Karl Rahner, "Marriage as Sacrament," in *Theological Investigations,* vol. 10 (London: Darton, Longman and Todd, 1973) 220.

31. Bernard J. Cooke, *Sacraments and Sacramentality* (Mystic, Conn.: Twenty-Third Publications, 1983), p. 20.

32. David M. Thomas, *Christian Marriage: A Journey Together* (Wilmington: M. Glazier, 1983), p. 203.

33. *Gaudium et Spes,* p. 48.

34. Matthias Joseph Scheeben, *The Mysteries of Christianity* (St. Louis: B. Herder, 1946), p. 601, n. 13. The work of this nineteenth-century German theologian still remains profound and modern.

35. Karl Rahner, "Marriage as a Sacrament," *Theology Digest* 17 (1969): 7.

36. Thomas Merton, *New Seeds of Contemplation* (New York: New Directions, 1961), p. 37.

37. Peter J. Elliot, *What God Has Joined* (New York: Alba House, 1990), p. 222.

38. Maurice Merleau-Ponty, *The Primacy of Perception* (London: Routledge and Kegan Paul, 1962), p. x.

39. Leonardo Boff, "The Sacrament of Marriage," in *The Sacraments,* ed. Michael J. Taylor (New York: Alba House, 1981), pp. 193–203.

40. O'Callaghan, "Marriage as Sacrament," p. 104.

41. Karl Rahner, *Theological Investigations,* vol. 14 (London: Darton, Longman and Todd, 1976), p. 166.

42. John Paul II cited in *L'Observatore Romano* (January 21, 1980).

43. Bernard Cooke, "What God Has Joined Together . . ." in *Perspectives on Marriage,* ed. K. Scott and M. Warren (New York: Oxford University Press, 1993), p. 358.

44. Patrick J. Brennan, *Re-Imagining the Parish* (New York: Crossroad, 1991), p. 121.

45. Patrick McDonald and Claudette McDonald, *The Soul of a Marriage* (New York: Paulist, 1995), p. 14.

PART THREE

Marriage: Meanings and Transition

CHAPTER 6

Marriage versus Living Together

Jo McGowan

⌖

Students will find the following essay interesting and controversial. Jo McGowan lays out the two positions—i.e., that marriage is an outdated formality and that it is for several reasons an important step. She makes clear her own position about the importance of marriage as a public and communal act.

Questions for Discussion

1. Why does the author claim that living together is like taking on all that is difficult in marriage without taking the helps that marriage offers?
2. The author says that living together implies that the central relationship of one's life is nobody's business but one's own. Why would you agree or disagree?
3. How accurate are the things the author says about the typical wedding?
4. How common in North America is the author's conviction that marriage (not just the wedding) is a communal matter?
5. What are your reasons for accepting or not accepting the author's conviction "What the community does not bless, it doesn't feel responsible for"?

Some months ago we had a beautiful young woman from India (my husband is also from India) staying with us. At dinner, the conversation turned to the question of marriage versus simply living together. Smita, the Indian woman, maintained that marriage was nothing more than a convenience, a way to avoid the censure of society; that if two people were willing to commit their lives to each other, then marriage was an unnecessary formality, signifying nothing.

To engage in the kind of discussion that followed is to risk sounding foolish. One talks of "marriage" as an institution and yet it is apparent that one is talking out of personal experience that cannot help but be narrow and unimposing compared to the subject itself. Having been married not very long myself, I realized how presumptuous it is to say almost anything (even at the dinner table, let alone in print) about marriage in general. But when will it become *not* presumptuous—after five years, ten, twenty, fifty? The more years pass, I also realize, the more changes in social and cultural conditions will separate me from those entering marriage then, and so perhaps my reflections would take on a presumptuousness of a different sort. In any case, the discussion that evening was so enlightening to me that I decided to risk my dignity and write down some of the thoughts that emerged.

Apart from anything else, marriage is simply a very practical institution. It is an institution which recognizes and makes allowances for human failings. Since constancy is a virtue that very few of us possess at all times, it is important that we see marriage as something beyond ourselves. The very nature of marriage insists that we see it so: when we marry, we create new life; we go beyond ourselves. We create responsibilities, the weight of which our marriages must be strong enough to bear. Marriage is one of those peculiar things (like God!) which make immense demands of us while simultaneously giving us the strength to meet those demands. It is precisely because marriage is so difficult that we must see it as permanent. It is precisely because we are so likely to give it up that we must promise—at the outset, when everything is wonderful—that we are in it for life. (This is one reason, then, why the extreme prevalence of divorce is so troubling. It not only destroys the marriages of those individuals who choose to separate, but it erodes the *concept* of the permanence of marriage. It makes it that much easier for the next couple to give up.)

Simply living together, without "benefit of marriage," does not provide the security of knowing that this is forever. But if you need that security, our friend Smita says, then the relationship can't be that strong to begin with. Smita and I are both in our early twenties, still young enough to believe in the power of love to overcome all odds. And I do believe that. What I don't believe is that a wife and husband always love each other enough to stay married. There are times when love fails, and in those times, many people just take a deep breath and stay married because they *are* married. And when they come through to the other side, their marriages are stronger and more firmly rooted in love.

Smita grew up in India where divorce is practically unheard of—I grew up in an America where *marriage* is practically unheard of. She can perhaps afford to take marriage for granted. I can't. I have seen far too many of my friends—and even my parents' friends—divorce. I have taken care of too many children whose parents are separated. I have seen the scars that divorce inevitably leaves—the pain and near-despair in grownups; the bewilderment and insecurity in the children. I'm not saying that these couples didn't have problems; I'm sure they did. But no human relation is without problems. And if one enters into marriage, one should do it knowing full well that this is the case and that *in spite of it*, the marriage is forever. Living together does not carry with it the weight of a centuries-old tradition. The content of the relationship—a woman and a man living together sexually—contains all the elements that are present in a marriage, but without its form. It is like taking on all that is difficult in a marriage without taking the helps that marriage can offer. Simply knowing that one is married, that one has promised—before God and the human community—that this is forever, puts a different light on the inevitable problems that one faces. One is more likely (given, of course, a belief in the permanence of marriage) to slog through, to get past whatever it is in the way, to stay together.

Constancy, of course, is not limited to those couples who are formally married. Many of my friends are living together. They have made serious commitments to each other, they have children and, for all practical purposes, they might as well be married. Indeed, several of them have relationships that I consider to be closer to the ideal of marriage than that of most of the married couples I know. But that, I think, is more a function of the kind of people they are, and not of the form of their living arrangements. They are extraordinary people who would probably make a success of any relationship.

Even so, there is, it seems to me, something missing. I wouldn't presume to judge what goes on between two people who have committed themselves to each other—in whatever form they have chosen. I can only look at their relationship as it is perceived by the rest of the human community. It is here, I think, that the strongest argument for marriage as opposed to living together can be made.

Let us assume two couples: One married, one living together. Both have promised a lifetime commitment, both have children, both are trying to live with each other as lovingly, gently, and non-violently as they can. What is the difference?

The difference, as Ravi and I pieced it together that night with Smita, is this: one is a community-building act from the very beginning and the other is not.

To marry, to celebrate a love and a commitment publicly, in the presence of family and friends, is to say that the meaning of one's life can only be found in the context of a community. It is to acknowledge one's part in the human family, to recognize that one's life is more than one's own, that one's actions affect more than oneself. It is to proclaim that marriage is more than a private affair between one woman and one man.

To live together seems to me to imply that the central relationship of one's life is nobody's business but one's own. To live together is a decision reached privately and put into motion alone. There is no community blessing or celebration of the decision.

And what the community does not bless, it does not feel responsible for. Couples who are living together often find themselves quite alone when problems arise in their relationships. Their community may quite properly feel that such problems are none of its business. It was not asked for advice, or even congratulations, at the outset; why should it feel any responsibility now that things are going badly? On the other hand, a community which is asked to witness and bless the beginning of a marriage is far more likely to feel a sense of responsibility to the couple as their marriage grows and develops. I grant that most couples who do actually marry do not ask this of their community. Indeed, most couples think of the people at their wedding simply as guests who have to be fed, and not as participants in a community celebration. More on that in a bit.

The need for privacy, for individualism, looms extraordinarily large in American culture. We have been brought up to believe that it is a sign of weakness to admit that we need others. We have made a virtue of going it alone. Our ideal family is composed of a mother, a father, and one or two children. Grandparents, aunts, uncles, and cousins are all kept at a safe distance, and even neighbors are required, by zoning laws, to be at least an acre away. That this should be reflected in young people's choosing to live together, an essentially private choice, is not surprising. What *is* perhaps surprising is the extent to which most *marriages* are also quite private affairs, all the while purporting to be community events.

Most weddings say very little about the two individuals marrying—or about the community witnessing the union. Most weddings say something about the amount of money the participants have to throw about. They say something about fashion. They say something about respect for authority, in the form of the State, which issues the license, for a fee.

Most wedding ceremonies take place on an altar—so far from the guests who, theoretically, are there to witness the union of these two, that no one but the priest can hear the vows they exchange.

Most weddings are the occasion for bitter arguments: over relatives one cannot abide but invite anyway, seating arrangements at the reception, who pays for what, how many guests each family is allowed. . . . It goes on and on until many couples wish they *had* just decided to live together and skip all the hassle.

What is most telling, though, is the fact that so many weddings do not welcome children. Indeed, many outright discourage them. The phrase "No children, please" can be found frequently on wedding invitations and hard are the judgments passed on parents who dare to bring them anyway. Children, the hope and the future of any community, are an interruption, a noisy distraction, an additional and unnecessary expense—they take away from what is really important.

And what is really important, apparently, is that two grownups want to live together, but before they can, they have to get married.

This alienation of the community from the wedding ceremony, this lack of identification with the bride and groom—who seem more like actors playing prearranged roles than two people expressing their love for each other— serves to depersonalize the celebration. There is a boring sameness to weddings—one goes because one has to, because it is expected. The community is not asked to take part, and it does not. And the wedding sets the tone for the community's role in the marriage itself. The message is clear: It should limit its involvement to making appearances at the appropriate times, giving gifts on the appropriate occasions. Nothing more.

When Ravi and I married, we wanted a community celebration, one involving as many of our friends and families as possible. We wanted our wedding to reflect our religious (Catholic/Hindu) and cultural backgrounds, as well as our social and political concerns; we wanted our wedding to be a celebration of our love, naturally, but also for the community who had come to share our joy.

And it was. What a diversity of talents went into that day—from the wedding invitations and programs we designed, Ravi's side in Hindi and mine in English, to the wedding clothes made by Ravi's cousin and the wedding cake made by my father and a close friend. Ravi's mother performed the Hindu wedding ceremony; two priest friends witnessed the Catholic ceremony. Ravi and I wrote our own vows and selected the readings (from the Hindu and Christian scriptures) that friends and relatives read at the ceremony. Two nuns who had taught me in high school provided their oceanside convent for the day. The vegetarian banquet (both Indian and American foods) was entirely prepared by friends who arrived a few days early to cook . . . and best of all were the children everywhere, behaving exactly as children should behave, especially at a wedding.

It seemed to us then, and it seems even more so now, that our wedding was a symbol of the way we want to live our lives: surrounded by family and friends; giving, and receiving the gifts of time, laughter, advice, and help; sharing food, work, prayer, and celebration; creating a world where children are free and full of joy.

But marriage is a community event. It expresses, in its ideal form, a belief in the goodness of community, a belief in the beauty of two people who love each other coming together to live in communion, a belief in the wonder of human life, a belief so strong that it expressed itself in the creation of new human life.

If two people who say they want to marry do not believe this, then perhaps they should not marry. If they want to "join America"—to live in the suburbs with themselves and their 1.7 genetically screened children, exactly one acre from the nearest neighbor—then perhaps what they want is not marriage but just to live with each other.

If they want to be part of the human community, to start building the kingdom of God here on earth, then marriage is probably what they are seeking. And if it is, then the wedding itself, which is the beginning of marriage, should be an expression of their belief in community.

CHAPTER 7

Marriage Preparation and Cohabiting Couples: Information Report

NCCB Marriage and Family Committee

The report that follows may be the most succinct and comprehensive treatment of what today is a trend among young people: living together (cohabiting), either as a step toward marriage or as a way of saying that a public legal marriage is no longer necessary. This report explores the growing prevalence of living together in North America.

On first reading this report, those students—convinced that marriage as an institution in the twenty-first century is as outmoded as the tooth fairy—may initially rejoice. The report does offer data about a growing trend toward living together outside of marriage, but such data are not the sum total of the report's disclosures.

The report offers facts that should give those involved in or contemplating a cohabiting relationship cause for serious concern, especially those seeking a lifelong relationship. Statistically, there is a greater rate of divorce for those who live together before marriage than for those who do not. Whether they live together as a step toward marriage or not, such persons divorce at a higher rate than those who get to know one another, go through an engagement, marry, and *then* live together.

Unwillingness to take one's time can spell disaster in a committed relationship. Actually, many students are quite aware of the perils of impetuousness, and class discussion often uncovers much wisdom about the issues raised in this report.

Only the report's first part containing social science research is presented here. The second part, which deals with pastoral issues and questions raised by cohabitation, has been omitted.

Questions for Discussion

1. How important is security as a base for growth in an intimate relationship?
2. If there are risks in a cohabiting arrangement, whose risk is greater, the man's or the woman's? If the relationship goes bad, who has the most to lose?
3. If lovers cohabit, who owns the lease? Who owns the furniture? If the relationship falters, who moves out?

4. Consider the following statement: People should do what suits them; they are old enough to make up their own minds and even make their own mistakes.

INTRODUCTION

Today almost half the couples who come for marriage preparation in the Catholic Church are in a cohabiting relationship.[1] Cohabitation, in a commonly understood sense, means living together in a sexual relationship without marriage. Living together in this way involves varying degrees of physical and emotional interaction. Such a relationship is a false sign. It contradicts the meaning of a sexual relationship in marriage as the total gift of one-self in fidelity, exclusivity and permanency.

Over the past 25 years cohabitation has become a major social phenomenon affecting the institution of marriage and family life.[2] It is also an extremely perplexing issue for priests, deacons and lay pastoral ministers who help couples prepare for marriage in the church.

In 1988 the National Conference of Catholic Bishops' Committee on Pastoral Practices published *Faithful to Each Other Forever: A Catholic Handbook of Pastoral Help for Marriage Preparation.* The intent of this volume was to be a resource for those involved in marriage-preparation work. It remains a very useful and comprehensive pastoral tool.

Faithful to Each Other Forever discussed (pp. 71–77) the question of cohabitation under two headings: (a) input on cohabitation from personal experiences and the behavioral sciences, and (b) pastoral approaches to cohabiting couples. In this latter section the handbook drew upon the written policies of a few dioceses to present a range of possible options for working with cohabiting couples who come seeking marriage in the church.

Now, nearly 12 years after the original work of *Faithful to Each Other Forever,* the cumulative pastoral experience of ministering to cohabiting couples has broadened and deepened. This is reflected, at least partially, in the increased number of dioceses that now include a treatment of the issue within their marriage-preparation policies.

In this present resource paper the NCCB Committee on Marriage and Family builds upon the foundation provided by *Faithful to Each Other Forever* when it first treated the question of cohabitation. . . .

This paper is neither an official statement of the Committee on Marriage and Family nor of the National Conference of Catholic Bishops. It does not offer formal recommendations for action. It is intended as a resource paper, offering a compilation of resources and a reflection of the present "state of the question" regarding certain issues of cohabitation.

In this way, it wishes to help:

1. Bishops and diocesan staff who are reviewing and possibly revising their marriage-preparation policies.

2. Priests, deacons, pastoral ministers and lay volunteers who want to become more informed and effective in working with cohabiting couples who come to marriage-preparation programs.

3. Those who are responsible for in-service and continuing education of clergy and laity who carry out the church's ministry of marriage preparation.

As pointed out in *Faithful to Each Other Forever* (p. 71), the committee acknowledges a distinction between sexual activity outside of marriage and cohabitation. They are not identical matters. One can exist without the other. Couples may engage in sexual intercourse without living together; other couples may share the same residence but not live in a sexual relationship. The focus of this paper, however, is on cohabitation understood as both having a sexual relationship and living together in the same residence.

EMPIRICAL INFORMATION ABOUT COHABITATION AND MARRIAGE

Those couples who are in a cohabiting relationship and who come to the church for marriage preparation represent only a percentage of the total cohabiting population. Nonetheless, to understand and respond to them one must appreciate some aspects of the broader phenomenon of cohabitation. This, in turn, is set within a context of widespread sexual activity outside of marriage. In this section we provide highlights of what social science has discovered about cohabitation in general and with specific reference to cohabiting couples who eventually marry.

1. HOW WIDESPREAD IS COHABITATION?

Cohabitation is a pervasive and growing phenomenon with a negative impact on the role of marriage as the foundation of family. The incidence of cohabitation is much greater than is indicated by the number of cohabiting couples presenting themselves for marriage. Slightly more than half of couples in first-time cohabitations ever marry; the overall percentage of those who marry is much lower when it includes those who cohabit more than once. Cohabitation as a permanent or temporary alternative to marriage is a major factor in the declining centrality of marriage in family structure. It is a phenomenon altering the face of family life in first-world countries.

• Eleven percent of couples in the United States cohabited in 1965–74; today, a little over half of all first marriages are preceded by cohabitation (Bumpass and Lu, 1998; Popenoe and Whitehead, 1999).

- Across all age groups there has been a 45 percent increase in cohabitation from 1970 to 1990. It is estimated that 60 percent to 80 percent of the couples coming to be married are cohabiting (Bumpass, Sweet, and Cherlin, 1991).

- Overall, fewer persons are choosing to be married today; the decision to cohabit as a permanent or temporary alternative to marriage is a primary reason (Bumpass, 1995). The percent of couples being married in the United States declined 25 percent from 1975 to 1995. The Official Catholic Directory reported 406,908 couples married in the Catholic Church in 1974; in 1995, it reported a 25 percent decline to 305,385 couples.

- Only 53 percent of first cohabiting unions result in marriage. The percentage of couples marrying from second and third cohabitations is even lower (Bumpass and Lu, 1998; Bumpass, 1990; Wu, 1995; Wineberg and McCarthy, 1998). Ten percent to 30 percent of cohabitors intend never to marry (Bumpass and Sweet, 1995).

- All first-world countries are experiencing the phenomenon of cohabitation and the corrosive impact it has on marriage as the center of family (Bumpass, 1995; Hall and Zhao, 1995; Thomasson, 1998; Haskey and Kiernan, 1989).

2. WHAT IS THE PROFILE OF THE COHABITING HOUSEHOLD?

The profile of the average cohabiting household is both expected and somewhat surprising. Persons with low levels of religious participation and those who have experienced disruption in their parents' marriages or a previous marriage or their own are likely candidates for cohabitation. Persons with lower levels of education and earning power cohabit more often and marry less often than those with higher education. The average cohabiting household stays together just over one year, and children are part of two-fifths of these households. Men are more often serial or repeat cohabitors, moving from woman to woman, while women tend to cohabit only one time.

- Forty percent of cohabiting households include children, either the children of the relationship or the children that one or both partners bring to the relationship (U.S. Bureau of Census, 1998; Wu, 1995; Schoen, 1992).

- Median duration of cohabitation is 1.3 years (Bumpass and Lu, 1998; Wu, 1995). Previously married persons cohabit more often than never-married [persons]; two-thirds of those separated or divorced and under age 35 cohabit. They are more likely than never-married cohabiting couples to have children in the household, and they are much less likely than never-married [persons] to marry their current partner or someone else (Wineberg and McCarthy, 1998; Wu, 1995; Bumpass and Sweet, 1989).

- Those not completing high school are almost twice as likely to cohabit as those who complete college. Forty percent of college graduates, however, do cohabit at some time. Only 26 percent of women with college degrees cohabit, compared to 41 percent of women without a high school diploma. The higher the level of education, the more likely the cohabitor is to marry the partner (Qian, 1998; Bumpass and Lu, 1998; Thornton, Axinn, and Teachman, 1995; Willis and Michael, 1994).

• Women are likely to cohabit only once, and that with the person they subsequently marry; men are more likely to cohabit with a series of partners (Bumpass and Sweet, 1989; Teachman and Polanko, 1990).

• Individuals, especially women, who experienced disruption in their parents' marriages are more likely to cohabit than those who had parents with stable marriages (Axinn and Thornton, 1992; Kiernan, 1992; Black and Sprenkle, 1991; Bumpass and Sweet, 1989).

• Persons with low levels of religious participation and who rate religion of low importance are more likely to cohabit and less likely to marry their partner than those who consider religion important and practice it. There is no difference in frequency of cohabitation by religious denomination; there is a significant difference in cohabitation frequency by level of religious participation (Krishnan, 1998; Lye and Waldron, 1997; Thornton, Axinn, and Hill, 1992; Liefbroer, 1991; Sweet, 1989).

• In general, those in cohabiting households are more independent, more liberal in attitude and more risk oriented than noncohabitors (Clarkberg, Stolzenberg, and Waite, 1995; Cunningham and Antill, 1994; Huffman, Chang, and Schaffer, 1994; DeMaris and MacDonald, 1993).

3. WHAT ARE THE REASONS FOR COHABITATION?

The declining significance of marriage as the center of family is in large part a result of growing secularization and individualization in first-world cultures. Aversion to long-term commitments is one of the identifying characteristics of these trends and a major reason for cohabitation. Key milestones previously associated with marriage, such as sexual relationships, childbearing, and establishing couple households, now occur without marriage. Individuals choose to cohabit under the influence of these cultural values but also for very individual reasons. Some are seeking to ensure a good future marriage and believe that a "trial marriage" will accomplish this; many are simply living together because it seems more economically feasible or because it has become the social norm. In general, cohabitors are not a homogenous or monolithic group, however fully their general characteristics can be described. The reasons for choosing cohabitation are usually mixed: Cohabitation may be in equal parts an alternative to marriage and an attempt to prepare for marriage.

There are both broad cultural reasons and a range of individual reasons for cohabitation.

• The cultural reasons are descriptive of most first-world countries: changing values on family and decline in the importance of marriage (Bumpass, 1995; Clarkberg, Stolzenberg, and Waite, 1995; Parker, 1990).

- Declining confidence in religious and social institutions to provide guidance (Nicole and Baldwin, 1995; Thornton, Axinn, and Hill, 1992).

- Delaying of marriage for economic or social reasons while sexual relationships begin earlier. Eighty-five percent of unmarried youth are sexually active by age 20. "Marriage no longer signifies the beginning of sexual relationship, the beginning of childbearing or the point at which couples establish joint households" (Bumpass, 1995; Popenoe and Whitehead, 1999; Peplau, Hill, and Rubin, 1993; Rindfuss and Van den Heuvel, 1990).

The individual reasons for cohabitation are varied:

- Fear of or disbelief in long-term commitment (Nicole and Baldwin, 1995).

- Desire to avoid divorce (Nicole and Baldwin, 1995; Thornton, 1991; Bumpass, 1990).

- Desire for economic security (Rindfuss and Van den Heuvel, 1990; Schoen and Owens, 1992).

- Stage of personal development, escape from home, "rite of passage" (Nicole and Baldwin, 1995).

- Desire for stability for raising of children (Wu, 1995; Bumpass, Sweet, and Cherlin, 1991; Manning and Lichter, 1996).

- Pressure to conform to current mores that having cohabiting partner is measure of social success, personal desirability, adult transition (Rindfuss, and Van den Heuvel, 1990; Schoen and Owens, 1992).

- Desire to test the relationship (Nicole and Baldwin, 1995; Bumpass, Sweet, and Cherlin, 1991; Bumpass, 1990).

- Rejection of the institution of marriage and desire for an alternative to marriage (Sweet and Bumpass, 1992; Rindfuss and Van den Heuvel, 1990).

4. WHAT ABOUT COHABITORS AND MARRIAGE?

Overall, less than half of cohabiting couples ever marry. Those who do choose to marry are in some part counterculture to the growing view that it is certainly not necessary and perhaps not good to marry. Those who choose to marry instead of continuing to cohabit are the "good news" in a culture that is increasingly anti-marriage. Those cohabiting couples who move to marriage seem to be the "best risk" of a high-risk group: They have fewer risk factors than those cohabitors who choose not to marry. Even so, they still divorce at a rate 50 percent higher than couples who have never cohabited. They are a high-risk group for divorce, and their special risk factors need to be identified and addressed, especially at the time of marriage preparation, if the couples are to build solid marriages.

Only 50 percent to 60 percent of cohabitors marry the persons with whom they cohabit at a given time. Seventy-six percent report plans to marry their partner, but only about half do. The percentage of couples marrying after second and third cohabitation is even lower (Brown and Booth, 1996; Bumpass and Sweet, 1989).

- Up to 30 percent of cohabitors intend never to marry (Bumpass and Sweet, 1995).
- Twenty percent of cohabiting partners disagree about whether or not they intend to marry (Bumpass, Sweet, and Cherlin, 1991).
- When cohabitors do marry, they are more at risk for subsequent divorce than those who did not cohabit before marriage. In the United States the risk of divorce is 50 percent higher for cohabitors than noncohabitors. In some Western European countries, it is estimated to be 80 percent higher (Bumpass and Sweet, 1995; Hall and Zhao, 1995; Bracher, Santow, Morgan, and Trussell, 1993; DeMaris and Rao, 1992; Glenn, 1990).
- When previously married cohabitors marry, their subsequent divorce rate is higher than that of cohabiting couples who have not been previously married (Wineberg and McCarthy, 1998; Wu, 1995; Bumpass and Sweet, 1989).
- Those who cohabit more than once prior to marriage, serial or repeat cohabitors, have higher divorce rates when they do marry than those who cohabit only once (Brown and Booth, 1996; Stets, 1993; Thomson and Colella, 1991).
- There is some indication that the divorce rate is higher for people who cohabit for a longer period of time, especially over three years. The data on this are mixed (Lillard, Brien, and Waite, 1995; Thomson and Colella, 1991; Bennett, Blanc, and Bloom, 1988).
- Cohabitors who marry break up in the earlier years of marriage. Cohabitors and noncohabitors have the same rate of marriage stability if the marriage remains intact over seven years (Bumpass, Sweet, and Cherlin, 1991; Bennett, Blanc, and Bloom, 1988).

5. WHAT ARE THE FACTORS THAT PUT COHABITORS WHO MARRY AT RISK?

Individuals who choose to cohabit have certain attitudes, issues and patterns that lead them to make the decision to cohabit. These same attitudes, issues, and patterns often become the predisposing factors to put them at high risk for divorce when they do choose to move from cohabitation to marriage. The cohabitation experience itself creates risk factors, bad habits, that can sabotage the subsequent marriage. These attitudes and patterns can be identified and brought to the couple preparing for marriage for examination, decision making, skill building, [and] change. Without creating "self-fulfilling prophecies," those preparing cohabiting couples for marriage can help them identify and work with issues around commitment, fidelity, individualism, pressure, [and] appropriate expectations.

Many studies explore why cohabitors are more at risk when they marry. The research suggests that there are two overlapping and reinforcing sources for risk:

- Predisposing attitudes and characteristics they take into the marriage.
- Experiences from the cohabitation itself that create problem patterns and behaviors.

PREDISPOSING ATTITUDES AND CHARACTERISTICS

- Cohabitors as a group are less committed to the institution of marriage and more accepting of divorce. As problems and issues arise to challenge the marriage, they are more likely to seek divorce as the solution (Lillard, Brien, and Waite, 1995; Bracher, Santow, Morgan, and Trussell, 1993; Thomson and Colella, 1991; Bennett, Blanc, and Bloom, 1988).

- "Sexual exclusivity" is less an indicator of commitment for cohabitors than for noncohabitors. In this regard, cohabitation is more like dating than marriage. After marriage, a woman who cohabited before marriage is 3.3 times more likely to be sexually unfaithful than a woman who had not cohabited before marriage (Forste and Tanfer, 1996).

- Cohabitors who do choose to marry appear to be of lesser risk for later divorce than those cohabitors who choose not to marry would be. They appear to be the best risk of a high-risk group (Thomson and Colella, 1991).

- Cohabitors identify themselves or the relationship as poor risk for long-term happiness more often than do noncohabitors. There is evidence that some cohabitors do have more problematic, lower-quality relationships with more individual and couple problems than noncohabitors. Often this is why they feel the need to test the relationship through cohabitation. There is the probability that some of these significant problems will carry over into the marriage relationship (Lillard, Brien, and Waite, 1995; Thomson and Colella, 1991; Booth and Johnson, 1988).

- Cohabitors tend to hold individualism as a more important value than noncohabitors do. While married persons generally value interdependence and the exchange of resources, cohabitors tend to value independence and economic equality. These values do not necessarily change just because a cohabiting couple decides to move into marriage (Clarkberg, Stolzenberg, and Waite, 1995; Waite and Joyner, 1996; Bumpass, Sweet, and Cherlin, 1991).

- Cohabitors can allow themselves to marry because of pressure from family and others, and because of pressure to provide a stable home for children. While it is generally better for the children in a cohabiting household or a child born to a cohabiting couple to be raised in a stable marriage, this is not by itself sufficient reason for the marriage. While family and friends are often right to encourage marriage for a cohabiting couple, a marriage made under such pressure is problematic unless the couple chooses it for more substantial reasons (Barber and Axinn, 1998; Wu, 1995; Mahler, 1996; Manning and Smock 1995; Teachman and Polanko, 1990).

• Cohabitors are demonstrated to have inappropriately high expectations of marriage that can lead them to be disillusioned with the ordinary problems or challenges of marriage. Cohabitors generally report lower satisfaction with marriage after they marry than do noncohabitors. There is danger that they think they have "worked out everything" and that any further challenges are the fault of the institution of marriage (Brown, 1998; Nock, 1995; Booth and Johnson, 1988).

EXPERIENCES FROM THE COHABITATION ITSELF

• The experience of cohabitation changes the attitudes about commitment and permanence, and makes couples more open to divorce (Axinn and Barber, 1997; Nock 1995; Schoen and Weinick, 1993; Axinn and Thornton, 1992).

• Cohabitors have more conflict over money after they marry than noncohabitors do. Often they have set patterns of autonomy or competition about making and handling money during the time of cohabitation, and this carries over to the marriage. Many couples have one pattern of money handling in the cohabitation household and have not discussed clearly how one or the other individual expects this pattern to change after marriage (Singh and Lindsay, 1996; Ressler and Walters, 1995; Waite, 1995).

• Domestic violence is a more common problem with cohabitors than with married persons, and this pattern will carry over to a subsequent marriage relationship. Cohabiting partners can have a lesser-felt need to protect the relationship while they are cohabiting because they do not see it as permanent. If this is the case, some will begin dysfunctional patterns of problem-solving. The existence of the partner's children in the relationship [and] stress over the permanency of the relationship are common causes of conflict and sometimes violence (Jackson, 1996; McLaughlin, Leonard, and Senchak 1992; Stets and Straus, 1989).

• Cohabitors who marry are less effective at conflict resolution than those who did not cohabit. Either a fear of upsetting an uncommitted relationship or the lack of need to protect a temporary relationship can be factors that lead cohabiting couples into poor patterns of conflict resolution which they then carry into marriage (Booth and Johnson, 1988).

• Using sex as a controlling factor can be a negative pattern, which cohabiting couples can bring to their subsequent marriage. Reinforcement of negative family of origin patterns can also have occurred in the cohabiting relationship and be carried over to marriage. Both of these patterns are common issues that dating couples carry into marriage, but they can be exaggerated by the cohabitation experience (Waite and Joyner, 1996; Waite, 1995; Thornton and Axinn, 1993).

NOTES

1. In 1995 a national study of Catholic-sponsored marriage preparation found that 43.6 percent of couples were living together at the time of their marriage preparation. The average length of cohabitation had been 15.6 months. See "Marriage Preparation in the Catholic Church: Getting It Right," Creighton University Center for Marriage and Family, 1995, p. 43.

2. In a report titled "The State of Our Unions: The Social Health of Marriage in America" (The National Marriage Project, Rutgers University, 1999), authors David Popenoe, Ph.D., and Barbara Dafoe Whitehead, Ph.D., identify the rise in unmarried cohabitation as partly responsible for the 43 percent decline, from 1960 to 1996, in the annual number of marriages per thousand unmarried women.

REFERENCES

Axinn, William G. and Barber, Jennifer S. "Living Arrangements and Family Formation Attitudes in Early Adulthood." *Journal of Marriage and the Family* 59 (1997) 595–611.

Axinn, William G. and Thorton, Arland. "The Relationship between Cohabation and Divorce: Selectivity or Causal Influence?" *Demography* 29 (1992) 357–374.

Barber, Jennifer S. and Axinn, William G. "Gender Role Attitudes and Marriage among Young Women." *The Sociological Quarterly* 39 (1998) 11–31.

Bennett, Neil G., Blanc, Ann Klimas, and Bloom, David E. "Commitment and the Modern Union: Assessing the Link between Premarital Cohabitation and Subsequent Marital Stability." *American Sociological Review* 53 (1988) 127–138.

Black, Lenora E. and Sprenkle, Douglas H. "Gender Differences in College Students' Attitudes toward Divorce and Their Willingness to Marry." *Journal of Divorce and Remarriage* 14 (1991) 47–60.

Booth, Alan and Johnson, David. "Premarital Cohabitation and Marital Success." *Journal of Family Issues* 9 (1988) 255–272.

Bracher, Michael, Santow, Gigi, Morgan, S. Philip, and Trussell, James R. "Marriage Dissolution in Australia: Models and Explanations." *Population Studies* 47 (1993) 403–425.

Brown, Susan L. "Cohabation as Marriage Prelude vs. Marriage Alternative: The Significance for Psychological Well-Being." Unpublished Paper, Bowling Green University, Ohio (1998).

Bumpass, Larry L., Sweet, James A., and Cherlin, Andrew. "The Role of Cohabitation in Declining Rates of Marriage." *Journal of Marriage and the Family* 53 (1991) 913–927.

Clarkberg, Marin, Stolzenberg, Ross M., and Waite, Linda J. "Attitudes, Values and Entrance into Cohabitational vs. Marital Unions." *Social Forces* 74 (1995) 609–634.

Committee on Pastoral Practices, National Conference of Catholic Bishops. *Faithful to Each Other Forever: A Catholic Handbook for Marriage Preparation.* Washington, D.C.: NCCB, 1988.

Creighton University Center for Marriage and Family. "Marriage Preparation in the Catholic Church: Getting It Right." Omaha, Neb.: Creighton University, 1995.

Cunningham, John D. and Antill, John K. "Cohabitation and Marriage: Retrospective and Predictive Comparisons." *Journal of Social and Personal Relationships* 11 (1994) 77–93.

DeMaris, Alfred and MacDonald, William. "Premarital Cohabitation and Marital Instability: A Test of the Unconventionality Hypothesis." *Journal of Marriage and the Family* 55 (1993) 399–407.

DeMaris, Alfred and Rao, K. Vaninadha. "Premarital Cohabitation and Subsequent Marital Stability in the United States: A Reassessment." *Journal of Marriage and the Family* 54 (1992) 179–190.

Forste, Renata and Tanfer, Koray. "Sexual Exclusivity among Dating, Cohabiting and Married Women." *Journal of Marriage and the Family* 58 (1996) 33–47.

Glenn, Norval D. "Quantitative Research on Marital Quality in the 1980s: A Critical Review." *Journal of Marriage and the Family* 52 (1990) 818–831.

Hall, David R. and Zhao, John Z. "Cohabitation and Divorce in Canada: Testing the Selectivity Hypotheses." *Journal of Marriage and the Family* 57 (1995) 421–427.

Haskey, John and Kiernan, Kathleen. "Cohabitation in Great Britain—Characteristics and Estimated Numbers of Cohabiting Partners." *Population Trends* 58 (1989).

Huffman, Terry, Chang, Karen Rausch, and Schaffer, Nora. "Gender Differences and Factors Related to the Disposition toward Cohabitation." *Family Therapy* 21 (1994) 171–184.

Jackson, Nicky Ali. "Observational Experiences of Interpersonal Conflict and Teenage Victimization: A Comprehensive Study among Spouses and Cohabitors." *Journal of Family Violence* 11 (1996) 191–203.

Kiernan, Kathleen. "The Impact of Family Disruption in Childhood and Transitions Made in Young Adult Life." *Population Studies* (1992) 46.

Krishnan, Bijaya. "Premarital Cohabitation and Marital Disruption." *Journal of Divorce and Remarriage* 28 (1998) 157–170.

Liefbroer, Aat C. "The Choice between a Married or Unmarried First Union by Young Adults." *European Journal of Population* 1 (1991) 273–298.

Lillard, Lee A., Brien, Michael J., and Waite, Linda. "Premarital Cohabitation and Subsequent Marital Dissolution: A Matter of Self-Selection?" *Demography* 32 (1995) 437–457.

Lye, Diane N. and Waldron, Ingrid. "Attitudes toward Cohabitation, Family, and Gender Roles: Relationships to Values and Political Ideology." *Sociological Perspectives* 40 (1997) 199–225.

Mahler, K. "Completed Premarital Pregnancies More Likely among Cohabiting Women Than among Singles." *Family Planning Perspectives* 28 (1996) 179–180.

Manning, Wendy and Smock, Pamela. "Why Marry?: Race and the Transition to Marriage among Cohabitors." *Demography* 32 (1995) 509–520.

McLaughlin, Iris G., Leonard, Kenneth E., and Senchak, Marilyn. "Prevalence and Distribution of Premarital Aggression among Couples Applying for a Marriage License." *Journal of Family Violence* 7 (1992) 309–319.

Nicole, Faith Monique and Baldwin, Cynthia. "Cohabitation as a Developmental Stage: Implications for Mental Health Counseling." *Journal of Mental Health Counseling* 17 (1995) 386–397.

Nock, Steven L. "A Comparison of Marriages and Cohabiting Relationships." *Journal of Family Issues* 16 (1995) 53–76.

Parker, Stephen. *Informal Marriage, Cohabitation and the Law, 1750–1989.* New York: St. Martin's Press, 1990.

Peplau, Letitia A., Hill, Charles T., and Rubin, Zick. "Sex Role Attitudes in Dating and Marriage: A 15-Year Follow-Up of the Boston Study." *Journal of Social Issues* 49 (1993) 31–52.

Popenoe, David and Whitehead, Barbara Dafoe. *Should We Live Together?: What Young Adults Need to Know about Cohabitation before Marriage.* New Brunswick, N.J.: The National Marriage Project (Rutgers University), 1999.

Qian, Zhenchao. "Changes in Assortative Mating: The Impact of Age and Education, 1970–1990." *Demography* 35 (1998) 279–292.

Ressler, Rand W. and Walters, Melissa S. "The Economics of Cohabitation." *Ayklos* 48 (1995) 577–592.

Rinfuss, Ronald R. and Van den Heuvel, Audrey. "Cohabitation: A Precursor to Marriage or an Alternative to Being Single?" *Population and Development Review* 16 (1990) 703–726.

Schoen, Robert. "First Unions and the Stability of First Marriages." *Journal of Marriage and the Family* 54 (1992) 281–284.

Schoen, Robert and Owens, Dawn. "A Further Look at First Unions and First Marriages." *The Changing American Family,* ed. Scott J. South and Stewart E. Tolany. Boulder, Colo.: Westview Press, 1992.

Schoen, Robert and Weinick, Robin. "Partner Choice in Marriages and Cohabitation." *Journal of Marriage and the Family* 55 (1993) 408–414.

Singh, Supriya and Lindsay, Jo. "Money in Heterosexual Relationship." *Australian and New Zealand Journal of Sociology* 32 (1996) 57–69.

Stets, Jan E. "The Link between Present and Past Intimate Relationship." *Journal of Family Issues* 14 (1993).

Stets, Jan E. and Straus, Murray A. "The Marriage License as a Hitting License: A Comparison of Assaults in Dating, Cohabiting and Married Couples." *Journal of Family Violence* 4 (1989) 161–180.

Sweet, James A. "Differentials in the Approval of Cohabitation." National Survey of Families and Households, Working Paper No. 8. Center for Demography and Ecology: University of Wisconsin-Madison, 1989.

Sweet, James A. and Bumpass, Larry L. "Young Adults' Views of Marriage, Cohabitation and Family." *The Changing American Family,* ed. Scott J. South and Stewart E. Tolany. Boulder, Colo.: Westview Press, 1992.

Teachman, Jay D. and Polanko, Karen A. "Cohabitation and Marital Stability in the United States." *Social Forces* 69 (1990) 207–220.

Thomasson, Richard. "Modern Swedes: The Declining Importance of Marriage." *Scandinavian Review,* August 1998.

Thomson, Elizabeth and Colella, Ugo. "Cohabitation and Marital Stability: Quality or Commitment." Center for Demography and Ecology: University of Wisconsin-Madison, 1991.

Thornton, Arland. "Influence of the Marital History of Parents on the Marital and Cohabitational Experience of Children." *American Journal of Sociology* 96 (1991) 868–894.

Thornton, Arland and Axinn, William G. "Mothers, Children and Cohabitation: The Intergenerational Effects of Attitudes and Behavior." *American Sociological Review* 58 (1993) 233–246.

Thornton, Arland, Axinn, William G., and Hill, Daniel H. "Reciprocal Effects of Religiosity, Cohabitation and Marriage." *American Journal of Sociology* 98 (1992) 628–651.

Thornton, Arland, Axinn, William G., and Teachman, Jay D. "The Influence of School Enrollment and Accumulation on Cohabitation and Marriage in Early Adulthood." *American Sociological Review* 60 (1995) 762–774.

U.S. Bureau of the Census. "Marital Status and Hiring Arrangements." March 1997 (1998).

Waite, Linda J. "Does Marriage Matter?" *Demography* 32 (1995) 483–507.

Waite, Linda J. and Joyner, Kara. "Men's and Women's General Happiness and Sexual Satisfaction in Marriage, Cohabitation, and Single Living." Unpublished Paper, Population Research Center: National Opinion Research Center and University of Chicago, 1996.

Willis, Robert J. and Michael, Robert T. "Innovation in Family Formation: Evidence on Cohabitation in the United States." *The Family, the Market, and the State in Aging Societies,* ed. J. Ermisch and N. Ogawa. London: Oxford, 1994. 119–145.

Wineberg, Howard and McCarthy, James. "Living Arrangements after Divorce: Cohabitation vs. Remarriage." *Journal of Divorce and Remarriage* 29 (1998) 131–146.

Wu, Zheng. "Premarital Cohabitation and Postmarital Cohabiting Union Formation." *Journal of Family Issues* 16 (1995) 212–232.

CHAPTER 8

A Case for Gay Marriage

Brent Hartinger

⌒⌒⌒

What is the meaning of marriage? The question *initially* appears simple and easy to answer. Our taken-for-granted assumption, however, is that the frame of reference is heterosexual union. This assumption is challenged and the complexity of the question emerges when homosexual unions insist on inclusion in the meaning of the term. This is the position of Brent Hartinger in this article.

An estimated 10 percent of the U.S. population—about 25 million people—is exclusively or predominantly homosexual in sexual orientation. Some data indicate that 50 percent of the men and about 70 percent of the women are in long-term, committed relationships. The concept of "domestic partnership" seems an inadequate classification for these enduring relationships. In spite of the benefits associated with the concept, it is seriously flawed. A simpler solution, according to Hartinger, is to allow gay civil marriage and to offer the support and endorsement of religious institutions to the bond.

This, in fact, would be a conservative move, the author claims. It would nurture long-term, committed, monogamous gay relationships and provide them with some measure of respect and social support. It would grant recognition to a significant cross-cultural minority and allow them to participate in an important social institution. The interests of the state would be served by legalizing gay bonding and the meaning of marriage enriched by the public celebration of this loving and committing union.

Questions for Discussion

1. Would homosexual marriage harmonize with our current underlying cultural values?
2. Would legalizing and legitimizing gay unions weaken or strengthen the family?
3. In view of the AIDS crisis, would gay marriage foster good public-health policy?
4. Is the meaning of marriage (as religious sacrament) consonant with the meaning of homosexuality?
5. Are all sexual forms equal with reference to specific social goods?
6. Are procreative heterosexual marriages a special and irreplaceable central symbol of the Jewish and Christian traditions?

In San Francisco this year, homosexuals won't just be registering for the draft and to vote. In November 1990, voters approved legislation which allows unmarried live-in partners—heterosexual or homosexual—to register themselves as "domestic partners," publicly agreeing to be jointly responsible for basic living expenses. Like a few other cities, including New York and Seattle, San Francisco had already allowed bereavement leave to the domestic partners of municipal employees. But San Francisco lesbians and gays had been trying for eight years to have some form of partnership registration— for symbolic reasons at least—ever since 1982 when then-mayor Diane Feinstein vetoed a similar ordinance. A smattering of other cities provide health benefits to the domestic partners of city employees. In 1989, a New York court ruled that a gay couple is a "family" in that state, at least in regard to their rent-controlled housing (the decision was reaffirmed late in 1990). And in October of 1989, Denmark became the first industrialized country to permit same-sex unions (since then, one-fifth of all marriages performed there have been homosexual ones).

However sporadic, these represent major victories for gay men and lesbians for whom legal marriage is not an option. Other challenges are coming fast and furious. Two women, Sandra Rovira and Majorie Forlini, lived together in a marriage-like relationship for twelve years—and now after her partner's death, Rovira is suing AT&T, Forlini's employer, for refusing to pay the death benefits the company usually provides surviving spouses. Craig Dean and Patrick Gill, a Washington, D.C., couple, have filed a $1 million discrimination suit against that city for denying them a marriage license and allegedly violating its human rights acts which outlaw discrimination on the basis of sexual orientation; the city's marriage laws explicitly prohibit polygamous and incestuous marriages, but not same-sex ones.

Legally and financially, much is at stake. Most employee benefit plans— which include health insurance, parental leave, and bereavement leave— extend only to legal spouses. Marriage also allows partners to file joint income taxes, usually saving them money. Social Security can give extra payment to qualified spouses. And assets left from one legal spouse to the other after death are not subject to estate taxes. If a couple splits up, there is the issue of visitation rights for adopted children or offspring conceived by artificial insemination. And then there are issues of jurisprudence (a legal spouse cannot be compelled to testify against his or her partner) and inheritance, tenancy, and conservatorship: pressing concerns for many gays as a result of AIDS.

In terms of numbers alone, a need exists. An estimated 10 percent of the population—about 25 million Americans—is exclusively or predominantly homosexual in sexual orientation, and upwards of 50 percent of the men and about 70 percent of the women are in long-term, committed relationships. A 1990 survey of 1,266 lesbian and gay couples found that 82 percent of the male couples and 75 percent of the female ones share all or part of their incomes.

As a result, many lesbians and gays have fought for "domestic partnership" legislation to extend some marital and family benefits to unmarried couples—cohabitating partners either unwilling or, in the case of homosexuals, unable to marry. In New York City, for example, unmarried municipal workers who have lived with their partners at least a year may register their relationships with the personnel department, attesting to a "close and committed" relationship "involving shared responsibilities," and are then entitled to bereavement leave.

But such a prescription is inadequate; the protections and benefits are only a fraction of those resulting from marriage—and are available to only a small percentage of gays in a handful of cities (in the above-mentioned survey, considerably less than 10 percent of lesbian and gay couples were eligible for any form of shared job benefits). Even the concept of "domestic partnership" is seriously flawed. What constitutes a "domestic partner"? Could roommates qualify? A woman and her live-in maid? It could take an array of judicial decision making to find out.

Further, because the benefits of "domestic partnership" are allotted to couples without much legal responsibility—and because the advantages of domestic partnership are necessarily allowed for unmarried heterosexual partners as well as homosexual ones—domestic partnership has the unwanted consequence of weakening traditional marriage. Society has a vested interest in stable, committed relationships—especially, as in the case of most heterosexual couples, when children are concerned. But by eliminating the financial and legal advantages to marriage, domestic partnership dilutes that institution.

Society already has a measure of relational union—it's called marriage, and it's not at all difficult to ascertain: you're either married or you're not.

Yet for unmarried heterosexual couples, marriage is at least an option. Gay couples have no such choice—and society also has an interest in committed, long-lasting relationships even between homosexuals. An estimated 3 to 5 million homosexuals have parented children within heterosexual relationships, and at least 1,000 children were born to lesbian or gay couples in the San Francisco area alone in just the last five years. None of the recent thirty-five studies on homosexual parents has shown that parental sexual orientation has any adverse effect on children (and the children of gays are no more likely to be gay themselves). Surely increased stability in the relationships of lesbians and gay men could only help the gays themselves and their many millions of children.

Some suggest that legal mechanisms already exist by which lesbian and gay couples could create some of the desired protections for their relationships: power-of-attorney agreements, proxies, wills, insurance policies, and joint tenancy arrangements. But even these can provide only a fraction of the benefits of marriage. And such an unwieldy checklist guarantees that many lesbian and gay couples will not employ even those available.

There is a simpler solution: Allow gay civil marriage. And throw the weight of our religious institutions behind such unions.

In 1959, Mildred Jeter and Richard Loving, a mixed-race Virginia couple married in Washington, D.C., pleaded guilty to violating Virginia's ban on interracial marriages. Jeter and Loving were given a suspended jail sentence on the condition that they leave the state. In passing the sentence, the judge said, "Almighty God created the races white, black, yellow, Malay, and red, and he placed them on separate continents. And but for the interference with his arrangements, there would be no cause for such marriages. The fact that he separated the races shows that he did not intend for the races to mix." A motion to overturn the decision was denied by two higher Virginia courts until the state's ban on interracial marriage was declared unconstitutional by the United State Supreme Court in 1967. At the time, fifteen other states also had such marital prohibitions.

Clearly, one's sexual orientation is different from one's race. While psychological consensus (and compelling identical and fraternal twin studies) force us to concede that the homosexual *orientation* is not a choice (nor is it subject to change), homosexual behavior definitely is a choice, very unlike race. Critics maintain that gays can marry—just not to members of their same sex.

But with regard to marriage, whether homosexual behavior is a choice or not is irrelevant, since one's marriage partner is *necessarily* a choice. In 1959, Richard Loving, a white man, could have chosen a different partner to marry other than Mildred Jeter, a black woman; the point is that he did not. The question is whether, in the absence of a compelling state interest, the state should be allowed to supersede the individual's choice.

Some maintain that there are compelling state interests to prohibiting same-sex marriages: that tolerance for gay marriages would open the door for any number of unconventional marital arrangements—group marriage, for example. In fact, most lesbian and gay relationships are probably far more conventional than most people think. In the vast majority of respects, gay relationships closely resemble heterosexual ones—or even actually improve upon them (gay relationships tend to be more egalitarian than heterosexual ones). And in a society where most cities have at least one openly gay bar and sizable gay communities—where lesbians and gays appear regularly on television and in the movies—a committed relationship between two people of the same sex is not nearly the break from convention that a polygamous one is. More important, easing the ban on same-sex marriage would make lesbians and gays, the vast majority of whom have not chosen celibacy, even more likely to live within long-term, committed partnerships. The result would be more people living more conventional lifestyles, not more people living less conventional ones. It's actually a conservative move, not a liberal one.

Similarly, there is little danger that giving legitimacy to gay marriages would undermine the legitimacy of heterosexual ones—cause "the breakdown of the family." Since heterosexuality appears to be at least as immutable as homo-sexuality (and since there's no evidence that the prevalence of homosexuality increases following the decriminalization of it), there's no chance heterosexu-als would opt for the "homosexual alternative." Heterosexual marriage would still be the ultimate social union for heterosexuals. Gay marriage would simply recognize a consistent crosscultural, transhistorical minority and allow that significant minority to also participate in an important social institution. And since marriage licenses are not rationed out, homosexual partnerships wouldn't deny anyone else the privilege.

Indeed, the compelling state interest lies in *permitting* gay unions. In the wake of AIDS, encouraging gay monogamy is simply rational public health policy. Just as important, gay marriage would reduce the number of closet gays who marry heterosexual partners, as an estimated 20 percent of all gays do, in an effort to conform to social pressure—but at enormous cost to them-selves, their children, and their opposite-sex spouses. It would reduce the atmosphere of ridicule and abuse in which the children of homosexual par-ents grow up. And it would reduce the number of shameful parents who dis-own their children or banish their gay teen-agers to lives of crime, prostitu-tion, and drug abuse, or to suicide (psychologists estimate that gay youth comprise up to 30 percent of all teen suicides, and one Seattle study found that a whopping 40 percent of that city's street kids may be lesbian or gay, most having run away or been expelled from intolerant homes). Gay mar-riage wouldn't weaken the family; it would *strengthen* it.

The unprecedented social legitimacy given gay partnerships—and homosexuality in general—would have other societal benefits as well: it would dramatically reduce the widespread housing and job discrimination, and verbal and physical violence experienced by most lesbians and gays, clear moral and social evils.

Of course, legal and religious gay marriage wouldn't, as some writers claim, "celebrate" or be "an endorsement" of homosexual sexual behavior— any more than heterosexual marriage celebrates heterosexual sex or endorses it; gay marriage would celebrate the loving, committed relationship between two individuals, a relationship in which sexual behavior is one small part. Still, the legalization of gay marriage, while not making homosexual sexual behavior any more prevalent, would remove much of the stigma concerning such behavior, at least that which takes place within the confines of "mar-riage." And if the church sanctions such unions, a further, moral legitimacy will be granted. In short, regardless of the potential societal gains, should society and the church reserve a centuries-old moral stand that condemns homosexual sexual behavior?

We have no choice; the premises upon which the moral stand are based have changed. Science now acknowledges the existence of a homosexual sex-ual *orientation*, like heterosexuality, a fundamental affectional predisposition. Unlike specific behaviors of, say, rape or incest, a homosexual's sexual behav-ior is the logical expression of his or her most basic, unchangeable sexual make-up. And unlike rape and incest, necessarily manifestations of destruction and abuse, sexual behavior resulting from one's sexual orientation can be an expression of love and unity (it is the complete denial of this love—indeed, an unsettling preoccupation with genital activity—that makes the inflammatory comparisons of homosexual sex to rape, incest, and alcoholism so frustrating for lesbians and gays).

Moral condemnation of homosexual sexual behavior is often founded on the belief that sex and marriage are—and should be—inexorably linked with childrearing; because lesbians and gay men are physiologically incapable of creating children alone, all such sexual behavior is deemed immoral—and gays are considered unsuitable to the institution of marriage. But since moral sanction is not withheld from infertile couples or those who intend to remain childless, this standard is clearly being inconsistently—and unfairly—applied.

Some cite the promiscuity of some male gays as if this is an indication that all homosexuals are incapable or undeserving of marriage. But this standard is also inconsistently applied; it has never been seriously suggested that the existence of promiscuous heterosexuals invalidate all heterosexuals from the privilege of marriage. And if homosexuals are more likely than heterosexuals to be promiscuous—and if continual, harsh condemnation hasn't altered that fact—the sensible solution would seem to be to try to lure gays back to the monogamous fold by providing efforts in that direction with some measure of respect and social support: something gay marriage would definitely provide.

Human beings are sexual creatures. It is simply not logical to say, as the church does, that while one's basic sexual outlook is neither chosen nor sinful, any activity taken as a result of that orientation is. One must then ask exactly where does the sin of "activity" begin anyway? Hugging a person of the same sex? Kissing? Same-sex sexual fantasy? Even apart from the practical impossibilities, what about the ramifications of such an attempt? How does the homosexual adolescent formulate self-esteem while being told that *any* expression of his or her sexuality *ever* is unacceptable—or downright evil? The priest chooses celibacy (asexuality isn't required), but this *is* a choice—one made well after adolescence.

Cultural condemnations and biblical prohibitions of (usually male) homosexual behavior were founded upon an incomplete understanding of human sexuality. To grant the existence of a homosexual orientation requires that there be some acceptable expression of it. Of course, there's no reason why lesbians and gays should be granted moral leniency over heterosexuals—which is why perhaps the most acceptable expression of same-sex sexuality should be within the context of a government sanctioned, religiously blessed marriage. But before we can talk about the proper way to get two brides or two grooms down a single church aisle, we have to first show there's an aisle wide enough to accommodate them.

CHAPTER 9

The Meaning of Marriage

Evelyn Eaton Whitehead
James D. Whitehead

Some unmarried people think of marriage only in terms of a relationship filled with romance, rejecting the social institution of marriage as too rigid, too filled with legal formalities and rigid rituals—basically, too "unromantic." In this essay Evelyn and James Whitehead look at three aspects of marriage: as a relationship, as a commitment, and as a lifestyle.

They see relationship as not one way but mutual. Once they use the term *mutual*, they put the marriage relationship in a line of continuity with all other mutual relationships, like friendship and family. Married love as a relationship of mutuality has these characteristics: romance, sex, friendship, and devotion. None of these characteristics maintains itself automatically. Each must be *intended* and then *attended to.*

It is worth noticing that the model they use for mutual relationships is friendship. They point out how there arise in any friendship tensions and pressures, but especially "the tensions and ambiguities that are inevitable as we attempt to live as complex a relationship as marriage."

This highlighting of "tensions and ambiguities" may be especially encouraging to those with the mistaken notion that "being in love means never having to say you're sorry," but who are going through the inevitable strains of any mutual relationship. These tensions and ambiguities are more a sign of mutuality than a sign of a relationship in danger.

The commitment side of marriage is the one that makes many people most nervous and raises the most questions about whether one is capable of such a commitment. The Whiteheads offer wisdom on two dimensions of commitment: our expectations of exclusivity and our expectations of permanence. This section of the essay might be read in conjunction with Margaret Farley's "The Meaning of Commitment" (chapter 28).

The final section is about the lifestyle of marriage. The authors wisely point out that a lifestyle comes from choices made in a marriage, but also from circumstances. Some choices—like parenthood—are permanent and can't be changed. However, many choices can and must be rethought and remade or unmade and shifted, like our choices about money and time. Readers of this collection may want to give special attention to this last section and the meaning it may have for the choices being made right now.

T he word "marriage" refers to many things. We can use the word to mean our own experience of the day-to-day relationship we share. The word can also mean the social institution of matrimony, which has legal definition and rights and duties that are regulated by the state and sanctioned in many religious traditions through special rites and ceremonies. Between these two senses of the word—marriage as my experience and marriage as a social institution—there are other meanings as well. Marriage is a relationship; marriage is a commitment; marriage is a lifestyle.

When we speak of marriage as a *relationship* we focus on the quality of the bond that exists between us, our mutual love. The *commitment* of marriage refers to the promises we make to do "whatever is necessary" to deepen and develop this love and, in this love, to move beyond ourselves in creativity and care. The *lifestyle* of marriage describes the patterns that we develop as we attempt to live out these promises—our choices among values and activities, the organization of our daily life, our patterns in the use of time and money and the other resources we have. These three facets of marriage are overlapping and interrelated. Each contributes richly to the complexity of our life together and to the satisfaction we experience in marriage. And, as we are becoming more aware, none of these aspects of our marriage is ever finished or static. Each is in movement, in an ongoing process of realization and development—or decline.

THE RELATIONSHIP OF MARRIAGE—MUTUAL LOVE

Mutual love is the heart of the process of marriage as we envision it today. This has not always been the case. In patriarchal understandings of marriage the wife is more property than partner. Vestiges of this "wife as possession" are still to be found (often embodied in laws and customs surrounding sexuality in marriage) but the movement toward mutuality continues in the way many married people choose to live and, gradually, in the larger social definitions of marriage as well.

The expectations for love in marriage today are high. The "ideal" of married love for most people includes romance, sex, friendship and devotion. Romance: We want the emotional and physical attraction that we experienced early in our relationship to continue through our married years. Sex: We want our lovemaking to be lively and mutually satisfying, enhanced by a deepening responsiveness to each other's preferences and needs. Friendship: We want to continue to like each other, to enjoy each other's company, to find in each other the sources of comfort and challenge, of solace and stimulation that we need for continuing growth. Devotion: We want to be able to "count on" one another, to give our trust in the deep conviction that it shall not be betrayed, to experience the awesome responsibility and transforming power of holding someone else's well-being as important to us as our own and to know that we, too, are held in such care.

These are not easy accomplishments. With these high expectations come equally high demands. In a relationship that is mutual, I must be ready to give these benefits as well as to receive them. And for many of us these emotional benefits are sought and expected only in marriage. We have no other so serious or so sustained an adult relationship.

Marriage did not always carry such high emotional demands. Wives and husbands did not generally expect to be one another's chief companion or best friend. Each could be expected to develop a range of social relationships—in the extended family, in the neighborhood, in the workplace, in clubs and churches and associations—that provided support and a sense of belonging to complement the marriage relationship. Today our involvement in these wider circles seems to have slipped. Economic and geographic mobility can cut into, even cut off, ties with family and neighborhood. The workplace is increasingly competitive; our relationships there seem of necessity to remain superficial. No one wants to take the risk of deeper friendship with a potential rival. And here, too, mobility plays a part in keeping these relationships light. We know it is likely that one or both of us may move to another job. Many associations—political parties, civic groups, churches—seem to have lost the consensus they formerly enjoyed. In these groupings today we are likely to experience polarization rather than a sense of belonging. Now it is often only from my spouse and, perhaps, my children that I expect any deep or continuing emotional response. This expectation has enriched the experience of mutuality in marriage, but it has also added to its strains. There are few of us today who would choose a style of marriage that did not include friendship and mutuality among its chief goals. But we have not given much attention to pressures that are inevitable in the companionate marriage or to the resources that may be required for us to live well this style of mutual love.

Marriage brings us in touch with our incompatible hopes for human life. It is useful to look at some of these incompatibles—the tensions and ambiguities that are inevitable as we attempt to live as complex a relationship as marriage. These tensions exist not simply because I am "selfish" or my spouse is "unreasonable" or "immature." These tensions are built into the experience of relationship—most relationships, but especially relationships as encompassing as marriage.

Security and adventure are both significant goals in adult life. We seek the stability of established patterns, and yet we are attracted by the new and the unknown. Often we sense these goals in opposition; life seems to force our choice of one over the other. To seek adventure means to risk some of the security I have known; to be secure means to turn away from some of life's invitations to novelty and change. Most of us learn to make these choices, but an ambivalence remains. At times, when the pull of security is strong, change may be seen as uninviting or even dangerous. A preference for stability is then easy to sustain. But at other times the appeal of change will be compelling and stability will seem a synonym for boredom and stagnation.

One of the ongoing tensions of marriage concerns this conflict between freedom and security, adventure and stability. I want to deepen the love and life we share, and I want to be able to pursue other possibilities that are open to me, unencumbered by the limits that come with my commitment to you. I need change and novelty and challenge; I need what is predictable and familiar and sure. I want to be close to you in a way that lets me share my weaknesses as well as my strengths, and I want to be strong enough to stand apart from you and from the relationship we share. Again, the presence of these incompatibles is not, of itself, cause for concern. These are normal, expectable, inevitable. But, then, neither is it surprising that the process of mediating among these needs generates considerable stress.

The commitment of marriage takes us to the heart of this ambivalence between stability and change. In marriage we say both "yes" and "no"—"yes" to each other and to the known and unknown possibilities that will be a part of our life together as it unfolds, "no" to the known and unknown possibilities that our life together will exclude. Marriage for a lifetime demands both stability (that we hold ourselves faithful to the promises we have made) and change (that we recognize the changing context in which our promises remain alive). We can anticipate that at different points in our marriage we will experience this ambivalence—sometimes celebrating the new developments in our life together, sometimes resisting these changes; sometimes grateful for the stability of our love, sometimes resenting its "sameness."

Marriage invites me to recognize these ambiguities of my own heart as I attempt to choose a style of life and love in which both to express myself and to hold myself accountable. Without commitment and choices, I know I remain a child, but that realization seldom makes the process of choice any easier.

THE COMMITMENTS OF MARRIAGE— PRIORITY AND PERMANENCE

The commitments of marriage are the promises we make. In many ways it is these mutual promises that transform our experience of love into marriage—an enduring relationship of mutual care and shared life-giving. Both by our choice and by the momentum of its own dynamics, marriage takes us beyond where we are now. It projects us into the future. Through the hopes we hold for our life together we condition the future—we begin to mold and shape it. We open ourselves to possibilities, we make demands, we place limits, we hold each other in trust.

Our commitments, of course, do not control the future. We learn this mighty lesson as we move through adult life, invited by the events of our days to give up one by one our adolescent images of omnipotence. An illusory sense of the degree to which we can control our own destinies may have once served us well, energizing us to move beyond indecision and enter the complex world of adult responsibility. But maturity modifies both our sense of power and our sense of control. We are both stronger and weaker than we had known. Our promises are fragile, but they still have force. It is on this vulnerable strength of human commitment that we base our hope. And it is through our commitments that we engage the future.

The commitments of marriage are the promises we make—to ourselves, to one another, to the world beyond—to do "whatever is necessary" so that the love that we experience may endure; even more, that it may flourish. Our own relationship of love is, we know, similar to that which other couples share. But it is in many ways special, unique to who we are, peculiar to the strengths and needs and history we have. Our commitments, then, will reflect features in common with most marriages as well as the demands and possibilities that are particularly our own.

Two of the commitments that have been seen to be at the core of marriage are sexual exclusivity and permanence. The social meaning of these commitments has fluctuated across time. Stress on the importance of the woman's virginity at marriage and her sexual availability only to her husband after marriage is particularly strong in cultures where property and social status are transferred according to the male line of descent. It is important here that there be no confusion about paternity. And strict regulation of the woman's sexual experience is one way to keep the facts of paternity clear.

There are other instances where the stress on sexual exclusivity is intended to regulate the wife's behavior but not, or not to the same degree, the husband's. This double standard of sexual morality, which looks with some leniency on a married man's "fooling around" while it castigates a married woman as a wanton or an adulteress, has been tied closely with those understandings of marriage that see the wife as, in some ways, the property or possession of her husband.

In many current marriages the commitment to sexual exclusivity has expanded toward an expectation that neither spouse shall have any emotional involvement outside the marriage itself. By conscious decision or simply by circumstances, the couple or the small family unit depend exclusively upon one another for emotional sustenance. They have become an emotional island, apart. Neither wife nor husband has any other substantive adult friendship; their network of social acquaintances is shifting and somewhat superficial. Each may also feel that to need or seek support from someone other than the spouse is itself a kind of "infidelity." Sometimes this caution in exploring wider friendship is rooted in a fear of the "inevitable" sexual overtones of relationships between women and men. "Better not to start anything than to find this friendship slipping into an affair." Sometimes it responds to real insecurity or jealousy in one or both spouses. Sometimes, however, this insistent emotional exclusivity is more an expression of what couples judge to be "expected" of marriage. Emotions and needs, personal values and concerns—these are of the substance of my "private life." Family is the unit of private life in our society. It is to my family, especially to my spouse, that I retreat from the arbitrary and impersonal "public world." Increasingly, colleagues at work, people in the neighborhood, fellow citizens are all seen as part of the "public world." My relations with them are limited, objective and often hostile. There is little opportunity and less ability to share with them any meaningful part of life. It is in marriage that I expect that my subjectivity will be nourished. Here, and possibly here alone, "who I am" is more important than "what I can do." As the polarization of the subjective and the objective worlds, the realms of the private and the public, increases, so do the pressures for emotional exclusivity in marriage.

Many judge that the pressures of the emotionally exclusive marriage ultimately work against its development and permanence. Permanence is the second of the commitments that have generally described marriage. Here, too, the promise has been experienced differently at different times. Seldom has this expectation been absolute. Cultures and legal systems, while stressing the significance of permanence to the interpersonal experience and the legal contract of marriage, have also stipulated a variety of circumstances under which this commitment can be set aside. Sometimes childlessness was justification, frequently adultery has been sufficient cause. Religious conversion, desertion, physical abuse, psychological immaturity, emotional illness—each has been seen as of sufficient weight to justify the dissolution of marriage, whether through annulment or divorce.

The commitment of permanence has also had different psychological meaning. As recently as a century ago "marriage for a lifetime" often did not last very long. The woman's death in childbirth ended many marriages. An average life expectancy of some fifty years meant that many marriages ended in mid-life. In 1870, for example, a married woman could expect that her husband would die before her youngest child would leave home. Today, increasingly, couples can anticipate some twenty or more years together, alone, after the children have left the family household and are on their own. Movement into this time of "post-parental intimacy" is hard on some marriages. Couples may be surprised to find that, without their shared concern for parenting, they have little left of mutuality. They face the challenge of developing anew a life in common, one that is adequate to the reality of each partner now and to the possibilities that are present in their relationship. Other couples have been aware of a deteriorating relationship and yet have chosen to remain together through the years of their most active family responsibilities. These past, they judge there is no further bond to hold them together.

The strains on permanence can be experienced earlier in marriage as well. The accelerated pace of social change today is reflected in the experience of personal change. As we approach marriage we judge—to some degree correctly, to some degree in error—that we "fit" together, that we shall be able to offer each other the resources of love and support and challenge that will enable us to find and to give life. And then we change, sometimes each of us and in ways that enrich our mutual commitment. Sometimes, though, there is not such synchrony. One of us changes in ways that are threatening or seem unfair to the other. Each of us develops—perhaps gradually, perhaps suddenly—in directions that lead us apart and leave us without a clear sense of how we can be together now. Are there ways we might stay better in touch over the course of change so that we are not so taken by surprise? Or must the loss of our relationship be the price we pay for growth?

There are those who suggest that the prevalence of divorce among us today has dissolved our expectations of permanence in marriage. Young people approaching marriage, it seems, do not expect it to last. And, so the argument goes, married people today consider divorce a ready option, one which they anticipate that they, too, will use. There are, obviously, people of whom this characterization is true. But the effect of the increasing incidence of divorce on the expectations of permanence in marriage is more complex than these attitudes suggest. Permanence is no longer a guarantee of marriage even when it is promised. This awareness permeates our consciousness today. This may lead us to question whether, or under what circumstances, permanence is possible. But it seldom leads us, whether we are beginning a relationship of marriage or ending one, to judge that permanence is not to be preferred. Permanence is not to be preferred to everything, so that under no circumstances will I consider the end of my own marriage. But permanence is to be preferred as the goal and intention of our life together. And it is to be preferred, if it is in any way possible, to the pain of divorce.

Most people want marriage to last. It is in the hope of an enduring relationship that we take the emotional and the practical, legal steps that lead us into marriage. Our standards are high for what constitutes the kind of relationship that we want to endure, and sometimes these criteria are not always clear or compatible. (We may want to be the central figure in each other's life and also want each to be open to continuing growth in new relationships. We may want to start our family now and yet to have each of us pursue the development of our own career without serious interruption.) Each of our goals for marriage, taken alone, may be worthy. But taken together they may place considerable strain on our resourcefulness. While no one of our goals may be incompatible with our marriage flourishing over a lifetime, the combination of goals and priorities that we establish may carry heavy costs. We may find, in living out these patterns that define our marriage, that the strain is taxing. This realization invites us to reconsider—to reexamine what it is we want together, to reassess the strengths and needs we bring to the relationship, to recommit ourselves to its development and continuation.

We may find, especially if it is through a period of pain or deprivation that we come to a sense of the costs of sustaining this relationship, that the price is too high. Our own goals are no longer fulfilled, our resources are spent, our trust is broken. The movement through legal divorce will seem the only reasonable option to terminate a relationship that has already died.

But for many people the prevalence of divorce set against their own hope of an enduring relationship in marriage leads not to taking marriage lightly but to approaching it with greater seriousness, even caution. The expectation of permanence, sometimes experienced as an all too fragile hope, remains. The concern becomes how we shall safeguard and make robust this fragile conviction of our love.

Each marriage today must come to terms with these two dimensions of commitment: our expectations of exclusivity (What is the meaning of the priority in which we hold each other in love? How is this priority expressed?) and our expectations of permanence (What is the significance of our hope that our love shall flourish for our lifetime? How does this hope influence our lives now?).

THE LIFESTYLE OF MARRIAGE

Marriage is love, marriage is commitment, marriage is also a lifestyle—not one lifestyle experienced universally but the many particular lifestyles through which married couples express their love and live out the promises that hold them in mutual care. The lifestyle of marriage is the design or pattern of our life together that emerges in the choices we make. Many people do not experience the patterns of their daily life as open to personal choice. By the time of marriage, and from long before, factors of poverty or class or personality have narrowed the range of those parts of my life over which I have much say. I live out life, but I do not see myself as influencing its design in many important ways. Things happen to me, to my marriage, to my family—and I make the best of them. But I have little conviction that I can initiate changes or take responsibility on my own.

But for most Americans today there is a heightened consciousness of choice. We are aware that there are different ways in which the possibilities of life and of marriage may be lived out. And while our choices are always limited, we are aware that we not only can but must choose among these options for ourselves. The lifestyle of our marriage thus results from both our choices and our circumstances.

The choices that construct the lifestyle of our marriage include the decisions we make about the practical details of living—the routine of our daily activities, how we allocate the recurrent tasks of family and household care. But more basic decisions are involved—the values we hold important, the goals we have for our life together, the ways we choose to invest ourselves in the world.

At the heart of our decision about lifestyle is the question: What is our marriage for? Are we married only for ourselves? Does our life together exist chiefly as a place of personal security and a source of mutual satisfaction? Or is our marriage also about more than just the two of us? Is it a way for us to engage ourselves—together—in a world that is bigger than ourselves?

In previous decades the expectable presence of children in marriage answered this question in part. One of the things our marriage is for is our children. A child is so concrete an expression of the love that exists between us and so insistent an invitation that this love now go beyond itself in care. In parenting we experience the scope of our love widening to include our children. Often this broadening of concern continues, expanding to include more of the world and even the future, in which "our children's children" shall have to find their own way. Married people have always been generously engaged in the world in ways other than as parents, as well. But the central connection between being married and having children has been so clear and so prevalent for centuries that it has been a defining characteristic of the lifestyle of marriage.

Today there is more choice involved in the link between marriage and parenthood. Couples come to the decision to have a child with more consideration given to how many children there shall be in the family, how the births of these children shall be spaced, when in the marriage the commitments of family life shall begin. Some couples who have been unable to have children of their own seek other ways to expand their life together as a family—through adoption or foster care or through the assistance of recent developments in the biological sciences and medical practice. Other couples decide not to have a family and, instead, to express their love beyond themselves in other forms of creativity and care.

A comparable challenge accompanies each of these options—to develop a way of being together in marriage that takes seriously the demands of mutuality in our own relationship as it takes seriously the challenge that we look beyond ourselves in genuine contribution and care. Thus a central choice in marriage concerns our progeny—how shall we give and nurture life beyond ourselves: in our own children? in our friendships and other relationships? in our creative work? in our generous concern for the world? And the decisions that we come to here do much to determine the design of our daily life together.

Beyond this central choice concerning the focus of our creative love, there are other decisions of lifestyle. How shall we use the resources we possess? How, especially, do we allocate our money and our time? Here, again, the questions can be stated simply: What is our money for? What has priority in our time? We can respond to these questions at the practical level, offering the balance sheet of the family budget and our calendar of weekly events. But as an issue in lifestyle the question is more to the core: How are our own deepest values expressed or obscured in how we spend our money and our time?

Most American families today experience both money and time as scarce. There is not enough of either to go around. There seem to be always more possibilities, more demands for each than we feel we can meet. We have little "discretionary" income and even less "free" time. But among the demands that seem both genuine and inevitable there are others that seem to squander us uselessly, leaving us no time to be together or to be at peace and leaving us few resources to use for any purpose beyond ourselves. This sense of overextension characterizes the lifestyle of many marriages. Its prevalence invites us to reflect on our own patterns of money and time, not looking to praise or blame but trying to come to a better sense of the motives and pressures that move us and, in that way, define our lives. How much does our use of money and time revolve around "us," somewhat narrowly conceived—as a couple or a family over against "others"? What are the ways in which our decisions about time and money are more reflective of what our society expects of us than of the values and activities and possessions that make sense to us? Couples and families will differ in their responses to these questions, as they will differ on other issues of value and lifestyle. But the reflective process can lead to a greater congruence between the goals we have for our life together in marriage and the ways that this life is lived on a day-to-day basis.

Establishing our lifestyle in marriage is not done once and for all, but is itself an ongoing process. The lifestyle of our marriage must respond to the movements of development and change in each of us, in our relationship and in our responsibilities.

Marriage for a lifetime, then, is constituted by the interaction of our relationship, our commitments and our lifestyle. Our mutual love is at the core of our marriage. But in marriage we experience our relationship as more than just our love here and now. Marriage is focused by the promises to which we hold ourselves. It is the commitments that we made to one another that ground our love and give it duration. These commitments give us courage to undertake the risks of creative and procreative activity together. It is these commitments that are expressed in the choices and behavior and attitudes that make up the patterns of our lifestyle. And it is, in turn, an important goal of the commitments of our marriage and the lifestyle to which these commitments give shape, to sustain and deepen and mature the relationship of love between us.

It is important to note, as we begin our consideration of marriage for a lifetime, that the relationship and commitment and lifestyle of marriage do not exist in a vacuum. For each of us our experience of marriage is influenced by legal and historical and cultural understandings of what marriage is. In the next chapter we shall examine more closely the ways in which these social understandings of marriage are themselves undergoing change.

REFLECTIVE EXERCISE

These sentence stems may help you to explore your own awareness of the relationship, the commitments and the lifestyle that are marriage today. Complete the sentence begun by each of these phrases. There is no need to force an answer, just respond with what comes to mind at the time. For some phrases you may have several responses; others may call up little for you right now.

The relationship of marriage . . .

For me, mutual love . . .

Romance is a part of marriage . . .

The commitments of married people . . .

Today permanence in marriage . . .

The lifestyle of married people today . . .

Children bring to marriage . . .

Marriage for a lifetime is . . .

After you have completed the sentences, read through your whole list a couple of times to see if there is a dominant theme or tone to your responses.

CHAPTER 10

Marriage Becomes a Journey

Evelyn Eaton Whitehead
James D. Whitehead

Overlooking the significance of the metaphor the authors use here would be a mistake: marriage as a journey. This metaphor suggests marriage as a much more fluid reality than when it is seen as an institution, an immobile and unmovable edifice, a building fixed in a single place. The new metaphor of journey helps focus on what the Whiteheads call "the necessary instability of marriage." Their explanation of the history of where the institutional image of marriage comes from and what its value has been, is helpful for understanding where the shifts in today's understanding of marriage come from.

Many have found the Whiteheads' explanation of the three psychological transitions in marriage to be a marvel of clarity and insight. When unmarried or newly married persons read it, they do well to ask if they are ready or willing to go through these transitions, which will shift their very sense of self. Looked at from the angle of each person in the marriage, the journey is toward a new way of being a human being, with new commitments and a growing, shifting set of priorities.

Questions for Discussion

1. Of the three psychological transitions in marriage, which one do you think people your own age resist most strongly and why?
2. If the resistance to the transitions is not just in one's head, but especially in one's behavior, what forms does the resistance take? Can you specify any specific resistant behaviors?

FROM INSTITUTION TO JOURNEY

Our view, as we have said, is about the dissolution of marriage as a state in life and its survival as a journey. More precisely it is about the growing awareness of the fluidity and movement that mark marriage today. The changes and transitions which are a necessary part of a maturing marriage give it less the appearance of a stable institution than of a complicated journey. Pope Paul VI turned, in a speech in 1970, to this metaphor of movement:

> The journey of married people, like that of all human lives, has its stages; difficult and sorrowful moments have their place in it, as you know from your experience through the years.

But the Pope then suggested that, though such a journey includes difficulty and sorrow, it ought not to entail anxiety or fear: "But it must be stated clearly that anxiety and fear should never be found in souls of good will." In our discussion of marriage as a journey in the following chapters, we will understand anxiety and fear, not as indicators of a failure of good will, but as expectable perils on the way.

An institution can be imagined as a building that one enters. It is a solid, fixed place. Most everyone is expected to enter this institution and to remain in it. Once inside, a person receives the traditional privileges and obligations that come with residence. The rules that apply here are well known and constant; everyone inside this institution is expected to follow them.

Understood as an institution, marriage has been a state that one either did or did not inhabit. Legally, a person is either married or not married; there is no in-between. The Christian Church, influenced by this legal orientation toward marriage, came to view matrimony as an either/or situation. Christian ambivalence about sexuality found a clear resolution in this institutional view of marriage. Outside this well-defined state no sexual sharing was permitted; once inside this institution, one could even demand one's sexual rights. There seemed no gradualness or development in this commitment; one was either in or out. The periods of engagement and of marriage preparation were anomalies; little effective attention and ministry could be given to these "borderline" events.

The shift in the image of marriage from that of an institution to that of a journey is in line with our experience of marriage today. The commitment of marriage is increasingly seen not as a contract between families but as a personal covenant between individuals. The *necessary instability* of marriage—the changes required as a person approaches it (and when a person must exit from it) and the transitions demanded within such a complex relationship—gives it less and less an institutional appearance.

The continuing shifts and challenges of a maturing marriage give it the appearance of a journey. Marriage as a journey suggests that this relationship is not a location in life but a pattern of movement. Marriage is not a place where we live but a way that we travel through life. The image of journey responds to our sense of the precariousness of marriage. Even after this trek is well begun, we continue to learn new things about ourself and our partner. These are often subtle and confusing things, not covered under the contract or the institutional warranty.

The change in our image of marriage reminds us that new skills and virtues will be needed: different strengths are required to live in an institution and to survive on a journey. More adaptable and even wily skills are called for on a trip that is only partly charted beforehand. The shift in our understanding of the virtues of marriage, once marriage becomes a journey, will be one of our concerns in Part Three of this book.

A second concern will be the patterns of movement discernible in this journey of marriage. Are we married people enough alike so that we can expect our marriages to be more than "private trips"? If so, what are the expectable turns, and detours, of this journey? What is the terrain of contemporary marriage? Is it similar enough that we can learn from one another how to become skillful travelers? In this section of the book we will examine the patterns of change in marriage today, especially under the rubric of marriage as a passage. But before turning to the transitions which bring us into marriage and would mature us there, let us recall that the images of institution and journey are both influential in our religious history.

Marriage was seen as an institution during the centuries when the Church itself was becoming a powerful social institution. Especially from the fourth century the Christian Church, originating as scattered groups of believers in Jesus Christ, increasingly pictured itself as an institution. At the beginning of the fifth century St. Augustine captured this self-understanding in the attractive image of the City of God. A city is a sort of institution: a stable, legal entity, it enjoys clear and certain boundaries. The citizens of the City of God were recognizable by their credential of Baptism. These citizens were expected to stay in the institution—to marry other Christians, their own kind. (This would get more complicated after the Reformation when Catholics would banish Protestants from their city, making them religiously "uncivilized" and therefore unmarriable.)

This institutionalizing of religious faith gave great clarity and stability to Christianity. Stability, unfortunately, is sometimes but a few steps from rigidity. The image of the City of God further solidified in the sixteenth-century hymn "A Mighty Fortress Is Our God." This hymn, still popular today, suggests a well-defended, institutional view of God and Christian faith. It also suggests, at least to many Christians today, that we know for certain where God is—with *us.* An institutional view of God tends to locate and even localize God in a definite, defended space. God is enshrined and "tabernacled" as ours. The legalistic management of this institution—be it the Church or marriage—naturally ensues.

Parallel to our recognition of marriage as a journey is our return to this primordial image as a description of our common religious faith. It was in the circuitous trek through the Sinai Desert that our religious ancestors came to their earliest encounters and covenant with God. Journey, then, should be an especially sacred image for us, whether describing our fragile and changing relationship with God or with our marriage partner. The metaphor of journey includes discovery and doubt, detours and new beginnings. It suggests the special set of virtues required for religious faith and for marriage—virtues which help us decide when to settle down and when to keep moving, which way to turn at a fork in the road, how to read the signs that tell us where we are.

The image of faith and of marriage as a journey also suggests a different understanding of our God. Not institutionalized in a shrine or other stable location, God is a presence sensed on the trip. God is a presence that visits our life in strange and unpredictable ways to give it meaning and direction. Religious faith and a Christian marriage require our attentiveness to this subtle and graceful presence.

Attractive as this image of the journey is, marriage today remains an institution as well. Marriage is too important for all of us for it to be reduced to a private affair. Every community has a stake in its marriages and so this commitment must remain public as a legal, social and religious institution. Yet today we are more conscious of marriage as a process, a path pursued, a journey which includes both expected and unexpected events.

THREE PSYCHOLOGICAL TRANSITIONS IN MARRIAGE

Of the many transitions which describe the journey of a growing marriage, three merit special attention here. The first of these is the gradual movement from "I" to "we," the transition into married mutuality.

A couple may bring to marriage very different histories and identities. You are Italian, from a large and demonstrative family; I am English, an only child and unaccustomed to emotional displays. Each of us has lived apart from our families for a few years, establishing our independent ways of work and recreation. Now we would bring together these very separate "I's" into the "we" of marriage. The commonness of this "we" involves more than having the same address and sharing bed and board. It involves the merging of our separate patterns of living into a shared life. The stakes here are high; the risks can be considerable. A life-in-common will involve practical questions of how we use time and money and how we shall establish together the rhythms that make up a lifestyle. And deeper issues are concerned—our priorities and values, our energies and enthusiasms, our patterns of emotional responsiveness and sexual expression. The establishment of such a new life together includes the lengthy process of mutual knowledge and mutual influence. The challenge here is to create a "we" that is an expression of both "I's," where the identity of each is tested and expanded, probably even changed, but not destroyed.

This movement from two separate "I's" toward a shared life as "we" has long been seen as essential to the relationship of marriage. The Bible speaks of this common life in powerful images of union: "bone from my bones and flesh from my flesh" (Genesis 2:23) and "a man leaves his father and mother and joins himself to his wife, and they become one body" (Genesis 2:24). This close union is stressed in English common law statements, an important part of our own legal heritage, that in marriage "the two shall become one."

But what does it mean, that we two shall become one? At one level this image captures a psychological experience that is strong in romantic love—the desire to be together, to share everything, to overcome whatever separates us and to merge ourselves as fully as we can. And this image of union is not limited to early romance. For many who are married, "two becoming one" describes their experience of love growing and tested over time. "And they become one body" may not say all we know about marriage but it expresses both a reality and a hope in which our love is grounded.

Psychologically, then, these images of union ring true, even where they express only part of the larger reality of married love. But marriage is more than a psychological reality; it takes on social forms as well. And these social forms both reflect and influence how we understand the union of woman and man in marriage. In a society in which patriarchy is strong the union of marriage will be understood in terms of the legal preeminence of the husband. Thus an early formulation of English common law states bluntly that "the husband and wife are as one and that one is the husband."

In earlier generations in our own country this union of two-in-one has often been achieved by incorporating the wife—her ambitions, her energies, her values and opinions, often her material resources as well—into the plan and plot of her husband's life. And many women have found personal meaning and genuine fulfillment in this experience of marriage: giving themselves—even somewhat exclusively—to tasks and roles that have served, and often been subservient to, their husbands. But today there are new expectations of mutuality in the "we" of marriage. It is less and less acceptable among women (and, to be sure, among many men) that the "we" of marriage be achieved primarily through the absorption of the wife into her husband's identity and life ambition. So today the process of marriage involves the more difficult—and more rewarding—effort to create a "we" that bears the stamp of both spouses, a "we" that moves beyond each into a larger reality of a common life.

To create a life in common in which both of us survive and continue to grow, together—it is in this hope that couples approach marriage today. To achieve this we must each bring to marriage some beginning sense of confidence and comfort in "who I am." Neither a defended nor an unclear identity can easily move toward mutuality. If I am largely unsure of who I am, I am not able easily to sustain a relationship. If I must defend a fragile sense of self against the demands of change, then flexibility and compromise will be hard. In either case, it will be difficult for me to come close to you without the fear that I will lose myself. And it is this fear, that "we" must mean a loss of "I," that complicates the transition into a common life in marriage.

COMPLEMENTARITY, EQUALITY, MUTUALITY

The mutuality that is a goal in marriage today takes us beyond the understanding of women and men as "complementary." Many couples experience themselves as complementing one another. We "fit" together well. Your dynamism enlivens me; my patience is a useful balance to your enthusiasm. Or, more pragmatically, I like to cook and you like to clean house. But as a cultural image "complementarity" does not celebrate these individual differences. Instead it reinforces the notion of the "innate" differences between all women and all men. In this understanding our complementarity in marriage is not something that we discover between us; it is rather a *given.* "After all, he's a man and she's a woman. It should be clear how their marriage should work." In this view it is not as two particular persons that we complement each other in our marriage; it is rather because each of us falls into one of the two "complementary" categories—male or female. Very often, then, as the image of complementarity actually functions, its appealing nuances of interdependence and exploration are lost. It becomes instead a restatement of a conventional notion of what marriage should be. Many critics judge that the impulse to understand women as "complementary" to men in marriage is similar to that which sees blacks as "separate but equal" in society. Both find their roots in a conviction of "the way things are" that owes more to ideology than to the evidence available.

If mutuality takes us beyond "complementarity" it takes us beyond "equality" as well. "Equality of opportunity" and "equality under the law" are appropriate statements of societal goals. But equality is a tricky objective in close relationships. This is not to say that intimacy always works itself out into some uneven dichotomy—leader-led or dominant-submissive. It suggests rather that quantitative images, such as equality, are not always useful in personal relations. It is difficult to determine "equality" in emotion or concern or generosity. It is hard to measure what is "enough" for each of us to give in order that our love might develop or survive. We must each nurture our own integrity in our marriage, but this will go beyond keeping count of who "gives in" the most. For many of us, these core issues of mutuality—the tension between integrity and interdependence, between autonomy and compromise—are not adequately covered by the term "equality."

Mutuality implies real engagement between people. I am open enough in this engagement to meet *you,* not just my stereotypes of you or my prejudices about *your kind.* In mutuality both of us experience ourselves giving and receiving. We can acknowledge our dependence on one another without guilt or shame; we can celebrate the ways we empower each other, without resentment or control. We each sense that our greatest strength is born of our being together. It is truly my strength, but I owe it to our love. And together *we* are more than either of us is alone.

Establishing this kind of mutuality in our marriage involves the ongoing process of learning more about each other and ourselves and of influencing each other as we develop toward a life together. It is not just a process of the first years of marriage but a continuing dynamic of growth and change over a lifetime. So the "we" of our marriage is to be celebrated now, but we know also that it is still becoming.

FROM ROMANCE TO COMMITTED LOVE

A second transition in marriage today is from romance to committed love. The dominant norm of marriage in America today is self-selection based on the criteria of romantic love. *I* choose whom I shall marry, and I choose to marry someone with whom I have fallen in love. The choice of romantic love is a complicated one, since romance often includes some element of projection. Part of what I see in you is my ideal of "man" or "woman," especially of the woman or man I shall marry. This ideal, itself partly a statement of my values and partly an expression of my needs, may correspond more or less closely to who you really are. So while romance may appear to be a highly personalized love, in many ways it is not. Romance often involves "falling in love with love." In the romantic stimulation of our discovery of love, we are likely to sense that we are perfectly suited to each other: we like the same things, we never argue, we share the same values of marriage and family life. As we live together in our marriage we will each have the chance to examine more closely this ideal. I will learn more about what I really want; I will learn more about who you really are.

The impact of romance in love may be described by the term "enchantment." I am enchanted by the one I love, enthralled by each detail and every mannerism. I am swept off my feet. *This* person, I am convinced, can rescue me at last—from my parents, from my dull job, even from myself. This marvelous power of romance appears in life as a most useful illusion. This larger-than-life, idealized view of the other energizes me to take on the commitments of married life. As an adult career often begins in larger-than-life ambitions of what I will be able to achieve, so romance leads me into marriage with powerful hopes of what our life together will be.

The route from romantic love toward a maturing marriage often goes by way of disenchantment. This is not to suggest that our prince (or princess) must always turn into a frog. It does mean that the enchanted, idealized view of my spouse will likely change as I come to know this person better. Practical decisions we must make about our children, our careers, even our housecleaning, can reveal unknown parts of who we are, to ourselves and to each other. As our life together matures, I am invited to love not just my ideal spouse, but the simultaneously lovely and limited person whom I have married.

"Disenchantment" is an ambiguous term, to be sure. While for many of us it is a necessary stage between romance and a matured love, it is for some an experience simply of falling out of love. Unable to tolerate a non-ideal lover or a growing realization that the person I married is not the person I dated, I may find that for me disenchantment leads to divorce. Or it may lead to my beginning the cycle of romance again, this time in an extramarital affair with a more exciting (because still unknown) partner. Here disenchantment is not part of the maturing of our love into a resilient and personalized commitment but an experience that sets off a cycle of immaturity: needing the enchantment of romance, I seek "someone new," leaving behind the demands and invitations that arise in the familiarity of my experience of my spouse.

The process of maturing in marriage thus requires a movement beyond the exhilarating but largely passive experience of falling in love, to the experience of love as a chosen and cultivated commitment. It is the added element of commitment that transforms romantic love into the love that is able to sustain marriage for a lifetime. Committed love grows as I am able to know and cherish my spouse "as is," beyond the idealized images that may have been a part of our early experience of romance. I come to know you more completely and more clearly, as perhaps more gifted than I had dreamed but also as more flawed than I had hoped. This is a maturing love of choice. In the light of this deepening awareness of who you are and who I really am, I choose anew to love you. I reaffirm the commitment to do "whatever is necessary" so that this relationship in which we hold each other may live and grow.

This is the movement from romantic love to the love of mutual devotion, strong enough to sustain us in the moments of strain and confusion that are inevitably associated with our continuing close contact. Such devotion is possible only if each of us is capable of generous self-disregard.

This dynamic of mutual devotion is one of the most profound movements in marriage. In it the "active" and "passive" sides of love seem to merge in an experience of both caring and being cared for. We are together deeply and we each feel this as a strength. You know me so well . . . and still you love me. You care for me in ways that go beyond what I could ask for. You call me out to what is best in myself. I know you hold my life as important to you as your own. And all these gifts I give to you as well.

Most of us are not capable of this quality of love in adolescence or even in young adulthood. In our twenties few of us have the resources of self-possession and self-transcendence that are needed. Mature inner commitment is the fruit of our married love, not its initial seed. Romance gives us the hope of mutual love, but only the test of time together can bring its realization.

For some this test is too difficult. Romance does not mature into commitment but simply fades, leaving us dissatisfied and disillusioned. The movement beyond romance is expectable—even inevitable—in marriage. But the loss of love is not. The expectation that the quality of our commitment to one another will change does not mean that we must fall out of love. It means rather that we must move into a love that is larger than romance.

THE PROCESS OF SEXUAL MATURING

While the commitment of marriage matures into a love that is larger than romance, it remains a love in which sexuality and affection are central. We approach sexual maturity in our marriage as we develop our capacity for sharing physical affection and genital pleasure. This sexual maturity, too, is more a process than a state. We learn to be good lovers and, for most of us, it takes time.

To give ourselves to this process of sexual maturing we must each be able to move beyond the experience of love play and intercourse as chiefly competitive—an experience of proving myself as a "real" woman or man or "winning out" over my partner. These interpretations of sex keep the focus on "me," making mutuality difficult. And without mutuality, sex is more often a barrier to, than a part of, the larger psychological experience of intimacy.

In contrast with many marriages of a generation ago, couples today generally approach marriage with greater awareness of their own bodies and with more information about genital sex. This intellectual sophistication is a boon to marriage, but it is, again, more a starting point of a satisfying sex life than its guarantee. Married sex is a process through which we both learn to contribute to what is, for us, mutually satisfying shared sexual experience. We learn the physical and emotional nuances that make lovemaking special for us. We develop the patterns of expression that fit us—patterns of frequency, of time and place, of initiation and response. We discover the ways in which passion and affection, humor and intensity, are a part of our own love life.

The exhilaration of sexual discovery is usually strong early in marriage, at least if we are able to move beyond an initial embarrassment. For most of us, it is our spouse who gives us the gift of knowing our sexuality to be beautiful. Loving me in my body, you invite me beyond the shame and guilt I carry still. With you, I am free to explore my passion and to expose my vulnerability and self-doubt. Having risked the self-revelation of sex—and survived—we can approach with greater confidence the other, even more threatening, processes of self-disclosure upon which the quality of our life together will depend.

After this early period of exploration, our sexual life may begin to level off. We have found a pattern that works for us and, especially in the press of the other responsibilities of our lives, this pattern can become routine.

It may be only gradually that we realize in our marriage that, though our love is strong, our lovemaking somehow falls short. Our early sexual sharing was surrounded with an aura of romance. Frequently, this romantic aura made our experiences of sex more satisfying than our lovemaking skills would otherwise justify! Now sex seems to have lost this savor. We know that the substance of our love is more important than our sexual style, but the questions of sexual style and satisfaction may begin to become more important than they were for us earlier in our marriage.

American culture's current interest in sexual techniques reinforces this concern over our own sex life. We are more aware of the richness of human sexuality and of the diversity of sexual expression. This new awareness can work destructively, setting up yet another standard of "success" against which to evaluate our own intimacy. But it need not have this negative effect. Instead it can remind us that the patterns of mutually satisfying sexual experience can be expected to differ from couple to couple. And that it is *we* who can best discover what these patterns are for us. In sex, as in most other aspects of our marriage, to be "mature" does not mean to fit some general criterion of performance but to have a developing (and, perhaps, changing) sense of what is appropriate *for us*, what works *for us*.

Sex research shows the contribution that diversity and surprise make to long-term sexual satisfaction. This realization can be liberating, inviting us to expand the ways in which we celebrate the sexuality of our marriage. This sense of exploration helps us move beyond a point of sexual boredom or routine, stimulating our own creativity in lovemaking. The expanding literature of sexual functioning can assist this process of sexual maturity in marriage, not by giving us a norm of what is "best" but by providing information that can enrich our own experimentation and choice.

THE MOVEMENT FROM "WE ARE" TO "WE CARE"

A third significant transition in the process of marriage is the movement from "we are" to "we care." Here we are involved in balancing the tensions between our own intimacy and the larger responsibilities of our lives. There is the challenge to move beyond our love as a couple in order that we may contribute to, and care for, a larger world. We can experience some strain as we try to learn ways to move beyond ourselves that do not destroy the experience and commitments of mutuality between us. The birth of the first child can be an early experience of this challenge. How shall we be for each other when we now must also be for our child? Job responsibilities and career choices also raise the challenge. Does marriage mean that only one of us may pursue a career? How do I, how do we, manage the multiple demands of being responsible citizen, financial provider, parent and spouse? The question can surface as an issue of social concern. How do we balance our commitments to each other and to our children alongside our responsibility to the needs of the world beyond ourselves?

The dilemma may be posed this way: What is our marriage for? Do we exist as a couple only for ourselves? Or does our being together go beyond ourselves? Are the resources of support and challenge that we generate in our family to be spent solely within our family? Or is there "enough" of us so that we can take the risk of sharing some of our resources (of love or concern or time or goods) with the world beyond? Is the love we share simply "a haven in a hostile world" or is it also a force that frees us to "love our neighbor as ourselves"?

Love is creative beyond itself and it must be so if it is to endure. A love that does not give life beyond itself risks becoming a caricature of intimacy. It is true that there is often a stage of mutual absorption in love, especially in the early experience of romance. The lovers are enthralled with each other. Everything about the other person is engrossing—and there is little beyond this relationship itself that seems worthy of attention. Job responsibilities, school activities, other friends and family—all pale to insignificance. In this timeless present of romance, "you and I" is all there is.

The world tends to be tolerant of this attitude in lovers—at least for a while. Recalling our own experience with romance we overlook much of the bizarre behavior of new love and excuse the rest. We know this shared obsession is but a phase of romance; soon it passes. The romance may mature into a deeper love or it may die from lack of any further substance. But in either case the charmed circle of exclusive fascination will be broken. Soon the lovers shall rejoin us—better, we trust, for the experience.

This early exclusivity in love is normal, an important dynamic of the process of exploration and self-disclosure that contributes to the possibility of commitment. But maturing love moderates this exclusivity. Being *for* one another does not require that each of us must be against everyone else. Indeed, the enrichment we experience in being for one another leads us to be for more than "just us." Our love for one another gives us more of what is best in each of us. We feel the impetus to move beyond ourselves, to share this wealth, to bring others into the power of what our love has given us. This movement of expansion is itself an expectable dynamic of love as it matures. Psychologists are aware of the importance to our love of this impulse beyond ourselves. They warn that the absence of any movement beyond "just us" imperils a love relationship. A "pseudo-intimacy" can result, turning the partners in upon themselves in a way that gradually impoverishes the relationship. What results from this failure to expand our concern is not an intimacy more protected and complete, but stagnation. Having failed to share our love beyond ourselves we soon find that we have little left to give each other.

This truth about love, of concern in current psychology, does not come as news to our religious tradition. Love that does not give life beyond itself will die—Christian wisdom has long proclaimed this sometimes fleeting insight of our own experience. There is an essential connection between loving and giving life. It is, in part, this abiding truth that the Church has tried to share in its celebration of the fruitfulness of marriage.

In our history there has been a tendency to understand this connection in an almost exclusively biological sense—that every act of genital love must be open to the creation of a child, that bearing children is the most important goal of marriage and married love. Many Catholics today, especially married lay persons, find these statements of the connection between marriage and generative love to be at odds with their own experience. But the larger truth, that a maturing love in marriage both wants to and needs to go beyond itself, is reinforced by our experience and our religious heritage.

PART FOUR

Attitudes toward Sexuality

CHAPTER 11

Passionate Attachments in the West in Historical Perspective

Lawrence Stone

Lawrence Stone, a historian at Princeton University, introduces the rich set of readings in this section with a historical examination of passionate attachments in the West. The two most common passionate attachments explored are: (1) romantic love between two adolescents or adults of different sex, and (2) the caring love-bond between mothers and children. We have undergone a revolution in both sets of attachments in the past century and find ourselves in a unique position today. Stone traces the historical trend in the spread of the cultural concept of romantic love in the West and the evolution in the mother-child relationship. This fascinating material gives us an educational reminder: We cannot assume people in the past thought about romance and parenting the way we do.

Questions for Discussion

1. What is the nature of romantic love?
2. Is it an adequate rationale and basis for marriage?
3. Is there a relationship between romantic love and permanence in marriage?
4. What is the distinction between romance, lust, and committed love?
5. Is there a gender gap in attitudes toward these diverse forms of passionate attachments in our culture?
6. What are some of the possible implications of changing sex roles in marriage on parent-child relationships?

Further Readings

The subject of romantic love is treated with skill and depth analysis by Robert Johnson in his book *We: The Psychology of Romantic Love* (San Francisco: Harper & Row, 1983).

Central to the argument of this chapter is a proposition put forward by my colleague Robert Darnton:

Reprinted with the permission of The Free Press, a Division of Simon & Schuster, Inc. from *Passionate Attachments: Thinking about Love*, edited by William Gaylin, M.D., and Ethel Person, M.D. Copyright © 1988 by Friends of Columbia Psychoanalytic Center, Inc.

One thing seems clear to everyone who returns from field work: other people are other. They do not think the way we do. And if we want to understand their way of thinking, we should set out with the idea of capturing otherness.[1]

What this means is that we cannot assume that people in the past—even in our own Western Judeo-Christian world—thought about and felt passionate attachments the way we do.

My remarks will be confined to the two most common of passionate attachments—between two adolescents or adults of different sexes, and between mothers and children. I know there are other attachments—between homosexuals, siblings, fathers and children—but they are not of such central importance as the first two. Before we can begin to examine the very complex issue of passionate attachments in the past, we therefore have to make a fundamental distinction between attachment between two sexually mature persons, usually of the opposite gender, and attachment to the child of one's body.

In the former case, the problem is how to distinguish what is generally known as falling in love from two other human conditions. The first of those conditions is an urgent desire for sexual intercourse with a particular individual, a passion for sexual access to the body of the person desired. In this particular instance the libido is for some reason closely focussed upon a specific body, rather than there being a general state of sexual excitement capable of satisfaction by any promiscuous coupling. The second condition is one of settled and well-tried ties which develop between two people who have known each other for a long time and have come to trust each other's judgment and have confidence in each other's loyalty and affection. This condition of caring may or may not be accompanied by exciting sexual bonding, and may or may not have begun with falling in love, a phase of violent and irrational psychological passion, which does not last very long.

Historians and anthropologists are in general agreement that romantic love—this usually brief but very intensely felt and all-consuming attraction toward another person—is culturally conditioned, and therefore common only in certain societies at certain times, or even in certain social groups within those societies—usually the elite, with the leisure to cultivate such feelings. They are, however, less certain whether or not romantic love is merely a culture-induced sublimated psychological overlay on top of the biological drive for sex, or whether it has biochemical roots which operate quite independently from the libido. Would anyone in fact "fall in love" if they had not read about it or heard it talked about? Did poetry invent love, or love poetry?

Some things can be said with certainty about the history of the phenomenon. The first is that cases of romantic love can be found at all times and places and have often been the subject of powerful poetic expression, from the Song of Solomon to Shakespeare. On the other hand, neither social approbation nor the actual experience of romantic love is at all common to all societies, as anthropologists have discovered. Second, historical evidence for romantic love before the age of printing is largely confined to elite groups, which of course does not mean that it may not have occurred lower down the social scale among illiterates. As a socially approved cultural artifact it began in Europe in the southern French aristocratic courts in the twelfth century, made fashionable by a group of poets, the troubadours. In this case the culture dictated that it should occur between an unmarried male and a married woman, and that it should either go sexually unconsummated or should be adulterous. This cultural ideal certainly spread into wider circles in the middle ages—witness the love story of Aucassin and Nicolette—but it should be noted that none of these models ends happily.

By the sixteenth and seventeenth centuries, our evidence for the first time becomes quite extensive, thanks to the spread of literacy and the printing press. We now have love poems, like Shakespeare's Sonnets, love letters, and autobiographies by women primarily concerned with their love life. All the courts of Europe were evidently hotbeds of passionate intrigues and liaisons, some romantic, some sexual. The printing press began to spread pornography to a wider public, thus stimulating the libido, while the plays of Shakespeare indicate that romantic love was a familiar concept to society at large, who composed his audience.

Whether this romantic love was approved of, however, is another question. We simply do not know how Shakespearean audiences reacted to Romeo and Juliet. Did they, like us, and as Shakespeare clearly intended, fully identify with the young lovers? Or, when they left the theatre, did they continue to act like the Montague and Capulet parents, who were trying to stop these irresponsible adolescents from allowing an ephemeral and irrational passion to interfere with the serious business of politics and patronage? What is certain is that every advice book, every medical treatise, every sermon and religious homily of the sixteenth and seventeenth centuries firmly rejected both romantic passion and lust as suitable bases for marriage.[2] In the sixteenth century marriage was thought to be best arranged by parents, who could be relied upon to choose socially and economically suitable partners who would enhance the prestige and importance of the kin group as a whole. It was believed that the sexual bond would automatically create the necessary harmony between the two strangers in order to maintain the stability of the new family unit. This, it seems, is not an unreasonable assumption, since recent investigations in Japan have shown that there is no difference in the rate of divorce between couples whose marriages were arranged by their parents and couples whose marriages were made by individual choice based on romantic love. The arranged and the romantic marriage each has an equal chance of turning out well, or breaking up.[3]

Public admiration for marriage-for-love is thus a fairly recent occurrence in Western society, arising out of the romantic movement of the late eighteenth century, and only winning general acceptance in the twentieth. In the eighteenth century orthodox opinion about marriage shifted away from subordinating the individual will to the interests of the group and away from economic or political considerations towards those of well-tried personal affection. The ideal marriage of the eighteenth century was one preceded by three to six months of intensive courting, between a couple from families roughly equal in social status and economic wealth, a courtship which only took place with the prior consent of parents on both sides. A sudden falling head over heels in love, although a familiar enough psychological phenomenon, was thought of as a mild form of insanity, in which judgment and prudence are cast aside, all the inevitable imperfections of the loved one become invisible, and wholly unrealistic dreams of everlasting happiness possess the mind of the afflicted victim. Fortunately, in most cases the disease is of short duration, and the patient normally makes a full recovery. To the eighteenth century, the main object of society—church, law, government, and parents— was to prevent the victim from taking some irrevocable step, particularly from getting married. This is why most European countries made marriage under the age of 21 or even later illegal and invalid unless carried out with the consent of parents or guardians. In England this became law in 1753. Runaway marriages based on passionate attachments still took place, but they were made as difficult as possible to carry out, and in most countries were virtually impossible.

It was not, therefore, until the romantic movement and the rise of the novel, especially the pulp novel, in the nineteenth century, that society at large accepted a new idea—that it was normal and indeed praiseworthy for young men and women to fall passionately in love, and that there must be something wrong with those who have failed to have such an overwhelming experience some time in late adolescence or early manhood. Once this new idea was publicly accepted, the dictation of marriage by parents came to be regarded as intolerable and immoral.

Today, the role of passionate attachments between adults in our society is obscured by a new development, the saturation of the whole culture— through every medium of communication—with sexuality as the predominant and overriding human drive, a doctrine whose theoretical foundations were provided by Freud. In no past society known to me has sex been given so prominent a role in the culture at large, nor has sexual fulfillment been elevated to such preeminence in the list of human aspirations—in a vain attempt to relieve civilization of its discontents. If Thomas Jefferson today was asked to rewrite the Declaration of Independence he would certainly have to add total sexual fulfillment to "Life, Liberty and Human Happiness" as one of the basic natural rights of every member of society. The traditional restraints upon sexual freedom—religious and social taboos, and the fear of pregnancy and venereal disease—have now been almost entirely removed. We find it scarcely credible today that in most of Western Europe in the seventeenth century, in a society whose marriage age was postponed into the late twenties, a degree of chastity was practiced that kept the illegitimacy rate—without contraceptives—as low as 2 or 3 percent. Only in Southern Ireland does such a situation still exist—according to one hypothesis, due to a lowering of the libido caused by large-scale consumption of Guinness Stout. Under these conditions, it seems to me almost impossible today to distinguish passionate attachment in the psychological sense—meaning love—from passionate attachment in the physical sense—meaning lust. But the enormous success today of pulp fiction concerned almost exclusively with romantic rather than physical love shows that women at least still hanker after the experience of falling in love. Whether the same applies to men is more doubtful, so that there may be a real gender gap on this subject today, which justifies this distinction I am making between love and lust.

To sum up, the historian can see a clear historical trend in the spread of the cultural concept of romantic love in the West, beginning in court circles in the twelfth century, and expanding outward from the sixteenth century on. It received an enormous boost with the rise of the romantic novel, and another boost with the achievement of near-total literacy by the end of the nineteenth century. Today, however, it is so intertwined with sexuality, that is is almost impossible to distinguish between the two. Both, however, remain clearly distinct from caring, that is, well-tried and settled affection based on long-term commitment and familiarity.

It is also possible to say something about the changing relationship of passionate love to marriage. For all classes who possessed property—that is, the top two-thirds economically—marriage before the seventeenth century was arranged by the parents, and the motives were the economic and political benefit of the kin group, not the emotional satisfaction of the individuals. As the concept of individualism grew in the seventeenth and eighteenth centuries, it slowly became accepted that the prime object was "holy matrimony," a sanctified state of monogamous married contentment. This was best achieved by allowing the couple to make their own choice, provided that both sets of parents agreed that the social and economic gap was not too wide, and that marriage was preceded by a long period of courtship. By the eighteenth and nineteenth centuries, individualism had so far taken precedence over the group interests of the kin that the couple were left more or less free to make their own decision, except in the highest aristocratic and royal circles. Today individualism is given such absolute priority in most Western societies, that the couple are virtually free to act as they please, to sleep with whom they please, and to marry and divorce when and whom they please to suit their own pleasure. The psychic cost of such behavior, and its self-defeating consequences, are becoming clear, however, and how long this situation will last is anybody's guess.

Here I should point out that the present-day family—I exclude the poor black family in America from this generalization—is not, as is generally supposed, disintegrating because of a very high divorce rate of up to 50 percent. It has to be remembered that the median duration of marriage today is almost exactly the same as it was 100 years ago. Divorce, in short, now acts as a functional substitute for death: both are means of terminating marriage at a premature stage. It may well be that the psychological effects on the survivor may be very different, although in most cases the catastrophic economic consequences for the woman remain the same. But the point to be emphasized is that broken marriages, stepchildren, and single-parent households were as common in the past as they are today, the only difference being the mechanism which has brought about this situation.

The most difficult historical problem concerns the role of romantic love among the propertyless poor, who comprised about one-third of the population. Since they were propertyless, their loves and marriages were of little concern to their kin, and they were therefore more or less free to choose their own mates. By the eighteenth century, and probably before, court records make it clear that these groups often married for love, combined with a confused set of motives including lust and the economic necessity to have a strong and healthy assistant to run the farm or the shop. It was generally expected that they would behave "lovingly" towards each other, but this often did not happen. In many a peasant marriage, the husband seems to have valued his cow more than his wife. Passionate attachments among the poor certainly occurred, but how often they took priority over material interests we may never know for certain.[4]

All that we do know is that courting among the poor normally lasted six months or more, and that it often involved all-night sessions alone together in the dark in a room with a bed, usually with the knowledge and consent of the parents or masters. Only relatively rarely, and only at a late stage after engagement, did full sexual intercourse commonly take place during these nights, but it is certain that affectionate conversation, and discussion of the possibilities of marriage, were accompanied by embracing and kissing, and probably also by what today is euphemistically called "heavy petting." This practice of "bundling," as it was called, occurred in what by our standards an extremely prudish, and indeed sexually innocent, society. When men and women went to bed together they almost invariably kept on a piece of clothing, a smock or a shirt, to conceal their nakedness. Moreover the sexual act itself was almost always carried out in the "missionary" position. The evidence offered in the courts in cases of divorce in the pre-modern period provide little evidence of that polymorphous perversity advocated in the sex manuals available in every bookstore today.

What is certain is that even after this process of intimate physical and verbal courtship had taken place, economic factors still loomed large in the final decision by both parties about whether or not to marry. Thus passion and material interest were in the end inextricably involved, but it is important to stress that, among the poor, material interest only became central at the *end* of the process of courtship instead of at the beginning, as was the case with the rich.

If an early modern peasant said "I love a woman with ten acres of land," just what did he mean? Did he lust after the body of the woman? Did he admire her good health, administrative and intellectual talents and strength of character as a potential housekeeper, income producer, and mother of his children? Was he romantically head over heels in love with her? Or did he above all prize her for her ten acres? Deconstruct the text as we wish, there is no way of getting a clear answer to that question; and in any case, if we could put that peasant on the couch today and interrogate him, it would probably turn out that he merely felt that he liked the woman more because of her ten acres.

Finally, we know that in the eighteenth century at least half of all brides in England and America were pregnant on their wedding day. But this tells us more about sexual customs than about passionate attachments: sex began at the moment of engagement, and marriage in church came later, often triggered by the pregnancy. We also know that if a poor servant girl was impregnated by her master, which often happened, the latter usually had no trouble finding a poor man who would marry her, in return for payment of ten pounds or so. Not much passionate attachment there, among any of the three persons involved.

The second type of passionate attachment is that which develops between the parent, especially the mother, and the child. Here again as historians we are faced with the intractable problem of nature versus nurture, of the respective roles of biology and culture. The survival of the species demands that the female adult should take optimum care of the child over a long period, to ensure its survival. This is particularly necessary among humans since the child is born prematurely compared with all other primates, because of its exaggerated cranial size, and so is peculiarly helpless for an exceptionally long period of time. Moreover, experiments with primates have shown that it is close body contact in the first weeks of life which creates the strong bond between mother and child. A passionate attachment of the mother for its child therefore seems to be both a biological necessity for survival and an emotional reality.

On the other hand recorded human behavior indicates that cultural traditions and economic necessity often override this biological drive. For over 90 percent of human history man has been a hunter-gatherer, and it is impossible for a woman to carry two babies and perform her daily task of gathering. Barring sexual abstention, which seems unlikely, some form of infanticide must therefore have been a necessity, dictated by economic conditions.

Other factors came into play in more recent times. From at least classical antiquity to the eighteenth century it was normal in northwest Europe to swaddle all babies at birth—that is, to tie them up head to foot in bandages, taken off only to remove the urine and feces. This automatically reduced body contact with the mother, and therefore presumably the bonding effect between mother and child. Secondly, all women who could afford to do so put their infants out to wet-nurse from birth to about the age of two. The prime reason for this among the more well-to-do was undoubtedly the accepted belief that sexual excitement spoils the milk. Few husbands were willing to do without the sexual services of their wives for that length of time; hence the reliance on a wet nurse. But this meant that for all except the tiny minority who could afford to take the nurse into the house, the child was removed within a few days of birth and put in the care of a village woman some distance from the home. Under these conditions affection between parents and children could not begin to grow until the child returned to the home at about the age of eighteen months or two years, and the child might well have a more passionate relationship with its nurse than with its mother—as was the case with Shakespeare's Juliet.

In any case, the child's return to its mother would only take place if it did not die while with the wet nurse. There is overwhelming evidence that the mortality rate of children being wet-nursed was very much higher than that of children being breast-fed by their mothers, and contemporaries were well aware of this. It is difficult to avoid the suspicion that one incentive for the practice, particularly for its enormous expansion in France in the nineteenth century, was as an indirect method of infanticide, out of sight and out of mind. This suspicion is reinforced by the huge numbers of children in the eighteenth and nineteenth centuries who were abandoned and deposited in workhouses or foundling hospitals, only a small fraction of whom survived the experience. Whatever the intention, in practice the foundling hospitals of London or Paris acted as a socially acceptable means of family limitation after birth. Few women other than those who gave birth to bastard children practiced infanticide themselves, if only because the risks were too great. But overlaying and stifling by accident while in the same bed during the nights, putting out to wet-nurse, abandoning to public authorities, or depositing in foundling hospitals served the same purpose. Unwanted children of the poor and not so poor were somehow or other got rid of in all these socially acceptable ways.[5]

These common eighteenth and even nineteenth century practices, especially prevalent in France, raise questions about the degree of maternal love in that society. This is not an easy question to answer, and historians are deeply divided on this issue. Some point to evidence of mothers who were devoted to their children and seriously disturbed by their premature deaths. Others point to the bleak statistics of infant mortality: about 25 percent dead before the age of two, a percentage deliberately increased by wet-nursing, abandonment, and infanticide by neglect—practices which have been described as "post-natal family planning." A mid-nineteenth century Bavarian woman summed up the emotional causes and consequences:

> The parents are glad to see the first and second child, especially if there is a boy amongst them. But all that come after aren't so heartily welcome. Anyway not many of these children live. Four out of a dozen at most, I suppose. The others very soon get to heaven. When little children die, it's not often that you have a lot of grief. They're little angels in heaven.[6]

Another question is how kindly children were treated if they did survive. I have suggested that sixteenth and early seventeenth century societies were cold and harsh, relatively indifferent to children, and resorting to frequent and brutal whippings from an early age as the only reliable method of discipline. Calvinism, with its grim insistence on original sin, encouraged parents and schoolmasters to whip children, in order quite literally to beat the Hell out of them. I have argued that only in the eighteenth century did there develop a more optimistic view of the infant as a plain sheet of paper upon which good or evil could be written by the process of cultural socialization.

The more extreme view of Rousseau, that the child is born good, in a state of innocence, was widely read, but not very widely accepted, so far as can be seen—for the rather obvious reason that it is contradicted by the direct experience of all observant parents.

To sum up, first there is ample evidence for the widespread practice of infanticide in societies ignorant of contraception, a practice which, disguised in socially acceptable forms, lasted well into the nineteenth century. Second, children, even of the rich, were often treated with calculated brutality in the sixteenth and seventeenth centuries, and again in the nineteenth, in order to eradicate original sin; the eighteenth and twentieth centuries are two rare periods of educational permissiveness. As for the poor, they have always regarded children very largely as potential economic assets and treated them accordingly. Their prime functions have been to help in the house, the workshop, and the field, to add to the family income, and to support their parents in old age. How much room was left over from these economic considerations for passionate attachment, even with the mother, remains an open question.

Passionate attachments between young people can and do happen in any society as a by-product of biological sexual attraction, but the social acceptability of the emotion has varied enormously over time and class and space, determined primarily by cultural norms and property arrangements. Furthermore, though there is a strong biological component in the passionate attachment of mothers to children, it too is often overlaid by economic necessities, by religious views about the nature of the child, and by accepted cultural practices such as wet-nursing. We are in a unique position today in that society, through social security and other devices, has taken over the economic responsibilities of children for their aged parents; contraception is normal and efficient; our culture is dominated by romantic notions of passionate love as the only socially admissible reason for marriage; and sexual fulfillment is accepted as the dominant human drive and a natural right for both sexes. Behind all this there lies a frenetic individualism, a restless search for the sexual and emotional ideal in human relationships, and a demand for instant ego gratification which is inevitably self-defeating and ultimately destructive.

Most of this is new and unique to our culture. It is, therefore, quite impossible to extrapolate from present values and behavior to those in the past. Historical others—even our own forefathers and mothers—were indeed other.

NOTES

1. Darnton, R. *The Great Cat Massacre and Other Episodes in French Cultural History* (New York: Basic Books, 1984), 4.

2. For further discussion of these issues, and references, see my book *The Family, Sex and Marriage in England, 1500–1800* (New York: Harper & Row, 1977).

3. *Journal of Family History*, 8, 1983, p. 100.

4. Flandrin, J. L. *Les Amours Paysannes* (XVI-XIX Siècles) (Paris: Gallimard, 1975).

5. The literature on infanticide (rare), infant abandonment, and early death by deliberate neglect or wet-nursing in Western Europe up to the nineteenth century is now enormous. See, for example:

de Mause, L. *The History of Childhood* (New York: Psychohistory Press, 1974).
Delasselle, C. "Les enfants abandonés à Paris au XVIII siécle," *Annales E.C.S.*, 30, Jan.–Feb. 1975.
Flandrin, J. L. "L'attitude devant le petit enfant . . . dans la Civilisation Occidentale," in *Annales de Demographie Historique,* 1973.
Sussman, G. D. *Selling Mother's Milk: The Wet-nursing Business in France, 1715–1914* (Champaign: University of Illinois Press, 1982).

6. Medick, H. and D. W. Sabean, eds. *Interest and Emotion* (New York: Cambridge University Press, 1984), 91.

CHAPTER 12

A Revolution's Broken Promises

Peter Marin

Sex has acquired a prominence in our society unrivaled in past time or in other cultures. Sexual fulfillment, likewise, has been elevated to the highest level in the list of human aspirations. We have witnessed, in the last quarter century, a sea change in sexual attitudes and behaviors. Peter Marin, in this essay, takes a critical look at what came ashore with this sexual revolution in the 1960s.

Marin is one of our favorite writers. He is an insightful and passionate cultural critic. His essay is a severe indictment of what passes for sexual liberation today. With the collapse of most traditional (social and religious) restraints upon sexual freedom, our human lives have become marred by pretense, desperation, and an immense amount of "bad faith." The author chronicles our culture's restless search for the ideal and the demand for instant gratification. The path is inevitably self-defeating and the results ultimately destructive. The essay will spark lively discussion, and its counterculture stance will challenge the student reader.

Questions for Discussion

1. Where do you see people acting out the sexual images and ideas provided for them, projected upon them, by others today?
2. Are these images/ideas liberating toward authentic personhood or a new form of imprisonment to selfishness?
3. Where are the casualties of the sexual revolution displayed today?
4. Are constraints, generosity, and kindness the new taboos in sexual relations?
5. Is sex a private affair, or does it have social and public dimensions?
6. What images/values can our religious traditions offer to the humanizing of sexual activity?

Further Reading

A similar analysis and critique of our sexual lives is made by Rollo May in his classic work *Love and Will* (New York: Norton, 1969), Chapter I.

Mention the sexual revolution to a dozen people, or to 100, and you get a dozen or 100 different analyses, conclusions, and complaints. And mixed in with these responses, there usually is a shrug or a grimace or a bitter smile: "What revolution?" people ask. The response does not mean that changes have not occurred. Obviously, they have. The rueful question means rather that the sexual freedom established during the past couple of decades has not been accompanied by the increase in happiness that many people assumed would follow from a freeing of sexual mores.

There have been obvious and important gains, of course. But there have been losses as well, many of which are suggested by the story of a friend of mine, Colin, who decided in the late '70s to have a sex change. He was then in his middle 30s, recently divorced from his wife, and separated from his son and daughter. One afternoon he showed up at our house and announced that he was going to have a sex change.

Years before, it turned out, he had idly picked up a book about sex and sex changes, and realized that he, too, like the subjects of the book, had felt since childhood as if he were a woman trapped in a man's body. Some time after that, he said, he made an agreement with his wife: When she went out with other men, as she often did, he would dress up in her clothes at home, pretending to be a woman. Then, after he and his wife separated, he met a woman who ran a clothing store for transvestites, and she taught him how to walk and talk and smile like a woman and to relearn, as a woman, all of the things that he did as a man. And now, he explained, he was going to have an operation to change his sex physically: He was going to become a woman.

A year later, one night in a bar in Los Angeles, a tanned, long-haired, muscular young man came up to me and said: "There's someone with me who knows you." At his table I saw a pretty, middle-aged woman, in a cashmere sweater, a string of pearls around her neck. "Hello, Peter," said the woman in a high, rather artificial voice, and I realized that it was my old friend Colin, now become Claire.

I saw him, or her, from time to time after that, and she seemed neither happy nor unhappy, only much the same as before. I remember once being taken aback when, in a discussion of how her sex change affected her children, she said: "Oh, but I just want to be a mother to them."

I did not see her for about a year, when she came again to the house one afternoon with a woman friend who might also once have been—I was not sure—a man. This time Claire was not happy. She was tired, and the feminine surface that she had so carefully cultivated seemed to be slipping. One could almost see through it, as if she was unable to muster the energy required to keep her femininity intact. Her voice kept sliding down into the lower registers; her hair kept coming undone; even her gestures had become again, at least for the moment, a man's. Her operation, it turned out, had not gone well. The doctor had botched it, though I did not get the details; and when I asked her how she was feeling in general, she said: "I had hoped I'd be happier. To tell the truth, I seem to be trapped in any body."

From *Psychology Today* (July 1983): 50–57. Reprinted by permission of the author.

I think of my friend now, and it seems to me that there is a sense in which he or she was trapped in a body—but not one of flesh and bone. It was, instead, an idea of a body that had been sold to him as surely as his car or house had been sold. He was acting out before the operation, and she was acting out afterward, not only a social role defined by others, but also a set of images imposed upon him. The mechanical devices that were now Claire's— the pumped-up silicone breasts, the carved vagina lined with the skin of what had been a penis—were no different, really, from the gadgets hawked in the marketplace: the various objects and accoutrements that we accept without question as a necessary part of our modern lives.

In essence, most of us are no different from Colin-Claire. Everywhere we act out the sexual images and ideas provided for us, projected upon us, by others. Whether it is men with their Marlboro mustaches, lesbians in their bull-dyke janitor's outfits, male homosexuals with their clone look, or adolescent girls in tight jeans, we move somnambulistically through roles and rituals, responding to every whim and wind in the cultural air. We have been liberated from the taboos of the past only to find ourselves imprisoned in a "freedom" that brings us no closer to our real nature or needs.

It is this that explains the grimaces and shrugs when one mentions liberation. For many people, the idea of liberation—whether it is sexual, political, or social—is synonymous with happiness or satisfaction. In the instance of sexual freedom, whether it is the work of Freud or that of myriad insistent sex-rebels exemplified by men and women as varied as Margaret Sanger, Havelock Ellis, John Cowper Powys, and Wilhelm Reich, everything said in support of sexual freedom implied that it would transform and restore all aspects of emotional and relational life. Since the absence of a successful sexual life was taken to be a cause of disease and pain, it followed that its presence would inevitably bring joy in its wake and, ultimately, social happiness.

There is something peculiarly bourgeois and hygienic about this line of thought. Sex, which in the culture's past had been associated with evil, was moved lock, stock, and barrel into the camp of goodness. It became an all-purpose healing instrument, a kind of glorifed patent medicine for everything that might ail us. Eventually, by a continuation of this logic, for Wilhelm Reich and the succeeding generation, the ideal orgasm itself became the wellspring of kindness and human decency.

What most of us currently seem to believe is that once restraints are removed from human behavior, "nature" simply asserts itself, like water filling an empty space. We forget that we bring with us, into any kind of freedom, the baggage of the past, our internalized cultural limits and weaknesses. Thus freedom—in this case sexual freedom—increases choice, but it guarantees nothing, delivers nothing. To the extent that it diversifies and expands experience, it also diversifies and multiplies the pain that accompanies experience, the kinds of errors that we can make, the kinds of harm that we can do to one another.

The simple fact is that many of the obstacles to sexual life are not merely the function of repressive attitudes or mores. They are grounded in the complexities of human nature and in the everyday difficulties of living together.

And all these natural—one is almost inclined to say "eternal"—difficulties are intensified by the disappearance of traditional sexual roles, the proliferation of sexual choices and styles, the permission to introduce, in public life, the full range of sexual fantasies and yearnings to which we are prey and heir.

I cannot here enumerate the various casualties of the sexual revolution, from the young men and women whom I once saw as a therapist and teacher, who, barely out of adolescence, had slept with so many people that they found themselves frigid or unresponsive beside those whom they genuinely loved, to the middle-aged couples who, spurred on by glowing reports of open marriage, pushed one another too far, into the jealousy and fury that they believed they could leave behind. But I think all of us must acknowledge, however reluctantly, that there was something to those "reactionaries"—starting with Freud's colleagues—who argued that deliberate, broad changes in our systems of sexual remissions and taboos would let loose among us as many troubles as they solved.

Sexual life, which ought to begin with, and deepen, a pervasive and genuine sympathy between men and women, seems instead to produce among us a set of altogether different emotions: rage, disappointment, suspicion, antagonism, a sense of betrayal, and sometimes contempt. It is not so much that one cannot find good feelings in many persons or between many lovers; it is, rather, that the sexual realm as a whole seems somehow corrupted. The general feel to it is one of perplexity, even anger; betrayal rather than gratitude pervades it; and though sex no longer seems to us a curse visited upon us by the devil, few of us seem to experience it continuously, or even often, as a gift. It remains for most men and women a world through which they move warily, cautiously, self-protectively—not a home but an alien land.

Ironically, much of this is the result of the shifting of sex from the private to the public world, which is the hallmark of the sexual revolution. Back in the '50s and early '60s, sex could be an alternative to the dominant culture. It constituted a world in which the mores and fashions of the public realm did not hold quite the power that they did elsewhere, and to enter that world on one's own was, in various small rebellious ways, to leave home, to mark out a territory where one could define oneself. Though that had its own costs (making a rebellion out of behavior that should be natural), it also had its advantages, not least of which was that it often made comrades and friends out of lovers; they were, after all, engaged together in creating a private world.

But the popularization of sex has changed much of that. Sex has become almost entirely socialized, invaded by manufactured images and experts; it is no longer a way of retreating from the public world but a way of entering it. The sexual realm has been corrupted by any number of absurd or destructive ideas, almost all of them put forward by people whose main interest is not sex but making money or names for themselves. The nonsense bruited about is unbelievable; the ignorance passing itself off as wisdom is endless; sexual ideas and techniques are hawked incessantly in the marketplace. Creative masturbation, the ideal orgasm, the clitoral orgasm, the G spot, the joys of sex, the virtues of homosexuality, the virtues of bisexuality, the virtues of sex with children, porpoises and disembodied spirits, the good old missionary virtues of heterosexuality—all of these now have their norms, their measures, their proprieties. We do sex filling in the squares laid out for us by others.

Whereas in the more puritanical past, the darkness and mysteries of sex remained outside the order of things, it has now become a sort of vast Club Med, a vacation paradise into which supposedly anyone can venture successfully and without cost. It is crowded with visitors, each of them seeking an identity and an experience that bears no more relation to things as they are than did the old idea of sex as the devil's playground.

Beneath all this there is one crucial point that we often ignore: that many people are far less driven or drawn by sex than we like to think. The cant and fashion of the age imply that sex is fundamentally important to everyone and a powerful, primary source of pleasure for everyone. But if you listen carefully to what moves beneath people's words, it does not really seem so.

The loneliness and dissatisfaction that most people express, the yearnings they articulate, have much less to do with sex than with an unfulfilled desire for good company or good conversation or the intimacy of shared perceptions and interests. I would say that friendship and community seem more important to most people than genuine sexual passion, and what they accept as a decent sexual life has little to do with the turbulence and confusion and adventurous risk required to live out, deeply and fully, the tendings of one's sexual nature. What seems to dominate their concerns about sex when they do surface is a sort of idealized and sugary notion, brought up to date with erotic trimmings—a child's drawing of security extended to include sex: a house with smoke curling from the chimney, a couple hand-in-hand at the door, and behind them, upstairs, the circular mirrored bed into which, after the day's work has been done and the front and back doors locked, they tumble for a riotous good time.

One does not usually find attached to sex these days the curiosity, adventurousness, and the tolerance for disappointment or capacity for camaraderie that once seemed to mark it and that must always accompany any genuine attempt to keep faith with one's nature. Where excitement does exist, it seems as often as not to come not from the pleasures of sex, but from the situation, the cinematic trappings of "affairs." One is tempted to say that we are a nation of romantics, using sex to create idealized scenarios for ourselves, but it is probably more accurate to say that we are sentimentalists, pining—as James Joyce puts it—for emotions for which we are not willing to pay the price of experience.

Do I exaggerate here? Perhaps a bit. There are moments, of course, for most men and women—both those who are genuinely concerned with sex and those who are not—in which the raw truth of some kind of love breaks through the preconceptions that have ringed it round, and desire sweeps all before it, even our notions of romance. Such moments have nothing to do with fantasy or even images. When they occur, they occur, as the wise Greeks understood, in forms and with consequences we have not anticipated or even wanted: A world is revealed—and with it a sweetness and a self we had not imagined.

But how often does it happen? Once, twice, half a dozen times in a life-

time. Sometimes, for some people, it does not happen at all. At my daughter's
school, for instance, they teach the children about sex with the help of a
child's picture book that describes orgasm as something akin to a sneeze. The
book tells its readers that the children can get an idea of sexual pleasure by
imagining first a terrible itch and then the relief of scratching it. What kind of
adults could have written such a book? Certainly not those for whom sex has
some importance. Perhaps the authors simply lack a talent for language, but
one suspects that there is more to it than that. The sneeze represents the head
and the itch stands for surface sensation, and these seem to be the ways in
which many men and women experience sex.

We are, after all, a puritanical people still, whose talent or capacity for
sexual feeling falls far short of the attention we pay to it. As a result—despite
all our rhetoric, all our manuals, all our universal make-believe—the sexual
realm is marred by pretense, desperation, and an immense amount of "bad
faith," which constitutes a simultaneous betrayal of both the other person
and oneself.

It was not always this bad; it was not this bad even recently. I remember
coming to California from the East in the very early '60s, a couple of years
before the sexual revolution burst into full bloom and "the greening of America" made adolescence into the model for all adult behavior. I was surprised
by the quality of sexual life I found there: men and women who seemed to
feel at ease with sexuality and with one another. This was true of men and
women in their 40s and 50s—something that I had not seen before.

I had grown up in Brooklyn in the '50s, when almost no one had much of
a sexual life—not, at least, in terms of real lovemaking. Our adolescence—
which was more openly sexual than the life of our elders—was not as terrible as it has since been made out to be. We were romantic, mildly driven,
somewhat frustrated, skewed in various trivial sexual ways, but nonetheless
we did not have a bad time of it. Sex for us was straightforward; desire was
almost always focused on a particular person. There were crushes, attrac-
tions, awkwardness, small fiascos, and though we never got to make love
(that came later, in college, for us), at least there was a genuine yearning,
accumulating and mixing with frustration, forming a preliminary sense of
what desire means, of how it might feel.

It was not until I got to California that I came upon large numbers of
grown men and women who had about them a casual sexual grace. Remember, these were the early '60s. This was not the California of cranks and
encounter groups, idealized sexual abandon, and foolish or apocalyptic zeal.
It was an easier and warmer world in which people drank rather than took
drugs, and somehow this gave a different tone to things than the one later
provided by drugs. There was not the driven sexuality or pornographic desperation back then that would later fill the air.

As a corollary, those who found themselves drawn to sex or one another
were more often than not comrades. That seems to me the most significant
difference from what now surrounds us. Of course, sex did not often have
attached to it, even back then, the deepest intensities, higher kinds of aware-

ness, or the transformative significance that Reich or D. H. Lawrence claimed for it. But it did have kindness and good humor attached, and to meet with someone in the flesh was to enter a shared community of flesh, as if one had met someone far from home with whom one could make at least a temporary home.

That happened to people—by their own accounts—even in casual encounters, not all of the time, but at least part of the time. Men and women seemed capable of tolerating their disappointments and mistakes without holding their failures—as we tend to do now—against those with whom they were involved. If things went wrong in or out of bed, there was little recrimination and much less rage. Expectations were lower, needs not as great; people did not yet think of sex as a panacea, did not expect it to make them whole or pure or healthy in any magical way.

Most important of all was that the only people who bothered with sex were, for the most part, those who liked it. Everyone else left it alone. The mild taboos still intact in those days were not strong enough to discourage those who were genuinely drawn to a sexual life. But they were strong enough to allow those not so drawn to stick to pleasures closer to their own natures. This left the sexual world to those who felt at home in it, whereas today, it is much like the ski slopes on a crowded weekend: mobbed with people who are there for a dozen reasons other than a genuine love of skiing or the slopes.

No doubt it was all too casual, and perhaps it was not all that it seemed. There must have been—there always is—cruelty, exploitation, and pretending, and at the heart of each privacy, the kinds of sorrow, estrangement, and pain familiar to us all. Perhaps women complained less because they did not then have the courage to speak out. But I think there was more to it than that. There was a kind of restraint, as if men and women still understood that what they owed one another, and the way to protect the sexual realm, was not to visit upon one another all of their sorrows and pain.

It is precisely that constraint, a minimal kindness connected to a naturalness of behavior, that is in large part what is missing from the sexual world today. What we have seen on a grand scale during the sexual revolution has been called in another context "the return of the repressed." But what has been repressed for so long is not only animal need. It is also, we have learned as it comes flooding upward to the surface, a raw mix of anger, frustration, bitter disappointment, sullen resentment—the whole underlying plane of feeling that forms itself in those whose world (despite all our talk of liberation) seems to have made no room for their deepest nature. How many, these days, turning to take another person in their arms, have not found themselves confronted by a range of accumulated disappointments, betrayals, and unfulfilled yearning—the living residue left behind not only by mothers, fathers, and lovers, but also the despair engendered by an unlived or falsely lived life?

Caught in the midst of this, people seem to have no one to blame but one another.

What I hear, everywhere around me, are complaints, descriptions of unmet demands, disappointments—that someone has failed them, let them down, is not what they ought to be. This is the strain that runs through much that I have heard as a therapist, teacher, or friend when men and women talk about one another (though men are less articulate, feel less justified than women in their public complaints). Many of these complaints are accurate, of course—we do fail one another. But their accuracy cannot hide the fact that the expectations have less to do with the world as it is or people as they are than with mistaken, preconceived, borrowed or inherited notions about what men and women ought to be or can be. The tone of all this is not merely one of sadness or unanswered yearning; more often than not it is a tone of judgment, impatience, even contempt. It is as if every lover is also an enemy, as if every companion is less an invited guest than an unwanted intruder.

We have come a long way in the sexual revolution. We have left behind us a great many old illusions and delusions; we know more than we did about the kinds of betrayal, guilt, and confusion that we can survive, and the kinds that we cannot. But what we have not learned—and this is the heart of the problem—is how to be kind to one another, how, in the midst of the confusions we ourselves have created, among the congeries of styles and pretenses of sex that surround us—how we can sustain those we find at our sides or in our arms.

The problem is not that sex has been separated from love, as many people have suggested (though there is some truth to this). The more general problem is that sex—along with countless other activities—has been emptied of generosity. There is nothing specifically sexual about such generosity, nor is there anything unique in the place it ought to play in sex. Yet the hardest thing of all in sexual life, more difficult by far than having the world's finest orgasm, is to leave images and dreams behind, and to learn that the person in one's arms is a poor forked creature, subject to the same confusions and alarms as oneself. Beyond all will, beyond all imagining, beyond all sensation—whether a sneeze or an itch—there remains a human reality that yields itself to a kindness of touch but which remains closed to us, despite all our yearnings, until we can somehow learn to bring to sex, through generosity, precisely what it is that we seek there from others, and without which the sexual world remains a kind of limbo.

Unfortunately for all of us, a capacity for generosity may be no more easily learned than a love of sexual life. Here too is an area where manuals or good advice are not likely to save us. It is one thing to be able to explain where the generosity in a particular culture comes from or what tends to destroy it (and I am not sure, really, that we can do even that). But nobody knows how to interject generosity into a culture whose members no longer seem to feel it on their own.

Of course, in spite of all this, the graces of flesh have not vanished completely and will not vanish. Like any other power rooted in nature, they seem capable of reasserting themselves in spite of anything we do or say. There will always be experiences that sweep away our notions derived from therapy or ideology and liberate us even from our notion of liberation.

It is the imperviousness of sex to ultimate understanding, the way it dissolves understanding, that gives rise to both its curses and gifts, its devils and angels. It remains, in the midst of that "revolution" which has provided neither much equality nor liberty nor fraternity, a troublesome but fecund darkness in which, like lost children, we call out to one another in both fear and delight.

CHAPTER 13

Four Mischievous Theories of Sex: Demonic, Divine, Casual, and Nuisance

William F. May

William May's article easily lends itself to constructive classroom discussion and clarification on the topic of sex. The author lays out four conflicting attitudes on sex. While the attitudes are loosely associated with the behavior of different cultural groups, the divergent views can be found in each one of us.

The author's typology is suggestive and stimulating: sex as demonic, divine, casual, and a nuisance. Each category contains an element of truth, but each is also ultimately fallacious. A theological interpretation and analysis is offered of the viewpoints on the basis of the biblical tradition and Christian heritage. The article is a valuable pedagogical tool to facilitate self-examination on this important topic.

Questions for Discussion

1. How do you account for the popularity of the playboy philosophy of sex in the United States? What is the root problem in this attitude? Is there a credible alternative?
2. Is there a place for discipline in sex? How would you justify it? Where does discipline end and repression begin?
3. What is the current dominant attitude toward sex in contemporary music, movies, church?

Several conflicting attitudes toward sex beset us today. We loosely associate these attitudes with the behavior of different cultural groups. Whether the groups actually behaved in these ways poses a descriptive question that will not preoccupy me for the moment. I am interested more in the attitudes than in the historical accuracy of the symbols. The Victorian prude feared sex as demonic; romantics, such as D. H. Lawrence, elevated sex to the divine; liberals tend to reduce sex to the casual; and the British, as the satirists relent-

Reprinted with the permission of The Free Press, a Division of Simon & Schuster, Inc. from *Passionate Attachments: Thinking about Love*, edited by William Gaylin, M.D., and Ethel Person, M.D. Copyright © 1988 by Friends of Columbia Psychoanalytic Center, Inc.

lessly portray them, pass it off as a nuisance. I will argue that all these views of sex contain an element of truth; all are ultimately mischievous; and most can be found conflicting and concurrent in ourselves.

SEX AS DEMONIC

Those who fear sex as the demon in the groin reckon with sex as a power which, once let loose, tends to grip and destroy its host; it is self-destructive and destructive of others, a loose cannon, as it were, in human affairs. Our movies and drugstore paperbacks relentlessly mock this view, which we tend to assign remotely to our Victorian forebears and proximately to our parents. While parents, in fact, may fear the explosive power of sex in their adolescent children, it is doubtful whether most parents are quite the Victorians their children assume them to be. Children impute this view to their elders because at some level of their being they partly hold to this attitude themselves.

In any event, this pessimism that emphasizes the runaway destructiveness of sex hardly originated with the Victorians. Religiously, it dates back to the Manichaean dualists of the Third Century of the Common Era. Manichaeans divided all reality and power into two rival kingdoms: the Kingdom of God pitted against the Kingdom of Satan, Good versus Evil, Light versus Darkness. They associated the Absolute Good with Spirit and Absolute Evil with Matter. Originally Spirit and Matter existed in an uneasy separation from one another; but through the aggressive strategies of Satan, the present world and humankind came into existence, a sad commingling of them both—Spirit and Flesh. The world is a kind of battleground between these two rival kingdoms. Man's only hope rests in disengaging himself from the pain and confusion and muck of life in the flesh, and allying himself with the Kingdom of Spirit. I say "man" deliberately because the Manichaeans tended to associate women with the intentions of the Devil; that is, with his strategy to perpetuate this present age of confusion and commingling through the device of sex and offspring. Quite literally, marriage in their view is an invention of the Devil, a scheme for perpetuating the human race and the messy world that we know. Man should achieve a final state of metaphysical *Apartheid*, a clean separation from the toils of the flesh, women, and all their issue.

Manichaean sex counselors thus urged on their followers a rigorous ethic of sexual denial—with, however, an antinomian escape clause since not everyone could lead the wholly ascetic life. If one couldn't totally abstain— here is the twist—the Manichaeans believed it was better to engage in "unnatural sex" so as to avoid the risk of progeny. In the Manichaean vision of things, sex is bad, but children are worse. Reproduction should be avoided at all costs, since it only perpetuates the grim, woe-beset world that we know. (The mythology sounds strange to the modern ear, but the Manichaeans have served as a symbol of pessimism in later Western theology, and rightly so. A reluctance to have children usually blurts out the pessimism—whatever its causes—of those who think little of the world's present and future prospects.)

Christianity rejected this Manichaean pessimism, and thereby confirmed the religious vision it derived largely from the Scriptures of Israel and from the New Testament. Its monotheism differs from a dualism that takes evil too seriously and that identifies evil too readily with the flesh. Its scriptures highly esteem sexual love (the erotic Song of Solomon would jar in a Manichaean scripture); it grants a sacramental status to marriage; and it describes the body as the temple of the Lord. The lowly, needy, hungering, flatulent body is nothing less than the real estate where the resurrection will occur.

But dualism kept reappearing in the Western tradition, often nesting in Christianity itself or appearing in an alluring alternative, the cult of romantic love. On the surface, the ideal of romantic love, Denis de Rougemont once shrewdly argued, appears to be sexually vigorous; it celebrates God's good green gift of sex. But, in fact, it secretly despairs of sex; it always directs itself to the faraway princess—not to the partner you've got, but to the dream person, the remote figure not yet yours. Sex slips its focus on actual contacts between people and transposes to the realm of the imagination. To possess her is to lose one's appetite for her. Love, therefore, feeds best on obstacles. "We love each other, but you're a Capulet and I'm a Montague." And so it goes from Romeo and Juliet, backward to the Tristan and Iseult myth, and forward to Noel Coward's "Brief Encounter" and the mawkish *Love Story*. The poignancy of passion depends upon separation, ultimately upon death. The cult of romantic love locates passion in the teased imagination. The flesh kills; the spirit alone endures; thus Manichaean pessimism hides in its alluring garb.

The post-Renaissance world offered a somewhat drabber version of this dualist suspicion of sex. Social diseases assaulted the Western countries and associated sex with forces that abuse the mind and body. Further, a concept of marriage emerged with middle-class careerism that encourages a Manichaean wariness toward sex. The bourgeois family depended for its stability and life on the career and the property of the male provider. Premarital sex, which distracts a man from his career and leads him prematurely into marriage, severely limits his prospects. Extramarital sex spoils the marriage itself and public reputation. And marital sex leads to too many children with a cramping effect on the careers of those already arrived. Thus, all told, sex severely inconveniences a careerist-oriented society that depends throughout on deferred gratification.

But not surprisingly, bourgeois culture produced not only repression, but also a pornographic fascination with sex. Sex became, at one and the same time, unmentionable in polite society but also an unshakable obsession in fantasy. Geoffrey Gorer, the English social anthropologist, in his often plagiarized article, "The Pornography of Death," nicely defined all such pornographic preoccupation with sex as an obsession with the sex act abstracted from its natural human emotion, which is *affection*. This definition helps explain the inevitable structure of pornographic novels and films. Invariably, they must proliferate and escalate the varieties of sexual performance. When the sex act separates from its natural human emotion of affection, it loses its tie with the concrete lives of the two persons performing the act; it becomes *boring*. Inevitably, one must reinvest one's interest in the variety of ways and techniques with which the act is performed—one on one, then two on one, then in all possible permutations and combinations, culminating in the orgy. When affection isn't there, it won't do to have bodies perform the act in the age-old ways. Sad variety alone compensates.

(The oft-cited pornographic preoccupation with death and violence today follows the same pattern of escalation. A pornography of death entails an obsession with death and violence abstracted from its natural human emotion, which is grief. Once again such violence, abstracted from persons, inevitably bores, and therefore one must reinvest interest in the technology with which the act is performed. It won't do for James Bond to drive an ordinary General Motors car (as though it weren't death-dealing an instrument enough); he must have a specially equipped vehicle that jets flames out its exhaust. Spies must be killed in all sorts of combinations and permutations. Violence inevitably excalates.)

This ambivalent attitude toward sex that generates both repression and obsession is basically religious—not Jewish or Christian, to be sure, but religious, specifically Manichaean—in its root. It religiously preoccupies itself with sex as a major evil in human affairs.

SEX AS DIVINE

The second of the four attitudes toward sex also qualifies as religious; in this case, however, one elevates sex from the demonic to the divine. D. H. Lawrence offers the definitive expression of this sex-mysticism; let his views stand for the type. *Lady Chatterley's Lover* is a religious book. That assessment didn't occur to people of my generation who, before laying hands on the book, assumed its title was *Lady Chatterley's Lovers,* and settled down for the inevitable orgy. The book offered, however, religion in a very traditional sense, for religion consists of some sort of experience of sacred power perceived in contest with other powers. The sacred grips the subject as overwhelming, alluring, and mysterious, and eventually orders the rest of life for the person or community so possessed. (Exodus 3, for example, describes the contest between Yahveh, God of the Jews, and the power of the Pharaoh. God liberates his people from Egypt and orders their life at Mt. Sinai; God prevails.)

Just so, the novel focuses on a woman who experiences in her own being a contest of the powers—those opposingly symbolized by Lord Clifford, her husband, and Oliver Mellors, her husband's gamekeeper. Her husband possessed those several powers which the English highly prized—status, money, and talent. He was at once an aristocrat, an industrial captain, and an author—an ironmonger and wordmonger. He wielded economic power and word power. Leaving such a man for his gamekeeper would utterly confound the commitments of Lady Chatterley's class. Lord Clifford's only trouble, his fatal trouble, however, was a war wound that left him dead from the waist down, a state of affairs which was but the natural issue of the kind of destructive power which he wields. Lady Chatterley discovers in the gamekeeper and in the grove where he breeds pheasants, a different kind of power, a growing power in the pheasant and the phallus, and this power prevails.

Lawrence's novel celebrates not random sex but a sex-mysticism. The grove where Lady Chatterley and Oliver meet serves as a sacred precinct removed from the grimy, profane, sooty, industrial midlands of England where men like Lord Clifford ruled. Lawrence explicitly uses the coronation Psalms of Israel to describe the act of sexual intercourse. "Open up, ye everlasting gates, and let the king of glory enter in." In using royal language, Lawrence advocated not sexual promiscuity, as the hungering undergraduates of my generation supposed. Far from it! Lawrence disdained the merely casual affair: he exalted sexual union into a sacred encounter. Tenderhearted sex is the closest we come to salvation in this life. It provides contact with all that nurtures and fulfills. Americans in the 1950s relied on a sentimental marital version of this religious expectation. As the song of the times put it, "love and marriage go together like a horse and carriage." In the oft-called "age of conformity" one tended to look to the sanctuary of marriage to provide respite from the loneliness and pressures of the outer world to which one conformed but which one found unfulfilling.

SEX AS CASUAL

W. H. Auden once observed that the modern liberal offended Lawrence more than the Puritan. The Puritan mistakenly viewed sex as an outsize evil, but the liberal made the even greater mistake of reducing sex to the casual—to one of the many incidental goods that in our liberty we take for granted. Some have called this the drink-of-water theory of sex.

This casual attitude toward sex reflects a liberal industrial culture that prizes autonomy above all else, that reduces nature to raw material to be manipulated and transformed into products of man's own choosing, and that correspondingly reduces the body to the incidental—not to the prison house of the dualists, or to the Lord's temple of the monotheists, or to the sacred grove of the mystics, but to a playground pure and simple.

Some observers argue that this third attitude toward sexual experience dominates our time. Is not D. H. Lawrence, despite his flamboyance, actually somewhat quaint and old-fashioned, the reverse side, if you will, of the Victorian prude? Don't both the prude and the romantic make the mistake of taking sex too seriously? One elevates sex into the satanic, and the other celebrates it as divine. Have we not succeeded in desacralyzing sex and reducing it now to the casual?

This third and apparently prevailing theory of sex today, the so-called new sex ethic, takes two forms. First and most notoriously, its earlier, male chauvinist version converts sex into an instrument of domination. It reduces sex to the casual, by converting women into bunnies and by replacing heterosexuality with a not so latent male orientation. In its magazine formula, it condemns women, flatters the young male, and lavishes on him advice on how to dress, talk, choose his cars, and handle his women—all without involvement. The women's movement has shown proper contempt for this view.

The second version of the new sex ethic avoids the more obvious criticisms of the woman's movement; indeed, it seeks to join it by offering easy access, easy departure, and no long-term ties, but with equal rights for both partners. One of our entertainers best summarized this casual, tentative, experimental attitude toward sex and marriage by referring to his decision to do the "marriage bit"—a phrase from show biz. It suggests that marriage offers a role one chooses to play rather than a relationship by which one is permanently altered—not necessarily a one-night stand, but then not likely, either, to run as long as "Life With Father."

This reading of the social history of our time—from the religious to the secular—only apparently persuades. We are not quite as casual about sex as this analysis would suggest. Our popular magazines—men's and women's—may have evangelized for a cool attitude toward sex; but they would not have sold millions of copies if, underneath it all, in the steamy depths of our desires, we could toy with it that easily.

Denis de Rougemont neatly skewers our irrepressible fascination with sex in *The Devil's Share,* a book that included chapters on such topics as the "Devil and Betrayal," the "Devil and War," and the "Devil and Lying." His first sentence in his essay on the "Devil and Sex" reads, in effect: "To the adolescent amongst my readers who have turned to this chapter first . . ." I read de Rougemont's book when I was 32, but the age makes little difference. There one is—young or old—caught red-handed, eyes riveted, imagination stirred, ready for fresh rivulets of knowledge on that most fascinating of topics. Casual curiosity? Yes. But the lure of mystery as well. Elements of the religious as well as the casual characterize our attitude toward the subject.

SEX AS A NUISANCE

So far, this essay has covered three views of sex; symmetry alone would demand a fourth to complete two sets of paired attitudes. Dualists inflate sex into a transcendent evil; mystics view it as a transcendent good; and casualists reduce it to a trivial good. The demands of symmetry, then, would posit the existence of a fourth group composed of those prosaic folk who dismiss sex as a minor evil, a nuisance. Comic writers have rounded up this particular population and located them in Great Britain under the marquee: "No Sex, Please. We're British." Copulation is, at best, a burdensome ritual to be endured for the sake of a few lackluster goods. One has visions therewith of an underblooded, overarticulate clutch of aristocrats in whom the life force runs thin.

But a report in one of the most popular of American syndicated newspaper columns (in the *Washington Post,* June 14 and 15, 1985) suggests that the number of people occupying the quadrant of petty pessimists may be surprisingly large. Ann Landers asked her reading audience to send a postcard or letter with a reply to the question: "Would you be content to be held close and treated tenderly and forget about 'the act'? Reply YES or NO and please add one line: 'I am over (or under) 40 years of age.' No signature is necessary." Even discounting for the fact that the disgruntled find more time to write than the contented, the percentage of those replying to Landers' inquiry who deemed themselves to be sexually burdened was impressive. More than 70 percent replied YES and 40 percent of those affirmatives were under 40 years of age. Clearly the people who find sex to be a burden transcend the boundaries of the British Isles. Over 90,000 letters poured in from the U.S. and other places where Landers' column appears (in Canada, Europe, Tokyo, Hong Kong, Bangkok, Mexico). This outpouring has exceeded every inquiry that Landers has directed to her readers, except for the pre-fab letter to be sent to President Reagan on the subject of nuclear war. "This sex survey beats . . . the poll asking parents, 'If you had to do it over again, would you have children?'" (Seventy percent said NO.) (Some astute historians of religion have argued that Manichaeaism persists as the ranking heresy in the West.)

Critics of the Landers report have warned that her results are not scientific. Her respondents are self-selective and her question tips the responses negatively. By placing the term for intercourse in quotation marks and calling it "the act," she tends to separate the sex act from tenderness. Still, the grammar of her question does not force an either/or response: tenderness or sex. However parsed, Landers uncovers a great deal of dissatisfaction amongst women . . . "it's a burden, a bore, no satisfaction . . ." Her letter-writers largely blame men for this state of affairs, but her survey and the ensuing discussion leave untouched the question as to whether the male failure to satisfy reflects a deeper masculine version of the experience of sex as a nuisance. One thinks here not of the occasionally impotent male who is agonizingly aware of sex as a nuisance, but, of the robust stallion who prides himself on his efficient performance but who finds foreplay, after-play, tenderness, and gratitude an incomprehensible and burdensome detail.

THEOLOGICAL INTERPRETATION

Since I am a trained Protestant theologian, not a social commentator, I will close with a few comments about each of these four attitudes on the basis of the biblical tradition. In these matters I don't think I stray too far from what my colleagues in the rabbinate and priesthood might say.

1. Whatever criticisms the biblical tradition might deliver against the casualist approach to sex, that approach has an element of truth to it. Not all sexual encounter should carry the weight of an ultimate significance. Sometimes sex is merely recreational, a way to fall asleep, a *jeu d'esprit*, to say nothing of a *jeu de corps*. But at the same time, the interpretation of a particular episode should not exhaust the full meaning of the activity. At first glance, the ideology of the casualist seems virile, optimistic, and pleasure-oriented. But a latent melancholy pervades it. The fantasy of transient pleasure as an interpretation of the full meaning of the act requires a systematic elimination of everything that might shadow the fantasy. The sacred grove trivializes into a playpen. Hugh Hefner's original policy of never accepting a story for his magazine on the subject of death betrays the pathos of the approach. The fact of human frailty and death shatters the illusion upon which Hefner's world depends. By comparison, a sturdy optimism underlies a tradition that invites a couple to exchange vows that can stretch across the stark events of plenty and want, sickness and health, until death parts them. Since life is no playpen, it lets the world as it is flood in upon the lovers in the very content of their pledge.

Further, the casual outlook tends to ignore the inevitable complications of most sexual relationships. It lapses into a kind of emotional prudery. We are inclined to apply the word prudish to those who deny their sexual being. The modern casualist, however, is an emotional prude; that is, he tries to deny those emotions that cluster around his sexual life: affection, but not affection alone, loneliness in absence, jealousy, envy, preoccupation, restlessness, anger, and hopes for the future. The emotional prude dismisses all these or assumes that sincerity and honesty provide a kind of solvent that breaks down chemically any and all inconvenient and messy feelings: You hope for the future? But I never promised you a future. Why complain? I am emotionally clean, drip-dry. Why not you? This antiseptic view overlooks the element of dirt farming in sex and marriage. Caesar ploughed her and she cropped. Put another way, this view overlooks the comic in sex; adopting the pose of the casual it lacks a comic sense. It overlooks the way sex gets out of control. Sex refuses to stay in the playpen. It tends to defy our advance formulae. It mires each side down in complications that need to be respected.

If sex is a great deal more important, complicated, and consequential for the destiny of each partner than the committed casualists are wont to pretend, then it may not be out of place to subject it to a deliberateness, to submit it to a discipline, to let sexual decisions be *decisions* instead of resolving sexual ties by the luck of the draw, opportunity, and drift. The Hebrew tradition emphasized and symbolized the element of deliberateness in sexual life when it imposed the rite of circumcision. The rite does not deny the natural (as castration does with a vengeance) but neither does it accept the natural vitalities without their conforming to purposes that transcend them. Human sexual life is properly itself only when it is drawn into the self's deeper identity. Thus, against those who reduce sex to the casual, the tradition says sex is *important,* and should be subjected to discipline like anything important and consequential in human affairs.

2. The approach of the dualists to sex, either those who elevate it to a transcendental evil or those who reduce it to a doggish burden, hold to an element of truth. Sometimes, sexual activity can be abysmally self-destructive and destructive of others; at other times, it is merely a burdensome obligation. But, from the biblical perspective, both approaches wrongly estimate sexual love: they confuse the abuse of an activity with the activity itself. Sexual love is a good rather than an evil. God created man in his own image, *male and female* created He them. Genesis provides quite an exalted theory of sexual identity. Not divine, but in the image of God.

This differing estimate of sexual love shifts dramatically the meaning and warrants for discipline in one's sexual life. The Manichaeans disciplined sexual activity in the sense that they sought to eradicate it altogether; they justified radical denial on the ground that sex is inherently *evil.* The Jew and Christian, on the other hand, justify discipline on the basis of the goodness of sexual power.

Unfortunately, most popular justifications of discipline, especially in the perspective of the young, rest on the evilness of an activity or a faculty. Discipline the child because he is evil. Renounce your sexuality because it corrupts. This is the Manichaean way.

We may need to recover the vastly more important warrant for discipline that we already recognize in education and that the biblical tradition largely supports. The goodness and promise of the human mind, not its evilness, justifies the lengthy discipline of an education. Because the child has worthwhile potentialities, we consider it worth our while to develop her to the maximum. Because the piano is a marvelously versatile and expressive instrument, we think it worth the labors of the talented person to realize the full potentialities of the instrument rather than trivialize its capabilities with "Chopsticks." Some sexual encounters are not so much wicked as trivial, less than the best.

3. Finally, the sex-mystics also have an element of truth on their side. The event of sexual intercourse does supply us with one of our privileged contacts with ecstasy—the possibility of being beside ourselves, of moving beyond ourselves, experiencing a level of energy and urgency that both suspends and restores the daily round. But when all is said and done, sexuality, though a good, is only a *human* good, not *divine* as such. Despite Lawrence's perorations on the subject of love and the mountains atremble for Robert Jordan and his mate in Hemingway's *For Whom the Bell Tolls,* the act of sexual intercourse falls short of Exodus–Mount Sinai, death-resurrection. Intercourse is not an event of salvation; neither is marriage another name for redemption.

Biblical realism requires us to acknowledge three ways of abusing sex—to malign it with the dualists, to underestimate it with the casualists, but also to overestimate it with the sentimentalists and therefore to get angry, frustrated, and retaliatory when it fails to transcend the merely human. As a sexologist, St. Augustine had his faults, but he recognized that people tend to engage in a double torture when they elevate the human into the divine—whether it be sex, marriage, children, or any other creaturely good.

First, they condemn themselves to disappointment; they torture themselves. If men and women look for the resolution to all their problems in marriage, if they look to it for salvation, they are bound to discover that neither sex nor marriage converts an ordinary human being into someone sublime. They let themselves in for a letdown. Second, one not only tortures oneself, one also tortures the partner to whom one has turned. One places on the mate too heavy a burden. Dostoevsky tells of a dream in which a driver flogs a horse, forcing it to drag an overloaded wagon until the horse collapses under too much weight. We similarly overburden another when we look to him for too much. We expect others to function as a surrogate for the divine. Thus parents drive their thwarted ambitions through their children like a stake through the heart. Some marriages break up not because people expected too little from marriage, but because they have expected too much.

This biblical realism need not produce the sort of pessimism that expects little of the world and savors even less. Indeed, it should free us a little for enjoyment. Once we free our relationships to others from the impossible pressure to rescue us or redeem us, perhaps we can be free to enjoy them for what they are. Specifically, we can enjoy without shame and with delight a sexual relationship for the pleasurable, companionable, and fertile human good that it is.

CHAPTER 14

The Neglected Heart: The Emotional Dangers of Premature Sexual Involvement

Thomas Lickona

Most young people I have met are very clear about the following principle: in order to be on a sport's team you have to show some skill at playing the game. You can't just walk onto the field, name yourself as a player, and expect to be handed a uniform. You have to go through tryouts to see if you have developed enough skill to qualify for the team. And then if you do get a spot on the team, you will face endless activities at strengthening your skills, at becoming a team player, and—and this is my main point here—at psychological conditioning for the sport, ensuring that your mind and heart are also ready when you take to the field or the court.

Not all people understand that by its very nature, "sex" is meant to be something more than a physical activity. Understanding this aspect of ourselves seems of great importance. I once heard an astute fifteen-year-old say this about her sex education class: "Today I found out that I was physically fully prepared to be a mother: to conceive a child, to carry that child to term, and to give birth to that child. And today I finally saw that that was the *only* sense in which I was prepared. I am not prepared emotionally, psychologically, educationally, financially, or socially."

The following essay argues that the "skills" of full human sexual functioning are not just the physical "skills" of "doing it." Many twelve-year-olds think that is all there is to it. One can understand that error in one so young. The problem comes when the person over seventeen lives out the same illusion. Thomas Lickona gives us something to think about.

The best way to read this essay may be to ask yourself where the author touches on matters you know to be true.

Questions for Discussion

1. Where does he tell it like it is? After all, some reading this book can tell their own stories about the dangers Lickona touches on.
2. What would I want to say to fourteen-year-olds to help them be aware of the dangers that may lie ahead?

3. Where does the author seem, in your view, to overstate "the dangers of premature sexual involvement."

4. What does that word *premature* mean? Could a particular involvement be premature for a twenty-five-year-old? What would be some examples?

You didn't get pregnant. You didn't get AIDS. So why do you feel so bad?

—*Leslee Unruh, abstinence educator*

There is no condom for the heart.

—*Sign at a sex education conference*

In discussions of teen sex, much is said about the dangers of pregnancy and disease—but far less about the emotional hazards. And that's a problem, because the destructive psychological consequences of temporary sexual relationships are very real. Being aware of them can help a young person make and stick to the decision to avoid premature sexual involvement.

That's not to say we should downplay the physical dangers of uncommitted sex. Pregnancy is a life-changing event. Sexually transmitted disease (STD)—and there are now more than 20 STDs—can rob you of your health and even your life. Condoms don't remove these dangers. Condoms have an annual failure rate of 10 percent to 30 percent in preventing pregnancy because of human error in using them and because they sometimes leak, break, or slip off. Condoms reduce but by no means eliminate the risk of AIDS. In a 1993 analysis of 11 different medical studies, condoms were found to have a 31 percent average failure rate in preventing the sexual transmission of the AIDS virus.[1] Finally, condoms do little or nothing to protect against the two STDs infecting at least one-third of sexually active teenage girls: human papilloma virus (the leading cause of cervical cancer) and chlamydia (the leading cause of infertility), both of which can be transmitted by skin-to-skin contact in the entire genital area, only a small part of which is covered by the condom.[2]

Why is it so much harder to discuss sex and emotional hurt—to name and talk about the damaging psychological effects that can come from premature sexual involvement? For one thing, most of us have never heard this aspect of sex discussed. Our parents didn't talk to us about it. The media don't talk about it. And the heated debate about condoms in schools typically doesn't say much about the fact that condoms do nothing to make sex *emotionally* safe. When it comes to trying to explain to their children or students

Reprinted with permission from the Summer 1994 issue of the *American Educator*, the quarterly journal of the American Federation of Teachers.

how early sexuality can do harm to one's personality and character as well as to one's health, many adults are simply at a loss for words, or reduced to vague generalities such as, "you're too young" or "you're not ready" or "you're not mature enough."

This relative silence about the emotional side of sex is ironic, because the emotional dimension of sex is what makes it distinctively human.

What in fact are the emotional or psychological consequences of premature, uncommitted sex? These consequences vary among individuals. Some emotional consequences are short-term but still serious. Some of them last a long time, sometimes even into marriage and parenting. Many of these psychological consequences are hard to imagine until they've been experienced. In all cases, the emotional consequences of sexual experiences are not to be taken lightly. A moment's reflection reminds us that emotional problems can have damaging, even crippling, effects on a person's ability to lead a happy and productive life.

Let's look at 10 negative psychological consequences of premature sexual involvement.

1. WORRY ABOUT PREGNANCY AND AIDS

For many sexually active young people, the fear of becoming pregnant or getting AIDS is a major emotional stress.

Russell Henke, health education coordinator in the Montgomery County (Maryland) Public Schools, says, "I see kids going to the nurses in schools, crying a day after their first sexual experience, and wanting to be tested for AIDS. They have done it, and now they are terrified. For some of them, that's enough. They say, 'I don't want to have to go through that experience anymore.'"[3]

A high school girl told a nurse: "I see some of my friends buying home pregnancy tests, and they are so worried and so distracted every month, afraid that they might be pregnant. It's a relief to me to be a virgin."

2. REGRET AND SELF-RECRIMINATION

Girls, especially, need to know in advance the sharp regret that so many young women feel after becoming sexually involved.

Says one high school girl: "I get upset when I see my friends losing their virginity to some guy they've just met. Later, after the guy's dumped them, they come to me and say, 'I wish I hadn't done it.'"[4] A ninth-grade girl who slept with eight boys in junior high says, "I'm young, but I feel old."

Girls are more vulnerable than boys because girls are more likely to think of sex as a way to "show you care." They're more likely to see sex as a sign of commitment in the relationship.

If a girl expects a sexual interlude to be loving, she may very well feel cheated and used when the boy doesn't show a greater romantic interest after the event. As one 15-year-old girl describes her experience: "I didn't expect the guy to marry me, but I never expected him to avoid me in school."

Bob Bartlett, who teaches a freshman sexuality class in a Richfield, Minn., high school, shares the following story of regret on the part of one of his students (we'll call her Sandy):

> Sandy, a bright and pretty girl, asked to see Mr. Bartlett during her lunch period. She explained that she had never had a boyfriend, so she was excited when a senior asked her out.
>
> After they dated for several weeks, the boy asked her to have sex with him. She was reluctant; he was persistent. She was afraid of appearing immature and losing him, so she consented.
>
> "Did it work?" Mr. Bartlett asked gently. "Did you keep him?"
>
> Sandy replied: "For another week. We had sex again, and then he dropped me. He said I wasn't good enough. There was no spark.
>
> "I know what you're going to say. I take your class. I know now that he didn't really love me. I feel so stupid, so cheap."[5]

Sandy hoped, naively, that sex would keep the guy. Here is another high school girl, writing to an advice column about a different kind of regret. She wishes she *could* lose the guy she's involved with, but she feels trapped by their sexual relationship.

> I am 16, a junior in high school, and like nearly all the other girls here, I have already lost my virginity. Although most people consider this subject very personal, I feel the need to share this part of my life with girls who are trying to decide whether to have sex for the first time.
>
> Sex does not live up to the glowing reports and hype you see in the movies. It's no big deal. In fact, it's pretty disappointing.
>
> I truly regret that my first time was with a guy that I didn't care that much about. I am still going out with him, which is getting to be a problem. I'd like to end this relationship and date others, but after being so intimate, it's awfully tough.
>
> Since that first night, he expects sex on every date, like we are married or something. When I don't feel like it, we end up in an argument. It's like I owe it to him. I don't think this guy is in love with me, at least he's never said so. I know deep down that I am not in love with him either, and this makes me feel sort of cheap.
>
> I realize now that this is a very big step in a girl's life. After you've done it, things are never the same. It changes everything.
>
> My advice is, don't be in such a rush. It's a headache and a worry. (Could I be pregnant?) Sex is not for entertainment. It should be a commitment. Be smart and save yourself for someone you wouldn't mind spending the rest of your life with.
>
> —Sorry I Didn't And Wish I Could Take It Back[6]

Regret over uncommitted sexual relationships can last for years. I recently received a letter from a 33-year-old woman, now a psychiatrist, who is very much concerned about the sexual pressures and temptations facing young people today. She wanted to share the lessons she had learned about sex the hard way. After high school, she says, she spent a year abroad as an exchange student:

> I was a virgin when I left, but I felt I was protected. I had gotten an IUD so I could make my own decisions if and when I wanted. I had steeled myself against commitment. I was never going to marry or have children; I was going to have a career. During that year abroad, from 17½ to 18½, I was very promiscuous.
>
> But the fact is, it cost me to be separated from myself. The longest-standing and deepest wound I gave myself was heartfelt. That sick, used feeling of having given a precious part of myself—my soul—to so many and for nothing, still aches. I never imagined I'd pay so dearly and for so long.

This woman is happily married now, she says, and has a good sexual relationship with her husband. But she still carries the emotional scar of those early sexual experiences. She wants young people to know that "sex without commitment is very risky for the heart."

3. GUILT

Guilt is a special form of regret—a strong sense of having done something morally wrong. Guilt is a normal and healthy moral response, a sign that one's conscience is working.

In his book for teenagers, *Love, Dating, and Sex,* George Eager tells the story of a well-known speaker who was addressing a high school assembly. The speaker was asked, "What do you most regret about your high school days?"

He answered, "The thing I most regret about high school is the time I singlehandedly destroyed a girl."

Eager offers this advice to young men: "When the breakup comes, it's usually a lot tougher on the girls than it is on the guys. It's not something you want on your conscience—that you caused a girl to have deep emotional problems."[7]

One 16-year-old boy says he stopped having sex with girls when he saw and felt guilty about the pain he was causing: "You see them crying and confused. They say they love you, but you don't love them."

Even in an age of sexual liberation, a lot of people who are having sex nevertheless have a guilty conscience about it. The guilt may come, as in the case of the young man just quoted, from seeing the hurt you've caused other people.

The guilt may come from knowing that your parents would be upset if they knew you were having sex. Or it may stem from your religious convictions. Christianity, Judaism, and Islam, for example, all teach that sex is a gift from God reserved for marriage and that sexual relations outside marriage are morally wrong.

Sometimes guilt about their sexual past ends up crippling people when they become parents by keeping them from advising their own children not to become sexually involved. According to counselor Dr. Carson Daly: "Because these parents can't bear to be considered hypocrites, or to consider themselves hypocrites, they don't give their children the sexual guidance they very much need."[8]

4. LOSS OF SELF-RESPECT AND SELF-ESTEEM

Many people suffer a loss of self-esteem when they find out they have a sexually transmitted disease. For example, according to the Austin, Texas-based Medical Institute for Sexual Health, more than 80 percent of people with herpes say they feel "less confident" and "less desirable sexually."[9]

But even if a person is fortunate enough to escape sexually transmitted disease, temporary sexual relationships can lower the self-respect of both the user and the used.

Sometimes casual sex lowers self-esteem, leading a person into further casual sex, which leads to further loss of self-esteem in an oppressive cycle from which it may be hard to break free. This pattern is described by a college senior, a young woman who works as a residence hall director:

> There are girls in our dorm who have had multiple pregnancies and multiple abortions. They tend to be filled with self-loathing. But because they have so little self-esteem, they will settle for any kind of attention from guys. So they keep going back to the same kind of destructive situations and relationships that got them into trouble in the first place.

On both sides of dehumanized sex, there is a loss of dignity and self-worth. One 20-year-old college male confides: "You feel pretty crummy when you get drunk at a party and have sex with some girl, and then the next morning you can't even remember who she was."

Another college student describes the loss of self-respect that followed his first sexual "conquest":

> I finally got a girl into bed—actually it was in a car—when I was 17. I thought it was the hottest thing there was, but then she started saying she loved me and getting clingy.
>
> I figured out that there had probably been a dozen guys before me who thought they had "conquered" her, but who were really just objects of her need for security. That realization took all the wind out of my sails. I couldn't respect someone who gave in as easily as she did.
>
> I was amazed to find that after four weeks of having sex as often as I wanted, I was tired of her. I didn't see any point in continuing the relation-

ship. I finally dumped her, which made me feel even worse, because I could see that she was hurting. I felt pretty low.[10]

People aren't things. When we treat them as if they were, we not only hurt them; we lose respect for ourselves.

5. THE CORRUPTION OF CHARACTER AND THE DEBASEMENT OF SEX

When people treat others as sexual objects and exploit them for their own pleasure, they not only lose self-respect; they corrupt their characters and debase their sexuality in the process.

Good character consists of virtues such as respect, responsibility, honesty, fairness, caring, and self-control. With regard to sex, the character trait of self-control is particularly crucial. The breakdown of sexual self-control is a big factor in many of the sex-related problems that plague our society: rape, promiscuity, pornography, addiction to sex, sexual harassment, the sexual abuse of children, sexual infidelity in marriage, and the serious damage to families many of these problems cause. It was Freud who said—and it is now obvious how right he was—that sexual self-control is essential for civilization.

Sex frequently corrupts character by leading people to tell lies in order to get sex. The Medical Institute for Sexual Health reports: "Almost all studies show that many sexually active people will lie if they think it will help them have sex."[11] Common lies: "I love you" and "I've never had a sexually transmitted disease."

Because sex is powerful, once sexual restraint is set aside, it easily takes over individuals and relationships. Consider the highly sexualized atmosphere that now characterizes many high schools. A high school teacher in Indiana says, "The air is thick with sex talk. Kids in the halls will say—boy to girl, girl to boy—'I want to f—you.'"

In a 1993 study by the American Association of University Women, four of five high school students—85 percent of girls and 75 percent of boys—said they have experienced "unwelcome sexual behavior that interferes with my life" in school.[12] An example: A boy backs a 14-year-old girl up against her locker, day after day. Says Nan Stein, a Wellesley College researcher: "There's a Tailhook happening in every school. Egregious behavior is going on."

Another recently reported example of this corruption of character is the Spur Posse club at Lakewood High School in suburban Los Angeles. Members of this club competed to see how many girls they could sleep with; one claimed he had slept with 63. Sadly, elementary school-age children are beginning to mimic such behavior. In a suburb of Pittsburgh, an assistant superintendent reports that sixth-grade boys were found playing a sexual contact game; the object of the game was to earn points by touching girls in private parts, the most points being awarded for "going all the way."

In this sex-out-of-control environment, even rape is judged permissible by many young people. In a 1988 survey of students in grades six through nine, the Rhode Island Rape Crisis Center found that two of three boys and 49 percent of the girls said it was "acceptable for a man to force sex on a woman if they have been dating for six months or more."[13] In view of attitudes like these, it's easy to understand why date rape has become such a widespread problem.

In short, sex that isn't tied to love and commitment undermines character by subverting self-control, respect, and responsibility. Unchecked, sexual desires and impulses easily run amok and lead to habits of hedonism and using others for one's personal pleasure. In the process, sexual intercourse loses its meaning, beauty, and specialness; instead of being a loving, uniquely intimate expression of two people's commitment to each other, sex is trivialized and degraded.

6. SHAKEN TRUST AND FEAR OF COMMITMENT

Young people who feel used or betrayed after the break-up of a sexual relationship may experience difficulty in future relationships.

Some sexually exploited people, as we've seen, develop such low self-esteem that they seek any kind of attention, even if it's another short-lived and demeaning sexual relationship. But other people, once burned, withdraw. They have trouble trusting; they don't want to get burned again.

Usually, this happens to the girl. She begins to see guys as interested in just one thing: Sex. Says one young woman: "Besides feeling cheap [after several sexual relationships], I began to wonder if there would ever be anyone who would love and accept me without demanding that I do something with my body to earn that love."[14]

However, boys can also experience loss of trust and fear of commitment as a result of a broken relationship that involved sex. Brian, a college senior, tells how this happened to him:

> I first had intercourse with my girlfriend when we were 15. I'd been going with her for almost a year, and I loved her very much. She was friendly, outgoing, charismatic. We'd done everything but have intercourse, and then one night she asked if we could go all the way.
>
> A few days later, we broke up. It was the most painful time of my life. I had opened myself up to her more than I had to anybody, even my parents.
>
> I was depressed, moody, nervous. My friends dropped me because I was so bummed out. I felt like a failure. I dropped out of sports. My grades weren't terrific.
>
> I didn't go out again until I got to college. I've had mostly one-night stands in the last couple of years.
>
> I'm afraid of falling in love.[15]

7. RAGE OVER BETRAYAL

Sometimes the emotional reaction to being "dumped" isn't just a lack of trust or fear of commitment. It's rage.

Every so often, the media carry a story about a person who had this rage reaction and then committed an act of violence against the former boyfriend or girlfriend. Read these accounts, and you'll find that sex was almost always a part of the broken relationship.

Of course, people often feel angry when somebody breaks up with them, even if sex has not been involved. But the sense of betrayal is usually much greater if sex has been part of the relationship. Sex can be emotional dynamite. It can lead a person to think that the relationship is really serious, that both people really love each other. It can create a very strong emotional bond that hurts terribly when it's ruptured—especially if it seems that the other person never had the same commitment. And the resulting sense of betrayal can give rise to rage, even violence.

8. DEPRESSION AND SUICIDE

In *Sex and the Teenager*, Kieran Sawyer writes: "The more the relationship seems like real love, the more the young person is likely to invest, and the deeper the pain and hurt if the relationship breaks up."[16] Sometimes the emotional turmoil caused by the rupture of a sexual relationship leads to deep depression. The depression, in turn, may lead some people to take their own lives.

In the past 25 years, teen suicide has tripled. In a 1988 survey by the U.S. Department of Health and Human Services, one in five adolescent girls said they have tried to kill themselves (the figure for boys was one in 10).

This is the same period during which the rate of teenage sexual activity has sharply increased, especially for girls. No doubt, the rise in youth suicide has multiple causes, but given what we know about the emotional aftermath of broken sexual relationships, it is reasonable to suspect that the pain from such break-ups is a factor in the suicide deaths of some young people.

9. RUINED RELATIONSHIPS

Sex can have another kind of emotional consequence: It can turn a good relationship bad. Other dimensions of the relationship stop developing. Pretty soon, negative emotions enter the picture. Eventually, they poison the relationship, and what had been a caring relationship comes to a bitter end.

One young woman shares her story, which illustrates the process:

> With each date, my boyfriend's requests for sex became more convincing. After all, we did love each other. Within two months, I gave in, because I had

justified the whole thing. Over the next six months, sex became the center of our relationship. . . .

At the same time, some new things entered our relationship—things like anger, impatience, jealousy, and selfishness. We just couldn't talk anymore. We grew very bored with each other. I desperately wanted a change.[17]

A young man who identified himself as a 22-year-old virgin echoes this warning about the damage premature sex can do to a relationship:

I've seen too many of my friends break up after their relationships turned physical. The emotional wreckage is horrendous because they have already shared something so powerful. When you use sex too early, it will block other means of communicating love and can stunt the balanced growth of a relationship.[18]

10. STUNTING PERSONAL DEVELOPMENT

Premature sexual involvement not only can stunt the development of a relationship; it also can stunt one's development as a person.

Just as some young people handle anxieties by turning to drugs and alcohol, others handle them by turning to sex. Sex becomes an escape. They aren't learning how to cope with life's pressures.

Teenagers who are absorbed in an intense sexual relationship are turning inward on one thing at the very time in their lives when they should be reaching out—forming new friendships, joining clubs and teams, developing their interests and skills, taking on bigger social responsibilities.

All of these are important nutrients for a teenager's development as a person. And this period of life is special because young people have both the time and the opportunities to develop their talents and interests. The growing they do during these years will affect them all their lives. If young people don't put these years to good use, they may never develop their full potential.

The risk appears to be greater for girls who get sexually involved and in so doing close the door on other interests and relationships. Says New York psychiatrist Samuel Kaufman:

A girl who enters into a serious relationship with a boy very early in life may find out later that her individuality was thwarted. She became part of him and failed to develop her own interests, her sense of independent identity.[19]

Reflecting on her long experience in counseling college students and others about sexual matters, Dr. Carson Daly comments:

I don't think I ever met a student who was sorry he or she had postponed sexual activity, but I certainly met many who deeply regretted their sexual involvements. Time and time again, I have seen the long-term emotional and spiritual desolation that results from casual sex and promiscuity.

No one tells students that it sometimes takes years to recover from the effects of these sexual involvements—if one ever fully recovers.

Sex certainly can be a source of great pleasure and joy. But as should be amply clear—and youngsters need our help and guidance in understanding this—sex also can be the source of deep wounds and suffering. What makes the difference is the relationship within which it occurs. Sex is most joyful and fulfilling—most emotionally safe as well as physically safe—when it occurs within a loving, total, and binding commitment. Historically, we have called that marriage. Sexual union is then part of something bigger—the union of two persons' lives.

NOTES

1. Susan Weller, "A Meta-Analysis of Condom Effectiveness in Reducing Sexually Transmitted HIV," *Social Science and Medicine,* June 1993, p. 12.

2. See, for example, Kenneth Noller, *OB/GYN Clinical Alert-t,* September 1992; for a thorough discussion of the dangers of human papilloma virus, see "Condoms Ineffective Against Human Papilloma Virus,"*Sexual Health Update* (April 1994), a publication of the Medical Institute for Sexual Health, P.O. Box 4919, Austin, Texas 78765.

3. "Some Teens Taking Vows of Virginity," *Washington Post* (November 21, 1993).

4. William Bennett, "Sex and the Education of Our Children," *America* (February 14, 1987), p. 124.

5. Bob Bartlett, "Going All the Way," *Momentum* (April/May, 1993), p. 36.

6. Abridged from Ann Landers, "A Not-So-Sweet Sixteen Story," *Daily News* (September 23, 1991), p. 20.

7. Eager's book is available from Mailbox Club Books, 404 Eager Rd., Valdosta, Ga. 31602.

8. Carson Daly, personal communication.

9. *Safe Sex: A Slide Program.* Medical Institute for Sexual Health, Austin, Texas: 1992.

10. Josh McDowell and Dick Day, *Why Wait: What You Need to Know About the Teen Sexuality Crisis* (Here's Life Publishers, San Bernardino, Calif.: 1987).

11. Medical Institute for Sexual Health, P.O. Box 4919, Austin Texas 78765.

12. *American Association of University Women Report on Sexual Harassment,* June 1993.

13. J. Kikuchi, "Rhode Island Develops Successful Intervention Program for Adolescents," *National Coalition Against Sexual Assault Newsletter* (Fall 1988).

14. McDowell and Day, op. cit.

15. Abridged from *Choosing the Best: A Values-Based Sex Education Curriculum,* 1993. (5500 Interstate North Parkway, Suite 515, Atlanta, Ga. 30328).

16. Kieran Sawyer, *Sex and the Teenager* (Ave Maria Press, Notre Dame, Ind.: 1990).

17. McDowell and Day, op. cit.

18. Ann Landers, "Despite Urgin', He's a Virgin." *Daily News* (January 15, 1994).

19. Quoted in Howard and Martha Lewis, *The Parent's Guide to Teenage Sex and Pregnancy* (St. Martin's Press, New York: 1980).

CHAPTER 15

Beyond Romance to Human Love

Robert A. Johnson

This chapter complements Lawrence Stone's essay (chapter 11) on the history of romantic love and its emergence as a mass phenomenon in the West. In *We,* Robert Johnson brings a profound Jungian analysis to our understanding of the dynamics of romantic love, the single greatest energy system in the Western psyche. It saturates every facet of popular culture and has become the rationale and basis for marriage. But, if we are honest with ourselves, we have to admit that our approach to romantic love is not working well. We have not yet learned to handle its tremendous power. More often than not, we turn it into tragedy and dead ends rather than enduring human relations.

In this excerpt, Johnson seeks to salvage love from the swamps of romance. The key is to distinguish between human love and romantic love. Romantic love is airy, fantasy, projection, an evanescent high. It is fundamentally egotistical—fixated on its own wants and whims. It can never lay the foundation for personal commitments. Human love, on the other hand, is "stirring-the-oatmeal" love. It is rooted in relatedness, directed toward the good, and attentive to small daily tasks in our lives. Human love affirms the wonderful and flawed person who is actually there. Romance, however, is blind, intoxicating, and illusionary. The question is: will we continue to drink the love potion of romantic love or sober up to establish a new/old substance and basis for enduring human relations?

Questions for Discussion

1. Where in popular culture (movies, music, novels, TV) do you see the ideology of romantic love influence the daily lives of people? Give examples.
2. Comment on the statement: Hindus love the woman they marry, rather than marry the woman they love.
3. Is our culture of divorce connected to the pervasive influence of romance in our society?
4. Compare Johnson's meaning of human love with the Christian meaning of *agape.*
5. What should be the rationale and basis for committed personal relations?
6. What does Johnson mean when he says: "the essence of love is not to use the other to make us happy"?

P eople become so wearied of the cycles and dead ends of romance that they begin to wonder if there is such a thing as "love." There is. But sometimes we have to make profound changes of attitude before we can see what love is and make room for love in our lives.

Love between human beings is one of the absolute realities of human nature. Just as soul—Psyche—was one of the gods of the Greek pantheon, so was Love: His name was Eros. For the Greeks understood that love, being an archetype of the collective unconscious, is both eternal and universal in humankind. And for the Greeks, that qualified Love as a god.

Because love is an archetype, it has its own character, its own traits, its own "personality." Like a god, love behaves as a "person" in the unconscious, a separate being in the psyche. Love is distinct from my ego; love was here before my ego came into the world, and love will be here after my ego departs. Yet love is something or "someone" who lives within me. Love is a force that acts from within, that enables my ego to look outside itself, to see my fellow humans as something to be valued and cherished, rather than used.

Therefore, when I say that "I love," it is not I who love, but, in reality, Love who acts through me. Love is not so much something I do as something that I am. Love is not a doing but a state of being—a relatedness, a connectedness to another mortal, an identification with her or him that simply flows within me and through me, independent of my intentions or my efforts.

This state of being may express itself in what I do or in how I treat people, but it can never be reduced to a set of "doings," or acts. It is a feeling within. More often than we realize, love works its divine alchemy best when we follow the advice of Shakespeare's Cordelia: "Love, and keep silent."

Love exists, regardless of our opinions about what it ought to be. No matter how many fabrications or how much selfishness we justify in the name of "love," love still keeps its unchanging character. Its existence and its nature do not depend on my illusions, my opinions, or my counterfeits. Love is different from what my culture has led me to expect, different from what my ego wants, different from the sentimental froth and inflated ecstasies I've been taught to hope for; but love turns out to be real; it turns out to be what I am, rather than what my ego demands.

We need to know this about love. Otherwise we could never stand to look honestly at our self-deceptions. At times people say: "Don't make me see my illusions; if you take away my illusions, there will be nothing left!" We seem to think of love as "man-made," as though we invented it in our minds. Even though romantic love has not turned out to be what we thought, there is still a human love that is inherent in us, and this love will be with us even after our projections, our illusions, and our artifices have all passed away.

Human love is so obscured by the inflations and commotions of romance that we almost never look for love in its own right, and we hardly know what to look for when we do search. But as we learn love's characteristics and attitudes, we can begin to see love within us—revealed in our feelings, in the spontaneous flow of warmth that surges toward another person, in the small, unnoticed acts of relatedness that make up the secret fabric of our daily lives.

Love is the power within us that affirms and values another human being as he or she is. Human love affirms that person who is actually there, rather than the ideal we would like him or her to be or the projection that flows from our minds. Love is the inner god who opens our blind eyes to the beauty, value, and quality of the other person. Love causes us to value that person as a total, individual self, and this means that we accept the negative side as well as the positive, the imperfections as well as the admirable qualities. When one truly loves the human being rather than the projection, one loves the shadow just as one loves the rest. One accepts the other person's totality.

Human love causes a man to see the intrinsic value in a woman; therefore love leads him to honor and serve her, rather than to try to use her for his ego's purposes. When love is guiding him, he is concerned with her needs and her well-being, not fixated on his own wants and whims.

Love alters our sense of importance. Through love we see that the other individual has as great a value in the cosmos as our own; it becomes just as important to us that he or she should be whole, should live fully, should find the joy of life, as that our own needs be met.

In the world of the unconscious, love is one of those great psychological forces that have the power to transform the ego. Love is the one power that awakens the ego to the existence of something outside itself, outside its plans, outside its empire, outside its security. Love relates the ego not only to the rest of the human race, but to the soul and to all the gods of the inner world.

Thus love is by its very nature the exact opposite of egocentricity. We use the word *love* loosely. We use it to dignify any number of demands for attention, power, security, or entertainment from other people. But when we are looking out for our own self-styled "needs," our own desires, our own dreams, and our power over people, this is not love. Love is utterly distinct from our ego's desires and power plays. It leads in a different direction: toward the goodness, the value, and the needs of the people around us.

In its very essence, love is an *appreciation*, a recognition of another's value: It moves a man to honor a woman rather than use her, to ask himself how he might serve her. And if this woman is relating to him through love, she will take the same attitude toward him.

The archetypal nature of love is perhaps nowhere better expressed than in the simple language of Saint Paul:

> Love suffers long and is kind; love does not envy; love does not vaunt itself, is not puffed up. . . . Love does not seek her own way, is not easily provoked, is not anxious to suspect evil. . . . bears all things, believes all things, hopes all things, endures all things.
>
> Love never fails: but whether there be prophecies, they shall fail, whether there be tongues, they shall cease, whether there be knowledge, it shall vanish away.

Here is a brief and eloquent statement of the difference between an ego left to its own devices and an ego under the influence of love. My ego is concerned only with itself; but "love suffers long and is kind." My ego is envious, always seeking to inflate itself with illusions of absolute power and control, but "love does not vaunt itself, is not puffed up." My ego, left to its ego-centeredness, will always betray, but "love never fails." My ego only knows how to affirm itself and its desires, but love "seeks not her own way." Love affirms all of life: "bears all things, believes all things, hopes all things."

This is why we have taken exception to romantic love, and this is the main distinction between human love and romantic love: Romance must, by its very nature, deteriorate into egotism. For romance is not a love that is directed at another human being; the passion of romance is always directed at our own projections, our own expectations, our own fantasies. In a very real sense, it is a love not of another person, but of ourselves.

> It should now be clear that to the extent that a relationship is founded on projection the element of human love is lacking. To be in love with someone we do not know as a person, but are attracted to because they reflect back to us the image of the god or goddess in our souls, is, in a sense, to be in love with oneself, not with the other person. In spite of the seeming beauty of the love fantasies we may have in this state of being in love, we can, in fact, be in a thoroughly selfish state of mind.
>
> Real love begins only when one person comes to know another for who he or she really is as a human being, and begins to like and care for that human being.
>
> . . . To be capable of real love means becoming mature, with realistic expectations of the other person. It means accepting responsibility for our own happiness or unhappiness, and neither expecting the other person to make us happy nor blaming that person for our bad moods and frustrations. (Sanford, pp. 19–20)

When we are focused on our projections, we are focused on ourselves. And the passion and love we feel for our projections is a reflexive, circular love that is directed inevitably back to ourselves.

But here, again, we run headlong into the paradox of romantic love. The paradox is that we *should* love our projections, and that we should also love ourselves. In romance the love of self becomes distorted; it becomes egocentric and its original nature is lost. But if we learn to seek it on the correct level, the love of self is a true and valid love: It is the second great stream of energy that flows into romantic love, human love's archetypal mate, the other face of Eros.

We need to revere the unconscious parts of ourselves that we project. When we love our projections, when we honor our romantic ideals and fantasies, we affirm infinitely precious dimensions of our total selves. The riddle is how to love one's self without falling into egotism.

As we learn the geography of the human psyche, with its islands of consciousness, its multilayered and multicentered structure, we see that the love of the total self can not be a centering of the universe on our egos. Love of self is the ego's seeking after the other "persons" of the inner world, who hide within us. It is ego's longing for the larger dimensions of the unconscious, its willingness to open itself to the other parts of our total being, and to their points of view, their values, and their needs.

Understood in this way, our love of self is also the "divine" love: our search for the ultimate meaning, for our souls, for the revelation of God. This understanding returns us to the words of Clement of Alexandria:

> Therefore, as it seems, it is the greatest of all disciplines to know oneself; for when a man knows himself, he knows God.

The fault in romantic love is not that we love our-selves, but that we love ourselves wrongly. By trying to revere the unconscious through our romantic projections on other people, we miss the reality hidden in those projections: We don't see that it is our own selves we are searching for.

The task of salvaging love from the swamps of romance begins with a shift of vision toward the inside; we have to wake up to the inner world; we have to learn how to live the "love of self" as an inner experience. But then it is time to redirect our gaze outward again, toward physical people and the relationships we make with them—we must learn the principles of the "human" love.

Many years ago a wise friend gave me a name for human love. She called it "stirring-the-oatmeal" love. She was right: Within this phrase, if we will humble ourselves enough to look, is the very essence of what human love is, and it shows us the principal differences between human love and romance.

Stirring oatmeal is an humble act—not exciting or thrilling. But it symbolizes a relatedness that brings love down to earth. It represents a willingness to share ordinary human life, to find meaning in the simple, unromantic tasks: earning a living, living within a budget, putting out the garbage, feeding the baby in the middle of the night. To "stir the oatmeal" means to find the relatedness, the value, even the beauty, in simple and ordinary things, not to eternally demand a cosmic drama, an entertainment, or an extraordinary intensity in everything. Like the rice hulling of the Zen monks, the spinning wheel of Ghandi, the tent making of Saint Paul, it represents the discovery of the sacred in the midst of the humble and ordinary.

Jung once said that feeling is a matter of the *small*. And in human love, we can see that it is true. The real relatedness between two people is experienced in the small tasks they do together: the quiet conversation when the day's upheavals are at rest, the soft word of understanding, the daily companionship, the encouragement offered in a difficult moment, the small gift when least expected, the spontaneous gesture of love.

When a couple are genuinely related to each other, they are willing to enter into the whole spectrum of human life together. They transform even the unexciting, difficult, and mundane things into a joyful and fulfilling component of life. By contrast, romantic love can only last so long as a couple are "high" on one another, so long as the money lasts and the entertainments are exciting. "Stirring the oatmeal" means that two people take their love off the airy level of exciting fantasy and convert it into earthy, practical immediacy.

Love is content to do many things that ego is bored with. Love is willing to work with the other person's moods and unreasonableness. Love is willing to fix breakfast and balance the checkbook. Love is willing to do these "oatmeal" things of life because it is related to a person, not a projection.

Human love sees another person as an individual and makes an individualized relationship to him or her. Romantic love sees the other person only as a role player in the drama.

A man's human love desires that a woman become a complete and independent person and encourages her to be herself. Romantic love only affirms what he would like her to be, so that she could be identical to anima. So long as romance rules a man, he affirms a woman only insofar as she is willing to change, so that she may reflect his projected ideal. Romance is never happy with the other person just as he or she is.

Human love necessarily includes friendship: friendship within relationship, within marriage, between husband and wife. When a man and a woman are truly friends, they know each other's difficult points and weaknesses, but they are not inclined to stand in judgment on them. They are more concerned with helping each other and enjoying each other than they are with finding fault.

Friends, genuine friends, are like Kaherdin: They want to affirm rather than to judge; they don't coddle, but neither do they dwell on our inadequacies. Friends back each other up in the tough times, help each other with the sordid and ordinary tasks of life. They don't impose impossible standards on each other, they don't ask for perfection, and they help each other rather than grind each other down with demands.

In romantic love there is no friendship. Romance and friendship are utterly opposed energies, natural enemies with completely opposing motives. Sometimes people say: "I don't want to be friends with my husband [or wife]; it would take all the romance out of our marriage." It is true: Friendship does take the artificial drama and intensity out of a relationship, but it also takes away the egocentricity and the impossibility and replaces the drama with something human and real.

If a man and woman are friends to each other, then they are "neighbors" as well as lovers; their relationship is suddenly subject to Christ's dictum: "Love thy neighbor as thyself." One of the glaring contradictions in romantic love is that so many couples treat their friends with so much more kindness, consideration, generosity, and forgiveness than they ever give to one another! When people are with their friends, they are charming, helpful, and courteous. But when they come home, they often vent all their anger, resentments, moods, and frustrations on each other. Strangely, they treat their friends better than they do each other.

When two people are "in love," people commonly say that they are "more than just friends." But in the long run, they seem to treat each other as *less* than friends. Most people think that being "in love" is a much more intimate, much more "meaningful," relationship than "mere" friendship. Why, then, do couples refuse each other the selfless love, the kindness and good will, that they readily give to their friends? People can't ask of their friends that they carry all their projections, be scapegoats for all their moods, keep them feeling happy, and make life complete for them. Why do couples impose these demands on each other? Because the cult of romance teaches us that we have the right to expect that all our projections will be borne—all our desires satisfied, and all our fantasies made to come true—in the person we are "in love" with. In one of the Hindu rites of marriage, the bride and groom make to each other a solemn statement: "You will be my *best friend*." Western couples need to learn to be friends, to live with each other in a spirit of friendship, to take the quality of friendship as a guide through the tangles we have made of love.

We can learn much of human love by learning to look with an open mind at Oriental cultures and their attitudes.

During the time I spent in India and Japan, I saw marriages and love relationships that are not based at all on romance but on a warm, devoted, and enduring love. Hindus are instinctive masters of the art of human love. I think this is because they have never taken on romantic love as a way of trying to relate to each other. Hindus automatically make the differentiation that we have completely muddled in the West: They know how to worship anima, the archetypes, the gods, as inner realities; they know how to keep their experience of the divine side of life distinct from their personal relationships and marriages.

Hindus take the inner world on a symbolic level; they translate the inner archetypes into images and external symbols through temple art and allegorical ritual. But they don't project the inner gods onto their husbands and wives. They take the personified archetypes as symbols of another world and take each other as human beings; as a result, they don't put impossible demands on each other and they don't disappoint each other.

A Hindu man does not ask of his wife that she be anima or that she take him off to another world or that she embody all the intensity and perfection of his inner life. Since lyrical religious experience is still part of their culture, Hindus do not try to make their marriages and human relationships into a substitute for communion with the soul. They find their gods in the temple, in meditation, or sometimes in the guru; they don't try to make the outer relationship serve the role of the inner one.

At first a Westerner is confused by the Hindu way; their love doesn't seem to be bubbling with enough heat and intensity to suit the Western romantic taste. But if one observes patiently, one is startled out of Western prejudices and begins to question the assumption that romance is the only "true love." There is a quiet but steady lovingness in Hindu marriages, a profound affection. There is stability: They are not caught in the dramatic oscillations between "in love" and "out of love," adoration and disillusionment, that Western couples are.

In the traditional Hindu marriage, a man's commitment to his wife does not depend on his staying "in love" with her. Since he was never "in love" in the first place, there is no way he can fall "out of love." His relationship to his wife is based on loving *her*, not on being "in love" with an ideal that he projects onto her. His relationship is not going to collapse because one day he falls "out of love," or because he meets another woman who catches his projection. He is committed to a woman and a family, not to a projection.

We think of ourselves as more sophisticated than the "simple" Hindus. But, by comparison with a Hindu, the average Western man is like an ox with a ring in his nose, following his projection around from one woman to another, making no true relationship or commitment to any. In the area of human feeling, love, and relationship, Hindus have evolved a highly differentiated, subtle, and refined consciousness. In these matters, they do better than we.

One of the most striking and surprising things I observed among traditional Hindus was how bright, happy, and psychologically healthy their children are. Children in Hindu families are not neurotic; they are not torn within themselves as so many Western children are. They are bathed constantly in human affection, and they sense a peaceful flow of affection between their mother and father. They sense the stability, the enduring quality of their family life. Their parents are committed permanently; they don't hear their parents asking themselves whether their marriage is "going to work out"; separation and divorce do not float as specters in the air.

For us Westerners there is no turning back of the clock. We can't go the way of the Hindus; we can't solve our Western dilemma by doing an imitation of other people's customs or other people's attitudes. We can't pretend that we have an Eastern psyche rather than a Western psyche. We have to deal with our own Western unconscious and our own Western wounds; we have to find the healing balm within our own Western soul. We have drunk the love potion and plunged into the romantic era of our evolution, and the only way out is by the path that leads straight ahead. We can't go back, and we may not linger.

But we can learn from the Eastern cultures to stand outside ourselves, outside our assumptions and our beliefs, just long enough to see ourselves in a new perspective. We can learn what it is to approach love with a different set of attitudes, unburdened by the dogmas of our culture.

We can learn that human relationship is inseparable from friendship and commitment. We can learn that the essence of love is not to use the other to make us happy but to serve and affirm the one we love. And we can discover, to our surprise, that what we have needed more than anything was not so much to be loved, as to love.

REFERENCE

Sanford, John A. *Invisible Partners: How the Male and Female in Each of Us Affects Our Relationships*. New York: Paulist, 1984.

CHAPTER 16

Where Are We? Seven Sinful Problems and Seven Virtuous Possibilities

James B. Nelson

Religious traditions have had a mixed record, to say the least, in relationship to human sexuality. The dynamics and power of sexuality have accentuated this volatile interplay. But this ambiguous intertwining of the creative and the destructive has been part of Christian history from its beginnings. Streams of perversion and distortion have found their way into our central teachings corrupting, at times, the core.

In this chapter, James Nelson, a United Church of Christ theologian and ethicist, lays out some contrasting sexual vices and virtues that should lend themselves to lively classroom discussions. He names seven deadly sins that have contributed to our sexual alienation (spiritualistic dualism, patriarchal dualism, heterosexism and homophobia, self-rejection, legalistic ethics, sexless spirituality, and privatized sexuality). These problems are all rooted in a fear of the body.

On the other hand, the road to sexual integration, sexual responsibility, and sexual justice requires a reclaiming of what is more authentic to the core of the Jewish and Christian traditions, namely, seven virtuous possibilities (body-self unity, human equality, gay and lesbian affirmation, self-love, love ethics, sexual spirituality, and personal/public sexuality). These are rooted in an incarnational theology. If embraced, these virtues can become the renewed wellspring for sexual health. They may also restore credibility to teachings of our religious traditions in their dealings with human sexuality.

Questions for Discussion

1. Where do you see the perpetuation of spiritualistic dualism today (a) within religious traditions, and (b) within our culture at large?
2. Sexist dualism is "dangerous to the health and well-being of women" (Nelson). Elaborate. Give concrete examples. What would you propose as a counterforce?
3. How does Nelson make the connection between homophobia (the irrational fear of same-sex feelings and expression) and fear of the body? Is his argument convincing to you?
4. Authentic self-love is a deep self-acceptance. How could this virtue release us from our desire to control others?

5. Discuss Nelson's position: an ethics of love affirms (a) blessing the union of same-sex couples, and (b) committed heterosexual relationships short of legal marriage.
6. How would a sexual spirituality manifest itself in the routine and rhythm of ordinary married life?

It is commonly observed that religion is a very ambiguous human enterprise. The creative power of religion is great, for the divine presence is, indeed, often mediated with life-giving power through religious patterns of doctrine, morals, worship, and spirituality. The religious enterprise is also one of the most dangerous of all human enterprises, since it is always tempted to claim ultimate sanction for its humanly constructed beliefs and practices. This ambiguous mix of the creative and the destructive in religion is particularly evident when it comes to religious dealings with human sexuality. That is because the dynamisms of human sexuality give it particular power for both good and ill. Thus, throughout history most religions have given unusual attention to this dimension of human life, have attempted to control it, and often have shown considerable fear of it.

Early in Christian history two lists arose: the seven deadly sins and the seven virtues.[1] The original contents of those early lists are not my concern at this point. I simply want to name seven deadly sins through which the Jewish and Christian traditions have contributed to our sexual alienation, countered by seven virtues or positive resources which these same traditions offer to nurture our sexual wholeness. I am assuming two things. First, the sexual distortions in these traditions have largely resulted from perversions of their own central teachings. Through reclaiming that which is more authentic to the core of these faiths, there may be sexual healing. Second, each of these seven sins betrays profound suspicions of the human body. The body, especially in its sexual dimensions, often evokes anxieties about mortality, loss of control, contamination, uncleanness, personal inadequacy, and a host of other fears. Thus, we sorely need body theologies that will illuminate our experience, and that is a concern of these chapters.

SPIRITUALISTIC DUALISM OR THE BODYSELF UNITY?

Spiritualistic dualism is the first deadly sin. With its counterpart, sexist or patriarchal dualism, spiritualistic dualism underlies and gives shaping power to all the other sins of the list. Any dualism is the radical breaking apart of two elements that essentially belong together, a rupture which sees the two coexisting in uneasy truce or in open warfare.

Though quite foreign to Jewish scriptures and practice, spiritualistic dualism was grounded in Hellenistic Greco-Roman culture and had a profound impact on the early Christian church. Continuing with power to the present, it sees life composed of two antagonistic elements: spirit, which is good and eternal, and flesh or matter, which is temporal, corruptible, and corrupting. The sexual aspects of the body are the particular locus of sin. With this perspective, escape from the snares of bodily life through the spirit's control is central to the religious life.

There is, however, a countervailing virtue in both Judaism and Christianity, one much more authentic to the roots of each faith. In Judaism it is a strong belief in the goodness of creation and with it an anthropology that proclaims the unity and goodness of the human bodyself. The Hebrew scriptures show little reticence about human bodies and their varied functions. Neither do they divide the person into parts or locate the core of personhood in some disembodied spirit. They take for granted the created goodness of sexuality, and at times display lyrical celebrations of the delights of robust, fleshly love.

Christianity also expresses this antidualistic virtue by affirming creation as good, and it adds to this its particular emphasis on divine incarnation. Incarnation proclaims that the most basic and decisive experience of God comes not in abstract doctrine or mystical otherworldly experiences, but *in flesh*. True, the faith's ongoing struggle with dualism has been evident in its marked discomfort over taking incarnation radically. Both Christian doctrine and practical piety have largely confined the incarnation of God to one, and only one, human figure—Jesus of Nazareth. Further, persisting body denial has made most Christians suspect Jesus' full humanity through silence about or actual denial of his sexuality.

There is another possibility, however implausible it may seem to some: without denigrating the significance of God's revelation in Jesus, incarnation might yet be understood more inclusively. Then the fleshly experience of each of us becomes vitally important to our experience of God. Then the fully physical, sweating, lubricating, menstruating, ejaculating, urinating, defecating bodies that we are—in sickness and in health—are the central vehicles of God's embodiment in our experience.

Nevertheless, Christian suspicions of the body and its pleasures continue. The sexual purity campaigns did not end with the Victorian era. But the authentic core of both religious traditions affirm the unity of spirit and body, mind and matter, spirituality and sexuality. The creation-affirming Jewish faith and the incarnational Christian faith attest to the goodness of the bodyself with all its rich sexuality as part of God's invitation into our full humanness and loving communion.

PATRIARCHAL DUALISM OR HUMAN EQUALITY?

The second deadly sin is sexist or patriarchal dualism. The systematic and systemic subordination of women is the counterpart of spiritualistic dualism, for men typically have defined themselves as essentially spirit or mind, and men have defined women as essentially body and emotion. The logic, of course, is that the higher reality must dominate and control the lower.

Patriarchal dualism pervades Jewish and Christian scriptures and their cultures as well. In Christianity, however, it has taken particular twists that powerfully join the male control of women to body denial. For example, classic understandings of the crucifixion and the atonement have given many Christians throughout the ages the sense that suffering is the necessary path to salvation. At the same time, Christian theology has often denigrated sensual pleasure, suggesting that deprivation and pain are mandatory if eternal joy is to be found. But *women's* suffering has particularly been encouraged, for in patriarchy it is they and not males who essentially represent the evil (the fleshly body) that needs redemption.[2] That sexist dualism is a deadly sin dangerous to the health and well-being of women needs no elaboration. That it is also enormously destructive for males, even while men continue to exercise dominant social power and privilege, needs to be recognized as well.

The *good news*, the countervailing virtue in these religious traditions, is the affirmation of human equality. In one of his better moments the apostle Paul wrote, "There is no longer Jew or Greek, there is no longer slave or free, there is no longer male and female; for all of you are one in Christ Jesus" (Gal. 3:28). The second great wave of feminism in our society, occurring in the latter third of the current century, has produced real gains in gender justice and inclusiveness—few would doubt this. That Jewish and Christian communities have far to go is also beyond question. Continuing resistance to women's religious leadership and ongoing religious justifications for male control of women's bodies are but two of many sad illustrations possible.

Nevertheless, gender equality is a truer expression of our common religious heritage. Sexism is the religious perversion. At the same time, the continuing power of sexist dualism displays a deep fear of the body, and sexism declares that the body is central to woman's being in a way that is not true for the man. All the issues about our bodies are enormously complicated by the interplay of these two faces of dualism, as are all the major moral issues of our day. Not only are the more obvious issues of body rejection, sexism, homophobia, and heterosexism rooted in dualistic dynamics, but so also are crucial dynamics of social violence, militarism, racism, economic oppression, and ecological abuse (about which I shall say more later).

HETEROSEXISM AND HOMOPHOBIA, OR GAY AND LESBIAN AFFIRMATION?

The third deadly sin is heterosexism (socially enforced compulsory heterosexuality) and its companion phenomenon homophobia (the irrational fear of same-sex feelings and expression). Tragically, this sin has pervaded both Jewish and Christian histories. Yet, it cannot be justified by careful biblical interpretation. The Bible does not even deal with homosexuality as a psycho-sexual orientation. Such understandings did not arise until the latter part of the nineteenth century. While scriptures do condemn certain homosexual *acts*, they appear to do so because of the lust, rape, idolatry, violation of religious purity obligations, or the pederasty expressed in those acts in specific contexts. We find no explicit biblical guidance on same-sex genital expression in relationships of mutual respect and love. On the other hand, the Bible pointedly celebrates instances of same-sex emotional intimacy, a fact often overlooked by fearful proof-texters.

The dynamics of homophobia are numerous and complex. Frequently they are deeply rooted in misogyny, in the fear of and contempt for the "failed male," in the fear of one's own bisexual capacities, in general erotophobia (the fear of sexuality itself), and in the alienation from one's own body and hence the desperate envy of anyone who appears to be more sexual than oneself.

The good news—the virtue—is that Jews and Christians have significant resources for dealing with these things. The same religious convictions that resist the spiritualistic and sexist dualisms also undercut heterosexism and homophobia. Central to each faith is God's radical affirmation of every person, each unique bodyself. Further, when we experience that grace that pervades the heart of biblical faith, there grows a sense of personal security that releases us from the anxious need to punish those who seem sexually different from ourselves. Then the issue becomes not sexual orientation as such, but rather whether, whatever our orientation, we can express our sexuality in life-giving ways.

That both faith communions are making some progress on issues of sexual orientation seems evident from a number of indications. That this subject is still the most divisive one for many congregations and judicatories is also evident—witness the passionate and often rancorous debate over lesbian and gay ordinations. In all of this one fact seems clear: fear of the body is a central dynamic in the resistance to equality in sexual orientation.

SELF-REJECTION OR SELF-LOVE?

The fourth deadly sin contributing to sexual dis-ease is guilt over self-love. Christian theologies and pieties have had a more difficult time with this than have Jewish. Dominant Christian interpretations all too frequently have understood self-love as equivalent to egocentrism, selfishness, and narcissism, and hence incompatible with the religious life. A sharp disjunction has been drawn between *agape* (selfless, self-giving love believed normative for the faithful) and *eros* (the desire for fulfillment).

When suspicion about self-love is combined with a suspicion of the body and of sexual feelings, the stage is set for sexual dis-ease. Masturbation is a case in point. To be sure, this subject is no longer inflamed by passions akin to those of the nineteenth-century sexual purity reformers. Sylvester Graham's "graham crackers" and John Kellogg's cornflakes are no longer persuasive as bland diets to prevent the solitary vice, though this was their original purpose. Yet, masturbation is still an obvious arena of guilt, simply because giving oneself sexual pleasure seems to be sheer self-centeredness. *Self-love*, in its larger sense, has had a bad press, particularly in Christianity. And when self-love is denigrated, authentic intimacy with a sexual partner is made more problematic, for true intimacy always is rooted in the solid sense of identity and self-worth of each of the partners.

The good news is that self-love is not a deadly sin. Both Hebrew and Christian scriptures bid us to love our neighbors as ourselves, not *instead of* ourselves. Both religious traditions at their best know that love is indivisible and nonquantifiable. It is not true that the more love we save for ourselves the less we have for others. Authentic self-love is not a grasping selfishness— which actually betrays the lack of self-love. Rather, it is a deep self-acceptance, which comes through the affirmation of one's own graciously given worth and creaturely fineness, our "warts and all."

Furthermore, genuine self-love personalizes the experience of one's own body. "My body *is* me, and I am worthful." When this is our experience, we are less inclined to exploit others sexually or, for that matter, to exploit ourselves. Genuine self-love is essential to our experience of fullest sexual pleasure as well as to an inner-directed sense of sexual responsibility for ourselves and toward others. When we are deeply self-affirming we lose the desire to control others, sexually or otherwise.

Better theological work in recent decades has brought corrections in earlier simplistic condemnations of self-love. Such theological shifts undoubtedly have been undergirded by a growing psychological sophistication within religious communities. Even more important, Christian and Jewish feminists, gay men, and lesbians have shown how dominant males have made the virtue of self-denial a means of controlling those whose sexuality was different from theirs.

Nevertheless, the battle about self-love is far from over, particularly in its sexual expressions. While theological treatises are beginning to give sexual pleasure some justification, most congregations would still be embarrassed by its open endorsement except, perhaps, in a discreet hint spoken during a wedding service. The affirmation of masturbation as a positive good for persons of all ages, partnered or unpartnered, is rarely found in religious writings and even more rarely mentioned aloud in synagogue or church. The sexual and body aspects of self-love surely are not the only dimensions, but they are barometers that remind us how our problems with genuine self-love appear intricately intertwined with our continuing bodily denial.

LEGALISTIC ETHICS OR LOVE ETHICS?

The fifth deadly sin is a legalistic sexual ethic. Many adherents of both Christian and Jewish faiths have fallen into more legalism about sexual morality than about any other arena of human behavior. Legalism is the attempt to apply precise rules and objective standards to whole classes of actions without regard to their unique contexts or the meanings those acts have to partic-

ular persons. Masturbation, homosexual expression, and nonmarital heterosexual intercourse are frequent targets for religio-moral absolutes. So also,
however, are numerous issues related to reproduction: contraception, abortion, and various new reproductive technologies such as in vitro fertilization.

The virtue that speaks to the deadly sin of legalism is *love*. Our body-
selves are intended to express the language of love. Our sexuality is God's
way of calling us into communion with others through our need to reach out,
to touch, to embrace—emotionally, intellectually, and physically. Since we
have been created with the desire for communion, the positive moral claim
upon us is that we become in fact what essentially we are: lovers, in the richest and deepest sense of that good word. A sexual ethic grounded in love
need not be devoid of clear values and sturdy guidelines. Indeed, such norms
are vitally important. The morality of sexual expression, however, cannot
adequately be measured by the physiological contours of certain types of
acts. For example, religious legalism typically has condemned genital sex
outside of heterosexual marriage and has blessed sex within marriage. Such
a morality consequently has prevented us from blessing the loving unions of
same-sex couples or finding ways to affirm committed heterosexual relationships short of legal marriage. At the same time, that morality (even if unwittingly) has given moral justification for unloving and exploitive sex *within*
marriages by insisting that the rightness of sex is measured not fundamentally by the quality of the relationship but by its external form.

The alternative to sexual legalism is not laxity and license, but an ethic
grounded in the centrality of love. Such an ethic is based on the conviction
that human sexuality finds its intended and most profound expression in the
kind of love that enriches the humanity of persons and expresses faithfulness
to God. Such an ethic cannot guarantee freedom from mistakes in the sexual
life, but it aims to serve and not to inhibit the maturation and human "becoming" of sexual persons.

Perhaps more than ever, many Christians and Jews are now open to a
nonlegalistic approach to sexual ethics. But sexual legalism is not a thing of
the past. The unbending stringency of Orthodox Judaism, the official Roman
Catholic retreat from Vatican II sexuality teachings, and the strident moral-
isms of fundamentalist Protestants are still with us. What we seldom recognize, however, is that religious legalism is much more commonly applied to
sexuality and body issues than to any other area of human morality. Many
people who customarily operate with more flexible and contextually applied
rules in other areas of life are wedded to exceptionless absolutes when it
comes to sex. That should not surprise us. The body is still a great source of
anxiety, and we typically want desperately to control that which we fear.

SEXLESS SPIRITUALITY OR SEXUAL SPIRITUALITY?

The sixth deadly sin of which our religious traditions are often guilty is a sexless image of spirituality. This has been a bane of Christianity more than of
Judaism, for the church more than the synagogue has been influenced by the

Neoplatonic split between spirit and body. In its more extreme forms, such a view perceived true spirituality as sexless, celibacy as meritorious, and bodily mortification and pain as conducive to spiritual purification. In the early centuries of the church, the pressures of the last imperial persecutions brought a new wave of anti-body thought, and an ethic of sexual renunciation took hold in the teachings of the church fathers. Thus, Origen spoke of two distinct creations, the spiritual and the material, one higher and one lower. Acting on his beliefs, Origen actually castrated himself "for the kingdom of God." Similarly, Jerome could say, "Blessed is the man who dashes his genitals against the stone." Tertullian typically connected antisex, anti-body perceptions with a misogynist, antiwoman bias. Speaking to women in one of his sermons, he proclaimed, "The sentence of God on this sex of yours lives on even in our times. . . . You are the one who first plucked the fruit of the forbidden tree; you are the first who deserted the divine law."[3]

While these negative extremes were not the whole story, even in that early period, they dramatically illustrate a significant current that has influenced the Christian sexual story and, unfortunately, still has its hold. In our more recent history it has been "sexual Victorianism." (H. L. Mencken was wrong in his quip about the Puritans. They were not really the ones tortured by the haunting fear that others somewhere else might be enjoying themselves. That was the Victorians—and many others since that time.)

Good news comes in the recognition that a sensuous, body-embracing, sexual spirituality is more authentic to both Jewish and Christian heritages. We are beginning to see that repressed sexuality "keeps the gods at bay" and does not bode well for the fullest, healthiest spirituality. We are beginning to recognize that the kind of erotic and bodily hungers celebrated in the Song of Solomon are human sharings in the passionate longings of God, the divine One who is shamelessly the earth's Lover.

The seventeenth-century Puritan bard John Milton expressed this "delicious Paradise" in his depiction of Adam and Eve beyond the Fall:

> half her swelling breast
> Naked met his under the flowing gold
> Of her loose tresses hid
>
> Thus these two
> Imparadised in one another's arms
> The happier Eden, shall enjoy their fill
> Of bliss on bliss.[4]

Similarly, incarnational theologians are reclaiming the sacramental possibilities of body experience. Thus Evgenii Lampert described the promise of sexual intercourse:

> It is the mystery of a sudden merging and union into a single indivisible being of flesh and spirit, of heaven and earth, of human and divine love. The

divine spirit touches human flesh ... in the burning moment of erotic ecstasy. We are witnessing to a true *sacrament:* the Spirit of God invades the cosmic element, without ceasing to be Spirit, and the flesh widens into the transcendence of the Spirit, without ceasing to be flesh.[5]

PRIVATIZED SEXUALITY OR PERSONAL AND PUBLIC SEXUALITY?

The seventh deadly sin of our religions has been the privatization of sexuality. My word play is intentional. Sexuality has been religiously consigned to the nonpublic world and narrowed to a genital matter—"the privates." To that extent, the public, institutional, and justice dimensions of human sexuality have often been neglected.

Yet one of the ironies of American history is that the nineteenth-century "sexual purity movements" most determined to push sex back into the confines and privacy of the marital bed frequently heightened its visibility and made sex a matter of more public discussion. Thus, early in the twentieth century even Anthony Comstock's war on obscenity unwittingly served Margaret Sanger's movement for birth control.[6]

"The personal is public." This familiar feminist affirmation is also a conviction of the Jewish and Christian religious traditions at their best. Sexuality issues are inevitably political, and the most deeply personal is at the same time connected with the social. Yet, there are different ways of understanding this. The radical religious right wing of Christianity exemplifies one. Clearly, sexuality issues are at the core of its public agenda: opposition to gender equality, sex education, abortion, homosexuality, pornography, the Equal Rights Amendment, and family planning, on the one hand, and support of those programs that would strengthen "the traditional family," on the other. Yet, for all its public emphasis on sexuality, the radical right exhibits a thinly veiled fear of it. The two familiar dualisms shape its agenda: patriarchy's hierarchical ordering of the sexes and spiritualism's denigration of the body. The message becomes clear. The right wing's current public sexual agenda is to get sexuality out of the public and back into the private sphere once again. And the private sphere is that of the male-controlled "traditional family."

There is a different way of seeing sexuality as a public issue. It is to recognize that the sharp distinction between private and public is a dualism directly growing out of the sexual dualisms. It is to see that sexual politics is inevitable, for politics (as Aristotle taught us) is the art of creating community, and human sexuality at its core deals with those intimate relationships that shape the larger communities of life. Thus, the bedroom cannot be confined to the bedroom. Justice issues for the sexually oppressed, sexual abuse, reproductive choice, population control, exploitation in commercialized sex, adequate sexuality education—these, among others, are now obviously public issues. Yet, we are only beginning to understand that there are important sexual dimensions to other vast social issues that previously we had not recognized. Social violence is a case in point. Whether it is crime on the city streets, or the arms race, or economic oppression, or the assumptions behind our foreign policies in Vietnam, Central America, or the Persian Gulf, such violence has important sexual dimensions.

To be sure, violence is complex in both causes and manifestations. No single explanation is adequate. But the sexual dimensions of social violence are present, and we have usually overlooked them. What, for example, of the competitiveness, the cult of winning, the armoring of emotions, the tendency to dichotomize reality into either-ors, the abstraction from bodily concreteness, the exaggerated fear of death manifested in a morbid fascination with death? All of these feed social violence, and all of these are deeply related to sexual distortions. Perhaps we are late in recognizing the sexuality embedded in these matters because of our continuing penchant for dualisms. Body anxiety still bids us to keep sex private, or to try to return it to the realm of the private, but it will not be so contained.

So, the seven (or more) deadly sexual sins are still very much with us. Nevertheless, they are neither the last nor the truest word about our religious traditions. I repeat my thesis: While Christianity and Judaism have often confounded good sexuality education and social policies, they have done so through the perversions and distortions of their own central teachings. What is more authentic to the core of both faiths can become the renewed wellspring for sexual health, sexual responsibility, and sexual justice, and for more adequate body theologies.

NOTES

1. See also James B. Nelson, "Religious Dimensions of Sexual Health," in *Readings in Primary Prevention of Psychopathology: Basic Concepts,* ed. Justin M. Joffe et al. (Hanover, N.H.: University Press of New England, 1984).

2. See Joanne Carlson Brown and Carole R. Bohn, eds., *Christianity, Patriarchy and Abuse: A Feminist Critique* (New York: Pilgrim Press, 1989).

3. Helpful documentations of these teachings of the church fathers can be found in Frank Bottomley, *Attitudes to the Body in Western Christendom* (London: Lepus Books, 1979), chs. 4–6; and in Raymond J. Lawrence, Jr., *The Poisoning of Eros* (New York: Augustine Moore Press, 1989), ch. 3.

4. John Milton, *Paradise Lost,* ed. Scott Elledge (New York: W.W. Norton & Co., 1975), Book IV, 91.

5. Evgenii Lampert, *The Divine Realm* (London: Faber & Faber, 1944), 97f.

6. See John D'Emilio and Estelle B. Freedman, *Intimate Matters: A History of Sexuality in America* (New York: Harper & Row, 1988), ch. 10.

CHAPTER 17

The Argument for Unlimited Procreative Liberty: A Feminist Critique

Maura A. Ryan

This much-acclaimed essay deals with one of the most controversial ethical and legal issues of our time, reproductive technologies. Maura Ryan, a professor of Christian Ethics, University of Notre Dame, draws our attention to the host of urgent questions raised by the "new reproduction." Can the components of parenting—genetic, gestational, and social—be separated at will? Are the foundations of the family threatened? Are there any "natural" limits to human intervention? If so, for whom, and under what circumstances? Some advocate the unlimited right of access to reproductive means. Ryan, however, challenges this view. It is the *basis* of her challenge that makes the essay unique.

Reproductive freedom has been a central issue in the contemporary women's movement. But feminists have not welcomed recent developments in reproductive technology without reservation. Ryan's essay is a brilliant critique of the underlying model of procreative liberty from the feminist perspective. In general, she challenges the view of offspring presupposed by the proponents, and their manipulation of reproduction in such a way as to foster oppression in society. Specifically, her concerns lie in three areas: (1) the tendency of the advocates to treat children as property, (2) a contractual model of family undergirding their position, and (3) a tendency to split ends from means, with undue attention given to ends.

From a feminist ethical viewpoint, according to Ryan, the proponents' position fails to consider the relational, contextual, and symbolic framework of the family. *How* we reproduce is as significant as *whether* we do it.

Questions for Discussion

1. Feminism suggests a middle road between technical domination and passivity toward nature. Do you agree? Do we have the moral right to reshape nature?
2. Ought artificial reproduction be permitted to become a commercial venture?
3. Is surrogate parenting a responsible moral option?
4. What is your perspective on the use of reproductive technologies to determine the sex or race of a child? Should we be permitted to determine what characteristics are "desirable"?

5. How would you balance the expense of the new reproductive technologies and services against the realities of poverty and overpopulation in certain areas of the world?

6. What is the potential for harm on various levels with the use of the "new reproductions"?

A s growing numbers of infertile heterosexual and gay and lesbian couples, along with single individuals, seek to parent through techniques that facilitate conception or permit the use of a genetic and/or gestational donor, and the boundaries of the "scientifically possible" enlarge, we are confronted with a host of increasingly urgent questions. Can the components of parenting—genetic, gestational, and social—be separated at will without harm to the participants? Do new forms of noncoital and donor-assisted reproduction threaten the foundations of the family, and hence, social existence as we know it? Are there "natural" limits to human intervention in the procreative process? Ought artificial reproduction be permitted to become a commercial venture? Does the right to engage in coital reproduction, protected for married couples under the U.S. Constitution, extend into a right to engage in noncoital reproduction; if so, for whom, and under what circumstances?

Questions of liberty and individual rights are emotionally charged ones in American public discourse. Moreover, family autonomy has long been held as a value worthy of such firm protection in our courts and legislatures that policies of minimal interference by the state into domestic life have been maintained even where it has meant a certain institutional blindness to the reality of spousal and child abuse. This context explains why the question of procreative liberty is important in current public policy debates surrounding the "new reproduction." Decisions with respect to the limits that may be placed on efforts to procreate, on which parties may be permitted to seek technological assistance in procreation, on the amount of public protection or funding to be extended, and on the conditions under which funding or protection might be warranted turn, many legal scholars believe, on the question of whether we have a right to procreate. Some maintain that the Constitution provides for virtually unlimited right of access to reproductive means.

The freedom to decide whether one will bear and nurture children, and under what circumstances, has been a central issue in the women's liberation movement. As persons whose self-identity and social role have been defined historically in relation to their procreative capacities, women have a great deal at stake in questions of reproductive freedom. Early feminists expended significant energy to secure the right to use contraceptive measures and to seek legal abortion, as well as to gain recognition of their rights as consumers of gynecological and obstetrical care. To say that feminism has promoted procreative liberty for women is not, however, to say that contemporary feminists have welcomed recent developments in reproductive technology without reservation.[1] Nor is it to say, despite the central importance given to the protection of women's autonomy in reproductive decisions, that feminists in general would treat procreative liberty as an unrestricted value. Rather, a feminist perspective includes commitments to human relationality as well as autonomy, and attention to the social context of personal choices. Thus questions of individual freedom, even in matters of reproduction, must be raised in conjunction with other equally compelling considerations about what is needed for human flourishing and what is required for a just society.

I want to highlight these themes by attending to the arguments for an unlimited right to procreate raised most cogently by John Robertson.[2] This position, based primarily on the importance of procreation for individuals, contains several elements that are troubling from a feminist perspective. My concern will not be with matters of constitutional law, but instead with the underlying model of procreative liberty, and its consequences for our understanding of reproduction and our attitudes toward human persons in general and children in particular.

THE CASE FOR FULL PROCREATIVE LIBERTY

Robertson's argument for the protection of a right to reproduce noncoitally or collaboratively (that is, with the participation of a gamete donor or gestator who is not one's spouse) is based on a historical protection of intramarital reproductive rights and the societal interest in safeguarding family autonomy. Since courts have recognized persons' rights to reproduce coitally, and not to reproduce coitally, their right to pursue those ends by noncoital means, if necessary, must also be protected. As a consequence of the natural lottery, infertility ought not prevent some from pursuing what has been recognized as of value to all.

Because childbearing and rearing have been viewed as experiences of great significance to persons, constitutive of individual identity and notions of a meaningful life, the courts have tended to take a position of noninterference in procreative decisions, particularly where married couples were involved. However, while an individual's right *not* to conceive, gestate, and rear has been explicitly protected in cases like *Griswold v. Connecticut* and *Roe v. Wade,* as has the right of parents to rear according to their own beliefs in cases like *Wisconsin v. Yoder,* the right to procreate has been addressed only implicitly. Robertson argues that one could and should infer from the right of couples to avoid procreation a correlative right to procreate, and from the unregulated freedom of married couples to add to their families coitally a freedom to do so noncoitally. No clear distinction should be allowed to stand, when procreative means exist, between fertile and infertile couples:

> The reason and values that support a right to reproduce coitally apply equally to noncoital activities involving external conception and collaborators. While the case is strongest for a couple's right to noncoital and external conception a strong argument for their right to enlist the aid of gamete and womb donors can also be made.[3]

Since reproductive rights are derived from the central importance of reproduction in an individual's life and are limited only by a capacity to participate meaningfully and an ability to accept or transfer rearing responsibilities, all those persons meeting this minimum criteria, whether married or not, ought to be free to pursue it.

Having argued that procreative autonomy is finally rooted in "the notion that individuals have a right to choose and live out the kind of life that they find meaningful and fulfilling," Robertson will allow for the use of technology for any reason that would realize the couple's "reproductive goals":

> The right of married persons to use noncoital and collaborative means of conception to overcome infertility must extend to any purpose, including selecting the gender or genetic characteristics of the child or transferring the burden of gestation to another.[4]

Because procreative interests are for some persons dependent on the offspring's having certain gender or genetic characteristics, procreative liberty includes, according to Robertson, the freedom to manipulate egg, sperm, or embryo to achieve the desired offspring, and the freedom to stop implantation or abort a fetus with undesirable characteristics. A couple is not free to alter genetic material in a way that would cause serious harm to the offspring (that is, harm so great as to make life not worth living), but they may do whatever else will facilitate the development of an offspring possessing those characteristics and traits that make having a child meaningful for them.[5] Claims of harm made in the name of society (threats to the ideal of the family, etc.) are not compelling enough in his view to override individual rights.

Many people have taken issue with this position on the grounds that a right to assistance in reproduction simply does not follow from the right not to be compelled to bear a child.[6] It is one thing to say that no one ought to be made to reproduce, or no one ought to be prevented from reproducing by decree; it is quite another to say that society ought to provide whatever is necessary for reproduction to occur.[7]

While sharing these reservations, I wish to raise a different set of objections: The view of offspring presupposed in such a position in unacceptable from a feminist perspective; further, treating the act of reproducing in such a way has serious implications for efforts to bring about a society free of oppression. My concerns lie chiefly in three areas: the tendency in this position to treat children as property; the use of "rights" language and a contract model to define the family; and an imbalance of concern for reproductive ends versus reproductive means.

ATTITUDES TOWARD CHILDREN

The success of Robertson's argument depends upon accepting the view that persons can be the object of another's right. Since he is not arguing for the protection of the right to engage in procreative activities, but the freedom to "acquire that sort of child that would make one willing to bring a child into the world in the first place,"[8] he is asserting the right to acquire a human being (and one with particular characteristics). Nor is Robertson referring simply to the right of persons to share in the experience of child nurture (since ability to adopt would satisfy that), but to have a genetically related child. As a feminist, I would agree that persons ought to be protected in their right to determine when and in what manner they will reproduce, and that they should be free to shape familial life in a way meaningful for them. But such a right should not be understood as unlimited, as extending as far as the acquisition of a concrete human being. Every exercise of freedom has a history and a context; our liberty is thus conditioned both by our potential for causing harm to others and by our responsibility for the quality of our common lives. A view of unlimited procreative liberty does not give sufficient attention to the ways in which not only individual offspring could be harmed, but the human community. Nor does it take seriously enough the possibilities for conflicts between claims.

First, such a position fails to respect offspring as autonomous beings, as ends in themselves. While a child's special dependency requires a condition of compromised autonomy vis-à-vis his or her caretakers, still that child comes into this world as a human person with the potential for self-determination. Although we might grant that the experience of reproduction appropriately fulfills needs and desires for the adults involved, advocating a model where children are brought into this world *chiefly* for that purpose gives too much weight to parental desires and too little to the protection of the offspring's essential autonomy. I am not saying that the desire to reproduce must be altruistic to be morally acceptable, nor that the experience of reproduction ought to be, or even could be, free of parental hopes and expectations for that offspring. My challenge is to a framework wherein the basis for unlimited procreative liberty is an individual desire for a particular type of child, a desire that is seldom weighed appropriately against the reality of the child-to-be as a potential autonomous human being. At what point does a being, who has been conceived, gestated, and born according to someone's specifications, become herself or himself? And if a child comes into the world primarily to fulfill parental need, are there limits to what a parent may do to ensure that the child will continue to meet the specified expectations?

With others, I share the fear that this understanding of procreative liberty incorporates a notion of children as products, on the assumption that individuals have a right to a particular kind of child and ought to be free, insofar as it is possible without causing grave physical harm, to manipulate the reproductive process so as to acquire the desired offspring. Currently, collaborative reproduction is a lengthy, arduous, and quite costly experience. How might parents look upon offspring when they enter the process with the belief that a certain kind of child is *owed* to them, and after they have paid a high price for that child? Certainly well-meaning people can bring children into the world through artificial reproduction and value them highly because of what they have gone through to have them. But this view of reproduction carries nonetheless the sense of "ordering" or "purchasing" children in accordance with specific parental desires, which in the end objectively devalues the child.

Not unlike, and just as dangerous as the thinking that makes women the property of their husbands, is the underlying view that children are not first and principally autonomous persons who also function as members of families and societies but rather the proper object of a parental right. We place our children at serious risk when we fail to see them first as existing for their own sakes and when we allow ourselves to think of them as malleable goods.

There are, in addition, serious problems in accepting as the standard for deciding how technology will be used to intervene in the reproductive process the adult initiator's definition of "procreative excellence." Since we are talking about a potentially autonomous human being, questions about the manipulation of genetic features, etc., ought to be asked first from the point of view of the offspring's best interests, not the prospective parents' desires. The decision then would be whether a certain genetic characteristic ought to be altered to facilitate that child's flourishing rather than whether a feature ought to be manipulated to make that offspring more acceptable to the parent.

A position of unlimited procreative liberty rooted in individual desire risks harming as well the quality of our lives together in community. Since reproduction in this view is tied so closely to one's private conception of a meaningful life, we are never talking about offspring per se, but a very specific type of offspring—a child with those genetic and gender characteristics that allow it to be incorporated into and contribute to the initiator's overall life project.

In a world where mixed-race and handicapped children are not now being adopted because they are "undesirable" we need to ask who determines, and should be permitted to so determine, what human characteristics are "desirable." My claim is not that parents are wrong to want a healthy, and genetically similar, child nor that persons may not have any good grounds for intervening in a pregnancy, for example one in which it is obvious that given certain characteristics the child will place great burdens on the parent or the family. My criticism is directed at an implied yardstick of acceptability, and the determination of reproductive standards based on personal whim. Such a model stands at odds with a feminist vision of community where all are welcome and persons are challenged to deal creatively with differences.

In addition, we need to weigh the consequences of using a model of reproductive desirability which includes choices about the preferred sex of one's offspring, for efforts to promote equality between persons in society. This is not to suggest that such a practice, if widespread, would result in more boys being chosen than girls. We have no way to know that nor reason necessarily to assume it. What is dangerous, in light of the reality of sexism in our society, is the perpetuation of the belief that an offspring's gender should be a determinative factor in her or his value to parents, or to anyone else. The primary question is whether the project to provide the subjectively desirable child is where social energies and resources in reproductive medicine ought to be directed.

The underlying ideal of perfection shaping this perspective and the belief that all so-called imperfection, even in so complex a process as reproduction, can or should be eliminated, needs thus to be questioned seriously. Reproduction and nurture are processes that are never totally within our control, no matter how sophisticated our technology. The formation of a child's character and personality, the development of his or her talents, have to do with a great deal more (such as education, historical events, significant role models) than genetic blueprint. A genetically normal, or "genetically perfect" offspring in this model can for a variety of reasons turn out to be the sort of person his or her parents would not have objectively speaking "been willing to bring into the world." Thus the claim that a parental right to a satisfying reproductive experience justifies the manipulation of genetic material is flawed, for the sort of guarantee sought cannot be provided by control of conception.

The attempt to exert this level of control over the creation of offspring is not only an illusory project but a mistaken one. I do not want to advocate a total passivity toward nature or to suggest that the use of technology in altering the conditions of conception and gestation is always inappropriate. But the feminist value of cooperation with and humility toward nature suggests a middle road between technical domination of the natural reproductive process and passivity. This middle road entails, at least, some attention to the essential elements of particular personhood, and thus a weighing of which features of our offspring we ought to attempt to determine in advance and which we should accept as characteristics of that unique being.

It is not only the sense of "reproducing for excellence" that is troubling about the case for unlimited procreative liberty but the presupposition that since children are property, all relationships between offspring and interested adults can be wholly a matter of contract. This way of thinking about the family is in some ways reflective of an old and familiar pattern, one about which feminists ought to be very cautious.

THE CONTRACTUAL MODEL OF FAMILY

Robertson admits that when we begin to have multiple participants in reproduction "it becomes unclear which participants hold parental rights and duties and will function socially and psychologically as members of the child's family."[9] Such confusion can be alleviated, however, by a presumption that the contract between the parties will determine obligations and entitlements toward the child, rather than the commonly held definitions of paternity and maternity. Whether collaborative arrangements can or will result in family disruption and identity confusion for the offspring or in productive and satisfying "alternative" family experiences will depend in part on the clarity and quality of these contracts. Experience with donor sperm, Robertson argues, suggests that the contract between parties will play the decisive role in determining rearing rights and duties to the offspring. Generally speaking, the presumption of rightful parentage ought to go to the initiating couple according to the agreements made prior to conception.

If these practices become institutionalized, there is no doubt that well-constructed contracts will be enormously helpful for clarifying parental rights and duties and that all the parties, including potential offspring, would benefit from legal protection. There are serious problems, however, with accepting a simple contract solution to the confusion of collaborative reproduction; it is both inadequate and perpetuates an ideologically dangerous model of the family. For example, claiming that the pre-conception contract can be sufficiently clear as to determine parental relationships in advance denies the complexity of reproduction as an affective and social experience as well as a biological one. Accounts of surrogate mothering, for example, suggest it can be quite difficult to decide the shape of one's reproductive role beforehand when we are engaged in a project about which we can come to have very deep feelings. In addition, the nature of what reproductive initiators are contracting about is qualitatively different than the object of ordinary contracts. We do not have at this time, and may never have, a good way to determine the value of specific reproductive contributions or to weigh conflicts between contributors (for example, what is the market value of gestation versus gamete donation?) At the very least, to use sperm donation as a paradigm for workable contracts reflects inattention to the vast differences, emotional as well as physical, in the nature of various collaborative roles. Moreover, it masks inequalities between parties with respect to risk and benefit. A contract that may well be sufficient to determine rearing duties and rights with respect to a sperm donor may not address at all the complex physical and affective situation of the surrogate mother.

Our understanding of the experience can perhaps be reinterpreted as Robertson suggests, so that what comes to count as reproduction is the donation of genetic material for one person, or the experience of gestation for another. Yet while there are very good reasons for preserving the freedom of individuals to choose their level of participation in procreation, to say that the meaning of reproduction can be reduced to one of these partial roles is to perpetuate an impoverished notion of what it means to be a parent. Assigning various rights and obligations to abstract roles may facilitate the execution of collaborative contracts, but risks treating the various components of reproduction as though they fit into neat compartments, and as though the conception-gestation-rearing relationship is entirely negotiable. Feminists do not want to affirm a view of reproduction that makes the moral connections between conception, gestation, and rearing such that conception generates an absolute duty to rear; at the same time, however, concerns for embodiment and thus for reproduction as a whole process mitigate against treating parental obligations and entitlements in isolation from the experiences of conception, pregnancy, and birth.

There is, of course, a kind of tacit agreement, at least in our society, involved in every gestation and birth with respect to the resultant offspring's nurture (and in a sense, also with respect to parental entitlements). Whatever model has been used thus far to understand the relationship, however, has not taken the form of an entirely free contract. Prior to the development of technology, we identified the mother as the woman giving birth to the child and the father as the man whose sperm initially fertilized the egg—those persons with biological and experiential connection, rather than those who have contracted for parental rights and duties. Even when we describe situations where another individual has taken over rearing responsibilities for a child not his or her issue, we continue to refer to that person as an "adoptive" or· "foster" parent. We do this not to say anything about the quality of rearing, but to preserve a truer sense of identity and biological continuity for the child, acknowledging that no matter what function the rearing adult serves, he or she cannot ever become the child's father or mother in the traditional sense. I do not want to hold that there could be no legitimate reasons for separating genetic, gestational, and rearing components of reproduction, or that persons who conceive a child will always be the best rearers of that child and that they must therefore be the rearers in all cases. Experience shows that children can be raised well in situations other than the traditional biologically related family. However, the genetic-gestation-rearing connection in procreation ought not be disregarded a priori in the way suggested by the contract model, both for the sake of protecting the offspring's sense of identity as a value and for preserving an awareness of the importance of the task involved when human life is created.

While "rights" and "entitlements" in childbearing do have much to do with an agreement to accept responsibility, the biological parent-child relationship is still deeply significant, particularly if we are speaking of the intimate mother-child bond in a normal gestation experience. It may be acceptable to say that a woman who has conceived, carried, and birthed a child may legitimately choose to transfer rearing obligations to another, but it does not seem correct to say then that this experience of procreation places *no* claim on her as a mother unless she chooses to assume one under the terms of a contract, or that her claim to this child is identical to the claims of all other contracting parties prior to the contract. Both the experience of having conceived and carried a child and the implicit agreement to nurture ground parental entitlements; these two dimensions must be seen as elements of the same experience even where a decision is made to separate them. Given the significant burdens and challenges of childbearing and the length of time the commitment ordinarily encompasses, this interconnection is important to protect when possible. Implicit in my critique is the great irony of collaborative reproduction: it is precisely the value of this biological connection, which must be open for renunciation on the part of the donor or gestator, that drives the search for new methods and justifies the infertile party's right to assistance.

THE INVOLUNTARY NATURE OF KINSHIP

The authority of the collaborative contract, coupled with a property view of children, generates a troubling picture of the parent-child bond. One of the false notions perpetuated in such a model of parental entitlement is that we are free to choose all obligations, and able to formulate all the conditions of our lives to meet our expectations. While most contracts and commitments are based on things such as shared purpose, equal benefit, common attraction, etc., and are entered into and terminated voluntarily, until recently, the agreement to conceive, gestate, and rear a child has been of a different nature. While in the best of circumstances we make a choice to parent, and a series of choices about how children will be raised and the shape our family life will take, a great deal of the experience of reproduction is not in our control. The common expression "This child has a face only a mother could love" speaks, of course, to the fact that a parent's bond to her child transcends all cultural standards of beauty, etc., but also alludes to a deeply entrenched understanding of the "givenness" and duration of parental responsibilities. These have included acceptance of a relatively unknown outcome, of inequalities in benefits and burdens, and also of a certain irrevocability. "A face only a mother could love" says something as well about acceptance and fidelity to children, even to those whose looks or gender or genetic characteristics are not what the parent would have desired or what meets society's standards. We have accepted the fact that, unlike a product in the market, children cannot be returned or exchanged if found to be other than what was expected.

The commitment a parent undertakes is not dependent on that child's behavior or the return of like affection or the fulfillment of expectations in life, although those factors can certainly influence a parent's subjective experience and may at times modify obligations. A child does not enter into a committed relationship with his or her parents in the same way that a parent, by virtue of the decision to bear offspring, does with the child; still, there is some measure of givenness in the child-parent relationship as well. We are free throughout life to choose friends, a mate, employers, etc. but not our family of origin. One of the things that family life can teach us is that we are born into some obligations, and some are born to us, and life includes the acceptance of those kinds of indissoluble and predefined obligations as well as the ones we freely incur. The involuntary quality of kinship can also teach us how to accept others as intimately connected to us, even when they fail to live up to our standards or when they do not possess the physical or personal qualities most attractive to us. To image reproduction as primarily a contractual process, where all the elements are open for negotiation, threatens to lose sight of this sense of transcendent commitment.

From the perspective of feminist ethics, the contractual view of procreative liberty assumes and perpetuates a traditional patriarchal model of the family (centered around rights and ownership), a model that has proven oppressive and sometimes dangerous for persons, especially women. A contract approach is initially attractive as it appears to bring about greater flexibility in the definition of family and the protection of procreative liberty (among the values feminists want to promote). But when persons are treated primarily as the object of another's right, and significant relationships are defined wholly according to legal arrangements rather than the experiences of nurture, the symbolic framework is that of the patriarchal family. Janet Farrell Smith has argued that this property model of parenting, having at its center a notion of rights, is inherently gender-biased and is protective of dangerous authority patterns. It is problematic in her view both because its structure of relationship is "male" in form and because males have traditionally been the exclusive holders of familial rights.[10]

What makes such a model destructively gender-biased, according to Smith, is its rootedness in an extractive view of power rather than a developmental one and its relation to the authority patterns of the traditional patriarchal family. The major elements of such a property model of human relations,

> namely ownership and proprietary control, have had more to do with fathering than with mothering. The realities of motherhood, on the other hand, have had more to do with care, nurturance and day-to-day responsibility. These represent a very different set of moral and political ideals.[11]

The concepts of right and entitlement used in the contractual model correspond to the values preserved in traditional notions of patriarchal fathering (control and ownership) rather than to those of care and responsibility associated with mothering. While many feminists would not want to posit "distinctively female" values or ideals, most would reject familiar structures that treat persons as property and would call instead for a style of parenting that is respectful of a child's autonomy and encourages individual flourishing. They would, as well, reject models of the family that attach authority to rigidly defined roles in favor of models based on equality between partners and cooperation in the performance of family tasks.

As Smith argues, promoting a property (or "rights-centered") model, whether through vigorous protection of familial autonomy or by the rhetoric of "right to procreate" can only reinforce an ideal of the family that not only does not encourage more respectful and cooperative parenting styles but may further facilitate the abuse of parental power. In the context of Robertson's argument, familial autonomy means a protection of parental control as rightful parent (owner) over minor children (a control that in the past has extended to wives). But this sort of familial autonomy underlying arguments for clarity of contract serves largely to protect proprietary interests rather than to facilitate intimacy or the development of creative, more humane forms of parenting for women and men.[12] Since the problem is not only that males have been the exclusive holders of rights to property (including their wives and children) but that this way of imaging the family denies the reality of women and children as fully human, it may not be enough simply for feminists to argue for equality between women and men in the holding of these rights. Rather, the very language of rights, implying as it does some exclusive access to property, must be seen as inappropriate when describing the structure of the family.

REPRODUCTIVE ENDS AND MEANS

One of the weaknesses of the argument for unlimited procreative liberty is a tendency to split ends from means, to overemphasize goals while giving little moral consideration to the methods employed to achieve them or to the price paid. Robertson's concern to promote the procreative initiator's interests is not adequately balanced, for example, by a concern for the persons who will participate as the means to the stated reproductive goals. Except where he discusses contract stipulations (requirements for informed consent, freedom from coercion, screening procedures, etc.) Robertson does not speak of donors and gestators as though they really have interests to be weighed; he argues, in fact, that unless grave harm is being done, their interests cannot override individual procreative liberty. As we saw earlier, the offspring as a particular child is treated not as an end in himself or herself, but as the means to a goal (a fulfilling parenting experience). The question of how such treatment may affect that child's quality of life, sense of identity, or development is hardly raised.

The problem is not that the holding of a reproductive end is wrong in itself, but that it may be mistaken to assume that an end-state can be clearly demarcated from the processes that lead up to it.[13] The primary assumption that reproduction is highly valued by individuals and therefore that freedom of access should be promoted treats reproductive freedom for the most part as a value that could be pursued in isolation of other claims (except the minimal obligation not to do grave harm to an offspring). Feminists reject such thinking as inadequately attentive to the reality of events as processes and to the fact that the means we use to bring about any end are part of the total reality of the event in question. Thus it is not enough to assert that providing genetically related children to infertile individuals is a good to be promoted; questions must be raised about the nature of the arrangement by which that might occur, the impact of that project on the individuals involved and on the larger human community, and the claims other goods are simultaneously exerting.

It is wrong to suppose that an individual procreative right can be posited and its unlimited exercise upheld without careful consideration of the moral nature of the means necessary to attain its end. Interest in a genetically related child cannot be seen as an independent end, the value of which automatically discounts concerns for the present and future state of the offspring, for the physical and emotional safety of the collaborators, or for the place of the experience of reproduction in our collective value system. In addition, the particular techniques used in collaborative reproduction need separate evaluation. We might accept the use of artificial insemination by a donor, for example, on particular grounds (as that the risks to donor are small and the benefit great), but have serious reservations about the practice of surrogacy. An adequate argument for procreative liberty as a good would have to include a fair description of the necessary means since they cannot be separated from the end-state.

Because reproduction has a social dimension, and reproductive practices have profound real and symbolic impacts on the community, the promotion of individual procreative liberty can never be an abstract end. The value of collaborative reproduction for individuals needs to be weighed against the costs these practices may exact, not only in the lives of those individuals directly involved, but also with respect to the promotion of full human community. An assessment of procreative liberty that takes seriously the contextual nature of our choices asks, in addition to whether the "new reproduction" is good for individuals, how it relates to social concerns (to efforts to secure an adequate standard of living for all persons, to progress in the quality of class, gender, and race relations, etc.).

A commitment to the creation of a just society requires that an individual desire for a genetically related child cannot be held up as an end commanding significant public resources and energy if as a "good" it encourages the exploitation of vulnerable persons or fosters negative attitudes toward persons or groups of persons. At a minimum, questions need to be raised about the influence of institutionalizing these practices on our views toward women: will opportunities to serve as egg donors or gestators facilitate progress toward equality with men for women, or does this type of service further identify women in an oppressive way with their reproductive capabilities? If individuals have a right to a genetically related child, do others have an obligation to donate genetic material, and how will the extent of the obligation be determined? What are the potential consequences of medicalizing reproduction in terms of women's right to control over their own bodies? And who will the women be who serve as donors?—will the poor, who have always been exploited by the rich, be used to perform even this form of domestic service?

To take account of the context in which individual procreative liberty is pursued, we also need to weigh the expense and energy channelled in the direction of these reproductive services against the realities of poverty and overpopulation. We need to ask whether we should support the right of individuals to go to any length to acquire the type of child they want when there are so many children already living who are not being taken care of. And, recognizing that collaborative reproduction ordinarily has as its object a white child, we need as well to examine the kind of racial attitudes being perpetuated. We cannot treat the pursuit of a genetically related child, or the protection of individual procreative liberty, as though they are abstract goods that are never in conflict with other relevant goods, nor can we consider procreative liberty from the point of view of its end alone. Given the nature of the procreative task, *how* we reproduce is as significant as *whether* we do.

PROMOTING FULL HUMANITY

The promotion of women's right to self-determination, especially in matters of reproduction, has indeed been a critical item on the feminist political agenda. But for most feminists, protection of individual autonomy is never treated as the single value to be considered in the analysis of a situation. A commitment to viewing persons as embodied and relational, as well as autonomous, mitigates against an abstract notion of freedom that does not take seriously enough the way in which personal choices alter the shape of the world in which they occur. Questions of personal liberty, including how far our right to procreate extends, can only properly be asked from the point of view of our reality as relational beings whose power for reproduction is a capacity with profound personal and social implications. It is never even theoretically unlimited.

The objectification of children, impoverishment of meaning in the experience of reproduction, damage to notions of kinship, the perpetuation of degrading views of women—all these concerns may be deemed "symbolic harms" that are not compelling enough to override personal liberty. But attention to women's experience has taught feminists that there are no "merely symbolic" harms; we interpret and shape experience through our symbols and therefore how we think about persons, events, and biological processes has a great deal to do with how we behave toward them. We need, then, to pay careful attention to what is being said of personhood, of parent-child relationships, of reproductive capacities, and so on in arguments for unlimited procreative liberty. If we hope to use reproductive technology in a way that promotes the full humanity of all persons, in a manner that is truly creative rather than destructive, then we must be attentive to the potential for harm on all levels. We have an ever-expanding power to reshape the experience of reproduction; whether we will prove in the future to have done so in the service of human life or not will have more than a little to do with how we came to think about it and what we allowed to be of value today.

NOTES

1. While a few feminists have heralded developments in technology as the ground of possibility for women's true liberation, most have remained more cautious, foreseeing potential for further oppression as clearly as hope of equality. See Shulamith Firestone, *The Dialectic of Sex: The Case for Feminist Revolution* (New York: Bantam Books, 1971), 238; Christine Overall, *Ethics and Human Reproduction: A Feminist Analysis* (Boston: Allen and Unwin, 1987).

2. John Robertson, "Procreative Liberty and the Control of Conception, Pregnancy and Childbirth," *Virginia Law Review* 69 (April 1983), 405–462; "Embryos, Families and Procreative Liberty: The Legal Structures of the New Reproduction," *Southern California Law Review* 59 (1986), 942–1041.

3. Robertson, "Embryos, Families and Procreative Liberty," 961.

4. Robertson, "Procreative Liberty," 450.

5. Robertson, "Procreative Liberty," 432.

6. See Overall, *Ethics and Human Reproduction,* chapter 8; also Richard L. Fern, "The Fundamental Right to Marry and Raise a Family," unpublished manuscript (1987).

7. The parallel would be marriage, that is, there is a recognized right to noninterference in the decision to marry but no obligation on society's part to provide a mate. See William J. Daniel, "Sexual Ethics in Relation to IVF and ET: The Fitting Use of Human Reproductive Power," in *Test-Tube Babies*, William Walters and Peter Singer, eds. (Melbourne: Oxford University Press, 1982), 73.

8. Robertson, "Procreative Liberty," 430.

9. Robertson, "Procreative Liberty," 424.

10. Janet Farrell Smith, "Parenting and Property," in *Mothering: Essays in Feminist Theory*, Joyce Treblicott, ed. (Totowa, NJ: Rowman and Allanheld, 1983), 199–210.

11. Smith, "Parenting," 208.

12. Smith, "Parenting," 206.

13. For a discussion of a feminist critique of dualistic means-ends reasoning, see Jean Grimshaw, *Philosophy and Feminist Thinking* (Minneapolis: University of Minnesota Press, 1986), 187–226.

CHAPTER 18

The Transmission of Life

Pope John Paul II

Pope Paul's Encyclical *Humanae Vitae* (1968) caused a firestorm of protest within Roman Catholicism. Its prohibition against artificial means of contraception was a marker point for millions of practicing Roman Catholics. Following one's conscience, continued reception of the sacraments, and informed dissent became the ecclesial way of life for many. And so it is today.

In this excerpt, from his Apostolic Exhortation on "Role of the Christian Family in the Modern World," Pope John Paul II vigorously defends the traditional Roman Catholic teaching. It is truly, he believes, prophetic proclamation. The fundamental task of family life is to serve life by the transmission of new life. The unitive and procreative meanings of the conjugal act can never be *artificially* separated. Natural family planning accepts the natural cycle of the person and expresses the total reciprocal self-giving of the couple. The artificial use of contraceptives, on the other hand, speaks an objectively contradictory language, namely, not giving oneself totally to the other.

In the current social and cultural context, Pope John Paul II acknowledges that this traditional teaching is difficult to understand. An array of forces fosters a contraceptive mentality and antilife dispositions. Some public authorities formulate public policies (contraception, sterilization, abortion) that support this outlook. The church, however, must say "yes" to life in the face of the "no" that assails and afflicts the world. John Paul II's stance is certainly countercultural. Will it win the hearts and minds of the faithful?

Questions for Discussion

1. Is John Paul II's argument against artificial contraception convincing for you? Why?
2. Is there some truth to the claim that a contraceptive mentality holds sway in the lives of some young married couples today?
3. John Paul II's position is: harmonizing conjugal love with the responsible transmission of life must be determined by *objective standards*. Are there objective standards to look to? If so, where?
4. What can you affirm in this papal perspective as a form of prophetic cultural resistance today?
5. Have human beings the right and/or responsibility to shape and reorder expressions of their sexuality? If so, when?

6. Would you agree or disagree with governmental support and financing of contraception, sterilization, and abortion?

COOPERATORS IN THE LOVE OF GOD THE CREATOR

With the creation of man and woman in His own image and likeness, God crowns and brings to perfection the work of His hands: He calls them to a special sharing in His love and in His power as Creator and Father, through their free and responsible cooperation in transmitting the gift of human life: "God blessed them, and God said to them, 'Be fruitful and multiply, and fill the earth and subdue it.'"[1]

Thus the fundamental task of the family is to serve life, to actualize in history the original blessing of the Creator—that of transmitting by procreation the divine image from person to person.[2]

Fecundity is the fruit and the sign of conjugal love, the living testimony of the full reciprocal self-giving of the spouses: "While not making the other purposes of matrimony of less account, the true practice of conjugal love, and the whole meaning of the family life which results from it, have this aim: that the couple be ready with stout hearts to cooperate with the love of the Creator and the Savior, who through them will enlarge and enrich His own family day by day."[3]

However, the fruitfulness of conjugal love is not restricted solely to the procreation of children, even understood in its specifically human dimension: it is enlarged and enriched by all those fruits of moral, spiritual and supernatural life which the father and mother are called to hand on to their children, and through the children to the Church and to the world.

THE CHURCH'S TEACHING AND NORM, ALWAYS OLD YET ALWAYS NEW

Precisely because the love of husband and wife is a unique participation in the mystery of life and of the love of God Himself, the Church knows that she has received the special mission of guarding and protecting the lofty dignity of marriage and the most serious responsibility of the transmission of human life.

Thus, in continuity with the living tradition of the ecclesial community throughout history, the recent Second Vatican Council and the magisterium of my predecessor Paul VI, expressed above all in the Encyclical *Humanae vitae*, have handed on to our times a truly prophetic proclamation, which reaffirms and reproposes with clarity the Church's teaching and norm, always old yet always new, regarding marriage and regarding the transmission of human life.

For this reason the Synod Fathers made the following declaration at their last assembly: "This Sacred Synod, gathered together with the Successor of Peter in the unity of faith, firmly holds what has been set forth in the Second Vatican Council (cf. *Gaudium et spes,* 50) and afterwards in the Encyclical *Humanae vitae,* particularly that love between husband and wife must be fully human, exclusive and open to new life (*Humanae vitae,* 11: cf. 9. 12)."[4]

THE CHURCH STANDS FOR LIFE

The teaching of the Church in our day is placed in a social and cultural context which renders it more difficult to understand and yet more urgent and irreplaceable for promoting the true good of men and women.

Scientific and technical progress, which contemporary man is continually expanding in his dominion over nature, not only offers the hope of creating a new and better humanity, but also causes ever greater anxiety regarding the future. Some ask themselves if it is a good thing to be alive or if it would be better never to have been born: they doubt therefore if it is right to bring others into life when perhaps they will curse their existence in a cruel world with unforeseeable terrors. Others consider themselves to be the only ones for whom the advantages of technology are intended and they exclude others by imposing on them contraceptives or even worse means. Still others, imprisoned in a consumer mentality and whose sole concern is to bring about a continual growth of material goods, finish by ceasing to understand, and thus by refusing, the spiritual riches of a new human life. The ultimate reason for these mentalities is the absence in people's hearts of God, whose love alone is stronger than all the world's fears and can conquer them.

Thus an anti-life mentality is born, as can be seen in many current issues: one thinks, for example, of a certain panic deriving from the studies of ecologists and futurologists on population growth, which sometimes exaggerate the danger of demographic increase to the quality of life.

But the Church firmly believes that human life, even if weak and suffering, is always a splendid gift of God's goodness. Against the pessimism and selfishness which cast a shadow over the world, the Church stands for life: in each human life she sees the splendor of that "Yes," that "Amen," who is Christ Himself.[5] To the "No" which assails and afflicts the world, she replies with this living "Yes," thus defending the human person and the world from all who plot against and harm life.

The Church is called upon to manifest anew to everyone, with clear and stronger conviction, her will to promote human life by every means and to defend it against all attacks, in whatever condition or state of development it is found.

Thus the Church condemns as a grave offense against human dignity and justice all those activities of governments or other public authorities which attempt to limit in any way the freedom of couples in deciding about children. Consequently, any violence applied by such authorities in favor of contraception or, still worse, of sterilization and procured abortion, must be altogether condemned and forcefully rejected. Likewise to be denounced as gravely unjust are cases where, in international relations, economic help given for the advancement of peoples is made conditional on programs of contraception, sterilization and procured abortion.[6]

THAT GOD'S DESIGN MAY BE EVER MORE COMPLETELY FULFILLED

The Church is certainly aware of the many complex problems which couples in many countries face today in their task of transmitting life in a responsible way. She also recognizes the serious problem of population growth in the form it has taken in many parts of the world and its moral implications.

However, she holds that consideration in depth of all the aspects of these problems offers a new and stronger confirmation of the importance of the authentic teaching on birth regulation reproposed in the Second Vatican Council and in the Encyclical *Humanae vitae*.

For this reason, together with the Synod Fathers I feel it is my duty to extend a pressing invitation to theologians, asking them to unite their efforts in order to collaborate with the hierarchical Magisterium and to commit themselves to the task of illustrating ever more clearly the biblical foundations, the ethical grounds and the personalistic reasons behind this doctrine. Thus it will be possible, in the context of an organic exposition, to render the teaching of the Church on this fundamental question truly accessible to all people of good will, fostering a daily more enlightened and profound understanding of it: in this way God's plan will be ever more completely fulfilled for the salvation of humanity and for the glory of the Creator.

A united effort by theologians in this regard, inspired by a convinced adherence to the Magisterium, which is the one authentic guide for the People of God, is particularly urgent for reasons that include the close link between Catholic teaching on this matter and the view of the human person that the Church proposes: doubt or error in the field of marriage or the family involves obscuring to a serious extent the integral truth about the human person, in a cultural situation that is already so often confused and contradictory. In fulfillment of their specific role, theologians are called upon to provide enlightenment and a deeper understanding, and their contribution is of incomparable value and represents a unique and highly meritorious service to the family and humanity.

IN AN INTEGRAL VISION OF THE HUMAN PERSON AND OF HIS OR HER VOCATION

In the context of a culture which seriously distorts or entirely misinterprets the true meaning of human sexuality, because it separates it from its essential reference to the person, the Church more urgently feels how irreplaceable is her mission of presenting sexuality as a value and task of the whole person, created male and female in the image of God.

In this perspective the Second Vatican Council clearly affirmed that "when there is a question of harmonizing conjugal love with the responsible transmission of life, the moral aspect of any procedure does not depend solely on sincere intentions or on an evaluation of motives. It must be determined by *objective standards.* These, *based on the nature of the human person and his or her acts,* preserve the full sense of mutual self-giving and human procreation in the context of true love. Such a goal cannot be achieved unless the virtue of conjugal chastity is sincerely practiced."[7]

It is precisely by moving from "an integral vision of man and of his vocation, not only his natural and earthly, but also his supernatural and eternal vocation."[8] that Paul VI affirmed that the teaching of the Church "is founded upon the inseparable connection, willed by God and unable to be broken by man on his own initiative, between the two meanings of the conjugal act: the unitive meaning and the procreative meaning."[9] And he concluded by re-emphasizing that there must be excluded as intrinsically immoral "every action which, either in anticipation of the conjugal act, or in its accomplishment, or in the development of its natural consequences, proposes, whether as an end or as a means, to render procreation impossible."[10]

When couples, by means of recourse to contraception, separate these two meanings that God the Creator has inscribed in the being of man and woman and in the dynamism of their sexual communion, they act as "arbiters" of the divine plan and they "manipulate" and degrade human sexuality—and with it themselves and their married partner—by altering its value of "total" self-giving. Thus the innate language that expresses the total reciprocal self-giving of husband and wife is overlaid, through contraception, by an objectively contradictory language, namely, that of not giving oneself totally to the other. This leads not only to a positive refusal to be open to life but also to a falsification of the inner truth of conjugal love, which is called upon to give itself in personal totality.

When, instead, by means of recourse to periods of infertility, the couple respect the inseparable connection between the unitive and procreative meanings of human sexuality, they are acting as "ministers" of God's plan and they "benefit from" their sexuality according to the original dynamism of "total" self-giving, without manipulation or alteration.[11]

In the light of the experience of many couples and of the data provided by the different human sciences, theological reflection is able to perceive and is called to study further *the difference, both anthropological and moral,* between contraception and recourse to the rhythm of the cycle: it is a difference which is much wider and deeper than is usually thought, one which involves in the final analysis two irreconcilable concepts of the human person and of human sexuality. The choice of the natural rhythms involves accepting the cycle of the person, that is the woman, and thereby accepting dialogue, reciprocal respect, shared responsibility and self-control. To accept the cycle and to enter into dialogue means to recognize both the spiritual and corporal character of conjugal communion, and to live personal love with its requirement of fidelity. In this context the couple comes to experience how conjugal communion is enriched with those values of tenderness and affection which constitute the inner soul of human sexuality, in its physical dimension also. In this way sexuality is respected and promoted in its truly and fully human dimension, and is never "used" as an "object" that, by breaking the personal unity of soul and body, strikes at God's creation itself at the level of the deepest interaction of nature and person.

NOTES

1. Gn 1:28.

2. Cf Gn 5:1–3.

3. Second Vatican Ecumenical Council, Pastoral Constitution on the Church in the Modern World, *Gaudium et Spes*, n. 50.

4. *Propositio* 21. Section 11 of the encyclical *Humanae Vitae* ends with the statement: "The Church, calling people back to the observance of the norms of the natural law, as interpreted by her constant doctrine, teaches that each and every marriage act must remain open to the transmission of life (*ut quilibet matrimonii usus ad vitam humanam procreandam per se destinatus permaneat*)": AAS 60 (1968), 488.

5. Cf 2 Cor 1:19; Rv 3:14.

6. Cf the Sixth Synod of Bishops' Message to Christian Families in the Modern World (Oct. 24, 1980), 5.

7. Pastoral Constitution on the Church in the Modern World, *Gaudium et Spes*, n. 51.

8. Encyclical *Humanae Vitae*, n. 7:AAS 60 (1968), 485.

9. Ibid., 12: loc. cit., 488–489.

10. Ibid., 14: loc. cit., 490.

11. Ibid., 13: loc. cit., 489.

PART FIVE

Communication, Conflict, and Change

CHAPTER 19

"Put Down That Paper and Talk to Me!": Rapport-Talk and Report-Talk

Deborah Tannen

In reading the following essay, men may find themselves fidgeting or their attention wandering, while women may read on with attentive fascination. Tannen puts a spotlight on habits men have rarely thought about but that may need changing, while women find Tannen naming things they themselves have noticed but never dared name or bring to attention. It is important to notice she is dealing here with *tendencies*, true enough in general, but not true of all men. However, if she is right about these tendencies, then the essay is especially important for men, because it can help men rethink how ordinary speech helps or hinders intimacy.

Another important point to notice is that Tannen is not blaming either men or women for the communication patterns she outlines. "The real problem is conversational style," she says. Men and women (especially boyfriends and girlfriends) do well to talk over these styles and the entire essay from their own points of view. As Tannen says, these differences in ways of speaking may never be perfectly adjusted for our partner's satisfaction, but *understanding them* takes the edge off complaints.

Some years ago, at the annual meetings of a professional association of professors, feminists began noting how many people of each gender were present at a particular session and how many women spoke and how many men. At the end of a session, they would announce their count. This procedure was transformative for many men in that association, who had never noticed the patterns. It was also transformative for women, who saw their need to speak up more often.

The marriage-course classroom might be an interesting lab for testing Tannen's claims. If someone agreed to do a regular speech analysis, giving at the end of class the ratio of women and men who volunteered observations, personal anecdotes, questions, and so on, all in class would become more conscious of "speaking out" as an important ongoing issue. Such consciousness could provide the spark to ignite very lively discussion of any issue that might arise.

Questions for Discussion

1. From your own point of view as a woman or a man, what single statement of Tannen's do you find most true of your own way of speaking? What statement do you find most true of the opposite sex's way of speaking?

2. What can you point to in her essay as most important for men to understand about their conversational styles? What do you find most important for women?
3. Where in her essay did you find she overstated or exaggerated?
4. If you were pushed to find one point that might change your own behavior, what would it be?

I was sitting in a suburban living room, speaking to a women's group that had invited men to join them for the occasion of my talk about communication between women and men. During the discussion, one man was particularly talkative, full of lengthy comments and explanations. When I made the observation that women often complain that their husbands don't talk to them enough, this man volunteered that he heartily agreed. He gestured toward his wife, who had sat silently beside him on the couch throughout the evening, and said, "She's the talker in our family."

Everyone in the room burst into laughter. The man looked puzzled and hurt. "It's true," he explained. "When I come home from work, I usually have nothing to say, but she never runs out. If it weren't for her, we'd spend the whole evening in silence." Another woman expressed a similar paradox about her husband: "When we go out, he's the life of the party. If I happen to be in another room, I can always hear his voice above the others. But when we're home, he doesn't have that much to say. I do most of the talking."

Who talks more, women or men? According to the stereotype, women talk too much. Linguist Jennifer Coates notes some proverbs:

> A woman's tongue wags like a lamb's tail.
>
> Foxes are all tail and women are all tongue.
>
> The North Sea will sooner be found wanting in water than a woman be at a loss for a word.

Throughout history, women have been punished for talking too much or in the wrong way. Linguist Connie Eble lists a variety of physical punishments used in Colonial America: Women were strapped to ducking stools and held underwater until they nearly drowned, put into the stocks with signs pinned to them, gagged, and silenced by a cleft stick applied to their tongues.

Though such institutionalized corporal punishments have given way to informal, often psychological ones, modern stereotypes are not much different from those expressed in the old proverbs. Women are believed to talk too much. Yet study after study finds that it is men who talk more—at meetings, in mixed-group discussions, and in classrooms where girls or young women sit next to boys or young men. For example, communications researchers Barbara and Gene Eakins tape-recorded and studied seven university faculty meetings. They found that, with one exception, men spoke more often and, without exception, spoke for a longer time. The men's turns ranged from 10.66 to 17.07 seconds, while the women's turns ranged from 3 to 10 seconds. In other words, the women's longest turns were still shorter than the men's shortest turns.

When a public lecture is followed by questions from the floor, or a talk show host opens the phones, the first voice to be heard asking a question is almost always a man's. And when they ask questions or offer comments from the audience, men tend to talk longer. Linguist Marjorie Swacker recorded question-and-answer sessions at academic conferences. Women were highly visible as speakers at the conferences studied; they presented 40.7 percent of the papers at the conferences studied and made up 42 percent of the audiences. But when it came to volunteering and being called on to ask questions, women contributed only 27.4 percent. Furthermore, the women's questions, on the average, took less than half as much time as the men's. (The mean was 23.1 seconds for women, 52.7 for men.) This happened, Swacker shows, because men (but not women) tended to preface their questions with statements, ask more than one question, and follow up the speaker's answer with another question or comment.

I have observed this pattern at my own lectures, which concern issues of direct relevance to women. Regardless of the proportion of women and men in the audience, men almost invariably ask the first question, more questions, and longer questions. In these situations, women often feel that men are talking too much. I recall one discussion period following a lecture I gave to a group assembled in a bookstore. The group was composed mostly of women, but most of the discussion was being conducted by men in the audience. At one point, a man sitting in the middle was talking at such great length that several women in the front rows began shifting in their seats and rolling their eyes at me. Ironically, what he was going on about was how frustrated he feels when he has to listen to women going on and on about topics he finds boring and unimportant.

RAPPORT-TALK AND REPORT-TALK

Who talks more, then, women or men? The seemingly contradictory evidence is reconciled by the difference between what I call *public* and *private* *speaking*. More men feel comfortable doing "public speaking," while more women feel comfortable doing "private" speaking. Another way of capturing these differences is by using the terms *report-talk* and *rapport-talk*.

For most women, the language of conversation is primarily a language of rapport: a way of establishing connections and negotiating relationships. Emphasis is placed on displaying similarities and matching experiences. From childhood, girls criticize peers who try to stand out or appear better than others. People feel their closest connections at home, or in settings where they *feel* at home—with one or a few people they feel close to and comfortable with—in other words, during private speaking. But even the most public situations can be approached like private speaking.

For most men, talk is primarily a means to preserve independence and negotiate and maintain status in a hierarchical social order. This is done by exhibiting knowledge and skill, and by holding center stage through verbal performance such as story-telling, joking, or imparting information. From childhood, men learn to use talking as a way to get and keep attention. So they are more comfortable speaking in larger groups made up of people they know less well—in the broadest sense, "public speaking." But even the most private situations can be approached like public speaking, more like giving a report than establishing rapport.

PRIVATE SPEAKING: THE WORDY WOMAN AND THE MUTE MAN

What is the source of the stereotype that women talk a lot? Dale Spender suggests that most people feel instinctively (if not consciously) that women, like children, should be seen and not heard, so any amount of talk from them seems like too much. Studies have shown that if women and men talk equally in a group, people think the women talked more. So there is truth to Spender's view. But another explanation is that men think women talk a lot because they hear women talking in situations where men would not: on the telephone; or in social situations with friends, when they are not discussing topics that men find inherently interesting; or, like the couple at the women's group, at home alone—in other words, in private speaking.

Home is the setting for an American icon that features the silent man and the talkative woman. And this icon, which grows out of the different goals and habits I have been describing, explains why the complaint most often voiced by women about the men with whom they are intimate is "He doesn't talk to me"—and the second most frequent is "He doesn't listen to me."

A woman who wrote to Ann Landers is typical:

> My husband never speaks to me when he comes home from work. When I ask, "How did everything go today?" he says, "Rough . . ." or "It's a jungle out there." (We live in Jersey and he works in New York City.)
>
> It's a different story when we have guests or go visiting. Paul is the gabbiest guy in the crowd—a real spellbinder. He comes up with the most interesting stories. People hang on every word. I think to myself, "Why doesn't he ever tell *me* these things?"
>
> This has been going on for 38 years. Paul started to go quiet on me after 10 years of marriage. I could never figure out why. Can you solve the mystery?
> —The Invisible Woman

Ann Landers suggests that the husband may not want to talk because he is tired when he comes home from work. Yet women who work come home tired too, and they are nonetheless eager to tell their partners or friends everything that happened to them during the day and what these fleeting, daily dramas made them think and feel.

Sources as lofty as studies conducted by psychologists, as down to earth as letters written to advice columnists, and as sophisticated as movies and plays come up with the same insight. Men's silence at home is a disappointment to women. Again and again, women complain, "He seems to have everything to say to everyone else, and nothing to say to me."

The film *Divorce American Style* opens with a conversation in which Debbie Reynolds is claiming that she and Dick Van Dyke don't communicate, and he is protesting that he tells her everything that's on his mind. The doorbell interrupts their quarrel, and husband and wife compose themselves before opening the door to greet their guests with cheerful smiles.

Behind closed doors, many couples are having conversations like this. Like the character played by Debbie Reynolds, women feel men don't communicate. Like the husband played by Dick Van Dyke, men feel wrongly accused. How can she be convinced that he doesn't tell her anything, while he is equally convinced he tells her everything that's on his mind? How can women and men have such different ideas about the same conversations?

When something goes wrong, people look around for a source to blame: either the person they are trying to communicate with ("You're demanding, stubborn, self-centered") or the group that the other person belongs to ("All women are demanding"; "All men are self-centered"). Some generous-minded people blame the relationship ("We just can't communicate"). But underneath, or overlaid on these types of blame cast outward, most people believe that something is wrong with them.

If individual people or particular relationships were to blame, there wouldn't be so many different people having the same problems. The real problem is conversational style. Women and men have different ways of talking. Even with the best intentions, trying to settle the problem through talk can only make things worse if it is ways of talking that are causing trouble in the first place.

BEST FRIENDS

Once again, the seeds of women's and men's styles are sown in the ways they learn to use language while growing up. In our culture, most people, but especially women, look to their closest relationships as havens in a hostile world. The center of a little girl's social life is her best friend. Girls' friendships are made and maintained by telling secrets. For grown women too, the essence of friendship is talk, telling each other what they're thinking and feeling, and what happened that day: who was at the bus stop, who called, what they said, how that made them feel. When asked who their best friends are, most women name other women they talk to regularly. When asked the same question, most men will say it's their wives. After that, many men name other men with whom they do things such as play tennis or baseball (but never just sit and talk) or a chum from high school whom they haven't spoken to in a year.

When Debbie Reynolds complained that Dick Van Dyke didn't tell her anything, and he protested that he did, both were right. She felt he didn't tell her anything because he didn't tell her the fleeting thoughts and feelings he experienced throughout the day—the kind of talk she would have with her best friend. He didn't tell her these things because to him they didn't seem like anything to tell. He told her anything that seemed important—anything he would tell his friends.

Men and women often have very different ideas of what's important—and at what point "important" topics should be raised. A woman told me, with lingering incredulity, of a conversation with her boyfriend. Knowing he had seen his friend Oliver, she asked, "What's new with Oliver?" He replied, "Nothing." But later in the conversation it came out that Oliver and his girl-friend had decided to get married. "That's nothing?" the woman gasped in frustration and disbelief.

For men, "Nothing" may be a ritual response at the start of a conversation. A college woman missed her brother but rarely called him because she found it difficult to get talk going. A typical conversation began with her asking, "What's up with you?" and his replying, "Nothing." Hearing his "Nothing" as meaning "There is nothing personal I want to talk about," she supplied talk by filling him in on her news and eventually hung up in frustration. But when she thought back, she remembered that later in the conversation he had mumbled, "Christie and I got into another fight." This came so late and so low that she didn't pick up on it. And he was probably equally frustrated that she didn't.

Many men honestly do not know what women want, and women honestly do not know why men find what they want so hard to comprehend and deliver.

"TALK TO ME!"

Women's dissatisfaction with men's silence at home is captured in the stock cartoon setting of a breakfast table at which a husband and wife are sitting: He's reading a newspaper; she's glaring at the back of the newspaper. In a Dagwood strip, Blondie complains, "Every morning all he sees is the news-paper! I'll bet you don't even know I'm here!" Dagwood reassures her, "Of course I know you're here. You're my wonderful wife and I love you very much." With this, he unseeingly pats the paw of the family dog, which the wife has put in her place before leaving the room. The cartoon strip shows that Blondie is justified in feeling like the woman who wrote to Ann Landers: invisible.

Another cartoon shows a husband opening a newspaper and asking his wife, "Is there anything you would like to say to me before I begin reading the newspaper?" The reader knows that there isn't—but that as soon as he begins reading the paper, she will think of something. The cartoon highlights the difference in what women and men think talk is for: To him, talk is for information. So when his wife interrupts his reading, it must be to inform him of something that he needs to know. This being the case, she might as well tell him what she thinks he needs to know before he starts reading. But to her, talk is for interaction. Telling things is a way to show involvement, and listening is a way to show interest and caring. It is not an odd coincidence that she always thinks of things to tell him when he is reading. She feels the need for verbal interaction most keenly when he is (unaccountably, from her point of view) buried in the newspaper instead of talking to her.

Yet another cartoon shows a wedding cake that has, on top, in place of the plastic statues of bride and groom in tuxedo and gown, a breakfast scene in which an unshaven husband reads a newspaper across the table from his disgruntled wife. The cartoon reflects the enormous gulf between the romantic expectations of marriage represented by the plastic couple in traditional wedding costume, and the often disappointing reality represented by the two sides of the newspaper at the breakfast table—the front, which he is reading, and the back, at which she is glaring.

These cartoons, and many others on the same theme, are funny because people recognize their own experience in them. What's not funny is that many women are deeply hurt when men don't talk to them at home, and many men are deeply frustrated by feeling they have disappointed their partners, without understanding how they failed or how else they could have behaved.

Some men are further frustrated because, as one put it, "When in the world am I supposed to read the morning paper?" If many women are incredulous that many men do not exchange personal information with their friends, this man is incredulous that many women do not bother to read the morning paper. To him, reading the paper is an essential part of his morning ritual, and his whole day is awry if he doesn't get to read it. In his words, reading the newspaper in the morning is as important to him as putting on makeup in the morning is to many women he knows. Yet many women, he observed, either don't subscribe to a paper or don't read it until they get home in the evening. "I find this very puzzling," he said. "I can't tell you how often I have picked up a woman's morning newspaper from her front door in the evening and handed it to her when she opened the door for me."

To this man (and I am sure many others), a woman who objects to his reading the morning paper is trying to keep him from doing something essential and harmless. It's a violation of his independence—his freedom of action. But when a woman who expects her partner to talk to her is disappointed that he doesn't she perceives his behavior as a failure of intimacy: He's keeping things from her; he's lost interest in her; he's pulling away. A woman I will call Rebecca, who is generally quite happily married, told me that this is the one source of serious dissatistaction with her husband, Stuart. Her term for his taciturnity is *stinginess of spirit.* She tells him what she is thinking, and he listens silently. She asks him what he is thinking, and he takes a long time to answer, "I don't know," In frustration she challenges, "Is there nothing on your mind?"

For Rebecca, who is accustomed to expressing her fleeting thoughts and opinions as they come to her, *saying* nothing means *thinking* nothing. But Stuart does not assume that his passing thoughts are worthy of utterance. He is not in the habit of uttering his fleeting ruminations, so just as Rebecca "naturally" speaks her thoughts, he "naturally" dismisses his as soon as they occur to him. Speaking them would give them more weight and significance than he feels they merit. All her life she has had practice in verbalizing her thoughts and feelings in private conversations with people she is close to; all his life he has had practice in dismissing his and keeping them to himself.

WHAT TO DO WITH DOUBTS

In the above example, Rebecca was not talking about any particular kind of thoughts or feelings, just whatever Stuart might have had in mind. But the matter of giving voice to thoughts and feelings becomes particularly significant in the case of negative feelings or doubts about a relationship. This difference was highlighted for me when a fifty-year-old divorced man told me about his experiences in forming new relationships with women. On this matter, he was clear: "I do not value my fleeting thoughts, and I do not value the fleeting thoughts of others." He felt that the relationship he was currently in had been endangered, even permanently weakened, by the woman's practice of tossing out her passing thoughts, because, early in their courtship, many of her thoughts were fears about their relationship. Not surprisingly, since they did not yet know each other well, she worried about whether she could trust him, whether their relationship would destroy her independence, whether this relationship was really right for her. He felt she should have kept these fears and doubts to herself and waited to see how things turned out.

As it happens, things turned out well. The woman decided that the relationship was right for her, she could trust him, and she did not have to give up her independence. But he felt, at the time that he told me of this, that he had still not recovered from the wear and tear of coping with her earlier doubts. As he put it, he was still dizzy from having been bounced around like a yo-yo tied to the string of her stream of consciousness.

In contrast, this man admitted, he himself goes to the other extreme: He never expresses his fears and misgivings about their relationship at all. If he's unhappy but doesn't say anything about it, his unhappiness expresses itself in a kind of distancing coldness. This response is just what women fear most, and just the reason they prefer to express dissatisfactions and doubts—as an antidote to the isolation and distance that would result from keeping them to themselves.

The different perspectives on expressing or concealing dissatisfactions and doubts may reflect a difference in men's and women's awareness of the power of their words to affect others. In repeatedly telling him what she feared about their relationship, this woman spoke as though she assumed he was invulnerable and could not be hurt by what she said; perhaps she was underestimating the power of her words to affect him. For his part when he refrains from expressing negative thoughts or feelings, he seems to be over-estimating the power of his words to hurt her, when, ironically, she is more likely to be hurt by his silence than his words.

These women and men are talking in ways they learned as children and reinforced as young adults and then adults, in their same-gender friendships. For girls, talk is the glue that holds relationships together. Boys' relationships are held together primarily by activities: doing things together, or talking about activities such as sports or, later, politics. The forums in which men are most inclined to talk are those in which they feel the need to impress, in situations where their status is in question.

MAKING ADJUSTMENTS

Such impasses will perhaps never be settled to the complete satisfaction of both parties, but understanding the differing views can help detoxify the situation, and both can make adjustments. Realizing that men and women have different assumptions about the place of talk in relationships, a woman can observe a man's desire to read the morning paper at the breakfast table without interpreting it as a rejection of her or a failure of their relationship. And a man can understand a woman's desire for talk without interpreting it as an unreasonable demand or a manipulative attempt to prevent him from doing what he wants to do.

A woman who had heard my interpretations of these differences between women and men told me how these insights helped her. Early in a promising relationship, a man spent the night at her apartment. It was a weeknight, and they both had to go to work the next day, so she was delighted when he made the rash and romantic suggestion that they have breakfast together and report late for work. She happily prepared breakfast, looking forward to the scene shaped in her mind: They would sit facing each other across her small table, look into each other's eyes, and say how much they liked each other and how happy they were about their growing friendship. It was against the backdrop of this heady expectation that she confronted an entirely different scene: As she placed on the table an array of lovingly prepared eggs, toast, and coffee, the man sat across her small table—and opened the newspaper in front of his face. If suggesting they have breakfast together had seemed like an invitation to get closer, in her view (or obstructing her view) the newspaper was now erected as a paper-thin but nonetheless impenetrable barrier between them.

Had she known nothing of the gender differences I discuss, she would simply have felt hurt and dismissed this man as yet another clunker. She would have concluded that, having enjoyed the night with her, he was now availing himself of her further services as a short-order cook. Instead, she realized that, unlike her, he did not feel the need for talk to reinforce their intimacy. The companionability of her presence was all he needed, and that did not mean that he didn't cherish her presence. By the same token, had he understood the essential role played by talk in women's definition of intimacy, he could have put off reading the paper—and avoided putting her off.

THE COMFORT OF HOME

For everyone, home is a place to be offstage. But the comfort of home can have opposite and incompatible meanings for women and men. For many men, the comfort of home means freedom from having to prove themselves and impress through verbal display. At last, they are in a situation where talk is not required. They are free to remain silent. But for women, home is a place where they are free to talk, and where they feel the greatest need for talk, with those they are closest to. For them, the comfort of home means the freedom to talk without worrying about how their talk will be judged.

This view emerged in a study by linguist Alice Greenwood of the conversations that took place among her three preadolescent children and their friends. Her daughters and son gave different reasons for their preferences in dinner guests. Her daughter Stacy said she would not want to invite people she didn't know well because then she would have to be "polite and quiet" and put on good manners. Greenwood's other daughter, Denise, said she liked to have her friend Meryl over because she could act crazy with Meryl and didn't have to worry about her manners, as she would with certain other friends who "would go around talking to people probably." But Denise's twin brother, Dennis, said nothing about having to watch his manners or worry about how others would judge his behavior. He simply said that he liked to have over friends with whom he could joke and laugh a lot. The girls' comments show that for them being close means being able to talk freely. And being with relative strangers means having to watch what they say and do. This insight holds a clue to the riddle of who talks more, women or men.

PUBLIC SPEAKING: THE TALKATIVE MAN
AND THE SILENT WOMAN

So far I have been discussing the private scenes in which many men are silent and many women are talkative. But there are other scenes in which the roles are reversed. Returning to Rebecca and Stuart, we saw that when they are home alone, Rebecca's thoughts find their way into words effortlessly, whereas Stuart finds he can't come up with anything to say. The reverse happens when they are in other situations. For example, at a meeting of the neighborhood council or the parents' association at their children's school, it is Stuart who stands up and speaks. In that situation, it is Rebecca who is silent, her tongue tied by an acute awareness of all the negative reactions people could have to what she might say, all the mistakes she might make in trying to express her ideas. If she musters her courage and prepares to say something, she needs time to formulate it and then waits to be recognized by the chair. She cannot just jump up and start talking the way Stuart and some other men can.

Eleanor Smeal, president of the Fund for the Feminist Majority, was a guest on a call-in radio talk show, discussing abortion. No subject could be of more direct concern to women, yet during the hour-long show, all the callers except two were men. Diane Rehm, host of a radio talk show, expresses puzzlement that although the audience for her show is evenly split between women and men, 90 percent of the callers to the show are men. I am convinced that the reason is not that women are uninterested in the subjects discussed on the show. I would wager that women listeners are bringing up the subjects they heard on *The Diane Rehm Show* to their friends and family over lunch, tea, and dinner. But fewer of them call in because to do so would be putting themselves on display, claiming public attention for what they have to say, catapulting themselves onto center stage.

I myself have been the guest on innumerable radio and television talk shows. Perhaps I am unusual in being completely at ease in this mode of display. But perhaps I am not unusual at all, because, although I am comfortable in the role of invited expert, I have never called in to a talk show I was listening to, although I have often had ideas to contribute. When I am the guest, my position of authority is granted before I begin to speak. Were I to call in, I would be claiming that right on my own. I would have to establish my credibility by explaining who I am, which might seem self-aggrandizing, or not explain who I am and risk having my comments ignored or not valued. For similar reasons, though I am comfortable lecturing to groups numbering in the thousands, I rarely ask questions following another lecturer's talk, unless I know both the subject and the group very well.

My own experience and that of talk show hosts seems to hold a clue to the difference in women's and men's attitudes toward talk: Many men are more comfortable than most women in using talk to claim attention. And this difference lies at the heart of the distinction between report-talk and rapport-talk.

REPORT-TALK IN PRIVATE

Report-talk, or what I am calling public speaking, does not arise only in the literally public situation of formal speeches delivered to a listening audience. The more people there are in a conversation, the less well you know them, and the more status differences among them, the more a conversation is *like* public speaking or report-talk. The fewer the people, the more intimately you know them, and the more equal their status, the more it is like private speaking or rapport-talk. Furthermore, women feel a situation is more "public"—in the sense that they have to be on good behavior—if there are men present, except perhaps for family members. Yet even in families, the mother and children may feel their home to be "backstage" when Father is not home, "onstage" when he is: Many children are instructed to be on good behavior when Daddy is home. This may be because he is not home often, or because Mother—or Father—doesn't want the children to disturb him when he is.

The difference between public and private speaking also explains the stereotype that women don't tell jokes. Although some women are great raconteurs who can keep a group spellbound by recounting jokes and funny stories, there are fewer such personalities among women than among men. Many women who do tell jokes to large groups of people come from ethnic backgrounds in which verbal performance is highly valued. For example, many of the great women stand-up comics, such as Fanny Brice and Joan Rivers, came from Jewish backgrounds.

Although it's not true that women don't tell jokes, it is true that many women are less likely than men to tell jokes in large groups, especially groups including men. So it's not surprising that men get the impression that women never tell jokes at all. Folklorist Carol Mitchell studied joke telling on a college campus. She found that men told most of their jokes to other men, but they also told many jokes to mixed groups and to women. Women, however, told most of their jokes to other women, fewer to men, and very few to groups that included men as well as women. Men preferred and were more likely to tell jokes when they had an audience: at least two, often four or more. Women preferred a small audience of one or two, rarely more than three. Unlike men, they were reluctant to tell jokes in front of people they didn't know well. Many women flatly refused to tell jokes they knew if there were four or more in the group, promising to tell them later in private. Men never refused the invitation to tell jokes.

All of Mitchell's results fit in with the picture I have been drawing of public and private speaking. In a situation in which there are more people in the audience, more men, or more strangers, joke telling, like any other form of verbal performance, requires speakers to claim center stage and prove their abilities. These are the situations in which many women are reluctant to talk. In a situation that is more private, because the audience is small, familiar, and perceived to be members of a community (for example, other women), they are more likely to talk.

The idea that telling jokes is a kind of self-display does not imply that it is selfish or self-centered. The situation of joke telling illustrates that status and connection entail each other. Entertaining others is a way of establishing connections with them, and telling jokes can be a kind of gift giving, where the joke is a gift that brings pleasure to receivers. The key issue is asymmetry: One person is the teller and the others are the audience. If these roles are later exchanged—for example, if the joke telling becomes a round in which one person after another takes the role of teller—then there is symmetry on the broad scale, if not in the individual act. However, if women habitually take the role of appreciative audience and never take the role of joke teller, the asymmetry of the individual joke telling is diffused through the larger inter-action as well. This is a hazard for women. A hazard for men is that continu-ally telling jokes can be distancing. This is the effect felt by a man who com-plained that when he talks to his father on the phone, all his father does is tell him jokes. An extreme instance of a similar phenomenon is the class clown, who, according to teachers, is nearly always a boy.

RAPPORT-TALK IN PUBLIC

Just as conversations that take place at home among friends can be like pub-lic speaking, even a public address can be like private speaking: for example, by giving a lecture full of personal examples and stories.

At the executive committee of a fledgling professional organization, the outgoing president, Fran, suggested that the organization adopt the policy of having presidents deliver a presidential address. To explain and support her proposal, she told a personal anecdote: Her cousin was the president of a more established professional organization at the time that Fran held the same position in this one. Fran's mother had been talking to her cousin's mother on the telephone. Her cousin's mother told Fran's mother that her daughter was preparing her presidential address, and she asked when Fran's presidential address was scheduled to be. Fran was embarrassed to admit to her mother that she was not giving one. This made her wonder whether the organization's professional identity might not be enhanced if it emulated the more established organizations.

Several men on the committee were embarrassed by Fran's reference to her personal situation and were not convinced by her argument. It seemed to them not only irrelevant but unseemly to talk about her mother's telephone conversations at an executive committee meeting. Fran had approached the meeting—a relatively public context—as an extension of the private kind. Many women's tendency to use personal experience and examples, rather than abstract argumentation, can be understood from the perspective of their orientation to language as it is used in private speaking.

A study by Celia Roberts and Tom Jupp of a faculty meeting at a second-ary school in England found that the women's arguments did not carry weight with their male colleagues because they tended to use their own expe-rience as evidence, or argue about the effect of policy on individual students. The men at the meeting argued from a completely different perspective, mak-ing categorical statements about right and wrong.

The same distinction is found in discussions at home. A man told me that he felt critical of what he perceived as his wife's lack of logic. For example, he recalled a conversation in which he had mentioned an article he had read in *The New York Times* claiming that today's college students are not as idealistic as students were in the 1960s. He was inclined to accept this claim. His wife questioned it, supporting her argument with the observation that her niece and her niece's friends were very idealistic indeed. He was incredulous and scornful of her faulty reasoning; it was obvious to him that a single personal example is neither evidence nor argumentation—it's just anecdote. It did not occur to him that he was dealing with a different logical system, rather than a lack of logic.

The logic this woman was employing was making sense of the world as a more private endeavor—observing and integrating her personal experience and drawing connections to the experiences of others. The logic the husband took for granted was a more public endeavor—more like gathering information, conducting a survey, or devising arguments by rules of formal logic as one might in doing research.

Another man complained about what he and his friends call women's "shifting sands" approach to discussion. These men feel that whereas they try to pursue an argument logically, step by step, until it is settled, women continually change course in midstream. He pointed to the short excerpt from *Divorce American Style* quoted above as a case in point. It seemed to him that when Debbie Reynolds said, "I can't argue now. I have to take the French bread out of the oven," she was evading the argument because she had made an accusation—"All you do is criticize" that she could not support.

This man also offered an example from his own experience. His girlfriend had told him of a problem she had because her boss wanted her to do one thing and she wanted to do another. Taking the boss's view for the sake of argumentation, he pointed out a negative consequence that would result if she did what she wanted. She countered that the same negative consequence would result if she did what the boss wanted. He complained that she was shifting over to the other field of battle—what would happen if she followed her boss's will—before they had made headway with the first—what would happen if she followed her own.

SPEAKING FOR THE TEAM

A final puzzle on the matter of public and private speaking is suggested by the experience I related at the opening of this chapter, in which a woman's group I addressed had invited men to participate, and a talkative man had referred to his silent wife as "the talker in our family." Following their laughter, other women in the group commented that this woman was not usually silent. When their meetings consisted of women only, she did her share of talking. Why, then, was she silent on this occasion?

One possibility is that my presence transformed the private-speaking group into a public-speaking event. Another transformation was that there were men in the group. In a sense, most women feel they are "backstage" when there are no men around. When men are present women are "onstage," insofar as they feel they must watch their behavior more. Another possibility is that it was not the presence of men in general that affected this woman's behavior, but the presence of *her husband*. One interpretation is that she was somehow cowed, or silenced, by her husband's presence. But another is that she felt they were a team. Since he was talking a lot, the team would be taking up too much time if she spoke too. She also may have felt that because he was representing their team, she didn't have to, much as many women let their husbands drive if they are in the car, but do the driving themselves if their husbands are not there.

Obviously, not every woman becomes silent when her husband joins a group; after all, there were many women in the group who talked a lot, and many had brought spouses. But several other couples told me of similar experiences. For example, when one couple took evening classes together, he was always an active participant in class discussion, while she said very little. But one semester they had decided to take different classes, and then she found that she was a talkative member of the class she attended alone.

Such a development can be viewed in two different ways. If talking in a group is a good thing—a privilege and a pleasure—then the silent woman will be seen as deprived of her right to speak, deprived of her voice. But the pleasures of report-talk are not universally admired. There are many who do not wish to speak in a group. In this view, a woman who feels she has no need to speak because her husband is doing it for her might feel privileged, just as a woman who does not like to drive might feel lucky that she doesn't have to when her husband is there—and a man who does not like to drive might feel unlucky that he has to, like it or not.

AVOIDING MUTUAL BLAME

The difference between public and private speaking, or report-talk and rapport-talk, can be understood in terms of status and connection. It is not surprising that women are most comfortable talking when they feel safe and close, among friends and equals whereas men feel comfortable talking when there is a need to establish and maintain their status in a group. But the situation is complex, because status and connection are bought with the same currency. What seems like a bid for status could be intended as a display of closeness, and what seems like distancing may have been intended to avoid the appearance of pulling rank. Hurtful and unjustified misinterpretations can be avoided by understanding the conversational styles of the other gender.

When men do all the talking at meetings, many women—including researchers—see them as "dominating" the meeting, intentionally preventing women from participating, publicly flexing their higher-status muscles. But the *result* that men do most of the talking does not necessarily mean that men *intend* to prevent women from speaking. Those who readily speak up assume that others are as free as they are to take the floor. In this sense, men's speaking out freely can be seen as evidence that they assume women are at the same level of status: "We are all equals," the metamessage of their behavior could be, "competing for the floor." If this is indeed the intention (and I believe it often, though not always, is), a woman can recognize women's lack of participation at meetings and take measures to redress the imbalance, without blaming men for intentionally locking them out.

The culprit, then, is not an individual man or even men's styles alone, but the difference between women's and men's styles. If that is the case, then both can make adjustments. A woman can push herself to speak up without being invited, or begin to speak without waiting for what seems a polite pause. But the adjustment should not be one-sided. A man can learn that a woman who is not accustomed to speaking up in groups is *not* as free as he is to do so. Someone who is waiting for a nice long pause before asking her question does not find the stage set for her appearance, as do those who are not awaiting a pause, the moment after (or before) another speaker stops talking. Someone who expects to be invited to speak ("You haven't said much, Millie. What do you think?") is not accustomed to leaping in and claiming the floor for herself. As in so many areas, being admitted as an equal is not in itself assurance of equal opportunity, if one is not accustomed to playing the game in the way it is being played. Being admitted to a dance does not ensure the participation of someone who has learned to dance to a different rhythm.

CHAPTER 20

Communication and Conflict

Evelyn Eaton Whitehead
James D. Whitehead

❧

Enriching this section on communication, conflict, and change is the following essay by Evelyn and James Whitehead. Like so many of the other writers in this section, they situate conflict within the context of intimacy. In other words, conflict can be a means for greater intimacy—or, if handled poorly, for greater distance and alienation. The Whiteheads state clearly that any couple "can get better at being married" by getting better at the skills of intimacy. One of these is skill with confrontation and conflict.

This essay may well be a classic for its helpful way of explaining conflict's connection with communication and intimacy. It deserves careful study.

Questions for Discussion

1. What are the skills of intimacy and which of them seems to you most crucial?
2. Why is premature judgment so dangerous in confrontation?
3. How common is it for people to grow up "assuming love does away with conflict, that love and conflict are mutually exclusive"?
4. Do you think most people accept that "conflict is a normal, expectable ingredient in any relationship," including marriage?

In marriage we see intimacy in both its most inviting and its most challenging face. Our daily patterns of life—living together, working together, sleeping together—these are the substance of intimacy. Here we feel ourselves being tested and getting better at being "up close." To live well these "up close" patterns of marriage we need the resources of psychological maturity: a sense of who I am, an openness to others, a capacity for commitment, some tolerance for the ambiguity both in myself and in other people. But these resources may not be enough. Aptitudes for intimacy must be expressed in behavior. We must be able, in the give-and-take of our life together, to develop a lifestyle that is mutually satisfying. Our desire to be close must be expressed in the way we act toward one another. It is encouraging to know that we can get better at being married. We can learn more satisfying ways *for us* to be close; we can learn more effective ways to give and receive the gift of ourselves that is at the core of our married love. And among the most valuable resources for this growth in marriage are the skills of intimate living.

THE SKILLS OF INTIMACY

Over the past two decades there has been much interest in psychology and other disciplines in understanding better what happens in communication between people. As a result we are more clearly aware today of both what helps and what frustrates understanding in close relationships. Values and attitudes are important in our ability to live up close to others, but so, especially, is our behavior. There are skillful—that is, effective—ways to be with and behave toward one another. Interpersonal skills that are especially important to the intimate life of marriage include empathy, self-disclosure and confrontation. Each involves both attitudes and behaviors; each can contribute significantly to marriage for a lifetime.

Empathy enables me to understand another person from within that person's frame of reference. Empathy begins in an attitude of openness which enables me to set aside my own concerns and turn myself toward you. But this basic openness is not always sufficient. My capacity for empathy can be enhanced by my developing a range of behavioral skills. An accepting posture, attentive listening, sensitive paraphrasing—each of these can contribute to my effective presence to you.

My posture can give you important information about who you are to me and how important I judge your communication to be. If I appear distracted or edgy, if I keep glancing at my watch or rush to take an incoming phone call, I am likely to let you feel that you are not very important to me now. In the midst of the hectic schedules of most married couples today, it is often necessary to take steps to ensure the postures of presence: taking the time to sit down together to talk, finding ways to give each other some undivided attention, learning when to hold a personal concern until later and when to "stop everything" in order to deal with an issue now.

Learning to listen well to each other can be the most important skill of our marriage. To listen well is to listen actively, alert to the full context of the message—the words and silences, the emotions and ideas, the context in which our conversation takes place. To listen is to pay attention: paying attention is a receptive, but not a passive, attitude. If I cannot pay attention, it will be difficult for me to hear; if I do not listen, it will be difficult for me to understand and to respond effectively to you. The skills of active listening are those behaviors which enable me to be aware of your full message. This includes my being alert to your words and their nuances. But equally and often even more important are the non-verbal factors involved. Your tone of voice, your gestures, the timing, the emotional content—these may tell me more than the words between us. To listen actively, then, calls for an awareness of the content, the feelings and the context of our communication.

Sensitive paraphrasing is a skill of empathy as well. I show you that I understand you by saying back to you the essence of your message. To paraphrase is not merely to "parrot"—to repeat mechanically what you have just said. Rather I want to show you that I have really heard *you*, that I have been present not just to your words but to their deeper meaning for you. I go beyond the simple assurance that "I understand" by offering you a statement of what I have understood. You can then confirm that, in fact, I have understood you—or clarify your message so that my understanding may be more accurate. In either case, I demonstrate my respect for you and for your message. It is important to me that I understand what you say, and it is to you that I come to check my understanding.

Empathy, then, is my ability to understand your ideas, feelings and values from within your frame of reference. The goal of empathy is to understand; as such, it precedes evaluation. Empathy does not mean that I will always agree with you; it does not require that I accept your point of view as my own or even as "best" for you. I may well have to evaluate your ideas. We may well have to discuss and negotiate as we move toward a decision we can share. But these movements of evaluation and judgment come later in our communication. My first goal is to accurately understand you and what you are trying to say to me. Judgment and decision are not secondary in our communication but they are subsequent to accurate understanding.

Empathy is the practical ability to be present to another person. Its exercise is a discipline: if I am distracted by fatigue or agitated by fear I cannot be present to my spouse. As virtuous behavior, empathy depends on a (relatively) strong sense of my identity and vocation. I do not have to defend myself: being aware of and comfortable with who I am, I can give my full attention to another person. Empathy thus is the stuff of intimacy. Without some skill, some virtue here, it will be difficult for me to express my love for my partner. Finally, to speak of empathy as both a skill and a virtue is to remind us again that we can get better at it. A Christian spirituality or asceticism of marriage will include these efforts to learn to be more effectively present to those we most love.

The open stance of empathy does much to enhance communication in marriage. But communication involves more than receptivity. I must be able to speak as well as to listen; to initiate as well as to understand. Self-disclosure thus becomes an essential skill of intimacy. To share myself with you I must be able to overcome the hesitancy suggested by fear or doubt or shame. But these inhibitions overcome, I must be able to act in a way that gives you access to my mind and heart, in a way that is fitting for me and for our relationship. Appropriate self-disclosure can seem complicated. But I am not limited to my current level of success. I can become more skillful, learning better ways to express my values and needs, my ideas and feelings.

Self-disclosure begins in self-awareness. I must *know* what I have experienced, what I think, how I feel, what I need, what I want to do. This knowledge is not likely to be full and finished; an unwillingness to speak until I am completely sure of myself can be a trap in communication. Self-awareness is rather an ability to know where I am now, to be in touch with the dense and ambiguous information of my own life. Beyond knowing my own insights, needs and purposes, I must value them. This need not mean that I am convinced that they are "the best." It means rather that I take them seriously as deserving of examination and respect, from myself and from others as well. My feelings, my perceptions of myself and of the world—these have worth and weight. By valuing them myself I contribute to the possibility that they can be appreciated by others as well. My needs and purposes exist in a context of those of other people, to be sure. But a conviction that my own ideas and goals are of value is basic to mature self-disclosure.

An important skill of self-disclosure is my ability to speak concretely. I must be able to say "I," to acknowledge my own ideas and feelings. Self-disclosure can be thwarted by a retreat into speaking about "most people"; "everybody knows . . ." instead of "I think that . . ."; "most people want . . ." instead of "I need . . ."; "people have a hard time . . ." instead of "it is difficult for me to . . ." Beyond this willingness to "own" my experience, I can learn to provide more specific details about my actions and emotions. To share myself with you in our marriage I will need, for example, a well-nuanced vocabulary of feelings—one that goes well beyond "I feel good" and "I feel bad." To tell you that "I feel good" is to share some important information about myself but not yet very much. What does this mean for me? Is this good feeling one of confidence? or affection? or physical vigor? Does it result from something I have done or something that has been done for me? Are you an important part of this good feeling for me or are you really incidental to it? My self-disclosure becomes more concrete when I can name my feelings more precisely and when I can describe the events and actions that are part of them for me.

Confrontation, too, makes a critical contribution to intimacy in marriage. For most of us the word "confrontation" implies conflict. And, as we shall see shortly, the ability to deal well with conflict between us is an important skill of marriage. But we use the word "confrontation" here in a meaning that goes beyond its narrow and, most often, negative connotation as interpersonal conflict. The ability to confront involves the psychological strength to give (and to receive) emotionally significant information in ways that lead to further exploration rather than to self-defense. Sometimes the emotionally significant information is more positive than negative. To say "I love you" is to share with you emotionally significant information. And many of us know how confrontive it is to learn of another's love for us. Similarly, to give a compliment is to share emotionally significant information, and there are people who defend themselves against this "good news" as strongly as others of us defend ourselves against an accusation of blame. But most often, to be sure, when confrontation becomes necessary and difficult in our marriage, it is because there is negative information we must share with our spouse. It may be some practical issue of daily life that we must face—the use of the automobile, our bank balance, plans for next summer's vacation. The issues, however, may be more sensitive—the way you discipline the children, my parents' influence in our home, how satisfying is our sex life.

Skills of confrontation are those behaviors that make it more likely that our sharing of significant negative information in these instances will lead us to explore the difficulty between us rather than to defend ourselves against one another. My ability to confront effectively is enhanced when I am able to speak descriptively rather than judgmentally. To tell you that I missed my meeting because you came home late is to *describe*; to call you a selfish and inconsiderate person is to *judge*. While both may be hard for you to hear from me, one is more likely to escalate into a quarrel than is the other. As we have noted before, judgment is not irrelevant in marriage, but premature judgment is likely to short-circuit the process of exploration and mutual understanding. Perhaps there are extenuating circumstances that caused you to be late; perhaps you are genuinely sorry that you inconvenienced me and want to do something to make amends. My attack on your selfishness is not likely to leave room for this kind of response on your side. It is more likely to lead you to defend yourself against my accusation, perhaps by calling up instances of my own selfishness, perhaps by leaving the scene altogether. In neither case has communication between us been furthered.

There are other behaviors that make our confrontation more effective, that is, more likely to further communication between us. These include the ability to accept feelings of anger in myself and in you and the ability to show respect for you even as I must disagree with you or challenge your position. These skills become especially important in dealing with conflict in marriage.

CONFLICT AND LOVE

Conflict is an aspect of Christian marriage about which our rhetoric can be misleading. In ceremonies and sermons about marriage, it is upon images of unity and peace and joy that we dwell. These images of life together in Christian marriage are important and true, but partial. When, as a believing community, we do not speak concretely to the more ambiguous experiences in marriage—experiences of anger, frustration, misunderstanding—we can leave many married people feeling that their marriages are somehow deficient.

Conflict and hostility are not goals of marriage, to be sure. But neither are they an indication that our marriage is "on the rocks." Conflict is a normal, expectable ingredient in any relationship—whether marriage, teamwork or friendship—that brings people "up close" and engages them at the level of their significant values and needs. The challenge in close relationships is not to do away with all signs of conflict or, worse, to refuse to admit that conflicts arise between us. Rather we can learn ways to recognize the potential areas of conflict *for us* and to deal with these issues and feelings in ways that strengthen rather than destroy the bonds between us.

Conflict is normal in interpersonal exchange; it is an expectable event in the intimate lifestyle of marriage. Whenever people come together in an ongoing way, especially if significant issues are involved, we can expect that they will become aware of differences that exist between them. Sometimes these differences will be simply noted as interesting. But often they will involve disagreements, misunderstanding and discord. It is here that the experience of conflict begins.

Marriage engages each of us at a level of our most significant values and needs. My sense of who I am, my convictions, my ideas and ideals, what I hope to make of my life—in our marriage all these are open to confirmation or to challenge and change. In addition, every marriage is a complex pattern of interaction and expectation. We develop our own way of being together and apart; we come to our own understanding of what each of us gives and receives in this relationship. The process through which we develop the patterns of our own marriage is ongoing. We can expect times of relative stability when the rhythms of our life together seem to fit especially well. We can also expect periods marked by significant adjustment and change. The process of marriage includes this continuing exploration, even trial and error, as we attempt to learn more about ourselves and our partner. It is these normal and even inevitable experiences of personal challenge and mutual change in marriage that set the stage for conflict.

Conflict is a response to discrepancy or disparity. "Things are not as I expected or as I want them to be." In interpersonal conflict the other person is seen as somehow involved in, or responsible for, this discrepancy. "You are not as I expected; it is your fault that things are not as I want them to be." Marriage brings us together in so many ways, as friends and lovers as parents and householders, in cooperation and competition, in practical decisions about our money and our time. These overlapping issues give us many opportunities both to meet and to fail each other's expectations. Thus discrepancy and conflict are predictable.

This predictability of conflict in marriage is not simply a cause for concern. Conflict is not "all bad." Its effects in intimacy are not simply or necessarily destructive. As many marriage counselors know, conflict is as often a sign of health in a relationship as it is a symptom of disease. The presence of conflict between us indicates that we are about something that is of value to us both. Conflict thus marks a relationship of some force. This energy can be harnessed; it need not always work against us. A marriage in which there is nothing important enough to fight about is more likely to die than one in which arguments occur. Indifference is a greater enemy of intimacy than is conflict.

Many of us have grown up assuming that love does away with conflict, that love and conflict are mutually exclusive. But this romantic view of love is challenged by our experience of tension in our own marriage. We come to know conflict as a powerful dynamic in our relationship and one with ambiguous effect. For most of us, it is the negative effects of conflict that we know best and fear. Conflict feels bad and seems to have bad results. To be in conflict seems like a move away from intimacy. I am angry or hurt, you feel rejected or resentful. And most often my own past experience reinforces the unpleasant conclusion that conflict leads to the disintegration of relationships. Sometimes the relationship ends immediately; sometimes it continues, but with a burden of bitterness and unhealed grievances that ultimately leads to its death. In the face of this negative sense of the power of conflict, the evidence that it is expectable and even inevitable in our marriage is likely to strike us with alarm.

CONFLICT CAN BE CONSTRUCTIVE

But these negative results of conflict do not give the full picture. Conflict can make a constructive contribution to our marriage. It can bring us to a more nuanced appreciation of who each of us is; it can test and strengthen the bonds that exist between us; it can deepen our capacity for mutual trust.

The experience of conflict points to an area of discrepancy between us. I am uncomfortable with the way you discipline our oldest child; you don't like me to let my new job interfere with our weekends together as a family; I no longer want to be "the perfect housewife and mother," though this is the way you have always seen me; you no longer want to be "the strong and self-sufficient male," though you know it frightens me to see your weakness.

If we are willing to face the conflict, we may be able to learn from the experience of discrepancy that is at its root. Exploring this discrepancy— between what I want from you and what you are able to give, or between who I am and who you need me to be, or between our differing views about money or privacy or sex or success—we can come to know one another more fully. We can grow toward a greater and more respectful mutuality, based on a greater awareness and respect for who each of us really is.

Conflict is not necessarily a part of every development in marriage. Some changes are accompanied more by a sense of fulfillment than frustration. Some couples are open to the processes of mutual exploration in such a way that there is little sense of discrepancy and little experience of conflict between them. But change is frequently a source of confusion and conflict, even if only temporarily. A relationship that cannot face at least the possibility of conflict will soon be in trouble. In order to ensure the conflict will not arise between us, we may decide that our relationship should touch us only minimally, in areas where we are not vitally concerned. Or we may believe that we must be willing to disown our response to the concerns that do matter to us. But to disown conflict does not strengthen a relationship. It tends instead to have us look away from part of the reality that exists between us. But the reality that is there—the troublesome concern that stands beneath the conflict—does not go away. The discrepancy remains, unattended, as a likely source of more serious trouble between us in the future.

We may know from previous experiences that conflict, faced poorly, can lead to resentment and recrimination. But not to face it does not ensure that our marriage will be free of these negative emotions. A more useful stance involves our willingness to face the conflicts that may arise between us, aware of their ambiguous power both to destroy and to deepen the love we share. This willingness to accept conflict as inevitable and even as potentially valuable need not mean that we find it pleasant to be at odds. But it does mean that we are willing to acknowledge and even tolerate this discomfort that conflict brings, in view of the valuable information it provides about our relationship and ourselves.

The experience of facing together the conflicts that arise between us can give greater confidence, an increased security in the strength and flexibility of the commitment between us, since we have it tested and found it sufficient to the test. Conflict can have this positive effect in a relationship but it remains a powerful and ambiguous dynamic. Just as the presence of conflict does not necessarily or automatically signal a relationship in trouble, neither does it necessarily or automatically result in new learning or growth. Whether the expectable event of conflict in our marriage will have positive or negative effect is due in large part to how we respond to it. To deal well with the ambiguous power of conflict we must first appreciate that conflict can be more than just negative between us. We must believe that the benefits of working through our conflict are worth the trouble and discomfort that attend. We must both have the resources of personal maturity that enable us to face strong emotion and to look at ourselves anew and possibly change. And we must have the skills that enable us to deal effectively with one another even in the heat of our disagreement.

CHAPTER 21

Communication

Thomas N. Hart and Kathleen Fischer Hart

⤫

Thomas and Kathleen Hart begin this essay on communication with a tale of conflict in Tony and Sue's marriage. Their conflicts are similar to those of many couples who are dating or even engaged.

Behind the Harts' eleven hints for communication lies an assumption that we can change our basic patterns of communicating if we are willing to try and if there are others to help us. One of the hardest lessons of life comes in realizing that nobody can force another person to change. You can encourage the person, but change can only come from the person him- or herself. This means that we ourselves have to face our own willingness to change so as to become a more trustworthy and loving gift to others.

The eleven techniques, or "hints," offered here need to be practiced. A person who wants to develop these as skills might ask a close friend to help. They could practice them together. This essay, like so many others in this book, is meant to be shared with those we love and with whom we are trying to improve communication.

Questions for Discussion

1. The authors stress that in marriage two people pledge to each other "the gift of the self," which "always involves the disclosure of feelings," including ones we may find difficult to communicate. This raises the question of whether the disclosure of feelings may be just as difficult before a marriage—say, during dating or engagement—as afterward. Which feelings would you say are most difficult to communicate in dating? Why are these particular feelings so difficult to express?

2. This essay offers eleven hints to help foster the art of communication in intimate relationships. If you were to pick a small number of these—say, five or fewer—that are more important than the others, what would they be and why do you pick them?

3. The Harts seek to make us much more aware of how we actually go about communicating to others. Considering that our patterns of communicating are learned as habits in childhood interaction with parents, what chances do you think we have of changing them? For example, how do you react to the common defense: "This is how I am; I can't change; you have to accept me as I am"?

When Tony and Sue came in for counseling, they had been married five years and had two children. But things were not going at all well. At a recent workshop for couples, the two of them had been asked to recall one or two of the peak experiences of their marriage, and Tony could not think of any. He wondered if he was just so angry that his recall of anything good was blocked. As we talked, the roots of the anger were gradually uncovered. Tony summed up the problem this way: "Sue never understands me, and so she always reacts in the wrong way. But you know, the reason she doesn't understand me is that I have never really let her know me." Sue chimed in and said: "Everything he said is true. What's worse, he doesn't understand me either. And that's my fault, because I've held back too. So you can imagine what our guessing-game interaction is like." They went on to say that it had been like this from the beginning.

This clear analysis of their problem, offered by the couple themselves, set the agenda for counseling. The task was to assist them to begin to talk to one another about what was going on deep inside, to open out their inner worlds to one another. The heart of that was to get them expressing how they felt about themselves, each other, and the myriad situations of their lives. Tony admitted that the reason he held himself in was that he did not like himself very much, and he found it much easier to remain crouched behind his wall sniping at Sue than to come out from behind it and let her see who he was. To do the latter would be to make himself vulnerable, to admit hurt, weakness, inadequacy, and need, and to put the truth in Sue's hands for her to deal with. That required a degree of courage he had long been unable to muster.

We talk in Christian terms of the gift of the self. In marriage, that is what two Christians pledge to one another. It is *the* great gift of love. Many married people stay with one another and serve each other in many ways. But this is not yet the gift of the *self*, which can only be given if one is willing to open one's heart to the other. One can do many external deeds of love and still hold back the really precious gift, the inner self. This gift can be given only through communication. It costs, like all of the better gifts. But union between two persons is hardly possible if they have not let each other into their inner worlds. This always involves the disclosure of feelings.

Some feelings are harder to communicate than others. Some people, for some reason, find it next to impossible to say "I love you." Many people, especially men, find it difficult to admit their fears, their sense of failure, or their sadness. Some find it hard to affirm others, to give positive feedback. Husbands stop telling their wives that they are beautiful, saying, "She already knows that," or "It would go to her head." We have yet to meet someone who does not need to be told the good things over and over (and even then still doubts it), or whose head is in much danger of an over-swell from too much affirmation. But there is another reason why people hold in their feelings in marriage. They care about their mates and do not want to hurt them. So they do not express dissatisfaction, irritation, or any other uncomfortable feelings.

What happens in an intimate relationship when unconfortable feelings are held in? Terrible outbursts from time to time, when feelings reach the breaking point. A note on the kitchen table announcing the divorce. Or, in milder forms, sarcasm, silence, and various forms of subtle punishment. One thing is certain. If people cannot deal with their anger, they cannot be intimate either. You either have a relationship in which there are angry exchanges at times and warm closeness at others (often shortly after the angry exchange), or you have a relationship in which all is smooth on the surface but the psychological distance is unbridged. In these latter relationships there are several forbidden subjects and an abundance of silence.

In intimate relationships, communication is the foundational skill. There is none more basic. It is the indispensable condition of union. It is the key to resolving conflict. It is the only way two people can continue growing together, or even living together.

The question is: How do you do it? It is an art, and it takes time to cultivate. The following are eleven hints to point the way.

1. *Use I-statements rather than You-statements.* Talk about yourself rather than your mate. Don't say things like, "*You* never care about anybody but yourself," or "*You* think you know everything all the time," or "*You* never do anything around here." Say instead, "*I* often feel lonely," or "Sometimes *I* feel put down by things you say," or "*I* feel overburdened with household chores and sometimes *I* resent it because it doesn't seem fair to me." Talk about yourself, in other words, and your feelings, in response to concrete behaviors for your mate. Do that instead of making judgments about your mate ("You're always flirting"; "You're so damn sure about everything") or giving commands ("Get out of here"; "Why don't you loosen up once in a while?").

The approach we are suggesting is risky because it exposes you. But it has many distinct advantages. It does not make your mate so defensive, and so it gives you a better chance of getting a hearing and an honest response. It lets your mate in on your inner world, and so reveals important information. It does not pronounce judgment about who is wrong, but leaves the question open. For instance, if I am bothered by the way you socialize at parties, it may indeed be your fault. But it could just as well be mine. Maybe I am very insecure, and cling too much, and am very easily threatened and jealous. Maybe I misinterpret what you are doing. If I find you overly emotional, it may be that you are. But it may also be that I am emotionally repressed and uncomfortable with the expression of feelings, or simply that I feel inadequate to meeting the needs you make known to me. When I stay with my own feelings, owning them and letting you know them, I let you know me and I leave the question open about who should do what. We can work on that together. "I feel uncomfortable around your dad" is not yet a comment about your dad, still less about you. So far, it is just an informative comment about me.

Talking about your mate is legitimate to this extent: As far as possible, tie your feeling statements to your mate's concrete *behaviors*. "When you come in without saying hello, I feel unloved." "I start to feel insecure when I see you having a good time with another man." You are talking here just about concrete *behaviors*, externally observable. You are not guessing at your mate's *feelings* or *intentions*, which are hidden from view.

There are four basic I-statements which carry most of the weight in an intimate relationship. They are: (1) I think, (2) I feel, (3) I want, and (4) I need. All of them are positive steps in self-assertion and indicate an underlying self-respect. All of them make me vulnerable to you. They do not state what is right, nor do they make a demand. They simply tell you who I am and what is going on with me right now. If you are willing to make a similar self-revelation, we have the materials for really learning to care for one another.

2. *Express feelings rather than thoughts.* Not that it is bad to express thoughts. There is plenty of scope for those too. But our feelings reveal more of who we are. One can sit for an entire course before many professors, and know a good deal of their thought and almost nothing of who they are. A wife expressed this eloquently once, saying that everything her husband said to her could be said on television. He was an engineer, and lived much more in the realm of thought than of feeling. He was not untalkative, but she was always left wondering what was going on inside. It is in expressing our feelings that we give the gift of the self. That was the gift she was still waiting for.

People sometimes hide their feelings behind their thoughts. "A woman's place is in the home" is an apparent statement of principle, but it may be a man's way of saying that he feels he has failed as a provider if his wife takes a job outside the home, or that he fears he will lose her if she has much occasion to be with other men. Those are feelings. "Should" statements can also be masks. "You should enjoy sex" is probably best translated "I enjoy sex," or "I feel inadequate as a lover when you don't seem to enjoy sex, or hurt when you turn me down." In more open communication, people just talk about their feelings, not about the eternal order of things (as they see it), or the commonsense truths embraced by all (but you). Most of our feelings, after all, come out of our cultural relativity.

Some people are not very aware of their feelings. You cannot communicate what you do not know. To develop a greater awareness of feelings, it is a helpful exercise to go inside yourself from time to time during the day, inquiring what you are feeling right now. Watch the variations in typical situations: talking with your child, talking with the boss, hearing the phone ring, approaching the front door at home, waking up in the morning, watching TV at night, going about your daily work, getting into bed at night. Move gradually from becoming more aware of feelings to becoming more expressive of them.

3. *Listen attentively without interrupting.* Good communication requires more than good talking. It demands good listening too. Listening is difficult. It requires setting other things aside, even the ruminations of the mind. It is

especially hard when we do not like what we are hearing, or when we think we have heard it all before. One of the things a marriage counselor does most frequently is stop married partners from interrupting each other, suggesting instead a three-step process which can revolutionize the way they talk to each other: (a) listen without interrupting; (b) say back what you heard, and check it out; (c) respond to it.

In poor communication, the listeners are working on their responses instead of listening, and cut in to make them as soon as they are ready. In the approach suggested here, you have to listen closely or you will not be able to say back what you heard. This is how you make sure you got the message. There are often surprises here, as the original speaker makes the necessary corrections. Then you can respond. This may seem cumbersome and time-consuming. But if you really get your mate's message, and respond to it rather than to something else, you end up saving time. And your mate has the gratifying feeling of being heard, even if you end up differing. If two people are in the habit of interrupting each other as they argue back and forth, the entire time is probably being wasted. Neither is listening. Neither is open. Nothing is being produced except more bad feeling.

4. *Check out what you see and hear.* Part of this is summarizing what you hear your mate saying and asking if that is the message. It keeps the conversation on track. But there are other parts to this checking out too. Listen for the feelings behind the words, and check those out. Listen for anger and frustration. Listen for loneliness. Listen for fear. And test what you think you hear, saying, for example, "You sound weary," or, "You sound as if this is really hard for you to tell me." This approach is especially useful with people who do not express feelings directly, but prefer to make statements of fact, pronounce judgments of good and bad, and give direct or indirect commands. You cannot get them to play by your rules. If you say, "Don't make judgments; tell me your feelings," you have given them a command instead of expressing your frustration and leaving them free. Even if they persist in their usual ways, you can listen for the feelings behind the words, and check those out.

Checking out can be useful outside of times of conversation. You come home, and seem tired, discouraged, or distant. But I am not sure. Mostly you are silent. If I want to relate to you appropriately—giving you space, encouraging you, or inviting you to unburden yourself—I have to know what you are feeling. I can ask the open question, "How are you doing?" Or I can check out my impressions: "You seem distant." Or, "You look as if you had a hard day."

Such an approach invites mates to express themselves. The ideal situation would be that they would volunteer this information, and ask for what they need. But the situation is not always ideal.

5. *Avoid mind-reading.* Mind-reading is the attempt to reach inside the sanctuary of the other person's psyche and declare what is going on there. You tell others what they are feeling or what their motives are. "You're say-

ing that because you're jealous." "You're just telling me what you think I want to hear." This kind of statement almost always gets an angry reaction. It deserves it. The statement is a violation of the other's privacy, and what is alleged is often inaccurate besides. We have *impressions* of other people's feelings, and *hunches* about their motives. It is legitimate to inquire. It is also all right to voice our impressions, if we do it tentatively, with recognition of our uncertainty. Mindreading is another matter. It is a violation of the person. It shows disrespect for that person's integrity, destroys trust, and invites retaliation.

6. *Make your needs known.* Sometimes those needs are general: "I need about half an hour's space when I get home from work before I can face any new challenges." "I need relief from child care at least one day a week." Sometimes they are particular: "I need a hug." "I need to get away some weekend soon."

A couple came for counseling. The problem they brought was that the husband was angry much of the time. What came to light was that he expected his wife to anticipate his needs and take care of them, and when she did not, he got angry. He expected her to know when he needed space, and not to talk to him then. He expected her to know when he needed affection, and to be affectionate then. When she guessed wrong and acted unsuitably, he was angry. This is an extreme form of a common fallacy: "If you really loved me, you would know what I am feeling and what I need." Not so. All of us are unfamiliar territory, often even to ourselves, certainly to others. Our only hope of getting our needs met is to be assertive in declaring them. They will not always get met, of course, because others have their needs too and some limitations in their ability to meet ours. But if needs are declared, they can at least be negotiated.

7. *Learn your mate's language of love.* All of us have a language in which we like to be told that we are loved. And one person's language differs from another's. What tells Randy that he is loved is a massage by Betty. But what tells Betty that she is loved is not a return massage by Randy, but just being held by him. What told your mother that your father was sorry was a single red rose, but what tells *your* wife you are sorry is not a rose at all but an apology and an explanation of what was going on inside you at the time of the incident. A woman might express her love by keeping a very clean house, but what would actually speak love to her husband would be her relaxing more with him.

There is usually a lot of love in the first two years of marriage, but sometimes it is spoken in your own language rather than your mate's, and so it does not have much impact. The trick is to learn your mate's language and to speak that. One very ironic situation of our acquaintance was that of a couple who differed in how they wanted to be treated when they were sick. She liked people to come into her room, freshen the air, bring her some orange juice, ask her how she was, and leave some flowers behind. He liked to be left completely alone so he could sleep. So when she was sick, he left her alone. And when he was sick, she visited him often and did all kinds of nice things for him. It took them a while to learn each other's language. It usually does. The Golden Rule here is "Do unto others as they would have you do unto them."

8. *Avoid the words "always" and "never."* This is an easy one to understand, but a hard one to do. "Always" and "never" are very tempting words, especially when you are angry. "You *never* listen." "You're *always* complaining." "You *never* want to do anything but watch TV." Because they are exaggerations, they provoke anger and invite a quick denial. And so the point is missed. Wouldn't "sometimes" be a better word than "always," more accurate and easier for the other person to hear? Then there is "often," and, when you really want to be emphatic, "usually." Never use "never."

9. *Avoid name-calling.* Names usually come into the game in the heat of anger. They hurt (which is why they are used). They stick. That is the problem. The fight ends, you make up, and things are supposed to be all right again. But your mate cannot forget that name you called her. Did you really mean that? If you didn't mean it, why did you say it? You have unwittingly planted a weed, and weeds are very hard to eradicate.

A couple once agreed in marriage counseling to just two contracts with one another. They would not read each other's minds and they would not call each other names. Seventy-five percent of their wrangling dropped away.

10. *Deal with painful situations as they arise.* Have you had the experience of setting off an angry tirade by some simple slip-up, like being five minutes late to pick up your mate? There has probably been some gunnysacking going on, and the sack has just burst. You take it over the head not just for the present offense but for several others stretching back over weeks and months. You didn't know your mate was carrying all this around. You can't even remember the incident they refer to.

If couples would be close, they must learn to deal with anger honestly and constructively. That means handling it by occasions, not allowing it to build. There is no point in trying not to hurt your mate with the bad news that you did not like something. You will harm your mate more in the long run if you hold these things back. You can soften the pain by telling the truth with love each time. That way you avoid the big outburst with white-hot anger, exaggerated statements, name-calling, and sometimes physical violence.

11. *Make time for talk that goes beyond practical problems.* Most couples manage to get the day-to-day problems solved. They communicate enough to get the bills paid, the food bought, the baby taken care of, the guests entertained, the car fixed. But many couples gradually neglect talking about themselves. The very thing that made the courting period such a deeply happy time, talking about you and about me and about us, gets pushed from the center to the periphery and sometimes dies out altogether. We make love less frequently, and I notice it, but I don't say anything. We do more things separately, and talk about them less. I go to work and muse a lot on the general drift of my life, but I keep these thoughts and feelings to myself. You go off to be with your parents. We keep solving the day-to-day problems, but we do

not talk about *ourselves*. And both of us notice in our interaction a growing distance and irritability.

Marriage Encounter has a simple idea to keep marriages going and growing. Each day the couple write each other a short letter, no more than ten minutes' worth, on some subject that draws out feelings. Some couples accomplish the same purpose in other ways. They keep an agreement to do something together one night a week, to be by themselves and talk about things that are important to each of them. It may be a dinner, or it may just be a walk. Other couples commit themselves to a weekend away every few months. These exercises in deliberate cultivation of the relationship are vital. Often all that is needed is to remove the obstacles, the challenges that ordinary living throws in the way of deeper communication. If we can free ourselves from these regularly, the deeper currents can keep flowing and joining. There is an amazing power of resurrection in marital relationships if they are not neglected too long. The coals may seem a little quiet at times, but don't call the fire out. Couples who make a little time and tend the embers see some amazing things happen. The habit of doing this needs to be formed in the first two years.

Communication is the foundational skill, and the key to all the rest of the elements that build a marriage. It is learned over time. Doing some reading about it, and attending marriage enrichment events that foster it, are very helpful in making it grow. It is actually possible for two people to be open and honest with each other, to entrust each other with nothing less than the gift of the whole self, and to become increasingly one instead of increasingly two. It takes courage, but it is one of the most satisfying experiences that life offers.

Anger Defused

Carol Tavris

Carol Tavris's research on anger offers helpful clues in understanding how anger can help or hinder our ability to communicate. As a way of communicating, anger can be important in any relationship, including intimate ones. While most people realize that anger is an important issue in interpersonal relationships, they tend to lack a way of thinking about anger and of directing their anger constructively, instead of destructively. Read the following pages carefully for some important insights on this often misunderstood emotion.

Questions for Discussion

1. What does Tavris mean by the ventilationist approach to anger, and what problem does she find in it?
2. What evidence does she offer to show that aggression inflames anger?
3. Why do you accept or reject the statement, "Talking out anger doesn't reduce it; it rehearses it"?
4. Tavris claims nothing she says makes the case for keeping quiet when you are angry. If not, then what is her main point?
5. Why does she advocate different rules on anger for women and men?
6. What is the reappraisal method of dealing with anger?

M y husband, my teenage stepson, and I were enjoying a lavish brunch with friends one August day, when a neighbor of the hosts dropped in to visit. She is a journalist, and when she heard that I was working on a study of anger her curiosity was whetted. I was reluctant to talk about it, which aroused her interest all the more.

"Is it about women and anger?" she asked.

"Not specifically," I said.

"Is it about work and anger?"

"Not entirely."

"Then is it a sociobiology of anger?"

"No," I said curtly, trying to discourage her.

"Is it political?"

"You could say so." But I was failing.

"Is it a clinical analysis of anger in intimate relationships?"

"NO!" shouted my stepson, slamming his hand on the table in mock fury. The woman visibly jumped, and then all of us laughed. The interrogation and my tension were over, and Matthew had demonstrated one of my major points. Anger has its uses.

The social perspective on anger, I believe, explains the persistence and variety of this emotion far better than reductionistic analyses of its biology or its inner psychological workings. Anger is not a disease, with a single cause; it is a process, a transaction, a way of communicating. With the possible exception of anger caused by organic abnormalities, most angry episodes are social events: They assume meaning only in terms of the social contract between participants.

This is a minority view in an era that celebrates medical and psychological models of the emotions. Research on the brain and hormones, after all, promises exciting possibilities for "cures" of emotional abnormalities, and of course many people are accustomed to hunting for the origins of their emotional conflicts within themselves, rummaging around in their psyches. It is not that I think that these approaches are entirely wrong; rather, they are insufficient. An emotion without social rules of containment and expression is like an egg without a shell: a gooey mess.

Our contemporary ideas about anger have been fed by the Anger Industry, psychotherapy, which too often is based on the belief that inside every tranquil soul a furious one is screaming to get out. Psychiatric theory refers to anger as if it were a fixed amount of energy that bounces through the system. If you pinch it in here, it is bound to pop out there—in bad dreams, neurosis, hysterical paralysis, hostile jokes, or stomachaches. Therapists are continually "uprooting" anger or "unearthing" it, as if it were a turnip. Canadian psychiatrist Hossain B. Danesh, for example, writes that his profession has "succeeded in unearthing" anger that is buried in psychosomatic disorders, depression, suicide, homicide, and family problems. Yale psychiatrist Albert Rothenberg is not so sure about this success:

> In depression we look for evidence of anger behind the saddened aspect; in hysteria we experience angry seductiveness; in homosexuality and sexual disorders we see angry dependency; in marital problems we unearth distorted patterns of communication, particularly involving anger. We interpret the presence of anger, we confront anger, we draw anger, we tranquilize anger, and we help the working through of anger. . . . We operate on the basis of a whole series of assumptions, none of which has been clearly spelled out.

ANGER-INS, ANGER-OUTS

One of the assumptions most prevalent in the anger business is that the physical or verbal ventilation of anger is basically healthy, and suppressed hostility medically dangerous. "There is a widespread belief that if a person can be allowed, or helped to express his feelings, he will in some way benefit from it," writes psychiatrist John R. Marshall.

> This conviction exists at all levels of psychological sophistication. Present in one or another form, it occupies a position of central importance in almost all psychotherapies. . . . The belief that to discharge one's feelings is beneficial is also prevalent among the general public. Friends are encouraged to "get if off their chests," helped to "blow off steam," or encouraged to "let it all hang out," Sports or strenuous physical activities are lauded as means of "working off" feelings, particularly hostility, and it is accepted that there is some value in hitting, throwing, or breaking something when frustrated.

But is there? It seems to me that the major effect of the ventilationist approach has been to raise the general noise level of our lives, not to lessen our problems. I notice that the people who are most prone to give vent to their rage get angrier, not less angry. I observe a lot of hurt feelings among the recipients of rage. And I can plot the stages in a typical "ventilating" marital argument: precipitating event, angry outburst, shouted recriminations, screaming or crying, the furious peak (sometimes accompanied by physical assault), exhaustion, sullen apology, or just sullenness. The cycle is replayed the next day or next week. What in this is "cathartic"? Screaming? Throwing a pot? Does either action cause the anger to vanish or the angry spouse to feel better? Not that I can see.

TRAINING MALE AND FEMALE RESPONSES

By looking at what happens, physically and psychologically, when people "let anger out," we can see that the ways that we express anger actually affect how we feel. The decision of whether or not to express anger rests on what you want to communicate and what you hope to accomplish, and these are not necessarily harmonious goals. You may want to use anger for retaliation and vengeance, or for improving a bad situation, or for restoring your rights. Your goals determine what you should do about anger. For example, consider the popular notions that aggression is the instinctive catharsis for anger and that talking anger out reduces it. Jack Hokanson, a social psychologist who is a veritable Sherlock Holmes of psychological sleuthing, has been tracking catharsis theories for the past 20 years, using clues from one experiment to pose questions for the next. In the early 1960s, for example, Hokanson found that aggression *was* cathartic: The blood pressure of angry students would return to normal more quickly when they could retaliate against the man who had angered them. But Hokanson noticed that this was true only when the man who had angered them was a fellow student; when he was a teacher, retaliation had no cathartic effect. Naturally. In those days, teachers were still regarded as legitimate authorities, and one did not snap back at them in a cavalier manner.

So, after a flurry of studies on the target of catharsis, the first modification of catharsis theory appeared: Aggression can be cathartic only against your peers and subordinates; it does not work when the target is your boss, another authority, or an innocent bystander. If the reservoir-of-energy model were correct, though, ventilating anger against anyone or anything would result in reduced tension. It does not.

Then Hokanson noticed something that most of his fellow psychologists were ignoring in the 1960s: women. They were not behaving like the men. When you insulted then, they didn't get belligerent, they generally said something friendly to try to calm you down. When Hokanson wired them up to a physiological monitor to see whether they were secretly seething in rage, he discovered that one man's meat was a woman's poison. For men, aggression was cathartic for anger; for women, *friendliness* was cathartic. For them, any aggression, even toward a classmate, was as arousing and upsetting as aggression toward authority was for the men.

This difference gave Hokanson the idea that aggressive catharsis is a learned reaction to anger, not an instinctive one. People find characteristic ways to try to handle obnoxious persons, he concluded. In the case of sex differences, what works has a lot to do with the requirements of one's role. When women react to attack or threat by smiling, being friendly, or making gestures of accommodation, they traditionally assuage the other person's anger (often, however, at the cost of their own rights); when they act angrily or aggressively, they typically provoke a critical reaction from others ("what a bitch"), which in turn increases their arousal and anxiety. The reverse is true for men: Aggression and anger typically bring respect and results, whereas friendly accommodation is a sign of "caving in" ("what a weakling").

But sex roles are not straitjackets, and Hokanson's next experiment was prescient of the women's movement.

Imagine that you are seated at a console, facing an array of impressive gizmos and gadgets. Your partner, a fellow student of your gender and age, is sitting at an identical console nearby. You will communicate by pressing one of two buttons marked "shock" and "reward." You are probably in a friendly mood—"Only an hour of this," you think, "and I'll be done with my psychology requirement"—when suddenly, ZOT! Your partner has sent you an unpleasant shock.

If you are male, you are instantly irritated. "What the hell did the SOB do *that* for?" you mutter. "I'll show him he can't do that to me." So you press your shock button to give him a taste of his own medicine. Relief surges through your veins, according to that damned machine you're hooked to.

If you are female, you are instantly puzzled. "I wonder why she did that?" you murmur. "Maybe she hit the wrong button. Maybe she got a bad grade on the intro exam. I'd better be kind." So you press your reward button, which awards her a point in whatever mysterious game the experimenters have up their sleeve. You feel so good about your forgiving response that relief surges through your veins, according to that interesting machine you're hooked up to.

This mechanical conversation between you and your partner goes on for 32 rounds, and half the time the partner responds to whatever you do with a shock and half the time with reward. (The shocks and rewards, of course, are really controlled by the experimenters.) If you are a man, you notice the shocks. "Why, the bastard," you say to yourself. "He persists in attacking me." If you are a woman, you notice the rewards. "She must be feeling better," you think. "She's not sending me as many shocks." In either case, your blood pressure is down and your spirits are up.

Little do you know that those 32 rounds are only to inform the experimenters about your typical reactions. Now you go 60 rounds with new rules. If you are a man, your partner will reward you every time you are friendly in response to his shock. If you are a woman, your partner will reward you every time you are aggressive in response to her shock. In short, a woman can stop being treated unfairly by being aggressive, and a man can shake the bully by being friendly.

Hokanson and his associates observed that two things happened as a result of this new situation. First, the women rapidly learned the value of being aggressive and so became aggressive in response to shock more frequently, whereas the men learned the value of a generous reaction to insult. Second, the traditional form of catharsis for each sex was reversed. Women showed catharsis-like reduction in blood pressure when they responded aggressively and had a slow vascular recovery when they were friendly. The opposite was the case for men: Catharsis now followed friendliness, not belligerence.

AGGRESSION ESCALATES ANGER

Some schools of therapy, such as Alexander Lowen's bioenergetics, recommend any form of aggressive anger release that comes to mind, or foot: shouting, biting, howling, kicking, or slapping (anything short of assault and battery). Such aggression is supposed to get us "in touch" with our feelings. But aggression frequently has precisely the opposite effect of catharsis: Instead of exorcising the anger, it can inflame it.

One of the first studies to quarrel with the Freudian ventilationist position was conducted by Seymour Feshbach in 1956. Feshbach gathered a group of little boys who were not aggressive or destructive and encouraged them to play with violent toys, kick the furniture and otherwise run amok during a series of freeplay hours. This freedom did not "drain" any of the boys' "instinctive aggression" or "pent-up anger"; what it did was lower their restraint against aggression. On later occasions, the boys behaved in much more hostile and destructive ways than they had previously.

When you permit children to play aggressively, they don't become less aggressive, as the catharsis theory would predict; they become more aggressive. Indeed, aggressive play has no cathartic value at all. In a study in which third-grade children were frustrated and irritated by another child (whom the experimenters had enlisted in their cause), the children were given one of three ways of "handling" their anger: Some were permitted to talk it out with the adult experimenters; some were allowed to play with guns for "cathartic release" or to "get even" with the frustrating child; and some were given a reasonable explanation from the adults for the child's annoying behavior. What reduced the children's anger? Not talking about it. Not playing with guns; that made them more hostile, and aggressive as well. The most successful way of dispelling their anger was to understand why their classmate had behaved as she did (she was sleepy, upset, not feeling well).

The same principles of anger and aggression apply to adults. Murray Straus, a sociologist in the field of family violence, finds that couples who yell at each other do not thereafter feel less angry but more angry. Verbal aggression and physical aggression were highly correlated in his studies, which means that it is a small step from bitter accusations to slaps. Leonard Berkowitz, who has studied the social causes of aggression for many years, likewise finds that ventilation by yelling has no effect on anger. "Telling someone we hate him supposedly will purge pent-up aggressive inclinations and will 'clear the air,'" he says. "Frequently, however, when we tell someone off, we stimulate ourselves to continued or even stronger aggression."

TALKING IT OUT REHEARSES ANGER

Like most people I know, I have always been a firm believer in the talk-it-out strategy. Talking things over makes you feel better. That's what friends are for. That's what bartenders are for. But that's not what the research shows. Talking out an emotion doesn't reduce it, it rehearses it.

Emotions are social constructions: The physiological arousal that we feel depends on cues from the environment to provide a label and a justification. Talking to friends is one way to find that label—to decide, for example, that you feel angry instead of hurt, or more sad than jealous. Sympathetic friends who agree with your self-diagnosis, or provide a diagnosis for you, are aiding that process of emotional definition.

The belief that talking it out is cathartic assumes that there is a single emotion to be released, but clinically you seldom find "pure" emotions. Most are combinations that reflect the complexity of the problem and of our lives: hurt and jealousy, rage and fear, sadness and desire, joy and guilt. Ventilating only one component of the mix, therefore, emphasizes it to the exclusion of the others. If you are upset with your spouse and you go off for a few drinks with a friend to mull the matter over, you may, in talking it out, decide that you are really furious after all. You aren't ventilating the anger; you're practicing it.

Three psychologists conducted a field experiment that showed just how this process works. Ebbe Ebbesen, Birt Duncan, and Vladimir Konecni were working in San Diego when the local aerospace-defense industry had to lay off many of its engineers and technicians. It was the right time to study anger. The employees were irate, and legitimately so, for they had been promised a three-year contract and the layoffs came after only one year. If this happened to you, at what or with whom would you be angry? Fate? The economy? The company? Your supervisor? Yourself?

The researchers seized this opportunity to interview 100 of the engineers who had been fired, comparing them with 48 who were voluntarily leaving the company at the same time. Birt Duncan conducted an exit interview with each man, during which he directed his questions—and the men's expressions of hostility—in one of three ways: toward the company (In what ways has the company not been fair with you? Are there aspects of the company you don't like?); toward the company supervisors (What action might your supervisor have taken to prevent you from being laid off? Are there things about your supervisor that you don't like?); or toward the man himself (Are there things about you that led your supervisor not to give you a higher performance review? What in your past performance might have been improved?). Some men in each group were asked neutral questions only, such as their opinion of the technical library.

Notice that Duncan was not telling the men what they *should* be angry about, but asking them what they *did* feel angry about. When the interview itself was over, he asked each man to fill out a report that included questions about what he now felt about the company, the supervisors, or himself. "Ventilation" of the anger during the interview did not act as a catharsis in any way. On the contrary, the men became more hostile toward the company or their supervisors if they had taken an angry public stance against them in conversation. And their anger increased only toward the target they had discussed, not the others. The men who were asked to criticize themselves, however, did not blame themselves more later—a result I was happy to see, since clearly the engineers' ability was not at issue in the layoffs, and the men knew it. But neither did the self-criticizers get as angry at the company or their supervisors as the men who outspokenly blamed these targets.

The simple act of pinpointing the cause of your anger makes you more likely to repeat the explanation, even at the risk of harmful consequences (in this case, not getting rehired). As you recite your grievances, your emotional arousal builds up again, making you feel as angry as you did when the infuriating event first happened, and, in addition, establishing an attitude about the source of your rage. Friends and therapists, of course, often do just what Birt Duncan did with the laid-off engineers: ask probing questions, innocent or intentional, that direct us to a particular explanation of our feelings ("In what ways was Sheila not fair to you?" "Could you have done something to keep Herb from leaving?").

LEARNING HOW TO THINK ABOUT ANGER

The psychological rationale for ventilating anger does not stand up under experimental scrutiny. The weight of the evidence indicates precisely the opposite: Expressing anger makes you angrier, solidifies an angry attitude, and establishes a hostile habit. If you keep quiet about momentary irritations and distract yourself with pleasant activity until your fury simmers down, chances are that you will feel better, and feel better faster, than if you let yourself go in a shouting match.

Now, none of this is to make a case for keeping quiet when you are angry, as some people seem to think whenever I talk about these research findings. The point is to understand what happens when you *do* decide to express anger, and to realize how our perceptions about the causes of anger can be affected just by talking about them and deciding on an interpretation. Each of us must find his or her own compromise among talking too much, expressing every little thing that irritates, and not talking at all, passively accepting injustices.

Silent sulking is a lousy and deadly weapon. Few people are magnanimous enough to never bear a grudge, nurse an indignity, or express their anger in devious ways—such as "forgetting" to do something they had promised to do, holding back sexually, or sulking irritably around the house. I argue, though, that these are not examples of "not talking"; they are examples of talking to yourself. You know that you feel angry, but in the guise of magnanimity or self-righteousness, or because you are afraid to announce your feelings, you pretend that everything is fine. Meanwhile, you are muttering imprecations to yourself and holding elaborate conversations in your head.

This is not going to reduce your feelings of anger either. The purpose of anger is to make a grievance known, and if the grievance is not confronted, it will not matter whether the anger is kept in, let out, or wrapped in red ribbons and dropped into the Erie Canal.

Of course, emotional release can feel awfully good. Telling off someone whom you believe has mistreated you is especially satisfying. Publishing the true story of how you were victimized by the bigwigs makes you feel vindicated. These cathartic experiences feel good not because they have emptied some physiological energy reservoir, but because they have accomplished a social goal: the redemption of justice, reinforcement of the social order. Further, some expressions of emotional release are morally and politically necessary. Bureaucracies, hospitals, and other large institutions have plenty of subtle and not-so-subtle ways to "cool out" the legitimate anger of mistreated customers and patients (by making them feel that they, the mistreated customers, are crazy, misguided, or stupid). People who sustain their anger under such circumstances often are taking a lonely but heroic course.

To know whether and how catharsis gets rid of anger, therefore, you have to know what you're angry about, and what the outside circumstances are. When you let out an emotion, it usually lands on somebody else, and how you feel—relieved, angrier, depressed—is going to depend on what the other person does. For example, the calm, nonaggressive reporting of your anger (those "I messages" that so many psychologists recommend) is the kindest, most civilized and usually most effective way to express anger, but even this mature method depends on its context.

Consider the predicament of Margie B., a 40-year-old mother of two, and a part-time decorator, who told me that, to her dismay, an abusive rage is the only way that she can convince her husband, a 32-year-old construction worker, that she is really angry. Calm discussion of her feelings, she said, may be the preferred middle-class way, but it gets her nowhere:

> The next day [after a furious argument], he ran around, and mowed the lawn, and cleaned the gutters, and washed the kitchen floor. And he said he was sorry he was so lazy. Then he said, "You'll never get me to do anything unless you get flat-out mad, like you did," which puts me in an awkward position because I hate getting angry.
>
> Usually our fights end in frustration all the way around and in a very empty feeling. For the next day or so I feel definitely terrible. I'm tempted to totally abase myself just to get rid of the feeling, the horrible emptiness. We don't make connection in our fights at all, and when they are over I feel so dead, so lonely.
>
> They say that expressing your anger is so good for you, so good for all concerned, but I don't think it has very good results at all. My therapist was always saying to me, "Well, can't you just say, in a calm but irate tone of voice, 'You know, it's driving me crazy that you're doing this'?" But I've never found that using that tone does any good, cuts any ice. Either people ignore you, or else you get a little *too* angry and they get angry back and you get in a fight that settles nothing.

There are no simple guidelines to determine when talking is better than yelling, because the choice depends as much on the receiver of the message as on the sender. Many of us know this intuitively, and tailor our communications to fit the purpose. A 42-year-old businessman, Jay S., described how his eyes were opened when he overheard his usually even-tempered boss on the phone one afternoon:

> I've never heard him so angry. He was enraged. His face was red and the veins were bulging on his neck. I tried to get his attention to calm him down, but he waved me away impatiently. As soon as the call was over, he turned to me and smiled. "There," he said. "That ought to do it." If I were the guy he'd been shouting at, let me tell you, it would have done it, too. But it was all put on.

The catharsis of anger, like its creation, depends on mind and body, if you want to "let go" of anger, you have to rearrange your thinking, not just lower your pulse rate. The most successful therapeutic methods for helping people who are quick to rage, therefore, take mind and body into consideration. Practitioners of yoga learn techniques to relax the heart rate and slow breathing, and they learn techniques to calm distracting, worrying, or infuriating thoughts. Western psychologists are catching on. For example, Ray Novaco, who teaches at the University of California at Irvine, works with people who have problems with chronic anger, teaching them two things: how to think about their anger, and how to reduce tension. Novaco reasons that anger is fomented, maintained, and inflamed by the statements we make to ourselves and others when we are provoked—"Who does he think he is to treat me like that?" "What a vile and thoughtless woman she is!"—so he teaches people how to control anger the same way, by showing them how to reinterpret a supposed provocation: "Maybe he's having a rough day"; "She must be very unhappy if she would do such a thing." (This is what people who are slow to anger do naturally: They empathize with the provoker's behavior and try to find justifications for it.) And then, because anger may have been an effective strategy for easily provoked people, they often have to learn new and gentler reactions that will bring them results as effectively as anger.

The reappraisal method is being used with people who are exposed to constant provocations as part of their jobs (or who believe that they are constantly provoked), such as police officers and bus drivers. New York City bus drivers, for example, may now see a film in which they learn that passengers who have irritating mannerisms may actually have hidden handicaps. Repeated questions ("Driver, is this 83d Street?") may indicate severe anxiety, which the passenger cannot control, apparent drunkenness may actually be cerebral palsy, mild epileptic seizures can make a passenger seem to be deliberately ignoring a driver's orders. "[The film] makes you feel funny about the way you've treated passengers in the past," says a bus driver from Queens. "Before I saw this film, if a passenger rang the bell five times, I'd take him five blocks to get even. Now I'll say, 'Maybe the person is sick.'"

There are, though, some events that cannot be reappraised. A gorgeous woman I know who has multiple sclerosis was asked to leave her elegant health club because she was, the manager said, not one of the "beautiful people," and beautiful people don't want to exercise with the disabled. (The extent of her disability at the time was a cane and brace, and, in fact, other women in the club were extremely helpful to her.) When she told me of this appalling experience, I found I had no desire to worry about the manager's personal life and woes to reduce my feeling of outrage.

But ventilating anger directly is cathartic only when it restores your sense of control, reducing both the rush of adrenaline that accompanies an unfamiliar and threatening situation and the belief that you are helpless or powerless. So the question is not "Should I ventilate anger?" or even "How should I ventilate anger?" but instead, "How should I behave in this situation to convince Harry that I'm angry—and get him to do something about it?"

A charming (if psychologically flawed) example of how to rethink a provocation to make yourself feel less angry comes from screenwriter Larry Gelbart. A friend of Gelbart's, who worked at a movie studio for a tyrannical employer, was irate because the boss had chewed him out for some insignificant matter once too often.

"I will not be treated like a worm," he raged to Gelbart. "I'm going to punch him out the next time he shouts at me like that. How dare he?"

"Hold on, hold on," Gelbart said, "I think I see the problem. You're not Jewish, are you?"

"What the hell has that got to do with anything?" his friend replied irritably. "We're talking about common courtesy, damn it."

"Listen," Gelbart said. "Relax. What any Jewish person would know is that he's not yelling at *you*, he's yelling for *himself*. Next time he shouts at you, this is what you do. You lean back in your chair, fold your arms, and let his screams wash over you. Tell yourself: 'Oy, such good it's doing him to get it out of his system!'"

The friend says that this advice works wonders. The mogul won't feel any better for yelling (in fact, as we now know, he's bound to feel worse), but Gelbart's friend will surely feel better for thinking that he does.

CHAPTER 23

Domestic Violence: The Long, Sad Silence

Gloria Durka

This chapter is the first of two essays on the topic of domestic violence. The topic has come to the fore in recent decades with the unmasking of its "ugly little secrets." Gloria Durka, professor of religion and religious education at Fordham University, sets the overall context for the discussion and links it to appropriate pastoral responses. Lenore Walker, in the following essay (chapter 24), separates myth from reality in the lives of battered women.

Durka's essay is a model of clarity and eminently practical. Various types of domestic violence are delineated—physical, sexual, psychological, and assaults against property and pets. Just as the victims come from all walks of life, so do the perpetrators.

The focus of Durka's study is violence against women. She lays out the causes and what can be done to break the cycle of violence. The causes spring from (1) personal and family traits, (2) religious and sociocultural factors, and (3) communal insensitivities. Durka then turns to spell out a moral and educational Christian response. Her recommendations are full of practical wisdom: (1) break the silence, (2) dispel the myths, and (3) take a systems approach to prevention and intervention.

All is not darkness and doom, she claims. There are rays of light on the horizon, some of them emerging in the most surprising places, namely, within our own religious traditions.

Questions for Discussion

1. Churches continue to play an ambivalent role regarding the abuse of women. Where do you see the teachings of churches serve (a) as a roadblock or (b) a resource in addressing domestic violence?

2. How would you deconstruct the myth: "Women bring domestic violence upon themselves"?

3. Imagine you were a member of a Pre-Cana team. How would you enable the engaged couples to examine their own family systems? Give examples.

4. How is patriarchy deeply entrenched behind sexual and domestic violence?

5. Where do you see signs of hope that the long, sad silence with regard to domestic violence is being broken in your community?

Have pity one me, O God, for I am in distress; with sorrow
my eye is consumed; my soul also, and my body. . . .
I am like a dish that is broken . . .
But my trust is in you, O God;
I say, "You are my God."

Psalm 31, 9–14

For Christian women who suffer from domestic violence, this passage is both a prayer and an image that embodies their predicament. It is a prayer and an image that presses us all for a response.

Domestic violence refers to a pattern of violent and coercive behavior exercised by one adult in an intimate relationship over another. It is *not* "marital conflict," "mutual abuse," "a lovers' quarrel," or "a private family matter." It may consist of repeated, severe beatings, or more subtle forms of abuse, including threats and control. There are four basic types of domestic violence:

- *Physical Assault*—this is understood as any act intended to inflict injury or that results in bodily harm. It includes shoving, pushing, restraining, hitting, or kicking. Physical assaults may occur frequently or infrequently, but in many cases they tend to escalate in severity and frequency over time.
- *Sexual Assault*—this occurs any time one partner forces sexual acts that are unwanted or declined by the other partner.
- *Psychological Assault*—this includes isolation from family and friends, forced financial dependence, verbal and emotional abuse, threats, intimidation, and control over where the partner can go and what she can do. Emotional and psychological abuse often inflicts the most long-lasting harm.
- *Attacks against Property and Pets*—this form of violence involves destruction of property which may include household objects or treasured objects belonging to the victim, hitting the walls, or abusing or killing beloved pets.

WHO ARE THE VICTIMS OF DOMESTIC VIOLENCE?

Statistics reflect that 95 percent of domestic violence victims are women, although men may also be victims (Center for the Prevention of Sexual and Domestic Violence, 1994). It cuts across all classes, religions, races, income groups, and geography. Its effect on the family unit and individuals involved is both devastating and lasting. Yet reliable statistics on different aspects of domestic violence are difficult to secure for several reasons:

- There is social stigma associated with reporting many aspects of domestic violence.
- If abuse is discovered, there is often an element of denial that surrounds the incidents.
- Many service organizations are small and isolated with no connections to research organizations.

But existing evidence suggests that domestic violence is widespread, even though perceptions about it are often based on myth rather than on reality. It is estimated that one out of six family units experience at least one violent episode per year. Despite controversy over definitions and research practices, most observers believe domestic violence in its various forms is a large and serious problem, pervasive yet still hidden from view in many ways. This essay focuses on one part of the grim fabric of domestic violence: violence against women.

During the past three decades, there has been significant progress made in increasing attention to the epidemic problem of domestic violence. Yet despite these advances, domestic violence against women remains as one of the most damaging problems facing contemporary U.S. society. Consider the following:

- In 1983, according to William French Smith, U.S. attorney general, battering was the single major cause of injury to women, exceeding rapes, muggings, and even auto accidents.
- In 1987, former U.S. Surgeon General C. Everett Koop identified domestic violence as the number one health problem for American women, causing more injuries than automobile accidents, muggings, and rapes combined.
- Thirty-one percent of all women killed in the United States are murdered by their husbands, ex-husbands, or boyfriends (National Criminal Justice Reference Service, 1989).
- Fifty percent of all homeless women and children are fleeing domestic violence (Legal Reform Efforts for Battered Women: Past, Present, and Future, July 1990).
- The rate of child abuse in homes where domestic violence occurs is 1,500% higher than the national average (Senate Judiciary Report on Violence against Women Act, 1990).

These staggering statistics raise several questions. For example, how can one recognize a victim of domestic violence? The answer is simple. Women who are being battered are as different from each other as nonbattered women. They come from all walks of life, all races, all educational backgrounds, and all religions. Anyone experiencing any of the patterns of abuse listed above is a victim of domestic violence. Another question is, why does she stay? She stays because she is terrified that the abuser will become more violent if she leaves, that he will try to take the children, and that she cannot make it on her own. Who are batterers? Just as with battered women, men who batter fall into no specific categories. They also come from all class backgrounds, races, religions, and walks of life. They may be unemployed or highly paid professionals. The batterer may be a good provider, a sober and upstanding member of the community, and a respected member of his church.

CAUSES OF DOMESTIC VIOLENCE

Understanding domestic violence requires scrutiny of both husband and wife, the relationships among members of the whole family, the larger society, and the overall cultural norms that permit or encourage violent behavior. A few causes quickly emerge.

PERSONAL AND FAMILY TRAITS

There are three common characteristics in families where spousal violence occurs: (1) high levels of stress, (2) high levels of verbal aggressiveness, and (3) the concentration of power in the hands of one person. Also, violence toward a spouse is more likely to occur within families that are isolated from larger supportive networks. Men who batter their wives are likely to come from homes in which their own parents were violent. They usually have low self-esteem and are frequently excessively jealous of their wives. Women who are battered also tend to come from battered households, and they too have low self-esteem.

RELIGIOUS AND SOCIOCULTURAL FACTORS

From the misogyny of church fathers such as Augustine, Jerome, and Tertullian to recent statements about the complementary role of women in the family, churches have continued to play an ambivalent role regarding the abuse of women, at times supporting wife-beating, and at other times suggesting moderation. In the fifteenth-century *Rules of Marriage*, Friar Cherubino gives the following advice:

> When you see your wife commit an offense . . . scold her sharply, bully and terrify her. And if this still doesn't work . . . take up a stick and beat her soundly, for it is better to punish the body and correct the soul. . . . Readily beat her, not in rage, but out of charity . . . so that the beating will redound to your merit and her good. (Okun 1986, p. 3)

Bernard of Siena, a predecessor of Cherubino, exhorted his parishioners to exercise more compassion for their wives by treating them with as much mercy as they would their hens and pigs.

The Reformation brought no great changes to the patriarchal structure for women. Martin Luther also believed that women are subject to men as punishment for sin: "The rule remains with the husband, and the wife is compelled to obey him by God's command" (*Lectures on Genesis*, 2:18). Nor did the views of the Calvinist John Knox hold out any promise for women. Reviewing the Bible and ideas of the earlier church fathers, Knox reiterated the natural and irrefutable inferiority of women's character, their sole place in the family, and their rightful subordination to their husbands, and God's decree that it be so.

The sixteenth to the eighteenth centuries were known as the "great age of flogging" as a way of controlling the powerless—children, women, and the lower classes. Wife-beating, in spite of the theologians' exhortations to the contrary, remained widespread. Community tolerance of such behavior was great as long as the physical force was suitable. It was the moderate use of physical punishment that separated the reasonable husband from the brute.

It is fair to conclude that religious teachings can serve as either a roadblock or a resource in addressing domestic violence even though there is nothing in Jewish or Christian teaching that can rightly be used to justify abuse. However, there are teachings that can be misused and distorted to suggest that domestic violence may be acceptable, or even God's will. When these teachings or interpretations of scripture are misused, they become roadblocks to ending the abuse. For example, an interpretation of *Shalom Bayit,* the Jewish teaching about peace in the home, which places the sole responsibility on the woman to "keep the peace" and obey her husband, would be a serious roadblock to addressing domestic violence for a battered woman. An understanding that *Shalom Bayit* is everyone's responsibility offers help for the woman and accountability for the abuser. Likewise, the Christian teaching that husbands are to love their wives as Christ loved the church is a challenge to husbands to treat their wives with respect and love, not with violence or control. This teaching can serve as a valuable resource to challenge and prevent domestic violence.

Many contemporary feminist theologians point out that insofar as the churches fail to challenge sexual stereotypes, they sanction the cultural system that has allowed domestic violence to exist. Some have argued that the socialization of males and females that is directly related to marital violence is embedded in and reinforced by such systems as church and family. The sex roles that women and men are socialized into often create a relationship that is unequal. In addition, there is much *cultural support* for men to exhibit physical aggressiveness, and a lack of support for nonviolent means of dealing with stress. On the other hand, women are expected to be passive, dependent, and weak. Thus, for a man to use force to gain compliance from his wife or companion is quite compatible with these role expectations. In fact, surveys find that about one-fourth of the U.S. population actually approves of a husband hitting his wife under some circumstances. This is not so surprising when we realize that legal traditions in the United States sanctioned the use of physical force by husband upon his wife. It was only in the latter part of the nineteenth century that reforms in the treatment of women and wives began in the United States. By the end of that century wife-beating was made illegal. A North Carolina Supreme Court ruling of 1874 reversed the long-accepted norm that a husband had the right to hit his wife as long as he did not use a switch that was any bigger than his thumb ("the rule of thumb"). But it went on to add:

> If no permanent injury has been inflicted, nor malice, cruelty, nor dangerous violence shown by the husband, it is better to draw the curtain, shut out the public gaze, and leave the parties to forget. (Moore 1979)

COMMUNITY FACTORS

Until recently, there has been very little societal support for victims of domestic violence. There have been few organized community efforts to help abused women. Somehow these matters were deemed best handled within the privacy of the family itself.

WHAT CAN BE DONE TO BREAK THE CYCLE OF DOMESTIC VIOLENCE?

A Christian response to domestic violence is rooted in the call to build the body of Christ—a body that is in need of at-one-ment. The following suggestions are basic.

BREAK THE SILENCE

Many people are available to break the cycle of violence. They include doctors, dentists, counselors, nurses, teachers, neighbors, friends, relatives, priests, and ministers, to mention the most obvious. One could begin by simply asking questions: "Are you feeling all right?" "Is anything the matter?" And by immediately following up with a simple offer of help: "Would you like to talk about it (or anything)?" Or, "If you need anything, or would like to talk later, just give me a call, or drop in."

Breaking the cycle of violence also requires that we know what is available in the local community, such as counseling services, shelters, hot lines, medical facilities, respite care programs, and support groups. The local telephone directory is an easy place to start.

DISPEL THE MYTHS

We can learn the facts and make them available to others through continuing education. Children should be included because they can be helped to recognize the signs of violence within their own homes, and they can be taught where to go for help. All of us can be taught to question our own assumptions about domestic violence. Some of the most commonly held myths that should be eliminated are the following.

ABUSERS ARE PSYCHOLOGICALLY ILL Abuse is not usually a total personality pattern. It is a behavior pattern. As such it is often learned from one's parents. Estimates are that only 10 percent of parents who abuse or neglect their children exhibit serious psychiatric disorders. Similarly, most wife abusers are not psychologically ill.

THE VICTIM CAUSES AND/OR DESERVES VIOLENT TREATMENT   Action by one family member affects other members of the family, but no action ever justifies abuse. Each person has a right to be treated with dignity. Victims of abuse are generally the most vulnerable members of the family system. For example, studies suggest there are disproportionate numbers of attacks by husbands on pregnant women resulting in serious injury to the unborn child. The greater physical strength of men over women and children makes it likely that women and children will be seriously injured when beaten up.

EVOKING EXPRESSIONS OF SORROW FROM THE ABUSER MEANS IT WON'T HAPPEN AGAIN   Being sorry is simply not enough. To counsel an abuse victim with words such as, "He (or she) didn't mean," is poor advice for the victim and unhelpful for the abuser. Abusers need to be helped to recognize their problem and to learn alternative behaviors. This is difficult because abusers share common characteristics such as denial, minimization, unrealistic expectations, and the need for a high degree of external control over others, and a lack of internal control over themselves. Violence is often a response made out of an experience of powerlessness.

ABUSED PERSONS CAN ESCAPE THE VIOLENT ENVIRONMENT   It is very difficult for those who are dependent on the abuser to leave home. Abused women may fear reprisals or rejection of self and children by others, especially if they are economically dependent on the abuser.

ASSUME A SYSTEMS APPROACH TO PREVENTION AND INTERVENTION

Just as *causes* of spouse abuse are found at several different levels (individual, family, community, and culture), *responses* to these causes are directed at all of these levels. If we want to change behavior, we have to change environment. Since the environment is a set of systems, each interconnected and impacting on one another, intervention at any point can be appropriate and effective. So interventions aimed at several systems simultaneously should effect more change over time.

INDIVIDUAL AND FAMILY LEVEL   Individual and couple counseling to assist couples in developing constructive ways of interacting can facilitate nonviolent settlements to disagreements. Workshops aimed at improving communication skills and raising the self-esteem of people can remove some root causes of physical violence. The staff members of Pre-Cana preparation programs could encourage couples to examine the family systems from which they come, and whose views they bring with themselves. Exercises such as these can expose many stereotypes and marital expectations. But raising questions before marriage is not enough. Older sponsor couples could share their wisdom with young married couples. Parenting classes can help expectant couples prepare to adjust to the addition of children to their family system, and to recognize and assume their roles as primary teachers of their children.

PARISH/COMMUNITY LEVEL   Family ministry could be recognized as a priority in terms of focus, vision, and resources. Teachers can become more aware of changes in patterns of family life, and critique their own assumptions about families. Those engaged in educating seminarians, in providing ongoing education for clergy, and in preparing pastoral ministers for new and developing ministries can keep the question alive of how to minister to victims of domestic violence. This requires that pastoral workers be made aware of the dynamics of violence as it affects the family system by increasing their own pool of information, as well as by refocusing their understanding of how behavior affects individuals and systems.

Concrete services could also be provided at the parish and community level. For example, emergency hot lines to offer advice and referrals can be established. Shelters for battered women can be opened and supported. Respite care for children whose parents are under pressure could provide short-term relief for weary spirits and physically exhausted bodies. This kind of service could be provided in the home or at a center. Quality day care also does much to relieve tension within the family unit. Parent-effectiveness training, support groups for hurting families, short-term economic help, and domestic support services are obvious needs as well. Pastoral workers can cooperate with secular resources to help both abused victims and the abusers. Of course, no one local church should be expected to provide all these services, but all local churches could provide complementary service to what already exists in their neighborhood. The rich resources for spiritual healing and support that already exist in parishes could be tapped even further. Marriage counseling, liturgical services (especially the rite of reconciliation), prayer groups, faith-sharing groups, scripture discussion groups, to name but a few, already provide contexts of trust, as well as pools of caring, committed persons who are interested in exploring the meaning and challenge of the Gospel in their lives.

Why is all of this necessary? Because doctors and social workers can respond to only part of the problem, since many victims do not seek help through traditional service channels. A broad network of other service institutions must be developed to meet the needs of the victims not seen in established social service organizations. Churches and schools could be part of such a referral or direct service network.

CULTURAL LEVEL   Since marital violence is related to the socialization of both women and men into traditional sex-role stereotypes that include dominance and submission, and because such stereotyping has been supported by religious beliefs that shaped our patriarchal Judeo-Christian heritage, religious belief and practice cannot be exempt from critical scrutiny and revision. Of course, this is difficult, since religious leaders themselves are as much a product of socialization as are the victims of abuse. Studies have shown, for example, that members of most U.S. religious denominations, unless they are mental health practitioners actively engaged in work with marital violence, see no connection between the belief system of their church and marital violence. Yet religion can be a countervailing force against the dominant culture. Religious attitudes and values form society's moral foundations, even as those same attitudes and values reflect that society's world view.

In a 1998 publication entitled, "Lutheran Theology Facing Sexual and Domestic Violence," feminist theologian Mary Pellauer suggests that as long as there is an active women's movement, patriarchy will be under attack from many directions. Like other feminist scholars, Pellauer points out that patriarchy stands deeply entrenched behind sexual and domestic violence. Rape and battering are weapons of male dominance. They keep women afraid in homes, sidewalks, workplaces, schools, and churches. Healing from them, or bearing the unhealed consequences of them, consume enormous amounts of energy and concern. Further, Pellauer indicates that subtler forms of patriarchy are being created to fit contemporary changing circumstances. For example, some women are encouraged to carry guns as a strategy for safety; professional women may be accepted as long as they behave exactly like their male colleagues.

HOPE ON THE HORIZON: RELIGIOUS RESPONSE TO DOMESTIC VIOLENCE

There are lights in the darkness: in the last decade several Christian churches have taken steps to articulate policies on domestic violence and sexual misconduct. The National Council of Catholic Bishops in the United States has joined bishops in other countries, notably Canada and New Zealand, in stating clearly and strongly that violence against women, in the home or outside the home, is *never* justified. They clearly and strongly reiterate that violence in any form—physical, sexual, psychological, or verbal—is *sinful;* many times it is a crime as well. Further, the bishops condemn the use of the Bible to condone abusive behavior. They point out that a correct reading of the Scriptures leads people to a relationship based on mutuality and love. In 1992, the U.S. Catholic Conference of Bishops published a book entitled, *When I Call for Help: A Pastoral Response to Domestic Violence against Women.* In it the bishops call on the Christian community to "join forces with and complement the work of those associations and groups that are already involved in preventing and fighting this form of violence." This call is consistent with the church's affirmation of the sacredness and dignity of the human body and the human spirit found in Scripture: ". . . the temple of God is sacred, and you are that temple" (1 Cor 3:17). To help all of us believe and experience the implications of these words, the prophet Isaiah can teach us what this work and promise entails:

> Is not this the fast that I choose: to loose the bonds of wickedness, to undo the thongs of the yoke, to let the oppressed go free, and to break every yoke? . . . Then shall your light break forth like the dawn, and your healing shall spring up speedily. (Isa 58:6, 8)

And the long, sad silence will be no more. Amen.

REFERENCES

Moore, Donna, ed. *Battered Women.* Beverly Hills, Calif.: Sage Publications, 1979.

Okun, Lewis. *Women Abuse: Facts Replacing Myths.* Albany, N.Y.: State University of New York Press, 1986.

Secretariat for Family, Laity, Women, and Youth. *When I Call for Help: A Pastoral Response to Domestic Violence against Women.* Washington, D.C.: U.S. Catholic Conference, 1992.

CHAPTER 24

The Battered Woman: Myths and Reality

Lenore E. Walker

Lenore Walker's report on her research on battered women is, to say the least, alarming. She is quite convincing as she tells of her own interviews with battered women and as she notes what other researchers have written. Her report is written in a very popular style, avoiding theoretical and technical language, in favor of an easy-to-understand style that can speak to those who have not thought much about the problem of physical abuse in intimate relationships. Interested students wishing more detailed statistical information will find ample evidence here to back up her claims.

Her report has interesting correlations with David James's "The Integration of Masculine Spirituality" (chapter 27). Also she mentions the Eisenberg and Micklow study that indicates that 90 percent of batterers had been in the military, a point some students may want to ponder.

Consider reading this essay with this hypothesis in mind: physical abuse rarely begins only after the marriage. In most cases, it is present before the wedding in one or other of the abuser's relationships with women. Some researchers have claimed that between 35 and 45 percent of teen women are physically abused by their boyfriends. To make the situation even more frightening, we have the official U.S. crime statistics. Each year the U.S. Department of Justice publishes its *Uniform Crime Statistics* Report, which can be found in most libraries. In the report are the yearly statistics on the number of women murdered that year in the United States, and also the gender of the murderers. In one recent year, 2,751 women were murdered; all but 243 were murdered by men, a total that year of 2,508. That comes out to men being responsible for 91 percent of murders of women that year.

Both women and men do well to consider these facts. And both may want to consider what they, as individuals and by working together, can do to counter the phenomenon of the battered woman.

Questions for Discussion

1. What single point in Walker's essay surprised you the most?
2. What point in her essay were you already convinced of?
3. What information do you, from your own observation and your own listening to what people say, know about this problem?
4. What action can you take about this problem?

The battering of women, like other crimes of violence against women, has been shrouded in myths. All of the myths have perpetuated the mistaken notion that the victim has precipitated her own assault. Some of them served as a protection against embarrassment. Others were created to protect rescuers from their own discouragement when they were unsuccessful in stopping the brutality. It is important to refute all the myths surrounding battered women in order to understand fully why battering happens, how it affects people, and how it can be stopped.

The battered woman is pictured by most people as a small, fragile, haggard person who might once have been pretty. She has several small children, no job skills, and is economically dependent on her husband. It is frequently assumed she is poor and from a minority group. She is accustomed to living in violence, and her fearfulness and passivity are emphasized above all. Although some battered women do fit this description, research proves it to be a false stereotype.

Most battered women are from middle-class and higher-income homes where the power of their wealth is in the hands of their husbands. Many of them are large women who could attempt to defend themselves physically. Not all of them have children; those who do do not necessarily have them in any particular age group. Although some battered women are jobless, many more are highly competent workers and successful career women. They include doctors, lawyers, corporation executives, nurses, secretaries, full-time homemakers, and others. Battered women are found in all age groups, races, ethnic and religious groups, educational levels, and socioeconomic groups. Who are the battered women? If you are a woman, there is a 50 percent chance it could be you!

MYTH NO. 1: THE BATTERED WOMAN SYNDROME AFFECTS ONLY A SMALL PERCENTAGE OF THE POPULATION

Like rape, the battering of American women is a seriously underreported crime. Data on wife beating are difficult to obtain because battering generally occurs at night, in the home, without witnesses. The statistics on battered women are buried in the records of family domestic disturbance calls to police departments, in emergency room records in hospitals, and in the records of social service agencies, private psychologists, and counselors. The United States Commission on Civil Rights recently completed an investigation which supports the suspicion that police records on battered women are inaccurately low owing to poor police reporting techniques. My personal estimate is that only one in ten women report battering assaults.

Marjory Fields, a New York City attorney who specializes in battered women, reports that of 500 women represented in divorce actions in Brooklyn in 1976, 57.4 percent complained of physical assaults by their husbands. They had suffered these assaults for approximately four years prior to seeking the divorce. Of 600 divorcing wives in Cleveland, according to a study by Levinger, 36.8 percent reported physical abuse by their husbands. The first epidemiological study of battered women undertaken in this country, by sociologists Murray Straus, Richard Gelles, and Susan Steinmetz, reported that a physical assault occurred in 28 percent of all American homes during 1976. This statistic, nearly one third of all families, is certainly evidence that the battered woman problem is a widespread one.

MYTH NO. 2: BATTERED WOMEN ARE MASOCHISTIC

The prevailing belief has always been that only women who "liked it and deserved it" were beaten. In a study of battered wives as recently as twenty years ago, it was suggested that beatings are solicited by women who suffer from negative personality characteristics, including masochism. "Good wives" were taught that the way to stop assaults was to examine their behavior and try to change it to please men: to be less provocative, less aggressive, and less frigid. There was no suggestion that provocation might occur from other than masochistic reasons, that aggressiveness might be an attempt to ward off further assault, and that frigidity might be a very natural result of subjection to severe physical and psychological pain. The burden of guilt for battering has fallen on the woman, and the violent behavior of the male has been perpetuated. The myth of the masochistic woman is a favorite of all who endeavor to understand the battered woman. No matter how sympathetic people may be, they frequently come to the conclusion that the reason a battered woman remains in such a relationship is that she is masochistic. By masochism, it is meant that she experiences some pleasure, often akin to sexual pleasure, through being beaten by the man she loves. Because this has been such a prevailing stereotype, many battered women begin to wonder if they are indeed masochistic.

MYTH NO. 3: BATTERED WOMEN ARE CRAZY

This myth is related to the masochism myth in that it places the blame for the battering on the woman's negative personality characteristics. Battered women's survival behaviors have often earned them the misdiagnosis of being crazy. Unusual actions which may help them to survive in the battering relationship have been taken out of context by unenlightened medical and mental health workers. Several of the women in this sample reported being hospitalized for schizophrenia, paranoia, and severe depression. One woman who told of hearing voices which told her to kill her husband had received numerous electroshock therapy treatments. But just listening to her describe her husband's brutal treatment made her hallucination very understandable. Many women reported being given heavy doses of anti-psychotic medications by doctors who were responding to their overt symptoms rather than attempting to understand their family situations. It is not clear whether these women were overtly psychotic at the time of their reported diagnoses. As a clinical psychologist, I can state that at the time I interviewed these women, there was insufficient evidence of such disorders. One woman was interviewed shortly after being released from a state hospital. Arrangements had been made for her to go to a temporary shelter, legal assistance was provided to initiate divorce proceedings, and her batterer was refused knowledge of her whereabouts. Her mental health improved markedly within days. I wonder how many other women who have been mislabeled as mentally ill were really attempting to cope with a batterer. After listening to their stories, I can only applaud their strength in retaining their sanity.

MYTH NO. 4: MIDDLE-CLASS WOMEN DO NOT GET BATTERED AS FREQUENTLY OR AS VIOLENTLY AS DO POORER WOMEN

Most previously recorded statistics of battering have come from lower-class families. However, lower-class women are more likely to come in contact with community agencies and so their problems are more visible. Middle- and upper-class women do not want to make their batterings public. They fear social embarrassment and harming their husbands' careers. Many also believe the respect in which their husbands are held in the community will cast doubt upon the credibility of their battering stories. The recent public focus on battered women has brought many of these middle- and upper-class women out of hiding. The publicity being given the problem is creating a climate in which they think they will finally be believed. They report an overwhelming sense of relief once they have told their stories and find that others will now believe them.

MYTH NO. 5: MINORITY-GROUP WOMEN ARE BATTERED MORE FREQUENTLY THAN ANGLOS

The battered women interviewed in this study were Hispanic, native American, black, Asian, and Pacific American, as well as Anglo. Although each grew up in a culture with different values and different attitudes about male and female roles, none of them was able to make any impact on the kind of violence she experienced. Anglo and minority women alike told similar battering stories and experienced similar embarrassment, guilt, and the inability to halt their men's assaults. Minority women, however, spoke of having even fewer resources than Anglos to turn to for assistance.

MYTH NO. 6: RELIGIOUS BELIEFS
WILL PREVENT BATTERING

The Catholic, Protestant, Mormon, Jewish, Eastern, and other religious women in this study all indicated that their religious beliefs did not protect them from their assaultive men. Most of the women in my study held religious beliefs. For some, belief in a deity helped them endure their suffering, offering comfort and solace. Sometimes attending services was the only safe outside contact they had. However, other women indicated they no longer practiced their religion, because giving it up eliminated a point of conflict with their batterer. Still others gave up their religion in disillusionment, feeling that a just and merciful God would not have let them suffer so. Others reported losing faith after having unsuccessfully sought help from a religious or spiritual leader.

Some women told stories in which their religious adviser suggested they pray for guidance, become better women, and go home and help their husbands "become more spiritual and find the Lord." Needless to say, these women did not have time to wait for their husbands to "find the Lord" while they continued to receive brutal beatings. Other women joyfully told of humane religious advisers who understood their problems and helped them break out of their disastrous relationships.

MYTH NO. 7: BATTERED WOMEN ARE
UNEDUCATED AND HAVE FEW JOB SKILLS

The education level of the women interviewed ranged from fifth grade through completion of professional and doctoral degrees. They were homemakers, teachers, real estate agents, lawyers, psychologists, nurses, physicians, businesswomen, politicians, and successful corporation executives. Some did well at their jobs and some performed poorly. Although many were successful career women, they stated they would give up their careers if it would eliminate the battering in their relationships. Most had tried changing jobs or staying home without any effect on their husbands' behavior. Those women who chose to be homemakers tried heroically to keep their lives from falling apart: they struggled to make financial ends meet, kept family chaos at a minimum, and tried to smooth life for their batterer. Most of them sought status in their home lives rather than in their careers. Thus, their self-esteem was dependent on their ability to be good wives and homemakers and was not well integrated with their successful professional activities.

MYTH NO. 8: BATTERERS ARE VIOLENT
IN ALL THEIR RELATIONSHIPS

Based on the women in my study, I estimate that only about 20 percent of battered women live with men who are violent not only to them but also to anyone else who gets in their way. Unfortunately, this violent group of men has been the most studied. They tend to be poorer and to live outside the mainstream of society's norms. They often have fewer resources or skills with which to cope with the world. Most street crime is committed by such men. They also have the most contact with society's institutions and seem always to be in trouble with the police. They often subsist on welfare payments; their children have behavioral and learning problems in school; they use hospital clinics. Courts send them to treatment facilities in lieu of jail sentences. Because so much of our resources is spent in dealing with these people, it often seems that they are representative of all of the violence in our culture. When it comes to battered women, this is simply not true. Most men who batter their wives are generally not violent in other aspects of their lives.

MYTH NO. 9: BATTERERS ARE UNSUCCESSFUL AND
LACK RESOURCES TO COPE WITH THE WORLD

It has been suggested that men who feel less capable than their women resort to violence. Contrary findings were reported in England, where physicians, service professionals, and police had the highest incidence of wife beating. Most of the professionally successful volunteers in this study have similarly successful husbands. Among the affluent batterers were physicians, attorneys, public officials, corporation executives, scientists, college professors, and salesmen. Many of these men donated a good deal of time and energy to community activities. Often they would be unable to maintain their high productivity level were it not for the support of their wives. In one town, the mayor's wife, whose layers of make-up concealed the serious bruises he had inflicted upon her, regularly assisted him with all his official duties. In some cases, previously successful men lost their effectiveness because of alcohol or emotional problems. Many men were reported as erratic in performance by the women. As a group, however, the batterers in this sample would be indistinguishable from any other group of men in terms of capability.

MYTH NO. 10: DRINKING CAUSES
BATTERING BEHAVIOR

Over half the battered women in this sample indicated a relationship between alcohol use and battering. Many tended to blame the battering incidents on their men's drinking. Upon further questioning, however, it became clear that the men beat them whether or not they had been drinking. But some association between drinking and battering cannot be denied. Exactly what it is is still not known. It does seem reasonable, however, to suggest that in many cases alcohol is blamed as the precipitating factor, whereas it is only a component in the battering relationship. But it is psychologically easier for the battered woman to blame the violence on the batterer's drunkenness. Often the men in this study drank as a way of calming their anxieties. Drinking seemed to give them a sense of power. Many of the women felt that if they could only get their men to stop drinking, the battering would cease. Unfortunately, it just did not happen.

The most violent physical abuse *was* suffered by women whose men were consistent drinkers. Much work still needs to be done on the association between drinking and battering. I strongly suspect that there are specific blood chemistry changes that occur under a generalized stress reaction such as battering. Furthermore, these may be the same chemicals that are found in the blood of alcoholics. It is entirely possible that fundamental changes in brain chemistry cause both cycles. It is hoped that as our scientific technology becomes more precise, we will be able to measure these chemical changes with more accuracy.

MYTH NO. 11: BATTERERS ARE PSYCHOPATHIC PERSONALITIES

If batterers could be considered antisocial and psychopathic personalities, then individual psychopathology could be used to differentiate batterers from normal men. Unfortunately, it is not that simple. The batterers in this sample were reported to have many kinds of personality disturbances other than just being psychopathic. One trait they *do* have in common with diagnosed psychopaths is their extraordinary ability to use charm as a manipulative technique.

The women interviewed all described their batterers as having a dual personality, much like Dr. Jekyll and Mr. Hyde. The batterer can be either very, very good or very, very horrid. Furthermore, he can swing back and forth between the two characters with the smoothness of a con artist. But, unlike the psychopath, the batterer feels a sense of guilt and shame at his uncontrollable actions. If he were able to cease his violence, he would.

MYTH NO. 12: POLICE CAN PROTECT THE BATTERED WOMEN

The women in this study manifestly do not believe this to be true. Only 10 percent ever called the police for help. Of these, most stated that the police were ineffective: when the police left, the assault was renewed with added vigor.

Sociologist Murray Straus, in his studies on violence in the family, labeled such assaults a crime and declared that were the violence to occur in any setting other than the home, it would warrant prosecution. He cites studies indicating that somewhere between 25 and 67 percent of all homicides occur within the family in all societies.

A recently completed study in Kansas City and Detroit indicates that in 80 percent of all homicides in those cities, the police had intervened from one to five times previously. Thus, homicide between man and woman is not a "crime of passion," but rather the end result of unchecked, long-standing violence.

MYTH NO. 13: THE BATTERER IS NOT A LOVING PARTNER

This myth has spawned others, most particularly that of the masochistic wife. Women have been accused of loving the batterers' brutality rather than their kindness because it has been difficult for society to comprehend the loving behavior of batterers. But batterers are often described by their victims as fun-loving little boys when they are not being coercive. They are playful, attentive, sensitive, exciting, and affectionate to their women. The cycle theory of battering described later on explains how the batterers' loving behavior keeps these women in the battering relationship.

MYTH NO. 14: A WIFE BATTERER ALSO BEATS HIS CHILDREN

This myth has some foundation in fact. In my sample, approximately one third of the batterers beat their children. These men were also suspected of seductive sexual behavior toward their daughters. In another third of the cases, battered women beat their children. Although the children of the final third were not physically abused, they suffered a more insidious form of child abuse because of living in a home where the fathers battered the mothers. Those women in my sample who had seen their fathers beat their mothers report psychological scars which never healed. Children whom I encountered while doing this study seemed to be undergoing similar traumas. The National Center for Child Abuse and Neglect has reported a higher percentage of men in battering relationships who also beat their children than those who do not. Their data show that when there is concurrent child abuse in these families, 70 percent is committed by the violent man.

MYTH NO. 15: ONCE A BATTERED WOMAN, ALWAYS A BATTERED WOMAN

This myth is the reason why many people have not encouraged women to leave their battering relationships. They think she will only seek out another violent man. Though several of the women in this sample had a series of vio-

lent relationships, this pattern did not hold true for most of those interviewed. While they wanted another intimate relationship with a man, they
were extremely careful not to choose another violent one. There was a low
rate of remarriage for older women who had left battering relationships.
Most of them had left a marriage by going against the advice of their families
and friends. They preferred being single rather than trying to make the male-
female relationship work again. Women who had received some beneficial
intervention rarely remarried another batterer.

MYTH NO. 16: ONCE A BATTERER, ALWAYS A BATTERER

If the psychosocial-learning theory of violent behavior is accurate, then batterers can be taught to relearn their aggressive responses. Assertion rather
than aggression, negotiation rather than coercion, is the goal. My theoretical
perspective, then, indicates that this myth of once a batterer, always a batterer
is just that. The data have not yet been analyzed to prove it false.

MYTH NO. 17: LONG-STANDING BATTERING RELATIONSHIPS CAN CHANGE FOR THE BETTER

Although everyone who believes in the positive nature of behavior change
wants to believe this myth, my research has not shown it to be true. Relationships that have been maintained by the man having power over the
woman are stubbornly resistant to an equal power-sharing arrangement.
Thus, even with the best help available, these relationships do not become
battering free. At best, the violent assaults are reduced in frequency and
severity. Unassisted, they simply escalate to homicidal and suicidal proportions. The best hope for such couples is to terminate the relationship. There is
a better chance that with another partner they can reorder the power structure and as equals can live in a nonviolent relationship.

MYTH NO. 18: BATTERED WOMEN DESERVE TO GET BEATEN

The myth that battered women provoke their beatings by pushing their men
beyond the breaking point is a popular one. Everyone can recount a story
where the woman seemed to deserve what she got: she was too bossy, too
insulting, too sloppy, too uppity, too angry, too obnoxious, too provocative,
or too something else. In a culture where everyone takes sides between win-
ners and losers, women who continuously get beaten are thought to deserve

it. It is assumed that if only they would change their behavior, the batterer could regain his self-control. The stories of the women in this study indicate that batterers lose self-control because of their own internal reasons, not because of what the women did or did not do. Furthermore, philosophically this myth robs the men of responsibility for their own actions. No one could deserve the kind of brutality reported in these pages.

MYTH NO. 19: BATTERED WOMEN CAN ALWAYS LEAVE HOME

In a society where women are culturally indoctrinated to believe that love and marriage are their true fulfillment, nothing is lost by pretending that they are free to leave home whenever the violence becomes too great. In truth, battered women do not have the freedom to leave after being assaulted. . . . A battered woman is not free to end her victimization without assistance.

MYTH NO. 20: BATTERERS WILL CEASE THEIR VIOLENCE "WHEN WE GET MARRIED"

A small number of women in this sample reported violence in their premarital relationships. They thought that their men would cease their abuse once they were married, because the men would then feel more secure and more confident of the women's exclusive love for them. In every case, the expected marital bliss did not happen. Rather, the batterer's suspiciousness and possessiveness increased along with his escalating rate of violence.

MYTH NO. 21: CHILDREN NEED THEIR FATHER EVEN IF HE IS VIOLENT—OR, "I'M ONLY STAYING FOR THE SAKE OF THE CHILDREN"

This myth shatters faster than some of the others when confronted with the data on the high number of children who are physically and sexually abused in homes where there is such domestic violence. There is no doubt that the ideal family includes both a mother and a father for their children. However, children of abusive parents, compared with children of single parents, all say they would choose to live with just one parent. The enormous relief in living with a single parent expressed by children who formerly lived in violent homes is universal. In this sample, young children from homes where the father beat the mother had severe emotional and educational problems. The women in this sample remained with their batterers long after the children left home, putting to rest the myth that they were staying because it was better for the children. They remained because of the symbiotic bonds of love established over a period of time in such relationships.

Who, then, are the battered women?

COMMON CHARACTERISTICS OF BATTERED WOMEN

As indicated earlier, the battered women interviewed for this book were a mixed group, representing all ages, races, religions (including no religion), educational levels, cultures, and socioeconomic groups. The youngest was seventeen years old, and the oldest was seventy-six years old. The shortest battering relationship was two months and the longest lasted fifty-three years, when the batterer died from natural causes.

The battered woman in this study commonly:

1. Has low self-esteem.
2. Believes all the myths about battering relationships.
3. Is a traditionalist about the home, strongly believes in family unity and the prescribed feminine sex-role stereotype.
4. Accepts responsibility for the batterer's actions.
5. Suffers from guilt, yet denies the terror and anger she feels.
6. Presents a passive face to the world but has the strength to manipulate her environment enough to prevent further violence and being killed.
7. Has severe stress reactions, with psychophysiological complaints.
8. Uses sex as a way to establish intimacy.
9. Believes that no one will be able to help her resolve her predicament except herself.

Although a few of the women were unmarried and not living with their batterers, most either lived with their batterers or had been legally married to them. Many women reported living with their batterers prior to marriage without experiencing abuse. Abuse usually began in the first six months of marriage. Some women had no children; several had seven or more; a few were interviewed during pregnancy. For many, this was their first marriage; for others, it was their second, third, and, in one case, her fifth. While some of the women were still living with the batterers, others had left the relationship prior to participating in this study. A number of the women began the process of terminating a battering relationship while the interviewers were still in contact with them. Several of the women interviewed were referred while in the hospital recuperating from injuries inflicted by the batterer. To the best of my knowledge, none of the women has died. Four killed their husbands and several others were arrested for assault on their men. The women who talked with us lived in urban environments, in suburbia, and in isolated rural areas. There seemed to be a high concentration of women living in areas which afford anonymity. Many Metropolitan Denver women lived in the foothills of the mountains, where they were isolated, especially in winter.

Low Self-Esteem

Because of their lowered sense of self-esteem, these women typically underestimated their abilities to do anything. They doubted their competence and underplayed any successes they had. Those battered women with activities outside the home evaluated their outside performance and skills more realistically than they could their wifely duties. They were in constant doubt about their abilities as housekeepers, cooks, or lovers. Thus, the man's constant criticism of them in these areas adversely affected their judgment. Women in general have not learned how to integrate their home lives and outside lives as men do. They tend to evaluate their performances at home and outside the home according to separate criteria. Battered women tend to be traditionalists about home performance, since that is the basis of their self-esteem. Activities outside the home simply do not figure in their evaluation of how they feel about themselves. Thus, when things are not going well at home, the battered woman considers herself a failure. She has internalized all the cultural myths and stereotypes and assumes the guilt for the batterer's behavior. She agrees with society's belief that the batterer would change his behavior if only she could change her behavior. If she has lived with him for a while, she is aware that although she can often manipulate him to some degree, she has, in truth, little control over his behavior. This makes her feel even more of a failure. Most of the women interviewed eventually got around to saying that they were still not completely sure that there was not something they could have done differently that might have made the batterer cease his abusive behavior.

Traditionalists

The traditionalist orientation of the battered woman is evident in her view of the woman's role in marriage. First, she readily accepts the notion that "a woman's proper place is in the home." No matter how important her career might be to her, she is ready to give it up if it will make the batterer happy. Often she does just that, resulting in economic hardship to the family. Even those who believe that women have a right to a career suspect that that very career might be causing the batterer's difficulties. Those women who cannot give up working feel guilty. Although many of the women work because the family needs the money, they also state that the time spent on the job provides a brief respite from the batterer's domination. But the batterer's need to possess his woman totally often causes her to lose or leave her job. The batterer batters her with a litany of suspicions about her supposed behavior on the job. Usually, he is jealous of her work relationships, especially those with other men.

Battered women who work often turn their money over to their husbands. Even those women who provide the family's financial stability feel their income belongs to their husband. Ultimately, she gives the man the right to make the final decisions as to how the family income is spent. The battered woman views the man as the head of the family, even though often she is the one actually keeping the family together; she makes the decisions concerning financial matters and the children's welfare; and she maintains the house and often a job as well. She goes out of her way to make sure that her man feels he is the head of the home. Some of the women interviewed revealed elaborate deceptions they resorted to to put aside some money—money they saved secretly in order to leave the marriage. Often they did not follow through, but their nest egg helped them cope. Others left the relationship when they had enough money.

KEEPERS OF THE PEACE

Another behavior common among battered women is the attempt to control other people and events in the environment to keep the batterer from losing his temper. The woman believes that if she can control all the factors in his life, she can keep him from becoming angry. She makes herself responsible for creating a safe environment for everyone. One woman interviewed spent an enormous amount of time talking about her efforts to control her mother, his mother, and their children so that none of them would upset her husband. She found that if she kept all these people in check through some interesting manipulations, life was pleasant in their home. The moment someone got out of line, her man began his beatings.

SEVERE STRESS REACTION

The battered women in this sample were hard workers who lived under constant stress and fear. This had physical and psychological effects on them. Although most battered women report being able to withstand enormous amounts of pain during a battering incident, at other times they are often seen by their doctors for a variety of minor physiological ailments. Battered women often complain of fatigue, backaches, headaches, general restlessness, and inability to sleep. Psychological complaints are, frequently, depression, anxiety, and general suspiciousness. Being suspicious and secretive often helps a battered woman to avoid further beatings. Many battered women go to great lengths to find a few moments of privacy from their very intrusive battering husbands. They will often hide things from their men that they fear might precipitate another battering incident.

CHILDHOOD VIOLENCE AND SEX-ROLE STEREOTYPING

I was curious to learn whether or not the women who lived in battering relationships with their husbands had also lived in battering relationships with their parents. Although this was true in a small number of cases, many more women reported that their first exposure to violent men was their husbands. Their fathers were described as traditionalists who treated their daughters like fragile dolls. The daughters were expected to be pretty and ladylike and to grow up to marry nice young men who would care for them as their fathers had. Doted upon as little girls, these women, in their fathers' eyes, could do no wrong. Such pampering and sex-role stereotyping unfortunately taught them that they were incompetent to take care of themselves and had to be dependent on men.

COMMON CHARACTERISTICS
OF MEN WHO BATTER

Who are the batterers?

The batterers described were also a mixed group. They represented all ages, races, religions (including no religion), educational levels, cultures, and socioeconomic groups. The youngest was described as sixteen years old and the oldest was seventy-six. They were unrecognizable to the uniformed observer and not distinguished by demographic data.

The batterer, according to the women in this sample, commonly:

1. Has low self-esteem.
2. Believes all the myths about battering relationships.
3. Is a traditionalist believing in male supremacy and the stereotyped masculine sex role in the family.
4. Blames others for his actions.
5. Is pathologically jealous.
6. Presents a dual personality.
7. Has severe stress reactions, during which he uses drinking and wife battering to cope.
8. Frequently uses sex as an act of aggression to enhance self-esteem in view of waning virility. May be bisexual.
9. Does not believe his violent behavior should have negative consequences.

The first three characteristics of the batterers are strikingly similar to those of the battered women. Batterers typically deny that they have a problem, although they are aware of it; and they become enraged if their women should reveal the true situation. These men do not want to discuss the problem, and attempts to learn more about batterers have not been successful. When these men do agree to be interviewed, often as a favor to their women during their contrite and loving phase, they cannot describe the details of an acute battering incident. They evade questions or claim not to remember very much of what did occur. Thus, the knowledge we have of these men comes from the battered women themselves and our few, meager observations.

Researchers Eisenberg and Micklow found 90 percent of the batterers in their study had been in the military. Twenty-five percent received dishonorable discharges. I did not systematically collect such data for this sample, but subjectively it appears that a similarly high percentage were also in the military. Del Martin, feminist author of *Battered Wives*, suggests a correlation between the military as a "school for violence" and subsequent battering behavior in males.

OVERKILL

There is always an element of overkill in the batterer's behavior. For example, he reports he does not set out to hurt his woman; rather, he sets out to "teach her a lesson." He may begin by slapping her once, twice, three times; before he knows it, he has slapped her ten or twelve times, with punches and kicks as well. Even when the woman is badly injured, the batterer often uncontrollably continues his brutal attack. The same is true for his generosity. During his loving periods, he showers the woman with affection, attention, and gifts. Rather than buying his woman a small bottle of perfume, one batterer bought her a three-ounce bottle. In another instance, the woman asked for a pocket calculator to help her to keep their checkbook balanced. The batterer bought her a calculator capable of performing mathematical computations neither of them understood. Several women complained of their husbands' extravagance, stating that they had to work longer and harder to pay off the charge accounts. This quality of overdoing things tends to be a standard characteristic of battering relationships.

EXCESSIVE POSSESSIVENESS AND JEALOUSY

Another staple characteristic is the batterer's possessiveness, jealousy, and intrusiveness. In order for him to feel secure, he must become overinvolved in the woman's life. In some instances, he may take her to work, to lunch, and bring her home at the end of the working day. In others, when he goes to work, he may require her to bring him coffee, lunch, his checkbook, and generally to account for every moment of her time. In one extreme case, the batterer escorted his wife to the door of the ladies' room in any public facility they visited. Despite this constant surveillance of her every activity, the batterer is still suspicious of his woman's possible relationships with other men and women.

A frequent subject for the batterer's verbal abuse is his suspicion that the battered woman is having an affair or affairs. Most of the women interviewed had not had other sexual liaisons. If they did engage in affairs, they were generally of very short duration and represented an attempt to alleviate some of their loneliness and stress. Most battered women do not expect another relationship to be any better than the one they are suffering through. If they had any such hopes, they probably would have left the batterer in search of a new Prince Charming long ago.

CHILDHOOD VIOLENCE AND SEX-ROLE STEREOTYPING

Although battered women typically do not come from violent homes, batterers frequently do. Many of the batterers saw their fathers beat their mothers; others were themselves beaten. In those homes where overt violence was not reported, a general lack of respect for women and children was evident. These men often experienced emotional deprivation. These reports support the notion of the generational cycle theory that is so popular in our child abuse literature today. Children who were abused or witnessed abuse are more likely to grow up to be tomorrow's abusers.

BATTERERS' RELATIONSHIP WITH THEIR MOTHERS

The women also reported that their batterers have unusual relationships with their mothers. It is often characterized as an ambivalent love-hate relationship. The batterer's mother seems to have a good deal of control over his behavior; yet he will often abuse her, too. In fact, many women report that acute battering incidents are triggered by a visit to the batterer's mother. Often their rages are reminiscent of infantile temper tantrums designed by angry little boys to provoke their mommies. Included in this study are several reports from women being battered by young sons. In one such case, a twenty-one-year-old college honor student beat his sixty-five-year-old mother several times a week. When the mother was ill or simply unavailable to him because of previous batterings, he would beat his twenty-year-old girl friend.

Much more research is needed before we can reach any definite conclusions about the relationship between the batterer and his mother. Psychology has done much damage by casting mothers in a negative light as being responsible for the emotional ills of their children. Still, we must look carefully at the role of the batterer's mother in this problem. Also, we must look at the role of the batterer's father and the father-son relationship. The information that we have collected can serve as a beginning to formulate new questions that need to be answered.

MENTAL STATUS OF BATTERERS

Psychological distress symptoms were often reported in batterers, particularly prior to an acute battering incident. Alcohol and other drugs were often said to calm his nervousness. Although many of the men seemed to have a need for alcohol, few of them were reported addicted to drugs. Those who were had become addicted to hard drugs while in the military, usually in Vietnam.

Personality distortions were frequently mentioned by the women. They said the batterers had a history of being loners and were socially involved with others only on a superficial level. They were constantly accomplishing feats that others might not be able to. They loved to impress their women. For example, one man took his future bride into a furniture store and handed the salesperson two thousand dollars in cash for a bedroom set she admired. This sort of behavior tended to reinforce their women's viewing them as possessing extraordinary abilities.

The men are further described as being extremely sensitive to nuances in other people's behavior. Their attention to minimal cues from others gives them the ability to predict reactions faster than most of us can. Thus, they are helping their women to deal with others in their world when they share their usually accurate predictions of others' behavior. When these men decompensate under stress, their sensitivity becomes paranoid in nature. When they are comfortable, however, the women appreciate and benefit from this protective behavior, since battered women tend to be overly gullible and trusting of others. Much of this seemingly self-protective behavior becomes homicidal and suicidal when the batterer's violence escalates beyond his control.

BRAIN DISEASES

Many of the battered women felt their husbands' violent behavior approximated some kind of brain seizure and that there might be a relationship between neurological disorders and violence. The most common disorder discussed was psychomotor epilepsy. This is a disorder of the brain manifested by sudden, unexplained outbursts of movement. Persons who suffer from such brain disorder often do not remember their episodes, especially if they result in violence. Sometimes an aura or feeling of an impending attack is identifiable but usually precipitation is unknown. Medication is often useful in controlling onset and frequency of attacks, although a cure is most times impossible.

Neurologists are studying the relationship of such brain diseases and violence. It is interesting, though, that seemingly only men, and not women, are so afflicted with such a physical disorder.

Another disease mentioned that may cause violent outbursts was hypoglycemia. This disease is characterized by low blood-sugar levels that cause starvation among body cells. The brain cells become irritable more rapidly than the rest of the body, and such irritability, it is theorized, can trigger violent outbursts. One woman reported that if she sensed a rising tension, she was able to avoid an acute battering incident by feeding her hypoglycemic husband. Although minor battering incidents still occurred, explosions disappeared. This improvement had been stable over the six months prior to her interview and followed a three-year battering history. I wonder how much her nurturing behavior of feeding him also helped to alleviate his explosiveness.

Further support for the theory of neurological or blood chemistry changes in batterers is found in the geriatric population. Some older women report dramatic changes in their husbands' behavior as they age. Senility or hardening of the arteries can cause previously nonviolent men to begin to abuse their wives. One sixty-eight-year-old woman told of her seventy-year-old husband's attacking her with his cane. Other stories indicate the cruel fate that can befall women who have devoted their lives to pleasing their husbands only to find that aging brings on organic brain syndromes that can impel them to violent behavior.

In conclusion, battered women and batterers come from all walks of life. This sample has indicated that they cannot be distinguished by demographic description or stereotypes. They do have some personality characteristics in common, but it is not known how much the victim/offender roles produce such personalities or whether they sought each other out first. Rather than concentrating on the study of individual personality, it appears that the study of the interrelatedness of the sociological and psychological factors may be the way to a solution.

PART SIX

Getting beyond
Stereotypes

CHAPTER 25

Western Religion and the Patriarchal Family

Christine E. Gudorf

This essay is packed with wisdom and rich in stimulating insight for classroom discussion. Christine E. Gudorf, professor of religious studies at Florida International University, meticulously details how the Jewish and Christian traditions have shaped, legitimized, and even sacralized the patriarchal family. Gudorf examines the effects of three specific aspects of the traditional model of family: the headship/breadwinner role of husband, the subordinate/motherhood role of wife, and the obedience role of children. These three aspects are explored in terms of their effects on the three groups of participants in the modern family: men, women, and children. Issues of power, identity, intimacy, work, and rights are uncovered in the dominant/subordinate model for each group. Disadvantages, and sometimes advantages, are noted for each. The analysis is incisive and revelatory.

If Gudorf's critical hermeneutics is correct, the traditional patriarchal family is not very conducive for men, women, or children to move toward adulthood. The greatest casualty may be the marital relationship itself.

There is, however, a constructive alternative: expose the internal contradictions in Western religious traditions and reclaim their liberating elements that counter dominant practices regarding the family. These resources can prophetically reshape the family toward being a household of hospitality for men, women, and children.

Questions for Discussion

1. What New Testament resources subvert the dominant/subordinate relationship prescribed for husbands and wives in patriarchy?
2. Do men and women sin differently? Men by control and abuse of power, women by manipulation and seduction? Or are these stereotypes?
3. How does patriarchal power operate against intimacy in marital relationships?
4. What alternative to patriarchal power would you propose? What form or design would that model take?
5. Are children ever freed from the obligation of parental obedience? Or is this biblical injunction without limits?

T he Judeo-Christian tradition has helped to shape, legitimate, and even sacralize the model of family characteristic of the western world: the patriarchal family. Though the Judeo-Christian tradition neither created nor exclusively controlled the patriarchal family—which both predated it and was manifested in areas outside the influence of both Judaism and Christianity—neither did the Judeo-Christian tradition merely passively accept the patriarchal family, but instead made it central to the religious tradition itself, and even based religious structures on patriarchal assumptions.

Within Christianity in particular, it is necessary to distinguish between the influence of the overall Christian tradition on the family, and the existence within the Christian gospel of a teaching on family contrary to the dominant patriarchal thrust, a teaching which seems to be rooted in the teachings of Jesus himself and to have exercised a great deal of influence in the first century or two of Christianity. In the New Testament, for example, in addition to the patriarchal household codes found in a number of epistles (especially Eph. 5:22–6:9 and Col. 3:18–4:1) which recapitulated prevailing family structure in the Roman empire and accorded with the patriarchal Jewish norms, there are also a number of countervailing passages. In the Gospels, Jesus opposed the generally accepted primacy of familial duty, especially filial duty, in his refusal to interrupt his teaching to see his mother and brothers (Mk 3:31–35), in his refusal to sanction burying one's father before taking up the duties of discipleship (Lk 9:59–62), and in rebutting the woman who blessed his mother for having birthed him ("Blessed rather are those who hear the word of God and keep it!" Lk 11:27–28). While Jesus never directly contravened the dominant/subordinate relationship prescribed for husbands and wives in patriarchy, he did give many examples extraordinary in his time of respect for women, and he demonstrated support for breaking the stereotypically servant role of women in the home (Mary and Martha, Lk 10:38–42). Perhaps the strongest evidence for a New Testament tendency to contravene patriarchy comes from Gal. 3:28 and the examples in Paul's epistles of the leadership roles given to women in the early church, some of whom, like Prisca, shared authority in the church with their husbands ([12], Ch. 5). Yet regardless of the existence of this potential for opposing the patriarchal family within the Christian tradition, from the second century onward such New Testament passages were overshadowed by the development of a patriarchal church that stressed those sections of the New Testament supporting patriarchal relations in the family, such as the household codes.

Today, the passages from the Gospels and the epistles which undermine the legitimacy of the patriarchal model are being lifted up in some quarters of Christianity as the basis for constructing alternative models of Christian family and community [12], [13], [5]. A similar movement is taking place within Judaism, though the primary texts of Judaism are somewhat less

Christine E. Gudorf, "Western Religion and the Patriarchal Family" in *Religion and Sexual Health* (Dordrecht: Kluwer, 1992), ed. Ronald M. Green, pp. 99–117. Reprinted with kind permission from Kluwer Adademic Publishers.

explicitly supportive of alternatives to patriarchy, due largely to their greater antiquity and their original social location [7], [38].

In this discussion I will restrict myself to suggesting some of the effects of three specific aspects of the traditional Judeo-Christian model of family: the headship/breadwinner role of husbands/fathers, wives' subordination to husbands and restriction to motherhood and the domestic hearth, and the imperative that children obey parents. These have been standard aspects in Judeo-Christian tradition, culled from the Genesis story of creation (men as bread-winners, women as childbearers subject to men) and from the commandments (children's obedience to parents), and embodied and elaborated in countless stories in both Hebrew and Christian scriptures. Both Jewish and Christian scripture scholars and religious writers have further discussed, elaborated, and confirmed these three aspects of religious teaching on family throughout history up to and including our century [9]. The effects of these three aspects of the traditional family on both contemporary individuals in the family and on society itself are enormous, and frequently destructive. I will examine the effects of these three aspects on the three groups of participants in the modern family: men, women and children.

EFFECTS ON MEN

The division of roles and power in the traditional family has both privileged and disadvantaged men in varying ways. Since the family has been understood as the primary and basic social unit, the power of men over women and children in the family also served to give men a power, a freedom, in wider society that women, and certainly children, did not have. For example, the chief reason that Thomas Aquinas gives for the impossibility of women becoming priests is that women were created subject to men in families, and for a much narrower purpose (reproduction), so that ordination could not be effective for women (*Summa Theologiae*, III Suppl. Q 39). Similarly Jewish women were not obligated by any of the time bound positive laws—such as on prayer and study of the law—since these would interfere with women's obligations in the home. Because women were ignorant of the law, they were excluded not only as judges, but as witnesses ([19], p. 191). Thus the power of men over women, and their comparative lack of restriction to assigned roles in the family, also conferred on men power outside the family itself. One result of this greater social power and freedom of men has been greater opportunity for personal development and for the formation of identity. Psychologists still find today that men of college age have usually reached a stage in identity formation that most women do not reach before middle age ([45], p. 175).

With social power for men came the power to name and define the world; the material world, the nature of men, women and children, as well as ultimacy itself came to be male-defined. One must be careful not to exaggerate this matter, since rigid hierarchies among men have, throughout history, severely restricted the number of men who exercised social power; for most men, rule over one's own home ("a man's home is his castle") was minimal compensation for exclusion from the male elites who ruled the wider society.

Within the family men's power over women and children tended at many periods in history to be absolute: he determined the place of residence, controlled all family resources regardless of their source, and had the right to use physical force—even to the point of death—to punish women or children or to compel obedience. In some periods and places he could sell them as property, whether in slavery, apprenticeship, or indenture. Within the marital relationship, the greater power of men allowed the sexual double standard, under which women, but not men, were held to celibacy before marriage and fidelity within marriage. Though both later Jewish and all Christian teaching included insistence on chastity, neither tradition rigorously or consistently attacked the double standard, often treating chastity as an impossible ideal for men due to their sexual nature and their social freedom ([33], pp. 227–228; [19], p. 198; [4], pp. 50–52).

To balance this great power of men, the traditional family imposed on men the responsibility of providing material support for the family. Until the modern era most people subsisted from agriculture, in which women and children participated as well. But the responsibility for family support was the husband's. This responsibility was usually onerous, and was made periodically impossible by droughts and floods, wars, epidemics or other social dislocations.

Besides the burden of responsibility for material support, the assignment of work to men, as means of providing family support, has resulted in some serious distortions in men's lives, especially in the contemporary era. Work ideally serves two other purposes in addition to material support. It is human beings' chief method for participating in and contributing to the larger human community. Work also serves as the major activity through which human persons create themselves by learning and developing their talents, encountering and overcoming challenges, and interacting co-operatively with others. In the modern world work is not only very specialized and therefore varied, but chosen by individuals rather than assigned by class or heredity. The emphasis on work as the means to support a man's family, as that which legitimates his participation and role in the family, has overshadowed for many men these other purposes of human work. Many men today do not feel free to choose work through which they can satisfy personal needs or contribute to their societies in ways meaningful to them. Many are trapped in jobs they actively dislike, some in jobs they feel detract from the broader social welfare; they feel obliged to choose work which provides as much material support as possible. Many workers dislike their work so intensely that they understand it as a sacrifice for their families, who in turn owe them respect and obedience—and greater success than the worker himself achieved ([46], Ch. 2; [40], Ch 7). This is a problem not only among the working class, where basic levels of support are often difficult to achieve, but is also true for many middle class men. Many middle class college men feel pressured to prepare for careers in accounting, law, medicine, finance and engineering, and to squelch any satisfaction they might feel in courses which might otherwise lead them to careers as poets, nurses, forest rangers, social workers or teachers. This is a common source of depression among college and university students. It is, of course, closely intertwined with more general social pressure to measure one's worth by the size of one's paycheck. Working women, socialized to think of their salaries as secondary to their spouse's (pin money), and who normally take their social status (and economic class) from their husband's job rather than their own, have not felt nearly the degree of pressure to choose work for its remuneration alone.

Today the breadwinner role of man in the West faces an additional pressure from the increased numbers of working women. In many countries the majority of women—even the majority of married women with children— now work. The reasons vary, and include career ambitions among more educated women, larger numbers of female headed households and ideological pressure in communist states, but the overwhelming majority of women work due to the inability of a single wage to support a family in adequate comfort.

The phenomenon of women working in large numbers causes anxiety in men at three levels: (1) it undermines the historic economic dependency of women and children on men on which men's authority in the family was based, (2) it forces men to work with women as co-workers, and sometimes with women as bosses, though they have been socialized to view women as subordinates, and (3) it calls into question the value of men's contribution to the family. This last is important, and often overlooked. Women's role in the family is much more secure than men's. Subordination to men and restriction to domestic work has often been difficult, and has sometimes resulted in abuse of women, but the role of mother and homemaintainer is comparatively impervious to becoming anachronistic. The tasks involved in women's role change, but they have never, despite some ideologically motivated attempts at collectivization, either been eliminated or successfully reassigned away from women. Thus economic depression and other social dislocations, for all their disastrous consequences on general family welfare, are much more devastating for men than for women, in that they steal from men the activity on which their identity, their place and authority in the family, as well as their livelihood, are based.

The greater security of women's role in the family has been augmented by the romanticization of the family in the last few centuries, which was aimed at camouflaging the power inequities in the family from a culture increasingly critical of power inequities. This romanticization described women's role in the family as being the heart of the family, as the center of warmth and as mediator of love and communication, as the primary source of nurture. The child was represented as innocent and carefree, protected and cherished. Men's role, however, did not require any romanticization, as men did not require convincing as to the benefits of the patriarchal family; their role was still presented in terms of headship and breadwinner. At times religious treatment of the burden of breadwinning suggested that this onerous

burden was men's admission price to the warm refuge of the family hearth—
a warmth generated by women and children.[1]

In the present when many women and children no longer are dependent
upon men's breadwinning, what do men have to offer as the admission price
of membership in the family? The relation between men and the rest of the
family in the traditional model was based on economic need, not emotional
ties, though emotional ties often developed. Mutual love as constitutive of
relationships, though advocated for the Christian community as a whole,
was not described as central to the family, but was assumed to be naturally
present in the relation between mother and children. In the household codes,
for example, the husband was to love, the wife to obey; the father was to
refrain from provoking children, the children to obey; the injunctions are
complementary, but not mutual.

A major effect of the traditional family on men, then, which is only highlighted by the loss of economic dependency of families on men, is the depiction, and consequent socialization of men as emotionally isolated persons
who relate to others primarily through power and provision.[2] Men's historic
roles of ruler and breadwinner in the family have never demanded interpersonal nurturance skills, though many men have developed these independently. In dominant/subordinate relations, it is always the subordinates who
need to develop sensitivity, tact, communication and solidarity skills, which,
under greatly unequal divisions of power, are actually survival skills.

Another explanation often given for the lesser relationality of men is the
different conditions under which male children deal with the task of gender
identity, which children face in their first and second years ([39], pp. 20–25; [8],
pp. 50, 274). Since virtually all child care during these early years is provided
by women, boys cannot use the modelling technique which girls use for
achieving gender identity. The absence of fathers or other males, and the fact
that the young boy's closest attachment is to a female, makes his task of gender identity much more anxiety-ridden. Boys' technique for reaching gender
identity is a combination of separation from the mother or mother-substitute,
and reliance on reinforcement and cognitive learning. In this explanation, the
restriction of child care to women (and the resulting absence of men in child
care) is an important factor forcing boys to renounce their earliest intimate
relation (with a women) in favor of more impersonal cognitive learning if they
are to feel themselves men. The implications for men's later capacity for intimacy and for later attitudes toward women are potentially serious.

Today we face massive evidence that at social-psychological levels men
are increasingly isolated, anxious, and emotionally repressed, and that these
conditions are potentially lethal. Their socialization in and for the traditional
family has not equipped them in great numbers for child nurturance or for
the emotional self-disclosure necessary for the close friendships and mutual,
intimate marriages which become more necessary in modern society as more
traditional forms of community and intimacy disintegrate under the influence of mobility and urban anonymity. There is a shift in the masculine paradigm now occurring in the West, largely under socio-economic pressure,

which emphasizes the co-operative teamwork required of labor in a mecha-
nized age rather than the stoic physical strength and endurance of traditional
masculinity ([39], Ch. 10). This shift, toward masculine interpersonal skills
and more mutual forms of relationship, which is now in its early stages and
is largely limited to middle class workers, is greeted warmly by many
women desirous of more mutuality and intimacy in relationships with men.
There is no better way to sell women's magazines then headlines promising:
"How to Get Your Man to Know and Share His Feelings"; "How Men Can
Learn to Parent Well"; "How Spouses Can Be Partners." Yet men's socialization in and for the traditional family is a primary obstacle to this paradigm
shift. The situation of many western men today bears eloquent witness to the
cliche that it is lonely at the top. Headship and responsibility for breadwinning have deprived many men of some important human experiences, pres-
suring them to find identity in power and responsibility.

At a social level, the headship of men in the family has been so accepted
that there have been few checks on the illegitimate use of men's power in the
family. Today we face horrendous statistics regarding men's abuse of women
and children, both inside and outside the family. In the U.S. domestic violence
occurs in 10–21 percent of all families, with men as the almost exclusive perpetrators of this violence ([32], p. 11; [42], pp. 21–22). Studies show that
between 20–48 percent of women are victims of serious sexual assault by
males,[3] with a marital rape rate of 14 percent ([42], pp. 57, 64). Over 30 percent
of girls and 10 percent of boys are sexually molested [43]—and the overwhelming majority of the offenders are men. 4.5 percent of all girls in this society are sexually abused by their fathers ([44], p. 10). While there are traditional
Jewish and Christian teachings on family which condemn such practices, the
religious legitimation of the power of men in families conditions some men to
understand wives and children as possessions they may use as they wish, thus
undermining the bans. Religious traditions have exhibited peculiar blind
spots which also promoted abuse. Christianity long understood marriage as
entailing the gift of one's body to the spouse in perpetuity,[4] so that the
churches, and the Christian states, until very recently failed to recognize the
possibility of rape in marriage. Still today not all the United States recognize
marital rape, the largest single type of violent rape, and until 15 years ago no
state recognized it. In Judaism also there has been some blindness to illegitimate exercise of men's power in families. The Mosaic law's list of relationships
covered by the incest ban includes bans on a man uncovering the nakedness
of his mother, his sisters, his granddaughters, his father's wives, his daugh-
ters-in-law, his aunts by blood and marriage, his sisters-in-law, but not his
own daughters (Lev. 18:7–16), though father-daughter incest is one of the most
prevalent, most violent, and most damaging type of adult-child incest ([44],
pp. 231–232). The women covered by the ban were understood as the property of another man, while his daughters were his. In the Decalogue, men are
forbidden to covet not only their neighbor's house, ox, ass, manservant or
maidservant, but also his wife—another piece of his property (Ex. 20:17). In
the Mosaic law, if a man rapes a betrothed virgin, he is sentenced to death; if

he rapes an unbetrothed virgin, he must pay her father the bride price and marry her (Deut. 22:25–29). The injury done is understood to be to the victim's father or betrothed, not to her; she can be married off to her rapist.

EFFECTS ON WOMEN

Just as there are some disadvantages to men in the power given to men in the patriarchal family, there are some limited benefits which accrue to women despite their subordination and restriction to home and motherhood. Chief among the positive benefits are a capacity for and interest in relationship with others which frequently produces among women intimate friendship, varying degrees of solidarity, and nurturing bonds to children. One must be careful not to understand these as inherent in women; just as some men resist male socialization to develop these qualities, so some women do not develop these qualities. But by comparison to men as a group, women are inclined to be much more relational and to develop skills for nurturing intimacy. For example, studies of conversation among male groups and female groups demonstrate that men are more likely to interrupt one another, discuss impersonal subjects and events rather than feelings or relationships, and to compete with one another for the speaker role. In contrast, women's groups demonstrate attempts to include women who have been silent, to share feelings and discuss relationships, and seem to lack the dominance hierarchy so central to men's groups ([2], pp. 292–299).

Yet for all the importance of these relational skills, the overall effects of women's role in the family have been negative. The understanding that women were created to be full time mothers and domestic workers has resulted in economic discrimination against women for millennia. Even today in the U.S. the average female wage for full time workers is less than ⅔ that of men, though women as a group are better educated than men. The channeling of the majority of women into "women's work," sometimes called pink collar work, makes "comparable worth" campaigns difficult to implement, and so women's work continues to be underpaid. Furthermore, the majority of married women who do work today find that they, compared to their husbands, carry a "double burden" [1]. They share the burden of supporting the family, in addition to virtually the entire burden of child care and domestic work. Working wives have a workday of ten to twelve hours; they average workweeks of 76 hours ([18], p. 379 in [1]). Studies of men's labor in the home report that husbands spend from .3 to 1.3 hours per day in child care or domestic labor ([37], p. 285 in [1]). Thus in the contemporary world what might once have been an equitable division of labor—though not of power—between men and women in the patriarchal family has become blatantly inequitable as women share the burden of men's traditional role, while men fail to share the burden of women's traditional role.

The definition of women as made to be mothers within the patriarchal family contributed to an understanding of women as body, as inherently carnal, during centuries when all things material, and especially the body, were understood as morally dangerous and inferior to the spiritual soul, which characterized men. It was the possession of the soul that was understood to make humans reflect the image and likeness of God; yet Christianity tended to follow Augustine's dictum that men possessed the image and likeness of God in themselves, women only when joined to a man (De Trinitate, IV, 6). The carnality which characterized women for most of Christian history was understood to justify men's control of female bodies. This not only allowed the sexual abuse of women described above, but produced many other variations of female loss of control of their bodies. It was decided that the evil seductiveness of female flesh (to men!) should be covered and kept out of sight; women who failed to heed this decision were considered to have invited random abuse. Women's carnality was considered to be redeemed only through childbirth (1 Tim. "Yet woman will be saved through childbearing, if she continues in faith and love and holiness, with modesty"). Because childbearing was women's function, until recently Christianity has forbidden women any reproductive control over their bodies: no contraception, no abortion, and no right to refuse intercourse in marriage, even though frequent childbearing endangered women's lives, and millions of women died in childbirth. Women still struggle for control over their bodies with a largely male medical establishment,[5] which, it is charged, has developed medical procedures contrary to women's interests, such as widespread caesarean sections, induced births, unnecessarily radical hysterectomies and mastectomies, not to mention the development of the horizontal birthing position which extends labor time [48], [16].

But perhaps the most negative effects of women's role in the family have been on women's personalities and identities. Many women in the West feel a lack of individual identity. Longer lives and shorter periods of child bearing and rearing have left many women feeling as if they have drifted through their lives fulfilling assigned roles without any sense of themselves as individuals. Universities, churches, and volunteer organizations benefit from attempts of middle class women to fill this void; marriages are strained as women seek to expand their interests and test their capacities in new ways. There is frequent feminist discussion of women as spiders sitting on a web and unable to distinguish themselves from their webs: they are daughters, sisters, wives and mothers, but they fear that apart from these relations they do not exist, and are therefore dependent [27]. The contemporary understanding of the human person as autonomous contributes to their dissatisfaction [27], [47]. This is the reverse of the situation of many men, who have constructed the identity which women feel the lack but are constrained from the relationality which women feel defines them.

Passivity is often described as characteristic of women. One element of passivity under increasing attention is fear. There is little doubt that most women live in fear, to greater or lesser degrees, of male anger and aggression. A cursory review of the statistics on domestic battering and sexual abuse makes this understandable. But we are coming to understand that the 20, or

30 or 40 percent of women who personally suffer the various types of male abuse are not the only women who live in fear. The knowledge that one's mother, sister, friend or neighbor (not to mention many anonymous women in the daily news) has been beaten, raped, or molested is sufficient to provoke fear of men's anger and aggression. Even fathers teach girls to fear violence, or at least coercion, from males; many end their warnings with "I know; I was once a young man." In fact, parents of both sexes teach women from the time that they are little girls that men are to be feared at some level. "Don't talk to strange men, don't accept rides, be careful to travel in groups, always carry money for a cab or phone." The very measures we teach our girl children to make them safe, alert young women that there is danger out there, and it is male. Mothers often counsel children to avoid or to appease Daddy when he is angry (whether the anger is appropriate or not), thus teaching children that Daddy's anger is potentially dangerous. Fear has a debilitating effect on persons; the greater the level of fear, the more energy must go to coping with the fear, and less is left for other activities. A great deal of many women's energy gets used coping with fear and attempting to avoid, deflect, or distract men from men's anger and violence, not to mention coping with the familial after-effects of anger and violence.

Is it any wonder that religious women are increasingly admitting to problems with relating to a male God we call Father? It seems clear that the Judeo-Christian tradition, so long as it continues to identify God as male and father, and so long as women's experience of males is tinged with fear of anger and violence, will have great difficulty in overcoming traditional understandings of God as strict judge, swift to anger and terrible in his wrath.

But explorations of anger have expanded from considerations of the effects of men's anger and violence to deal with the phenomenon of anger in women. Many writers increasingly point to anger as both having beneficial effects, and as being absent in women ([17]; [34], Chs. 6, 12). Many encourage women to experience their anger, rather than repress it, with the understanding that anger arises from injury, form a slight to their personhood, or that of someone they care about. If the anger is not expressed toward the cause of the injury, but is repressed and unrecognized, it takes other more destructive forms. One common form that repressed anger at injury takes in women is self-blame. Victims of rape and child sexual abuse frequently come to accept responsibility for their own victimization, rationalizing that such atrocities do not happen to the innocent, that they must have done something to attract or set off the abuser ([13], Chs. 7, 8, 10). Victims of marital rape and child incest abuse are often so dependent both emotionally and materially on their abusers that they fear the loss of love and support if they vent their anger by accusing the abuser. Even women victims of strangers frequently fear a lack of support from relatives, friends, and social agencies—a fear which is all too often realistic—and interpret this to mean that there is no basis for their anger; that it is appropriately aimed inward.

Anger aimed inward in the form of self-blame is terribly destructive, and often begins a process of loss of respect and concern for one's self as not worthy of care and protection. The fact that many victims of sexual abuse, especially young victims, are frequently revictimized later in life, is often explained through this learned failure to care for, and therefore to protect, themselves ([44], Ch. 11).

But all injuries to women are not sexual. Parents and teachers who steer top ranking girl students into nursing schools instead of medical schools, secretarial programs instead of academic tracks, companies who routinely pass over women for promotion, personnel directors who ask women applicants what form of contraception they use and do they plan to have children, all do women injury. The anger at this injury is often repressed because women know that such behavior is not intentionally vindictive, and is often well meant. But repression of such anger does not eliminate it.

All persons yearn for power, not necessarily power over others, but personal power—the power to choose and direct one's course, to make a difference, to achieve, to earn recognition. Many women in the traditional family have been denied freedom and opportunities to fulfill their yearning for power in legitimate ways. The role ascribed to them is supportive, with little room for independence. Denied legitimate methods of exercising personal power, some women, like some in other suppressed groups, choose illegitimate ways of exercising personal power, usually through manipulation of those to whom they are bonded in the family ([36], pp. 13–20). In the nineteenth and early twentieth century, middle and upper class women frequently used illness as a means of gaining attention and controlling other family members. The nagging wife, the controlling mother, are contemporary stereotypes not true of women as a whole, but nonetheless all too often real. They result at least in part from the restriction of women to a narrow role in which they are unable to recognize or satisfy their own ambitions.

Such responses of women to the restrictions of women's roles in the family are still present in our world, but as opportunities for some women open up we have become aware of another type of damage done to women by socialization for the patriarchal family, and that is fear of success ([14], pp. 238–241; [36], pp. 29–32, 119–122). Many women fear success in a variety of forms. Adult women sometimes fear job success out of concern that their husbands cannot accept wives who earn more or who have higher status positions; this fear may be well grounded, as such situations frequently figure in reasons given for divorce. Many young women deliberately fail to succeed both in school and in sports, especially when directly competing with men, for fear this will turn off boyfriends, or boys in general. Some women exhibit a more generalized fear of success as something not feminine, something they are unable to reconcile with themselves as women. Women seem to achieve best when they understand the endeavor in terms of developing or testing social skills. Women are least likely to achieve when success is achieved in direct competition; studies show that while competition raises achievement for boys, it decreases success for girls, even when the competitors are same sex ([31], pp. 247–254; [20]).

Women's repressed anger and the fear women carry of men take their toll on women's relations with men, even men they have no reason to fear, men who have not injured them. They create real tension in women who want to love and trust their husbands, but cannot entirely banish the whispered warnings of male violence and male failure to take women seriously which echo in women's heads every time their husband curses a reckless driver or complains about his secretary's incompetence.

All of this leads us to one of the greatest casualties of the patriarchal family structure: the marital relationship itself. There seems little doubt that the interpersonal intimacy which can characterize marriage is rendered infinitely less possible within the structure of patriarchal marriage. Both spouses suffer this lack of intimacy, though differently. Women seem to have greater resources for intimacy outside marriage than men, who are more dependent on wives for intimacy than wives are on them. But wives are much more likely to feel a conscious need for intimacy, and to mourn or resent low levels of intimacy in marriage. It is the power relation in patriarchal marriage which operates against intimacy. When one person has power over another—and the greater the power, the more profound the effect—trust becomes difficult. The powerless party is unlikely to fully trust the powerful party, and therefore avoids complete vulnerability. Who of us chooses to confess our fears and failures on the job to our boss? Co-workers are more likely confidants, and, especially for men, only when the co-workers are not in any way competitors. We are more likely to confide in fellow students than teachers, siblings than parents, unless the object of our confiding is to enlist the powerful one on our side against another. True marital intimacy requires trust so total that it allows us to abandon self-consciousness—to fail to consider how we appear to the other—and to merge with the other at some level. To merge with someone of superior power is dangerous, for we can disappear completely, be swallowed up by the other—which has been women's experience of the legal, political and economic consequence of marriage historically understood as "two in one flesh."

While the powerful person may have no fear of being controlled, punished, abandoned, swallowed or otherwise hurt, the role division in the traditional family leaves men also wary of marital intimacy. For the nature of power over others, which men are conditioned to see as central to masculinity, is that it is never vulnerable, never allows the lowering of the barrier of self-consciousness, lest power be lost. Fear of intimacy, especially with women, as an obstacle to identity, which may be left over from boys' early struggle for gender identity, may also contribute to men's resistance to marital intimacy, and to men's tendency to understand marital intimacy in terms of physical sharing in sex ([6], p. 364) rather than as an integration of physical with emotional intimacy.

EFFECTS ON CHILDREN

The area in which the traditional family's effects have received the least scrutiny is that of effects on children. The ideological right today bemoans the demise of the traditional patriarchal family; their argument that children are the foremost victims of its demise is widely accepted. Even liberals, who support the changes in women's role opposed by the right, often approach the issue of the family by asking how to compromise the legitimate aspirations of women with the real needs of children for the protective nurture of the traditional family. There is little systematic attempt to assess the positive and negative effects of the traditional family on children.

The most commonly posited benefit of the traditional family for children is the full time presence of mothers. In fact, this supposed benefit does not withstand much historical scrutiny, as it seems to suppose a modern, stable, two parent household with a full time female homemaker. For thousands of years women in the home worked—in the fields, in animal care, weaving, slaughtering, candle and soap making, not to mention cooking, washing and cleaning. Among the poor, married women were often employed outside the home as cooks, laundresses, in factories and mines, as seamstresses and maids, and in raising the children of the rich. It has probably been historically accurate to posit that contemporary working mothers with a 40 hour work-week spend more time interacting with their children than their ancestresses did.

We also need to look at the psychological research on the effect of female child care on young children referred to above, which leads girls and boys to different strategies for reaching gender identity—strategies which promote later deficiencies in intimacy and relationship for boys, and in individual identity for girls.

Liberal rights language is just beginning to be applied to children. It can be helpful to probe the rights of children, and the extent to which children's rights are recognized in the traditional patriarchal family. Children obviously have at least equal rights to material subsistence with adults. The role of fathers as breadwinners in the traditional family is assumed to supply the material needs of children. When fathers are adequately remunerated for work, children are usually benefitted.[6] However, the material dependence of children on fathers is often experienced by children—and often consciously presented by parents—as the basis of fathers' authority in the family, the reason that obedience is due to father: "So long as you live in my house, and I feed you, you do as I say." The dependence of the child on father's control of resources (or in female-headed households on mother's) conditions children to view reality as a realm where those with material resources call the shots. While this can stimulate in children a positive desire to aspire to economic self-sufficiency as an adult, it can also have very negative effects. It is a very real factor in children leaving home before they are prepared for independence, either as runaways or in order to marry too early. It can lead children to see the amassing of material resources as the means of being in total control of one's life (especially when fathers are not only powerful but non-expressive of feelings of failure, dependency, and anxiety), when in fact such freedom is impossible; all humans must learn to deal with dependency and the unavoidable arbitrariness of accidents, sickness, and death. This link between father's resources and father's authority can also lead children to desire control over others, to be as powerful as, or more powerful than, father. Worse, it can condition children to be deferential to those in later life who have more resources than they, as if those persons have a right to authority over them. Interestingly enough, the Judeo-Christian tradition has from its beginnings criticized attempts by the rich to use their wealth to manipulate and control the less fortunate, to deny them justice and rights, but has never recognized that the identification of the headship role with the breadwinner role of men predisposes children to resign themselves to the real power—if not the just right—of the rich to manipulate others less well endowed.

The emphasis on the obedience of children to parents, in the absence of any elaboration of the rights of children, fails to prepare children to recognize parental wrongdoing, whether towards them or others. Thus child victims of parental physical or sexual abuse, even when they consciously hate the abusive parent, frequently have no consciousness that the parental action is objectively wrong and could be condemned by, or much less stopped by, outside authorities. The difference in age and status between parents and children, not to mention the tremendous emotional and material dependence of children on parents, will always make it difficult for children to challenge parents' wrongdoing. But the model of the traditional family actually encourages the child to see the parent as the ultimate authority, incapable of wrongdoing. Even when children as adults could otherwise expect to be freed from obligations of parental obedience, the religious tradition has insisted that adult children honor and respect parents, without specifying any limits on that honor and respect (Ex. 20:12, 21:17; Mt. 19:18–19; Eph. 6:1–3). While it is one thing to demand that children provide material support for dependent elderly or disabled parents, unlimited honor and respect, as indicated in the Exodus condemnation of anyone who curses his parents, is quite another.

The terror and trauma of children trapped in physical, sexual or emotional abuse by parents cries to heaven, but because children have been silenced by our failure to instill in them a sense of their own right to freedom from abuse, only heaven hears their largely unspoken cries. We often read that many of these abused children grow up to be abusers, which is true. But we need to add to this picture the hundreds of thousands of child runaways whose chief reason for flight was abuse, and who all too often end up further exploited in our urban underworlds. We need to add to the picture the thousands of victims of parental incest who become self-destructive out of internalized anger and hatred, and commit suicide, or choose the slow death of drugs, alcohol, or the daily death of self-punishing sexual exploitation by others. We have a tendency to think that these cases, despite burgeoning statistics, are only exceptions to a general rule of parental nurture. But we have a great deal of psychoanalytic literature that describes other, more subtle but also disabling consequences on children of the power roles embedded in the traditional family.

Alice Miller, a German psychoanalyst, writes of her work with many "successful" persons whose parents have demanded and received the surrender of the child's self to meet the parents' needs. The loss of the self in such children cripples them emotionally:

> Children who fulfill their parents' conscious and unconscious wishes are "good," but if they ever refuse to do so, or express wishes of their own that go against those of their parents, they are called egoistic and inconsiderate. It usually does not occur to the parents that they might need and use the child to fulfill their own egoistic wishes. They often are convinced that they must teach their child how to behave because it is their duty to help them along the road to socialization. If a child brought up this way does not wish to lose his parents' love (and what child can risk that?) he must learn very early to share, to give, to make sacrifices and to be willing to "do without" and forego gratification—long before he is capable of true sharing or of the real willingness to "do without." Frequently such children use their own children, satisfying the needs of the suppressed child in themselves at the expense of their child, just as their parent did. ([35], p. xii)

The very language we use to describe many of the reasons for having children are revealing, for they say little of respect for the dignity and identity of the child her/himself: to insure our immortality, to succeed more than I did; to be the —— I never got to be; for company and security in my old age; to see myself in another person; to have someone who will love me; to have someone I can pour out my love on; to be a real woman (man). All of these reasons are based on the needs of the parent, and on using the child to fulfill one's need. The very description of women in the traditional family as necessarily mothers—and the long millennia that barren women have been despised or pitied—encourages women, in particular, to see children as fulfilling a basic need for women.

In many ways we do see children as property, a special kind of property which fulfills a variety of intimate needs for us. We give very little thought to the process by which children become adults (and later parents themselves), to how they are to move from being dependent objects to becoming subjects with free agency. Marriage counselors tell us that many of the most common marital problems stem from relationships between parent and child that remain unresolved ([15] Ch. 3). Most persons in our society marry long before having reached adulthood in terms of seeing themselves as peers of their parents. Most remain trapped by the emotional authority they were socialized to grant parents. One problem for marital intimacy resulting from this failure to throw off the emotional authority of parents takes the form of fearing to achieve greater emotional intimacy in one's marriage than one's parents achieved. The adult child has accepted the parents as the norm which cannot be surpassed; to attempt to do so is to be disloyal. Such disloyalty implies a recognition of parental failure at intimacy, not only within the parental marriage, but also a failure to satisfy the intimacy and affection needs of the child. Such recognition is often painful for the child, a festering sore that has often been long repressed. A failure on the part of the adult child to face parental failure in intimacy and one's own resentment toward the parent for such failure (and all parents some-times fail their children) produces resistance to intimacy with one's spouse, often most obviously in the presence of one's parents.

Another obstacle to marital intimacy reported by marriage counselors stemming from the failure of adult children to understand themselves as peers, and not emotional dependents, of their parents, concerns identifying one's spouse with the parent of the same sex. We often marry seeking in a spouse the positive qualities we see in our opposite sex parent without the negative qualities we resent in that parent. Frequently, after marriage, we come to see in the spouse the negative qualities we most resent in the par-ent—whether or not the spouse really exhibits such qualities. When we have never resolved with the parent the resentments which linger from our child-hood, when we have never recognized and forgiven the parent their failures with us, we often read into and resent in the spouse the qualities we resented and feared in the parent but could never openly face in the parent due to dependency and fear/reverence for parental authority. The wife who resented her father's consistent failure to listen to her, to take her seriously, may explode in anger at her husband's momentary preoccupation which causes him to miss some more or less inconsequential remark of hers, and may see a few such incidents over a period of years as evidence that he is just like her father: uncaring. The husband who resented his mother's attempts to control his every action and relationship through guilt and emotional manip-ulation may flare up at a wife who expresses a preference regarding some decision they face; he interprets her statement not as a preference, but as an attempt to control his decision, as his mother did.

In conclusion, the emphasis on children's obedience to parents in the Judeo-Christian tradition, and the underlying assumption that parents are natural protectors guided by the best interests of the child, have worked against any recognition of the rights of children. The absence of treatment of children's rights has failed to restrain parental abuse of children, helped pre-vent children from resisting parental abuse, and caused social blindness to the abuse of children. In addition, because within the tradition children are always children of their parents, subject to some degree of obedience, and never become peers, children are hindered in resolving the very real and pow-erful resentments against parents that they carry from childhood. These resentments are often pre-rational, deeply rooted angers (sometimes unrea-sonable) at the ways in which they were weaned, toilet trained, disciplined, and touched or not touched with affection, or even actually abused. Religious communities could be a source of real support for children in becoming adults if they encouraged children to see their parents as humans, not as god-like authorities, humans who are themselves wounded, who make mistakes and fail to love enough. For only if children can see their parents realistically, and forgive them their inadequacies, can they move on to the real issues of adult-hood without projecting the problems of childhood on their adult relation-ships and situations. Such a resolution of our childhood resentments affects also our relationship with God, since the Judeo-Christian tradition presents

God as parent. If we so often project our problems with our parents on our spouses, how easy it is to project these same problems onto our divine parent.

CONCLUSION

It is clear that the patriarchal understanding of the family within western religion is not merely an issue for theologians. Religion shapes both individuals and social relationships. Many different kinds of contemporary professionals—doctors, psychotherapists, social workers, and marriage counselors, among others—as well as a variety of non-religious institutions deal on an everyday basis with unhealthy effects of religious understandings of the family. Their concern is one source of support for the growing interest within many religious communities both in revamping the family in directions which would allow for healthier individuals and relationships among men, women and children, and in using social scientific criteria to give shape to these new directions.

The greatest obstacle to such revamping is ingrained reverence for religious tradition, which manifests itself in opposition to all changes in what is perceived as the revealed tradition. The best rebuttal to such opposition seems to be a demonstration of the internal contradictions within western religious traditions, in particular the existence within these traditions of potentially liberating perspectives which counter dominant practice regarding the family. Within Judaism, we can look to the nature of Yahweh as revealed both in divine intervention to liberate the suffering. Hebrews enslaved in Egypt and in the law given to Moses, which took such pains to establish a strong community rooted in justice and concern for the weak. From this grounding, both Talmud and Mishnah elaborated further protections for women and children. In Christianity, Jesus's treatment of women, children, work, and power, together with the evidence of how the early church in Acts and the epistles implemented some of these teachings, from the basis for rethinking the family. This work has only barely begun.

NOTES

1. See the speeches of twentieth century Roman Catholic popes, for example, [21], [22], [23]. In Protestantism, Martin Luther himself is often pointed to as the initiator of this romanticizing of the family ([29], pp. 89, 160–161, 191) though his appreciation of the joys of the family hearth and the conjugal bed are less fulsome than in the twentieth century popes, and seem a welcome relief from the often legalistic and ascetic treatment of family in the theology of his own day.

2. Mirra Komorovsky writes: "The need to maintain a 'manly' facade, the fear of acknowledging 'feminine' traits—all generate in the male a constant vigilance against the spontaneous expression of feelings. . . . Such guardedness adds stress to the ever-present external sources of tension" [28]. Jourard argues that being manly requires men to wear a kind of neuromuscular armor against expressiveness. He goes so far as

to consider that the chronic stress thus generated is a possible factor in the relatively shorter lifespan of men as compared with women. But the deleterious effects of such self-control do not end with stress. A man who does not reveal himself to others is not likely to receive their confidences. It is precisely in the course of such interaction, however, that a person learns to recognize his own motivations, to label emotions, and to become sensitive to the inner world of his associates. Without an experience of psychological intimacy a person becomes deficient in self-awareness and empathy [26], [3]. Still another recent writer ([11], p. 210) alleges that men are threatened by psychological probings of feelings. What passes for confidence in their relationships with women is nothing but their need for uncritical reassurance ([28], p. 158).

3. This range is based on two studies: ([25], p. 145) for the conservative figure of 20–30 percent, and ([44], p. 158) for the 48 percent, which is conservative in its own way: Russell's survey found that 82 percent of the victims of child incest were later victims of serious sexual assault as adults, whereas *only* 48 percent of those who had not been victims of child incest suffered serious sexual assault as adults. Thus the figure of 48 percent is not for the population as a whole, but for the population who were not victims of child incest. Figuring in the victims of child incest would raise the figure even higher.

4. As found, for example, in 1 Cor. 7:3–4: "The husband should give to his wife her conjugal rights, and likewise the wife to the husband. For the wife does not rule over her own body, but the husband; likewise the husband does not rule over his own body, but the wife."

5. This male medical establishment itself used Christianity in its bid to replace the midwives who preceded the male physicians: midwives were accused by the male physicians of pagan superstition because of their refusal to use the new mechanical forceps and their insistence on working with, and not against nature. As a result, thousands of midwives were burned at the stake as witches by the church [10]. The struggle over women's bodies continues [41].

6. For example, there is continuing emphasis through one hundred years of Catholic social teaching on the just wage as one sufficient for the support of the wage earner and his family in adequate comfort and security, without the necessity of his wife or children working ([29], p. 662; [26], pp. 626–629).

BIBLIOGRAPHY

1. Andolsen, B.: 1985, "A Woman's Work Is Never Done," in B. Andolsen et al. (eds.), *Women's Consciousness, Women's Conscience: A Reader in Feminist Ethics*, Winston, Minneapolis, pp. 3–18.

2. Aries, E.: 1977, "Male-Female Interpersonal Styles in All Male, All Female, and Mixed Groups," in A. Sargent (ed.), *Beyond Sex Roles*, West, St. Paul, MN, pp. 292–299.

3. Balswick, J. O. and Peek. C. W.: 1971. "The Inexpressive Male: A Tragedy of American Society," *Family Co-ordinator* 20, 263–268.

4. Bird, P.: 1974 "Images of Women in the Old Testament," in R. Reuther (ed.), *Women and Sexism*, Simon and Schuster, New York, pp. 41–88.

5. Brown, J. C. and Bohn, C. R. (eds.): 1989, *Christianity, Patriarchy, and Abuse: A Feminist Critique*, Pilgrim, New York.

6. Bunker, B. B. and Seashore, E. W.: 1977, "Power, Collusion, Intimacy/Sexuality, Support: Breaking the Sex-Role Stereotypes in Social and Organizational Settings," in A. Sargent (ed.), *Beyond Sex Roles*, West, St. Paul, pp. 356–370.

7. Cantor, A.: 1976, "Jewish Women's Haggadah." in C. Christ and J. Plaskow (eds.),

Womanspirit Rising: A Feminist Reader in Religion, Harper and Row, San Francisco, pp. 185–192.

8. Chodorow, N.: 1978, *The Reproduction of Mothering: Psychoanalysis and the Sociology of Gender*, University of California Press. Berkeley.

9. Clark, E. and Richardson, H. (eds.): 1977, *Women and Religion*. Harper and Row, San Francisco.

10. Ehrenreich, B. and English, D.: 1972. *Witches, Midwives, and Nurses*, Feminist Press, Old Westbury, NY.

11. Fasteau, M. F.: 1974, "Why Aren't We Talking?" in J. Pleck and J. Sawyer (eds.), *Men and Masculinity*, Prentice-Hall, Englewood Cliffs, NJ, pp. 19–21.

12. Fiorenza, E. S.: 1983, *In Memory of Her: A Feminist Theological Reconstruction of Christian Origins*, Crossroad, New York.

13. Fortune, M. M.: 1983, *Sexual Violence: The Unmentionable Sin*, Pilgrim, New York.

14. Frieze, I. et al.: 1974, "Achievement and Nonachievement in Women," in I. Frieze et al. (eds.), *Women and Sex Roles*, W. W. Norton, New York, pp. 234–254.

15. Gallagher, C. et al.: 1986, *Embodied in Love: Sacramental Spirituality and Sexual Intimacy*, Crossroad, New York.

16. Gordon, L.: 1977, *Woman's Body, Woman's Right: A Social History of Birth Control in America*, Penguin, New York.

17. Harrison, B. W.: 1985, "The Power of Anger in the Work of Love: Christian Ethics for Women and Other Strangers," in C. Robb (ed.), *Making the Connections: Essays in Feminist Social Ethics*, Beacon, Boston, pp. 3–21.

18. Hartman, H.: 1981, "The Family as the Locus of Gender, Class and Political Study: The Example of Housework," *Signs* 6, 366–394.

19. Hauptman, J.: 1974, "Images of Women in the Talmud," in R. Ruether (ed.), *Women and Sexism*, Simon and Schuster, New York, pp. 184–212.

20. Horner, M. S.: 1970, "Femininity and Successful Achievement: Basic Inconsistency," in J. M. Bardwick et al., *Feminine Personality and Conflict*, Brooks-Cole, Belmont, CA, pp. 40–74.

21. John XXIII: 1960, "Ci e gradito," *Osservatore Romano*, 8 December 60.

22. John Paul II: 1979, "All'indirizzo," *The Pope Speaks* 24, pp. 168–174.

23. John Paul II: 1979, "Chi troviamo," *The Pope Speaks* 24, pp. 165–167.

24. John Paul II: 1981, "Laborem exercens," *Acta Apostolicae Sedis* 73, pp. 577–647.

25. Johnson, A. G.: 1980, "On the Prevalence of Rape in the U.S.," *Signs* 6, 136–146.

26. Jourard, S. M.: 1971, *Self-Disclosure*, Wiley-Interscience, New York.

27. Keller, C.: 1986, *From a Broken Web: Separation, Sexism and Self*, Beacon, Boston.

28. Komorovsky, M.: 1976, *Dilemmas of Masculinity*, W.W. Norton, New York.

29. Leo XIII: 1891, "Rerum novarum," *Acta Sanctae Sedis* 23 [William Gibbon (ed. and transl.), *Seven Great Encyclicals*, Paulist, New York, pp. 1–30)].

30. Luther, M.: 1967, *Table Talk*, in T. S. Tappert (ed. and trans.), *Luther's Works*, Vol. 54, Fortress, Philadelphia.

31. Maccoby, E. and Jacklin, C.: 1974, *The Psychology of Sex Differences*, Stanford University Press, Berkeley.

32. Martin, D.: 1976, *Battered Wives*, Glide, San Francisco.

33. McLaughlin, E.C.: 1974, "Equality of Souls, Inequality of Sexes: Women in Medieval Theology," in R. Ruether (ed.), *Women and Sexism*, Simon and Schuster, New York, pp. 213–266.

34. Milhaven, J. G.: 1989, *Good Anger,* Sheed and Ward, Kansas City.

35. Miller, A.: 1981, *The Drama of the Gifted Child* [1979 *Das Drama des begabten Kindes*], Basic, New York.

36. Miller, J. B.: 1986, *Toward a New Psychology of Women,* 2nd ed., Beacon, Boston.

37. Minge-Klevana, W.: 1980, "Does Labor Time Decrease with Industrialization? A Survey of Time Allocation Studies." *Current Anthropology* 21 (3), 279–298.

38. Plaskow, J.: 1976, "Bringing a Daughter into the Covenant," in C. Christ and J. Plaskow (eds.), *Womanspirit Rising: A Feminist Reader in Religion,* Harper and Row, San Francisco, pp. 179–184.

39. Pleck, J. H.: 1981. *The Myth of Masculinity,* MIT Press. Cambridge, MA.

40. Raines, J. C. and Day-Lower, D.: 1986. *Modern Work and Human Meaning,* Westminster, Philadelphia.

41. Rothman, B.K.: 1982, *In Labor: Women and Power in the Birthplace,* W. W. Norton, New York.

42. Russell. D.: 1983, *Rape in Marriage,* Macmillan, New York.

43. Russell, D.: 1984, *Sexual Exploitation: Child Sexual Abuse and Workplace Harassment,* Sage, Beverly Hills, CA.

44. Russell, D. E. H.: 1986, *The Secret Trauma,* Basic, New York.

45. Sales, E.: 1974, "Women's Adult Development," in I. Frieze et al. (eds.), *Women and Sex Roles,* W. W. Norton, New York, pp. 157–190.

46. Sennett, R. and Cobb, J.: 1972, *The Hidden Injuries of Class,* Vintage, New York.

47. Smith, R.: 1985, "Feminism and the Moral Subject," in B. Andolsen et al. (eds.), *Women's Consciousness, Women's Conscience: A Reader in Feminist Ethics,* Winston, Minneapolis, pp. 235–250.

48. Wertz, R. and Wertz, D.: 1979, *Lying-In: A History of Childbirth in America,* Schocken, New York.

CHAPTER 26

Men Who Make Women Want to Scream

Connell Cowan
Melvyn Kinder

The state of men's lives is troubling and problematic. We seem confused, direc-
tionless, and stuck in patriarchal patterns. It has become fashionable in the current situation to engage in male bashing and blame men for all the ills of the
world. This is neither therapeutic for men nor helpful to women who may be
seeking a suitable life-partner.

The Cowan and Kinder essay offers a suggestive typology that acts as a critical examination of four types of men. Each of the men is initially charming,
attractive and intriguing—but all end up infuriating women: The Clam radiates
a tough outer mystique; the Pseudo-Liberated male is disarmingly expressive; the Perpetual Adolescent shuns adult responsibilities: and the Walking
Wounded wallows in self-pity and vulnerability.

Exploration of the various types should make for interesting, if not provocative, classroom discussion.

Questions for Discussion

1. What is initially attractive about men who display a tough, macho mystique? What is the dark side of this type of masculinity?
2. Emotional expressivity can be a form of narcissism. Why is this so? How can
   it be a false form of liberation for men?
3. Why do so many men resist adult responsibilities and commitments today?
4. Men carrying a mixture of hurt, bitterness, and rejection can make foolish
   choices. Why? Is a healing and healthy relationship possible for them?

There are several types of men who very predictably end up infuriating
women. Some are charming in the beginning and then change. Others
are attractive because of the qualities women hope to find in them. All, sooner
or later, make women want to scream in frustration.

THE CLAM

Some men radiate a tough mystique that grows out of a basically selfish, withholding, and guarded nature. This kind of man can be as dangerous as he is attractive and intriguing. A woman can be drawn to what she sees as strength in this man's insensitive toughness and may also feel potentially reassured by that "strength." We say "potentially," because she never quite feels part of such a man's strength, since the man doesn't really share or even truly open himself to the woman. He makes the woman do the emotional work for the two of them. He sets the stage and she dances around, attempting to read his mind. She knows she wants the security of feeling close to his strength. But he doesn't ever allow her to get too close. She loves it, she hates it. She knows she is drawn by the very characteristic she is bound and determined to change.

Arlene, 28, is a warm, gregarious bank loan officer. When she met Tom she knew this relationship was "it" for her. She described him as "a bit too emotionally guarded" for her tastes, but she thought all that would change once he realized he could trust her. She thought that she understood Tom's secretive tendencies, which she saw as reflecting his self-control or perhaps shielding an old hurt. He wasn't the least sensitive to her needs, but she talked herself into believing it was only because she hadn't communicated them to him clearly enough, and so it must be her fault.

They married eight months after they met. Arlene felt sure the kind of commitment they were making would open the door to at last feeling loved by Tom. She was absolutely convinced that if she loved him enough, with no holds barred, he would open himself to her. With love as the key, she would open his heart and finally reap the treasure that surely lay within. Tom's tough, controlled outer shell concealed a tough, controlled inner core. Tom claimed he loved Arlene, but she never felt it and he never showed the demonstrative affection she wanted and needed. She divorced him after one painful year.

Arlene made a mistake in the choice of her relationship with Tom. She interpreted his guarded, withholding nature as mystique. What she found was that instead of standing guard over some hidden treasure, he in fact was desperately trying to protect his insecurity from exposure. When Arlene realized this, Tom's strength was transformed in her eyes to brittle crumbling defenses. His wonderful mystique turned to fear.

The Clam either fears his dependency needs or has managed to convince himself that he doesn't have any. He is very attractive to many women, who mistake this trait for strength and self-containment. But problems soon emerge as the woman begins to want more. We all experience love, at least in part, through feeling needed by our partner, "needed" emotionally. The Clam can't allow himself to need anyone enough to form an intimate, satisfying bond. To do so would require confronting his fears of weakness and vulnerability. Ancient, scarred-over hurts may have destroyed his capacity to feel that deeply.

We all need, in a love relationship, to have our partners dependent upon us—not bloodsuckingly so, but needing us emotionally nevertheless. And this man will never allow himself to be dependent enough to be able to form a close, sharing relationship. He functions as a self-contained system. No matter how warm a woman's love, it will never melt his protective shield. It is too tough, too old.

Another necessary bonding agent in the man/woman relationship is trust. Trusting and being trusted. The Clam is recognized by his secretive qualities. The secretive person is protecting something he fears may be lost, betrayed, taken away. Women need to keep in mind when they meet a secretive man that his concealment is a result of his past and has nothing to do with them.

Trust develops through a process of give and take. It involves mutually disclosing deeper and more complex aspects of ourselves. The Clam cannot take a chance on important emotional exposure. He will not risk the danger of looking into old wounds stored away in the locked file of forgotten, painful memories. Most often, he doesn't even know just what it is he is protecting or even that he is, in fact, behaving in a self-protective and distrustful fashion. The Clam cannot trust and he does not open up.

He doesn't know how to love, for the process of giving and loving means exposing his needs and vulnerabilities. If he hasn't learned to love by the time he is an adult, a woman won't be able to teach him—no matter how patient she is. It's foolish to believe otherwise.

What is misguided in the pursuit of this man is the failure to correctly identify his real strengths and weaknesses. If you find yourself with this type, you may believe you possess the magic potion to change him, to release in him what you believe to be a capacity to love, but you don't. In fact, the more a woman loves and cares for this kind of man, the better the chances of driving him away. Intimacy is his enemy—it scares the hell out of him. If he doesn't run away first, you will become so frustrated with having to do all the emotional work, provide all the tenderness, that eventually you will end the relationship—if you're smart.

THE PSEUDO-LIBERATED MALE

At the outset of a relationship, the Pseudo-Liberated Male can be disarmingly attractive to women. He is the living embodiment of the liberated man, the perfect and natural complement to today's woman. He accepts her changes, even encourages them. He seems gentle and sensitive, vulnerable, expressive, revealing—a real dream come true! But it's a dream that frequently turns into a nightmare.

This type of man interpreted the women's movement as an invitation to become more expressive emotionally. He distorts this new "freedom" as a license to whine and a rationalization to express endless fears and personal insecurities, often to the point of utter distraction. The Pseudo-Liberated

Male is certainly quite different from the withholding man described earlier. Many women see him as a welcome change—someone who will share himself, be open with his feelings. That's great, but some of these men go overboard. Even when women begin to get a whiff of his excesses, they frequently don't trust their own instincts—they don't run.

In a way, women have been encouraged and made to feel as if they should like this man. After all, if they expect to be able to explore new and unfamiliar "masculine" parts of themselves, and if they expect men to accept and love them for it, then they, in turn, should be tolerant of men's becoming more expressive and vulnerable.

When Marv and Marlena came in for couples therapy, Marv said they were not having any specific problems living together—they wanted rather to make their relationship as dynamic and positive as possible, and they were both interested in the therapy process as a means of personal growth.

Marv, 32, is a free-lance carpenter and unpublished novelist. Marlena, 34, is an office administrator for an import-export company and the steady wage earner in their household. They're both active in antinuclear and liberal political causes, Marv more so than Marlena because he doesn't work steadily and has more time.

Marv and Marlena are both bright, attractive, and personable. But what became clear in the very first session, as Marv talked on and on, with occasional glances at Marlena for approval, was that Marv is a narcissistic Pseudo-Liberated Male. He wasn't interested in making his relationship with Marlena better. What he wanted was a fresh, larger audience for his seemingly inexhaustible insights about himself.

Marlena revealed that Marv preferred talking about their relationship and himself to just about any other activity. Marlena eventually confessed that she felt exhausted by the constant talk and by his incessant demands for attention and analysis of "where we're at with each other now."

This man hides the fact that he is an emotional drain, that he's a taker. He is so happy and relieved to have a chance to legitimize his insecurity and neediness that he doesn't realize that he is taking without giving. He sincerely believes that his emotional diarrhea is a gift. He hides his fears and passivity beneath a deceptive costume of gentleness and sensitivity—and hopes the woman won't see through his disguises.

During the early stages of the relationship, this man performs dazzlingly. He is a master with words—he may even be poetic. His verbal output is such that a woman thinks she sould feel nourished. Instead, she feels drained. He wraps his need for reassurance in a pretty package, one that can make a woman feel privileged, needed. Eventually, she may become aware that all he ever seems interested in talking about is the relationship—or himself! She wants to like him. She thinks she should like him. After all, he is expressive, isn't he? "In touch" with his feelings? Why does he make her want to scream? Perhaps it's because she finally realizes that he would rather talk about a relationship than have one.

These men are sensitive, and that can be a refreshing experience. The problem is that as time goes by, it becomes increasingly apparent that their sensitivity is one-sided, directed consistently toward themselves.

We believe women do want to know how a man feels, but they don't want to hear about it all the time. A relationship with one of these overly emotional types can eventually make them feel crazy. Somewhere along the way, these women may sense they are drawing a curtain of insensitivity about themselves, much as they have accused men of doing in the past. They want to shout, "Will you just shut up and make love to me and stop this endless discussion about us?" "Where we're at" with this man is all too frequently talking about his feelings toward you, toward himself, and toward the relationship—"talking about" rather than letting it just happen.

The Clam is too contained, while the overly sensitive Pseudo-Liberated Male is too uncontained. He wears his insecurities like medals on his chest.

Trying to free this man from his emotional problem can make a woman feel powerful, but it's a trap. They are better left alone. You might even be doing them a favor, for then they would be forced to deal with their insecurities themselves, from the inside out, rather than attempting to foist the responsibility on some woman who will indulge them.

Some men who make women want to scream are fundamentally unredeemable. The smart woman passes on these men, regardless of how interesting or intriguing they may appear on the surface. The Clam and the Pseudo-Liberated Male are such men. Then there are two other types of men who are terribly frustrating to women, but who do have very redeemable features if a woman can tolerate the frustration and make her way through the obstacles they place in her way: the Perpetual Adolescent and the Walking Wounded.

THE PERPETUAL ADOLESCENT

The Perpetual Adolescent stopped developing in what is late adolescence for a man—around the mid-twenties. This man's unspoken and unconscious credo is "I'm going to be 25 forever." This stunted growth is not always easy to detect. It is reflected in his emotional construction and in his diminished capacity to participate fully in relationships rather than in the external surface features of his life.

Outwardly, he has many disarmingly attractive qualities. He may be boyish in a confident, brash way. This man often works with the public and is articulate, with an easy, charming manner. He makes people feel comfortable.

Greg, a handsome, athletic yacht broker, lives in an expensive condominium overlooking a marina. From his sundeck, he can see his sailboat bobbing in its slip as well as the pool and tennis courts crowded with tanned single men and women. At 36, Greg still considers himself young and needing to devote most of his time and energy to building his career. He feels no pressure to marry. In fact, he tells himself, as well as more than an occasional woman, that he needs more time before settling down—time for his work, time for travel, time to "have fun."

Greg describes his life-style as "fun." He jogs and works out daily. He looks youthful, tanned and toned. He dresses fashionably. He tells himself there's no hurry, plenty of time to find his "ideal woman."

Actually, these are excuses for Greg to live in a perpetual adolescence. He talks about responsibility and commitment but runs when a woman starts to demand it. He can be affectionate to a woman and mean it, but he is not willing to grow up and relate to her as an adult. When his relationships get to the stage where it is natural for them to move to a deeper level, Greg becomes frightened and pulls away. He typically dismisses the woman as "dependent, clingy, possessive, demanding," rather than facing his own fear and reluctance to enter adulthood. He is blind to his profound reluctance to mature, for his youthful posture serves as a shield and defense against intimacy.

The Perpetual Adolescent's greatest fear is entrapment, for he doesn't fully trust his own autonomy. "To have to give" and "to be able to receive" both detonate deep, underlying fears of dependency in him. This man hides his fears of intimacy from himself by coming very close to committing in a relationship. But he ultimately wards off those fears by always making sure that "very close" is only that, not marriage.

The Perpetual Adolescent has rather shallow views and interactions with women. For that matter, his friendships with men are equally shallow. He often perceives himself as an adventurer. But the greatest adventure of all—marriage—is an event he is never quite yet ready for.

Initially, he can be captivating, for he has fine-tuned many aspects of his external presence. He can trot out all the phrases that make him sound wonderful and make a woman feel wonderful. The trouble is, he's a deal opener, not a deal closer. The Perpetual Adolescent is extremely frustrating to women, for as they naturally want to deepen what seems like a nicely developing relationship, he slowly pulls away. If he only did something truly rotten, she could free herself and be glad to be rid of him. But he doesn't—maddeningly, his only real flaw is his unwillingness to grow up.

We have said that this man is redeemable, and he is. Given enough time and patience, most men eventually do grow up, marry, and have families. For this type of man, the critical age seems to be about 39. He begins to panic when he is unable to deny being middle-aged. Having learned to trust his own independence more solidly, he is less afraid of entrapment and connection. He has become acutely aware of his own mortality, and he doesn't want to become a lonely old man.

While we wouldn't recommend the younger version of this man, the older model isn't bad at all. Should you know someone like this and want to deepen the relationship, there are a couple of important factors to keep in mind.

This man, even though he fears it, is capable of becoming healthily dependent on a woman. The mistake most women make is in not understanding that he does need a woman and can make a connection. Typically, the woman pushes too quickly and succeeds only in pushing him away. It is not that the impulse to move forward is inappropriate on the woman's part, for it isn't, but the timing is critical. This man is most likely to connect deeply to the woman who has patience to let him develop a strong need for her first. Then, and only then, should she begin to make her healthy demands for commitment. By then, he is so involved that he wants to stay.

THE WALKING WOUNDED

After a separation or divorce, both men and women naturally feel a mixture of hurt, bitterness, and rejection. Fortunately for most of us, these wounds heal over time, and the best medicine is eventually to love again.

Men and women usually suffer equally, but there are wounds unique to men that merit understanding. The Walking Wounded man can drive women crazy for a time, but he does heal and definitely is redeemable. In fact, these men often make fine mates precisely because they are committed to long-term relationships.

There are two basic types of wounds. The most painful is, of course, the loss of one's mate and most likely the loss of family. The other is the loss of financial security resulting from the divorce. The loss of a family structure is devastating to most divorced men. Suddenly, he finds himself alone in an apartment or hotel room, feeling lost, disoriented, and forlorn. He envies his wife, who frequently continues living in the family home, in familiar and, at least in his mind, secure surroundings. For the first time, some men will sadly and poignantly realize how important it was to hear "Daddy" when they came home from work.

Contributing to this sense of isolation that divorced men experience is the constant apprehension that even in his grief, he must continue working hard to make money. There is a line from a western song that goes, "I can't halve my half again." For many men, a divorce means money: the destruction of the financial security and comfortable life-style which they worked so long and hard to create. Women suffer equally from the financial fallout from divorce, but it is our purpose here to acquaint you with the male point of view.

Most men feel "ripped off" after a divorce. Regardless of the validity of this attitude, they are nevertheless embittered by the helplessness they felt during the process of marital dissolution. This helplessness is often in combination with the sense of futility they have regarding child custody. In addition, they have increased financial anxieties related to the demand of separate living expenses. In their anxious and dark moments, they're not sure they can make it.

Even though they may be freer to date than are their wives, they have a sense that it's all a dream. They tend to drink and to abuse drugs, which compounds their depression.

How do these men appear to the women who encounter them? If they are newly separated, they can actually appear quite attractive, because they haven't yet assumed the guarded mantle of men who have been single for a while. They may be vulnerable too, which can be appealing to women, especially those who like to nurture men.

The newly separated man is open, eager to talk and to reveal himself, though too often this evolves into a tedious self-pity which will eventually drive a woman crazy. Even so, his eagerness for contact and relationships is quite appealing to many women.

The recently separated man tends to talk about his ex-wife and bitch about any number of injustices he feels. This facet of him can become so boring that women quickly feel the urge to run. A word of advice: After a while, don't be such a good listener. It's bad for him to wallow in self-pity and definitely not romantic for any woman.

There is a common problem with the Walking Wounded that can break a woman's heart. A woman may be age 32 to 40 and childless and find herself involved with a divorced man of the same age or older who already has children. It is vitally important for that woman, if she wants children of her own, to make this desire known to the man early in the relationship. Many divorced men are well-meaning but frankly have no desire to start another family. Yet they will mutter vaguely, "Well, if it's really going well, I guess I might want to have another kid." That's not good enough. A woman needs a clear answer or else it's time to move on. To invest precious years in a relationship only to end up with a man who has very different dreams is tragic indeed.

Men who have been separated for a year or more are usually less appealing than the very vulnerable, freshly separated ones we've been exploring. But they often have another kind of attractiveness: They're ripe for the picking. This is true in spite of their seemingly hardened outer shell. Though wary and a bit suspicious about being hurt again, they will become involved. They can make good mates, and do wish genuine intimacy, but they are scared. The solution is simple: Don't push for commitment in the beginning, even in the first six months. Women who need reassurances right away will not do well with this type of man. He does need extra time, but not forever. After a period of exclusive involvement, it is appropriate for the relationship to deepen and become more involved. He will commit himself if the woman really means it. But in some cases it may take an ultimatum. The woman who acts as if she will wait forever is making a real mistake, because she will be taken for granted.

One final word on the Walking Wounded. There are women who advise friends and say to themselves, "Stay away from any man who has just come out of a relationship. They just want a nursemaid. As soon as they heal a little, they'll leave you to play the field." It is true that they may be overly dependent at first or need to date around a bit, but some of the best men are not out there very long. Men who have been in a marriage, even a bad marriage, want to be in a relationship again. The best men are not single for long, and shouldn't be dismissed foolishly.

CHAPTER 27

The Integration of Masculine Spirituality

David James

Male students who read this essay may find themselves inwardly scoffing at the some of its initial claims about men. Some may perceive what they are reading as an attack on men, which is far from its intent. David James is examining the pain and hurts of men in order to get at the underlying causes. His aim is to invite men to consider the conditions under which their own lives are dehumanized. Men do well to pay attention.

A helpful approach men might take in this reading is to ask, "To what extent is any of this applicable to my friends, those I care most about?" or, "Which of my friends shows these signs of alienation?" Another helpful strategy might be to ask women friends what truth or value they find in the author's description of men's alienation.

No matter what approach readers take to this essay, some, both women and men, will find themselves resisting the ideas James asks us to consider. "This is boring" or "how ridiculous" or "too many generalizations" are some of the resistant stances other readers have taken to these ideas. However, those willing to bring an open mind to these questions will find much to consider about the situation of men in our culture and how a process of healing might begin.

The main claim the essay makes is that "most men are alienated from themselves, their relationships, their environment, and ultimately their God." Among the evidence offered for this claim are the following tendencies: workaholism, emotional numbness, and a tendency toward various kinds of addiction. These compulsions are attempts to heal emotional pain. If the claim is true in any degree, then attentive men—and the women who love them—will recognize the pain behind the compulsions and the call for change within them. The author also provides specific steps toward healing change.

Questions for Discussion

1. What statements in this essay strike you as true or probably true, based on your own observations?
2. What statements do you find either false or exaggerated? What evidence would you give to back up your position?
3. What do you find to be the most important point made in the essay?
4. Though the essay is about "men" of all ages, is there anything James writes here that you find particularly true of men your own age?

5. If you were to suggest a very first step toward the integration of masculine personhood, what would it be?

Further Reading

Harriet Goldhor Lerner. *The Dance of Anger: A Guide to Changing the Patterns of Intimate Relationships* (New York: Perennial Library, 1989).

———. *The Dance of Intimacy: A Guide to Courageous Acts of Change in Key Relationships* (New York: Perennial Library, 1990).

THE ALIENATION OF MEN

The western male is in a state of alienation. Most men are alienated from themselves, their relationships, their environment, and ultimately their God. Reflecting upon the effects of the current crisis of masculinity, Sam Keen asks:

> Why has the gender that gave us the Sistine Chapel brought us to the edge of cosmocide? Why have the best and brightest exercised their intelligence, imagination, and energy and managed only to create a world where starvation and warfare are more common than they were in neolithic times? Why has the history of what we dare to call "progress" been marked by an increase in the quantity of human suffering?[1]

Men experience deficits in personality development due to child rearing practices which tend to foster a boy's alienation from himself and others.[2] Men have been reared with a limited range of socially acceptable models of masculinity.[3] As such, a stunted and dominating masculine is a common expression of manhood for most in the west.[4] Such developmental defects become more evident when a boy grows up and enters the world of men. The symptoms of men's disconnection are socially manifest in increasing rates of male violence, delinquency, divorce and the abandonment of children. Statistics indicate that males overwhelmingly account for the majority of assault and homicide victims, persons with AIDS, and those homeless, or killed on the job.[5] The field of addictions research shows an abundance of data which point to men's disconnection from themselves. Jed Diamond, a licensed clinical social worker, notes:

> Untreated addictions continue to grow like cancer. Twenty-eight years ago, when I first began working in the field, men were dealing mostly with alcohol and heroin addictions. In recent years, there has been an addictions explosion. Men are now struggling with everything from homemade amphetamines to designer drugs, compulsive sex to destructive work, overspending to overeating.[6]

Many men suffer some significant degree of estrangement from relationships. Dwight H. Judy notes:

> There are problems for men in the area of aggression and violence and in a limited understanding of the potential for creative relationships with women in many diverse roles. We also find the male struggling with his relationships with men in authority and with men as coequals in companionship. We find a negative view of emotions and the human passions. We find men in many ways cut off from others, as well as from their sources of both passionate energy and creative vision.[7]

Whether the divide is between a man and his own being, or a man and others, most possess a limited capacity to engage in the challenges and satisfactions of relationships. Aaron Kipnis cites the following as evidence of men's disconnection:

- Co-dependency
- Workaholism
- Emotional Numbness
- Addiction to Excitement
- Sexual Addictions
- Loss of Soul[8]

This inventory of masculine wounds resonates with many authors writing in the field of masculine psychology/spirituality. In his work, *The Intimate Connection*, James B. Nelson suggests that men are wounded at the very essence of their masculinity. These wounds result in an inability to embrace intimate relationships, friendships, or their own mortality.[9] Sam Keen labels the post-modern man the "concupiscent consumer,"[10] who lives life by aesthetic or sensual whim rather than from a moral or spiritual center. This betrays evidence of men's disconnection to their own depths, as they make decisions based on fancy or feeling.

Those involved in the field of masculine psychology or spirituality agree that this fracture of the male psyche is evident in men's addictions. Jed Diamond calls addictions the "disease of lost self-hood . . . a loss of the primal connection with the masculine self."[11] He notes that through addictions men attempt to substitute an attachment to a person, object or feeling for authentic experiences of being—"of living life for its own sake."[12] In recovery work, men unearth reservoirs of anger, shame and despair that addictions previously masked. Diamond suggests that addictions are often the result of attempts to deal with the pain of parental shaming or childhood abuse. In other words, "Our addictions became our way of dealing with our wounds."[13]

Diamond identifies alcohol, cocaine, narcotics, steroids, food, work, and money as the most common "masculine compulsions."[14] Attachment to any of these provides enough sensual stimulation to keep a man from being confronted with his emotional pain. He also notes that in addition to compulsive behavior, most men suffer from sex and love addictions, commonly called co-dependency.[15] Given men's inability to form authentic relationships, it is not surprising to discover that they look to others to provide them with feelings of acceptance, passion and significance. In a culture that places such a high value on sexuality, men have been socialized to view sexual activity as the chief means of receiving intimacy and tenderness. I will examine the issues of sexuality in greater detail later in this chapter. At this point, however, it is important to note that sexuality is a major source of addiction for men.

Diamond suggests that the study of addictions in men demonstrate that (1) all men are addicted to something or to someone; (2) recovery and restoration should begin sooner and continue longer than current practice dictates; (3) all addictions have a positive aspect that must be acknowledged; and (4) developing a mature masculine personality and recovering from addictive behavior are correlative tasks.[16]

There are a number of challenges necessary for men to address in their quest for wholeness. For the purpose of these reflections, I have categorized these challenges as "The Father Wound," "Warped Sexuality," and "Hatred of the Feminine." Each plays a crucial role in developing an authentic spirituality for men. Unless men successfully engage each of these challenges to psychological development, they will be forever alienated to some degree from God and others.

THE FATHER WOUND

The relationship between father and son is perhaps the most ruptured relationship of our time. A popular notion of child rearing is that it is "the woman's responsibility." But the father is the boy's first significant non-maternal influence. One of the father's primary roles is to free a boy from his mother's influence. Jed Diamond notes:

> We need help in separating from the force field of the Woman or we will never make it to manhood. Her gravitational pull is too strong to resist on our own. Older males must be there to exert an even greater pull or we will always be afraid of being sucked back into our mother's orbit . . . we may grow physically, and do all the "manly" things, but inside we still feel like mama's boy.[17]

Consequently a father's responsibility is to assist his son in establishing a cohesive psychic structure. When this doesn't happen, the boy's ability to develop psychologically is hampered.

A memory common to many contemporary men is that their father was either absent or abusive. In men's gatherings there is little talk of the presence and support of the father. Instead, great sadness overtakes these groups as men speak about their unrealized hopes and dreams for relationships with their fathers. Robert Bly calls grief the "primary masculine emotion,"[18] based in large part upon his conversation with thousands of men still yearning for their father's love. In his work, *Iron John: A Book About Men*, Bly suggests that fathers need to pass on to their sons masculine energy, a "cellular knowledge." If this doesn't occur, then boys are unable to learn "at which frequency the masculine body emanates." He notes:

> Sons who have not received this retuning will have father-hunger all their lives. I think calling the longing "hunger" is accurate: the young man's body lacks salt, water, or protein, just as a starving person's body and lower digestive tract lack protein. If it finds none, the stomach will eventually eat up the muscles themselves. Such hungry young men hang around older men like the homeless do around a soup kitchen. Like the homeless, they feel shame over their condition, and it is nameless, bitter, unexpungeable shame.[19]

In his book, *Absent Fathers, Lost Sons*, Guy Corneau reflects upon the consequence of the father's absence. He notes that the crisis of absent fathers is reaching epidemic proportions. In 1988, one in five children lived in a fatherless home and eighty-nine percent of these homes were headed by women.[20] Even when a man lives in the home, Corneau suggests that there is no guarantee of effective fathering:

> The term absent fathers . . . refers to both the psychological and physical absence of fathers and implies both spiritual and emotional absence. It also suggests the notion of fathers who, although physically present, behave in ways that are unacceptable: authoritarian fathers, for example, are oppressive and jealous of their sons' talents and smother their sons' attempts at creativity or self-affirmation. Alcoholic fathers' emotional instability keeps their sons in a permanent state of insecurity.[21]

Corneau notes that when a breach exists between a father and his son, the child is at a loss for a means of establishing his own masculine identity and is "unable to advance to adulthood."[22] Violence, should it occur, intensifies this fracture, and the boy's identity becomes even more fragile. Corneau suggests that the father plays the following developmental tasks in the life of his son:

- The father teaches his son how to become independent from his mother.
- The father makes it possible for his son to develop his own capacity for self-affirmation and self-defense.
- The father provides his son with the psychic safety to develop his sense of exploration, sexuality, and independence.
- The father encourages his son's achievements and teaches him responsibility.[23]

He submits that fathers vitiate the necessary link to masculine energy when they are absent for a prolonged period of time, neglect their son's need for affection, threaten to abandon him, shame or cling to him.[24] This is often evidenced when a father demands that his son "follow in his footsteps" or be successful in ways that the father couldn't. This type of abusive behavior creates a son who lacks self-confidence, has adjustment disorders, is "given to anxieties, depression, obsessions, compulsions and phobias."[25] Corneau notes that a boy who has experienced such paternal neglect struggles with sexual identity, represses aggression, lacks healthy ambition, suffers from learning disorders, has a diminished sense of moral value and personal responsibility, and often turns to some form of substance abuse in an attempt to quench his inner psychic turmoil.[26] Patrick Arnold notes that "psychologists and counselors tell us that many American men bear these father-wounds all their lives, never understanding them much less finding healing with their fathers."[27] To summarize the depths of the problem, Corneau writes:

> The father's absence results in the child's lack of internal structure. . . . His ideas are confused; he has trouble setting himself goals, making choices, deciding what is good for him, and identifying his own needs. For him, everything gets mixed up: love and reason, sexual appetites and the simple need for affection. He sometimes has problems concentrating, he is distracted by all sorts of insignificant details. . . . Basically he never feels sure about anything.[28]

One of the deleterious effects of the father wound is the effect that it has on society at large. As noted previously, sociologists indicate that a disproportionate number of delinquent boys come from homes where the father was either absent or abusive. In order to compensate for a lack of healthy male energy or role models, boys become hyper-masculine and violent. Male violence is then perpetuated upon other men, women, children, and animals and ultimately the environment. This cycle of violence continues to the next generation as the latest batch of wounded men produce alienated sons, who in turn do the same to their sons. This poisonous pedagogy is self-perpetuating unless something breaks the effects of this abusive chain.[29]

To summarize, the lack of effective fathering is one of the most profound deficits that a boy can experience. A review of the literature demonstrates that boys who experience either abusive or absent fathers lack the ability to develop coherent psychic structures. This deficiency leads to a host of psychological, relational, sexual and spiritual challenges that boys are unable to meet. This type of fathering (or lack of it) is perpetuated generationally, and the damage to the corporate masculine psyche is evident in the addictions, compulsions and disorders noted above.

WARPED SEXUALITY

Patrick Arnold asserts that "sexuality gives our personal as well as our faith relationships depth, color, excitement, and vivacity."[30] Counselors tell us that one of the disastrous effects of the "father wound" is the warping of a boy's sexual identity. Those who work with men don't need statistics to understand that male sexuality is in trouble. What was designed by God as a gift and means of life has become a source of deep pain for men. Many men have little understanding of the difference between sex and love, intimacy and intercourse. The richness of a man's sexuality is usually shrouded in ignorance, fear and despair. Men know that something is missing, but the socialization of young men creates more questions than answers. Until the last thirty years, boys were not offered any formal education in sexual matters, and today's contemporary sexual pedagogy tends toward a mechanical view of sexual activity. Accordingly, those authors who work with men indicate that confusion and shame are two pervasive wounds to a man's sexuality.

James B. Nelson's book, *The Intimate Connection*, offers helpful reflections in the domain of masculine sexuality and spirituality. Nelson notes that the Christian faith holds that sexuality is a constitutive part of a man.[31] A man's sexuality is one way that God expresses incarnational love and presence in the world. According to Nelson, Christianity inspires a belief that sexuality is about more than a physical act leading to ejaculation and orgasm. Rather, it views sexuality as a part of a person's constitutive psychic makeup which leads to expressions of vulnerability, passion, love and connection.[32]

A review of the contemporary sexual landscape reveals a far different picture. Sex for the sake of sex is commonplace, as are the plethora of diseases and disorders that accompany it. Movies and television shows portray little relationship between love, commitment, vulnerability and sex. Instead, messages of recreational sexual activity are commonplace in the entertainment industry. Pornography is no longer restricted to seedy movie theaters on the edge of town. The sale and rental of pornographic home video is a multi-billion dollar industry in America in the 1990s. Steven Hill notes:

> In the United States, 22 million men spend $2 billion a year on a range of 105 pornographic magazines. Porn films gross $5 million per day and the porn industry earns over-the-counter profits of $8 billion per year.[33]

To the extent that this distorted and commercialized view of sex dominates the cultural landscape, it robs men of the power and beauty of their sexuality.

A particular mythology of sexuality has developed, and men are seemingly driven to live the myth. Don Sabo submits that the common masculine mythology for sex revolves around men as the "sexual athlete." This myth views sex as a sport, has its own language, involves score-keeping and conquest, and is oriented toward performance and reward.[34] Sam Keen identifies two predominant roles of men within the sexual myth. Men are expected to (1) fulfill the role of the "sexual warrior"—to conquer and possess as many women as possible as a proof of his potency, and (2) to fulfill the role of the "sexual worker," to "make love, perform, to produce the intended result— satisfying the woman."[35] This banal sexual mythology objectifies both parties. The love, commitment and appreciation of the "other" has no place in contemporary sexual expression. The sex partner, whether a woman, another man, a child, or an animal, become a means for personal gratification. Beauty, dignity, and intimacy are lost as performance, success, prestige, anger, fear and power become the common denominators in men's sexual experience.

The effect of the current sexual pedagogy is devastating to the psychic and moral health of young men. Men experience a dualistic split as they feel driven to sexual experience, and yet react to prevailing cultural mores and trends. Depending on the cultural voices that a man chooses to listen to, sexuality is either celebrated or condemned. He is encouraged to "score" as often as he can, or he is instructed that he must remain chaste in anticipation of his honeymoon. This denies the vast middle ground of sexuality. First, it reinforces a dualistic notion that a man's body is separate from his soul and spirit. Second, it limits sexuality to mechanical action alone. Third, it keeps the focus of sexual expression in the realms of either performance or gratification. Finally, it keeps a man's sexuality wrapped within a mantle of shame.[36]

Several authors note that a man's sexual shaming begins very early in life and continues throughout adolescence. Wounding the sexual organ at birth, such as through circumcision, inaugurates the shaming process.[37] As the boy matures he is told in subtle ways that his body is "dirty" and animal, and that his sexual urges and desires are to be avoided at all costs. Philip Culbertson notes:

> In reality, many men experience conflict about sex, partly due to the double message we learned as children: sex is dirty, and sex should be saved for someone you love. In other words, spend your youth accumulating the worst dose of self-loathing and repression you can think of, and then dump it on the most special person in your life.[38]

The degree to which sexuality is a source of shame is evidenced by society's preoccupation with it. As noted above, boys are routinely socialized toward either blatant promiscuity or repressed chastity. Sigmund Freud once noted that a person's denials tell as much about the person as do one's affirmations. The vast amount of money and energy spent demonizing or defending sexuality in our culture is indicative of the inordinate social fixation upon sexuality. Rather than being celebrated as a gift of God given to enhance and enrich life, sex has become a source of great pain for men.

The shame that men experience about their sexuality is multiplied when it comes to homosexual men. Centuries of prejudice and oppression have convinced many gay men that they are flawed at the essence of their being. This results in an ever downward spiral of shame as they struggle with the same need that every man has: for love, tenderness, erotic interaction and intimacy. Daniel Helminiak notes, "Much human potential is squashed and wasted in people who live for years in secret self-hatred, taught to be afraid of their own hearts."[39] He observes the results of societal intolerance of homosexuality:

- Thirty to forty percent of children living on the streets were thrown out or left their homes because they are homosexual.

- Thirty percent of teenage suicides, two to three times higher than the national norm, are among homosexual youth.

- The employment status of homosexual people is at risk when their orientation becomes known.

- Homosexual parents lose custody of their children, are evicted from their homes, are routinely beaten up or murdered, and in some instances are denied adequate medical care and die alone: all due to the inability of society to tolerate their presence.[40]

In light of ever expanding evidence about the nature of psycho-sexual orientation,[41] the damage that heterosexism generates takes on a more sinister character. "Gay bashing" is at an all time high as men, afraid of the implications of homosexuality, resort to violence and, in some cases, murder to stamp out its "plague."

This brief review demonstrates some aspects of the warped sexuality that contemporary men experience. Whether gay or straight, men live with confusion and shame relative to their sexuality. A review of the literature available on this topic demonstrates that an underdeveloped sexuality inhibits men's ability to love themselves, others or God.[42] Rather than having companions, lovers or spouses, men look for sex objects to satisfy cravings for intimacy, tenderness or passion.

HATRED OF THE FEMININE

"Women, you can't live with them and you can't live without them," or so says traditional masculine lore. Women remain a source of constant fascination for men. The woman is the one where men first reside in amniotic bliss, she is the one who brings men into the world, and she is the first one to whom men look for nourishment and life. To some degree, men never separate from the world of women. In contemporary culture this assessment seems ever more apt, as there are fewer older men walking boys through initiation rituals designed to break the hold of the woman upon the man. Men remain under WOMAN's spell for most of their lives. Keen writes:

> It was slow in dawning on me that WOMAN had an overwhelming influence on my life and on the lives of all the men I knew. I am not talking about women, the actual flesh-and-blood creatures, but about WOMEN, those larger-than-life shadowy female figures who inhabit our imaginations, inform our emotions, and indirectly give shape to many of our actions.[43]

An abundance of multi-disciplinary literature indicates that young boys must differentiate not only physically from the feminine, but psychologically as well. As noted above, one of the most devastating results of the "father wound" is that men remain trapped in the control of the feminine, unable to rescue themselves. Anthropologists and mythologists propose that tribal initiatory rituals were designed to facilitate the differentiation process for boys. Robert Bly notes:

When initiation is in place, the old men help the boys to move from the mother's world to the father's world. Boys have lived happily since birth in the mother's world, and the father's world naturally seems to them danger-ous, unsteady, and full of unknowns. We recall that most cultures describe the first stage of initiation as a clean and sharp break with the mother. Old men simply go into the women's compound one day with spears when the boys are between eight and twelve and take the boys away.[44]

Many authors posit that since older men have abdicated their responsi-bility as initiators, younger men have not been effectively introduced to hearty masculine ways of knowing and loving. As a result, men remain in bondage to WOMAN. When one is struggling to break free from WOMAN, one cannot respect, honor and love women. Psychologists note that an inability to sepa-rate from WOMAN results in a bondage which enslaves a man to the feminine. This terrifying servitude has many faces to it. Men worship women, while abusing them. They entice women, charm them, sometimes even purchase them, all the while experiencing fear and anxiety about their relationship to them. This fear is not limited to women, but also to a man's own latent femi-nine characteristics. Philip Culbertson writes of the "fear of the feminine":

> Many men have been taught to shun whatever smacks of "playing the woman's role," for they do not know how to define masculinity other than be a sequence of "nots": not feminine, not womanly, not passive-receptive, not soft, not "on the bottom."[45]

This fear of the feminine is not limited to heterosexual men. In some facets of the gay community there tends to be a misogynist paradigm, where women are spurned, not only as sexual partners, but as friends, confidantes, and sisters in faith. Regardless of psycho-sexual orientation, the fear or hatred of the feminine is a consequence of a man's inability to integrate psy-chologically.

In his book, *He: Understanding Masculine Psychology,* Robert Johnson points to the tragic results of a man's failure to differentiate between the dif-ferent parts of his own psyche. When he is unable to integrate the feminine elements of his own psyche, a man projects his feminine presence into the outer world, onto flesh and blood women. Patrick Arnold notes:

> Many men are completely unaware that the "ideal woman"—soft, gentle, and mysterious—that they can never find, or sweeps them off their feet when they do, is within themselves. The only kind of women "out there" in the real world are real, flesh-and-blood women.[46]

This projection will be either highly positive or extremely negative, but never neutral. In other words, men expect women to provide what they are unable to: men expect women to feel for them, to provide them with comfort and nourishment, softness and empathy, to demonstrate depth of feeling and animation.[47]

This projection explains men's bondage to WOMAN. A man cannot live without a connection to the inner and outer feminine.[48] To compensate, women are objectified and, hence, controlled by men, both gay and straight. Women become queens or whores, goddesses or servants, all in an attempt to maintain some sense of distance and mastery over them.

To summarize, feminists have long pointed to the dangers of men's inability to co-exist with the feminine. Historically men have viewed women as their property, as objects of their sexual fantasies, and as servants who perform a variety of tasks upon demand. Psychological theory has demonstrated that this is primarily due to a man's fear and hatred of all that is feminine within himself. This fear and hatred is projected onto flesh and blood women who unnecessarily bear the burden and violence of men.

MATURE MASCULINITY

A formidable challenge exists for the men's movement as it seeks to guide men through processes of integration and recovery. As noted above, recovery work for men necessarily involves healing the personal, relational and environmental facets of a man's life. There are a number of authors who have identified a series of tasks that men must undertake if they hope to heal the split in their lives and relationships. Aaron Kipnis has identified the following tasks which heal the masculine soul.

- To admit woundedness.
- Begin healing by examining wounds.
- Rebuild self-esteem on deep masculine foundations.
- Break out of old stereotypes and claim diversity.
- Reclaim ancient sacred images of masculinity.
- Apply the myths of masculine soul to daily living.
- Rediscover male initiation and heal wounds between father and son.
- Love and work in ways that heal the masculine life.
- Restore connecting with ancestors and come to terms with mortality.
- Build male community and begin healing wounds between sexes.
- Develop a masculine affirming psychology.
- Continue reawakening the masculine soul.[49]

Kipnis is not alone in appreciating the value of formational tasks for men. Sam Keen suggests that there are ten movements toward maturity,[50] Dwight Judy identifies five goals for the quest of male healing,[51] and Philip Culbertson proposes a threefold agenda for masculine development.[52]

While other authors might vary their approach, the consensus of the literature is that men must intentionally participate in this journey of growth and integration. Men must first examine the roots of their ambivalence and hostility toward themselves and others. Next, they need to recognize flawed parental influences and stereotypical patterns of masculinity, and then break free from them. Finally, men must explore and embody new models of masculinity and manly living.

In his work, *The Warrior's Journey Home: Healing Men, Healing the Planet*, Jed Diamond offers a helpful model for men's healing and integration. Diamond's "Ten Tasks of the Mature Masculine" resonate with the other models of development noted above. For the purposes of these reflections, a brief review of Diamond's work will provide practical insight into the healing process for men. To summarize the work, Diamond suggests that men must:

1. *Balance the desire to "do" with the need to "be."* Men are socialized in ways that are oriented toward action and accomplishment. For authentic growth to occur, Diamond suggests that men must heal the rift in their psyche that values action over essence, doing over being.[53]

2. *Understand and heal confusions about sex and love.* Men have a distorted view of sexuality and love. As noted above, physical sexual expression is often the only way that men have been taught to "feel love." Mature masculine development points men toward "understanding, accepting, and integrating sex and love."[54]

3. *Transform ambivalent feelings toward women and children.* Men experience a love/hate relationship toward women and children. This ambivalence is often rooted in unresolved psychic and emotional conflict. Any effort toward masculine wholeness must address these sources of conflict and teach men how to appreciate women and children as individuals in their own right and not as property of men.[55]

4. *Express grief over the absence of the father and risk getting close to other men.* As previously noted, the absence of the father leaves deep wounds in many men. This lack of a strong, centered masculine presence inhibits a man's ability to develop relationships with other men. Men's work necessarily involves walking men through the grief of the "Father Wound" and teaching men how to form relationships that are rooted in mutuality, and not in competition.[56]

5. *Change self-hatred to self-actualization.* Given the lack of wholesome male role models, it is commonplace for men to develop an insecure personality which leads to self-loathing. Masculine development offers men the ability to relinquish self-hatred and to learn expressions of self-love and care.[57]

6. *Acknowledge wounds and heal body and soul.* In a society that seems to be focused on the physical beauty of women, it comes as a surprise that men are often ashamed of their bodies. "Shame, in all its various forms, manifests itself on a physical level."[58] Accordingly, if a man is ashamed of his body, he will not likely care for it. The task of the man is to acknowledge his wounds, provide better self-care and move toward a more healthy lifestyle.[59]

7. *Uncover the basic roots of insecurity.* The separation that men experience in the physical world is evidence of their insecurity within their psychic

world. Men today experience little connection to a place, a tribe, or a culture. As such, they must learn to develop a communitarian ethic which provides a safe environment in which to grow.[60]

8. *Acknowledge and heal hidden childhood abuse.* As noted above, many current disciplinary practices of parents are abusive at their core. Parental violence, whether physical or verbal, is a commonplace experience for many boys. The invitation of mature masculinity is to recognize the historical evidence of childhood abuse and heal the wounds that abuse left behind.[61]

9. *Explore the origins of violence and change destructive behavior.* The socialization of men often encourages the use of violence as an effective means of conflict resolution. Diamond notes that the rage that is present in many men makes masculine ferocity commonplace. Authentic growth calls for an analysis and repudiation of the way that men were trained to rely first on violence, and then to change the way that boys resolve conflict.[62]

10. *Return to the spirit of true warriors.* Anthropological studies indicate that for the majority of human history men lived as a hunter-gatherer, that is, in partnership with the earth. It has only been in most recent history that men have lost the ability to act as a "Sacred Warrior," one who has great respect for every facet of life. Diamond suggests that men now live as "dominators," viewing creation as a commodity for their consumption. He suggests that returning to the spirit of the sacred warrior and achieving mature masculine self-esteem are correlative tasks.[63]

This review demonstrates a possible direction for men to take in their quest for wholeness and integration. The strength of these models is their holistic approach to the developmental process. Rather than focusing only on alleviating addictive relationships or compulsive behaviors, these developmental tasks encourage a lifelong process of becoming a mature masculine personality.

MASCULINE SPIRITUALITY AND THE *VIA POSITIVA*

Christian spirituality is specifically concerned with human-kind's relationship with God. As such, it takes seriously the full spectrum of ways that men and women encounter God. In this light, masculine spirituality is attentive to the "God path" for men. Masculine spirituality is concerned with every aspect of a man's life—his prayers, emotions, body, and relationships. As noted in the beginning of this chapter, the development of a healthy spirituality depends on the degree to which they are able to participate in the process of integration called for in these pages.

While masculine spirituality affirms the value of the developmental or formational tasks of the authors noted above, it also recognizes that they don't answer the question of how to integrate spirituality and a man's life. Each of these authors illustrates necessary steps for men to take toward integration and healing, but they don't address the central question of this work:

How does masculine spirituality participate in the integration of a man? The remainder of this chapter seeks to address that question.

Dwight H. Judy proposes that spiritual practices and philosophies of the past are counter-productive in the quest to heal contemporary men because they dismiss much of the human personality. He notes that the development of Christian practice has been rooted in paradigms that are decidedly opposed to the experience of passion, emotion and embodiment. While Christianity seeks to provide spiritual practices which enliven its adherents, the ascetic and purgative style of monasticism seems to be idealized. As an example of this thought, Judy recognizes:

> The aim of the spiritual life was to become transformed within this body. One of the primary gauges of this transformation process was the degree to which the passions ceased to trouble one. The underlying assumption is that one cannot attain the insights of the spiritual realm while also being involved in the body's passions. Passionlessness is a goal for spiritual growth.[64]

Judy suggests that, historically, the goal of western spirituality has been one of "purity of heart, involving a perfection of emotions as well as of actions. "[65] This *via negativa,* or way of purgation, viewed emotionality and physicality with suspicion. He notes that there are three harmful assumptions that emerge from the *via negativa.* The first implication that emerges from this type of spiritual practice is that it distrusts human emotion. Contrary to sound psychological evidence, this spirituality holds that the emotions are somehow tainted by the influence of sin and untrustworthy. Second, the *via negativa* has a negative perception of the physical world. Creation has become warped through "Adam's fall," and, as such, has limited value. This warped view of creation legitimates the consumeristic attitude that has developed in western culture. Third, the *via negativa* enshrines mental practice over physical awareness as the most reliable source of interaction with God.[66]

Judy appreciates the solid emphasis on discipline and cognitive practice, but he calls for the development of a paradigm of spiritual practice which heals the male soul. Building upon the creation spirituality of Matthew Fox,[67] Judy labels this emerging spirituality as the *via positiva.* This *via positiva* celebrates every dimension of a man's life and experience as conduits of relationship with an incarnational God. This *via positiva* is a resolution of the ancient split between matter and spirit. In other words, "If God truly is flesh, then through flesh one finds God."[68] Practically, the *via positiva* suggests that the intersection between God and man occurs in the realm of emotion, passion, body and psyche.

There are three implications that spring from this position. First, the *via positiva* recognizes the value of human emotions. Instead of devising methods to quash the presence of a man's emotional life, he is encouraged to "listen" to those emotions for traces of God's connection. Second, creation and the physical world are highly valued in the *via positiva*. Creation is good and there is a vibrant presence of God to be discovered there. Accordingly, "matter" or things human have an intrinsic value to them and can be a locus of God's presence. Third, the *via positiva* encourages a man's physical awareness as a complementary partner to the development of the cognitive faculty. God speaks through the mind, but God also speaks through somatic awareness, emotional reactions and sensual passions.

As noted above, the *via positiva* is highly incarnational in its orientation. It celebrates God's divinizing presence in the world, in men and in women. When God "became flesh" in Jesus Christ, the evolution of spiritual consciousness reached a new level of awareness and possibility.[69] This increased awareness embraces universal experiences of wisdom and insight as legitimate disclosures of God's presence and love for humankind.

This is not to suggest that the *via positiva* is a spiritual practice given to physical excess. It is a call to restore a proper balance between all created energies within the human person. For most men, it is an invitation to befriend instinctual and passionate energies that have been repressed in the name of a "perfect spiritual life." It is a quest of discovering God through movements into their own personality. This pilgrimage recognizes the value of boundaries, of common morality, and of the primacy of love. But it asks men to reconnect with dimensions of their own being where God has long been waiting to embrace them. Judy reflects on this process:

> A primary path for me in coming to know my soul has been the body. Learning to live with the energies of the body, particularly its lower passions: sexual and aggressive. . . . What wholeness required of me was to come into contact with the warrior energies. . . . In liberating these lower energies, however, the higher energies have also awakened: the energies of the spiritual radiance as well as direct communion with the inner Christ.[70]

The *via positiva* is a path of both spiritual and psychological liberation and integration. All the sound psychological practices identified in these pages can be direct experiences of a healing quest into the love of God. Men can develop integrated and holistic personalities knowing that such freedom is a gift of God.

Men can grieve the loss of their fathers and experience the love of God through self-parenting and the reparenting of other men.[71] Instead of living with body-shame, men can participate in prayerful exercises designed to heal the distortions of the body image.[72] Rather than experiencing confusion, addiction and shame about sexuality, men can come to know that "sexuality is intrinsic to the divine-human experience."[73] Gay men can learn that an authentic Christian life is possible because "masculinity is not about whom you sleep with; it is about who you are and who you wish to become . . . it is about becoming your own man and following your bliss."[74] Men can come to know women for the actual people that they are, rather than remain entranced by undifferentiated psychological forces. They can tap into their own feminine essence and discover creativity, passion, sensitivity and tenderness.[75] In other words, they can learn to love *SOPHIA* within them.[76]

Finally, Judy suggests that through the practice of the *via positiva* men can learn to appreciate their strengths and gifts, not in opposition to the desire of others, but rather as an expression of their own fullness in relationship to God. "Stand up, take on your full capacity as a man, the capacity for power, the capacity for vision, and then God will address you face to face."[77]

SUMMARY

The aim of this chapter has been to demonstrate the disconnection that characterizes contemporary men. First, I examined the symptoms of men's alienation from themselves and others: co-dependency, workaholism, emotional numbness, addictions, violence and anger. Then I examined the "Father Wound," "Warped Sexuality," and a "Hatred of the Feminine" as challenges to a man's physical, emotional and spiritual well-being. Next, I surveyed the work of various authors engaged in leading men through a quest for wholeness. I identified some of the tasks that men must undertake if they are to move into mature masculinity. Finally, I sketched a *via positiva* for masculine spirituality. There I showed that such a spiritual practice could lead contemporary men into an encounter with God by physical, emotional and psychological awareness. It is not an understatement to suggest that men need to undertake the journey of healing and integration for themselves, for others, for the world, and for their relationship with their God.

NOTES

1. Sam Keen, *Fire in the Belly: On Being a Man* (San Francisco: Bantam Books, 1991), p. 35.

2. Alice Miller, *For Your Own Good: Hidden Cruelty in Child-Rearing and the Roots of Violence* (New York: Farrar, Straus, Giroux, 1983), notes that most commonly accepted methods of raising children in general, and boys in particular, are abusive at their core.

3. Keen, *Fire in the Belly*, pp. 35–36.

4. Dwight H. Judy, *Healing the Male Soul: Christianity and the Mythic Journey* (New York: Crossroad Publishing Company, 1992), p. 119.

5. Aaron Kipnis, *Knights Without Armor: A Practical Guide for Men in Quest of Masculine Soul* (New York: Tarcher/Pedigree Press, 1991), p. 37.

6. Jed Diamond, *The Warrior's Journey Home: Healing Men, Healing the Planet* (Oakland: New Harbinger Publications, 1994), p. 2.

7. Ibid., p. 156.

8. Kipnis, *Knights Without Armor*, pp. 15–18.

9. James B. Nelson, *The Intimate Connection: Male Sexuality and Masculine Spirituality* (Philadelphia: Westminster Press, 1988).

10. Keen, *Fire in the Belly*, p. 110.

11. Diamond, *The Warrior's Journey Home*, p. 17.

12. Ibid., p. 55.

13. Ibid., p. 74.

14. Ibid., p. 75.

15. Ibid., pp. 78–81.

16. Ibid., pp. 28–31.

17. Ibid., p. 107.

18. Interview with Bill Moyers, *A Gathering of Men with Robert Bly,* video (New York: Public Television Corporation, 1990).

19. Robert Bly, *Iron John: A Book About Men* (New York: Vintage Books/Random House, 1992), p. 94.

20. Guy Corneau, *Absent Fathers, Lost Sons: The Search for a New Masculine Identity* (Boston: Shambhala Publications, 1991), p. 11.

21. Ibid., pp. 12–13.

22. Ibid., p. 13.

23. Ibid., pp. 17–18.

24. Ibid., pp. 18–19.

25. Ibid., p. 19.

26. Ibid., pp. 19–21.

27. Patrick J. Arnold, *Wildmen, Warriors and Kings: Masculine Spirituality and the Bible* (New York: Crossroad, 1992), p. 96.

28. Ibid., p. 37.

29. "The Kronos in each of us has the tendency to 'eat' our children, to devour the younger generation in order to maintain our own hard-fought security." Judy, *Healing the Male Soul,* p. 139.

30. Ibid., p. 200.

31. Nelson, *The Intimate Connection,* pp. 116–118.

32. Ibid., p. 116.

33. Steven Hill, *A Man Thinks About Pornography: Beauty, Images, and Totalitarianism* (Bellingham: Tow Hill, 1988), p. 117.

34. Don Sabo, "The Myth of the Sexual Athlete," in *Men and Intimacy: Personal Accounts Exploring the Dilemmas of Modern Male Sexuality,* edited by Franklin Abbot (Freedom: Crossing Press, 1990), pp. 16–20.

35. Keen, *Fire in the Belly*, p. 75.

36. Diamond, *The Warrior's Journey Home*, pp. 80–81.

37. The number of authors who condemn circumcision as a warrant-less attack are profound. See ibid., pp. 139–149, for a helpful discussion in this regard.

38. Philip Culbertson, *The New Adam: The Future of Male Spirituality* (Minneapolis: Augsburg Fortress Press, 1992), pp. 23–25.

39. Daniel A. Helminiak, *What the Bible Really Says About Homosexuality* (San Francisco: Alamo Square Press, 1994), p. 12.

40. Ibid., pp. 12–13.

41. John J. McNeill, *The Church and the Homosexual* (Kansas City: Sheed Andrews and McMeel, 1976), p. 121.

42. Nelson, *The Intimate Connection,* p. 116.

43. Ibid., p. 13.

44. Bly, *Iron John,* p. 86.

45. Culbertson, *The New Adam,* p. 113.

46. Arnold, *Wildmen, Warriors and Kings,* p. 45.

47. Johnson, *He: Understanding Masculine Psychology,* Revised Edition (New York: Harper and Row Publishers, 1989), p. 36.

48. Robert Johnson, *Lying with the Heavenly Woman* (San Francisco: HarperCollins, 1994), pp. 19–32.

49. Kipnis, *Knights Without Armor,* pp. vii–x.

50. Keen, *Fire in the Belly,* pp. 128–149.

51. Judy, *Healing the Male Soul,* pp. 156–181.

52. Culbertson, *The New Adam,* pp. 23–25.

53. Diamond, *The Warrior's Journey Home,* pp. 55–69.

54. Ibid., p. 20.

55. Ibid., pp. 100–106.

56. Ibid., pp. 107–116.

57. Ibid., pp. 118–127.

58. Ibid., p. 22.

59. Ibid., pp. 137–164.

60. Ibid., pp. 166–170.

61. Ibid., pp. 171–180.

62. Ibid., pp. 190–200.

63. Ibid., pp. 235–240.

64. Judy, *Healing the Male Soul,* p. 114.

65. Ibid., p. 118.

66. Ibid., p. 119.

67. Matthew Fox, *Original Blessing: A Primer in Creation Spirituality* (Santa Fe: Bear & Co., 1980).

68. Judy, *Healing the Male Soul,* p. 133.

69. Ibid., pp. 125–126.

70. Ibid., p. 169.

71. Diamond, *The Warrior's Journey Home,* pp. 111–113.

72. Carl Koch and Joyce Heil, *Created in God's Image: Meditating on Our Body* (Winona: St. Mary's Press, 1991). See pp. 46–50 for a prayer/meditation exercise designed to heal a man's body shame.

73. Nelson, *The Intimate Connection,* p. 116.

74. Arnold, *Wildmen, Warriors and Kings,* p. 49.

75. Johnson, *He: Understanding Masculine Psychology,* pp. 34–37.

76. "In our age, the time has come to embrace all opposites and to cherish our passions. It is a time to embrace our full natures, physical as well as spiritual, and in this new embrace with the earth to profoundly embrace woman, as well." Judy, *Healing the Male Soul,* p. 158.

77. Ibid., p. 179.

PART SEVEN

Divorce and Annulment

CHAPTER 28

The Meaning of Commitment

Margaret Farley

During the 1960s and 1970s, it became fashionable in the United States to call commitment into question. Not only were specific forms and concrete situations critiqued, but commitment "in principle" itself came under challenge. We have never been the same as a society since that social and cultural upheaval. Psychologists, sociologists, philosophers, and novelists have attempted to name and shed some light on our area of "the uncommitted." Farley's essay, from a theological perspective, is the most systematic, sophisticated, and sober treatment of the topic available today.

The author sets the question of commitment in the widest social context. The many different forms of commitment, their complex interconnection, and the elements common to them all are laid out with balance and clarity. But what, precisely, is commitment? What purpose does it service? Are there limitations on its binding force? Are there conditions for release from its promise? These are the foundational questions pursued in this essay. The prime case of the purpose of commitment in human love is presented and brings the issue to the center of marital relations.

Questions for Discussion

1. What is the relation of commitment to the experience of genital sexuality?
2. What counts as a legitimate degree of commitment during the engagement period?
3. What new dimension of commitment is required between partners if they decide also to become parents?
4. What situations or conditions would allow for the release from one's marital commitment-relationship?

The reason why commitment is such a problem to us is that by it we attempt to influence the future, and by it we bind ourselves to someone or something. Two quite different customs in contemporary society illustrate dramatically how this is done. If I am arrested by the police and wish not to be in jail while I wait for my trial, I may be able to post bail and so be free until my date in court. In giving money as bail, I am declaring my intention to return for my trial at a future time, and I am binding myself to do so on penalty of forfeiting my bail money. In a wholly different setting, when two persons marry in our society, it is the practice of many to exchange rings. "With this ring, I thee wed . . ." symbolizes the express intention of each to love and to share the life of the other into the future. It symbolizes, moreover, a bonding whereby each gives to the other a claim to the fulfillment of that intention. These examples hold a key to the meaning of commitment. If we look at them closely, we can come to understand what we are doing when we make a commitment.

I find myself hesitant, however, to narrow our focus so quickly to these examples. We need a wider perspective from which to view them. There is, I suspect, something important to be gained from letting our minds roam a bit, trying to see the broadest possible sweep of the forms commitment can take in our lives. This will have the advantage of preventing premature closure on just one meaning for commitment. It will also help to keep any one dilemma of commitment from overwhelming us, or any one celebration of commitment from seducing us into complacency about it.

Indeed, the history of the human race, as well as the story of any one life, might be told in terms of commitments. Civilization's history tends to be written in terms of human discoveries and inventions, wars, artistic creations, laws, forms of government, customs, the cultivation of land, and the conquering of seas. At the heart of this history, however, lies a sometimes hidden narrative of promises, pledges, oaths, compacts, committed beliefs, and projected visions. At the heart of any individual's story, too, lies the tale of her or his commitments—wise or foolish, sustained or broken, fragmented or integrated into one whole.

SURVEYING THE HORIZON

Think again, then, of all the ways in which we experience what we with some seriousness call "commitment." Sometimes these are not immediately evident in one person's life at any one given time. When Sheila, for example, thinks of commitment, she tends to focus only on the one area of commitment which right now is difficult for her. Every day she lives with the more and more pressing question of whether or not she should persuade Joshua that they must divorce. Every day she agonizes over her responsibilities, through marriage, to her husband and to their children, to God, and to herself. But she has many more commitments than these, some that intersect with them, some that compete with them, and some that are not in question in relation to them at all. For instance, Sheila is committed to certain truths, to certain principles. From the day she had her first insight into what she now describes as the "equality" of women and men, her conviction has grown regarding this truth. She can no longer act as if she did not believe it. She cannot turn back and live out the roles in her life as if she had never seen the reality of herself and all women in a new way.

Sheila also believes deeply in the obligation of persons not to harm one another unjustly. Her perception of the value, and the need, of persons in relation to one another goes beyond this, to a desire and a sense of responsibility positively to help others. She has often said, "Life is hard enough for anyone to get through. I figure we can't do it alone. We have to help one another." Her compassion is based on conviction, and it does violence to her not to take account of others' needs—especially Joshua's, her children's, the people she meets in her volunteer work and in the political action groups to which she belongs. Genuine caring and compassion serve to motivate her involvement in organizations that oppose racism and violence and that promote economic rights and peace.

There is a sense, also, in which Sheila is committed to herself, though she is almost afraid to think in these terms. Her growing anger at what she perceives to be Joshua's indifference to her and to the children keeps generating in her mind the question of whether this is how she is meant to live. The frightening realization of how destructive her marriage has been to her keeps pushing her imagination to find alternatives, "ways out."

The story of Sheila's life and commitments could go on and on. But even a brief glimpse into it enables us to begin to see the many different forms, and complex interconnections, possible in our commitments. There are, of course, commitments to other persons—some made explicitly, some assumed implicitly. But there are other kinds of commitments, too. For example, there are what can be called "intellectual" commitments—to specific truths, sometimes to "truth" in general (a commitment that can undergird a pursuit of truth wherever it is to be found). There are commitments to values—the value of an institution, or the life of a family, or to so-called "abstract" values like justice, beauty, peace. There are commitments to plans of action, whether specific projects, or life-plans such as "living in accordance with the Gospel," or programs of vengeance, peaceful revolutions, or "being a good mother."

The appearance of commitment in our lives is even more extensive and nuanced than this, however, and more elusive when we try to encompass it in our overall perspective. There is, for example, a kind of unrecognized commitment, one that serves as an important background for almost everything we do. We are not explicitly aware of it (or of them, for there may be many such commitments). We may never bring it to a level of consciousness where we can reflect on it. This kind of commitment serves to *constitute* part of the very horizon against which we interpret everything. It may be a commitment that psychologists could describe as "basic trust," or one that philosophers could name a "presupposition." It may be one that any of us might recognize, if and when it is brought into focus—as, for example, taking for granted that the law is to be respected, or valuing without question the progress of human education, or assuming that things should "make sense" whether we understand them or not. These kinds of commitments, prior to any explicit recognition of them in our conscious awareness, can be called "pre-reflective" commitments.

But if "commitment" can appear in all these forms, what *is* the common meaning that keeps it from being empty as a term? Some clues emerge from what we have just seen. Commitment seems, in our ordinary language, to include a notion of *willingness to do something* for or about whatever it is we are committed to (at least to protect it or affirm it when it is threatened). Suppose I ask, for example, what truths I am committed to. I soon discover that there are many truths that I hold, affirm, am convinced of, but am not "committed" to. What can this mean? I may say, of some insight of mine or some conviction regarding a state of affairs or a direction to be taken, that "I would not stake my life on it." This could mean that I am not completely certain about it. Or it could mean that, though I am certain, it just is not important enough to me to *do* anything about it. It is not important enough to me to let go of anything else for the sake of it (let alone lay down my life for it); it is not important to me even to use my energy trying to defend it through argument.

A willingness to do something seems, moreover, to follow upon our sense of *being bound* to whomever or whatever is the object of our commitment. Our very selves (in greater or lesser degree) are tied up with this object, so that we do not just appreciate it or desire it, but we are in some way "identified" with it. Our own *integrity* seems to demand that, under certain circumstances, we do something. The object of our commitment has a kind of claim on us, not one that is forced upon us, but that is somehow addressed to our *freedom*. Even when we do not feel very free regarding our commitments, when we feel bound "in spite of ourselves" or against our other desires, there is still a sense in which our own initiative is involved when we act because of that commitment.

We could continue to survey the many forms of commitment and to probe the elements common to them all. We need to ask further about the relation of free choice to commitment and the importance of prereflective commitments for the commitments we are aware of making. Now, however, may be the time when it is more useful to take seriously my lantern metaphor and enter the deeper regions of but one form of commitment. To do that, it helps to identify a kind of "prime case," a central form of commitment—one from which all other forms derive some meaning. *Commitment to persons,* when it is *explicit and expressed,* offers just such a "prime case." And it will bring us back to our two examples: the posting of bail and the exchanging of wedding rings.

"PROMISES TO KEEP . . ."

By explicit, expressed, interpersonal commitment I mean promises, contracts, covenants, vows, etc. These commitments provide a prime case for understanding all of the forms of commitment because the elements of commitment appear more clearly in them. We recognize an obligation to act in a certain way within these commitments more frequently than in any others. Moreover, here we most often confront dilemmas and the inescapability of wrenching decisions. It is in these commitments that questions of love, of time and change, of competing obligations, seem more acute. The very explicitness of promises, or covenants and contracts, places the experience of commitment in bold relief and offers the best chance for understanding it.

There are interpersonal commitments, of course, that are not expressed in any explicit way (at least not in the making of them). For example, some roles that we fill or relationships in which we participate entail commitments, but they become ours without an original choice on our part. We are born into roles such as daughter or son, sister or brother. Some friendships grow spontaneously and seem to need no promises. Other roles we assume by explicit choice and usually through some external expression—familial roles such as husband or wife, sometimes mother or father, and professional roles like physician or teacher. Even roles we do not at first choose, however, can be understood in great part through understanding the roles we explicitly choose; for roles of whatever kind usually at some point require free and explicit "ratification" or "acceptance."

THE MAKING OF PROMISES

The first thing we must do in exploring explicit, expressed commitments is to ask: "What takes place when we commit ourselves in this way?" What did Sheila *do* when she married Joshua? What will actually *happen* in the moment when Karen vows to live a celibate and simple life within a community dedicated to God? What does Ruth *effect* when she signs a business contract? What *takes place* when Dan speaks the Hippocratic Oath as he begins his career as a doctor? What *happens* when heads of state sign an international agreement regarding the law of the seas? What *happens* when Jill and Sharon pledge love and friendship for their whole lives long? What do Barbara and Tim *do* when they place their names on the lease whereby they rent their new apartment for a year? What do any of us do whenever we make a commitment to one another, whenever we promise, whenever we enter or ratify a covenant?

We can ask this question of our examples of posting bail and exchanging wedding rings. What is happening in each of these cases? In both, I am "giving my word" to do something in the future. But what can it mean to "give my word"? It is surely not like other things I could do regarding future actions. It is not, for example, like a *prediction*. If it were, I would not be *responsible* for the future's turning out as I said it would (except perhaps in some limited situations like that of the weather forecaster, who is not responsible in the sense of being able to control the weather, but who might be considered irresponsible if she did not show professional competence in forecasting). "Giving my word" is also not like making a *resolution*, where I may indeed feel responsible to do what I resolved, but where my obligation would be only to myself (to be consistent in carrying out my decisions), not to another to whom I had given my word.

When I post bail, I give my word that I will return for trial. I declare to someone that I will do this in the future, and I bind myself to do so by giving my money as a guarantee of my word. When two persons exchange rings in a marriage ceremony, they declare to each other their intention to act and to be in a certain way in the future, and they give a ring as a sign that their word has been given and that they are thereby obligated to it.

To give my word is to "place" a part of myself, or something that belongs to me, into another person's "keeping." It is to give the other person a claim over me, a claim to perform the action that I have committed myself to perform.[1] When I "give my word," I do not simply give it away. It is given not as a gift (or paid like a fine), but as a pledge. It still belongs to me, but now it is held by the one to whom I have yielded it. It claims my faithfulness, my constancy, not just because I have spoken it to myself, but because it now calls to me from the other person who has received it. My money is still my money when I give it as bail. That is why it binds me to come to trial, lest I lose what is still mine. A wedding ring is not just "given away." It belongs somehow to both partners, for it signifies a word that is "the real" in the speaker, begotten, spoken, first in the heart. Belonging to the speaker, the word now calls from the one who has heard it and who holds it. "What is mine becomes thine," but it is also still mine. It is still mine, or it is still my own self, though I have entrusted it to another. That is why I am bound by it, bound to it, and bound to the other.

What happens, then, when I make a commitment is that I enter a new form of relationship. The root meaning of "commitment" lies in the Latin *mittere*—"to send." I "send" my word into another. Ordinary dictionary uses for "commitment" include "to place" somewhere (as "to commit to the earth," or "to commit to prison," or "to commit to memory"); and "to give in charge," "to entrust," "to consign to a person's care" (as in "to commit all thy cares to God"). When I make a commitment to another person, I dwell in the other by means of my word.

Much of the time "all" that we give is our word—not money, not rings, not special tokens that "stand for" us. We stand in our word. Still, when we give just our word, we search for ways to "incarnate," to "concretize," to make tangible, the word itself. It is as if we need to see the reality of what is happening. For example, we sign our name. Our word within a contract is sealed by placing ourselves—in the form of our name, written by our own hand—on the document. In an ancient Syrian form of blood covenanting, a man was required to write his name in blood on material which was then encased in leather and worn on the arm of his covenant partner.[2] Other rites of blood covenanting went even further, attempting to mingle the blood of one with another. For blood was the sign of life, and it was one's own life that was entrusted to the other in a scared self-binding ritual.

When words seem too weak to carry the whole meaning of a commitment, sometimes we turn the words into chants, as if by repetition they become more solid, more visible in transfer. There is an old betrothal ceremony among the Berber tribes, where the couple alternates in a song that continues for hours:

> I have asked you, I have asked you, I have asked from God and from you.
> I have given you, I have given you, I have given you if you accept my condition.
> I have accepted, I have accepted, I have accepted and agreed. . . . [3]

Commitment, then, entails a new relation in the *present*—a relation of binding and being-bound, giving and being-claimed. But commitment points to the *future*. The whole reason for the present relation as "obligating" is to try to influence the future, to try to determine ourselves to do the actions we intend and promise. Since we cannot completely do away with our freedom in the future (think of the gambler who must choose again and again to keep his promise or not), we seek by commitment to bind our freedom, though not destroy it. How can commitment do this?

By yielding to someone a claim over my future free actions, I give to that person the power to limit my future freedom. The limitation consists in the fact that I stand to lose what I have given in pledge if I fail to be faithful to my promise. I stand to lose the property I have mortgaged, or the bail money I have posted, or my freedom to travel if I am imprisoned for breach of legal agreement. I stand to lose my reputation, or the trust of others, or my own self-respect, if I am unfaithful to even an ordinary and fairly insignificant promise. I stand to lose another's love, or my home, or strong family support, or my sense of honesty and integrity, or my sense of continuity within a culture and religion, if I betray or finally break a profound commitment that is central to my life. I stand to risk the happiness of someone I love, if my fidelity is needed in a commitment made for the sake of another. Sometimes we know fully what we stand to lose, what binds us to our commitments; sometimes we learn what it is or has become only when our fidelity is seriously in question. It is clear that commitments vary, so that in some commitments we stand to lose little but in others we stand to lose everything. Above all, however, as we take our own word seriously, we always stand to lose a part of ourselves if we betray that word.[4]

If we stop here, accepting this as the full meaning of commitment, we are liable to all the dangers regarding commitment. On the one hand, we can see the glorious possibilities of commitment—of gathering up our future in a great love, of belonging to another in a self-expansive way; and we may move too hastily into commitment for commitment's sake. In so doing, our one great commitment can end in a grand, but empty and finally destructive, gesture. On the other hand, the thought of yielding to another a claim over us—great or small—may intimidate us, make us afraid that any commitment we make will narrow our possibilities, leave us with no "way out," give us claustrophobia in a life walled in by obligations and duties.

The essential elements of interpersonal commitment *are* an intention regarding future action and the undertaking of an obligation to another regarding that intended action. But in order to see a reasonable place for it in our lives, and to be able to discern *how* and *when* commitment obligates in specific circumstances, we need to think about the purposes that commitment can reasonably serve and the limitations that it must necessarily have.

A REMEDY AND A WAGER

The primary purpose of explicit, expressed interpersonal commitments is to provide some reliability of expectation regarding the actions of free persons whose wills are shakable. It is to allow us some grounds for counting on one another. As Hannah Arendt observed, "The remedy for unpredictability, for the chaotic uncertainty of the future, is contained in the faculty to make and keep promises."[5]

Commitment as it appears in the human community implies a state of affairs in which there is doubt about our future actions. It implies the possibility of failure to perform acts in the future that are intended, however intensely and whatever firmness, now. "Without being bound to the fulfillment of promises, we would never be able to keep our identities; we would be condemned to wander helplessly and without direction in the darkness of each man's [sic] lonely heart, caught in its contradictions. . . . "[6] Ours is not the instinctually specified and determined course of animals insofar as they have no freedom; ours is not the unshakable course of the freedom of God.

Because our wills are indeed shakable, we need a way to *assure others* that we will be consistent. Because we know our own inconsistencies, we need a way to *strengthen ourselves* for fulfilling our present intentions in an otherwise uncertain future. Yielding to someone else a claim over our future actions provides a barrier against our fickle changes of heart, our losses of vision, our weaknesses and our duplicity. By commitment we give ourselves bonds (and give others a power) which will help us to do what we truly want to do, but might otherwise not be able to do, in the future. A remedy for inconsistency and uncertainty, commitment is our wager on the truth of our present insight and the hope of our present love.

Insofar as promise-making provides assurance to others and strength to ourselves, it facilitates important aspects of human living. It is a device upon which personal relationships depend (in one form or another) and which political life (short of tyranny and total domination by force) requires. It undergirds the very possibility of human communication, for it is the implicit guarantor of truth-telling. As Erik Erikson insisted, "A spoken word is a pact. There is an irrevocably committing aspect to an utterance remembered by others. . . . "[7] It is interpersonal commitment (in a social contract of one kind or another) that has been the instrument of structures designed negatively for *mutual protection*—each person from the other, or a group from an outside threat; or designed positively for *mutual gain*—economic or cultural, through shared labor or property, shared knowledge or aesthetic enjoyment. I need not say again that it is commitment that serves to initiate (sometimes) and sustain (sometimes) *companionship and love*. It is commitment, too, that resides at the center of much of the history of religion, whether in the form of primitive bargainings with feared and hidden gods or of a personally offered covenant: God giving God's word, assuring a people of a divine unshakable will, calling a people to their own consistency in freedom and love.

LIMITATIONS ON BINDING

If we are ever to sort out how and when we are obligated by our commitments, we must have some way of determining their limits. Unless Sheila, for example, decides that there is no way, ever, under any circumstances, that she can justify divorcing Joshua, she needs to be clear about the *extent* of her obligation to him and to their marriage. If all of our commitments are absolutely binding, then we shall expect to be overwhelmed by their competing claims, with no way to resolve them or, ironically, to live them faithfully in peace.

Obviously, not every commitment that we make is of equal importance to us or equally comprehensive in its claim on us. We do set limits to the obligations we undertake. Almost all of our commitments, for example, are provisional in some sense; almost all are partial, conditional, relative. It must be so. In fact, we might well ask whether more than one commitment (at least at one time) can ever be, without contradiction, absolute.

Sometimes there are limits within our commitments of which we are not aware. That is, it is possible for us to think mistakenly that we are committed wholly to something or someone when, in fact, we are not; or the depth of our commitment may be much less than we thought it to be. We are in these instances, like the apostle Peter, surprised at our easy betrayal of what we presumed was our one unquestionable commitment. On the other hand, sometimes we are surprised in the opposite way when we discover, like Judas, that we are more committed, more bound, to someone than we realized; what we assumed was relatively superficial or marginal to our lives, shows itself to be profound and unforgettable. In either case, we may weep bitterly at our discovery and be filled with remorse or with gratitude for what it reveals.

There is perhaps no remedy except time and experience for deficiencies in our own self-knowledge. It is, however, possible to be more reflective about the limits we *intend* (legitimately and necessarily) to include in our commitments. To understand limits is not always to diminish a commitment but may, rather, serve to focus it, to allow it to share in the overall power and hope of a committed life.

It is too soon to try to work out all of the ways in which our commitment-obligations relate to one another. But we can see some general ways in this regard, and at the same time gain an understanding of the possible limits of commitments. The terms that are useful for this are terms like "conditional" and "unconditional," "partial" and "total," and "relative" and "absolute." These pairs of terms are not mutually exclusive, so that they tend to blur into one another at times. Nonetheless, they help to articulate how much we yield in claim to another.

If a commitment is *conditional*, it obligates only under certain conditions. Sometimes we make commitments where we very clearly stipulate the conditions under which they will be binding. I promise to do something *only if*, for example, you reciprocate in kind; or *only when* the building code is met; or *only until* another worker can be transferred to this position; or *only if* my insurance policy will cover my expenses. An *unconditional* commitment, of course, is one in which I commit myself to another "no matter what" conditions prevail. Thus, for example, I may commit myself to "go where you go and stay where you stay," allowing no conditions to justify changing my mind or my sense of being obligated. We may discover that while it is the nature of every commitment to refuse to count some conditions as justifying a change in the commitment, yet most commitments are at least subject to sheer conditions of *possibility* of fulfillment.

A commitment is either *partial* or *total* depending on what is yielded for claim. It may be partial because of a limitation in time: until next week, or until the weather changes, or when I reach retirement age. It may be partial because it simply is "part" of something larger—as a vow of poverty may constitute part of a total commitment to service of one's neighbor. It may be partial because it yields a claim only to my property and not to my person.

We think of commitment as *total* when it somehow involves the whole person of the one who makes it. These are the commitments that constitute fundamental life-options. These may be some of the commitments we make to love other persons. When we try to describe commitments in this way, however, we soon meet difficulties in expressing our complex experiences. For example, how shall we describe the commitment to love another person that arises from the whole of our being, that is affirmed totally with our very lives, and yet does not entail a total availability to the other for the deeds of love? We hesitate to call such a commitment a partial commitment, and the hesitation has its own rich truth.

The notion of "relative" and "absolute" can be extremely helpful for understanding the nature and limits of our commitments. But they, too, hold a variety of possibilities that are not always easy to keep clear. Thus, a *relative* commitment is just that—*related to* another commitment. It is, at least to some extent, dependent for its meaning on the other commitment. It may be derivative from, instrumental to, or a participation in the other commitment. But even these terms, describing modes of relation between commitments, conceal complex possibilities.

There is a vast difference, for example, between purely instrumental commitments (commitments that are solely a means to some other end, some larger commitment) and commitments to love someone who is perceived as an end in herself, though an end (not a means) whose deepest reality is in relation to God. For example, Joshua may be committed to his wife and children purely because they are necessary to him if he is to sustain a certain status with his business associates. Or he may be committed to them because he sees himself as a dependable, responsible husband and father, and he knows that they need his financial and personal support. Or he may be committed to them because he loves them in themselves; but since he believes them to "live and move and have their being" in relation to God, his commitment to them is an intrinsic part of his commitment to God.

The easiest way to think of an "absolute" commitment is to equate it with an "unconditional" commitment. In this sense, however, some relative commitments could be called absolute (if what they are related to is the object of an unconditional commitment, and if the relationship is intrinsic and necessary). We might also equate absolute commitments with "total" commitments; but here we encounter the same sort of uncertainty that we met with the partial/total distinction. To keep the category pure, we might reserve it for commitments that are both unconditional and total. This would be the kind of commitment Gabriel Marcel describes as "entered upon by the whole of myself, or at least by something real in myself which could not be repudiated without repudiating the whole—and which would be addressed to the whole of Being and would be made in the presence of that whole."[8] However Marcel's way of putting it may strike us, it is not difficult to catch the central point of what he is describing.

I could, of course, simply stipulate meanings for these terms. That would be helpful for my use of them hereafter. However, since my real concern is to show the many ways in which we must and do set limits to our commitments. I prefer to leave the terms open to various correlations and to continuing refinement that accords with the many possibilities in our experience.

Distinctions such as I have suggested thus far may seem already overly refined when all we want to do is to live out our commitments faithfully or discern when they no longer bind. Fidelity and betrayal are not simple matters, however, and our lives always prove more complicated than we wish. Not every giving of our word to another is an unlimited yielding of an unlimited claim. Nor is every commitment as circumscribed as our vague promises to "drop in sometime" to visit old friends. Through distinctions we may be surprised by some simple clearings in the forests of complication.

COMMITMENT AND LOVE

Like any other commitment, a commitment to love is not a prediction, not just a resolution. It is the yielding of a claim, the giving of my word, to the one I love—promising what? It can only be promising that I will do all that is possible to keep alive my love and to act faithfully in accordance with it. Like any other commitment, its purpose is to assure the one I love of my ongoing love and to strengthen me in actually loving. Given the challenges we have seen to the wisdom, if not the possibility, of commitments to love, this purpose bears fuller examination.

PURPOSES OF COMMITMENTS TO LOVE

Why should I want commitment if love rises spontaneously, and if I can identify with it by my freedom at every moment? Why should I promise to love if there are risks to the love itself in making it a matter of obligation? Only something at the heart of our experience of loving can explain this.

There are some loves whose very power in us moves us to commitment. "Love's reasons" for commitment are at least threefold, and they go something like this. First, like all commitments, a commitment to love seeks to *safeguard* us against our own inconsistencies, what we perceive to be our possibilities of failure. If we are not naively confident that our love can never die, we sense the dangers of our forgetfulness, the contradictions of intervening desires, the brokenness and fragmentation in even our greatest loves. We sense, too, the powerful forces in our milieu—the social and economic pressures that militate against as well as support our love. We need and want a way to be held to the word of our deepest self, a way to prevent ourselves from destroying everything in the inevitable moments when we are less than this. To give to the one we love our word, to yield to her or him a claim over our love, offers a way.

Love seeks more than this, however. We know that freedom cannot once and for all determine its future affirmation of love. No free choice can settle all future free choices for the continuation of love. Yet sometimes we love in a way that makes us yearn to gather up our *whole future* and place it in affirmation of the one we love. Though we know it is impossible because our lives are stretched out in time, we long to seal our love now and forever. By commitment to unconditional love we attempt to make love irrevocable and to communicate it so. This is the one thing we can do: initiate in the present a new form of relationship that will endure in the form of fidelity or betrayal. We do this by giving a new law to our love. Kierkegaard points to this when he says, "When we talk more solemnly we do not say of two friends: 'They love one another'; we say 'They pledged fidelity' or 'They pledged friendship to one another.'"[9] Commitment is love's way of being whole while it still grows into wholeness.

Finally, love sometimes desires commitment because love wants to express itself as clearly as it can. Commitment is destructive if it aims to provide the only remedy for distrust in a loving relationship. But it can be a ground for *trust* if its aim is honesty about intention, communication of how great are the stakes if intention fails. The decision to give my word about my future love can be part of converting my heart, part of going out of myself truly to meet the one I love (not part of hardening my heart because of excessive fear of sanctions if I break the law that I give to my love). My promise, then, not only verbally assures the one I love of my desire for constancy, but it helps to effect what it assures.

NOTES

1. Of course, not all theorists would describe the meaning of commitment, or of promise-making, in the way I do here. What a promise *is* is closely tied to one's view of how it obligates. There are at least three major positions on this that appear in the history of philosophy and in contemporary discussion of promises: (a) the obligation to keep promises is purely conventional—an agreed upon "practice," or "game" in a given community, sometimes a matter of pretense until it is taken for granted and believed (Hume), sometimes a matter of violent discipline until behavioral conditioning gives it lasting status (Nietzsche); (b) the obligation is produced by the promise itself, for the words of promise are "performative," or "commissive," actually *doing* what they say (Austin, Searle, Melden, Sartre); (c) the obligation to keep promises is ultimately grounded in a more general obligation to respect persons, or to sustain moral community, etc. (Aquinas, Kant, Hegel, Hare). Many philosophers hold a combination of these views—for example, asserting that promising produces its own

obligation, but only in a context where the conventions are such that this is possible (in other words, the "performative" depends on there being a "practice" of promising). My description of what "happens" when we make a commitment can be understood as a description of commitment as a performative. But it also assumes a fundamental ground of moral obligation in the reality of persons. Key treatments of these questions include historical works such as David Hume, *Treatise of Human Nature*, ed. L. A. Selby-Bigge (Oxford: Clarendon Press, 1968), Book III, Part 2, Sec. 5; Georg Hegel, *Philosophy of Right*, trans. T. M. Knox (New York: Oxford University Press, 1967), 57–63; Friedrich Nietzsche, *On a Genealogy of Morals*, trans. W. Kaufman and R. J. Hollingdale (New York: Vintage Books, 1967), 57–61; linguistic approaches such as J. L. Austin, *How To Do Things With Words*, ed. J. O. Urmson (New York: Oxford University Press, 1962); John R. Searle, *Speech Acts* (Cambridge: Harvard University Press, 1970), esp. chaps. 2 and 3; contemporary philosophical discussions such as Pall S. Ardal, "'And That's a Promise'" and "Reply to New on Promises," *The Philosophical Quarterly* 18 and 19 (July 1968 and July 1969); John Rawls, "Two Concepts of Rules," *Philosophical Review* 64 (1955): 3–32; Joseph Raz, "Promises and Obligations," in *Law, Morality and Society: Essays in Honour of H. L. A. Hart*, ed. P. M. S. Hacker and J. Raz (Oxford, 1977); G. J. Warnock, *The Object of Morality* (London: 1971), chap. 7; relevant to contract law, Patrick Atiyah, *The Rise and Fall of Freedom of Contract* (Oxford: Clarendon Press, 1979); Charles Fried, *Contract as Promise: A Theory of Contractual Obligation* (Cambridge: Harvard University Press, 1981). A key treatment important for the whole question of promise-making and promise-keeping is the classic study of Josiah Royce on loyalty: *The Philosophy of Loyalty* (New York: Macmillan, 1924).

2. H. Clay Trumbull, *Blood Covenant: A Primitive Rite and Its Bearings on Scripture* (London: George Redway, 1887), 5 and passim.

3. As quoted in Edward Westermarck, *Marriage Ceremonies in Morocco* (London: Macmillan, 1914), 40–41. This same kind of repetition occurs in pre-1965 ceremonies of vows in Roman Catholic religious communities. "Suscipe me, Domine," sang those making their vows, and they repeated this three times.

4. A further discussion of the nature of this obligation, and of what one risks losing, appears in chap. 7, of *Personal Commitments* (San Francisco: HarperCollins, 1987).

5. Hannah Arendt, *The Human Condition* (Chicago: University of Chicago Press, 1958), 237.

6. Arendt, ibid.

7. Erik Erikson, *Identity, Youth and Crisis* (New York: Norton, 1968), 162.

8. Gabriel Marcel, *Being and Having* (New York: Harper Torchbooks, 1965), 45–46.

9. Søren Kierkegaard, *Works of Love*, trans. Howard and Edna Hong (New York: Harper Torchbooks, 1962), 45.

CHAPTER 29

What God Has Joined Together . . .

Bernard Cooke

One of the most important essays in this collection is the following one by Bernard Cooke. It deserves and probably will require more than one reading. In addition, most students will probably need to be introduced to some of its technical language and to the process thought on which it is partly based.

Cooke looks at marriage from the points of view of biology, social institution, distinctive personal relationship, and biblically based covenant. He also brings to his discussion the three theological shifts outlined at the start of his essay. Basically, he proposes that marriage as the paradigm form of human friendship should at its best mature into an increasingly indissoluble bond between persons. It is his argument for this position that calls for study. Two sets of questions will aid in examining it, those Cooke himself asks at the very end of his essay and the questions for discussion.

Questions for Discussion

1. Cooke takes very seriously the deep sacramental value of marriage. Which of his statements were for you the clearest expression of this value?
2. What does Cooke mean by saying "The source of whatever indissolubility attaches to a particular marriage must be the character of the marriage itself" and its symbolic import as a Christian sacrament?
3. What do you say to Cooke's point that a marriage becomes increasingly indissoluble as it becomes increasingly Christian?
4. Is Cooke contradicting himself when he says that a couple can be truly married but at the same time still in the process of becoming married to each other?
5. How would you summarize Cooke's position on indissolubility?
6. How would you summarize his position on sexual intercourse?

Among the pastoral problems to which Catholic theology should address attention, few have as widespread impact as the question of the indissolubility of Christian marriages. That we are seriously reexamining this element of Catholic teaching reflects pastoral anxiety for the well-being of the millions of women and men in situations that have separated them from their Catholic roots. But it reflects also the broadened context of doing theology today, and it is to this aspect of reflection on indissolubility that I wish to direct my remarks.

Today's developments in theology constitute a multifaceted phenomenon; within this complex change, it seems to me that three shifts are of special relevance to the topic of our discussion. ① Today we are using the life experience of believing Christians, as individuals and as communities, as the starting point of our theological reflection. While other sources of insight— Scripture, traditional teaching, liturgy, etc.—enter in as principles of interpretation, it is the providential action of God in people's lives that provides the immediate "word" of revelation with which we must deal as theologians. ② We are gradually absorbing into our theological process the historical consciousness, the awareness of *process*, and the general acceptance of evolution that are hallmarks of modern Western thought. In doing so, we have rediscovered the eschatological perspective that characterizes biblical thought. ③ We are beginning to theologize ecumenically, realizing that we cannot ignore other Christian traditions—for that matter, religious traditions other than Christian—in our attempts to understand more deeply and accurately the workings of the divine with humans.

Let us, then, draw upon the first of these methodological shifts, namely the use of Christian experience as a basis for reflection. Here we are faced with the concrete and unavoidable reality: according to every ordinary observable measure, large numbers of Catholic marriages do, in fact, dissolve. Can we in the face of this widespread experience justifiably say that these marriages continue to exist?

Any response to that question must distinguish among several meanings of "marriage." For example, at the most elemental biological level, where marriage involves two people mating for the continuation of the race, it is undeniable that in many cases such a strictly biological relationship does not and need not continue beyond a certain point. As a social institution providing stability for the process of begetting and raising children, marriage can take various forms, including, in modern societies, persons being involved in a sequence of marriage-divorce-remarriage. As a distinctive personal relationship involving a unique sexual commitment, marriage does suggest some aspect of indissolubility—at least many people do believe and hope as they marry that this special self-giving is "forever." Nonetheless, the large number of people who have given up this attitude for one of remaining together "as long as things work out" suggests that there is no self-evident and adequate grounding for indissolubility in some promise intrinsic to marital sexual self-giving.

Finally, as a paradigm form of human friendship, marriage at its best should certainly mature into an increasingly indissoluble bond between persons; but human experience teaches us the bitter lesson that friendships, even long-standing and treasured ones, do not always stand the test of time. While it may always be "eternally true" that two married persons *were* close friends, if the friendship does cease, one simply cannot assert that it continues and constitutes indissolubility.

The reproductive drive of the species, society's concern for successful childbearing, marital sexual intimacy, human friendship—all these dimensions of marriage certainly point to some degree of permanence, but not to sufficient grounds for universally attributing indissolubility to all marriages, including Catholic marriages.

We enter a somewhat different realm, however, when we regard Catholic marriage in the light of the bibilical/theological category of covenant. In this context, the contractual aspect of the pledge between woman and man in marriage takes on added dimensions: the couple commit themselves to one another, but they also commit themselves *as a couple* to participate sacramentally and ministerially in the life of the Christian community; they commit themselves to shared discipleship and a life together of working for the establishment of the Kingdom of God. Not that all Catholic couples as they begin their married life are conscious of and open to this broader meaning of their marital contract, but this is the intrinsic reality of Christian marriage which we can hope will become understood and appreciated by people.

Certainly, we are closer to a grounding for indissolubility when we regard Catholic marriage as Christian covenant, for the promise involved has a clearly eschatological orientation; it reaches in its significance to the divine. But what are we to say when the contract has been broken by one or both parties? We might in some cases say that there has been infidelity that extends beyond the two persons to the Christian community and to God, that there has been sinful negligence or malice, that some responsibilities may still remain from the earlier covenant commitment. But can we say, for example, that an innocent and betrayed person in a marriage, a person who has, clearly been irrevocably deserted, is still involved in a one-sided contract? Can a person remain committed to the Christian community to live out a sacramental relationship that is existentially impossible?

One can, of course, give an essentially legal response to this question: we have a law, a law that gives expression to a view of Catholic marriage which we are not free to abandon. Much as it pains us, the overall common good requires that exceptions not be made, so that the indissoluble character of Christian marriage will be safeguarded. But does the preservation of this ideal demand the absolutely universal implementation of this rule? Perhaps this law itself is meant to be the statement of an ideal toward which Catholics should strive with varying degrees of success or failure. Having raised that question, let us bracket it for the moment and come back to it after we have treated some other elements of sacramental theology.

A final possibility for grounding the indissolubility of Christian marriage lies in the sacramentality of the two Christian persons as they live in relationship to one another. They are the sacrament, not simply because they are recognizable in the community as the two who publicly bound themselves by marital contract, but because and *to the extent* that they can be recognized as translating Christian faith into their married and family life. For Christians the parameters, of personal destiny, of personal responsibility and commitment, of personal development and achievement, in brief of human life, are broadened by the revelation contained in the life and death and resurrection of Jesus of Nazareth. This is true of individual human existence; it is true of the shared existence that is marriage.

When two Christians are married they commit not only their growth as persons to one another; they commit their faith, their relation to God in Christ to one another—obviously, not totally, but to a very considerable degree. The concrete interaction with one another in their daily life will unavoidably serve as "word of God" in the light of which they will develop their self-image, their freedom, their values, their faith and hope and love.

But God's word, no matter what the medium of its transmission, has always been a promise of unconditioned divine fidelity. No characteristic is more emphasized in the biblical literature; Israel's God is a faithful God. When we come to the New Testament, the raising of Jesus from the dead is seen as the culminating fulfillment of God's promises, the supreme proof of divine fidelity. And the question comes then: Can a Christian marriage truly sacramentalize, i.e., both speak of and make present, this divine fidelity unless it itself bears the mark of unfailing, irrevocable endurance? Can a marriage speak experientially about a divine love that never fails, unless it itself is lived as a relationship that is indissoluble? Or—to change the question slightly, but perhaps importantly—if it is not lived this way can one speak of it as sacramental?

In this context, we can return to the questions raised earlier about the commitment implicit in marital intercourse. That there is some special personal commitment signified by this action is hard to deny, but it is also hard to deny that it is signified only to the extent that this act is one of genuine personal love, expressive of each person's selfhood and honest respect of the other's selfhood. The extent to which an actual situation of sexual interchange symbolizes an irrevocable, i.e., indissoluble, commitment of each to the other seems, then, to be commensurate with the attitudes, understandings, etc., of the two people engaged in marital intercourse. Apparently we must ask, in a somewhat more restricted form, the question we just raised about the broader reality of Catholic marriage: When are we justified in applying the term "sacramental"?

Without suggesting any final answer to these questions, it does seem that we can associate the indissolubility of Christian marriage more satisfactorily with the sacramentality of marriage than with any other aspect. Historical studies have pointed out how the meaning of "sacrament" as applied to marriage has shifted from the emphasis on "binding promise" which it had in Augustine's explanation of Christian marriage to greater stress in medieval and subsequent centuries on the meaning of "Christian symbol." On the other hand, comtemporary sacramental theology has increasingly broadened the scope of sacrament beyond simply the liturgical ritual; and it has moved away from the "automatic effect" mentality that characterized so much post-Tridentine explanation of sacraments and has instead re-emphasized the extent to which the sanctifying effectiveness of sacraments depends on the awareness and decisions of the Christian people involved in one or other sacramental context.

Inadequate as our understanding of the sacramentality of Christian marriage is, it does seem to provide some focus for the practical pastoral judgments about indissolubility that we face at this moment in Christian history. Perhaps we can sharpen the focus a bit by raising the question: If indissolubility is in some way and to some degree "intrinsic" to Christian marriage, what is the source of this indissolubility *in a particular case?*

Is God the source—or, to put it more bluntly, is God doing something extra to make a particular Christian marriage indissoluble? Unless I misread present theological developments, it seems that we are presently moving toward a reinterpretation of "providence" in terms of the divine *presence* in the lives of humans. But if this is so, and if we then apply this to marriage, it would accentuate the importance of awareness and free decision in the sacramentality of any given marriage, for God's presence to humans is conditioned by their conscious and free acceptance of the divine saving love.

Is the church the source? Does the Christian community, more specifically do the bearers of authority in the church, have the power to make Catholic marriages dissoluble? And if they do have such power, is their exercise of this power the cause of Catholic marriages being indissoluble? I know of no theological voice that would clearly respond "yes," that would go beyond claiming for the church the power to proclaim and defend and socially implement (within the church's own internal life) an indissolubility that already exists in Christian marriage prior to any church action or regulation.

But has not the official church, at least as far back as Trent, claimed the power to govern the *existence* of Catholic marriages by its legal activity? Despite the most Christian self-giving on the part of two devoted Catholics, the absence of the legally established form or of proper delegation on the part of the witnessing cleric rendered their marriage invalid.

For example, years ago, when I was studying the canon law of marriage, the teacher highlighted the importance of "proper form" by repeating a canonical "horror story"—whether factual or not, the story quite clearly made its point. According to the account, a socially prominent young couple, wishing to avoid all the fuss of a big public wedding celebration, went for advice to the chancellor of a large U.S. diocese, since he was a close friend of the woman's family. Sympathetic to the young people's desire, he offered to marry them privately in his office; so, he requested his secretary to join them as witness to the marriage, the marriage was performed, and the young couple on their honeymoon informed their respective families of the fait accompli. However, the next day the chancellor—obviously with great embarrassment—realized the lack of due form because there had been only the one witness to the marriage. Clearly, it would have been catastrophic to contact the newly married in the midst of their honeymoon and ask them to return so that they could be married. Legalism was able, however, to triumph: the chancellor obtained a "sanatio in radice" and the young couple never had to know that they began their married life in a state of material sin.

Common sense seems to say that there is something wrong here. Let us suppose that the diocesan chancellor had never realized his error, and that without any legal "sanation" the two people had lived a life together that reflected to their children and to all who knew them the transforming presence of God's love. Could one truly say that there did not exist a deeply sacramental Christian marriage? My purpose in citing this example is not to ridicule canonical arrangements in the church; rather, it is to raise some basic questions about ecclesiastical claims to make things be or not be. More precisely, it is to question ecclesiastical power to condition the indissolubility of marriages.

We seem to be left, then, with no other clear alternative than the one we have already discovered; the source of whatever indissolubility attaches to a particular marriage must be the character of the marriage itself, more specifically its symbolic import as a Christian sacrament.

Up to this point our reflection together could quite justifiably be faulted for the static way in which it has treated marriage, so let us examine the indissolubility of Christian marriage from the perspective of *marriage as process*. Marriages come into existence over a considerable length of time, conditioned by any number of occurrences and experiences and choices, progressing—if they do progress—through stages of change that find their Christian explanation in terms of the mystery of death and resurrection. Men and women are gradually initiated into marriage as a human relationship and a Christian sacrament; the initiation is never completed in this life—no more than is a person's lifelong initiation into Christianity, for becoming married is for most Christians a major element in the broader initiation into the Christ.

It would seem, then, that one should not talk about a marriage as being completely or absolutely indissoluble but as becoming increasingly indissoluble as it becomes increasingly Christian; the more profoundly Christian a marriage relationship becomes, the more inseparable are the two persons as loving human beings, and the more does their relationship sacramentalize the absolute indissolubility of the divine-human relationship as it finds expression in the crucified and risen Christ. Exactly how all this will occur in a given instance is as diverse and distinctive as are the people involved and the overall social situation of a given culture or historical period.

To put it in biblical terms, a Christian marriage, like any other created realities, does not exist absolutely; like anything in creation, particularly anything in human history, a marriage exists eschatologically; it is tending toward its fulfillment beyond this world. However, the fact that it does not yet have in full fashion the modalities—such as indissolubility—that should characterize it does not mean that it is devoid of them. A Christian marriage is indissoluble, but short of the eschaton it is *incompletely indissoluble*. Perhaps we could profitably borrow a notion from recent New Testament scholarship, namely "realized eschatology." Christian marriage already realizes to some degree the indissolubility which can mirror the divine fidelity to humans, but it cannot yet lay claim to the absoluteness which will come with the fullness of the Kingdom. Similarly, two Christians can be very genuinely and sacramentally married, but they are still being married to one another; their union can become yet richer and stronger.

One wonders if the understanding of Christian marriage has not for centuries suffered the fate of being overly structured and frozen by the use of Greek categories of thought with their presumptions of universality and absoluteness. Since "absolute" is a characteristic reserved to divinity, one cannot strictly speaking apply it to any created reality or to any bit of human knowledge. On the other hand, the view of all creation as eschatological accords with the first of all biblical commands, "I alone am the Lord, your God."

Indissolubility is an aspect of the intrinsic finality of any marriage, more so of a Christian marriage because of its amplified significance. As such, it shares in the responsibility to fulfill that finality which a woman and a man undertake when they enter upon a marriage. Indissolubility is something they should strive to intensify in their shared life. But that does not say that it is impossible for them to fail at this task, impossible for the actual indissolubility of a marriage to gradually weaken and ultimately disappear.

Perhaps we can and must say that the *promise* not to engage in marital intimacy with any other person, the promise that each party made at the time of beginning their marriage, remains in force no matter what happens. Perhaps we can and must say the *responsibility* for the other rests permanently on each of them. But how can we say that a relationship that in its human and existential aspects, and therefore in its sacramentality, has dissolved is indissoluble?

The contemporary church is rapidly regaining its sense of Christian existence as a process, a lifelong initiation into relationship with the Christian community and with the risen Lord. This is the clear import of the post–Vatican II revision of the rite for the initiation of adults. As in the past, liturgical action points the way for our theological reflection and our doctrinal clarification: *lex orandi, lex credendi*. "Being Christian" is something a person only gradually and incompletely achieves.

For Christians, married life is meant to share in this initiation into Christ. The clear conclusion is that an individual Christian marriage does not from its first moments completely reflect the Christ-mystery, completely reflect the indissoluble bond of saving love that links Christ with his spouse, the church, any more than a person is completely Christian with baptism. One *becomes* Christian; one *becomes* married.

By way of corollary, it might be well to extend these remarks to the notion of marital consummation. There is a long history of the role of first sexual intercourse between a couple as establishing a societal bond, and along with this a long history of Christianity considering first marital intercourse as somehow intrinsic to the marriage contract and therefore to the very existence of the marriage. I have no intention of summarizing, even briefly, that history. Suffice it to recall the operative church law that regards a marriage soluble if it is only *ratum* and not *consummatum*.

What I do wish to do is suggest the impropriety of such an abstract understanding of sexual intercourse, especially of marital intercourse. It is true that for two people deeply in love, there is often profound meaning in their first full sexual intimacy, but theirs will be a sad married life if they do not progress in their self-giving far beyond this first experience. Too much of the discussion of sexual intercourse among moral theologians and canonists has forgotten that it is a *human* activity, even though they have verbally nodded in that direction. Precisely because it is so human—distinctive with each couple, fragilely linked with all the other elements of a couple's relationship to one another, symbolically expressive of so much that cannot find explicit verbalization yet is itself in need of communication between persons to make its meaning clear—truly human sexual intercourse needs to be learned over a long period of time. And when one introduces Christian significance into this action so that it can become the heart of the marriage's sacramentality, the need for lifelong learning becomes only too apparent. Sexual intercourse does consummate Christian marriage, but only in this context of ongoing personal intimacy, for it can only authentically say what the two Christians honestly are for one another.

Tragically, very many marriages are scarcely consummated as personal relationships; they do not grow. Among these are many that begin in a Catholic wedding ceremony. If consummation is intrinsic to the establishment of a Christian marriage, one can only wonder how many marriages qualify as "Christian," and therefore how much claim they can lay to indissolubility.

What can one say by way of conclusion? A list of questions:

- To what extent does modern process view of reality affect the way in which we consider a particular Christian marriage as indissoluble?

- If Christian couples themselves are the sacrament of Christian marriage, and couples obviously differ greatly in the extent to which they are genuinely Christian, to what extent is a particular marriage truly sacramental, to what extent does it actually symbolize the love between Christ and the church?

- And if the special indissolubility of *Christian* marriage is tied to sacramentality, in what way does indissolubility pertain to marriages that seem to have lost all operative sacramentality?

- Or are we to say that the covenant pledge, with one's partner and with the Christian community, which one took at the wedding ceremony remains a promise to the community even if the actual human marriage relationship dissolves? In this case the indissolubility attaches to the overall ecclesial sacramentality of the institution of Christian mar-

riage rather than to the sacramentality of this or that particular marriage union.

- But, to return to our emphasis on doing theology out of experience, is
  not the experience of "getting married" and the significance (sacramentality) attached to it one of promise to the other person rather than
  to the community?

- Finally, it seems that we need a somewhat new though tradition-
  respecting look at indissolubility to discover whether we are justified
  in applying it as absolutely as we Catholics have done in more recent
  centuries. It strikes me that a more flexible and individualized
  approach will still continue to honor the teaching that Christian marriage is of its nature indissoluble.

CHAPTER 30

Changes in the Ethos of Marriage, Faithfulness, and Divorce

Hans Kramer

The first three selections in this reader deal with the history of marriage. Those who have read them will not be surprised at the basic thesis of Kramer's essay on changes in marriage over the centuries. However, they may indeed be surprised at his insistence that the fact of change be better honored by official church teaching today. Right off he points out how church teaching of 1965 broke new ground in seeing marriage as a "personal covenant between the marriage partners," while insisting, almost in the same breath, that the marriage relationship is basically unchangeable, created by God as an aspect of human nature. Kramer finds these positions contradictory. In his own words, "A coherent and unbroken interpretation of the personal concept of marriage on the one side and the institutional concept held by the Council on the other is not possible." He implies these two poles of the argument come from two different ways of conceiving reality, two different metaphysics.

Basically Kramer is asking whether the "nature of marriage" is unchangeable, that is, a part of human nature as created by God. In this connection he asks whether Jesus' rejection of divorce is a statement of the law inscribed in human nature by God or is it a juridical statement, a communal statement of norms that should be followed faithfully, with some consideration of circumstances, like those of Matt 19:9 and 1 Corinthians. Kramer examines interesting variations in the way marriage has been understood over even the relatively short span of the past four centuries. His point is that today marriage is being viewed differently, with a changed set of expectations of what it is about. Here he adds an examination of four current aspects of "faithfulness." Readers will find echoes here of parts of Margaret Farley's "The Meaning of Commitment" (chapter 28).

Though Kramer's essay is brief, his questions are deep ones, needing wise pondering.

Questions for Discussion

1. Which position would you hold (and why): that Kramer's essay is defending divorce or defending commitment in marriage?
2. Which of the four shifts in the understanding of marriage in Europe made the most sense to you and why?
3. In the section on faithfulness, is he saying that faithfulness is no longer as important today as it was in earlier times, or is he saying something different from that? How would you state in a paragraph what his is saying to those who read his essay?

There is a naive view in the Catholic Church that the concept of marriage has remained constant and unchanging since NT times. In theology, this view has been abandoned and is considered contrary to the facts.

GAUDIUM ET SPES

The Pastoral Constitution on the Church in the Modern World (1965) gave currency to the personal view of marriage. Never before had a church document valued marriage as a personal covenant between the marriage partners. Nevertheless, it appears that Vatican II also provided strong theological emphases that oppose the legitimate cultural-historical variations in the concept of marriage in world history and the history of our civilization. Vatican II argues from a static concept of the institution of marriage:

> The intimate partnership of married life and love has been established by the Creator and qualified by His laws. It is rooted in the conjugal covenant of irrevocable personal consent. Hence, by that human act whereby spouses mutually bestow and accept each other, a relationship arises which by divine will and in the eyes of society too is a lasting one. For the good of the spouses and their offspring as well as of society, the existence of this sacred bond no longer depends on human decisions alone. For God Himself is the author of matrimony, endowed as it is with various benefits and purposes. (GS 48)

Following these statements, GS 48 points out that marriage in its entirety, and not merely the single sexual act, serves procreation and the rearing of children. GS 48 also emphasizes that

Reprinted with permission from *Theology Digest* 45: 2 (Summer 1998): 108–116. Originally published in *Stimmen der Zeit* 122:1 (1997).

> As a mutual gift of two persons, this intimate union, as well as the good of
> the children, imposes total fidelity on the spouses and argues for an unbreak-
> able oneness between them.

A coherent and unbroken interpretation of the personal concept of marriage on the one side and the institutional concept held by the Council on the
other is not possible. At the end of the above quote from GS 48, there is a foot-
note reference to the encyclical *Casti connubii* (1930). This reference is of decisive importance for the theme of the "change of marriage." *Casti connubii* is a
document conceived entirely in the horizon of Neo-Scholasticism. It evalu-
ates marriage on the basis of nature and sees marriage in the church as an
unchangeable reality.

NEO-SCHOLASTICISM

Since the 19th century, Neo-Scholasticism as a theological method has hardened ecclesial ethics. Neo-Scholasticism presents a static concept of marriage,
developing the idea of an enduring nature to marriage that is relatively recent
in theological history. Nonetheless, it is still favored by office-holders in the
Catholic Church. *The Catechism of the Catholic Church*, the so-called *World Catechism* of 1993, is decidedly Neo-Scholastic. The catechism, without discussion, considers marriage an historically static whole and does not take
account of the historical changes in European marriage for Catholic ethics
that have been pointed out by the historical and social sciences. The theological attempt to provide a new formulation of the ethos of marriage, faithfulness, and divorce in modern times has been rejected officially by papal
encyclicals like *Veritatis Splendor* (1993) as well as the *World Catechism.*

Neo-Scholasticism was established prior to the middle of the 19th century. At this time, Thomas Aquinas, Albertus Magnus, Bonaventure, and
other great scholastics had been forgotten. What church leaders desired was
something weighty that could counter the philosophical systems of idealism
and the Enlightenment. Above all, one referred back to Thomas, facilely citing him and simplifying him, especially in the manuals. The real phenomena
of life and the problems of 1850 were not considered. The only important
thing was the "transmitted body of thought," and only that body of thought
could be the truth. Even sacred scripture was subordinate to the "tradition."

In addition, Neo-Scholasticism established an unhistorical relationship
to history. One simply cited the ancients, especially Thomas. The fact that
Thomas himself was still full of life and that during and after his time there
were lively debates and discoveries of new truth in his writings, was not
seen. The magisterium spoke in favor of Neo-Scholasticism first in 1857, then
in 1879 against Modernism, later in the 1917 Code of Canon Law, and then
again in the marriage encyclical of 1930. The 1993 *World Catechism* also stands
in this Neo-Scholastic tradition.

THOMAS AQUINAS

As a church teacher, Thomas Aquinas, whose theological prominence was underscored in Neo-Scholasticism, was open to change on the ethic of marriage. Rejecting the inflexible view, he questioned whether marriage was something natural and determined by the laws of nature, and he concluded that it is not established by necessity from the principles of nature. Hot air over the fire must rise, according to the necessary laws of nature. Marriage, however, is not such a compelling necessity. It is worked out according to free will (*mediante libero arbitrio*). Furthermore, it is a given cultural and ethical freedom. Thomas even warns against a divinization of natural law with respect to marriage. Such a divinization would happen if one conceived the structural law of marriage rigidly. Thomas wrote concerning marriage,

> Human nature, unlike divine nature, is not unchanging. Thus, matters of nature have to be distinguished according to the various stages and life situations of human beings.

Thomas would also have argued that marriage, in culture and in time, should and must change. For him, it was unquestioned that the form of marriage is variable.

In this respect, Thomas agrees with Augustine (d. 430), who saw that the ethical norms of marriage were subject to cultural change. Concerning the polygamy of the OT patriarchs, Augustine wrote: "Having many wives was not a crime because it was customary and usual. Today, however, it is a crime because it is no longer customary and usual."

The NT demands faithfulness in marriage and is aware of divorce. Still, some Christians, by recourse to Jesus himself, exclude any change in the ethos of marriage, at least where divorce is concerned. Those who hold this position emphasize that Jesus formulates as law the new covenant of marriage, in which one partner can no longer, as previously, dismiss the other. Jesus' provocative formula is true and should not be overlooked. But did he proclaim a "law" in the sense of natural law, or in the juridical sense? Even Matthew did not accept Jesus' word as law. According to Mt 19:9 (cf. 5:32), divorce is prohibited "except for unchastity." This means that if faithfulness is decisively broken and the woman has established a living relationship with another, divorce in the Matthean community is legitimate. Human beings also bring changes into the Christian reality of marriage. Paul sees this when he cites Jesus' radical word in 1 Cor 7:10f. But in 1 Cor 7:12–16, he accedes to divorce if, in a specific marriage, "peace" is not established.

A further attempt to assert dogmatically that marriage is for all time is made by an appeal to Eph 5:32. The marital unity between husband and wife is "a great mystery; and I am applying it to Christ and the church." Here, however, it is not marriage that is the stated mystery (*mysterion, sacramentum*), but the "living and organic union of the head and bridegroom, Christ, with his bride, the church." The church is spoken about theologically here, but no marriage law is promulgated, above all no establishment of an eternal form of marriage.

VARIANTS

In conjunction with the change of ethos, the structure of marriage and the division of labor in marriage have changed significantly in the West over the last four centuries. Research in social and psychological history, two relatively recent historical disciplines, have provided reliable information. A brief look at the changes that have taken place can provide perspectives for the needs of today's ethos. What can be seen is how extensive is the freedom concerning the concrete forms of marriage of which Thomas spoke. The terminologies used to designate the forms of marriage, which differ historically, are at variance in the literature. But there is agreement in the historical and social sciences that there are important differences among the forms of marriage.

Originally in Europe, marriage was economically oriented. Until about 1800, marriage belonged to the status of farmers, craftsmen and shopkeepers, as well as some noblemen and office holders who had social status. Only those who had possessions could marry. Marriages were arranged; families promised partners to other families. The worldviews and religious horizons of the partners were similar. The social connection, like residency in the city or village, was secured and controlled. Knowledge of obligations and evidence of the ability to carry out the responsibilities of the profession and the house were presumed.

What was required, for and in marriage, was an ethos of specified, cooperative roles. The human life span and the length of marriage were short. Love was the motivating and creative force in housework and in work for the house. Emotions, eroticism, and what today is referred to as dialogical life, were non-existent. Faithfulness meant fulfilling one's obligations and roles. In the language of today's psychology of couples, one can call that a "love of serving and functioning," but the historical form should not be devalued unjustifiably. The experience of "domestic bliss" in this kind of marriage was essentially the process of toiling together hand in hand.

Divorce in such a system was unthinkable. It would have destroyed social existence as well as the lives of the partners. It would have been a kind of death sentence, increasing the already great numbers of beggars and leading to the possibility of divorced people being expelled from the cities.

MIDDLE-CLASS MARRIAGE AROUND 1800

In the 19th century a new form of middle-class marriage became possible, though the previous basic economic model of marriage still remained. Therefore, it is incorrect to speak here of the concept of a romantic love-marriage. However, marriage at this time was perhaps more emotionally open, and the sexual roles were more complementary. Marriage offered the wife economic security but also circumscribed her status. The husband was placed in the position of business leadership. He found security for his emotional and sexual needs.

The idea of love now begins to change, but not to the personal and individual love between partners that is known today. What was loved was not the person but the person's ability to carry out his or her expected role. This model was societally oriented. The wife had to be a good housewife, a rational planner, socially active, frugal, selfless, unpretentious, kind, tolerant, and totally understanding. The husband had to be professionally successful, resolute, strong, courageous, self-conscious, and principled.

Success in this type of marriage meant the guarantee of social prestige—but above all, business leadership on the part of the husband, and organization of the household and the rearing of children by the wife. Emotionality was directed toward mutual dependence and respect as gratitude for social support. The required ethos here was the ethos of activity and emotional support in fulfilling designated social roles.

WORKING-CLASS MARRIAGE IN THE NINETEENTH CENTURY

Historically, working-class marriage or, more accurately, marriage that was dependent on earning a salary, came with 19th-century industrialization. Increasingly, people from the poor classes who had previously been excluded from marriage and family leadership could now get married. Still, people lived in great financial straits and uncertainty. The role expectations between the sexes had to be maintained rigidly. The wife was forced into a dual role of caring for the family but also caring for the elderly and sick in the household. The average laborer around 1840 worked 83 hours a week—6 days a week, 14 hours a day. The 60-hour week of 10-hour days first appeared around 1900. Sundays were meant for washing work clothes, fixing the house, and repairing tools. Room for feelings and emotional interaction in this form of marriage was minimal. Work was exhausting and destroyed people's health. Domestic bliss in this kind of marriage resulted from mutually avoiding catastrophes.

Getting married was probably initiated by erotic fascination and personal inclination. Both partners, however, were inundated by domestic needs and shared the difficult fight for survival. The success of the couple was the common effort to secure food and a place to live.

The ethical maxim for this form of marriage was, in the literal sense of the word, necessity. Love in this type of marriage, and perhaps an approach to the middle-class ideal, meant survival with the marriage partner.

THE MODERN MARRIAGE FOR LOVE

Changing economic and social conditions provided room for the change to the modern marriage for love. In the 1950s and '60s, this type of marriage became more prevalent. The partners shared personal, intellectual, and sexual interests. The person, with his or her unique qualities, came to the forefront. Fascination, charm, delight, and the expectation of complementarity in all realms of life was what led to marriage. Material needs were decisively less important. Marriage changed from a work and economic community to one of feelings and freedom. Domestic bliss in marriage now was experienced when the partnership was successful in the personal sense of interchange, cooperation, and conversation. This personal concept of marriage has developed since World War II and is essentially still in effect.

The marriage ethos that obtains now is markedly that of a partnership that involves listening and speaking, giving and receiving at all levels of life, as well as the readiness to work out conflicts and frustrations, above all in the personal realm. But if such conflicts and disappointments cannot be worked out, it is ethically legitimate or even obligatory to consult an attorney in order to end the marriage by separation. Since 1992 in Europe, in one year, at least one of every three marriages has ended in divorce, and the trend is growing. In cities and industrial areas, the numbers of divorces and weddings in a year are almost the same. For the general population as well as for Christians, there is considerable worry about this trend, but for the most part ethical judgment of individuals and couples is restrained.

SOCIOLOGICAL VIEWS

Ethical considerations concerning the changes in marriage should not overlook sociological views. Sociology cannot and should not replace ethics, but ethics has to be supported by sociology. The signs of the times, to which theology must pay attention, are first indicated by sociology.

Marriage as an institution is not endangered. In 1969, René König's empirical sociological research maintained that because marriage had become so important for the individual and because one did not give up hope for a successful partnership in negative situations, the marriage was dissolved if its conflicts and dissonances could not be worked out. In the majority of cases, the partners enter new marriages; thus the growing number of divorces is no sign of a general rejection of marriage, but it does signal the special meaning and high value that people place on marriage. Still, there are some typically new personal, psychic, and ethical standards at work.

PERSONALIZING MARITAL PROBLEMS

After 1976, interviews with 68.4% of divorced couples showed that their marriages ended because of the conduct and qualities of the partners, as well as relational problems between the partners. Only 6.2% gave the classical reason for divorce—extramarital relationships—and 9% cited some form of addiction. There is documented proof that the growing psychical demands of marriage, and the highly affective-emotional demands on marriage, are what lead to the dissolution of the marriage partnership. In 60% of the cases, it is the wife who requests the separation.

SOCIETY AND MARRIAGE

The sociological study by H. Schelsky and H. Rosenbaum has refuted the claim that marriage and the family are "counter-structures to society," i.e., rejected by the outside world as an affectively charged private realm where emotionality, the discovery of identity, and relaxation are experienced. If the outside world did reject marriage and the family, change would not be necessary. Indeed, it would not be possible. What is more true and sociologically verifiable is that a wide range of external relationships in the world of work, free time, consumerism, social activity, and politics can now deeply affect a marriage. The dominant images of what it means to be human and live life in a practical way have an influence on the inner realm, and that induces change. There are sociologists who have indicated for more than a century that marriage and the family do not possess characteristically innate qualities, but that their structures and forms of life are directly shaped and changed by the forms of society's life. In earlier centuries in Europe, economic need shaped and influenced the ethos of marriage. Today cultural and social developments have influenced it—above all, the Enlightenment, secularization, industrialization, rationalism, urbanization, the growth of the middle class, and individualism. These developments have resulted in new expectations, forms of association, and ethical behavior with respect to marriage in modern times.

MARRIAGE TODAY—CHECKS AND BALANCES

Sociologists have formulated what they call a theoretical thesis of interchange: the duration of a marriage is bound up with the availability of the marriage's benefits and conveniences for the partners. The marriage partners seek to strike a balance, or one of the partners asks, under the load of his or her disappointments and burdens, whether this marriage is still worth it. A negative balance results in the termination of that marriage community.

In the discussion of this societal fact, the idea of "no-fault divorce" has been introduced. What is often inferred is that the divorce has insignificant but agreed-upon reasons and causes. While this kind of divorce cautions against ethical judgment, it also raises the question of whether or not hidden behind the terminology is the desire to gain a hasty adjudication of the divorce. Nevertheless, what may seem inconsequential or of little importance to those outside the marriage can have great implications for the couple.

The "theoretical perspective of interchange" which is part of the sociological consideration leads to the general observation that the partners test and weigh the qualities of the marriage community. The partners must do this because marriage is something they do in freedom. A marriage entered into in freedom in modern times must be conducted meaningfully and responsibly. Thus, the basic right or even the responsibility to seek balance in the marital partnership cannot immediately be called into question ethically.

THE ETHOS OF FAITHFULNESS

Not only do many families and individuals have a new attitude toward divorce and divorced people, so also do many Christian leaders. In 1993 German bishops in the Upper Rhine provided pastoral advice concerning the admission to the eucharist of remarried divorced people to the eucharist. The bishops said that priests should respect people who have examined their consciences and who are convinced that, before God, they can responsibly have access to the holy eucharist. Does this attitude of the bishops show a new conception of the ethos of faithfulness which is more versatile than that which the Catholic Church has advocated for marriage up until now?

TRADITION AND NEW QUESTIONS CONCERNING FAITHFULNESS IN MARRIAGE

Though little known, the gratifying and clear Neo-Scholastic idea of the "virtue and responsibility of faithfulness" can be helpful. In their textbook on moral theology (1961), J. Mausbach and E. Ermecke state that

> the responsibility of faithfulness is permanent . . . and at the same time gives people a sense of security and reliability. . . . But the entire situation can change to such an extent that the literal content of the word [faithfulness] goes counter to the actual sense of the promise made, so that the situation is injurious and unethical. In such cases the responsibility of faithfulness ceases because the promise is the most important element.

It is well known that this broad interpretation of faithfulness was applied without delay to church membership, vows, and marriage. Divorce, however, was not so legitimated. But the basic idea of the limit to the responsibility of faithfulness is part of the oldest ethical tradition.

Christians must ask whether the contemporary image of human beings and marriage, and the new possibilities for lifestyles, does not mean that the virtue of faithfulness needs to be examined anew. Faithfulness is a Christian virtue. It is undeniable that human destructiveness and unchristian infidelity must be avoided. But equally to be avoided is a destructive enslavement of people to an ideological concept of faithfulness. Virtues exist for the sake of human beings. Human and Christian reason and sensibility show that faithfulness is a form of love. Faithfulness is love, care, and support for the benefit of a person, even in the midst of disappointments, burdens, and hardships.

In the past, faithfulness was seen above all from the standpoint of a legal contract. One was to keep one's word and promise so that one person could rely on the other, and thus social relationships could remain stable and secure. This corresponds to the earlier social model of marriage, where marriage was a community of social need which had to overcome economic problems in order to maintain life. Faithfulness was the necessary social stabilizer and sole guarantor of survival. In the modern context of marriage, must not marriage and faithfulness have a more personal perspective?

NEW ANALYSES OF FAITHFULNESS

The phenomenon of faithfulness contains a variety of complementary elements. Faithfulness is formed concentrically by mutually interacting forms of faithfulness: faithfulness to oneself, faithfulness to you, faithfulness to us, and faithfulness to belief.

FAITHFULNESS TO ONESELF

Faithfulness to oneself says that a person accepts responsibility for him or herself. One has to care for oneself and shape life on the basis of its possibilities. Faithfulness to oneself means making promises and binding commitments. The basic ethical principle here is *ultra posse nemo tenetur*—no one can demand something beyond what one is able to do. Out of faithfulness to oneself, out of responsibility for one's own existence, the responsibility for faithfulness to a contract or promise is no longer binding if the emotional costs are too high.

FAITHFULNESS TO YOU

Faithfulness to you says that an "I," myself, has responsibility to another person. Thus one speaks of love for the other and of the marital community. Faithfulness is practiced dialogically. People justifiably have expectations of others. But this faithfulness also contains a burden because it needs to be preserved. If, however, the other person changes to the extent that one can no longer presume to be the recipient of the earlier promise of faithfulness, then faithfulness to the other reaches a limit. If the relationship changes decisively, faithfulness to the other, to the "you," must be examined. Classically such examination went on during marriage in cases of adultery, threat to the body and life, and threat to faith. The church legally acknowledges a dissolution of the partnership as separation from table and bed. Does not the new image of the world and human beings, also among Christians, indicate other limits to this kind of faithfulness? Some instances of separation or divorce after essential changes or radical disappointments are not to be evaluated as the rejection of faithfulness.

FAITHFULNESS TO US

This form of social or institutional faithfulness refers to basic adherence to social "givens" such as family relationships, neighborliness, membership in associations and parties, and even marriage. Marriage is a meaningful social institution. As such it deserves respect, which can assume the form of faithfulness. People do not deal frivolously with meaningful social values. But if the institution, good and meaningful in itself, demands an unreasonably high sacrifice from a person, that institution in this case loses its dignity and claim. The affected is then no longer bound by a responsibility to social faithfulness. In this scenario, examination is required as to whether the Catholic Church should demand religious-social faithfulness, to the extent that it has up until now, over against the sacrament of marriage, which is a sacral institution.

FAITHFULNESS TO BELIEF

This kind of faithfulness is a constant activity that is nourished by the sources of faith. Christians see their God as a faithful God. They have before their eyes Jesus of Nazareth, who, in loving faithfulness to his Father, surrendered his life. God and Christ, through the mediation of believing in the church, can be experienced by the individual in faithful loving. In the church, which lives by the power of the Holy Spirit, new power is unleashed. Through the sacrament of marriage, faithfulness to myself, to "you," and to "us," "in the Lord," becomes livable. Still, all magical notions must be excluded from this kind of faithfulness. It is more possible for Christians than for non-believers to live out this faithfulness to belief in marriage, but not everything is possible. The abandonment of responsibility to myself, or rejection of responsibility to the other, to you, can annul the aspect of faithfulness to belief. Then divorce might be not only possible but perhaps inevitable. And if the bishops mentioned above, as well as many theologians and ordinary Christians, think that some people in a second marriage should not be excluded from the eucharist, then in certain definite cases, as well as for divorced people in acute situations, it is legitimate as Christians to strive toward a prospective for remarriage—in a word, to seek a new partner.

PUBLIC AND INSTITUTIONAL HELP

It is a human fact of our time, from which Christians are not excepted, that problems concerning faithfulness are programmed into the growing psychical demands on marriage and the highly affective-emotional claims that are made on the marriage partners. There are also the further problems of staying together or getting divorced.

First, in the public arena it is helpful from both a human and a Christian perspective to propose that it is obvious that partnerships will experience problems and conflicts. There should be a clear public consciousness that it is necessary to discuss marital conflicts between one another and, where possible, to settle conflicts appropriately. It is important to strike a balance. Furthermore, one can also argue vehemently about the conflict without violating justice and love.

Second, the expectations of partnerships in the world and the church have to be seen realistically. Only after a divorce do many people today reexamine their romantic or ideal notions of a marital relationship. Only then are they capable of partnership. But the human costs are too high. More realistic images of marriage are needed today than we presently have, and such images would be helpful to ethics.

In the church and in the public square, there should be the perception, obviously with all good will and without discrimination, that couples have a claim to institutional help. This help has to be available early so that a solution to marital problems can be worked out. Institutional help for working out problems in marriage and the family should be available from the Catholic Church with open perspectives, even now when money is scarce. By providing such help the church today takes its place in the change of ethos concerning marriage, faithfulness, and divorce.

CHAPTER 31

Children after Divorce: Wounds That Don't Heal

Judith S. Wallerstein

In many discussions of divorce, the question of a breakup's effect on children does not arise. The discussion centers on what divorce means for the divorcing couple. In this section on divorce and annulment, we have put the question of children in divorce first, for two reasons. First of all, some students using this book will themselves be children of divorce or may be dating or engaged to a child of divorce. They may find in the following essay by Judith Wallerstein insight into their own reactions or those of their beloved. Secondly, it seems important to name all those wounded by divorce. Doing so raises the stakes involved in careful preparation for marriage.

Wallerstein reports research among the sons and daughters of divorce, where she finds far more emotional pain than many expected. Apparently, healing the wounds of divorce in children can take many years.

Questions for Discussion

1. Which of the findings of the follow-up studies of children of divorce were for you the most surprising?
2. What is the difference between seeing divorce as a single circumscribed event and seeing it as a process?
3. What does Wallerstein mean by the "sleeper effect" of divorce?
4. What is the diminished parenting consequence and how is it related to the overburdened child?
5. What interpretation do you give to the incident of the boy who piled all the furniture on top of the baby dolls?

As recently as the 1970s, when the American divorce rate began to soar, divorce was thought to be a brief crisis that soon resolved itself. Young children might have difficulty falling asleep and older children might have

From *The New York Times Magazine*, 22 January 1989, pp. 19–21, 41–44. Copyright © 1989 by Judith Wallerstein and Sandra Blakeslee. Reprinted by arrangement with Virginia Barber Literary Agency, Inc. All rights reserved.

trouble at school. Men and women might become depressed or frenetic, throwing themselves into sexual affairs or immersing themselves in work.

But after a year or two, it was expected, most would get their lives back on track, at least outwardly. Parents and children would get on with new routines, new friends and new schools, taking full opportunity of the second chances that divorce brings in its wake.

These views, I have come to realize, were wishful thinking. In 1971, working with a small group of colleagues and with funding from San Francisco's Zellerbach Family Fund, I began a study of the effects of divorce on middle-class people who continue to function despite the stress of a marriage breakup.

That is, we chose families in which, despite the failing marriage, the children were doing well at school and the parents were not in clinical treatment for psychiatric disorders. Half of the families attended church or synagogue. Most of the parents were college educated. This was, in other words, divorce under the best of circumstances.

Our study, which would become the first ever made over an extended period of time, eventually tracked 60 families, most of them white, with a total of 131 children, for 10, and in some cases 15, years after divorce. We found that although some divorces work well—some adults are happier in the long run, and some children do better than they would have been expected to in an unhappy intact family—more often than not divorce is a wrenching, long-lasting experience for at least one of the former partners. Perhaps most important, we found that for virtually all the children, it exerts powerful and wholly unanticipated effects.

Our study began with modest aspirations. With a colleague, Joan Berlin Kelly—who headed a community mental-health program in the San Francisco area—I planned to examine the short-term effects of divorce on these middle-class families.

We spent many hours with each member of each of our 60 families— hearing their firsthand reports from the battleground of divorce. At the core of our research was the case study, which has been the main source of the fundamental insights of clinical psychology and of psychoanalysis. Many important changes, especially in the long run, would be neither directly observable nor easily measured. They would become accessible only through case studies: by examining the way each of these people processed, responded to and integrated the events and relationships that divorce brings in its wake.

We planned to interview families at the time of decisive separation and filing for divorce, and again 12 to 18 months later, expecting to chart recoveries among men and women and to look at how the children were mastering troubling family events.

We were stunned when, at the second series of visits, we found family after family still in crisis, their wounds wide open. Turmoil and distress had not noticeably subsided. Many adults were angry, and felt humiliated and rejected, and most had not gotten their lives back together. An unexpectedly large number of children were on a downward course. Their symptoms were worse than they had been immediately after the divorce. Our findings were absolutely contradictory to our expectations.

Dismayed, we asked the Zellerbach Fund to support a follow-up study in the fifth year after divorce. To our surprise, interviewing 56 of the 60 families in our original study, we found that although half the men and two thirds of the women (even many of those suffering economically) said they were more content with their lives, only 34 percent of the children were clearly doing well.

Another 37 percent were depressed, could not concentrate in school, had trouble making friends and suffered a wide range of other behavior problems. While able to function on a daily basis, these children were not recovering, as everyone thought they would. Indeed most of them were on a downward course. This is a powerful statistic, considering that these were children who were functioning well five years before. It would be hard to find any other group of children—except, perhaps, the victims of a natural disaster—who suffered such a rate of sudden serious psychological problems.

The remaining children showed a mixed picture of good achievement in some areas and faltering achievement in others; it was hard to know which way they would eventually tilt.

The psychological condition of these children and adolescents, we found, was related in large part to the overall quality of life in the post-divorce family, to what the adults had been able to build in place of the failed marriage. Children tended to do well if their mothers and fathers, whether or not they remarried, resumed their parenting roles, managed to put their differences aside, and allowed the children a continuing relationship with both parents. Only a handful of kids had all these advantages.

We went back to these families again in 1980 and 1981 to conduct a 10-year follow-up. Many of those we had first interviewed as children were now adults. Overall, 45 percent were doing well; they had emerged as competent, compassionate and courageous people. But 41 percent were doing poorly; they were entering adulthood as worried, underachieving, self-deprecating and sometimes angry young men and women. The rest were strikingly uneven in how they adjusted to the world; it is too soon to say how they will turn out.

At around this time, I founded the Center for the Family in Transition, in Marin County, near San Francisco, which provides counseling to people who are separating, divorcing or remarrying. Over the years, my colleagues and I have seen more than 2,000 families—an experience that has amplified my concern about divorce. Through our work at the center and in the study, we have come to see divorce not as a single circumscribed event but as a continuum of changing family relationships—as a process that begins during the failing marriage and extends over many years. Things are not getting better, and divorce is not getting easier. It's too soon to call our conclusions definitive, but they point to an urgent need to learn more.

It was only at the 10-year point that two of our most unexpected findings became apparent. The first of these is something we call the sleeper effect.

The first youngster in our study to be interviewed at the 10-year mark was one who had always been a favorite of mine. As I waited for her to arrive for this interview, I remembered her innocence at age 16, when we had last met. It was she who alerted us to the fact that many young women experience a delayed effect of divorce.

As she entered my office, she greeted me warmly. With a flourishing sweep of one arm, she said. "You called me at just the right time. I just turned 21!" Then she startled me by turning immediately serious. She was in pain, she said.

She was the one child in our study who we all thought was a prime candidate for full recovery. She had denied some of her feelings at the time of divorce, I felt, but she had much going for her, including high intelligence, many friends, supportive parents, plenty of money.

As she told her story, I found myself drawn into unexpected intricacies of her life. Her trouble began, typically, in her late teens. After graduating from high school with honors, she was admitted to a respected university and did very well her freshman year. Then she fell apart. As she told it, "I met my first true love."

The young man, her age, so captivated her that she decided it was time to have a fully committed love affair. But on her way to spend summer vacation with him, her courage failed. "I went to New York instead. I hitchhiked across the country. I didn't know what I was looking for. I thought I was just passing time. I didn't stop and ponder. I just kept going, recklessly, all the time waiting for some word from my parents. I guess I was testing them. But no one—not my dad, not my mom—ever asked me what I was doing there on the road alone."

She also revealed that her weight dropped to 94 pounds from 128 and that she had not menstruated for a year and a half.

"I began to get angry," she said. "I'm angry at my parents for not facing up to the emotions, to the feelings in their lives, and for not helping me face up to the feelings in mine. I have a hard time forgiving them."

I asked if I should have pushed her to express her anger earlier.

She smiled patiently and said, "I don't think so. That was exactly the point. All those years I denied feelings. I thought I could live without love, without sorrow, without anger, without pain. That's how I coped with the unhappiness in my parents' marriage. Only when I met my boyfriend did I become aware of how much feeling I was sitting on all those years. I'm afraid I'll lose him."

It was no coincidence that her acute depression and anorexia occurred just as she was on her way to consummate her first love affair, as she was entering the kind of relationship in which her parents failed. For the first time, she confronted the fears, anxieties, guilt and concerns that she had suppressed over the years.

Sometimes with the sleeper effect the fear is of betrayal rather than commitment. I was shocked when another young woman—at the age of 24, sophisticated, warm and friendly—told me she worried if her boyfriend was even 30 minutes late, wondering who he was with and if he was having an affair with another woman. This fear of betrayal occurs at a frequency that far exceeds what one might expect from a group of people randomly selected from the population. They suffer minute to minute, even though their partners may be faithful.

In these two girls we saw a pattern that we documented in 66 percent of the young women in our study between the ages of 19 and 23; half of them were seriously derailed by it. The sleeper effect occurs at a time when these young women are making decisions with long-term implications for their lives. Faced with issues of commitment, love and sex in an adult context, they are aware that the game is serious. If they tie in with the wrong man, have children too soon, or choose harmful life styles, the effects can be tragic. Overcome by fears and anxieties, they begin to make connections between these feelings and their parents' divorce:

"I'm so afraid I'll marry someone like my dad."

"How can you believe in commitment when anyone can change his mind anytime?"

"I am in awe of people who stay together."

We can no longer say—as most experts have held in recent years—that girls are generally less troubled by the divorce experience than boys. Our study strongly indicates, for the first time, that girls experience serious effects of divorce at the time they are entering young adulthood. Perhaps the risk for girls and boys is equalized over the long term.

When a marriage breaks down, men and women alike often experience a diminished capacity to parent. They may give less time, provide less discipline and be less sensitive to their children, since they are themselves caught up in the maelstrom of divorce and its aftermath. Many researchers and clinicians find that parents are temporarily unable to separate their children's needs from their own.

In a second major unexpected finding of our 10-year study, we found that fully a quarter of the mothers and a fifth of the fathers had not gotten their lives back on track a decade after divorce. The diminished parenting continued, permanently disrupting the child-rearing functions of the family. These parents were chronically disorganized and, unable to meet the challenges of being a parent, often leaned heavily on their children. The child's role became one of warding off the serious depression that threatened the parents' psychological functioning. The divorce itself may not be solely to blame but, rather, may aggravate emotional difficulties that had been masked in the marriage. Some studies have found that emotionally disturbed parents within a marriage produce similar kinds of problems in children.

These new roles played by the children of divorce are complex and unfamiliar. They are not simple role reversals, as some have claimed, because the child's role becomes one of holding the parent together psychologically. It is more than a caretaking role. This phenomenon merits our careful attention, for it affected 15 percent of the children in our study, which means many youngsters in our society. I propose that we identify as a distinct psychological syndrome the "overburdened child," in the hope that people will begin to recognize the problems and take steps to help these children, just as they help battered and abused children.

One of our subjects, in whom we saw this syndrome, was a sweet 5-year-old girl who clearly felt that she was her father's favorite. Indeed, she was the only person in the family he never hit. Preoccupied with being good and helping to calm both parents, she opposed the divorce because she knew it would take her father away from her. As it turned out, she also lost her mother who, soon after the divorce, turned to liquor and sex, a combination that left little time for mothering.

A year after the divorce, at the age of 6, she was getting herself dressed, making her own meals and putting herself to bed. A teacher noticed the dark circles under her eyes, and asked why she looked so tired. "We have a new baby at home," the girl explained. The teacher, worried, visited the house and discovered there was no baby. The girl's story was designed to explain her fatigue but also enabled her to fantasize endlessly about a caring, loving mother.

Shortly after this episode, her father moved to another state. He wrote to her once or twice a year, and when we saw her at the five-year follow-up she pulled out a packet of letters from him. She explained how worried she was that he might get into trouble, as if she were the parent and he the child who had left home.

"I always knew he was O.K. if he drew pictures on the letters," she said. "The last two really worried me because he stopped drawing."

Now 15, she has taken care of her mother for the past 10 years. "I felt it was my responsibility to make sure that Mom was O.K.," she says. "I stayed home with her instead of playing or going to school. When she got mad, I'd let her take it out on me."

I asked what her mother would do when she was angry.

"She'd hit me or scream. It scared me more when she screamed. I'd rather be hit. She always seemed so much bigger when she screamed. Once Mom got drunk and passed out on the street. I called my brothers, but they hung up. So I did it. I've done a lot of things I've never told anyone. There were many times she was so upset I was sure she would take her own life. Sometimes I held both her hands and talked to her for hours I was so afraid."

In truth, few children can rescue a troubled parent. Many become angry at being trapped by the parent's demands, at being robbed of their separate identity and denied their childhood. And they are saddened, sometimes beyond repair, at seeing so few of their own needs gratified.

Since this is a newly identified condition that is just being described, we cannot know its true incidence. I suspect that the number of overburdened children runs much higher than the 15 percent we saw in our study and that we will begin to see rising reports in the next few years—just as the reported incidence of child abuse has risen since it was first identified as a syndrome in 1962.

The sleeper effect and the overburdened-child syndrome were but two of many findings in our study. Perhaps most important, overall, was our finding that divorce has a lasting psychological effect on many children, one that, in fact, may turn out to be permanent.

Children of divorce have vivid memories about their parents' separation. The details are etched firmly in their minds, more so than those of any other experiences in their lives. They refer to themselves as children of divorce, as if they share an experience that sets them apart from all others. Although many have come to agree that their parents were wise to part company, they nevertheless feel that they suffered from their parents' mistakes. In many instances, conditions in the post-divorce family were more stressful and less supportive to the child than conditions in the failing marriage.

If the finding that 66 percent of the 19- to 23-year-old young women experienced the sleeper effect was most unexpected, others were no less dramatic. Boys, too, were found to suffer unforeseen long-lasting effects. Forty percent of the 19- to 23-year-old young men in our study 10 years after divorce, still had no set goals, a limited education and a sense of having little control over their lives.

In comparing the post-divorce lives of former husbands and wives, we saw that 50 percent of the women and 30 percent of the men were still intensely angry at their former spouses a decade after divorce. For women over 40 at divorce, life was lonely throughout the decade; not one in our study remarried or sustained a loving relationship. Half the men over 40 had the same problem.

In the decade after divorce, three in five children felt rejected by one of their parents, usually the father—whether or not it was true. The frequency and duration of visiting made no difference. Children longed for their fathers, and the need increased during adolescence. Thirty-four percent of the youngsters went to live with their fathers during adolescence for at least a year. Half returned to the mother's home disappointed with what they had found. Only one in seven saw both mother and father happily remarried after 10 years. One in two saw their mother or their father undergo a second divorce. One in four suffered a severe and enduring drop in the family's standard of living and went on to observe a lasting discrepancy between their parents' standards of living.

We found that the children who were best adjusted 10 years later were those who showed the most distress at the time of the divorce—the youngest. In general, preschoolers are the most frightened and show the most dramatic symptoms when marriages break up. Many are afraid that they will be abandoned by both parents and they have trouble sleeping or staying by themselves. It is therefore surprising to find that the same children 10 years later seem better adjusted than their older siblings. Now in early and mid-adolescence, they were rated better on a wide range of psychological dimensions than the older children. Sixty-eight percent were doing well, compared with less than 40 percent of older children. But whether having been young at the time of divorce will continue to protect them as they enter young adulthood is an open question.

Our study shows that adolescence is a period of particularly grave risk for children in divorced families. Through rigorous analysis, statistical and otherwise, we were able to see clearly that we weren't dealing simply with the routine angst of young people going through transition but rather that, for most of them, divorce was the single most important cause of enduring pain and anomie in their lives. The young people told us time and again how much they needed a family structure, how much they wanted to be protected, and how much they yearned for clear guidelines for moral behavior. An alarming number of teen-agers felt abandoned, physically and emotionally.

For children, divorce occurs during the formative years. What they see and experience becomes a part of their inner world, influencing their own relationships 10 and 15 years later, especially when they have witnessed violence between the parents. It is then, as these young men and women face the developmental task of establishing love and intimacy, that they most feel the lack of a template for a loving relationship between a man and a woman. It is here that their anxiety threatens their ability to create new, enduring families of their own.

As these anxieties peak in the children of divorce throughout our society, the full legacy of the rising divorce rate is beginning to hit home. The new families being formed today by these children as they reach adulthood appear particularly vulnerable.

Because our study was such an early inquiry, we did not set out to compare children of divorce with children from intact families. Lacking fundamental knowledge about life after the breakup of a marriage, we could not know on what basis to build a comparison or control group. Was the central issue one of economics, age, sex, a happy intact marriage—or would any intact marriage do? We began, therefore, with a question—What is the nature of the divorce experience?—and in answering it we would generate hypotheses that could be tested in subsequent studies.

This has indeed been the case. Numerous studies have been conducted in different regions of the country, using control groups, that have further explored and validated our findings as they have emerged over the years. For example, one national study of 699 elementary school children carefully compared children six years after their parents' divorce with children from intact families. It found—as we did—that elementary-age boys from divorced families show marked discrepancies in peer relationships, school achievements and social adjustment. Girls in this group, as expected, were hardly distinguishable based on the experience of divorce, but, as we later found out, this would not always hold up. Moreover, our findings are supported by a litany of modern-day statistics. Although one in three children are from divorced families, they account for an inordinately high proportion of children in mental-health treatment, in special-education classes, or referred by teachers to school psychologists. Children of divorce make up an estimated 60 percent of child patients in clinical treatment and 80 percent—in some cases, 100 percent—of adolescents in inpatient mental hospital settings. While no one would claim that a cause and effect relationship has been established in all of these cases, no one would deny that the role of divorce is so persuasively suggested that it is time to sound the alarm.

All studies have limitations in what they can accomplish. Longitudinal studies, designed to establish the impact of a major event or series of events on the course of a subsequent life, must always allow for the influence of many interrelated factors. They must deal with chance and the uncontrolled factors that so often modify the sequences being followed. This is particularly true of children, whose lives are influenced by developmental changes, only some of which are predictable, and by the problem of individual differences, about which we know so little.

Our sample, besides being quite small, was also drawn from a particular population slice—predominantly white, middle class and relatively privileged suburbanites.

Despite these limitations, our data have generated working hypotheses about the effects of divorce that can now be tested with more precise methods, including appropriate control groups. Future research should be aimed at testing, correcting or modifying our initial findings, with larger and more diverse segments of the population. For example, we found that children—especially boys and young men—continued to need their fathers after divorce and suffered feelings of rejection even when they were visited regularly. I would like to see a study comparing boys and girls in sole and joint custody, spanning different developmental stages, to see if greater access to both parents counteracts these feelings of rejection. Or, does joint custody lead to a different sense of rejection—of feeling peripheral in both homes?

It is time to take a long, hard look at divorce in America. Divorce is not an event that stands alone in children's or adults' experience. It is a continuum that begins in the unhappy marriage and extends through the separation, divorce and any remarriages and second divorces. Divorce is not necessarily the sole culprit. It may be no more than one of the many experiences that occur in this broad continuum.

Profound changes in the family can only mean profound changes in society as a whole. All children in today's world feel less protected. They sense that the institution of the family is weaker than it has ever been before. Even those children raised in happy, intact families worry that their families may come undone. The task for society in its true and proper perspective is to strengthen the family—all families.

A biblical phrase I have not thought of for many years has recently kept running through my head: "Watchman, what of the night?" We are not, I'm afraid, doing very well on our watch—at least for our children. We are allowing them to bear the psychological, economic and moral brunt of divorce.

And they recognize the burdens. When one 6-year-old boy came to our center shortly after his parents' divorce, he would not answer questions; he played games instead. First he hunted all over the playroom for the sturdy Swedish-designed dolls that we use in therapy. When he found a good number of them, he stood the baby dolls firmly on their feet and placed the miniature tables, chairs, beds and, eventually, all the playhouse furniture on top of them. He looked at me, satisfied. The babies were supporting a great deal. Then wordlessly, he placed all the mother and father dolls in precarious positions on the steep roof of the doll house. As a father doll slid off the roof, the boy caught him and, looking up at me, said, "He might die," Soon, all the mother and father dolls began sliding off the roof. He caught them gently, one by one. "The babies are holding up the world," he said.

Although our overall findings are troubling and serious, we should not point the finger of blame at divorce per se. Indeed, divorce is often the only rational solution to a bad marriage. When people ask whether they should stay married for the sake of the children, I have to say, "Of course not." All our evidence shows that children exposed to open conflict, where parents terrorize or strike one another, turn out less well-adjusted than do children from divorced families. And although we lack systematic studies comparing children in divorced families with those in unhappy intact families, I am convinced that it is not useful to provide children with a model of adult behavior that avoids problem-solving and that stresses martyrdom, violence or apathy. A divorce undertaken thoughtfully and realistically can teach children how to confront serious life problems with compassion, wisdom and appropriate action.

Our findings do not support those who would turn back the clock. As family issues are flung to the center of our political arena, nostalgic voices from the right argue for a return to a time when divorce was more difficult to obtain. But they do not offer solutions to the wretchedness and humiliation within many marriages.

Still, we need to understand that divorce has consequences—we need to go into the experience with our eyes open. We need to know that many children will suffer for many years. As a society, we need to take steps to preserve for the children as much as possible of the social, economic and emotional security that existed while their parents' marriage was intact.

Like it or not, we are witnessing family changes which are an integral part of the wider changes in our society. We are on a wholly new course, one that gives us unprecedented opportunities for creating better relationships and stronger families—but one that also brings unprecedented dangers for society, especially for our children.

CHAPTER 32

Annulment: The Process and Its Meaning

Patrick R. Lagges

༺༄༅༻

The annulment process in the Roman Catholic Church remains laden with controversy in spite of some reforms since the Second Vatican Council. It is, as Patrick Lagges writes, a source of healing for some, and a source of scandal for others. It evokes anger and confusion or freedom and reconciliation. Once a rare event in Roman Catholicism, annulments during the past twenty-five years have climbed from fifteen thousand to sixty thousand worldwide—with the majority of those in the United States.

Lagges's essay accepts the current structure and process of annulments. The task he undertakes is to explain it. This he does admirably with clarity and precision.

"Annulment," he believes, is an unfortunate choice of terms. An annulment does not deny a marriage or a relationship existed, or that children born from the union are legitimate. It seeks to indicate that some key elements were missing from the relationship from the very beginning, which prevented a true marriage. The discussion, if it is to shed light rather than heat, then, must take place within the new framework of the church's teaching about marriage and its description of a "true marriage" as an exchange of persons rather than rights.

Lagges lays out the current canonical grounds for annulments and walks us through the process. How well does it work? It varies, he says, from tribunal to tribunal based on available personnel and resources—and we would add competencies.

Questions for Discussion

1. In the popular imagination, is the current annulment process a source of healing or a source of scandal? Give examples.
2. Is there an alternative structure or process you would propose?
3. Is the current process a form of Catholic divorce?
4. How would you compare the process to the Orthodox and the Protestant perspectives on the ending of a marital relationship?

For some, it is a source of healing; for others, a source of scandal. For most, it remains a dark, murky process that is heard about only through rumor and gossip.

The subject of declarations of nullity in the Roman Catholic Church has been a source of misunderstanding for many Catholics, especially those who grew up in the Church prior to the Second Vatican Council. For many people with a traditional Catholic education, annulments were rarely, if ever, obtained, and then only for the most serious reasons. Marriages which produced children or lasted for any length of time were believed to be incapable of being declared null. Much of that had to do with the Church's teaching about the nature of marriage. With the advent of the Second Vatican Council, however, that teaching was re-examined and formulated in a different way.

AN UNFORTUNATE CHOICE OF TERMS

To say that the Church annuls a marriage is not quite correct—for several reasons. First, the term "annulment" implies that the Church is doing something to a marriage. In reality, by granting an annulment, the Church is simply declaring something about a marriage. It says that some key element was missing from the very beginning which rendered the marriage invalid.

Second, the term "annulment" implies that a relationship is being denied or done away with. This is the source of most people's question: "How can you deny that our marriage ever existed?" Once again, declaration of nullity does not mean this. The Church, or anyone else, could never deny that a relationship existed. At the very least, there is a civil document and a Church document that state that these two people joined themselves together on a certain date and in a certain place. However, in declaring a marriage null, the Church states that something was there in the beginning which prevented a true marriage in the first place. Although the relationship resembled a marriage and may have produced children (who, according to Church law, are considered legitimate), there was some key element missing that prevented a real marriage from taking place.

WHAT IS A "TRUE MARRIAGE"?

The Church's description of a "true marriage" has changed in the wake of the Second Vatican Council. Prior to the Council, the Church described marriage as an exchange of rights. Both parties were to bind themselves to the right of their partner to sexual intercourse, to the procreation and education of children, to the permanence and indissolubility of the union, and to fidelity to

Reprinted from *Marriage and Family*, 73, 4 (April 1991): 18–24. Reprinted with permission of Abbey Press.

their spouse. A marriage could be declared null only if something impeded that exchange of rights: if the person excluded the right to sexual acts proper to the procreation of children or the right to permanence or fidelity. Marriages could be declared null if one of the parties entered into the union placing some sort of condition on their consent, was forced into the marriage, or was in error about the person they were marrying. In addition, marriages could be dissolved if they had not been consummated or if one or both of the parties had not been baptized.

In the Second Vatican Council, however, the Church's description of marriage changed. Instead of considering marriage as an exchange of rights, it was talked about as an exchange of persons. In Christian marriage, the parties give and accept each other in a permanent, faithful, fruitful union which is to mirror Christ's relationship to the Church.

Thus, the Council spoke of marriage as an "intimate partnership of life and love," and referred to the marriage covenant rather than the marriage contract. It described marriage as ". . . a means by which a man and a woman render mutual help and service to each other through an intimate union of their persons and of their actions; by which they experience the meaning of their oneness and attain to it with perfection day by day"; and by which "they increasingly advance their own perfection, as well as their mutual sanctification and hence contribute jointly to the glory of God." (These quotations are from paragraph 48 of the *Pastoral Constitution on the Church in the Modern World, Gaudium et spes.*)

In speaking of marriage in this way, the Church acknowledges that marriage is a far more complex reality than had been described previously. It was far more encompassing than two people merely exchanging certain rights and far more personally demanding than we had seen before. It now involves the whole person and is described in terms of the faithful, fruitful love of Yahweh toward the people Israel, and the total self-giving love of Jesus for his people, the Church.

This teaching about marriage forms the whole basis for any discussion about annulments in the Church. It is impossible to understand the concept of annulment unless at the same time you understand the Church's teaching on marriage. This may account for the fact that many people today are confused about the high number of annulments that are granted. The Church's teaching on marriage has changed and unless we understand what the Church teaches about marriage, our understanding of annulments will always be cloudy.

MARRIAGES THAT ARE NULL

In declaring a marriage null, the Church states that there was some key element missing at the time the two people exchanged their consent.

At times, it was the canonical form of marriage that was missing. For Latin-rite Catholics, that means exchanging their consent before a properly delegated priest, deacon, or lay person and two witnesses. For members of the Eastern Orthodox Churches, it means receiving the blessing of the priest within the marriage liturgy. However, these laws apply only to Catholics and to the Eastern Orthodox. The Church recognizes all other marriages as valid, regardless of where they take place. For example, when two non-Catholic Christians marry before a judge or a justice of the peace, the Church looks upon that marriage as a valid, sacramental union. To state otherwise would be to imply that marriages of non-Catholics were of less significance than marriages of Catholics. It would also deny the fact that marriage is first and foremost a human reality which, in the presence of the Lord, becomes the sign of a divine reality.

Sometimes, though, the person's freedom to marry is lacking. This would include people who are bound to a previous valid marriage, those who were not of a certain age, those who were related in certain ways or who had professed permanent vows in a religious community, or received the sacrament of orders. These facts, as well as several others called impediments, restrict a person's freedom to marry within the Church. Some of these impediments, such as a previous bond of marriage, are considered to be of divine law and hence bind all people. Others, like age, are merely Church laws and do not affect those who are not marrying in the Catholic Church.

At still other times, it is the person's actual consent that is called into question. These are the cases that are usually lumped together when people speak of annulments. They are handled by a judicial process which usually takes place over a period of time and requires certain legal procedures.

WHEN CONSENT IS IMPAIRED

The overwhelming majority of cases before Marriage Tribunals in the United States involve some form of defect of consent. Father William Woestman, O.M.I., of Saint Paul University, Ottawa, Ontario, writing in *Studia canonica*, noted that this is a world-wide phenomenon. His statistics indicate the percentages of cases decided in 1987 on the grounds of defect of consent: Australia, Great Britain, and the Republic of South Africa, 100 percent; Canada, the Federal Republic of Germany, Ireland, and the Netherlands, 99 percent; France and the United States, 98 percent; Italy, 96 percent; Poland and Spain, 91 percent. These cases deal with a person's ability to understand and choose marriage—an actual understanding of the commitment and what it is they are choosing. If marriage involves the pledge of two people to commit themselves to each other in an intimate union of life and love, then certain things are necessary. Both parties have to have an adequate understanding of themselves before they give themselves to each other. They have to have an adequate understanding of each other so that they know the person they are accepting as their marriage partner. They have to have a basic capacity for intimacy since this forms the essence of marriage. If either of the parties is seriously lacking in one of these areas, the marriage could be declared null.

Tribunals generally state these reasons as the "grounds" for the case. What follows is a brief explanation of what those grounds might be.

GROUNDS FOR AN ANNULMENT

According to canon law, a person is incapable of entering into marriage if he or she suffers from a "grave lack of discretion of judgment concerning essential matrimonial rights and duties which are to be mutually given and accepted" (Canon 1095.3). Cases heard under these grounds usually deal with a person's maturity, motivation, and understanding of marriage.

Because the commitment to marriage is so all-encompassing, a person has to have a maturity that is proportionate to the decision he or she is making. In a normal developmental process, a child gains the ability to make more and more complex choices based on an ability to understand the consequences of one's actions. Thus, there's usually a certain point when a parent allows the child to cross the street alone or go to the grocery store. Another point is reached when the adolescent is allowed to date or use the family car. Society, too, recognizes this development process when it states certain ages before a person can vote or purchase alcoholic beverages.

A far greater maturity is needed for marriage because the decision to marry has far greater consequences than some of the other choices that people make. It involves a person's whole life and is a commitment to the future as well as to the present. Until a person is able to understand that and is mature enough to make that commitment, he or she is not capable of entering into a valid marriage.

In other cases, though, the person's motivation comes into question. Canon 1057.2 states that the parties mutually give and accept each other "in order to establish marriage." This means that when a person exchanges consent with their partner, it must be motivated by the desire to enter into marriage and not for some other reason. At times, though, people have a different idea in mind. Some people view marriage as a "rite of passage" in society. It's something you do when you're too old to live at home or need to do before you start on a career. Other people marry for the purpose of escaping from a dysfunctional home environment. They suffer the physical or sexual abuse of one of their family members, they've been thrown out of their home, or they can no longer live with the unpredictability of alcoholism or other drug abuse. This consent is not "in order to establish marriage," but "in order to escape from home." Hence, they have not entered into a valid union.

In still other cases, a person fails to understand the implications of their commitment. They see part of the picture and mistake it for the whole thing. A person may see marriage as freedom but fail to see the responsibilities that go along with that. Another person may look to the good times they share with their partner but never realize they must share the struggles as well. They see the good aspects of their partner but overlook the fact that he drinks too much, has been violent on occasion, or has been unable to follow through on his commitments to school or to work. They may see the bad aspects of their partner but believe that marriage changes people and makes them into something they are not. In these cases, too, the person is gravely lacking in discretion of judgment about essential marital rights and duties. They have not formed a correct judgment about those rights and duties, and hence enter into marriage invalidly.

INCAPACITY TO ASSUME THE OBLIGATIONS

A second category of cases is heard under the grounds of one of the parties being "not capable of assuming the essential obligations of matrimony due to causes of a psychic nature" (Canon 1095.3). Some tribunals refer to this as a "lack of due competence" or "lack of canonical competence."

There is some psychological ability needed to enter into Christian marriage. In some cases, the person does not have the psychological ability to enter into Christian marriage. There is some psychological factor in their personality which makes them incapable of establishing a life of intimacy with their partner or of committing themselves to a permanent union or to one that essentially involves fidelity to one's spouse, or to the generation of new life.

For the most part, this includes people who suffer from personality disorders which produce characteristics directly opposed to the nature of marriage. For example, someone suffering from a narcissistic personality would not be capable of entering a relationship which is essentially directed toward the good of another. A person with an anti-social personality would not be capable of forming a relationship which essentially involves permanence, fidelity, and responsibility. And people with a paranoid personality or a schizoid personality would not be capable of the trust or the intimacy essential for a valid marriage. These people, along with those suffering from some of the other personality disorders, would be judged incapable of assuming the essential obligations of marriage. Also included in this category would be those psychosexual disorders or dispositions which would make a normal, heterosexual relationship impossible.

It's important to realize, though, that these must be serious psychological problems. All people have certain quirks and idiosyncrasies. All of us have isolated characteristics associated with certain personality disorders. It's only when those characteristics describe a person's major mode of acting, though, that it can be said that the person is incapable of assuming the essential obligations of marriage. In these cases, the tribunal relies heavily on psychological experts for their understanding of the human personality.

LACK OF INTENTION

Tribunals in the United States use less frequently the grounds that involve the intention of the parties when entering into marriage. These are some of the more traditional grounds used in the past. They include an intention against forming a union that can be dissolved only by the death of one's spouse, an intention against remaining faithful to one's partner, an intention against allowing the marriage to be fruitful or against fulfilling the responsibilities of parenthood, or an intention against working for the mutual good of each other. This also includes an intention against marriage altogether; for example, those who marry to regularize their immigration status, or to get their child baptized or enrolled in a Catholic school. Such people lack the proper intention for marriage since they exclude something essential from the marital commitment.

OTHER FACTORS

Other factors can also influence a person's consent. These include such things as placing a condition on one's consent, entering marriage because of force or fear, entering marriage deceived by fraud, or being in error about the person you are marrying. These factors, however, are difficult to establish. Tribunals use these less frequently, especially when other grounds are clearly evident.

THE PROCESS

One of the unfortunate parts of the 1983 Code of Canon Law is the fact that marriage nullity cases are still treated as contentious cases, even though it's not entirely clear about who the contending parties are. Treating these as contentious trials, the law presumes there are opposing parties. This is not true in most instances. In the majority of the cases before marriage tribunals, both parties agree that the marriage was null from the beginning. This produces the anomaly of having a contentious case with no contending parties. However, since these are the procedures that must be followed at the present time, most tribunals seek to apply these laws as pastorally and as sensitively as possible in order to find just and equitable solutions to the pain of marital breakdown.

The nullity process usually begins within the local parish. This is always going to be the key contact for the person seeking to have a marriage declared null. While at one time, divorced people were excluded from participation in the life of the Church, this is no longer true today. Pope John Paul II, in his *Apostolic Exhortation on the Christian Family in the Life of the World*, has stated: "I earnestly call upon pastors and the whole community of the faithful to help the divorced and with solicitous care to make sure that they do not consider themselves as separated from the Church, for as baptized persons they can, and indeed must, share in her life" (n. 84). Therefore, those who are divorced have a right to be part of their local community of faith. It is for this reason that most tribunals start the nullity process on that level. It helps pastoral ministers become more aware of the needs of their people and helps people become more integrated into their parish community. In many parishes, support groups allow those who have gone through the experience of divorce to come together to share those experiences and to support one another. These groups also assist people in the nullity process. Through sharing their experience of marriage and divorce, people gain a greater understanding of the factors that entered into their decision to marry in the first place.

Once the initial contact is made, tribunals differ on procedure. In some, the person contacts the tribunal directly for an interview; in others, much of the preliminary work is done through a written questionnaire. In either case, the main goal of the tribunal is to have the person tell the story of their relationship with their former spouse from beginning to end, to tell their own life story, and what they know of their former spouse's family history. Through this process, the tribunal gets a better understanding of these two people who entered into marriage: the families, their early life experiences, when and how their relationship began to develop, the factors that entered into their decision to marry, the ways they lived out their marital commitment to each other, and the factors which caused the breakdown of the union.

This is usually the most difficult part of the procedure since it requires the person to reflect upon the events of the past and to see how those events influenced the choices they made. At times, this involves re-living painful experiences of marriage or family life and gives the person the opportunity to gain greater personal insight, understanding, and appreciation for the complexity of Christian marriage. It also gives the Christian community the opportunity to support the person who is going through this process. The sensitive questioning of an interviewer or the discussions in support groups help to share burdens and so fulfill the command of the Lord.

The names of witnesses are also required. Like the term "annulment," the term "witness" is not exactly correct. Unlike the witness in a civil trial who generally testifies for one person and against another, the witnesses in a marriage nullity case are asked to describe the marriage as they saw it. Often, the witnesses can give the tribunal greater insight about the parties in the marriage and into the dynamics of that relationship as they lived it out. Witnesses are usually family members, but they can be nearly anyone who know the parties during the course of their marriage. Since the tribunal focuses on the parties at the time of their marriage, however, it is essential that the witnesses have some knowledge of the marriage from its inception. Tribunals differ in the way they obtain witness testimony. Some require the witnesses to be interviewed in person while others send out written questionnaires. Some tribunals seek the witness testimony before they begin the formal procedure; others wait until the case is actually accepted.

To begin a case, the person presents a formal petition to a tribunal which has jurisdiction over the marriage case. The case is then assigned to a judge, who accepts or rejects the petition. If he accepts it, he must also determine the grounds under which the case will be heard.

At this point, the judge informs both parties that a case has begun. Since there is a presumption in law that the marriage is valid, and since the other party (usually called the respondent or the defendant) has the right to uphold the validity of that union, it is absolutely essential that he or she be contacted and given an opportunity to participate. Failure to do so results in the whole process being null. At times, petitioners have requested that respondents not be contacted because of previous violence or harassment and the fear of a respondent's reaction when informed of the proceedings. This may seem reasonable but the fact is that respondents will generally hear about these proceedings from other sources in addition to the tribunal. Children of the marriage or relatives of one of the parties usually talk about the case long before the tribunal accepts it. Keeping it a secret is not an option that is open to the petitioner. The respondent has a right to know about the proceedings and to participate in them.

In some cases, though, the respondent has disappeared. This is especially true of a marriage which ended a number of years before. The petitioner has no knowledge of the respondent's whereabouts and has made every effort to find a current address. In these cases, the tribunals can proceed with the case but usually appoint an advocate to protect the rights of the respondent.

The judge may also need additional information from the petitioner and will request an additional interview for a psychological evaluation. In addition, he may ask the person to sign a release form so that he has psychological records available. Since many cases today involve psychological grounds, the judge may ask the psychologist specific questions about the maturity of the parties and their ability to enter into marriage.

Once the judge has all this testimony, the case is presented to the advocates (if there are any) and to the defender of the bond, who presents arguments upholding the validity of the marriage. After that, the judge writes his decision and states his reasons for declaring the marriage null or upholding its validity. An affirmative decision is automatically appealed, however, and must pass through a review process where the decision is either confirmed or the case is opened to a new process. If the appeal court confirms the affirmative decision or reaches an affirmative decision on its own, the case is concluded and the parties are free to marry in the Church. If the appeal court overturns the affirmative decision, the case can be appealed to Rome for a third hearing.

The length of time that this takes varies from tribunal to tribunal, based upon available personnel. Some tribunals can conclude cases within eight months while others take several years. Lack of cooperation on the part of the petitioner or the witnesses can also impede the progress of a case. A lack of cooperation on the part of a respondent should not impede the progress of a case. Although the respondent has a right to participate, no one can be forced to exercise a right. Furthermore, the petitioner has a right to have the case heard, and to have it concluded in a timely fashion.

The fees that tribunals request also vary widely. Some tribunals are subsidized through the diocesan tax on parishes or through a special collection for diocesan needs. Other tribunals have a fee based on the petitioner's income, while still others ask the petitioner to determine how much he or she can contribute toward the total cost of the case. Most tribunals have liberal policies for the reduction or total waiver of the fee.

CONCLUSION

It is no secret that more declarations of nullity are being granted today than in the past. Twenty years ago, tribunals heard slightly more than fifteen thousand marriage nullity cases throughout the world. In the present year, the number of affirmative decisions will approach sixty thousand. There are many reasons for this including better staffing of marriage tribunals throughout the world and a greater number of dioceses with functional tribunals. But, in large part, it is due to a greater understanding of the nature of Christian marriage and a greater appreciation of the commitment that couples make to each other when they marry "in the Lord."

CHAPTER 33

Remarried Catholics: Searching for Church Belonging

James J. Young

⚛

Paulist Father James Young explains here why so many divorced and remarried Catholics are still living as active Roman Catholics practicing their faith in Catholic parishes. Some of these persons—but far from all—have remarried after receiving annulments declaring their former marriages invalid. Young cites Pope John Paul II's letter, *On the Family,* encouraging divorced and remarried Catholics to remain members of the Church, though officially not allowed to receive communion.

Young points out a way such Catholics may still claim their right to the Eucharist. His discussion of this question deserves careful study.

Questions for Discussion

1. What are the deep conflicts Young claims beset Catholics who remarry without the Church's approval?
2. What are the reasons Catholic parishes are reaching out to divorced Catholics?
3. If the Pope says divorced and remarried Catholics may not receive Communion, what is the path of good conscience by which they may receive?
4. Explain the theological thinking that permits communion even to those clearly in invalid second marriages?
5. What is your overall reaction to Young's essay?

Note: Jim Young died suddenly in 1987 at a relatively young age. Most of his priestly life, he had worked with tireless creativity in ministry to divorced Catholics.

Sometimes they come to the parish house with a child to be baptized, or appear at parent classes for First Communion preparation. They may volunteer to help with the parish feeding program or sign up to visit the elderly. A husband or wife may be met on a hospital call or at a prayer meeting. At first, they may seem awkward and ill-at-ease, even evasive. They're remarried Catholics, and more of them are surfacing every day in American parishes.

Understandably, they often make other Catholics or those in positions of leadership somewhat nervous. They carry with them the suggestion of marriages abandoned, vows violated, and Church discipline ignored. Some Catholics are anxious that being too friendly or too accommodating to the remarried may undermine the Church's teaching on marital permanence and even encourage divorce. As predictable as these concerns may be, our pastoral experience is painting a far more complex and challenging portrait of remarried Catholics.

We are learning that they typically are men and women who exhausted every resource available to save a failing marriage, and only decided to divorce after prolonged consultation with counsellors and pastors. None divorced easily; the guilt, stress and upset that follows every broken marriage testifies to that. It may well be that because they were so Catholic, shaped by the Church's high valuation of lasting marriage, the pain was even more intense. Even though all divorce recovery programs hold up establishing an autonomous single existence as the major goal for the separated person, it is easy to understand why remarriage emerges so early as the obvious solution to this painful transition. For most people, a new marriage provides the only imaginable way of finding love again, of being happy again, or having a place in society again. Further, somewhat paradoxically, the best parts of a bad marriage may provide the appetite for a better marriage. Daily we meet divorced men and women who have put together a satisfying single life after divorce, but most admit that they would readily marry again if a suitable partner appeared.

The limited surveys we have suggest that, by and large, Catholics are much like the population at large. This means that almost three-fourths of divorced Catholics are dating seriously within a year, and half of them are remarried within three years of the civil divorce. Eventually as many as five out of six of the men and three out of four of the women will remarry.

The benefits of remarriage seem obvious to most. A new marriage brings a new partner with the companionship, sexual intimacy and support marriage provides. For most women, only remarriage helps them return to the financial security they knew in their former marriage. Most single parents are convinced that their children will be better off with a stepfather or stepmother, which is why fully 60% of remarriages bring children into the new household. Even though remarried living and stepparenting are unfamiliar situations with few accepted models of behavior, most will risk the unknown when the opportunity appears rather than continue raising children alone or living alone.

There may be as many as a million Catholics who have remarried over the past fifteen years with the Church's blessing. The increased availability of expeditious annulment procedures has allowed some 800,000 Catholics to receive annulments; many more, who never married as required in a Church ceremony the first time, have been able to marry again with the Church's approval. The Catholic community has worked very hard in recent years, using all the remedies available, to help Catholics remarry and remain in good standing in the community. Yet our best estimates are that well over 75% of remarried Catholics live in presumably invalid second marriages. They are the men and women who are presenting such difficult pastoral problems in Catholic parishes today.

Catholics who remarry without the Church's approval are usually caught in deep conflict. Many of them of lifelong devout Catholics, who attend Mass regularly, pray regularly, and live good Christian lives. When asked how they could go against the Church's discipline which does not provide for such second marriages, they often answer, "I hated to get married outside the Church, but I knew God would understand. I knew he didn't want me to be so lonely, and I knew he wanted my children to have a mother." Others say that though they loved the Church and being Catholic was in their bones, they felt the Church was too strict on divorce and remarriage and didn't appreciate the hardships people endure. Most say they agonized for months, sought spiritual counsel, and prayed at length before deciding to go ahead with a prohibited second marriage. Afterwards many were tormented by fears of "living in sin" and mistaken notions of being excommunicated from the Church. For some such guilt became a burdensome factor working against the success of the second marriage.

Those who have ministered extensively to divorced Catholics insist that the remarried are not men and women who have rejected the Church's teaching on the permanence and indissolubility of marriage. They are not people who promote divorce. Almost unanimously they profess a high regard for lifelong marriage, and insist they would never wish a divorce on anyone. "At times I still can't believe I'm divorced and remarried," a woman told me, "I'm sure if I was still caught in that first marriage, I'd be in a mental hospital now."

Further, surveys indicate that widespread divorce and remarriage among Catholics does not reflect a lessening of traditional Catholic family values among remarried Catholics. Recently, the Notre Dame Study of Parish Life found remarrying Catholics reapproaching and reidentifying with Catholic parishes. The remarried are "normal" again and want to live like ordinary families again. For traditional Catholics that means being part of a parish and raising children in the Church. Social critic Michael Novak believes that widespread divorce among Catholics stems more from the increased pressure on the family rather than lack of commitment to family values. Many commentators cite such contemporary factors as emotional problems, joblessness, addiction, mobility and loss of supportive family relationship, poverty, crime, and effects of Viet Nam—all of which tear marriages apart. To come close to divorced people is to look through a painful window at the dark underside of American life and the many forces that make lasting marriage difficult. For most, remarriage is a second chance to live and love again; another chance to salvage a broken life.

For this reason including these remarried couples in parish life may be an important way of helping the parish ground its life in the realities of Christian living today. The Catholic community has always been close to its people and their pain, and that basic pastoral instinct may be dramatized no more clearly today than in the ever-widening process of reconciliation of the remarried. And as this reconciliation has grown, rather than causing scandal and promoting more divorce and remarriage, the opposite actually has been the case. Since 1981 the U.S. divorce rate has been declining and the remarriage rate slowing. Could it be that understanding divorce better and the difficulties of remarriage has challenged more persons in troubled marriages to work harder at making them last?

The most important reason, however, for reaching out to remarried Catholics is the fact that they remain baptized members of the Church and deserve our pastoral care. Pope John Paul II clearly made this point in his 1980 letter *On the Family.* "I earnestly call upon pastors and the whole community of the faithful to help the divorced (and remarried) and with solicitous care to make sure that they do not consider themselves as separated from the Church, for as baptized persons they can and indeed must share in her life." He calls upon pastors to be especially sensitive to those "who have sincerely tried to save their first marriages and have been unjustly abandoned" and "those who have entered into a second union for the sake of the children's upbringing and who are sometimes subjectively certain in conscience that their previous and irreparably destroyed marriage had never been valid." (*On the Family,* 84) He goes on to say that remarried Catholics should be encouraged to attend Mass, listen to the word of God, persevere in prayer, contribute to works of charity and to community efforts in favor of justice, and to bring up their children in the faith.

In 1977 the American Bishops removed the American Church law which had attached a penalty of automatic excommunication to second marriage for Catholics who had previously been married in a Catholic ceremony and had not obtained an annulment of their first marriage. They wrote about their action, "It welcomes back to the community of believers in Christ all who may have been separated by excommunication. It offers them a share in all the public prayers of the Church community. It restores their right to take part in church services. It removes certain canonical restrictions upon their participation in church life. It is a promise of help and support in the resolution of the burden of family life. Perhaps above all, it is a gesture of love and reconciliation from the other members of the Church."

That love and reconciliation, of which the bishops wrote, is surfacing daily in American Catholic parishes. The papal and episcopal statements indicate the clear pastoral responsibility on the diocesan and parish level to search out and find such alienated remarried Catholics. Sadly some may have no interest in being an active Catholic again, but in recent years diocesan and parish efforts have turned up thousands of married Catholics most interested in being part of the Catholic community again. Pulpit appeals for reconciliation which clarify the place of remarried Catholics in the Church today continue to be needed; some parishes have deputized lay visitors to call on remarried couples who may be alienated and invite them back. There may be several million alienated remarried Catholics in the United States.

In his same 1980 letter, the Pope reaffirmed the Church's general practice of not admitting the remarried to Eucharistic communion. "They are unable to be admitted thereto from the fact that their state and condition of life objectively contradict that union of love between Christ and the Church which is signified and effected by the Eucharist." He added a second reason for the traditional exclusion. "If these people were admitted to the Eucharist the faithful would be led into error and confusion regarding the Church's teaching about the indissolubility of marriage." It must be noted that the Pope has already affirmed the place of remarried Catholics in the Church community and stressed the goodness of many of their lives with a most approving statement of their position in the Church. Yet he feels that the continuing existence of a prior marriage assumed to be binding until death bars them from the Eucharist. Since Eucharistic reception is a sign of accepting the teaching of the Church and living up to that teaching, those who have married a second time without Church approval are not properly disposed to take Communion.

There are two paths which make Eucharistic reception for the remarried possible. The first is an annulment of a prior marriage. Fortunately, this healing remedy is readily available in all of our American dioceses. Where properly explained to remarried Catholics, most choose to pursue an annulment since they have a strong desire to have their new marriage accepted by the Church community and restored to Communion. Catholic belonging always seems incomplete without Eucharist.

The second path is the "good conscience" solution by which a pastoral minister helps the remarried make a judgment about the appropriateness of their taking Communion when an annulment has not been possible. If the Catholics involved have a moral certitude that their first marriage was invalid, i.e., not a true Catholic marriage, then they are not bound by that prior marriage. This means that the second marriage can be considered a true Catholic marriage even though it cannot be publicly celebrated in the Church. This practice was urged on pastors by Cardinal Seper, then Prefect of the Congregation for the Doctrine of the Faith in Rome in 1973.

Where this solution has been applied and where couples in marriages not blessed by the Church have been encouraged by their pastors to take Communion, a compassionate readiness on the part of the Catholic people to welcome them to the Lord's table seems quite common. Even though there is always the danger of scandal in such cases, there seems to be little evidence of such scandal. It may be that given the mobility of our society and the largeness of our congregations people are not well-known enough for their personal marital circumstances to be public knowledge. Or it may be that now that most Catholics know someone who has struggled through divorce and remarriage, often their own family members, there is an understandable desire to see such remarried welcomed and accepted by the Church. Many pastors report a charitable openness on the part of most parishioners in supporting the Church's outreach to the remarried.

All Catholics in second marriages are not covered by the "good conscience" solution. A distinction is made between those who are morally certain that their first marriage was invalid and those who are certain that their first marriage was valid. There are many persons who insist that their first marriage was never a marriage; it was undermined by emotional illness or serious personality defects from the start. Yet others insist that they had a very good Catholic marriage for many years, but it died. Dramatic personality changes in mid-life, some personal tragedy which seemed to destroy the husband-wife relationship, or another person who wins away a spouse—all destroy marriages and lead to divorce. Many sincere Catholics, after the breakup of such marriages, refuse to apply for annulments, convinced they had a good marriage and would still be married, if only . . . The traditional position is that those who are sure their marriage was not a good one from the start, not ever valid, may receive Communion even if they do not have an annulment. Whereas those who are convinced that their first marriage was a good one for a long time, may not. Those in the second category, it is proposed, are bound by the first marriage, and so the second marriage is certainly invalid. Those in invalid second marriages, as we have seen, may not receive Communion.

As might be expected that latter position is being questioned by theologians and canonists today. Must those who have been unable to live up to the Church's teaching and laws on marriage always be excluded from Eucharistic sharing? Those open to the reception of Communion by such remarried persons suggest that where a first marriage is irretrievably lost, and where one or both parties have entered into a stable new marriage where he or she is faithful to obligations which remain from that first marriage—such as raising children in the faith or financial support—they should be offered the Eucharist as a spiritual resource to help them handle the demands of a new marriage. The Pope and bishops have insisted that the remarried are to live up to all the obligations of Christian life. How can they be asked to bear such burdens and not be offered the ordinary food of Christians? There is growing evidence that some pastors are supporting such remarrieds in taking the Eucharist, convinced that they are good people and need the Eucharist. Further, they ask, is not the Eucharist a meal of reconciliation for the flawed and imperfect? Did not the Lord share meals in the Gospels with the outcast and the suffering?

This is the frontier area of ministry to the remarried in the Church today. An enormous amount of progress has been made in cleansing the Catholic community of negative, condemnatory attitudes towards the remarried and a process of reconciliation is underway. How many of these people, and for what reason, can be offered the Eucharist needs much further reflection and lived experience.

Reconciling the remarried has many pastoral benefits for the parish community. It has also saved whole families for the Church; a decade ago many of these families would have been cut off with their children. Further, there are numerous reports of Catholics remarried to persons of no prior religious affiliation who are now coming forward and requesting to be baptized or received into the Catholic Church. Most of all, it brings into the life of the parish the rich Christian experience of men and women who have endured the heartbreak of broken marriage in faith and dared to love again.

PART EIGHT

Spirituality of Marriage

CHAPTER 34

A Spirituality of Resistance for Marriage

Kieran Scott

⌒◟◞⌒

What should we make of the resurgent interest in spirituality? It is difficult to avoid bumping into it today. It has reached far into the popular consciousness of many people. Even in academic circles, new courses and degrees in spirituality are flourishing. At times, it seems we are in the midst of a great new awakening!

This essay starts with the premise that the current spirituality phenomenon is in need of careful examination. Is it an unqualified good, or is there a dark and dangerous side to it? Is it one more self-help process? A middle-class consumer luxury? Or could spirituality address questions of money, sex, drugs, justice, and lifestyle? The answer, of course, depends on the *meaning* of spirituality and the *form* or shape it takes.

In this previously unpublished essay, Kieran Scott proposes a meaning of spirituality as a form of cultural resistance. Competing world views (or gospels) are contrasted so as to illuminate the daily life choices we face. The essay concludes with the application of a spirituality of resistance to marriage and family life. The spiritual, as a prophetic form of resistance, can give the deepest and richest context to our covenantal relations.

Questions for Discussion

1. How would you characterize your own spirituality? What spiritual practices form a regular part of your life? What practices are missing?
2. How would you connect household economics to the economy of salvation?
3. What spiritual issues come to the fore in a young marriage? In midlife? In elderly life?
4. Does your local faith community foster a consumerism spirituality or is it a "community of resistance and solidarity"?
5. What (forgotten) spiritual practices have you recovered from your own religious tradition? From the religious traditions of others?
6. How could a spirituality of resistance invite an alternative set of attitudes and practices toward food shopping, purchasing a car, taking a vacation, or offering hospitality?

Tolerance is regarded as the *highest good* in contemporary U.S. culture. The sociologist Alan Wolfe (1998) found something close to a consensus in this regard among the middle class. The U.S. style is averse to conflict. Wolfe suggests that most middle-class Americans have effectively added an 11th commandment to the biblical decalogue: "Thou shalt not judge thy neighbor." The prevailing stance and ethos seems to be "live and let live." This high valuing of tolerance is evident in middle-class attitudes toward religious belief, gender roles, immigration, multiculturalism, and race. The one notable exception is homosexuality. Still, the average American is nonjudgmental and unwilling to get pulled into ideological battles that might tear the country apart. They prefer what Wolfe calls "morality writ small" rather than the larger goals of social justice and equality.

We can take some comfort and encouragement from the high value we place on tolerance. Tolerance can be a virtue. It can be a strength in enabling us to navigate diversity and difference. This can be invaluable in our world today. Ask the people of Bosnia, Kosovo, or Northern Ireland. However, tolerance is a virtue among a cluster of virtues. The question I wish to address in this essay is: is it enough? Can tolerance be our highest good in married life? Can tolerance adequately respond to the all-consuming nature of a consumerist culture? Can it address questions of familial justice? Can it deal with fundamental issues of lifestyle? I believe the answer to all the above is negative. Tolerance alone, notes David Hollenbach (1999), cannot produce an adequate response to the cruel realities of urban poverty. We need, he believes, a stronger vision of the common good to address them. The times we live in may, in fact, call for a *form of intolerance*. The name I give to this form of life is a spirituality of resistance.

This essay will explore: (1) the meaning of spirituality as resistance; (2) two competing gospels: commodity form versus personal form; and (3) challenging and resisting the commodity form in marriage and family life.

SPIRITUALITY AS RESISTANCE

Spirituality is undergoing a widespread renaissance. The interest is phenomenal and touches multiple levels in our society. On the academic level, there has been a resurgence of interest in historical figures such as Julian of Norwich and Hildegard of Bingen. Among popular audiences, books on spirituality regularly hit the best-seller list. Every large bookstore has a wall that is stacked full of the most recent books on the new spirituality. TV audiences can tune in daily to Oprah, Suzie Orman, or Deepak Chopra for discussions on how to integrate the spiritual with love, sex, marriage, monetary success, and world peace. According to postmodern cultural critics, religion is fading, but spirituality is an inherent postmodern sensibility.

Is this interest in spirituality just a passing fad? Is it good or bad? Is it a complement to marriage and family life or could it be a chief competitor? Does it offer (long-neglected) resources for the contemporary world or is it dangerous and illusionary? And why the sudden burst of interest in spirituality in the 1990s? What caused this eruption?

My interest here is the linkage between spirituality and the practice of a disciplined and responsible married life. Before we can move in this direction, however, some *historical* lessons need to be learned and some current *misconceived* spiritualities need unmasking.

The new spirituality wishes to address the novel situation of the present. There is a hunger, a quest beyond materiality. Vaclav Havel, president of the Czech Republic, noticed this rapid spiritual awakening and spread of religious feeling among young people in his country. "This is not an accidental phenomenon," he writes, "it is an inevitable one: the endless, unchanging wasteland of the herd life in a consumer society, its intellectual and spiritual vacuity, its moral sterility, necessarily causes young people to turn their attentions somewhere further and higher; it compels them to ask questions about the meaning of life, to look for a more meaningful system of values and standards, to seek, among the diffuse and fragmented world of frenzied consumerism for a point that will hold firm—all this awakens in them a longing for a genuine moral 'vanishing point,' for something purer and more authentic" (1990, pp. 184–185). The new literature on spirituality attempts to respond to these deep yearnings of contemporary men and women. The books and TV discussions explore these desires and sentiments that speak to ordinary human experience. Ironically, it is the very lack of attention of church officials, preachers, and liturgists to the concrete daily lives of people that sends them outside institutionalized religion to have their spiritual thirst quenched.

Spirituality today is seen as the great unifier. The vague all-inclusive meaning of the term is seen as an advantage. The driving force behind its reemergence is the desire for a unifying idea. Contemporary life is fragmented. Dualisms abound: body-soul, East-West, religious-secular, science-philosophy. There is a deeply felt need to overcome this fragmentation. The "new spirituality" holds the promise of healing the world's splits. Historically, however, the spiritual represented the opposite: the inner as opposed to the outer, and the nonmaterial as opposed to the material or body. While contemporary writers may not *intend* that meaning today, at the same time they cannot ignore it. A premature jump into unity may be an illusion. High-level generalities may be deceptive. And, vague all-inclusive meanings float into abstractions. This is one of the dangers in the current spirituality craze. It lends itself to a Disneyland or cafeteria-style choosing, a fuzzy concern and love for the whole world but for no one or place in particular. This is a rootless spirituality. This is the result of the divorce, in much of the current literature and popular discussions, of spirituality from religion. It leads to disastrous escapism. On the other hand, spirituality is in critical need of religion. Religion, with all its flaws, can act as a wise restraint upon our spiritual drive, and at the same time nourish us with centuries of (external) religious practices.

A second cautionary note, with regard to some forms of contemporary spirituality, is sounded by L. Gregory Jones (1997). Jones offers a scathing critique of popular spiritual works. Too often, he observes, popular spirituality is prone to present the spiritual journey as an individual quest tailored to the individual's privatized needs and desires. The individual is invited, like a good tourist, to go on brief forays, sampling exotic "lands" of ideas, so as to discover the sacred in their midst. The journey, however, is without *telos,* except the ceaseless motion of self-discovery or self-invention. What it offers is "a synthetic substitute of vague, self-referential religiosity." "I am convinced," writes Jones, "that much contemporary spirituality is shaped by consumer impulses and captive to a therapeutic culture. It systematically avoids the disciplined practices necessary for engagement with God . . . [it] separates spirituality both from theological convictions and practices on the one hand, and social and political realities and commitment on the other" (p. 4). Jones acknowledges that the interest in popular spirituality reflects important yearnings *and* is a judgment on the failure of Christian communities. At the same time, he cautions us to be wary of "spirituality" as we nurture people in their often inchoate desires and yearnings. This can only be done, he claims, if we recognize the dramatic differences between Christian spiritual practices and a generic or consumerist spirituality. He identifies and explains five significant differences:

1. Contemporary popular spirituality has become a new commodity to consume in an increasingly commodified world. It plays right into the prevalent consumer mentality. People have (authentic) needs and desires. They are desperately searching for a new commodity that can satisfy the desires other commodities have failed to quench. Let them choose what they prefer: "the consumer is always right."

2. Contemporary spirituality celebrates the individuality over-against (external) other authority. The focus is almost exclusively on the self-sufficiency of one's interior life. It is a journey of self-knowledge and self-salvation. There is little sense of being part of something greater. It is the "triumph of the therapeutic" self. The individual becomes the ultimate authority for cultivating and evaluating spiritual progress. No external authority, institution, or official ministerial representative is necessary.

3. Contemporary spirituality has a syncretic approach to religious commitment. Everything is compounded—a little piece of Zen, a dash of animism, a sprinkling of Oriental mythologies, mixed with some elements of Jewish and Christian traditions. In this supermarket of spiritual selection, anything can be employed to meet individual needs.

4. Contemporary spirituality is lured by the idea to unite people around the world beyond political or institutional divisions. Social and political realities and commitments are not addressed. What really matters is the inner experiences of isolated individuals. The bifurcation of the spiritual and the political allows the spiritual to be a luxury consumer good. Massive suffering around the world will not be confronted.

5. Contemporary spirituality has severed itself from centuries of Christian practices. This gap between Christian practices and consumer spirituality is one of the reasons for the popularity of the "new spirituality," and yet one of its most dangerous elements. The Christian churches, however, have

done an abysmal job in sustaining the sort of practices and spiritual disciplines necessary for an authentic communal life.

Jones's incisive analysis insightfully sketches our contemporary drift or tour into misconceived spiritualities. The spiritual life, on the other hand, rooted in religious (Christian) traditions is "shaped by both the *absence* and the *presence* of God" (p. 6). We are called to repentance and conversion. There can be no self-knowledge without knowledge of God. We cannot save ourselves. Sin is self-deceptive, and all our life decisions are entangled in it. Christian spiritual practices teach us to become *detached* from those features of our world that separate us from God and free us to cling to the One who alone can satisfy our desires. They transform our desire from selfish acquisition into self-giving love.

Gabriel Moran and Maria Harris are in accord with these sentiments. Harris refers to spirituality as "our *way* of *being in the world* in *light of the Mystery at the core of the universe*" (1998, p. 109; emphasis added). Her choice of language is very instructive for us. Several elements stand out. Spirituality is conceived as:

1. *This Worldly.* It is not a flight from history or a disengagement from matter/body. Rather, today's spirituality is rooted in the concrete personal/communal/ecological relations that envelop our daily lives.

2. *Being.* Here spirituality breaks with a mere pragmatic or utilitarian approach to life. It broadens existence in the world beyond doing to being. It is not a commodity to give satisfaction.

3. *A Way.* Spirituality is connected to a "way" of life or a set of ways (or disciplines). This links it to an historical tradition, to a disciplined communal life.

4. *The Sacred.* This element stresses the sacred character of existence. We journey through life with a profound sense of the Mystery at the core of the universe. Notice the location of the sacred. The Holy One will be encountered in the depths (core) of all our relatedness.

This meaning and practice of spirituality as a daily lifestyle can have profound implications for marriage and family life. In the context of our mass culture, it is a countervailing force against the addiction of consumerism. This is a spiritual (way) life that makes decisions against the tide. It is a prophetic form of cultural resistance. It is a protest against a meaningless, self-centered, commodity-driven life. God is the Other who interrupts our lives and offers judgment on what we lack and need. Spirituality here is a shield or a defense against what destroys our integrity as persons. It allows us to say no to what destroys our dignity. It offers us a set of forms and teaches us a set of disciplines so that we will be able to resist evil. This language may seem peculiarly negative. However, if we look closely we will find a language of double negatives and thus a language of affirmation in the real and concrete world. The protest (no) takes place within the context of a life affirming (yes) quest for justice and peace.

TWO COMPETING GOSPELS: COMMODITY FORM VERSUS PERSONAL FORM

In order for us to move a step closer to establish a firm linkage between spirituality and the daily lived experience of marriage, the issue must be placed in the context of time and place. We are at the dawn of a new millennium. The United States is the only remaining superpower in the world. The Dow Jones reaches toward twelve thousand. Sports-utility vehicles fly out of dealers' parking lots. Luxury homes are mushrooming throughout suburbia. Unemployment is at an all-time low, and the economy at an unprecedented high. By some standards, these are very good times to live in this place. And yet for all our success in the modern United States, there is a sense that something has gone terribly awry.

In spite of repeated dire predictions, marriage and family are not about to fade into oblivion. They remain the most fundamental form of civil association and an anchor in turbulent seas. Contemporary "cultural wars," however, revolve around marriage and family. Left and right wing remain devoted to a strong picture of family life. Family imagery permeates our deepest hopes, fears, and aspirations. In her writings, Barbara Dafoe Whitehead (1997) argues that our national debate on the family is being conducted in two separate languages. These languages are foreign to each other and speak past each other. The first is the official language, spoken by experts, academics, liberal politicians, and the media. The focus of this official debate is how to get both parents into full-time work and fund child care. The second is family language, spoken by ordinary middle-class families (and sometimes coopted by right-wing religious and political ideologues). The preoccupation of this grassroots conversation is how parents can raise their kids in a culture unfriendly to parents and children. The focus is on contemporary culture and how it has made it almost impossible for families to flourish. There is a pervasive fear that our children are succumbing to the dominant mores and adopting the values of an aggressively materialistic, individualistic, and consumerist culture. Families are clearly stressed, but simply getting more partners into the workforce so that we can buy more goods and services misses the factor of moral formation. It also creates further needs and expectations and traps us in a pressure-filled economic treadmill.

Jean Bethke Elshtain has some sympathy for this latter conversation. "Who do we serve?" she asks. "The current American answer seems to be neither family, nor friends, nor church, nor civic society. Where, then, are we putting our energies? What takes our time, occupies our attention, diverts our minds? If the available data affords an accurate representation of the complexities of the moment, it must be said that Americans are working longer and harder than they ever did to earn a living, to 'get ahead,' save money, to buy goods, to live out one version of the American dream" (1998, p. 31). And after we have done all that, "there is nothing left to give." So we retreat to privacy and creature comforts.

The nature of the stark and fundamental choices confronting us in our daily lives in the United States is strikingly portrayed by John Kavanaugh in his book *Following Christ in a Consumer Society* (1981). In Kavanaugh's terms, our fundamental option is between two opposing forms of life, namely, the "commodity form" and the "personal form." Each represents a style of life, a formation system, a worldview, a way of journeying. They are, in effect, two competing gospels. "These gospels," he notes, "differ as radically as light and darkness, life and death, freedom and slavery, fidelity and unfaithfulness" (pp. 20–21). They serve as ultimate and competing hermeneutical lens on reality. One gospel reveals men and women as replaceable and marketable commodities; another gospel reveals persons as irreplaceable and unique free beings. One is a gospel of life; the other a culture of death.

The commodity form reveals the spiritual crisis at the heart of our social, political, and economic evils. It is aptly summed up in the bumper sticker: "I Shop, Therefore I Am." It is not things, material possessions, technology, or capitalism, in and of themselves, however, that are problematic. Rather, it is the idolatry of them and submission to them in terms of seeking meaning and fulfillment of our existence through them. The present consumer society in the United States runs on the producing, purchasing, and consuming of objects. But the formation and information system that is commodity culture does not just affect the way we shop. It affects the way we think and feel, the way we work and play, the way we relate to our spouses and children. It is "systemic." Its influence is felt in every dimension of our lives and provides, for some, their ultimate horizon of meaning. Marketing and consuming, then, become the standard of our final worth and ultimately reveal us to ourselves as things.

The commodity form is formation to a life of fragmented relatedness. The interior self is lost and this parallels the dissolution of mutuality and relationship. Free commitments and questioning are shut out. When we perceive ourselves and others as things, we invariably produce lives of manipulation, utility, domination, and violence. This personal and interpersonal breakdown is reflected in our lives through a flight from human vulnerability and channeling our desires into the amassing of possessions. In effect, the consumerist gospel offers a practically lived atheism. It embodies the most fundamental of human sins: idolatry.

The personal form of life, as revealed in Jesus of Nazareth, calls for a massive personal resistance to the values of the commodity form. Kavanaugh describes it as "a mode of perceiving and valuing men and women as irreplaceable persons whose fundamental identities are fulfilled in covenantal relationship." This gospel is countercultural. It offers a model of humanity that is personalistic, liberating, and ultimately exalting of human life. It is captured in Martin Buber's term *I-Thou* (1958), and in his statement: "All real living is meeting" (p. 11). Pope John Paul II has reiterated this theme through-

(handwritten marginalia: "SYSTEM WILL not take care of us if we conform & of us & COUNTER CULTURAL")

out his papacy. In his first encyclical, *Redemptor Hominis* (1979) he warned us in the West of the danger in achieving high economic success and productivity. We might fall into a form of unfreedom: a slavery to consumerism itself. "Humans," he writes, "cannot relinquish themselves or the place in the visible world that belongs to them; they cannot become slaves to things, the slaves of economic systems, the slaves of production, the slaves of their own production" (p. 25). Our vocation is to *negate* the negations, and to *affirm* a deeper communal life in justice and peace.

For Kavanaugh, the commodity form and the personal form stand in opposition to each other on every level. They elicit from us, whether we are conscious of it or not, a final and totalized allegiance. Each presents itself as the ultimate explanatory principle of life. Consequently, we are faced with a conscious choice. The choice is: what god to believe in. The implications for marriage and family are monumental.

CHALLENGING AND RESISTING THE COMMODITY FORM IN MARRIAGE AND FAMILY

The practicing Christian should look like a Martian. This metaphor suggested by Kavanaugh (1981) indicates the sense of otherness or foreignness that characterizes a Christian style of life. He or she will never feel fully at home in a commodity culture. And, if we do, something is drastically wrong. "Christians are called up," notes Jean Bethke Elshtain, "not to conform to the world's ways but to challenge them. If the world dictates that men and women are most human when they are buying and consuming, why should Christians follow suit?" (1998, p. 32). Are we not called to be signs of contradiction amidst the distorted values of the present moment? The Christian way places us in a *dialectical* relation with the economic, political, and institutional forms of contemporary culture. It is profoundly countercultural.

Marriage and family life can be a living testimony to this swimming against the tide. As a pivotal social form it can be a base for resistance to the commodity form. It can provide a zone of freedom where the deepest experiences of fidelity, trust, self-acceptance, intimacy, and selfless love can occur. When married couples and parents embody these qualities of personhood, they can be the most primal and resilient support for resistance to dehumanization. Thus understood, marriage and family is a modern parable, a cultural protest and a subversive force that undermines the gods of consumerism.

However, married couples and families need protective shields if they are to live as a counterforce. If they are to fully respond to this prophetic call, they must put on a set of practices rooted in the wisdom of religious traditions and modeled in the corporate life of a people. In Christian communities, these practices of spiritual disciplines teach. They are a form of divine pedagogy. The pedagogy shows us how to do two things: (1) they teach us how to become *detached* from things that clutter our lives and, consequently, leave no room for God, and (2) they teach us how to *transform* our desire so that our restless hearts will find human fulfillment in the Holy One. In other words, they offer an alternative way.

As a way of highlighting these disciplines, I will take the framework proposed by John Kavanaugh in some later writings (1984) and fill it with some of my own commentary and insights. Kavanaugh examines five areas of our lives where the economic gospel of our culture tries to establish its hegemony. In each of these areas, he counterposes spiritual practices as a living alternative to the cultural tyranny of consumerism. The framework and dialectic proposed is very instructive for marriage and family life today. The five areas and their counterpoints are:

1. the loss of *interiority* and (the unmarketability of) solitude
2. the loss of *solidarity* and the resistance of *covenantal life*
3. systematically legitimated *injustice* and *social commitment*
4. craving *consumption* and *simplicity* of life
5. the flight from *vulnerability* and (the counter-economics of) *compassion.*

On the one side, we have the wounds of consumerism; on the other side, the healing power of grace. Both are frequently intertwined on our marriages. It is the spiritual disciplines, however, that teach us how to resist evil in the daily routine of our family lives. Let us briefly examine the five areas and their interplay with spiritual practices.

THE LOSS OF INTERIORITY AND (THE UNMARKETABILITY) OF SOLITUDE

As a formation system, commodity culture cultivates a false inner self. Buying becomes our most interior experience. The self is now available for purchase. Our identities collapse into possessions and appearances. We *are* how we look, what we eat, and the way we buy. Economics becomes the gauge of our personhood. But basically this is a spiritual phenomenon. We are taught to fear who we are in solitary. We live by pretense and external appearance. Image is everything.

Maria Harris and Gabriel Moran (1997), however, direct us back to the basic question: "And what is a person?" "A person," they reply, "is one who listens inwardly and responds outwardly" (p. 61). Two characteristics stand out here. The first reminds us that as persons we possess characteristics for interiority and inwardness: an inner life. The second is: one cannot be a person alone. Relationality is necessary for personhood. The first characteristic is the focus of our attention here.

Harris and Moran write about education as a process of formation of the inner life. People are nourished, they note, by three deep springs: silence, listening, and Sabbath. These three forms are critical to the recovery and transformation of the self. *Silence* is a discipline learned by setting aside regular periods of time in which to move away from distraction and noise. It is the art of "centering down" where other forms of knowing become possible. It is an art absent in many homes today. The primary concern of parents in the United States today is time: loss of time with their children. This loss is also felt in the absence of zones of quiet and periods of silence in households.

The second nurturing spring is *listening*. Silence is for the sake of listening. A person listens inwardly as a condition for outward response. This art of listening demands attention to the voices of wisdom in our heritage, to the cries of the wounded in our midst, and to the calls for re-creation. Profound silence can break through the psychic and emotional numbness that conspicuous consumption fosters.

Sabbath is the third component in educating the inner life. It remains a central practice in both Jewish and Christian traditions. Sabbath begins as a cessation of labor. It is a "covenantal work stoppage" (Brueggemann cited in Harris and Moran 1997, p. 66). "Remember the sabbath day" is a reminder that our world is not a place of endless productivity, ambition, and stress. Couples and families need freeing from the burdens of labor periodically. They need rest for renewal.

These three springs of living water are prayer forms. They extricate us from patterns of behavior that have become normative in commodity culture. They center us in ourselves as persons and free us for engagement in the other arenas of life. Prayer may be perceived as lacking pragmatics, as a waste of time, as self-deception. On the contrary, it is an exercise in self-revelation, an act of economic resistance, and a radical alternative to the commercial imperative of our culture. It is a social and political act, and profoundly countercultural. Every couple and family needs it at the center of their daily lives.

THE LOSS OF SOLIDARITY AND THE RESISTANCE OF COVENANTAL LIFE

Cultural commentators in recent decades have raised the issue of the need for a new public philosophy in the United States. There is a weak sense of the common good. Private rights triumph over public purpose. The basic operating principle in our social, economic, and political structures is competition rather than cooperation, individualism rather than solidarity, self-sufficiency instead of interdependence. Most middle-class Americans live in neighborhoods that isolate them, not only from themselves, but from people of different socioeconomic backgrounds. They hunker down, as Robert Bellah and colleagues (1985) note, in "lifestyle enclaves" and find their identities in interaction with other persons with similar patterns of appearance, consumption, and leisure. It's a form of Club Med writ large. It pits the suburbs against the city, upstate against downstate, the middle class against the very poor, and frequently white against people of color. Authentic communities are hard to find. Rugged individualism holds sway. The economic myths that drive the engine of our culture have massive influence on our relationships. Our passions and desires are directed into things. We buy ourselves to death. What we experience in return is fragmentation, loss of solidarity, and the painful absence of covenantal intimacies in our lives.

Martin Buber (1966) writes: the first injunction in life is to begin with oneself. The second is not to be preoccupied with oneself. The key, he observed, is "To begin with oneself, but not to end with oneself; to start from oneself, but not to aim at oneself; to comprehend oneself, but not to be preoccupied with oneself" (pp. 31–32). This advice, penned some fifty years ago, is wisdom in an age of narcissism. I-Thou is potentially subversive. Friendship, family intimacy, and community are powerful forms of cultural resistance. They are countervalues. They represent a protest for the riches of a shared life.

Covenantal relations, then, carry within their very identities the seeds of prophetic resistance. Only in these relations can our truth be known and our personhood emerge. These relationships, however, take time. We cannot dignify one another or be fully present to one another if our calendars are bursting with activities and we are busy racing around with no time to pause. A committed relationship, on the other hand, is a courageous act of economic disengagement. Kavanaugh advises, "If we spend one half hour a day more in relationship talking with a community friend, walking for a while with our spouse, 'wasting time' with our children, speaking the truth to a brother or sister, we will find ourselves empowered to resist much of the institutionalized craving of our acculturated appetites" (1984, p. 608). Couples and families need less busyness and more presence in the rhythm of their lives.

SYSTEMATICALLY LEGITIMATED INJUSTICE AND SOCIAL COMMITMENT

Commodity culture makes things of us all. And we become as helpless as the things we worship. This reification of life spills over into a utilitarian disposition toward work, an instrumentalist attitude in our social commerce, and an objectification of our sexual partners. This depersonalization is intrinsically related to injustice. Violence and injustice fundamentally "thingify" the other: the poor, the homeless, the imprisoned, the unemployed, the undocumented immigrant, the ethnic minority, the gay. Our culture remains mired in these social deaths. The systematizing of these prejudices, in all of their subtle—and not so subtle—institutional, political, and interpersonal forms, is the real culture of death. Are we naive enough to believe there is no relationship between our divorce culture and our commodity culture in the United States? No connection between domestic violence and market economy? No link between mass advertising and hoarding more and more possessions?

Walter Brueggemann (1986) writes, "Justice is to sort out what belongs to whom, and to return it to them. . . . the work of liberation, redemption, salvation is the work of giving things back" (p. 5). This is the other side that completes our personhood. The inner life must be expressed in outward activity. In fact, the deeper the inwardness, the wider the external effect. This is the paradox at the heart of the Christian (as well as Jewish and Muslim) religion. Justice is not some bleeding-heart liberal program. It is a constituent element of faith and love. The issues of economic injustice, hunger, home-lessness, and powerlessness are the very flesh of faith. Judgment will be rendered on how we have responded to the other.

Social commitments are an alternative way of life. In a culture where human value is measured by beauty, wealth, gender, or race, social commitment shatters all of that. Our convictions must be given concrete expression. We must act. We must resist the plague (Camus).

In our marriages and families, justice begins with fidelity to our relationships. We are partners with our spouses, our children, our dogs and our cats, and the earth. All require responsive justice. Domestic violence must be negated. Familial structures need reshaping away from dominant and subordinate roles toward mutuality and collaboration. Commitments must be honored to ensure family stability. And justice in the family is inextricably connected to the struggle to repair a wounded world.

CRAVING CONSUMPTION AND SIMPLICITY OF LIFE

The story of commodity culture is the story of creating false needs. As a total formation system, it stimulates desires, cultivates needs, and inflates expectations. Our sense of belonging and well-being is increasingly defined by access to goods and services. The market has become ubiquitous, affecting our way of life, and burdening us with what early Quakers called "cumber." Our spent energy goes in circles: we crave, we accumulate, we secure, we maintain, and finally, we discard. Jean Bethke Elshtain writes, "We cannot offer the gift of self to one another if we ourselves are entirely consumed by consumption—wholly given over to a relentless fast-paced life in which the more we earn, the more we need to earn . . . on and on without any apparent oasis in sight" (1998, p. 34). "Can we," she asks, "glimpse an alternative?"

Voluntary simplicity is such an alternative. Simplicity is the desire for faithful living. It is as Sharon Daloz Parks (1997, p. 50) notes, "an orientation to life that can, over time, foster a sense of right proportion and right relation" in our households and the whole earth community. We *choose* to "travel light," not because of guilt, some trendy asceticism, or frugality, but because we value persons over things. The practice of simplicity is a lifestyle choice that touches every aspect of our lives—food, money, time, property, goods, and services. It is not simply a question of "cutting back" on these gifts, but rather the proper integration of them into our lives. Craving consumption chokes off fullness of life. Simplicity, on the other hand, is learning to say no to what crowds out God and our fellow travelers. It is a lifestyle form of resistance.

The implications for marriage and family are simply profound. "When we live simply," John Kavanaugh (1984, p. 610) writes, "we have more time for solitude, more time to savor and appreciate the things that we actually have. We are less cluttered by assaults from the media. We have more time for each other, more time to 'waste' in relationships, more time to appropriate our lives together in family and community. When we live more simply, we are more able to respond to the problems of injustice in the world—not only by sharing what we do not need, but also by time for greater availability in service and social action." Cutting back, then, on television viewing, on luxury purchasing, on excessive alcohol consumption, on working hours simply leaves more room for others and for God.

THE FLIGHT FROM VULNERABILITY AND (THE COUNTERECONOMICS OF) COMPASSION

Two economies operate in our world and are inextricably intertwined in our lives: the market economy and the gift economy. Both are necessary, potentially complementary but frequently conflictual. The market or cash economy consumes us in our work. This is the world of buying and selling, of supply and demand. It exists to produce abundance—more cars and computers, better medicine and services. These are valuable elements in our social life. We lose our equilibrium, however, when we allow market forces to control our lives and preoccupy our attention. This is the face of the commodity form. It distracts our attention from other vital arenas of life. We flee from the cries of the poor, the suffering of the dispossessed, the plight of the wretched of the earth. We become numb and anesthetized to vulnerability.

The gift economy also encircles us in our daily lives, even if it is less obvious at times. It operates according to different rules. For Christians, Jesus of Nazareth is the paradigm of the gift economy. The Christian gift economy holds that in giving we are enriched. It is a schooling in how to give oneself away. We volunteer our time, we engage in social outreach, we work pro bono, we serve on a citizen's committee. This economy also seeks abundance, fullness of life. What is given enriches both the giver and the receiver. Evelyn and James Whitehead note: "In our families and friendships, in public service and generative care, we experience an exchange in which giving is not loosing" (1998, 10). We discover that it is in giving our lives away that we receive our life back in abundance.

Marriage is a meeting place of the cash and gift economies. The two intersect and overlap in the daily routine of family life. However, vigilance is required. We must work hard to prevent the market from dominating and consuming our lifestyle. We must resist the collapse of the two into one. This will allow us to be open to vulnerability. It will foster compassion and call us to engage in the work of repairing our broken world.

Marriage is a covenant of love, care, and compassion. In the midst of these godly works, we must resist the ungodly. The resistance, however, takes place within the larger context of a life-affirming yes. Home is a place where we find anchor and where we craft the disciplines to live a life of integrity. These spiritual disciplines allow us to (1) affirm the goodness of marriage and family, (2) negate the intolerable evil that threatens to destroy it, and (3) affirm a deeper communal life together in justice and peace. A spirituality of resistance calls us to reclaim this center in our lives. And at this center, our hearts will find rest and be at home in the mystery.

REFERENCES

Bellah, Robert et al. *Habits of the Heart: Individualism and Commitment in American Life* (Berkeley: University of California, 1985).

Brueggemann, Walter. *The Prophetic Imagination* (Philadelphia: Fortress, 1978).

Brueggemann, Walter, Sharon Parks, and Thomas H. Groome. *To Act Justly, Love Tenderly, Walk Humbly* (New York: Paulist, 1986).

Buber, Martin. *I and Thou* (New York: Charles Scribner's Sons, 1958).

———. *The Way of Man according to the Teaching of Hasidism* (Secaucus, N.J.: Citadel Press, 1966).

Elshtain, Jean Bethke. "Families and Trust: Connecting Private Lives to Civic Good," in *Journal of Family Ministry* 12 (1): 31–40 (Spring 1998).

Harris, Maria, and Gabriel Moran. *Reshaping Religious Education: Conversations on Contemporary Practice* (Louisville: Westminster John Knox, 1998).

———. "Educating Persons," in *Mapping Christian Education,* ed. Jack L Seymour (Nashville: Abingdon, 1997), 58–73.

Havel, Vaclav. *Disturbing the Peace* (New York: Vintage, 1990).

Hollenbach, David. "The Common Good and Urban Poverty," *America,* 180 (20): 8–11 (June 5–12, 1999).

Jones, L. Gregory. "A Thirst for God or Consumer Spirituality? Cultivating Discipline Practices of Being Engaged by God," *Modern Theology,* 13 (1): 3–28 (January, 1997).

Kavanaugh, John F. *Following Christ in a Consumer Society: The Spirituality of Cultural Resistance* (Maryknoll, N. Y.: Orbis, 1981).

———. "Challenging a Commodity Culture," *Commonweal* (November 2–16, 1984): 606–612.

Parks, Sharon Daloz. "Household Economics," in *Practicing Our Faith,* ed. Dorothy C. Bass (San Francisco: Jossey-Bass, 1997), 43–58.

Pope John Paul II, *Redemptor Hominis,* (May 1979).

Whitehead, Barbara Dafoe. *Divorce Culture* (New York: Alfred Knopf, 1997).

Whitehead, Evelyn, and James Whitehead. "Making a Living, Making a Life: Toward a Spirituality of Work," *New Theology Review* 11 (3): 5–13 (August 1998).

Wolfe, Alan. *One Nation, After All: What Middle-Class Americans Really Think about God, Country, Family, Racism, Welfare, Immigration, Homosexuality, Work, the Right, the Left and Each Other* (New York: Viking, 1998).

CHAPTER 35

Spirituality and Lifestyle

Evelyn Eaton Whitehead
James D. Whitehead

When some people think about their future marriage, their fantasy is not one of "erotic flourishing" in a household with a beloved partner, but this: having in the marriage household all the things they could not afford in the parental household. If this statement is true, it means that the fantasy of marriage is not a relational one at all but a consumerist one, not one of loving but one of having.

There is much in the following essay that may seem to some readers as, to use the authors' own words, "illusory or naive." Here the Whiteheads deal with the sort of attitudes or sense of things that comes from the life and teaching of Jesus of Nazareth. The authors use the word *spirituality* to name the attitudes they describe. Not everyone understands the meaning of this term. The best way of understanding it is this: not thoughts about God but rather a way of living that shows what a person stands for. This can be positive or negative. Some people live out the motto: "Never give a sucker a break" or "Grab all the gusto you can get." Living out either motto gives us a negative dehumanized kind of spirit. Living out the kind of loving stance toward the world and its people that Jesus showed us gives us a very different kind of spirit. You understand a person's spirituality when you stand next to a coffin and ask: what was this person all about; what did this person stand for in his or her life?

One student who read this essay, a young woman, found its proposals so "far out" that she called the authors "religious fanatics." Seen against the depiction of family life found in TV sitcoms, the essay is indeed "far out." However, the authors are proposing that a particular couple have a definite kind of "agency," that is, the power to bring into their home a particular set of values and attitudes that become spelled out in deeds: in ways of speaking to one another; in ways of eating; in the kinds of issues that come up around the dinner table; in the sorts of people invited to gather around that table; in the patterns of prayer or of not praying.

No matter how you see these particular patterns, *there will be patterns of speaking and doing* that will characterize the household. What will they be? Will they be patterns of consumerism, of racism, of sexism, of homophobia, of greed, of hate. Will our attitudes be formed by sitcoms or will there be an alternate set of attitudes? Will the conviction that we are for more than ourselves be basic in our household, or will our conviction be "look out for number one"?

The fanatic is grim, determined, and funless. The proposal here is for a playful marriage. The core of the playful is "a light grasp on things," the opposite of the closed-fist grab for all the gusto you can get. These are the important matters needing discussion that arise in the final pages of this essay.

Questions for Discussion

1. What do you find "way out" in this essay?
2. Are there any particular attitudes or "spirit" you would want your home to have? What might they be?
3. Are there any attitudes you would *not want* your children to pick up in your home?
4. Which of the following do you want to give more thought to:
   - prayer together
   - action for justice
   - the use of time
   - the use of money
   - our participation in the life of a religious group?

The choices that influence our lifestyle are part of the spirituality of our marriage. It is in these choices that we express the values that shape our life together. And we sense that Christianity's most significant contribution to our marriage is in the values to which it calls us. That unselfish love is possible, that sacrifice can have value beyond itself, that pleasure is to be celebrated but not idolized, that I am not for myself alone—these profound truths of human life are not always apparent. There is much in contemporary society, perhaps even much in our own experience, to suggest that these convictions are illusory or naive. Alone, we may feel how fragile is their hold on us. In community with other believers, we can face our doubts with less fear because we do not face them alone. We can nourish the religious vision of life that sustains us in our journey of marriage for a lifetime.

Christianity does not give married love its value; rather it celebrates the deeper meaning of married love that can sometimes be lost or obscured in the hectic pace of life. Christianity gives us insight, vision into what is ordinarily invisible—the power and presence of God's redeeming love all around us and especially in certain privileged, sacramental experiences. And for most Christians, married love and the life commitments that flow from and surround this love are instances of this privileged experience of the power and presence of God. In this chapter we will explore several of the values which help to shape the lifestyle of Christian marriage.

The lifestyle of our marriage is influenced by many forces. Some of these seem beyond our immediate control—economic factors that bring inflation, political factors that shape national policy on child care, cultural factors that affect what is "expected" of women and men. In some marriages the influence of these external factors is so strong that there seems little room for choice. If I am poor, undereducated or chronically unemployed, it will be difficult for me to feel that I am in control of my own life. These burdens of social inequity weigh heavily on many Americans, adding stress in their marriages. A high incidence of divorce and desertion results.

But for most Americans, the lifestyle of marriage is not simply a product of external forces. We are conscious of ourselves as agents. Within certain limits we choose how we shall live. Some of our "choices" may be illusory, more influenced than we would like to admit by factors outside our awareness, but we are nevertheless conscious of ourselves as making decisions that influence the shape of our marriage.

The choices that are most important for our lifestyle are those that touch on the use of our resources. Our resources of concern, of time and of money are the "stuff" of our life together. The choices we make about these resources are not incidental; they are close to the substance of what our marriage is. What do we care about together? What is our money for? How do we spend the time of our life? It is in our response to these questions that we discover the values of our marriage and express them in our lifestyle.

PRAYER AND JUSTICE

Prayer is part of the lifestyle of Christian marriage. This will include the ways that we as a couple, as a family, participate in the prayer of the Church, especially the celebration of the Eucharist. But it will involve as well our developing suitable ways for us to pray together, to share—sometimes as a couple, sometimes with the children as well—the intimate experience of coming into the presence of God in prayer. In recent decades the devotional life of many Catholic homes included the family rosary or prayers honoring the Sacred Heart. Family prayer today is more likely to focus on the reading of Scripture, reflecting together on its meaning for our lives and our actions in the world.

Prayer has been urged in marriage as one of the ways for the family to deepen its own unity: "The family that prays together, stays together." To pray together as a couple and as a family can reinforce, sometimes powerfully, our experience of being together in the ways that matter most. But the prayer of Christians is not simply about unity among us; it is about our community with humankind in the presence of God. Liturgical prayer especially celebrates this larger awareness. It is as the people of God that, in the name of Jesus and through the power of his abiding Spirit, we pray. But family prayer, too, should open us beyond "just us." The needs of the world, concretely the ways in which pain and loss and injustice are part of the world that we can influence, are part of our prayer.

In fall 1978 Archbishop Jean Jadot delivered an address on the implementation of the pastoral plan for family ministry that had been developed by the bishops of the United States. In his talk he spoke of prayer, faith and justice as these touch the family. He said, "The prayer I am speaking about is not so much the recitation of prayers as a shared experience of prayer. This finds its origins in a common reading of the Holy Scriptures and in a concern for those who are in need, for justice and peace in the world, for the coming of the Kingdom of God . . . such prayer quite naturally evokes an awareness of the family's mission to service. It also raises the family's social consciousness."

The conviction that we are for more than ourselves is basic to the Christian world view. This value must find its expression not only in our prayer but in our lifestyle. Most of us know . . . that our marriage is about more than "just us." We need more than "just us" if our family is to thrive. We are aware of how much, as a couple and as a family, we depend on contact with certain relatives and support from special friends. But as Christians we go beyond ourselves not just in what we need but also in what we contribute.

Our life as a family and especially our children carry us into the larger world. As our children grow, we sense how much more they belong to the world and its future than they do to us. Thus, our care for them cannot end at our doorstep. Our first movements to contribute to the world beyond may well be for their sake—to make the world a better place for them, a place worthy of their hopes and conducive to their growth. But it is possible for this initial impulse of generative care, our concern for our children and their future, to stagnate. Our preoccupation with what is good for our family can become a new form of selfishness. The boundaries may be broadened slightly, but it is still "us" against "them."

But for many of us the movement of concern for our children invites us into a concern for the children of the world, for the future of humankind. I become more deeply aware that, by emotion and by action, I am involved in the lives of others. As parent, as worker, as citizen, I am in my own way somehow responsible for the future. The world—its hopes and problems—has a claim on me.

As Christians we hear this invitation to generativity reinforced in the call of Jesus. I am not only my brother's keeper; the category of brother and sister has expanded to include whoever is in need. "I was a stranger and you made me welcome, naked and you clothed me, sick and you visited me, in prison and you came to see me" (Matthew 25:35–36). Christianity expands the boundaries of our concern. We find we belong to a larger community. We hold our resources as stewards: these are not simply our "possessions," but the means of our contribution to a more just world.

Most of us sense, increasingly, that the issues of social value and justice that we face in our own lives are complex. There are not many questions where the "one right answer" emerges quickly and clearly. In any particular case, persons of good will and intelligence may come to different conclusions about what should be done. When the issues at stake touch directly on our own lives or our family's welfare—as in questions of job security or property values or tax reform—it can be even more difficult to determine the just response.

In these situations Christian awareness does not give easy answers but it does give us a starting point. We are not for ourselves alone. Action for justice and the transformation of the world is, as Pope Paul VI proclaimed, constitutive of our response to the gospel. We stand under the gospel challenge that we share the burdens of humankind and participate in its liberation. The way in which we, as a couple and as a family, participate in this mission of Christ may well have to be worked out on our own. But it can be expected that our maturing as Christian adults will involve our developing a lifestyle which expresses our understanding of the mission to which Jesus calls us and supports us in our response.

THE MEANING OF MONEY

Money is a central issue in marriage. What money means to us influences our relationship; how we use money shapes our lifestyle. And in many marriages decisions about money are among the most complex the couple face. Disagreements about money (how to manage it; how to spend it; who should make these decisions) and distress over money (living beyond our means; bills coming due; not having enough money to meet an unexpected expense) are significant sources of marital strain.

Money issues in marriage are troublesome in part because money carries so many different meanings. What is money for? My response here influences the way I answer the other questions. How much money does our family need? Can we ever have enough? How would we even go about determining what would be "enough" money for us?

For some of us, money is mainly for the practical necessities of life—food, clothing, shelter. For others, it is for enjoyment—for leisure or luxury or fun. Sometimes money is for our children's future, their education or financial security. Sometimes it is for self-esteem: "Surely I am worthwhile, just look at how much money I make." Sometimes money is for power: "I can buy anything and anyone I need." And sometimes it is a resource we have to be used for the good of the world.

Most practical decisions about money carry some larger emotional significance. These decisions say something important to us about who we are in the world. If, as a couple, we see money differently, if we each act out of a different sense of "what our money is for," we can anticipate that money issues will be troublesome to bring up between us and difficult to resolve.

The emotional significance of money is not the only source of strain. Inflation and the threat of economic recession are very real factors in the lifestyle of most families. Young couples find they can no longer afford to buy a house and so delay their decision to have a child. Couples with children realize that they both must bring in a paycheck if they wish to send their children to college. Couples who had resolved to retire early now plan to continue to work, unsure that their retirement benefits will remain adequate to living costs. Faced with rising prices, high interest rates and, for some, even unemployment, many families must make difficult decisions about money—decisions that significantly influence the lifestyle of their marriage.

But admitting the reality of these financially uncertain times, the money strain in many marriages is as much influenced by consumerism as by inflation. Even in this inflationary period, American families enjoy one of the highest levels of affluence in the world. We want and expect "the best that money can buy" for ourselves and our families. Advertising expands our sense of what we need, assuring us that "we owe it to ourselves" because "we're worth it." Perhaps especially as Americans we find ourselves susceptible to the temptation to judge our value by what we have—our material possessions, our standard of living, our buying power. This preoccupation with "the things of this world" has always been in tension with deeper religious intuitions: being is more than having; our worth is not grounded in our wealth; we are not "saved" by what we accumulate. The Christian vision has always called us to a certain detachment from wealth. As believers, we know we hold the goods of this world as stewards. Our responsibility is to care for the person in need, even out of our own substance. Today we see that this challenge has even broader scope. We are more aware of the connections between the prosperity of the United States and the poverty that exists elsewhere. It is often at the expense of other peoples that we have enjoyed, as a nation, the abundant resources of food and energy and technology that constitute "the good life." The patterns of this structural injustice are complicated, to be sure. It is not easy to trace our personal responsibility in this or to determine what we, as a family, can do to right the balance in world economics. But the complexity of the problem does not relieve us of responsibility. As Christians, we need to examine our family's standard of living not only in view of the shrinking dollar but in view of our accountability in the world. How we spend our money and where we invest our savings—for the Christian today these are more than practical financial questions to be resolved in terms of prices and interest rates alone. They are issues of religious significance that give shape to a Christian lifestyle.

MARRIAGE AND MINISTRY

For us as Christians, the question of lifestyle ultimately brings us to a discussion of ministry. Ministry is the action of believers undertaken in pursuit of the mission which Jesus entrusted to the Church—the coming of the Kingdom. Formal ministry is activity that is recognized or commissioned by the community of faith. Alongside this formal ministry is that ministry expected of all believers—the daily efforts to shape the world according to Christian values of love and mercy. Some Catholics who are married are part of the Church's formal ministry. The expanding involvement of lay persons in roles of official ministry is a fruit of the new vitality in the Church since the Second Vatican Council. Lay women and men serve in liturgical ministries in parishes as lectors and musicians and ministers of communion. Increasingly, the teaching ministry of parishes and dioceses is carried out by lay persons, some through full-time careers in religious education programs or Catholic school systems, others serving in a volunteer capacity as catechtists, conveners of an adult discussion group or members of the parish school board. There has been a comparable increase in the number of lay persons staffing the service agencies and social policy programs that operate under Church auspices or support.

This expansion of "approved" or "recognized" ministries over the past two decades has blurred many of the earlier distinctions among religious, clergy and lay persons in our Church. Married men ordained to the permanent diaconate, women religious serving as pastoral associates in parishes, women and married men studying in Catholic seminaries in preparation for careers of fulltime ministry—these persons do not fit easily into former categories. In some cases the openness to lay persons in roles of service and leadership has been more a response to personnel shortages ("There just aren't enough brothers, sisters and priests to go around anymore!") than a sign of a deeper appreciation of the scope of the Christian call to ministry. But in any case, a significant number of Catholic lay persons—both married and single— understand their life vocation to be in the formal ministry of the Church.

The involvement of married Catholics as formal ministers in the Church's ministry *to* marriage—as planners and leaders in programs of marriage preparation, marriage enrichment, marriage counseling, and as part of the liturgical celebration of marriage—is on the increase and is good. In our discussion here, however, we wish to look at the relationship of marriage and the general Christian call to ministry.

For some Christians, both those ordained and others who are not, the immediate focus of their own religious action is within the community of faith, a ministry to and through the formal Church. But for most believers the call to live and act in response to the Christian vision will find expression in their family and their work and their other involvements in society. How is the religious experience of marriage related to the religious action or ministry of an adult Christian life? We have discussed this ministry of the mature Christian in terms of religious generativity. Psychological maturity leads me beyond myself and my intimates toward genuine care for the world. So, too, religious generativity leads me beyond the celebration of the "Good News" for myself, toward religious action—ministry—for a world beyond myself and my religious "intimates." We have seen that intimacy can either contribute to generativity (when the experience of our love releases in each of us the psychological resources we need for generosity and self-transcendence) or detract from it (when our love seems so fragile that we must spend our energy and other resources on ourselves, with none to spare for the world beyond). So marriage can have an ambiguous effect in Christian maturity and ministry. There are Christians for whom their own marriage and family occupy their full concern, not only in moments of crisis such as serious illness or the loss of a job, not just during periods of predictable stress like the birth of a child or, for some, the event of retirement—but characteristically. "We are for ourselves—alone." They may take quite seriously their responsibilities as spouses and parents. Their marriage is stable, their children have as many educational opportunities and social advantages as the couple can afford. They may participate actively in the parish. They are regular churchgoers who contribute financially and see to it that their children take part in the religious education program. But through it all, they are "for themselves." They may see the parish in terms of what it has to give them—a satisfying experience of worship, a program of moral education for their children, perhaps even a sense of security and some status in the community. But to be an adult Christian has not brought with it for them the motivating conviction: I am, our family is, for more than ourselves.

Among many other Christians marriage is just such an opening to God and to the world. The lessons of our marriage teach us to care beyond ourselves; our concern for our children links us to the concerns of the world. We sense that our life together as a family not only "uses up" our strengths, but also generates new resources that we can share and spend beyond ourselves. Our home, our love, our joy together, our time, our insights, our concerns, even our money—these resources of our life together do not exist for ourselves alone. At any one point in our marriage we may be overwhelmed with a sense that there is not enough of us to go around, that our resources are deficient, not just in the face of the needs of the world but even for the needs of our own family. But over its life course, if not at every moment, our marriage as maturing Christians will be marked by openness to needs beyond the family and by an active sense of our own contribution to the coming of the Kingdom, the presence of God in justice and love.

There are, of course, many different ways in which this ministry of maturing Christians will be expressed, and so many ways in which the relationship between marriage and ministry will be seen. For some couples, their ministry is through their family life. They open their home to foster children or adopt a handicapped child. In another family the kitchen is always open to the teenagers in the neighborhood and the couple have time to listen to the concerns of their neighbors and friends. A third couple decide in retirement to devote two days a week together to visiting shut-ins or to welcome a recently widowed neighbor to live with them until she can make other plans. Other couples will sense that their involvement in issues of social concern is crucial to the religious education of their children. To take an unpopular stand on a question of racial justice, to become involved in a political campaign, to use part of their family's vacation money to assist those who have suffered in a disaster—these couples see such actions as of religious significance and encourage their children to share this practical understanding of faith.

For many lay Christians the arena of their ministry is the world of their employment. In my professional responsibilities, in my union activities, in a business decision I can influence, in the way I deal with my company subordinates and superiors, I try to bring to bear the convictions of my religious faith. On the job I take a stand that I know is right, even at the risk there may be repercussions. Or as a couple we decide to change jobs and move across country, so that we can participate in a project for economic justice. For many of us, then, our efforts to contribute to the world and to justice among people happen here, in the work that we do in the world. It is here that a sense of personal vocation takes shape. It is here that we work to hasten the coming of the Kingdom.

A PLAYFUL MARRIAGE

The lifestyle of our marriage has much to do with how we are involved beyond ourselves. But our lifestyle also influences and expresses how we are together. Many of the values of Christianity contribute to the way we live our life together by urging us to take marriage seriously. Marriage is for grownups; its responsibilities are significant; the honeymoon does not last forever. These sober truths are important for us to hear and the Church serves us well in giving voice to this wisdom. But Christian wisdom also speaks to another side of marriage—the intimate connections between love and play. As our marriage matures, it becomes more playful. Here we will consider several elements that are part of the lifestyle of a playful marriage.

THE TIME OF OUR LIFE

A playful marriage depends on how we spend time together. The demands of careers, children and other involvements can easily overwhelm a marriage relationship. The fatigue and distraction that result can seriously erode our presence to each other. We learn that the playfulness that marked our carefree relationship at the start of our marriage does not endure easily or automatically. We learn, paradoxically, that if we would have a playful marriage we must work at it. Playfulness between us, like our other experiences of intimacy, will have to be cultivated. It will require a discipline in our lifestyle, especially a discipline of our time.

If marriage is a vocation that begins in a resounding "yes," it matures in many "no's." To have quality time for my partner and our family I find I have to say "no" to many outside demands and requests. This discipline helps us structure time for these central commitments of our life. Such disciplined planning and foresight can be experienced as cold calculation or as a canny response to life's multiple demands. Without such an asceticism, we become subject to the endless demands (all of them "worthwhile") of contemporary married life. Gradually exhaustion takes the play out of our marriage, both its flexibility and its fun. Our playfulness can be fostered by planning special times for just the two of us. We set aside times and places with protective boundaries. On our vacation, in days of rest or retreat, we give ourselves permission to play again. Apart from the seriousness of the rest of our life, these occasions invite us to play together and enliven our love.

COMPETITION AND PLAY

A playful marriage also recognizes the connection between competition and play. Our competitiveness can be acknowledged. We can accept the fact that marriage is a contact sport, one in which injury, anger and even loss are some-times to be expected. But our competitiveness can also enliven us. As we identify together how and when we feel competitive toward one another, these feelings lose some of their force over us. We can share more concretely some of our fears about conflict between us and even feel some of the exhil-aration of our struggles.

Competition is often an act of intimacy. It brings us "up close" and engages us with one another, however ambiguously. In competition, as in wrestling, we can come in touch with each other in ways that both excite and threaten us. In our competitive encounters we can learn much about our-selves and each other. We can find unsuspected strengths; we can also come upon unacknowledged weaknesses. To compete does not mean that we must use these strengths to dominate or must exploit these weaknesses. My aware-ness of your weakness can help me love better, help me to protect or at least not take advantage of your vulnerability. Awareness of a strength can help me love better as well, enabling me to use it to foster rather than control our marriage.

The thought of competition in marriage may still disturb us. It may con-jure up images of the professional athlete, concerned only with performance and rating, and with coming out ahead in this encounter. But this is only one narrow interpretation of competition. We may also see competition in our marriage as not necessarily setting us against one another but as bringing us closer together. This "closer together" is, of course, threatening. It may well, on occasion, produce hurt and injury. In love and in competition we take the risk of a very close encounter, trusting that we will both play fair. But when we do—overcoming our fear of being crushed and our need to dominate— we are exhilarated *together*; the winner is our marriage and our intimate lifestyle.

PLAYFUL SEX

Our sexual life together will be part of a playful marriage. Here the Christian tradition has not always been helpful. A central characteristic of play is its uselessness; it is "just for fun." Christians have learned, on the other hand, that sex is very serious business. It has a specific and (even) exclusive pur-pose: the begetting of children. Only when this goal is dutifully pursued is our sexual activity to be enjoyed. Thus the seriousness and sacredness of sex-uality has, for many Christians, overpowered its playfulness. Is not "playful sex" for playmates and libertines? The ambiguity here parallels that of com-petition. As competition is neither simply destructive nor simply creative, human sexual activity is neither simply purposeful nor simply playful. As Christians we know that sex is sacred: in our sexual sharing we create more life; through it we confirm and increase our love for one another. But this sacredness does not exclude its playfulness. Sex is for Christians very respon-sible play. The sexual embrace, sometimes generative of new life and much more often generative of our own love, is also fun. Christianity has, to be sure, been cautious in recognizing the value of playfulness in sex. Only recently and even then reluctantly have many of the official voices within the Church been willing to acknowledge the legitimacy of a sexual love whose every act is not intended to bring children into the world. But these developments are happening in our time, in part through the testimony of married Christians. And as they do, it becomes easier for us to celebrate in the lifestyles of Christian marriage the variety and playfulness of sexual love. Sex is not the only place for play in a maturing marriage. But if there is little or no play in our sexual sharing we are likely to find it more difficult to play in the other areas of our common life.

LEARNING TO PLAY FAIR

Another element of a playful marriage is learning to play fair. This means learning the rules that can help our competitiveness and our other intimacies contribute to our marriage, not destroy it. A first rule is that we *need* to contest with one another. To regularly repress our anger, our confusion or disagreement will not reduce these feelings but only store them for later use. Being "a good sport" in our marriage does not mean choosing not to compete with or confront my partner. It means actively engaging in this relationship. "Poor sports" are those who choose not to contest anything with their partners. They may stand on the sidelines and complain, but they do not compete. A marriage in which the partners no longer contest, no longer struggle with each other in any significant way, can be called a stalemate. The partners in such a marriage are likely to experience each other as "stale mates."

If the first rule is simply to play—to compete, to get engaged—the second rule is to play fair. This means playing skillfully, knowing when and how to confront my partner. In marriage, as in every other kind of play, timing is important. And our experience of each other in marriage, the years we have been playing together, should help us to determine the timing of our confrontations. I bring up a sensitive issue when I sense the time is right: when *we* can handle it, not just when I want to take it on. Playing fair is likely to be a part of our lifestyle in marriage the more we are each able to display the skillful behaviors of communication and conflict resolution.

Learning to play fair is a complex virtue, one that most of us acquire only gradually as we mature. Its growth is likely to include the discipline of identifying and cutting away habits of ours that are destructive in our marriage— belittling the other person, striking back indirectly rather than confronting a troublesome issue, using the children as weapons in an effort to win or be right. Finally, play can teach us the importance of compromise and the value of being a good loser. Compromise means finding our way around questions and concerns that threaten a standoff or seem insoluble. The strategies of barter and negotiation will, at times, help us sustain our love and commitment. Learning how to be a good loser is also a sign of maturity. Each of us can expect to fail, even repeatedly, in our efforts at love and mutuality. Play reminds us that we need not be ashamed. Love does not mean never having to say I'm sorry; it means becoming good at it.

In all these ways we mature in love. We learn that play is not just for kids, that being able to trust one another is more important than always being right. In his study of adult maturity, *Adaptation to Life*, George Vaillant summarizes these connections among love, trust and play:

> It is hard to separate capacity to trust from capacity to play, for play is dangerous until we can trust both ourselves and our opponents to harness rage. In play, we must trust enough and love enough to risk losing without despair, to bear winning without guilt, and to laugh at error without mockery. (p. 309)

In our own marriage we can expect to know winning and losing, risk and error, laughter and love. These are the stuff of a playful marriage, the building blocks of a lifestyle of marriage for a lifetime.

PART NINE

Interreligious Perspectives on Marriage

CHAPTER 36

Marriage in the Jewish Tradition

Blu Greenberg

᷇᷇᷇᷇᷇᷇

To this point, the readings in this volume have been an exploration of marriage (and its set of related issues) mainly from a Christian perspective. This is apt, in light of our primary reading audience. However, a rich examination of marriage today cannot remain sealed within a narrow denominational context. There are two reasons for this: (1) interreligious marriages are flourishing across all boundaries, and (2) viewing marriage from diverse perspectives can foster tolerance, understanding, and appreciation. This section teaches us that comparison and contrast is the spice of life!

Blu Greenberg begins with a detailed sketch of marriage in the Jewish tradition. Marriage is the Jewish way. It is considered an ideal state, a primary community norm, the optimal way to live. It is good, very good. In fact, it is the ultimate paradigm for the relationship between God and the Jewish people.

Greenberg wisely requests a temporary suspension of a feminist critique of the tradition so as to examine the essence of the (biblical and rabbinic) sources—i.e., the centrality of marriage in the literature and life of the people. The voyage is intriguing and illuminating. It is all the more interesting when one compares the Jewish sources, ceremonies, and laws with Christian marital forms, rituals, and codes. Likewise, the impact of the women's movement and intermarriage on Jewish marriage can be seen to bear striking resemblances to the reshaping of marital forms in Christian circles today.

Questions for Discussion

1. What constitutes the core of the traditional Jewish ideal of marriage?
2. What impact has the contemporary women's movement had on Jewish marriages?
3. Name some of the factors involved in the rapid rise in the intermarriage rate for Jews in the United States.
4. If marriage is the primary communal model and norm in Judaism (and the only legitimate adult union), what implications does this hold for other sexual forms that fall outside the marital paradigm?

In Judaism, and from the very moment of origins of the Jewish people, marriage was considered to be the ideal state. Although the institution of marriage has been newly called into question by a marginal few whose values are shaped first and foremost by contemporary culture,[1] marriage nevertheless continues to be a fundamental socio-religious principle of Judaism and a primary community norm. Almost from birth, all things work toward marriage. The greeting recited at a boy's circumcision ceremony, on the eighth day of life, is: "As this child has been entered into the covenant, so may he be entered into a life of Torah study, the wedding canopy, and good deeds."[2]

The marital relationship takes precedence over every other human connection. For example, the Fifth Commandment—filial piety—is of ultimate value and reaches into many areas of life. There is much in the ethical and halachic literature that urges that a child not marry against the parents' will or without consent, but the law is unequivocal: "If the father objects to his son's marriage or woman of his choice, the son is not obliged to listen to his father . . . for the belovedness of the partners is of paramount value."[3]

Marriage is not only the optimal way to live, but it is also central to the theology of Judaism. The entire success of the covenant rests on the marriage premise and its procreative impulse. The biological family, born of marriage, is the unit that carries the promises and the covenant, one generation at a time, toward their full completion and realization.[4]

In this regard—the centrality of marriage—Judaism can be said to be an earthy religion, dealing with intimate relationships, sex, procreation, and the powerful though often untidy bonds of family life. In this regard, too, Judaism differs from more spiritually oriented religions. Or, to put it another way, the spirit comes as much through marriage and family life in Judaism as it does through the individual's experience of *mysterium tremendum.*

Having said all these lovely things about marriage and family in the Jewish tradition, I find myself in an unenviable position, for much of the literature, law, and language surrounding marriage and divorce reflects hierarchy and sexism. As a feminist writing to my own faith cohorts, I feel perfectly uninhibited to point up and critique inherent sexism in the tradition. As a Jew writing to Christians, Muslims, and members of Far Eastern religions—persons who would not naturally feel the love and appreciation an insider feels and who would, therefore, come away with a one-sided and uncorrected view—I feel somewhat constrained.

So I ask the reader to grant me two requests: First, I ask that you suspend for the moment a feminist critique, that you set aside questions of sexism, inequity, and noninclusive language. Let us assume these givens: that imbalance did exist, that patriarchy was the social and psychic mode, that role distinctiveness lent itself too easily to hierarchy. To all this we shall soon return. Second, I ask that you bear in mind these general truths: that the tradition was sexist more in theory than in practice, more in certain cultures than in others, more in the past than in the present, more in legal formulation than in actual relationships, more in ancient law than in scriptural narrative.[5]

Now, having temporarily set aside this issue, let us proceed to examine the essence of the sources—the centrality of marriage in the literature and life of the people as it moved through 4,000 years of human history.

THE SOURCES

Oddly enough, although marriage is undeniably the only legitimate adult union, we find throughout the Scriptures not a single explicit command to marry. Procreate? Yes. Marry? Not one commandment. Rather, the information comes to us in the form of description and recommendation.[6] In what is surely among the most romantic verses in the Bible, we read: "It is not good that man should live alone . . . therefore, shall a man leave his mother and father and cleave unto his wife, and they shall become as one flesh" (Gen. 2:18, 24). The use of the word "cleave" (*davok*) signifies sensuality, intimacy, interdependency, and a long-term relationship—staples, I would say, of a good marriage.[7]

In contrast to law, biblical narrative is very rich in details of marriage. More than the sacred literature of any other people, the Torah is the story of family, of marriages, and not prettied-up versions, either, but the stuff of real marriages—love, romance, anger, deceit, honor, faithfulness, distrust, infidelity, companionship, intimacy. There is not a single idealized version of marriage in the entire Bible—not one marriage without some flaw or weakness. Perhaps that explains why marriage becomes the ultimate paradigm for the relationship between God and the Jewish people.[8] Just as a good marriage has its high and low points, yet the partners do not sever the bonds, so does a covenantal relationship. This theme—of the lasting marriage between God and the Jewish people despite the latter's backsliding—is sounded repeatedly by the Prophets.

Jewish tradition is often referred to as halacha—the Jewish way. It is the sum of several parts: (a) divine revelation, (b) the Jewish historical experience, and (c) the exegetical enterprise of connecting (a) to (b). What is the process whereby this remarkable feat—of connecting revelation to people's lives through the sweep of generations and in a diversity of cultures—is achieved? That process is none other than rabbinic interpretation, explication, and expansion of the law. Rabbinic literature (Talmud and Midrash), in contrast to the Bible, is much more explicit on all matters concerning marriage and divorce. In fact, six of the sixty-three tractates of the Talmud deal in whole or in large part with such matters.[9]

THE OBLIGATION TO MARRY

Responsibility for marriage rests on everyone—parents, community, and individual:[10]

> What are the essential duties of father to son? . . . to circumcise, redeem,
> teach him Torah, take a wife for him, and teach him a craft. (Kid. 29A)

The tradition goes so far as to say:

> If an orphan wishes to marry [and has no means] the community should
> purchase for him a dwelling, a bed, and all necessary household utensils and
> then marry him off. (Ket. 67B)

CHOICE OF MATE

The marriage had to be characterized by *shalom bayit* (a peaceful and harmonious household); consequently, great care had to be taken in selecting a mate:

> A man should be matched to a woman according to the measure of his deeds.
> (Sot. 2A)

All measures of compatibility were to be considered: character, background,
values, the extended family, even genetic makeup.[11] Wealth, however, was
not to be a consideration,[12] but mutual desire was a requisite:

> A father is forbidden to betroth his daughter to another while she is a minor.
> He must wait until she grows up and says, "I want to marry So-and-so."
> (Kid. 41A)[13]

PREDESTINATION

Still, mere mortals cannot succeed in mate selection without a measure of
divine assistance:

> . . . What has God been occupied with since the six days of creation? . . . with
> the task of finding appropriate life mates for his earthly creatures . . . Though
> it looks easy to make a match, even for God the task is as difficult as splitting
> the Red Sea. (Gen. Rab. 67.3)[14]

DUTIES IN MARRIAGE

Many of the obligations of husband to wife were spelled out in the Talmud;
some of these were detailed in the *ketubah*, the marriage contract. Though
equality did not fully exist, and role distinctions were clearcut, there was nevertheless a kind of complementarianism to the Jewish marriage:

> These are the tasks that a wife must carry out for her husband: She must
> grind corn, bake, cook, suckle her child, make his bed, and work in wool.
> (Ket. 5:5)
>
> Her husband is liable for her support, her ransom, and her burial, Rabbi
> Judah says even the poorest in Israel must not furnish less than two flutes
> and one woman wailer [at his wife's funeral]. (Ket. 4:4)

One must always observe the honor due to his wife, because blessings rest on a man's home only on account of his wife. (B.M. 59A)

SEXUALITY

Sex, in the context of marriage, was of positive value. In contrast to Christianity (Mt. 19:10; 1 Cor. 7), celibates were frowned upon, even if they were considered to be among the greatest scholars (Yev. 63B). The sexual urge was considered a basic and normal need that required satisfaction:

> Should a man marry first, or devote himself to Torah and then marry . . . Marry first . . . for one who is not married will be possessed the day long with sexual thoughts . . . and be unable to concentrate on his studies. (Kid. 29B)[15]

PROCREATION

The very first biblical commandment, "Be fruitful and multiply" (Gen. 1:28), was a fundamental obligation of the marriage partners.[16] The institutions of polygyny and levirate marriage (a man's obligation to marry his deceased brother's widow if the brother died childless) can be understood only in the context of procreation.[17] But procreation had to be balanced with sexual passion in marriage, and mutual desire at that. This explains why (a) polygyny rarely was practiced and eventually was forbidden; (b) levirate marriages could be circumvented by a release ceremony of *halitza*; and (c) marital rape was explicitly forbidden.[18] It also explained why divorce, though not a popular or esteemed option, nevertheless was permitted, for divorce was deemed to be better than a marriage of unhappy or ill-suited partners.[19] In sum, then, the ideal was a relationship characterized by romance, sexuality, compatibility, harmony, fidelity, mutual care, and the business of raising children. The midrashist summed it up well:

> He who has no wife lives without peace, without help, without joy, without forgiveness, without life itself. He is not a whole person; he diminishes the image of God in the world. (Gen. Rab. 17:3)

THE ACT OF MARRIAGE

In its most technical sense, marriage in Judaism is a change in personal status. Neither sacrament nor mere legal transaction, it enjoys the trappings of both: an aura of sacredness, the language of sanctification, the richness of ceremony and rite, the sanction of religious leaders. It also involves a contract, a formal declaration, witnesses, signatures, and an exchange of monetary value. To understand how this conglomerate nature came to be, one must examine the Jewish wedding ceremony from its very beginnings.

The Bible provides relatively few clues to the act of creating a marriage. About all we know is that it is a man's initiative. A man "takes" a woman in marriage (Gen. 29:27; Ex. 2:1; Dt. 22:13). There is hint of preparation, feasting, and celebration (Gen. 24; Gen. 29; Jg. 14:12), but no description whatsoever of an actual ceremony, and no explanation of the verb "take."

The Talmud,[20] reflecting inherited tradition and building upon it, explains the procedures. The Mishnah teaches: "A woman is acquired [in marriage] in three ways and acquires herself [her independence] in two. She is acquired by means of money, deed [document] or cohabitation; she acquires herself by divorce or death of her husband" (Kid. 1:1). In a lengthy discussion of this Mishnah, the Gemara explains that the biblical "take" refers to money; however, this money does not signify purchase but rather is the symbol of a legal transaction.[21] What, then, does acquisition mean? For that, we turn to the next chapter in the Mishnah: "A man betrothes a woman . . ." (Kid. 2:1). The Hebrew for betrothal is *kiddushin*, derived from the root word *kadosh*—holy, set apart, off limits to all others. A woman is set aside for her husband and her husband alone. It is not merely a social commitment such as an engagement is today; rather, it is a halachic procedure. The transfer of an item of monetary value, however small, symbolizes this "setting aside."

A marriage, as mentioned above, can be constituted in two other ways: first, through a deed, a written document drawn to the satisfaction of all parties concerned; second, through cohabitation. What these three methods have in common is a certain privatism for the marriage partners: a man initiates, and a woman consents.[22] Technically, in each instance marriage can be effected in the absence of any sort of control or sanction by community. The sages of Gemara, however, point to the inadmissability of such methods. An exchange of coin of insignificant value was considered inappropriate and hasty for something as serious as marriage; intercourse as a means of betrothal carried the taint of licentious behavior. Thus, the rabbis forbade these procedures as means of effecting a marriage, not by striking the laws from the books, but by interpreting and circumscribing them to bring them more in line with community norms. Those who disregarded community norms could be subject to fines, flogging, and even annulment of the marriage (Yev. 110A). In tracing development of the law, then, we see that control over procedures of marriage was legally shifted from parties of the first part onto the community—probably as it had always been in ancient Jewish life.

Part of this ongoing process was the introduction (circa third century B.C.E. of the *ketubah*—the marriage contract that stipulated obligations of husband to wife during the course of the marriage as well as financial protections in the event of divorce. The *ketubah* was drawn between the parties prior to the betrothal and was witnessed as any other legal document.

To further prevent marriages of whim, the wedding ceremony was divided by rabbinic fiat into two parts: *erusin* (or *kiddushin*), the betrothal; and *nisuin*, the completion of the marriage procedures. The two parts were separated by a period of time, of up to a year. In *erusin* (or *kiddushin*), the groom gave the bride an object of value, in the presence of witnesses, then made a formal declaration to her: "Behold, thou art consecrated unto me, with this ring, according to the law of Moses [inherited tradition] and of Israel [sanction of community]."[23] After the set period of time had elapsed, the couple was joined in *nisuin* under the wedding canopy, and a series of blessings was recited in the presence of a quorum of ten men, the unit that technically constitutes a Jewish congregation. In time, it was observed that the arbitrary separation between betrothal and marriage could lead to problems, so it became standard procedure, and then law (twelfth century), to perform the two ceremonies at the same time. In order to maintain the distinctiveness of each, the *ketubah* was now read aloud between *erusin* and *nisuin*.

Increasingly, then, marriage came under religious control and communal sanction and celebration. Still, it retained its original bi-party transactional nature as described in the Mishnah: a ring as symbol of transaction, the marriage declaration in the presence of witnesses as oral deed, and the bridal canopy as suggestive of intimate relations.

THE WEDDING CEREMONY

A traditional wedding ceremony performed today would likely consist of the following order of events:

1. *Kabbulat Khyun* (acquisition): Prior to the ceremony the groom formally undertakes the obligations specified in the *ketubah*. He signifies this by holding aloft for a moment a handkerchief held out to him by the officiating rabbi, who stands in for the bride. This action is witnessed by two men who sign their names to the *ketubah*, certifying that the conditions therein were accepted by the parties involved.

2. *Bedeken* (veiling the bride): The groom, accompanied by male family and friends, is escorted to the room where the bride is seated with female members of her party standing about her. The groom and his entourage approach in song. He gently draws the bridal veil over her face. Often, at this moment, the fathers of the couple will each in turn bless the bride, laying their hands on her head as they give blessing. Family and friends look on. It is an indescribably sweet moment, and many eyes glisten in joy.

3. *Chuppah* (bridal canopy): The Jewish wedding has taken on the full coloration of Western culture—including the processional with bridesmaids, ushers, ringbearer, etc. But there are some differences: First, the ceremony must be performed under a *chuppah*, which symbolizes their intimate household. Second, bride and groom do not stand alone during the ceremony; they are accompanied down the aisle by their parents, a symbol that bride and groom do not marry in isolation, nor will they construct their future home in absence of familial or communal support. Third, the last part of the processional at a traditional Jewish wedding is a most unusual one—the bride's

encirclement of the groom. When she reaches the *chuppah,* she walks around the groom seven times, with her mother and mother-in-law following her. Various interpretations have grown around this custom: by drawing a circle with her own body, she creates an invisible wall and then steps inside—a symbol of togetherness and distinctiveness from the rest of society.[24] This tradition is also based on a messianic reference in Jeremiah: "a woman shall encircle a man" (31:22). (Though some consider it a sexist ritual, to me it has always seemed a wonderfully sexual one, as if she is wrapping him up to take him home with her!)

4. *Erusin:* The two betrothal blessings, one over wine and one over the act of betrothal that will follow, are recited by a rabbi. The rabbi does not drink the wine, but gives the goblet to the groom and then to the bride, for each to take a sip. The rabbi is known as the *mesader kiddushin,* one who "arranges" the betrothal rather than performs it. Unlike civil law, where a Justice of the Peace pronounces them husband and wife, Jewish marriage is an act between two partners. The core element of a Jewish marriage remains as it was from the very beginning: man taking woman in marriage. The groom places a ring on the bride's right index finger and recites the ancient declaration, "Behold, thou art consecrated unto me, according to the laws of Moses and of Israel." Her acceptance of the ring is considered assent.

5. *The ketubah:* The marriage contract is read aloud in its original Aramaic. Often, it is read also in translation. The person who reads the *ketubah*—an honored guest—hands it to the groom, who hands it to his bride. It is hers for safekeeping, but for the moment she will likely pass it to a parent or friend during the ceremony. At this juncture, the officiating rabbi often will address the bride and groom.

6. *Nisuin* (marriage): The final part of the ceremony consists of seven different blessings of celebration and hope. Customarily, seven different guests are given the honor, each reciting one blessing. The seventh blessing is as follows:

> Blessed art Thou, Lord our God, creator of the universe Who has created joy and gladness, bridegroom and bride, laughter and exultation, pleasure and delight, love, brotherhood, peace, and fellowship. May it be soon, O Lord our God, that there be heard in the cities of Judah and in the streets of Jerusalem the voice of joy and gladness, the voice of bridegroom and of bride, the jubilant voice of bridegrooms from their canopies and of youths from their feasts of song. Blessed art Thou, O Lord, Who enables bridegroom to rejoice with the bride.

Upon completion of the blessings, of which the first is the benediction over wine, the couple drinks from the wine goblet. Again, in order to distinguish between *erusin* and *nisuin,* a new goblet of wine is used.

Before the couple leaves the *chuppah,* one additional ritual is performed. A glass is wrapped in a napkin and placed on the floor, where the groom shatters it with a well-placed stomp. The breaking of the glass reminds Jews of the destruction of Jerusalem and its ancient holy Temple in the year 70 C.E. The act also suggests to all present that the world is not yet redeemed, and, therefore, our great joy on this day is incomplete—but only for a moment, for now everyone in the audience calls out, "Mazel tov! Congratulations, good luck."

7. *Yichud:* The public ceremony is completed. After the couple return down the aisle, they are escorted to a private room for *yichud,* a few moments of precious privacy. Two witnesses are posted at the door to ensure that no one disturbs them. *Yichud* has both historical and halachic referents. In biblical times, the bride and groom would have their first intercourse immediately after marriage, and the bride would bring forth tokens of her virginity—the sheet with bloodstains—which her family would then display as a badge of honor (Dt. 22:13–17).[25] The reader will remember that according to the Mishnah there were three ways to effect a marriage. Intercourse, the third, was rejected by the rabbis as not being a legitimate mode of marrying and could only consummate a properly performed marriage. Today, of course, no couple consummates marriage at this time, but the privacy of *yichud* symbolically represents consummation and thus finalizes the halachic requirements of a Jewish marriage.

8. *Seudah:* A wedding feast is required. It is a characteristic of Judaism that ritual and rite are formally celebrated with feasting.

9. *Shevah berachot:* The wedding feast closes with a special grace, which includes a repetition of the seven *nisuin* marriage blessings. Here, too, the honors are distributed among the guests.

So what have we in a Jewish wedding? As in much else in Judaism, a dialectic: ancient, yet overlaid with custom that grew in stages; a private transaction, yet one that requires full participation of others and is subject to broad communal norms; a joyous occasion, yet allowing the intrusion of reality and the memory of sorrowful times; straightforward legal procedures, yet replete with rituals of sanctification and tones of sacredness; sexist in structure, yet according honor and deference to the bride. Perhaps it could be no other way in a rite that was shaped over the course of several millennia.

The ceremony I have described is a traditional one. Conservative, Reconstructionist, and Reform Jews observe these procedures in varying degrees. Some assimilated Jews marry in a civil ceremony, but any person who chooses to be married in a Jewish ceremony will follow the core rituals of *erusin* and *nisuin.*

MARRIAGE AND DIVORCE IN RELATION TO THE STATE

Marriage and divorce come wholly under the jurisdiction of the religious courts. In a Jewish state, such as existed prior to the Hurban in 70 B.C.E., and again after 1948 with the rebirth of modern-day Israel, the religious courts were/are an integral part of state machinery. As such, they enjoy a natural autonomy and control in matters of family law.

What about the broad and extensive Diaspora experience, Jews living among the nations of the world as part of, yet distinct from, the host culture? Varied though that experience was, whether under the Zoroastrians of Persia, the Visigoths of Spain, the Muslims of Turkey, or the Roman Catholics of Italy, Jews performed and were married in Jewish marriages.

Under Julius Caesar, Jews were granted status as a *religio licita,* to live according to their own laws.[26] Gradually, as Christianity became the established church throughout Europe, the Jews were relegated increasingly to subordinate status. Life became more difficult and often more oppressive for Jews, but in many areas they were left largely to their own internal devices. Even where their rights and freedoms, including religious ones, were circumscribed, the privilege of regulating marriage was never taken from them.[27]

While internal autonomy was the rule regarding performance of marriage, there were instances where hostile governments imposed their will. In Germany, Austria, and Russia, at various intervals during the eighteenth and nineteenth centuries, the Jews feared the dreaded *familiaten,* government edicts which controlled the number of Jewish marriages that could be contracted in any given locale. Not to be able to marry or to marry off one's children was considered a great tragedy and deprivation. In some communities, child marriages were arranged, for who knew what the morrow would bring?[28]

With emancipation, Jews became citizens of the state and no longer members of a sub-national group with chartered rights, "a state within a state." While emancipation brought with it an end to diabilities, it also brought an end to rights and privileges of self-government and the internal control that this implies. Modern nation-states have continued to respect religious freedoms, and marriage and divorce have continued to be the prerogative of religious corporations. But now there was an alternative—civil procedures. For some Western Jews, emancipation provided the sanction "to reject Jewish civilization in its wider ethnic and cultural implications."[29] Emancipation also spawned the denominations—Reform, Conservative, and Orthodox Judaism—each taking a position regarding the binding nature of religious codes versus civil law. By the 1870's, the liberal branch of Reform Judaism placed marriage in the hands of the civil authorities.[30] In matters of divorce, too, the debate raged loudly between the liberal and traditional wings, the former accepting civil divorce as adequate and legitimate, the Orthodox and Conservative totally rejecting such a view.[31]

MARRIAGE AS A CHANGING INSTITUTION

Many of the halachic dictates regarding marriage come to us as ethical guidelines rather than commandments or prohibitions. Not every Jewish male married, nor did every woman bring joy and light into the home, nor did all couples marry compatibly or forever. Each person is an individual and therefore cannot be pressed into a mold; each relationship has its own dynamic and chemistry. With all its structure, Jewish law accommodated this reality. That is why there is no specific commandment to marry, and why the nondogmatic regulations and prescriptions could be subject to different interpretations in later generations.

In addition to personal variations, cultural factors affected the nature of Jewish marriage in any given generation. For example, there was greater sexism in Moslem than in Christian cultures. It was Maimonides of Spanish-Arabic culture, and not Rabbi Moses Isserles of the North European Christian one, who enacted more restrictive legislation regarding wives.[32] Polygyny persisted among Yemenite Jews until the twentieth century, for they lived among a people for whom several wives was a sign of status and success. Ashkenazic Jews, living in Christian Europe, never practiced polygamy, and it was formally outlawed in the Middle Ages.[33] Similarly, levirate marriages continued to be enacted in Oriental cultures long after they ceased elsewhere.

What about today? The primary cultural influence on marriage has been the women's movement. Jewish marriages are no less subject to redefinition in light of its far-reaching impact. I will mention five differences in Jewish marriage today.

First, except for the most traditional sectors of a community, Jewish women are now marrying later than ever before, often acquiring professional degrees and securing themselves in a career before they enter into marriage. No more biding one's time, no more waiting around for "Mr. Right" to come along and chart the future. On the one hand, this is a healthy sign of independence; on the other, there is some cause for concern in the Jewish community, because later marriages and the growing number of singles affect population growth. Second, marriages—whether early or late—are producing fewer children. The Jewish community suffers not from zero population growth but from negative population growth, with approximately 1.6 children per couple. This is far below replacement levels, producing a crisis in the community. Birth control is permitted in Jewish law. There are certain restrictions as to method and family requirements, but there is a great deal of room for choice,[34] and many couples make it in favor of smaller and smaller families. Population has always been a serious matter for Jews, particularly so in this generation after the Holocaust.[35]

Third, in view of the fact that most Jewish women also work, there has been an increasing fluidity of roles. Though there is a strong tradition of Jewish women in the workplace, for the past few generations these models were the exception, not the rule.[36] No one wants to rewrite the Mishnah to read, "And *his* duties are to cook, wash, and . . . weave in wool," but this greater sharing of breadwinning and nurturing roles is a fact of life. While the father was an ever-present figure in the medieval Jewish home, and Jewish fathers always instructed their children in a very personal way, the typical nurturing and homemaking tasks were left to the mother.[37] Today, like their non-Jewish counterparts, Jewish couples are restructuring these roles. Fourth, Jews are not much more immune to living in a divorce culture than are other modern Western people. Estimates of divorce among Jews are close to forty percent, compared with a nationwide rate of fifty percent. That represents a body-blow to the once-stable Jewish family. Feminism is surely not the cause, but its emphasis on independence has served as a catalyst—to wit, the great rise in female-initiated divorce.

Fifth, there is a call for equality in religious structures, including those relating to marriage. For example, in the traditional marriage ceremony the woman is a silent partner. In Reform and Conservative Judaism, this has been altered somewhat to incorporate a woman's voice. There are those among the Orthodox who have experimented in this area as well. Without changing the traditional ceremony, they have opened a place for women, such as a female guest reading the *ketubah* or the bride reciting several verses to the groom under the *chuppah*. Similarly, new strides are being made in an attempt to equalize men and women in Jewish divorce law; also, there is increased sharing of rituals in the home. These are relatively small changes, but they are not insignificant in the process of moving toward equality within traditional structures of marriage and divorce.

As the reader can see, it is a two-edged matter. Not all the winds of change blow kindly on Jewish marriages of today. Like all other people, Jews are affected by the erosive forces of contemporary values on marriage and family. And, like all other religious groups, those more anchored to tradition are most resistant to changes. Nevertheless, a balance must be found. Judaism must continue to search for ways to integrate into its permanent structures new rituals that represent the new equity in marriage today.

INTERMARRIAGE

From earliest times, intermarriage was explicitly forbidden to Jews (Dt. 7:3–4, Av. Zar. 36B). Because Judaism, the religion, took root in a family, the concept of Jewish peoplehood was perhaps more central than for most other religions. But it was not purity of bloodlines that was the issue; rather, it was the integrity of the faith community. One could join the faith community through conversion; one could not enter Judaism simply through the act of marrying a Jew. For Jews, exogamy represented not only a violation of halacha but also a dilution of Jewishness of the community. Throughout Jewish history, intermarriage was kept to a minimum. Several forces were at work. Aside from the laws—which were made very clear—the response that followed such a marriage was an even more powerful preventive. If a Jew married out of the faith, he or she knew what to expect: total banishment from family and community. Parents and siblings would rend their garments and observe the shiva mourning period, as if the child were no longer alive.

Non-Jewish society was similarly opposed to intermarriage. In almost every official Christian document on the Jews throughout the Middle Ages, the injunction against intermarriage with "perfidious Jews" appears.[38] Often, punishment for offenders was harsh. Nor was there any opportunity. In most Christian lands, Jews and non-Jews lived apart, either by mutual desire or by imposed ghettoes. Social interchange between Jews and Christians in non-business settings was the exception, not the rule.

With the dawn of emancipation, the ghetto walls came tumbling down. Jews mainstreamed into the social, cultural, and political life of the nations in which they lived. Intermarriage grew as social contacts grew and as the stigma against Jews was muted. Equality and fraternity were the new and ideal ways to view the "other." Romantic love took precedence over issues of group survival and cohesion. Civil marriages were convenient, for one did not need to convert out of one's own religion to marry a person of another faith.

Until recently, the intermarriage rate for Jews was quite low in the United States. In the decades before 1960, the rate was only six percent. Between 1960 and 1966, it rose to seventeen percent, and by 1971 it had jumped to thirty-two percent.[39] Adjusting for conversion and other factors, the number of Jews in America in 1980 having non-Jewish spouses was approximately 300,000—or five percent of the total Jewish population. Today, it is thought to be considerably higher. The rise is due to many factors: a new age of pluralism and ecumenism has dawned, in which value is placed on every other faith, belief, and style of life; the new fascination with, and therefore desirability of, ethnics; the intense relationships constructed by humanists of all faiths in the course of sharing a crusade such as civil rights, anti-nuclear protest, or feminism; the vast number of Jews on the college campuses[40]; the loss of enforcement power in religious communities; the increasing number of Jews in all professions; and feminism and the increase of female out-marriage.[41] Finally, because of the sheer numbers, the old response of total cut-off is no longer a viable threat.

There are certain new facts about intermarriage that make it no less forbidden according to Jewish law but help to explain some of the contemporary communal responses: First, there is a not-insignificant phenomenon of conversion into Judaism—in fact, more into than out of Judaism. In approximately thirty percent of the intermarriages, the non-Jewish spouse converts to Judaism, either before or after the wedding.[42] Second, even where there is no conversion, intermarriage seems no longer to represent to exogamous Jews a negation of Judaism. Most of them continue to think of themselves as Jews—which they are—and to maintain family and community links.[43] Third, in a recent study of a sample of intermarried couples across the United States, it was found that twenty percent of the families with no conversion had, nonetheless, provided some formal Jewish education for their children, and thirty percent of them celebrated the bar or bat mitzvah rite as well.[44]

The denominational responses to intermarriage are varied. In 1983, the Reform rabbinate formally adopted the principle of Jewishness by patrilineal descent (as well as matrilineal). This is a de jure statement of what Reform Judaism has de facto accepted all along, but the statement represents a more aggressive outreach to the acceptance of intermarried couples. Conservative and Orthodox Jews have strongly objected to the patrilineal-descent motion on the basis of its halachic inadmissibility.

The leaders of Reform Judaism have also called for greater outreach in the area of conversion, and this would apply particularly to non-Jewish spouses. While conversion has always existed in Judaism—and many converts were given the appellation "righteous convert"—there was a controlling ambivalence in tradition and community. Today, Reform Judaism has deemed it the right moment to extend its hand to the "unchurched"; simultaneously, the Central Conference of American Rabbis (Reform) voted to censure rabbis performing a mixed marriage.

Conservative Jews have expanded their educational and rabbinic resources available to potential converts. The procedure for conversion involves several months of study preceding conversion rites, often on a one-to-one basis. This study takes a great deal of time in the life of a rabbi.

In the Orthodox community, the primary response has been one of prevention—to raise children more intensively Jewish, in educational and social settings not conducive to intermarriage, such as yeshiva high school, Jewish summer camps, etc. Orthodox Jews tend also to live in communities that are identifiably Jewish. With community reinforcing home environment, intermarriage remains extremely rare in the Orthodox community. Still, it occasionally does happen, for Orthodox Jews go to college and enter the workplace and are geographically mobile, like everyone else. Moreover, while converts rarely come via an Orthodox partner, many wish to convert through an Orthodox conversion, so that later there will be no questions of acceptability. And, for many, Orthodoxy signifies a certain authenticity of tradition. Once one makes the effort to convert, the rationale seems to be to want to do it in the most "kosher" manner.

Thus, there is today a less resistant attitude to conversion in the Orthodox community. The law has always been that an ulterior motive, such as marriage, is not a valid reason for conversion, which must be based on love of Judaism and not love of a particular Jew. Most rabbis, recognizing reality, have tended to work around that obstacle. More recently, there has been an attempt to point up halachic precedents that validate conversion for the sake of marriage.[45] On the personal level, traumatic though a mixed marriage is in an Orthodox family, the old response of sitting shiva and cutting off all ties no longer seems to be the common response. While an Orthodox Jew would not participate in or attend the wedding ceremony, and while the relationship is surely affected, the connections are often maintained—in part, to encourage that the grandchildren be raised as Jews (converted, if the mother is not Jewish); in part, hoping that with love, time, and familiarity with Judaism the non-Jew will eventually want to convert; in part, because we all live in a culture that places human values above all other claims.

SEXISM IN THE TRADITION

How is one to deal with sexism in sacred and quasi-sacred literature? One cannot rewrite the sources any more than one can rewrite history, nor does one like to tinker excessively with issues of divinity and ancient authority. But neither can one let sexist sources stand uncorrected. One answer lies in the hermeneutic: to teach the richness of tradition and the essence of its message—whether that be the sanctity of marriage or the caring nature of a relationship—yet apply the yardstick of equality. It is possible to point out where the sources, for reasons of sociology, culture, and timing, fall short. It is possible to explain certain texts in the context of those times—hierarchies in all pre-feminist cultures. And because of the conglomerate and cumulative nature of Jewish tradition, it is often possible to find a benign precedent or principle to substitute or counterbalance a sexist one. In other words, it is possible to engage a critical eye and a loving heart at one and the same moment.

Moreover, tradition has much of value to teach—including something important about role distinctiveness in male/female relationships. Role distinctiveness does not necessarily imply hierarchy or inequity. In the long run, role distinctions may be quite healthy for psyche and society. But there are limits to such a gentle and respectful approach. These are reached when outright discrimination affects the lives of real people. In such a case, the second answer lies in the area of politics and power. For example, Jewish divorce law is unequivocally sexist. However, before we explain the law, let us examine the procedure: After all attempts at reconciliation have failed, the couple appear before a *bet din,* a Jewish court of law, consisting of three rabbis who are experts in Jewish divorce law. A scribe and two witnesses are also present. At the instruction of the husband, the scribe hand-letters the *get* (the writ of divorce), filling in name, location, time, and the standard text of the divorce. The core of the *get* is the husband's attestation to divorcing his wife and setting her free to marry any other man. The witnesses sign the *get,* and the rabbi reads it aloud; then the man places it into the woman's hands, acclaiming, "This is your *get.* You are now free to marry another."

No divorce, no matter how amicable, is problem-free. To some extent, Jewish divorce action with its routine methodical procedures and its absence of interpersonal negotiations helps to keep the tensions low; the *get* proceedings lend a note of closure to the relationship, which speeds up the process of psychological closure as well. In that sense, a Jewish divorce proceeding has some positive impact. Moreover, the fact that divorce is permitted at all in Judaism is a fundamental recognition of the human right to happiness.

But, for all that, Jewish divorce law poses problems for women. First, only the husband can issue the *get.* There are cases where the recalcitrant husband, for reasons of spite or blackmail, withholds the *get* from his wife and thereby does not release her to marry. Her life is in limbo. In the closed society of former times, a Jewish court could compel him to authorize the *get* or could punish him under rules of internal autonomy until he acquiesced. Paradoxically, in an open society, the problem is exacerbated. A recalcitrant husband can slip through the cracks between civil and religious jurisdiction.[46] He can refuse to show up at the rabbinic court. A woman faithful to Jewish law is most vulnerable in this situation. Second, if a husband disappears and his whereabouts are not known, his wife remains an *agunah*—a woman anchored to an absentee husband. She, too, is in limbo and cannot get on with her life. While the rabbis in every generation bent their efforts to resolving the problem of an *agunah,* they could do so only within limits, and their efforts were not always successful. Third, the liberal branches of Judaism—Reform and secular Jews—operate by civil law. Jews of Orthodox and Conservative denominations cannot marry Jews divorced according to the laws of the secular state who lack a *get.*

The problems grow directly out of the original sources: "If a man finds something unseemly in his wife, he writes her a writ of divorce, delivers it into her hands, and sends her away" (Dt. 24:1). This principle, the absolute right of the husband in matters of divorce, has been diminished, circum-scribed, and, through the process of rabbinic interpretation, whittled away from generation to generation. Moreover, the rights of women in family law have grown through the centuries. A woman may not be divorced against her will, and she has legitimate rights to sue in court for divorce. Yet, despite the many improvements instituted by the rabbis throughout the generations, and despite the new pre-nuptial clauses to prevent abuse, a woman still remains dependent on her husband's willingness to authorize and deliver a *get.* In fact, there are instances of blackmail on the part of recalcitrant hus-bands. And the community remains divided.

Until such time as Jewish law undergoes reinterpretation, in order to eliminate potential abuse and to incorporate the principle of equity into Jew-ish divorce proceedings, Jewish law will be subject to charges of sexism. Unless the potential for discrimination is rooted out, much of the credibility of what is good in the tradition, though sexist in language will be eroded.

CONCLUSION

Life in Western society as we approach the year 2000 has indeed changed. Whereas choosing a traditional marriage and family was the ultimate and only legitimate choice, today it is no longer the rule. With a divorce rate of fifty percent, a singles lifestyle, serial marriages—only twenty-four percent of all adult Americans fit the old model! But Judaism, while not forcing every-one into that mold, makes a strong case for traditional marriages: a long-term relationship characterized by love and the bonds of nurturing each other and children, and also bounded by traditional parameters of fidelity, mutual respect, and steadfastness.

I, for one, would hope that these teachings will never be muted, that this paradigm for living will never be replaced by another—no matter how mod-ern or au coruant a view of adult relationships might prevail at any given moment in history. I believe a covenantal model works for human relation-ships. And—just as we have all learned from ecumenism that it is possible for people of different faiths to experience the gifts, the promises, and the covenant uniquely, and without putting down all others—so I believe it is possible to posit a primary model of marriage without demoting to the status of pariah all those who fall outside of it.

What does Judaism teach? That marriage is good, very good: that it is the Jewish way.

NOTES

1. See Ellen Willis' review of *The Second Stage* by Betty Friedan in *The Village Voice*, Literary Supplement, November, 1981, p. 1.

2. The traditional greeting for an infant girl differs: "May she be raised to the wedding canopy and to a life of good deeds." Now that women also study Torah, many modern Jews add that to the female greeting as well.

3. Yoreh Deah 240:25. Yoreh Deah is one of the four tractates of the *Shulkhan Arukh,* which is the most authoritative Jewish legal compendium of the Middle Ages.

4. Irving Greenberg, "The Jewish Family and the Covenant," unpublished manuscript, 1983.

5. For two different approaches to the issue of sexism in the sources, see Leonard Swidlet, *Women in Judaism* (Methuchen, NJ: Scarecrow Press, 1976); and Blu Greenberg, *On Women and Judaism* (Philadelphia: Jewish Publication Society, 1982).

6. There are several other nonnarrative references in the Torah to marriage; among them, see Ex. 21:7–10; Dt. 24:1, 5.

7. It is interesting to note that the Hebrew root, *davok,* to cleave, is the word used to describe the relationship between God and the Jewish people: "And you who cleave unto the Lord your God . . ." (Dt. 4:4).

8. Is. 61:10, 62:5; Ez. 16; Hos. 2:21; Song of Songs.

9. *Yevamot, Kiddushin, Ketubot, Gittin, Niddah, Sotah.*

10. See also Kid. 29B, 30A; Yev. 62b, 113a.

11. Bav. Bat. 110A, Bech 45B, Pes. 49a.

12. Kid. 70A.

13. See further Kid. 41A, Ket. 102B.

14. See also Sot. 2A on predestination of partners.

15. Cf. Yev. 63B; Ket. 63A; Sot. 4B. See also Swidler, *Women in Judaism,* pp. 111–113, for a fuller discussion of wives as a distraction to Torah study.

16. Oddly enough, the formal obligation, "Be fruitful and multiply" (Gen. 1:28), was interpreted by the rabbis to apply only to men, with the defense that a woman could not be commanded to do something that might cause her physical pain.

17. See Chaim Pearl, "Marriage Forms," in Peter Elman, ed., *Jewish Marriage* (London: Soncino, 1967), p. 17. See also Gen. 38 and Ruth 2–3.

18. On circumscribing and then forbidding polygyny, see Yev. 65b and Pes. 113A; also *Shulkhan Aruch.* Even Ha'ezer 1:9–11. On halitzah, see the fine article by Menachem Elon in *Encyclopedia Judaica* (Jerusalem: Keter Publishing, 1971), vol. 11, pp. 122–130. On marital rape, see Eruvin 100b.

19. See Yev. 63B; Git. 90B.

20. The Talmud consists of two layers: the earliest, the Mishnah, is largely a detailed exposition of the law; the second, the Gemara, is an elaboration and explication of the Mishnah, and includes law, history, theology, aphorisms, narrative, debate, etc. The Mishnah was closed in the year 250 C.E.; the Gemara, in 499 C.E.

21. Such a conclusion is derived from two facts: (a) the money specified was so minimal as to eliminate any possibility of constituting a financial transaction; (b) unlike other acquisitions, a wife could not be resold or transferred.

22. The language in rabbinic literature shifts from "he takes" or "he acquires" to "is required," teaching us that the woman has the power of consent or refusal.

23. This declaration is found in the Talmud and is most likely the oral version of what originally constituted "deed" in the Mishnaic reference.

24. Maurice Lamm, *The Jewish Way in Love and Marriage* (San Francisco: Harper & Row, 1982), pp. 213–215.

25. Though it seems primitive to Western sensibilities, the custom of examining the bride's linen after the first night of marriage for spots of blood as proof of her virginity is still practiced in some Oriental communities. See *Encyclopedia Judaica,* vol. 11, p. 1045.

26. See James Parkes, *The Conflict of the Church and the Synagogue* (New York: Atheneum, 1969), ch. 1.

27. See Jacob R. Marcus, *The Jew in the Medieval World* (New York: Harper and Row, 1938), particularly sections 1 and 2. See also Philip and Hanna Goodman, eds., *The Jewish Marriage Anthology* (Philadelphia: Jewish Publication Society, 1965), p. 171; Louis M. Epstein, *The Jewish Marriage Contract* (New York: Jewish Theology Seminary, 1927), pp. 281 ff.; and Zev Falk, *Jewish Matrimonial Law in the Middle Ages* (Oxford: Oxford University Press, 1966).

28. See also Rachel Biale, *Women and Jewish Law* (New York: Schocken Books, 1984), p. 66.

29. See Howard M. Sachar, *The Course of Modern Jewish History* (New York: Dell Publishing, 1957), p. 63.

30. See A. Mielziner, *The Jewish Law of Marriage and Divorce in Ancient and Modern Times and Its Relation to the Law of the State* (Cincinnati: Bloch Publishing, 1884), p. 94.

31. Ibid., chap. 16.

32. See Maimonides, *Mishneh Torah,* Book IV, Laws of Women.

33. In approximately 1025, Rabbenu Gershom, a leading rabbinic light of the Diaspora, formally banned polygamy.

34. It is interesting to note that the responsibility falls upon women; the condom is not permitted. See David M. Feldman, *Marital Relations, Birth Control, and Abortion in Jewish Law* (New York: Schocken Books, 1974).

35. It has been reliably estimated that 6,000,000 Jews were killed in the Holocaust. This represented one-third of world Jewish population. It is now forty years after the Holocaust, and the losses have nowhere been made up.

36. See Paula Hyman, "The Jewish Family: Looking for a Useable Past," in Susannah Heschel, ed., *On Being a Jewish Feminist* (New York: Schocken Books, 1983).

37. See Israel Abrahams, *Jewish Life in the Middle Ages* (New York: Atheneum, 1969), particularly chap. 7, "Monogamy and the Home."

38. See Marcus, *The Jew in the Medieval World,* pp. 4–5, 139.

39. The National Jewish Population Study, Council of Jewish Federations and Welfare Funds, 1972.

40. See Irving Greenberg, "Jewish Survival and the College Campus," in *Judaism* 17 (Summer, 1968): 259–281.

41. Prior to the 1970's, the Jewish male/female outmarriage ratio was three to one. As women have moved increasingly into professional settings, the female outmarriage rate has risen.

42. Egon Mayer, "Intermarriage among American Jews: Consequences, Prospects and Policies" (New York: National Jewish Resource Center, 1979).

43. Ibid., p. 3.

44. Ibid.

45. See Marc Angel, unpublished paper presented at Chevra, National Jewish Resource Center, Spring, 1983, New York City.

46. Normon Solomon, "Jewish Divorce Law in Contemporary Society," *Journal of Jewish Social Sciences*, vol. 25, no. 2 (December, 1983).

CHAPTER 37

The Protestant View of Marriage

Wilson Yates

⁓ ❡ ⁓

Wilson Yates's essay represents the very best of the contemporary Protestant theology of marriage. Protestantism, of course, includes a wide range of denominations, but most mainline Protestant bodies, he claims, share a similar focus and meaning. That focal point revolves around the conventional image of marriage. It lies at the heart of its theology, its denominational statements and rituals, and its core meanings. Yes, differences exist among Protestants themselves, but when they gather to celebrate marriage, they are united in a common covenantal perspective.

Yates uses the metaphor of covenant to examine and interpret the major characteristics he deems central to Protestant marriage. He lays out six characteristics that define the contours and meaning of marriage as covenant: (1) to create a life of intimate companionship, (2) to create and sustain a fabric of honesty, trust, openness, and acceptance, (3) to explore and respond to the religious and moral issue in their life's pilgrimage, (4) to live an ethnic of covenantal wholeness, (5) to create appropriate boundaries of behavior, and (6) to break the covenant only as a last resort. Yates acknowledges a contemporary theological convergence in understandings of marriage between Roman Catholic, Orthodox, and Protestant perspectives, but this commonality, however, should be seen within a framework of genuine differences and contrasting emphases.

Questions for Discussion

1. Are the six characteristics of a covenantal marriage, as outlined by Yates, distinctive and unique to Protestant bodies?
2. The principle of intimate companionship lays the basis for a positive ethic of sexual love. What practical implications do you see in this statement for couples?
3. Is the family a "haven in a heartless world" (Lasch) or a "Little Commonwealth"(Morgan)? Discuss in light of an ethic of family social responsibility.
4. What does love expressed as justice mean for marital relations in terms of role patterns and institutional expectations?
5. Yates claims the covenant means breaking the covenant (as a last resort) when the internal life of the relationship has died. Do you agree? Is divorce a moral option?

P rotestantism includes a wide range of denominations, each with its own history and theology, but most mainline Protestant bodies that are rooted in the Continental and English Reformation traditions articulate views of marriage which are quite similar in focus and meaning.[1] It is possible, therefore, to speak of a Protestant view of marriage that is in large part shared by all mainline Protestant groups. In this discussion I shall set forth that common perspective while noting major points of divergence.

With the Reformation, Protestant marriage theory began to take shape: the legitimacy and significance of civil authority over the institution was recognized; the sacramental status which the Roman Catholic Church accorded the institution was removed; the biblical basis of marriage was lifted up with frequent references to the wedding at Cana; and certain theological affirmations were made regarding the nature and significance of the institution. Martin Luther considered marriage an order of creation whose origin transcended both church and state. The importance he accorded to the institution, if not his particular view of creation, has remained central to much of Protestant thought. Thus, services speak of marriage as an institution "ordained by God," as a "holy estate," as an institution "established by God." as "an institution of divine origin."

John Calvin and Martin Bucer viewed marriage as a covenant, and down through Protestant history the covenantal nature of marriage has been accented as the pivotal meaning of the relationship. Most important in this history was the work of the English and American Puritans who largely shaped early Protestant understanding in North America: Protestant theology and services of marriage pick up the covenantal character of the institution in our own time. For example, the new, proposed United Church of Christ service states, "God has called you to the covenant of marriage," and the marriage service from *The Lutheran Book of Worship* reflects the essence of the covenant in these words:

> With high praise we recall your acts of unfailing love for the human family, for the house of Israel, and for your people the church. . . . Pour down your grace upon (this couple) that they may fulfill the vows they have made this day and reflect your steadfast love in their lifelong faithfulness to each other.

In this discussion of the Protestant view, I want to examine the metaphor of covenant and to use it to interpret the major characteristics deemed central to Protestant marriage. The concept is deeply embedded in Scripture. God invited the people of Israel to become partners in a divine/human covenant—to become partners in a relationship marked by trust, fidelity, steadfast love, justice, and obedience to the will of God. While the people time and again broke that covenantal relationship, it remained at the heart of their religious calling. In the Hebrew Bible, the covenant had a patriarchal parent/child character. God was the authoritarian Father and the people of

Israel God's children. When early Protestants interpreted the marriage bond as a covenant, they applied the concept to both the husband/wife relationship and the parent/child relationship, with both types of relationship understood to be patriarchal and authoritarian in character.

Down through the history of Protestantism, however, the covenantal bond has taken on a more egalitarian form; the character of both husband/wife and parent/child bonds has accented companionship, love, justice, and intimacy as the moral shape God desires for the relationship. This more egalitarian form, with its emphasis on mutuality and intimacy, is now assumed in modern Protestant services when they speak of "the bond and covenant of marriage" and call the couple to "consider the holy covenant you are about to make." The contemporary United Methodist statement on marriage is typical:

> We affirm the sanctity of the marriage covenant which is expressed in love, mutual support, personal commitment, and shared fidelity, between a man and a woman. We believe that God's blessing rests upon such marriage, whether or not there are children of the union. We reject social norms that assume different standards for women than for men in marriage.[2]

To appreciate more fully the nature of the Protestant covenantal view of the marriage bond, I want to set forth six characteristics that define its contours and meaning. These characteristics constitute the major threads that move through Protestant theories of marriage. In doing so I will touch upon a range of related issues including sexuality and the primary ethical principles which are central to the Protestant image of marriage and the family.

1. The first characteristic is a *commitment by the partners to create a life of intimate companionship*. Companionship lies at the heart of the Protestant view of the marriage covenant. Luther pointed to its importance in his attack on celibacy and his affirmation of the marital relationship. Calvin, in his development of a Protestant theology of marriage, insisted that the essence of the marriage bond was moral and spiritual companionship between two partners; in effect, the primary purpose of marriage was companionship. This Calvinist perspective in the history of the churches' understanding of marriage was a watershed in its theory of marriage: before Calvin the primary purpose of marriage was considered to be procreation; with Calvin, procreation was reinterpreted to be a blessing flowing from companionship; after Calvin the idea of companionship emerged as a central theological focus in all the major Protestant traditions.[3] The Puritans and left-wing sectarian groups such as the Quakers and Congregationalists spoke out most boldly on the significance of companionship, and John Milton set forth the notion that a vital marriage should be a companionable and compatible relationship: "In God's intention a meet and happy conversation is the chiefest and noblest end of marriage." Milton also developed the first major case in Western theology for considering incompatibility, that is, the absence of true companionship, as grounds for divorce.[4]

In this development of the concept, companionship came to mean more than simply moral and spiritual unity, for Puritan writers insisted that love, intimacy, romance, and emotional depth be given due honor. This is delightfully portrayed in a poem by the American Puritan poet, Anne Bradstreet. Writing about her longing for her husband who was away on business, she expressed how she missed him as her romantic partner and companion and friend. She said it all with a touch of humor and irritation at his delay in returning to their home and bed:

My head, my heart, mine eyes, my life—nay more,
My joy, my magazine of earthly store:
If two be one, as surely thou and I,
How stayest thou there, whilst I at Ipswich lie?
So many steps from the heart to sever,
If but a neck, soon should we be together.
I like the earth this season mourn in black;
My sun is gone so far in's Zodiac,
Whom whilst I' joyed, nor storms nor frosts I felt,
His warmth such frigid colds did cause to melt.
My chilled limbs now numbed lie forlorn:
Return, return, sweet sol, from Capricorn.
In this dead time, alas, what can I more
Than view those fruits which through thy heat I bore?
Which sweet contentment yields me for a space
True living pictures of their father's face.
O strange effect! Now thou art southward gone,
I weary grow, the tedious day so long:
But when thou northward to me shalt return,
I wish my sun may never set, but burn
With the Cancer of my glowing breast.
The welcome house of him, my dearest guest.
Where ever, ever, stay, and go not thence
Til nature's sad decree shall call thee hence:
Flesh of thy flesh, bone of thy bone,
I here, thou there, yet both but one.[5]

The value of companionship continued to develop from the seventeenth century to the present, serving as the cornerstone of Protestant covenantal views of marriage. The love and intimacy expressed in Bradstreet's poem became increasingly identified as the inner spirit of companionship. This introduction of companionate love by that rather small community of Puritans in the seventeenth and eighteenth centuries was the major beginning point for Christian theology's accent on the primacy of love and intimacy as the heart of the marriage relationship.[6]

In this development, a positive understanding of sexuality as a means of expressing marital love, as well as a means of procreation, also emerged. Major Protestant theology at the time of the Reformation readily affirmed sexuality as a part of the goodness of creation and denied that the celibate calling and "spiritual" marriage were of a higher moral order than a marriage in which the "two became one flesh." But sexual expression was still held under suspicion by early Protestant theologians, with most insisting that the only positive purpose of sexual pleasure was the role it played in the procreative process. Thinkers in the late seventeenth and eighteenth centuries, however, linked sexual pleasure with marital love and companionship and thereby gave sexual companionship a positive function apart from procreation. Protestantism then had the basis for a positive ethic of sexual love and, in the early twentieth century, a major rationale for accepting contraception, which, by freeing persons from the fear of pregnancy, permitted fuller enjoyment of marital sexual love.[7]

Recently, a great deal of work has been done in further developing a Protestant sexual ethic. Such writers as Derrick Sherwin Bailey, Norman Pittenger, Daniel Day Williams, Letty Russell, Phyllis Trible, and, foremost, James B. Nelson have made major contributions in shaping this ethic.[8] In their work, they have made a concerted effort at overcoming the remnants of a body/soul dualism by setting forth a holistic view in which body and spirit are seen as an integrated whole. Sex is no longer identified as simply a body function, for it is as much an experience of the spirit as of the body. In turn, *eros* is related in an integral way to *agape*. As the British theologian Charles Williams has written, *eros* need "no longer stand on its knees before *agape*." James B. Nelson summarizes this integrated holistic understanding of the different dimensions of love in these terms:

> Agape is not another kind of love. Nor is it, as Tillich rightly notes, a dimension strictly comparable to the other three dimensions of our loving. It is the transformative quality essential to any true expression of any of love's modes. If we define Christian love as agape or self-giving alone—without elements of desire, attraction, self-fulfillment, receiving—we are describing love which is both impoverished and impoverishing. But the other elements of love without agape are ultimately self-destructive. Agape present with sexual desire, erotic aspiration and mutuality releases these from self-centeredness and possessiveness into a relationship that is humanly enriching and creative. It does not annihilate or replace the other modes of our loving. It undergirds and transforms. And faith knows that agape is a gift, and not of our own making.[9]

This important new work in Protestant theology indicates a further recognition of the importance of intimate, loving companionship and of the role of sexual expression in manifesting that intimacy within the marital relationship. The ability of persons to use sex for alienating and destructive ends is certainly recognized, but the accent rests on the way in which sexual expression can become a means by which intimate companionship is known and the grace of love experienced.

In the development of the meaning of companionship, there was also an insistence that such companionship include not only a depth of love and intimacy but also a breadth in its range of experiences. Hence, popular Protestant marriage manuals of the nineteenth and early twentieth centuries lifted up the encompassing nature of intimate companionship, insisting that the Christian marriage should realize religious, moral, social, sexual, parental, and intellectual companionship.[10] This perspective remains prominent in contemporary Protestant thought. Charlotte and Howard J. Clinebell's *Intimate Marriage*, for example, holds up sexual, emotional, intellectual, creative, recreational, work, crisis, commitment, and spiritual forms of intimacy as central to a healthy marriage.[11] The Episcopal Church's marriage service picks up in representative fashion this dimension of companionship: "The union of husband and wife in heart, body and mind is intended for their mutual joy, for the help and comfort given one another in prosperity and diversity, and when it is God's will, for the procreation of children and their nurture in the knowledge and love of the Lord."[12] Later in a prayer are the words: "Let their love for each other be a seal upon their hearts, a mantle upon their shoulders, and a crown upon their foreheads. Bless them in their work and in their companionship, in their sleeping and in their waking, in their joys and in their sorrows, in their life and in their death."[13]

2. A second characteristic of a covenantal marriage is *a commitment on the part of the couple to create and sustain a fabric of honesty, trust, openness, and acceptance.* Each of these virtues in Protestant theologies of marriage has its own history, with the latter two a part of more recent marriage theory.

Honesty, in its simplest terms, means truthtelling; it means telling the facts. But there is a deeper level of honesty that is also expected in a religiously shaped marriage, a level at which each person expresses an understanding of a situation with sensitivity for the impact it will have on the other person. In the language of ethics, which is such a dominant part of the Protestant language about marriage, this means being sensitive not only to the factual nature of our truthtelling but also to why we are honest, i.e., our motivations; what we hope to accomplish, i.e., our intentions or aims; and what effect our "telling the truth will have on the other person, i.e., what consequences will result. Dietrich Bonhoeffer expressed this deeper level of truthtelling: "Telling the truth is not solely a matter of moral character, it is also a matter of correct appreciation of real situations and of serious reflection upon them."[14] In Protestant thought, expressed in both theological statements and marriage rituals, such honesty is deemed a significant attribute of a morally mature marriage.

Trust is a second virtue that the literature accents as crucial to the covenantal fabric of marriage. Without it, the marital relationship can easily unravel. Thus, all services of marriage acknowledge the virtue of trust or fidelity, and the theological literature spells out its meaning. In nineteenth-century Protestant thought, the discussion of trust focused primarily on marital fidelity, but in more contemporary literature the concept has been given a much richer meaning. Norman Pittenger, a Protestant theologian who has written widely and representatively on issues of marriage relationships and sexuality, offers an understanding of trust which includes its reciprocity, its life as both trusting and entrusting, and its venturesome nature, its dependence on a leap of faith to reach its fullest depths:

> When I say that I "trust" someone, I am saying that I have a complete confidence in him, certain that what he does and is will never "let me down." And when I "entrust" myself to another, I am saying that I put myself in the other's hands, such that in those hands I am ultimately entirely *safe*, precisely because the other is known to be "trustworthy." Yet it is not quite correct to say that the other is known to be such, for that might suggest that I have some logical proof that such is the case. On the contrary, the situation is much more venturesome. For what I am doing is giving myself into the other's hands in a great act of faith; I do not *know* in any demonstrable fashion that he is what I take him to be. I cannot prove to you that someone to whom in love I thus entrust myself is in very fact what I am confident he is.[15]

The emphasis on trust as dependent, finally, on a "leap of faith" is rooted deeply in Protestant theology and especially its theology of marriage. The partners ought to risk such trust—make such a leap—for trust is a part of the bedrock of their covenant with God. God is trustworthy, and persons are called to trust in God. Equally, in the covenant of marriage, the partners are called to ground their relationship on a steadfast and abiding trust.

A third virtue is that of *openness:* being willing to be self-revelatory and open to the self-revelation of others, to be free to express needs, hopes, feelings, and thoughts in a process of mutual self-disclosure. This understanding of the marital relationship is rooted in a larger theological framework of values, particularly those of individualism and relationality. The Reformers insisted upon the significance of a direct relationship between the individual and God, which offered the individual knowledge about God and a deeper understanding of the person's own soul. Through such a relationship one grew in the love of God and, through the love of God, in the love of self and other. This perspective had a direct bearing on later marriage theology, where it is assumed that marital love and intimacy both help create and depend upon a mutual sharing of the couple's deepest feelings and thoughts. Theologically, then, love—a gift of grace—involves an openness both to receiving disclosure of the other and to disclosing the self to the other.

The virtue of *acceptance* follows from the commitment to openness, for one must accept the other and know that one is accepted. Once again, the model is a larger theological doctrine, that of justifying grace. Justification is the affirmation, as Tillich suggests, that we are accepted by God in spite of what we are. In a marriage neither partner is God, and neither partner is expected to accept unconditionally. Yet, the married couple is called to transcend a limited acceptance that is conditional and calculative and to realize a full and rich acceptance of one another. The couple is called to express in human terms what God offers in divine terms—pardon and acceptance. Such acceptance annuls neither the need for nor the possibility of judgment and forgiveness. Rather, acceptance is that underlying quality in a relationship which frees the partners both to judge and to criticize, to forgive and allow oneself to be forgiven. If such underlying acceptance and affirmation are lacking, judgment takes on the character of rejection, and the possibilities of forgiveness are frozen in the power struggle that follows. Thus, acceptance "for better, for worse, for richer, for poorer, in sickness and in health," as the marriage rituals state, is essential to the health of the marriage covenant.

3. A third element of the covenantal relationship is *the commitment to explore and respond to the religious and moral depths of human existence in light of the affirmations of the Christian faith*. For Protestant theology, one of the major metaphors for interpreting the religious journey is that of "pilgrimage." In this pilgrimage, the Christian encounters religious questions about the meaning of human existence and grapples with the affirmations and doctrines of the Christian faith that can help make sense out of those questions. Marriage is seen as a primary path on which this pilgrimage unfolds, and within its borders Christians are expected to "wrestle with the angels" in their struggle to understand and live out a life of faithfulness to God. Within marriage and the family, those ultimate issues of life and death are confronted; grief over death, suffering from illness, joy from loving, alienation over differences, happiness over success, fear from the threat of loneliness, and sustenance from the routines of marital rhythms are experienced; and the moral issues of truthfulness, promise-keeping, fair play, just dealings, loving acts, protection of freedoms, and demands for social responsibility are encountered and responded to. Thus, marriage is a time and place of pilgrimage, casting its partners into the arena of religious and moral issues which shock them into an awareness of their own limitations and invite them into the experience of fulfillment and wholeness. Marriage demands that some sense be made out of these encounters, that some faith response be given by Christians in light of the Christian faith.

Protestant marriage theory, then, calls married persons to see the relationship of their own marriage to the larger pilgrimage of faith and to accept the responsibility to take seriously the religious and moral issues marriage poses. Such theory goes further, however, for it asks married couples not only to call upon the resources of faith but also to nurture and strengthen one another in the roles of Christian pilgrim and disciple. The eighteenth-century Puritans and sectarians saw marriage as a means by which both partners would be strengthened in their spiritual and moral resolve. It was a vocation whose final goal was to give glory to God through the shaping of the religious and moral life—a theme picked up in the words of a contemporary Presbyterian service of marriage:

> As God's picked representatives of the new humanity, purified and beloved of God himself, be merciful in action, kindly in heart, humble in mind. Accept life, and be most patient and tolerant with one another. Forgive as freely as the Lord has forgiven you. And, above everything else, be truly loving. Let the peace of Christ rule in your hearts, remembering that as mem-

bers of the one body you are called to live in harmony, and never forget to be thankful for what God has done for you.[16]

The married couple also has a responsibility to the larger community to bear children, when such is possible and wise, and to nurture them in the Christian faith. Although contemporary theology and services of marriage lift up the importance of procreation and the nurturance of children, reflecting a certain expectation and goal for marriage, none considers it essential for fulfillment of the marriage covenant or suggests that the primary purpose of marriage is procreation. This is, in part, a recognition that some persons cannot have children; that other persons, given their own personal emotional and social means in life, should not have children; and that all persons should respect the fact that in an overpopulated world the vocation of marriage need not necessarily include bearing or nurturing children.

Finally, the married couple has a responsibility to the larger community to participate actively both in the life of the church which serves the community and as citizens of the community in those actions that contribute to the greatest realization of the common good. Again, it was the Puritans who developed the most elaborate ethic of family social responsibility, seeing the family as a commonwealth writ small which was to care for the larger commonwealth of which it was a part. While nineteenth- and twentieth-century marriage and family literature has highlighted the family's responsibility to its own members, there still remains that strong theme that the couple will "make their life together a sign of Christ's love to this sinful and broken world," will bring up their children "to know you, to love you, and to serve you," and will "reach out in love and concern for others."[17] Thereby, the religious pilgrimage becomes a Christian pilgrimage, and the couple and their family fulfill the vocation they have been given.

4. A fourth element of the covenant is *a commitment to live out an ethic of covenantal wholeness*. The covenantal relationship God created with the people of Israel was interwoven with ethical principles and moral expectations. The Protestant understanding of the marriage covenant is similar. In modern marriage theory, four dominant principles emerge: *love, justice, freedom,* and *order*. As the covenant is interpreted, God calls people to live within the bonds of a loving relationship, to relate in a just and fair manner, to claim and accept the judgment that we are created as free and self-transcending creatures who are responsible for giving moral shape and depth to the covenantal relationship, and to recognize the necessity both for order in life and for the importance of stability and change in maintaining that order.

I referred above to the significance which Protestant marriage theory attributes to the principle of love. Most significantly, contemporary writing recognizes that a healthy marriage needs both romantic and companionate experiences of love (*eros* and *philia*). Romantic love, as the attraction and desire for union with the other, is experienced most intensely in the sexual relationship of the couple, but it should also be present in a full range of relationships as spontaneous and empathetic responsiveness marked by a sense of emotional excitement and heightened awareness. Yet, such romantic love must be complemented or balanced by companionate love, which expresses itself as an ongoing responsiveness in the routines of life together. It is love embued with a respect for the other's privacy, an appreciation for the other's life as a unique blend of limitation and possibility, and a desire for an encompassing relationship of sharing. It is companionate love with its own special respect, appreciation, patience, and steadfastness that provides a foundation for the more emotionally charged expressions of love.

In the past, romantic love was often seen in an unfavorable light, especially in Victorian Protestant writings,[18] but in an earlier Puritan period romance was clearly accepted as a part of the marital relationship, one closely interwoven with companionship. Theologian Thomas Hooker wrote:

> The man whose heart is endeared to the woman he loves, he dreams of her in the night in his eye and apprehension when he awakes, museth on her as he sits at table, talks with her when he travels and parties with her in each place he comes. . . .
>   That the husband tenders his spouse with an endeared affection above all mortal creatures: This appears by the expressions of his respect, that all he hath, is of her command, all he can do, is wholly improved for her content and comfort, she lies in his bosom and his heart trusts in her, which forceth all to confess, that the stream of his affection, like a mighty current, runs with full tide and strength.[19]

In modern times there is again an appreciation, though in a different voice, of the romantic character of marriage and its importance alongside the extensive emphasis on companionate love.

Justice, and justice as fairness, is a principle which has recently become a very important part of Protestant writings on marriage and the family, paralleling the general cultural interest in justice and equality in the twentieth century, and which is informed by a larger social-justice concern of the church.[20] Justice is concerned with "each receiving his or her due." Its focus, therefore, is on distribution—whether of economic resources, time, work, roles, or other aspects of marital life—which can be seen in terms of either simple equity or special need. In the first, distribution is made on the basis that all receive an equal part or amount of whatever is being distributed; for example, marital roles or money. Creative justice based on special need is concerned with distribution in light of unique needs one partner may have; for example, special medical or career needs.

The question of justice in our own time is particularly manifest in feminist concerns about sexist role patterns and institutional expectations. In response, Protestant thought ranges from a more traditional to a more egalitarian understanding of roles men and women play, with more conservative denominations remaining traditional and more mainline denominations developing egalitarian perspectives. The egalitarian position holds that justice requires us to take very seriously the feminist critique of the traditional division of roles and lift up a new image of marriage in which both parties are invited to choose their own marital and vocational roles in light of their talents, interests, time, and possibilities—rather than simply on the basis of gender. Thus, each partner should be free to choose roles regardless of whether they have been traditionally considered masculine or feminine (with the obvious exceptions of bearing and nursing children). The literature also assumes that married men and women should be free of stereotypes in which women are seen as more relational and men as more autonomous, women as more emotional and men as more rational, women as more passive and men as more active.

There is, then, a new egalitarian image of marriage which has emerged in marriage theory and is making its way into marriage services in such details as the shift from the phrase "man and wife" to "husband and wife." This perspective is an attempt by denominations to grapple with the issue of sexism within marriage and the family. This concern roughly parallels denominational efforts to confront the issue of sexism in other aspects of its life (such as the status and role of women in leadership positions, the use of inclusive language in worship services, and support of the Equal Rights Amendment to the U.S. Constitution). Justice, then, has become an important principle in reasoning about the character of the covenantal relationship.

Freedom is the third principle. Central to Protestant understandings of human nature is the assumption that we are created, as Reinhold Niebuhr has written, both "finite and free." We are limited by the vicissitudes of our natural experience, and yet we are self-transcendent creatures with the power of reflection and choice. We are free to act. This freedom, in turn, implies that persons are responsible for their own actions, since they have chosen them. In terms of a covenantal relationship, a couple is free to respond to that relationship, change it, shape it, violate it, or destroy it. Accordingly, the couple should be held responsible for the quality of relationship that is created.

In marriage theology, freedom is translated in a twofold way: Couples are responsible for exercising their freedom in such a way that they enable each other to realize their own possibilities; at the same time, they are responsible for enabling the marriage to be actualized. Nineteenth-century Protestant marriage theory developed an understanding of marriage as an organic reality with a certain life of its own, a life that is greater than and transcends its individual members. Thus, a marriage has three parties: the two partners and the marriage itself. This theory has developed in late-twentieth-century thought partly in response to the fear that in our time too many couples have exercised their freedom in their own interest rather than that of the marriage. In recent writings, the issue of responsible freedom is often treated in terms of the rights of the individual partners (and children) and the rights of the marriage. Couples are expected to understand and balance these rights.

The fourth principle is that of *order*. The covenant is understood to be a structural order including both stability and change. Within this equation, stability is that sense of ongoingness and predictability within the relationship, undergirded by some significant degree of social, emotional, personal, and economic security. The couple commits itself to realizing such stability. At the same time, order implies change. Order, and its stability, must be dynamic; it must allow for growth so that the life of the relationship will be sustained and developed. The partners, therefore, should attempt to realize a balance between stability and change, such that the covenantal order may avoid either chaos or rigidity.

5. A fifth characteristic of the covenantal relationship is *a commitment to create boundaries or rules of behavior.* When persons marry, they should create certain agreements regarding their common life—agreements that have to do with all significant areas of activity from the personal to the social, from the economic to the parental. These agreements are responses to questions of how the marriage will maintain itself economically; how it will govern itself; how it will express itself sexually; how it will allocate the roles its members shall play; how it will function in the social arena; how it will define its goals regarding vocations, procreation, lifestyles, and social responsibilities; and what values it will hold as central to its life as a marriage.

Protestant marriage theory holds that a couple should take seriously not only the need for such boundaries, rules, or agreements regarding the form and style of their own relationship but also the need to rethink them as the marriage relationship changes, for such rules are necessary if the basic purpose and vision of the marriage covenant are to be realized in concrete patterns of behavior. While Protestant literature does not tend to spell out in detail such rules or guidelines, it does offer concrete advice in such areas of marital life as sex-role fairness, sexual conduct, procreation, church participation, interfaith marriage, and responsible citizenship. Denominations offer guidance on what constitutes responsible boundaries for healthy marital behavior.

6. The sixth element of the covenant has to do with its possible demise. It is that *the couple should commit themselves to breaking the covenant only if its life of intimacy has ceased to exist and all available means have been exhausted in an effort to renew it.* The breakdown of a covenant relationship seldom comes quickly or over a single issue but is the result of a range of negative experiences which increasingly damage and finally destroy the relationship. A couple, therefore, are expected to seek help when negative experiences begin to undercut their intimacy or prevent it from developing.

A breakdown, of course, does not necessarily entail an end to the legal relationship of the marriage nor an end to living together; rather, breakdown occurs when the internal life of the relationship has died. The covenant involves an inner quality of relationship, an internal life of commitment and purpose, an inward expression of virtues and feelings with its own spirit and spirituality. This may be expressed externally, for the covenant is also an external reality, but its life and death are determined by the health of its inner life. When a marriage has reached the point where its members say that "there is no health in us," that the spirit is no more, then the covenant is no longer a "living" reality. In light of this understanding of the covenant, persons should do all in their power to nurture its health and care for it so that it might live—and they should end its life only as a last resort.[21]

It should be noted that Protestantism has shifted over the centuries on the question of divorce. While John Milton's treatise, *On Divorce*, built a case for divorce as early as the seventeenth century, it was not until the twentieth century that Protestant denominations were willing to acknowledge that divorce could be a morally responsible action. It is also significant that there is a growing attempt to develop church rituals that recognize divorce and offer support and hope to the partners in their search for new beginnings, though no denomination has yet formally adopted such a ritual.[22]

I have set forth here a covenantal image of marriage that lies at the heart of Protestantism's theology of marriage and its denominational statements and rituals about the purpose and meaning of marriage.[23] Much of that understanding will also be found in Roman Catholic and Orthodox perspectives. We find in the Vatican II documents on marriage and the family the substantive use and interpretation of the covenantal nature of marriage, and in Protestant writings we discover an appreciation for the sacramental character of marriage insofar as its bonds of love and intimacy are seen as a means of grace. Thus, a certain slow convergence in the understandings of marriage does unfold, albeit within a framework of genuine differences and contrasting emphases among the three major divisions of Christianity.

There are, of course, differences among Protestants themselves. The more liberal mainline groups accent the egalitarian nature of the covenantal bond which has been described here, while conservative and fundamentalist groups tend to accent a more traditional image in which marital and family roles are defined by gender, with the man considered the "head" of the household. Similarly, different positions exist on intermarriage, with more liberal groups counseling the couple to find a church home in which both parties can share, and more conservative groups insisting on marriage "within the fold." Divorce is also treated differently, with all groups accepting divorce but some refusing to remarry divorced members. Sexuality tends to be interpreted differently, with a much stronger emphasis on the procreative function of sex within fundamentalism and less consideration of sexual expression as a means of love and grace. Among those mainline Protestant groups which have given shape to the covenantal image discussed here, however, the bonds of commonality dominate. When Protestants gather together to celebrate a marriage, therefore, their shared commitment to a covenantal perspective unites them.

NOTES

1. Primary source material includes representative Protestant marriage services and official statements from the following mainline denominations: the American Baptist Churches in the U.S.A., the Southern Baptist Convention, the Christian Church (Disciples of Christ), the Episcopal Church, the Lutheran churches (A.L.C., L.C.A.,

A.E.L.C., and Missouri Synod), the Presbyterian Church, U.S.A., the United Church of Canada, the United Church of Christ, and the United Methodist Church.

2. "Social Principles of the United Methodist Church," *The Discipline* (Nashville: The United Methodist Publishing House, 1984).

3. Richard Fagley, *The Population Explosion and Christian Responsibility* (New York: Oxford, 1960). Fagley offers a contrast between and comparison of Luther and Calvin regarding the purposes of marriage and the place of procreation.

4. Roland Bainton, *Sex, Love, and Marriage* (Glasgow: Fontana, 1964), chap. 4–5. See also John Halkett, *Milton and the Idea of Matrimony* (New Haven: Yale University Press, 1970), for an excellent study of Milton's ideas on marriage and divorce.

5. Anne Bradstreet, "A Letter to Her Husband, Absent Upon Publick Employment," in Perry Miller, ed., *The American Puritans* (New York: Doubleday, 1956), pp. 271–272.

6. Two major works explore the role Puritanism played in giving shape to a theory of marriage in which love and companionship are viewed as central to the Christian understanding of marriage: Lawrence Stone, *The Family, Sex, and Marriage in England, 1500–1800* (New York: Harper and Row, 1977); and Edmund Morgan, *The Puritan Family* (New York: Harper and Row, 1966). See also Steven Ozment, *When Fathers Ruled* (Cambridge: Harvard University Press, 1983).

7. Wilson Yates, "Population Ethics: Religious Traditions—Protestant Perspectives," in *Encyclopedia of Bioethics*, vol. 3 (New York: The Free Press, 1978), pp. 1259–1260.

8. E.g., see D. S. Bailey, *The Mystery of Love and Marriage* (New York: Harper and Row, 1952); N. Pittenger, *Making Sexuality Human* (Philadelphia: Pilgrim Press, 1970); D. D. Williams, *The Spirit and Forms of Love* (New York: Harper and Row, 1968); L. Russell, *The Future of Partnership* (Philadelphia: Westminster Press, 1979); P. Trible, "Eve and Adam: Genesis 2–3 Reread," *Andover Newton Quarterly* 13 (March, 1973), and "Two Women in a Man's World." *Soundings* 59 (Fall, 1976); and J. B. Nelson, *Embodiment* (Minneapolis: Ausburg Publishing House; New York: Pilgrim Press, 1978), and *Between Two Gardens* (New York: Pilgrim Press, 1983).

9. Nelson, *Embodiment*, p. 113.

10. Examples of nineteenth-century Protestant marriage manuals include: William Makepeace Thayer, *Hints for the Household* (Boston: John Jewett and Co., 1853); George Weaver, *The Christian Household* (Boston: A. Tompkins and B. B. Mussey, 1856); John Wesley Smith, *Courtship, Love, and Marriage* (New York: Nelson's and Phillip's, 1874); and Charles Hudson, *The Marriage Guide* (Boston: Jewett and Co., 1882).

11. Charlotte and Howard J. Clinebell, Jr., *The Intimate Marriage* (New York: Harper and Row, 1970), pp. 29–33.

12. *The Book of Common Prayer* (New York: Seabury Press, 1977), p. 423.

13. Ibid., p. 430.

14. Dietrich Bonhoeffer, "What Is Meant by Telling the Truth?" in his *Ethics* (New York: The Macmillan Company, 1965), pp. 363–373.

15. Pittenger, *Making Sexuality Human*, p. 43. See also Joseph L. Allen, *Love and Conflict* (Nashville: Abingdon, 1984), pp. 231–234.

16. *The Worshipbook, Services* (Philadelphia: Westminster Press, 1970), p. 67.

17. *Book of Common Prayer*, p. 429.

18. See Charles Franklin Thwing and Carrie F. Butler Thwing, *The Family* (Boston: Lothrop, Lee and Shepard Co., 1886, 1913), for an excellent study that reflects the concerns of the Victorian era regarding "modern" marriage and, particularly, concern over the focus in secular society on romance and individualism.

19. Quoted in Bainton, *Sex, Love, and Marriage*, pp. 104–105.

20. See Jane Cary Peck, *Self and Family* (Philadelphia: Westminster Press, 1984), and William Everett, *Blessed Be the Tie That Binds* (Philadelphia: Fortress Press, 1985).

21. See Allen, *Love and Conflict*, pp. 243–253.

22. The United Church of Christ includes in its proposed marriage services a proposed "Order for Recognition of the End of a Marriage" (*Proposed Services of Marriage* [St. Louis: Office for Church Life and Leadership, United Church of Christ, 1982]).

23. Allen (*Love and Conflict*) provides a good example of a contemporary theologian who uses a covenantal model to interpret a Christian view of marriage. See also Peck, *Self and Family,* and Everett, *Blessed Be the Tie.*

CHAPTER 38

Marriage in Islam

Lois Lamyā' Ibsen al Faruqi

There are a billion Muslims in the world today. Somewhere between two million and three million of that number are in the United States. Islam, currently, is also the fastest-growing religion in the United States and is expected early in the twenty-first century to surpass Judaism as the third-largest religion in the country.

Stereotypes abound in the public perception of Islam in the West. The emergence of a revivalistic Islam strikes bewilderment and terror in many minds and hearts. Prejudice is fueled also by mass ignorance. The result is intolerance, misunderstanding, and chauvinism. This essay should go a long way toward alleviating misperceptions and positively affirming the wisdom of Islam in its marriage teachings and traditions.

The essay falls neatly into four major divisions: (1) the dominant influence of religion on Islamic marriage and the avowed purposes it serves; (2) specific requirements and codes necessary for its legitimacy; (3) mechanisms for the dissolution of marriage are detailed; and, (4) a brief look at the changes and challenges facing Islamic marriage in the future. The essay is a model of clarity and a reservoir of knowledge about our Muslim sisters and brothers.

Questions for Discussion

1. What distinctive differences do you find between the Islamic and the Roman Catholic views of marriage? What common ground do they share?
2. Compare the purposes of marriage in Islam with the twofold purpose as stated in contemporary Roman Catholic theology.
3. Will the meeting of Islam and feminism be confrontation or cooperation in relation to marriage?
4. In what areas will Islamic marriage show resistance and/or assimilation to secular modernity?

In order to explain how marriage is regarded and manifested in Islamic society, an organization of four major divisions has been utilized here. The first discusses general characteristics and purposes of Islamic marriage; a second outlines the specific requirements which legitimize marriage; and a third details the mechanisms for its dissolution. A fourth and final section discusses briefly the issue of change and the future.

GENERAL CHARACTERISTICS OF MARRIAGE IN ISLAM

RELIGION AS DOMINANT FACTOR

Probably the most dominant factor that influences or has influenced Islamic marriage is religion. This is due in part to the Islamic idea that religion (*dīn*) is not a body of ideas and practices which should be practiced or which should influence only that part of human life generally designated as dealing with the sacred. In Islamic culture there is little or no conception of a bifurcation between that which is sacred and that which is secular. Instead, since every aspect of life is the creation of Allah, it carries religious significance. It is the matériel with which humanity works to fulfill the will of God on earth, the ultimate human purpose in creation. Thus, for the Muslim, the ritual prayer conducted in any clean place is as equally valid and acceptable as that performed in the mosque; the commitment to political and social awareness and activity is as much a religious duty as the recitation of prayers; economic pursuits are equally regulated in accordance with religio-ethical pronouncements as the *zakāt* (Islamic levy for social welfare) and the *hajj* (pilgrimage to Makkah). Aesthetic products present not art for art's sake, but art for religion's sake: they are restatements and reminders of religious truth. In fact, every aspect of Islamic life is permeated with the effects of qur'ānic and religious teachings. Marriage is no less affected.

In Islamic society, however, marriage is not a religious sacrament. In other words, it is not a ceremony which necessitates the involvement of any clergy, presupposes a numinous or divine involvement, or, as a consequence, tends to be regarded as an indissoluble commitment.[1] In Islam there are no priests and little notion of sacredness in marriage which surpasses that of any other similarly recommended institution of the culture. Consequently, the religion has delineated accepted procedures for its dissolution.

Although marriage is not regarded as a religious sacrament, Islam recommends it for every Muslim. Commendations are to be found for it in the Qur'ān (4:1, 29; 7:107; 13:38; 24:32–33; 30:20), and the *hadīth* literature—recording sayings and events from the life of the Prophet—contains numerous passages in which celibacy is discouraged and marriage encouraged. For example, "Marriage is of my ways," the Prophet is reported to have taught, as well as, "When a man has married, he has completed one half of his religion," and "Whoever is able to marry, should marry."[2] Such stimulus from religious teachings has made marriage the goal of every Muslim and caused a considerable amount of social pressure to achieve that end for every member of the society.[3] Parents, relatives, and friends all feel committed to assist actively in the process, and few are the individuals who "escape the system."

Religion also guarantees certain rights and imposes certain responsibilities on the participants in marriage. Both men and women are regarded as deriving substantial benefits from the institution of marriage, but they are also bound to its obligations by actual qur'ānic prescriptives and by the legal elaboration and interpretation of the scriptural passages.[4] The religious laws of personal status are therefore crucial to any understanding of Islamic marriage. It is in these laws that the most detailed enunciation of both the woman's and the man's rights and obligations is to be found. Complying with the fulfillment of those mutual responsibilities is therefore regarded as a religious obligation for both parties. The acquiescence of the failure to comply is regarded as an act carrying divine reward or punishment, and therefore it is not a matter to be taken lightly.

Also important is the fact that matrimony in Islam is as much a joining of two families as it is a joining of two individuals. Given the level of interdependence in the Islamic family,[5] Muslims are especially likely to believe marriage necessitates a consideration of the welfare of the familial groups involved rather than merely the desires of the two individuals. For this reason a much larger participation in the choice of marriage partners is regarded as proper and beneficial than would be acceptable in a contemporary Western environment. Even after the marriage, the extended family organization reduces dependence on the single adult relationship of husband and wife and stimulates equally strong relationships between the wife or husband and other members of the family. Despite this heavily "familial" character of the Islamic marriage, the woman maintains her separate legal identity after marriage, her maiden name, her adherence to a particular school of law, and her right to separate ownership of her money, property, or financial holdings.

THE PURPOSES OF MARRIAGE

The importance of marriage in Islamic society and its advocacy by the religious teachings rest on the avowed purposes it serves. First, Muslims regard marriage as providing a balance between individualistic needs and the welfare of the group to which the individual belongs. As such, it is regarded as a social and psychological necessity for every member of the community.

Second, marriage is a mechanism for the moral and mutually beneficial control of sexual behavior and procreation. Islam regards sexual activity as an important and perfectly healthy drive of both males and females. Thus, it is not shameful and should not be denied to members of either sex. Lack of sexual satisfaction is believed to cause personality maladjustments and to "endanger the mental health and efficiency of the society."[6] Islam, therefore, commends sex as natural and good but restricts it to participants of a union which insures responsibility for its consequences.[7]

A third purpose of marriage is its provision of a stable atmosphere for the rearing of children. Islam sees this purpose as inextricably tied to an extended family system. The extended family may vary in size, even in residential proximity, as is evidenced in different regions of the Muslim world, but the cohesion of its members is inextricably bound to qur'ānic prescriptions and Islamic law. These explicity enunciate the rights and obligations of its members and the legal extent of those benefits and responsibilities.[8]

Fourth, marriage assures crucial economic benefits for women during their child-bearing and child-rearing years. Self-support during this period is difficult, if not impossible, for mothers who have no outside help. Even if sustained by the "supermom," of which we hear so much in recent times, the physical and emotional toll on such persons is beyond what most individuals can tolerate.

Fifth, the close companionship of the marital partners provides emotional gratification for both men and women. The importance of this purpose of marriage in Islam is evidenced by repeated references in the Qur'ān and *ḥadīth* literature to the quiescence (Qur'ān 30:21; 7:189) and protective nature (Qur'ān 9:71) of the bond between the husband and wife. The man and woman are considered to be so close that they are described as garments of one another (Qur'ān 2:187). The kindness, love, and consideration enjoined on the partners appears repeatedly in both religious and legal texts.

SPECIFIC REQUIREMENTS FOR MARRIAGE IN ISLAM

Given its general characteristics and purposes as outlined above, Islamic marriage also entails certain specific features which are regarded necessary for its legitimacy. Let us first specify the criteria which must be met by the participants themselves.

LIMITATION OF PARTICIPANTS

Applying to both parties are the Islamic boundaries of incestuous union. The list of acceptable persons whom one can marry rests on a firm ground of conformity since the basic exogamy/endogamy[9] patterns are fixed by the Qur'ān and *ḥadīth*.[10] Islam prescribes limits on marriages between certain blood (consanguine) relatives, between others closely related through marriage (affinal relatives), and between lactational relatives, that is, those who have been nursed by the same woman.[11] Since the institution of the wet nurse and the reciprocal nursing of their babies by women with close familial or affinal ties have often been widespread, the lactational limits have proved very influential for discouraging inbreeding. The jurists of the different schools have unanimously adhered to that prohibition and accepted the authenticity of the *ḥadīth*s on this matter,[12] although the details of how much nursing and how much milk constitutes a prohibiting amount, the ages of affected children, etc., were sometimes disputed.

The definition of allowable marriage partners is considered by Muslims to fulfill two major purposes: to prevent the biological effects of inbreeding, and to guard against excessive familiarity between sexual partners. Such familiarity is regarded as cause for sexual indifference in the partners. Therefore, marriage with someone as close as a mother, sister, daughter, or aunt would result, in most cases, in a denial of sexual gratification for the marriage partners. In the Muslim village, young people of the opposite sex are separated from the age of puberty or before. If they are to realize a sexually successful marriage in the village, the possibilities for familiarity must be limited and the aura of mystery and excitement engendered by marriage candidates of the opposite sex preserved. Whether consciously or unconsciously pursued by the Muslim peoples, this concern seems to be at the base of the preference—or, in some parts of the Muslim world, the demand—for segregation of the sexes. That is a much more logical underlying purpose for segregation than the need to curb sexual promiscuity. The latter is almost an impossibility in the close quarters and intensive interaction of the village.[13]

There are also religious affiliation boundaries for participation in an Islamic marriage. The male must be a Muslim; the female may be a Muslim, Jew, or Christian (Qur'ān 5:6). Sometimes the religious requirements for the female have been interpreted more widely to include anyone who is not idolatrous. The prohibition against a non-Muslim man's marrying a Muslim woman is, however, qur'ānic and has been unequivocally adhered to by all the legal schools.

Though a few early jurists rejected completely the idea of intermarriage, most Muslims have considered it permissible under certain conditions.[14] The qur'ānic and legal directives on intermarriage tended to be reinforced by the circumstances of the early centuries of Islamic history. As traders, warriors, missionaries, teachers, administrators, and religious or education-seeking pilgrims, many Muslim men traveled to live in different parts of the world. They often lived in predominantly non-Muslim societies where Muslim women were not available for marriage partners. Women, on the other hand, tended to remain in their predominantly Muslim societies and therefore had access to Muslim male partners.

There were no age limitations for marriage partners in Islamic culture until recent times. Since the individuals remained part of a larger family structure which did not call upon them to support themselves, to set up their own home, or to cope unaided with the problems of parenting children, Islam held a much more relaxed view of the prior preparedness for marriage. As the extended family of certain urban environments has been weakened in recent times, a greater emphasis has been placed on the readiness of the married couple to live a more isolated and self-sufficient existence. This has stimulated an appeal by certain individuals and groups in a number of Muslim countries to call for the setting of minimum age limits for marriage.[15] Since marriage in Islam means the signing of a contract, with consummation following perhaps at a much later time, marriage of minors did not raise the same sort of problems it might in another societal complex. This does not mean that the custom of child marriage was never abused; it does mean that this Islamic custom need not be detrimental if practiced in tandem with a properly functioning Islamic society. Not its use but its misuse in an Islamically inconsistent social complex has generated Muslim concern and the recent need for a minimum-age limitation for marriage partners.

Some writers have attributed the recent calls for minimum-age requirements to Western influences on Islamic thinking and customs. In fact, that

argument has been the main thrust of conservative opposition to the initiation of age restrictions on marriage. It seems much more likely that this so-
called Westernization would not have taken root unless the misuse and/or
imbalance within the system had not made some sort of change necessary.

Another requirement which relates to the qualifications of the marriage
participants is that the Muslim woman must be unmarried. If she has formerly been married, she should not be pregnant or in the first three months
following her previous marriage, a period known as *'iddah,* in which she may
not be aware of a possible pregnancy. The former husband is obliged to support her during the *'iddah* or until the birth of her child, after which she may
remarry. Such restrictions help verify paternity of a child resulting from the
earlier marriage.

The male partner in marriage, however, is not limited to a single marriage. Islam can be described as permitting polygynous marriage, that is, it is
a society in which plural marriages for males are possible. In Islamic society,
however, only a small portion of the males practice polygyny. If those that do
are known to have no valid reason for taking another wife,[16] or do not treat
their wives with the complete equality commanded by the Qur'ān (4:3; 129),
Muslims judge such instantiation of this form of marriage as unIslamic and
religiously and morally reprehensible. As an excuse for sexual promiscuity,
the practice is unconditionally condemned, but, if practiced according to
Islamic moral exhortations and legal provisions, Muslims regard polygyny
as a more equitable and humane solution to certain situations than the
unconditional demand for monogamy.[17] In some schools of law, a woman
who wishes to prevent her husband's future second marriage can ask that
such a stipulation be written into the marriage agreement.

MECHANISTIC REQUIREMENTS

Other specific requirements of Islamic marriage pertain to the actual execution of the marriage rather than to the qualities of its participants. These are
designated here as "mechanistic requirements."

A WRITTEN CONTRACT Marriage in Islam constitutes an agreement
between a man and a woman which is embodied in a written contract. The
marriage agreement includes specification of the dower (both an initial and
delayed portion, see the section on Dower, below), signatures of the two participants and of their respective witnesses, and other terms agreed upon by
the parties concerned. The contract is a legal document, which is filed with
the local Islamic registry of the government and upholdable in a court of law.

The occasion for the signing of the contract is called *'aqd nikāh* ("marriage
contract"). It usually takes place at the home of the bride's parents, in the
presence of members of the family and close friends. The *'nikāh* is accompanied by the surrender of the agreed-upon initial dower and the exchange of
gifts by the marriage partners. It also marks the beginning of preparations for
the consummation of the marriage. The actual marriage requirements are fulfilled in the *'aqd nikāh,* and the marriage is complete, but it is not until the *'urs*

or actual wedding party that the marriage is consummated and the bride moves to the home of her husband. This may take place shortly after the contract signing or at a much later time, as the parties desire.

The 'urs may be a simple party or an elaborate occasion. Refreshments, activities, and entertainment vary according to tastes, financial capabilities, and regional preferences. It may take place at the groom's home or at a public place reserved for the occasion. It is the common practice not only for gifts to be presented to the bride and groom by guests on this occasion but also for the couple to reciprocate with a token of their gratitude—usually a small dish or platter for carrying sweets or an item of clothing for closer relatives. These vary in extravagance to match the economic situation of the wedding participants.

The clothing of the bride and groom varies from one level of society to another and from one region to another. In the Arab Mashriq (near the eastern end of the Mediterranean Sea), for example, the wedding dress may be a white gown and headcovering similar to that common in Western societies or an elaborate example of the local style. Men wear Western-style suits or traditional dress. In the Indian subcontinent, brides are clothed in crimson saris elaborately decorated with gold, while grooms don the traditional "Nehru jacket" with its high collar and buttoned front. In Malaysia the typical attire for both bride and groom is a traditionally styled outfit made of the locally produced brocade woven with gold threads. If the wedding couple come from wealthy families, the clothing may be so heavily decorated with the precious metal that the pair have difficulty in moving. But this does not present too much of a problem since the function of the 'urs is an elaborate reception at which the bride and groom and their families accept the congratulations and best wishes of friends and relatives.

TWO ADULT WITNESSES   Two witnesses—one representing the bride, the other representing the groom—are a necessary feature of the marriage-contract signing. Where possible, these are the two fathers of the couple, but any other adult Muslim could legitimately fill this role. No other intermediary is required for the performance of a marriage. Any person who is chosen by the parties may make and accept the marriage proposal. Often, however, a qāḍī or Muslim lawyer attends as a registrar of the marriage.

SU'ĀL AND ĪJĀB ("QUESTION AND CONSENT")   Another element of a legitimate marriage in Islamic society is an explicit request by the groom and his family or representatives and an explicit consent to marriage by the bride and her family or representatives, which may be either in writing or oral. The Qur'ān does not deal specifically with this matter, but there are a number of instances from the ḥadīth literature which pertain to this question.[18] The story is told of a woman in the time of Muhammad who demanded and was accorded by the Prophet the right to repudiate her marriage because she had not been asked and therefore had not given her consent to the bond.[19] Despite strongly authenticated instances in the sunnah ("example") of the Prophet Muhammad, Muslim jurists have varied in their interpretations of the guardian's powers in arranging marriage for his wards or children. Some deem it a necessary condition for the father to seek the consent of his daughter before he gives her in marriage. Others argue that it is commendable rather than necessary. Still others limit the need for the consent of the bride to the mature woman who is a widow or divorcee.[20]

DOWER   A fourth requirement of the Islamic marriage is a marriage gift or dower to the bride by the groom. This gift may consist of anything deemed suitable by the participants—money, real estate, or other valuable items. In some cases it has entailed the transfer of great wealth to the bride; in others, it has been as modest as an iron ring or a token coin.[21] No maximum has been set by Islamic law, though some schools have specified minimums.[22] Such details are worked out by the representatives of the bride and groom prior to the *'aqd nikāḥ* and are specified in the written contract.

The dower may be immediate, that is, given at the time of signing the *'aqd nikāḥ.* More often, the parties agree that the dower be divided into two parts: one portion (the *mahr*) surrendered to the bride at the time of marriage, and another delayed portion (the *mu' akhkhar*) which falls due in case of death or divorce. If a man dies, Islamic law provides that his widow's *mu' akhkhar* settlement be paid before any other commitment on his estate is honored.

The immediate dower may be used for the trousseau and the household purchases needed for the newly married couple. At other times it is a kind of economic insurance for the future welfare of the bride, in which case she invests it and draws benefits from it. In the case of poor people, the amounts are so negligible that they can be viewed as little more than a symbol of the groom's willingness to take on financial responsibility for this future wife. Amounts of dower vary not only with the difference in the economic capabilities of different grooms and their families but also according to regional practices and social levels within a particular society.

It is clear that the Islamic marriage is not a "ceremony." Although it may be associated with a number of elaborate activities (procession of the bride to her new husband's home, beautification of the bride prior to marriage with henna decorations, gift-giving and well-wishing of friends and relatives, elaborate clothing, refreshments, and entertainment), marriage in Islam is essentially a legal agreement between two individuals and two families. While carrying the sanction and blessing of the religion, it cannot be considered a sacred ceremony. Marriage, like so many other aspects of Islamic culture, is neither wholly sacred nor wholly secular, neither religious nor nonreligious.

DISSOLUTION OF MARRIAGE

DISSOLUTION THROUGH DEATH

Dissolution of marriage occurs either by death of one of the parties or by divorce. In the case of the woman's death, there are inheritance laws which pertain to her wealth since her property remains separate from that of her husband. There are similarly specific requirements for the distribution of his wealth following the death of the husband. Other requirements pertain to the female survivor. These include payment of the *mu' akhkhar* dower to the widow and the illegality of the widow's remarriage before completion of the three-month *'iddah* period in which the possibility of pregnancy can be determined. During this time, the widow is financially supported by her late husband's estate. If she is pregnant, maintenance is guaranteed until birth of the child or the end of the nursing period, but she must not remarry until the birth of her child.

DIVORCE

More complicated is the dissolution of marriage through legal divorce. Although it is generally believed that dissolution of marriage takes place in Islam only by male repudiation of the wife—that is, by his pronouncing three times, "I divorce you"—the fact is that Islamic law provides various mechanisms and channels for ending a marriage. Despite the variety of means for divorce, it has remained a repugnant act in Islamic society,[23] to be invoked only when all methods of reconciliation have been exhausted. Some types of divorce are male-instigated, others female-instigated; still others are the result of mutual agreement or judicial process.

MALE-INSTIGATED DIVORCE   The most common form of divorce initiated by Muslim males is known as *ṭalāq* ("letting go free"), which involves a series of three statements by the husband that he divorces his wife. Contrary to common opinion, these repudiation statements cannot legally be rendered at a single time. In fact, very strict rules have been established in Islamic law to prevent misuse.[24] Unfortunately, these laws have not always been enforced.

Ṭalāq is to be pronounced with specific terms before two qualified witnesses. Each pronouncement must be made at a time when the wife is not incapacitated for sexual activity by menstrual flow. Having made the first statement of divorce, the man must wait to make the second statement until the woman completes her next monthly period. The third pronouncement must be similarly spaced. Only after the third repudiation is the divorce considered final. Each of the other two statements is revocable. The wife continues to live in her home, and she is provided full maintenance throughout the divorce proceedings. During this time, attempts are made to achieve reconciliation through the counseling and arbitration of family and friends. Only if this is not possible is the final pronouncement made and the marriage considered irrevocably broken. From that point, husband and wife are forbidden to live together or to remarry each other unless and until the woman has remarried someone else from whom she becomes widowed or divorced. Any Islamic divorce, like the dissolution of marriage by death, requires a three-months' waiting period in order to determine whether the divorcee is pregnant. She is not free to remarry until that period is completed or, in case of pregnancy, until she gives birth. As in the case of dissolution of marriage by death, maintenance of the wife is incumbent upon the husband for the *'iddah* the period of child-bearing.

Any *ṭalāq* divorce not made in accordance with these rules is considered to be an aberration, or *bid'ah*. Such practice is regarded as sinful, but unfortunately the actions of some Muslims and the positions of certain jurists have not always accorded with the ideal.[25]

FEMALE-INSTIGATED DIVORCE   In the Qur'ān it is stated that women have equitable rights in divorce to those of men (2:228). As in other Islamic matters, equitable does not mean equivalence or identity. Therefore, there are different procedures which apply to women in their initiation of divorce proceedings. The wife is entitled to originate dissolution of her marriage under four circumstances.

First, in a delegated divorce, the right of *ṭalāq*, or repudiation, by the wife may be agreed upon prior to marriage and stipulated as a condition of the marriage contract.[26] Second is a conditional divorce, a stipulation in the marriage contract that the wife will be free to divorce her husband if he does certain things contrary to his pre-marriage promises. This type of divorce is accepted by some jurists but rejected by others.[27] Third is a court divorce, in which freedom from the marriage bond is granted to a woman for any of the inadequacies of the husband which are generally regarded as legitimate causes for divorce: long absence or desertion, impotence, failure to provide adequate support, physical or mental mistreatment, serious physical or mental illness, apostasy, and proved debauchery. As noted earlier, a wife may also be granted a divorce if, upon reaching maturity, she rejects a marriage contracted by a guardian on her behalf while she was still a child. A fourth type of divorce instigated by the wife is known as *khul'*. It involves a release of the wife from the marriage contract on her agreement to pay compensation to the husband.

MUTUAL CONSENT OR *MUBĀRA'AH*   When a husband and wife reach mutual agreement to dissolve their marriage, it is called *mubāra'ah*. It differs from the *khul'* in being effected by mutual desire on the part of the marriage partners.[28]

JUDICIAL PROCESS   *Li'ān* or "double testimony" is the dissolution of marriage which results from the husband's accusation that his wife has committed adultery. If he proves his case (four eye-witnesses are necessary in Islamic law!), it it considered valid reason for divorce. If he has no witnesses other than himself, he must swear by God four times that his statement is true. The wife is called upon to admit her guilt or to testify in a similar way that her husband has lied about her. Both also invoke divine curses for false swearing. If no further proof either for or against the accusation can be substantiated, reconciliation between the two parties is deemed impossible, and the marriage is dissolved by judicial process.[29] Certain types of divorce instigated by women are also dealt with by the Islamic courts (see "court divorce," above).

CHANGE AND THE FUTURE

An increase in the number of women in the work force, increased education for women and men, the development of Islamic awareness and identity among Muslims in all parts of the world, increased mobility, concentration of populations in urban centers, increased contact with alien cultures, as well as many other contemporary facts of life may require certain adjustments in marriage practice in any society. Whether such adjustments will prove disastrous to the institution of Islamic marriage as it is now known—and, therefore, to Muslim society—or merely productive of a new synthesis of twentieth- and twenty-first-century influences with the core premises depends on the ability of society to react with a strong and intelligent social conscience. Social change as such need not be unduly disruptive of Islamic marriage practices. In fact, the magnitude of the Muslim identity (nearly 1,000,000,000 persons) and the diversity of geographic, ethnic, linguistic, and cultural backgrounds out of which these people moved toward Islamization have resulted in an extremely rich and varied tradition in marriage as in all other aspects of the civilization.

Islam has been particularly tolerant of its new converts, and those converts have been particularly ingenious in adapting their local customs to basic Islamic premises wherever possible. At the same time, there were basic premises of the faith as expressed in the Qur'ān and exemplified in the teachings and example of Muhammad which provided a religio-cultural core with which the more superficial variations could be sympathetically related. History has confirmed that, along with a maintenance of the core, Islamic society has been flexible enough to allow regional variations as well as changes accompanying the passage of time and the variation of circumstances. Each period has had to make its "peace" with those variations of circumstances, to take that which was acceptable and combinable with the Islamic core, to reject those which were culturally and religiously "indigestible," and to adapt—that is, to Islamize—still others before adopting them. This process must, of course, be carried on in the present day and into the future. To rule it out would be to kill the culture and the religion.

A society's proper reaction to change implies two prerequisites. First, it needs a study and awareness of the total societal complex, each of whose institutions and factors is integrally interwoven with and dependent upon the others. Any suggestion for change regarding marriage practices, therefore, should not be investigated in isolation. It should be studied in relation to the other factors of individual and group welfare which those factors may affect. It might be argued, for instance, that, because of increased participation of women in the work force in many Muslim countries, the Islamic custom of mandatory male support for women should be abolished; yet such a shortsighted view fails to take into account anything but the material aspects of the question. It might be counter-argued that much more important in this Islamic stipulation is the reinforcement it gives to the interdependence of the marriage partners; to break those bonds of rights for women and obligations for men would cut deeply into the strength of the marriage bond.

Similarly, some contemporaries might argue that Islam is old-fashioned in its unshakable condemnation of sex outside of marriage. They would cite contraceptive devices and new attitudes toward the sexual freedom of women as demanding a reappraisal of an old Islamic "fixation." But Islam's reason for rejecting greater sexual freedom was not that no adequate contraceptives were available in earlier times to prevent children born out of wedlock, nor did it insist on the importance of female virginity in order to discriminate against women or set a "double standard." Rather, Islam promoted this idea in order to strengthen the institutions of marriage and the family by making them carry benefits that could not be achieved elsewhere. To destroy the uniqueness of such marital benefits in an attempt to provide complete sexual equity would carry widespread and debilitating effects, not only for those institutions, but equally for the individuals who make up those institutions. We do not have to surmise about the effect on women that this innovation might have, for a living example is available in Western society. The consequences are already glaringly apparent. The increased sexual dispensability of the wife which this new promiscuity produces is one of the factors leading to the increased divorce rate. It also has drastically adverse effects on both the financial and emotional security of middle-aged and older women. Proper reaction of a society to change, therefore, demands a careful screening of the elements of change and their results for compatibility with the rest of the culture's goals and institutions.

Second, in order for Muslims to avoid rash acceptance of drastic and harmful changes in their marriage laws and customs, they must purge their society of the misuse of existent laws and customs. Often it is the widespread neglect or circumvention of the qur'ānic or legal prescriptives which are at the root of the problem, rather than the institutions and practices themselves. A case in point is the misuse of the institution of *ṭalāq*, many instances of which fail to comply with the regulations and restrictions which have been established for it. Adherence to those regulations and restrictions would obviate the need for drastic changes in the institution.

The imbalances caused by rapid social change are probably inevitable factors in any society. At this period of history, they are particularly challenging. Without careful reappraisal of the side-effects of contemplated innovation and its compatibility with other aspects of the religion and culture, and without a purging of misapplications of extant institutions, massive social disorientation and deleterious effects on the members of any society are inevitable. This is the contemporary challenge, not only for Muslim society, but also for every other society in the world.

NOTES

1. In Christianity, marriage was first recognized as a sacrament in the twelfth century, when Peter Lombard's "Sentences" (Book 4, dist. 1, num. 2) enumerated marriage as one of the seven sacraments. That work became the standard textbook of Catholic theology during the Middle Ages and was formally accepted by the Councils of Florence (1439) and Trent (1545–1563).

2. Muhammad ibn Isma'il al Bukhārī, *Sahih Al-Bukhārī*, tr. Muhammad Muhsin Khān, Al-Medina al-Munauwara: Islamic University, 1974, Vol. 7, pp. 2–5, 8.

3. To this day, in the highly Westernized society of Beirut, Lebanon, unmarried young people are often embarrassed by the constant social pressures on them to marry.

4. The Muslim maintains that the Qur'ān is the word of God dictated verbatim to the Prophet Muhammad. Its basic ethical principles and prescriptive laws, therefore, carry the authenticity of divine provenance. These principles and laws are designated as the *sharī'ah* ("path"). The human elaboration and interpretation of the *sharī'ah*, i.e., its development into specific laws by the jurists of the five schools of law (four Sunnī and one Shī'ī *madhāhib*, s. *madhhab*), is the subject matter of Islamic jurisprudence or *fiqh*.

5. See Lois Lamyā' (Ibsen) al Faruqi, "An Extended Family Model from Islamic Culture," *Journal of Comparative Family Studies* 9 (Summer, 1978): 243–256; and "Islamic Traditions and the Feminist Movement: Confrontation or Cooperation?" *The Islamic Quarterly*, vol. 27, no. 3 (1983), pp. 132–139.

6. Hammūdah 'Abd al 'Atī, *The Family Structure in Islam* (Indianapolis: American Trust Publications, 1977), p. 50.

7. The Qur'ān and Islamic law, reflecting the practice of slavery which existed in the pre- and early Islamic periods, also condoned cohabitation of a master with his slave girls (Qur'ān 23:5–7; 70:29–31). Although most Muslims would try to rationalize the existence of the passages sanctioning this form of extramarital sex (see 'Abd al 'Atī, *Family Structures*, pp. 41–49) and draw attention to the companion mechanisms which legitimized the children of such unions, enjoined emancipation for the mothers, and generally controlled and regulated the practice, few, if any, Muslims today would regard sex as legitimate except within the bonds of marriage.

8. The Qur'ān contains not only repeated references to the rights of kin (17:23–26; 4:7–9; 8:41; etc.) but also inheritance and support provisions which are stipulated as reaching far beyond the nuclear family (2:180–182; 4:33, 176; eitc.). Dire punishment is threatened for those who ignore these measures for intra-family support (4:7–12).

9. Exogamy is the custom of marrying only outside one's own tribe, clan, or family, i.e., outbreeding; endogamy is the opposite, i.e., inbreeding.

10.
>   Prohibited to you
>   (For marriage) are:
>   Your mothers, daughters,
>   Sisters; father's sisters,
>   Mother's sisters; brother's daughters,
>   Sister's daughters; foster-mothers;
>   (Who gave you suck), foster-sisters;
>   Your wives' mothers;
>   Your step-daughters under your
>   Guardianship, born of your wives
>   To whom ye have gone in,
>   No prohibition if ye have not gone in;
>   (Those who have been)
>   wives of your sons proceeding
>   From your loins;
>   And two sisters in wedlock
>   At one and the same time,
>   Except for what is past;
>   For God is Oft-forgiving
>   Most Merciful. (Qur'ān 4:23)

See also al Bukhārī, *Sahih Al-Bukhārī*, pp. 28–34.

11. The qur'ānic passage stating that it is unlawful for men to marry their "milk rela-

tives" is to be found in 4:23. See note 10 above and al Bukhārī, *Ṣaḥiḥ Al-Bukhārī*, pp. 24–28.

12. 'Abd al 'Aṭī, *Family Structure*, p. 131; al Bukhārī, *Ṣaḥiḥ Al-Bukhārī*, pp. 28–34.

13. The ever-widening problems of impotence in contemporary males may in large part be a result of the excessive sexual freedom and familiarity which pertains in many of the societies of this century. See G. L. Ginsberg, et al., "The New Impotency," *Archives of General Psychology* 28 (1972): 218; and G. F. Gilder, *Sexual Suicide* (New York: Quadrangle/The New York Times Book Co., 1973).

14. See 'Abd al 'Aṭī, *Family Structure*, p. 139.

15. In Turkey and Pakistan, men and women can marry at eighteen and sixteen years of age, respectively; in Egypt, at nineteen and seventeen; in Jordan, at eighteen and seventeen; in Morocco and Iran, at eighteen and fifteen; and in Tunisia, at twenty for both sexes. Marriage of younger persons must have the consent of guardians and the permission of the court.

16. E.g., barrenness of the first wife, disbalance of male/female population, chronic illness of the wife, large numbers of helpless widows and orphans in the community, etc.

17. See Tanzil-ur-Rahman, *A Code of Muslim Personal Law* (Karachi: Hamdard Academy, 1978), pp. 94–101, for a summary of modern legislation pertaining to polygyny. The Tunisian Law of 1956 prohibits it outright, while other countries have placed various restrictions on having more than one wife—e.g., financial ability of the husband, just cause, consent of the first wife or wives, and/or permission of a court or ad hoc council.

18. Al Bukhārī, *Ṣaḥiḥ Al-Bukhārī, Al-Bukhārī*, pp. 51–53.

19. Tanzil-ur-Rahman, *Code*, pp. 51–52.

20. 'Abd al 'Aṭī, *Family Structure*, pp. 76–84. Tanzil-ur-Rahman, *Code*, chap. 3, see especially pp. 71–74, for modern legislation in various Muslim countries relating to consent to marriage.

21. Al Bukhārī, *Ṣaḥiḥ Al-Bukhārī*, pp. 51, 55, 59–61.

22. Asaf A. A. Fyzee, *Outlines of Muhammadan Law*, 2nd ed. (London: Oxford University Press, 1955), pp. 112–113; Tanzil-ur-Rahman, *Code*, pp. 218–221.

23. This paraphrases a *ḥadīth* from the life of the Prophet Muhammad: "Of all the permitted acts the one disliked most by God is divorce" (S. Ameenul Hasan Rizvi, "Women and Marriage in Islam," *The Muslim World League Journal*, vol. 12, no. 1 (Muharram. 1404 A. H. [October, 1984], p. 26).

24. Tanzil-ur-Rahman, *Code*, pp. 313–316; Fyzee, *Outlines*, pp. 128–130.

25. Fyzee, *Outlines*, pp. 130–131.

26. Tanzil-ur-Rahman, *Code*, chap. 12, pp. 339ff.; Fyzee, *Outlines*, pp. 134–135.

27. Tanzil-ur-Rahman, *Code*, pp. 346–350.

28. Ibid., pp. 552ff.; Fyzee, *Outlines*, pp. 138–139; Alhaji A. D. Ajijola, *Introduction to Islamic Law* (Karachi: International Islamic Publishers for Ajijola Memorial Islamic Publishing Co. [Nigeria], 1981), pp. 172ff.

29. Tanzil-ur-Rahman, *Code*, pp. 504ff.; Ajijola, *Introduction*, pp. 176–177; Fyzee, *Outlines*, pp. 141–142.